# contents

**July 1998**

# Strengthening families for life

Final report of the Commission on the Family to the
Minister for Social, Community and Family Affairs

BAILE ÁTHA CLIATH
ARNA FHOILSIÚ AG OIFIG AN tSOLÁTHAIR
Le ceannach díreach ón
OIFIG DHÍOLTA FOILSEACHÁN RIALTAIS,
TEACH SUN ALLIANCE, SRÁID THEACH LAIGHEAN, BAILE ÁTHA CLIATH 2,
nó tríd an bpost ó
FOILSEACHÁN RIALTAIS, AN RANNÓG POST-TRÁCHTA,
4 - 5 BÓTHAR FHEARCHAIR, BAILE ÁTHA CLIATH 2,
(Teil: 01 661 3111 - Fo-líne 4040/4045; Fax 01 4752760)
nó trí aon díoltóir leabhar.

DUBLIN
PUBLISHED BY THE STATIONERY OFFICE
To be purchased directly from the
GOVERNMENT PUBLICATIONS SALE OFFICE,
SUN ALLIANCE HOUSE, MOLESWORTH STREET, DUBLIN 2,
or by mail order from
GOVERNMENT PUBLICATIONS, POSTAL TRADE SECTION,
4 - 5 HARCOURT ROAD, DUBLIN 2
(Tel: 01 661 3111 - ext. 4040/4045; Fax 01 4752760)
or through any bookseller

£6.00

(Pn 5818)

ISBN 0-7076-6102-1
Dublin

Deigned by Red Dog
Printed by Brunswick Press Ltd

# foreword

I welcome the publication of the final Report of the Commission on the Family.

The report "Strengthening Families for Life" contains a comprehensive and in-depth analysis of the issues affecting families and wide-ranging recommendations across several different policy areas. The report also contains some original and significant research work which the Commission has undertaken, including a national survey on the childcare arrangements which families make, socio-logical research on fathers and their role in family life and an overview of family policy in Ireland.

The Government is committed to adopting a families first approach by putting the family at the centre of all its policies.

A new Family Affairs Unit has been established in the Department of Social, Community and Family Affairs to co-ordinate family policy, pursue the findings in the Commission's final report following their consideration by the Government, to undertake research, and promote awareness about family issues. The Unit has responsibility for a number of family services including: support for the marriage and child counselling services, the Family Mediation Service, a pilot programme in relation to the local offices of the Department building on the one-stop-shop concept, with the aim of providing improved support at local level to families and an information programme on parenting issues.

I wish to record my appreciation of the time, effort and expertise of members of the Commission in the preparation of this important document. I am confident that the Commission's report will make a positive contribution to developing coherent progressive and effective policies for families as promised in the Action Programme for the Millennium.

Dermot Ahern, T.D.
Minister for Social, Community and Family Affairs

July 1998

# preface

It is with great pleasure that I present the final report of the Commission on the Family.

The Commission since its inception in October 1995 has endeavoured, within its terms of reference, to achieve three broad aims.

First, to outline the parameters within which Family Policy should be formed.

Second, to present an up to date comprehensive picture of matters relating to family well-being in this country and place this in an international context where appropriate.

Third, to present a detailed analysis and assessment of particular areas of concern as highlighted by the many submissions which were received from the public, and the extensive consultation which took place with experts and interested parties.

In pursuit of our terms of reference we have undertaken some original and significant research work which details the factual situation as regards childcare in the under twelve age group on a national basis. For the first time we know the arrangements under which children are minded, the numbers which attend crèches and nurseries and those looked after by relatives and childminders. We feel that this new information will play a significant part in informing policy in this area.

A review which traces the development of family policy in Ireland has contributed to the Commission's deliberations in relation to the principles which should underlie and guide future policy development.

We also have a considerable body of sociological research on the position of fathers and their role in family life, both in an Irish and international context. We expect it will make a valuable contribution to our understanding of family dynamics and help us to support and strengthen family relationships, particularly from the child's point of view. Significant abstracts of these works are included in this report.

It would be presumptuous on the part of the Commission to assume that this report though labelled "Final" is anything but a beginning. Consequently we would particularly like to emphasise the Chapter within the Report which proposes structures and institutions which we recommend be set up to develop and progress the work. We also hope that policy development will be cognisant of the principles which we believe are the bedrock for future development of family support.

We are aware of the important areas not dealt with in-depth by this report and in mitigation plead time constraints. However we have included areas of importance which came to the attention of the Commission but which we were unable to develop and have documented these for future work.

The consensus in relation to the need to prioritise support for families across all parties in the lead up to the 1997 general election was very much welcomed by the Commission and we were considerably encouraged by the new remit of the Department of Social, Community and Family Affairs and the new responsibilities which it has been given in the family area.

The views of the many people and organisations who made submissions to the Commission have made an important contribution to our understanding of the concerns of families today. We thank everyone for the time they took to give the Commission the benefit of their experience.

We are also indebted to the many experts who contributed their time and expertise to assist in the Commission's examination of the complex issues which are of vital importance to families.

On behalf of the Commission I would like to thank the Minister for Social, Community and Family Affairs for his continued interest, encouragement and support and also express our appreciation to his predecessor Mr. Proinsias De Rossa, T.D., who set up the Commission and who encouraged and guided our first tentative steps.

I would like to thank the Department of Social, Community and Family Affairs for its continued generous support and help throughout, and in particular the secretary to the Commission, Catherine Hazlett and the secretariat whose contribution was invaluable.

On a personal note may I thank my fellow Commission members for their hard work, attention to detail and commitment, and particularly the balance and restraint which they brought to many complex and contentious issues. It was a privilege to work with them.

Dr. Michael Dunne
Chairman

# réamhrá

Is breá liom tuarascáil chríochnaithe an Choimisiún um an Teaghlach a chur i bhur láthair.

Ó bunaíodh i nDeireadh Fómhair 1995 é, d'fhéach an Coimisiún le trí chuspóir ghinearálta a bhaint amach, laistigh dá gcuid téarmaí tagartha féin.

Is é an chéad chuspóir ná paraiméadair a leagan amach maidir le Polasaí i leith an Teaghlaigh a cheapadh.

Is é an dara cuspóir ná eolas freacnairceach maidir le gnéithe de staid an teaghlaigh sa tír seo a chur ar fáil agus an méid sin a chur i gcomhthéacs idirnáisiúnta san áit ar cuí sin.

An tríú cuspóir ná mionanailís agus measúnú a dhéanamh ar na hábhair a tháinig chun cinn san iliomad aighneachtaí a chuir an pobal ar fáil agus fós tar éis dúinn dul i gcomhairle le saineolaithe agus le dreamanna ar suim leo an t-ábhar.

Faoi bhun ár gcuid téarmaí tagartha, rinneamar roinnt taighde a léiríonn conas atá an scéal náisiúnta maidir le cúram leanaí san aoisghrúpa faoi dhá bhliain déag, taighde nua shuntasach. Den chéad uair riamh, tá eolas againn ar na socruithe atá i bhfeidhm maidir le cúram leanaí, an líon leanaí a fhreastalaíonn ar crèches agus ar naíonraí agus an líon sin a bhfuil aire á tabhairt dóibh ag daoine muinteartha agus ag feighilithe leanaí. Táimid den bharúil go mbeidh tionchar nach beag ag an eolas seo ar cheapadh polasaí sa réimse.

Chomh maith leis sin, rinneadh taighde a chaith súil siar ar fhorbairt pholasaí i leith an teaghlaigh in Éirinn, taighde a raibh tionchar aige ar mhachnamh an Choimisiáin maidir leis na prionsabail ba cheart a bheith mar bhunús le forbairt pholasaí san am atá le teacht.

Anuas air sin tá saothar suntasach socheolaíoch ann maidir le ról an athar agus a pháirt i saol an teaghlaigh, in Éirinn agus go hidirnáisiúnta. Is dóigh linn go gcuirfidh seo go mór lenár dtuiscint ar na slite a fheidhmíonn an teaghlach, go gcabhróidh sé linn tacaíocht a thabhairt do chaidrimh laistigh den teaghlach agus na caidrimh sin a neartú, go háirithe ó thaobh pháirt an linbh de. Foilsítear coimrithe sách fada de na saothair seo sa tuarascáil chríochnaithe.

Ba dhána an mhaise don Choimisiún ligean orainn féin gurb ionann 'Tuarascáil Chríochnaithe' a thabhairt ar an gcáipéis seo agus a mhaíomh go bhfuil gach sórt curtha i gcrích. Níl an obair ach ina tús. Dá bhrí sin, is mian linn béim faoi leith a chur ar an gcaibidil sin de chuid na Tuarascála ina moltar struchtúir agus institiúidí a theastaíonn, dar linn, chun an obair a fhorbairt agus a chur ar aghaidh. Tá súil againn freisin nach mbeidh lucht ceaptha polasaí dall ar na prionsabail sin a gcreidimid gur cheart tacaíocht agus forbairt an teaghlaigh a bhunú orthu san am atá le teacht.

Tuigimid go bhfuil ábhair thromchúiseacha nach gcíoraítear sa Tuarascáil seo. Is é ár gcosaint ar aon achas á n a d'Èireodh as sin ná nach raibh an t-am againn. Mar sin féin, luaitear roinnt ábhar tromchúiseach nach raibh deis againn iad a phlé mar ba cheart, ach a mbeidh gá le tuilleadh oibre a dhéanamh orthu amach anseo.

Le linn aimsir olltoghchán 1997, bhíothas ar aon aigne maidir leis an ngá a bhí ann go mbeadh cabhair don teaghlach go hard ar chlár oibre gach páirtí polaitiúil. Thaitin an méid sin leis an gCoimisiún agus ba ábhar misnigh againn na dualgais nua a cuireadh ar an Roinn Gnóthaí Sóisialacha, Pobail agus Teaghlaigh maidir leis an teaghlach de.

Is iomaí dream a nocht a gcuid barúlacha agus a sheol aighneachtaí faoi bhráid an Choimisiúin. Chuir siad go mór lenár dtuiscint ar na rudaí is mó a bhíonn ag cur imní ar theaghlaigh inniu. Gabhaimid buíochas le gach duine as ucht an ama a chaith siad agus an taithí a roinn siad leis an gCoimisiún.

Táimid faoi chomaoin mar an gcéanna don iliomad saineolaithe a chaith a gcuid ama go fial agus a roinn a gcuid eolais leis an gCoimisiún agus muid ag fiosrú na n-ábhar ilghnéitheach úd atá barrthábhachtach i saol an teaghlaigh.

Ar son an Choimisiúin, ba mhaith liom buíochas a ghabháil leis an Aire Gnóthaí Sóisialacha, Pobail agus Teaghlaigh as ucht na spéise a léiríonn sé i gcónaí, an spreagadh agus an tacaíocht a thugann sé dúinn agus fós ár mbuíochas a chur in iúl don té a tháinig roimhe, an tUas Proinsias De Rossa, a bhunaigh an Coimisiún agus a spreag is a threoraigh muid sna laethanta tosaigh.

Ba mhaith liom fós mo bhuíochas a chur in iúl don Roinn Gnóthaí Sóisialacha, Pobail agus Teaghlaigh as ucht na tacaíochta falithiúla a thug siad dúinn ón tús, agus go háirithe rúnaí an Choimisiúin, Catherine Hazlett agus an rúnaíocht sin a raibh páirt chomh láranach acu san obair.

Ar mo shon féin, ba mhaith liom buíochas a thabhairt do mo chuid comhbhall ar an gCoimisiún as ucht na dianoibre agus an dua a chaith siad le gach mionghné den obair. Molaim go háirithe an stuaim agus an fhoighne a léirigh siad agus iad ag plé le hábhair chonspóideacha, ilghnéitheacha. Ba onóir bheith ag obair lena dtaobh.

*Michael Dunne*

An Dr. Michael Dunne
Cathaoirleach

# acknowledgements

In the preparation of this report, the contribution of many individuals has to be acknowledged.

The Commission wishes to thank all those who made submissions, individuals, families and organisations. These have made an important contribution to the Commission's work.

The Commission would like to thank in particular the Minister for Social, Community and Family Affairs, Mr. Dermot Ahern, T.D. and the former Minister for Social Welfare, Mr. Proinsias De Rossa, T.D. who established the Commission.

The Commission gratefully acknowledges the assistance of government departments and their agencies in its examination of the policies and programmes which impact on families, in particular the departments of Social, Community and Family Affairs, Education and Science, Health and Children and Justice, Equality and Law Reform whose Ministers were represented on the Commission.

Many people generously gave of their time and expertise to the Commission.

Dr. Anne McKenna, Psychologist, EU Network for Childcare; Ms. Nóirín Hayes, Dublin Institute of Technology; Mr. Robbie Gilligan, Senior Lecturer in Social Work and Head of Department, Trinity College Dublin, Mr. Barry Cullen, The Childrens Centre, Trinity College Dublin, Dr. Margret Fine-Davis, Trinity College Dublin; Dr. Finola Kennedy, Professor William Duncan, University of Dublin, Dr. Eileen Drew, Trinity College Dublin , Dr Carol Fitzpatrick, Dr Sean Denyer, Ms. Maureen Gaffney, and Dr. Michael Creedon, Johns Hopkins University U.S.A.

Mr. Brian Kenny, Mr. Owen Keenan, Ms. Grainne Burke, Barnardos; Ms. Patricia Murray, National Childminders Association, Dublin, Ms. Margaret Dromey and Ms. Margot Doherty, TREOIR, Federation of Services for Unmarried Parents and their children, Mr. Frank Brady and Ms. Elizabeth Agnew, Legal Aid Board; Ms. Rosemary Horgan, The Law Society of Ireland; Mr. Gerard Hogan, Senior Counsel; Bar Counsel of Ireland ; Dr. T.K. Whitaker (Chairman), and Mr. John Conlon (Assistant Secretary), Constitution Review Group,; Ms. Regina Martin, Irish Countrywomen's Association; Ms. Ceridwen Roberts, Director, Family Policy Studies Centre, London. Mr. Bob Carroll, National Council on Ageing and Older People; Ms. Berni Brady, AONTAS, Ms. Siobhán Lynam, Area Development Management Limited; Ms. Eileen Proctor, Life President, National Association of Widows in Ireland; Ms. Norah Gibbons and Ms. Geraldine French, Barnardos. The Commission also thanks the Health Boards and the Community Care Programme Managers, who offered advice and guidance in relation to family support services. Officers of the health boards were most helpful, in particular the Commission would like to thank Mr. Pat Dolan and Mr. Brian O'Donnell of the Western Health Board, Ms. Máire Bolger (Community Mothers), Ms. Yvonne Milner, Sr. Eileen Mullin and Ms. Chris Byrne, Parenting Skills Unit, Eastern Health Board and many others who gave advice.

Mr. Hugh Frazer, Ms. Joan O' Flynn Combat Poverty Agency, advised the Commission about poverty issues. The Honorary David Wotton MP, (South Australia) Minister for the Environment and Natural Resources, Minister for Family and Community Services and Minister for the Ageing; Mr. Steve Ramsey, Director, Office for Families and Children, (South Australia); Mr. Michael Player (Department of Social Welfare, New Zealand) gave valuable information on family initiatives from Australia and New Zealand.

Ms. Tina Roche and Ms. Marie Bourke of the National Gallery of Ireland, arranged the exhibition of the winning entries in the Transition Year competition on family studies on UN Day of Families 1997.

Dr. Edmund McHale, Clanwilliam Institute; Mr. Ed Boyne, Ms. Daria Parke, Irish Association for Counselling and Therapy; Ms. Ruth Barror, Marriage and Relationship Counselling Services Ltd.; Mr. Colm O' Connor, Cork Marriage Counselling Centre; Fr. Daniel Cavanagh, Mr. Eamonn McElwee, ACCORD; Mr. Peter Kieran, St. Catherine's Community Services Centre, Carlow; Ms Jane McColgan, AIM Family Services; Ms. Kathleen Kelleher, Teen Counselling, Mater Dei Counselling Centre; Ms. Joan Srennan, Clinical Psychologist and Counsellor, Dr. Gabriel Kiely, UCD and Mr. Barre Fitzpatrick, gave assistance in framing recommendations in relation to the future development of the marriage and relationship counselling services.

Many individual civil servants have made a significant contribution to the Commission's examination of policies and programmes for families. These include Mr. Gerry Mangan, Ms. Anne McManus, Ms. Anne Vaughan, Mr. Liam Walsh, Mr. Deaglán Ó Briain, Ms. Bernadette Lacey, Mr. Cyril Havelin, Mr. Brian Ó Raghallaigh, Mr. Brian Flynn and Ms. Deirdre Hogan, Ms. Mary Lynam, Ms. Doreen Keenan, Department of Social, Community and Family Affairs; Mr. Paul Haran, Ms. Melanie Pyne and Mr. Pat Nolan Department of Enterprise, Trade and Employment; Mr. Dominic Kelly, Mr. Michael Gleeson, Ms. Sylda Langford, Ms. Margaret O' Connor, Mr. Mairtín De Burca and Mr. Donal Costello, Department of Justice, Equality and Law Reform. Ms. Mary Moylan, Mr. Tom Corcoran, Mr. Joe Allen Department of the Environment and Rural Development.

Mr. Noel Usher, Mr. Bernard Carey, Dr. Ruth Barrington, Ms. Frances Spillane, Ms. Moira Staunton, Mr. Joe Gavin and Mr. Fergal Goodman, Department of Health and Children; Ms. Deirdre Fitzsimons, Public Health Nurse, Department of Health and Children; Mr. Dermot McCarthy, Ms. Mary Doyle, Department of an Taoiseach; Mr. Joe Mooney, Department of Finance.

The Commission thanks Ms. Mary Lloyd and Ms. Eileen Fitzgerald of the Family Mediation Service, and Ms. Leonie Lunny and Ms. Eva Creely of the National Social Service Board, and Mr. Dermot

Quish, Ms. Phil Halpin, Ms. Máire Corkery, Ms. Heather Faris, Ms. Lynda O' Toole, Mr. Billy Reidy and Ms. Maura Clancy Department of Education and Science, for their time and expertise in developing the module on family studies for Transition Year students; Mr. Albert Ó Ceallaigh, National Council for Curriculum and Assessment; Mr. Colm O' Maoláin and Ms. Concepta Conaty, Department of Education and Science for their contribution in relation to educational disadvantage and Ms. Anne Nolan who assisted the Commission.

Many other people sent helpful information. To these people and the many others who assisted in different ways the Commission extends its gratitude. Thank you all.

part 1

**Commission on the Family**

The Commission on the Family, its terms of reference and membership and the approach it has taken to completing its task.

## 1.1 Background

The Commission on the Family was established by the Minister for Social Welfare in October 1995

*" to examine the effects of legislation and policies on families and make recommendations to the Government on proposals which would strengthen the capacity of families to carry out their functions in a changing economic and social environment."*

The setting up of the Commission followed a series of initiatives at national and international level which brought about a new awareness of the changing role of families and the challenges they are facing in today's society.

In Ireland, the successful UN designated International Year of the Family in 1994 was the catalyst for much of this new focus on family issues. Events to mark the UN year in Ireland were co-ordinated by a National Steering Committee comprising representatives of organisations with an interest in families. [1] At a national level, the Oireachtas set up the Joint Committee on the Family. At an international level, the concerns expressed in the context of the UN International Year of the Family carried through to the UN World Summit for Social Development in 1995. The plan of action which followed contained a number of commitments regarding the obligation of the State to help families in their education, support and nurturing roles.

The work of the Commission received a new impetus when the Government, on taking office in June 1997, expanded the remit of the Department of Social Welfare to make family policy and family services central to its activities. The new title of the Department of Social, Community and Family Affairs indicates the new role of the Department in reflecting a modern society in which the family and community are key elements.

The Commission very much welcomed the consensus in relation to the need to prioritise support for families across all parties in the lead up to the 1997 general election.

---

1   The National Steering Committee comprised representatives from Barnardo's, C.O.F.A.C.E., Combat Poverty Agency, Department of Social Welfare, E.U. Childcare Network, TREOIR Federation of Services for Unmarried Parents and their Children, International Federation for Home Economists, Irish Association of Social Workers, Irish Countrywomen's Association, National Parents Council -Post Primary, St. Angela's College of Education for Home Economics (Sr. Anne Harte-Barry), Catholic Marriage Advisory Council, Clanwilliam Institute, Council for the Status of Women, Disability Federation of Ireland, Family Studies Centre, UCD, Institute of Public Administration, Irish Congress of Trade Unions, Irish Farm Families Committee, National Council for the Elderly, National Parents Council - Primary, St. Catherines College of Education, Society of St. Vincent de Paul, Women in the Home.

## 1.2    Terms of reference

The terms of reference of the Commission were wide-ranging. They include examining how Government policies, programmes and services affect family life.

The terms of reference are:

- to raise public awareness and improve understanding of issues affecting families;

- to examine the effects of legislation and policies on families and make recommendations to the Government on proposals which would strengthen the capacity of families to carry out their functions in a changing economic and social environment. The Commission would also be expected to make proposals to the All Party Committee on the Constitution on any changes which it believes might be necessary in the constitutional provisions in relation to the family. Proposals involving expenditure should be as far as practicable costed;

- to analyse recent economic and social changes affecting the position of families, taking account of relevant research already carried out, including reports of Commissions (e.g. Social Welfare, Taxation, Status of Women) and relevant working groups (e.g. Expert Working Group on Integration of Taxation and Social Welfare, Anti-Poverty Strategy Policy Committee); and carry out limited research as necessary.

In carrying out its work, the Commission, while having due regard to the provisions on the family in the Constitution intended to support the family unit, should reflect also in its deliberations the definition of the family outlined by the United Nations.

The Commission will liaise with the Joint Committee on the Family.


## 1.3    Members of the Commission

The Commission, among its members, reflects the following areas of expertise:

- social policy, specifically in health, education and social welfare
- family law, mediation, marriage and relationship counselling
- medical expertise at both G.P. and psychological level
- social work and community work
- economics, taxation and income support policies.

| | |
|---|---|
| **Chairman** | Dr Michael Dunne G P |
| | Former Chairman, Irish College of General Practitioners |
| **Professor Tim Callan** | Research Professor, Economic and Social Research Institute |
| **Ms. Deirdre Carroll** | Assistant Secretary, Department of Social, Community and Family Affairs |
| **Professor Michael Fitzgerald** | Henry Marsh Professor of Child and Adolescent Psychiatry, Trinity College, Dublin, Consultant Child Psychiatry, Eastern Health Board |
| **Mr. John Hurley** | Principal Officer, Department of Justice, Equality and Law Reform |
| **Ms. Yvonne Jacobson** | Supervisor and Counsellor, Marriage and Relationship Counselling Services Ltd. |
| **Ms. Augusta McCabe** | Social Work Adviser, Department of Health and Children |
| **Cllr. Catherine Murphy** | Public Representative, Leixlip, Co. Kildare |
| **Ms. Marie-Therese Naismith** | Administrator, AIM Family Services, Family Law Information, Mediation and Counselling Centre |
| **Dr. Deirdre O' Keeffe** | Principal Officer, Department of Education and Science |
| **Ms. Gemma Rowley** | Co-ordinator Health and Social Education, Mount Anville School, member of the Council of Barnardos, Chairperson, TREOIR |
| **Ms. Clare Tuohy** | Psychiatric Social Worker, St. Loman's Hospital, Palmerstown |
| **Ms. Bridín Twist** | Former President, Irish Countrywomen's Association |
| **Ms. Anne Waters** | Waterford Area President, Society of St. Vincent de Paul |
| **Secretary** | Ms. Catherine Hazlett, Assistant Principal Officer, Department of Social, Community and Family Affairs |

Ms. Éadaoin Collins and Ms. Catherine Walker were members of the secretariat which was provided by the Department of Social, Community and Family Affairs.

---

Ms. Margaret O' Connor, Department of Justice, Equality and Law Reform attended on behalf of Mr. John Hurley from January 1998.

Ms. Augusta McCabe replaced Mr. Noel Usher and Mr. Bernard Carey, Department of Health and Children, November 1996.

Ms. Mary Nolan of the ICA attended on behalf of Ms. Bridín Twist from May 1997.

## 1.4 Approach to the task

The Commission met at least once a month since it was established, with more frequent meetings of working groups. Much of the detailed work was initially prepared for the Commission by working groups comprised of Commission members with relevant expertise.

The Commission developed practical liaison arrangements with the Joint Committee on the Family, established by the Oireachtas in 1995.[2]

Early on, the Commission adopted an open and inclusive approach to its work. The objective was to encourage participation by those who have an interest in families and the challenges they are facing today.

The Commission received 536 submissions from every part of the country. The majority of submissions were from individuals, families and small groups. National organisations that work with families and voluntary and community groups also made submissions. The overriding concern of families and organisations was to promote family life and tackle the problems families are facing. Submissions acknowledged the partnership role among families, the statutory services and the voluntary sector in achieving these objectives. There was unanimous acknowledgement of the importance of families to society. People wrote about changes in society and in individual values and the impact these could have on families. A summary of the issues arising in the submissions made to the Commission is contained in Part 8 of this report.

Leading experts in the fields of family law, the Constitution, child care and services for children, employment and workplace policies, poverty and healthcare made valuable contributions to the Commission's work. In addition, there were a number of oral submissions made to the Commission at the Forum held to celebrate UN International Day of Families in 1996.

The Commission welcomed the many excellent submissions received and was pleased to have the contributions from experts. The Commission would like to express its gratitude to everybody who took the time and trouble to contribute to its work in a positive way.

## 1.5 Interim Reports

In November 1996, the Commission submitted an Interim Report to the Government. This report, sets out the progress in the work of the Commission at that time, a summary of the issues and concerns raised in the submissions received by the Commission and some preliminary recommendations.

In October 1997, the Commission made a submission to the Minister for Social, Community and Family Affairs in advance of the 1998 budget. The submission contained extracts from the draft final report and a number of recommendations which were brought forward for the consideration of the Government in the preparations for the 1998 budget. In preparing the submission, the Commission was considerably encouraged by the new remit of the Department of Social, Community and Family Affairs and the new responsibilities which it had been given in developing family services.

---

2    The term of office of the Committee ended in March 1997.

The Commission welcomed the Government's response to the recommendations in the pre-budget submission. In the 1998 budget, the following additional provision was made:

- £700,000 was allocated in 1998 for the phased introduction of Family and Community Services Resource Centres (25 centres in 1998)

- funding was allocated for a pilot programme for the transformation of local offices of the Department of Social, Community and Family Affairs, building on the one-stop-shop concept, to provide families with improved services at local level

- an allocation was provided for the introduction of an information programme on parenting and family issues by the Department of Social, Community and Family Affairs

- an additional £600,000 was allocated for marriage counselling services

- an extra £600,000 was allocated for the Family Mediation Service, to extend the service

- provision was made for the establishment of a Family Affairs Unit in the Department of Social, Community and Family Affairs.

### 1.6    Family Policy-Some findings[3]

In this report the Commission makes the point that family policy has never been co-ordinated or separately identified in any way. There are a range of policies in relation to families. Mostly these relate to provision for an individual family member with recognition of the dependency aspect of family relationships. Different policies cover social welfare, health services, child protection and family law.

These policies can be described under two broad headings. The first is *resource distribution:* that is the allocation of material resources or services to families. Resource distribution can be designed to serve a range of purposes including promoting social equity and supporting minimum living standards. This includes child benefit, one-parent family payment, social housing or programmes to address certain kinds of family problems. The second major form of State action is the regulation of family matters. This includes the legal rules governing family practices such as the law on marriage, marital breakdown and family property legislation.

The different policy areas are united by virtue of their common relevance in the lives of families. The responsibilities for them rest with various government departments.

In this report, the Commission makes the point that, while separately different areas of policy can be effective in meeting distinct needs of families, *the individuality and the different objectives which underpin policies mean that in particular situations the impact of various policies may not promote family well-being in the most effective way* (e.g. the dependency status of one partner in social welfare households and the disincentives in relation to joint parenting of children in the social welfare system). Neither are existing

3    This section draws on research work undertaken by Tony Fahey of the ESRI for the Commission on the Family. See Chapter 17.

structures designed to respond to new and emerging needs; for example, the need for parent education and information in local communities.

## 1.7 The need to clarify the objectives

The Commission suggests that this lack of coherence and clarity of objectives in relation to family policy should be rectified so that the valid role of the State in supporting family life and in promoting family well-being can be more effective.

As a first step, the Commission considers that the *foundations of family policy,* the *principles* and *objectives* which underlie and guide it *need to be set out clearly.* What the State is trying to achieve for and with families - the strategic dimension of family policy - should be clarified and made explicit.

Second, the Commission considers that there is a need to *strengthen the institutional framework of family policy* so that the various manifestations of family policy acquire a greater degree of coherence and rationality.

## 1.8 Principles to underpin the development of family policy

The Commission has presented for consideration a number of "principles ", which in its view are fundamental to the development of a coherent, progressive and effective family policy. These principles can be explained as the essential truths about families which should underlie the formulation of policy in relation to families. The principles have been developed through research work[4] undertaken on behalf of the Commission. They have emerged from a process of clarification and they draw on the overwhelming desire of the hundreds of families who wrote to the Commission to promote family life and tackle the problems families are facing.

The "principles" are:

### Principle No. 1
Recognition that the family unit is a fundamental unit providing stability and well-being in our society.

### Principle No. 2
The unique and essential family function is that of caring for and nurturing all its members.

### Principle No. 3
Continuity and stability are major requirements in family relationships.

### Principle No. 4
An equality of well-being is recognised between individual family members.

### Principle No. 5
Family membership confers rights, duties and responsibilities.

---

4    "Family Policy in Ireland, a Strategic Overview", from a report to the Commission on the Family by Tony Fahey of the ESRI. An abstract of the report is contained in Chapter 17.

**Principle No. 6**
A diversity of family forms and relationships should be recognised.

The extent to which these principles are supported in policies and services for families has been an important indicator for the Commission of whether or not family well-being is central to thinking in the formulation of policy.

**1.9    An overall objective of family well-being**

An important conclusion of the Commission's examination is that a new approach to policy formulation based on co-ordination, where responsibilities are spread across a number of agencies, would enhance the effectiveness of state policy working towards an overall objective of family well-being. Co-ordination and collaboration between state and community services at local level where services are delivered would go a long way towards achieving desirable outcomes for families. Moves towards a customised service for individual families (a "case management approach") and a focus on outcomes (i.e. family well-being) as well as outputs (i.e. the delivery of a service) are features of a radical reform of public services in New Zealand and Australia; countries which are considered to be at the forefront of public services reform. The refocusing of policies and services to achieve improved outcomes for families will involve exciting new ways of working with families and with their communities for the State agencies.

**1.10    A strong institutional framework for families**

It is the Commission's view that the success of this radical new approach to family well-being depends on a strong institutional framework, within which the State's response to families in the future can be developed and delivered.

In Chapter 24 the Commission sets out its views as to how this might be achieved through singling out family well-being as a matter of critical importance to the Government Programme and in the Houses of the Oireachtas; and the establishment of a Family Affairs Unit in the Department of Social, Community and Family Affairs.

The Commission proposes that the Family Affairs Unit would co-ordinate and facilitate the effort across different departments and agencies, including the voluntary and community sector, to achieve shared objectives in relation to the outcome for families. It is envisaged that the Unit will be responsible for pursuing the work in support of families initiated by the Commission and that it will provide a forum for raising awareness about the new and emerging needs of families into the new century.

Critical to placing families centre stage is the adoption by Government of a Family Impact Statement[5] which would set out clearly the consequence of policies, programmes and services for families in all major fields of Government activity, central and local. The Family Impact Statement would serve to highlight awareness of how Government affects families and would be a means of auditing the impact of programmes and services on family life.

5    See Chapter 24 for the Commission's recommendations in relation to the introduction of a Family Impact Statement.

## 1.11    This report - the beginning

In its final report to the Government, the Commission has concentrated on the welfare of children and vulnerable families and how public policy can best strengthen and support families in carrying out their important functions. It is the Commission's view that a task such as theirs is the beginning. The report therefore aims to lay the foundations of future policy development to strengthen families in our society.

The report contains the findings of the Commission following examination of the issues affecting family life. The overall thrust of the Commission's recommendations centres on the need for public policy to focus on **preventive and supportive measures to strengthen families in carrying out their functions.**

The Commission's main findings and recommendations are presented in terms of desirable outcomes for families. The pursuit of these desirable outcomes are the core themes of this report. They relate to:

- **Building strengths in families (Part 2)**
- **Supporting families in carrying out their functions - the care and nurturing of children (Part 3)**
- **Promoting continuity and stability in family life (Part 4)**
- **Protecting and enhancing the position of children and vulnerable dependent family members (Part 5)**

The Commission sets out its views on the **policy approach** which should be pursued in the various areas in the years ahead. Some preliminary recommendations are also presented in terms of **making a start.**

Other family concerns which were raised in submissions to the Commission and the importance of acknowledging the Irish Diaspora as part of the wider Irish family are explored in Part 6. Part 7 gives an overview of the research projects relating to aspects of family life in Ireland today which were undertaken by the Commission. Highlights of the Commission's programme to promote awareness about the issues affecting families are contained in Part 8. The Commission's views in relation to the family provisions in the Constitution are set out in Part 9. Part 10 contains the Commission's recommendations in relation to putting in place strong institutional mechanisms to follow the work of the Commission and to pursue an overall objective of strengthening families for life.

part 2

**Building strengths in families**

**Desired outcome:**

- The well-being of children and families who are managing in difficult circumstances.

**To be achieved through:**

- Greater investment in Family and Community Services Resource Centres funded by the Department of Social, Community and Family Affairs
- A refocusing of social welfare services to provide a "customised" local service for families in their own communities
- A priority for family support services at a preventive level.

**In Part 2 the Commission examines:**

- The potential of Family and Community Services Resource Centres for empowering and strengthening families and building capacities within local communities.
- The transformation of social welfare local offices building on the "one stop shop" concept to provide a gateway to a range of services for families.
- The prioritisation at policy level and in the health boards of family support services at a preventive level.
- The potential of the school setting as a focal point for the delivery of health and social services for children and their families.

# Overview of Part 2

**The Commission has a particular concern to prioritise the needs of families that are trying to do the best they can for their children in difficult circumstances. These circumstances may arise because of unemployment or low incomes, parenting alone or living in communities that are contending with social and economic disadvantage.**

In Part 2 of the report, the Commission discusses ways of supporting these families by meeting their specific needs and the role of local community based responses in building strengths in families.

The Commission notes the gap in current provision in relation to supporting community based responses to families' needs and makes recommendations for the development of a nation-wide network of Family and Community Services Resource Centres through the expansion of the existing programme administered by the Department of Social, Community and Family Affairs.

The Commission goes on to recommend that the development of Family and Community Services Resource Centres be matched by a refocusing of the State social welfare services to provide a customised local service for families, building on the concept of the "one stop shop" as a gateway to all services for families. The recommendation suggests that local offices of the Department of Social, Community and Family Affairs be transformed to provide this service to families.

Close co-operative links between the community-based Family and Community Services Resource Centres and the transformed local offices will underpin the provision of a programme of integrated and co-ordinated services.

The Commission considers the range of supports for families which have been introduced by health boards. These supports include the work of the family support workers, who provide practical support and guidance to families who are having difficulties in caring for their children and the work of community mothers helping new mothers in their child's early days. Other supports include programmes for adolescents aimed at raising self-esteem and social skills and support programmes in child behaviour management for parents.

The constraints in relation to the provision of more family support services at a preventive or developmental level provided by health boards are examined.

The Commission recommends that this type of family support, which is essential for families who are coping with considerable disadvantage, be prioritised and a mechanism developed to ring-fence resources, money and professional time for family support work at this level. The case for increased investment in the development of these family support services at a preventive level in the health boards is presented. The importance is highlighted of ongoing evaluation of initiatives and of encouraging the development of new responses to changing needs. Recommendations are made in relation to the extension of the Community Mothers programme in each health board area and for the extension of Family Support Workers to all areas.

The Commission makes recommendations in relation to strengthening the primary supports offered by the Public Health Nurse and the GP and highlights the potential of the community welfare officer in family support. In the main, the Commission's comments relate to the realisation of the potential of these services in an integrated and comprehensive programme of support for families.

The Commission highlights the potential of the school setting as a focal point for the delivery of a range of health and social services for children and their families.

**2.1    Introduction**

Family support covers a range of supports and services intended to meet the various needs of families.[1]

**Developmental family support** might include community-based services such as personal development groups for women and men, recreational projects, youth programmes, parent education or other adult education relevant to family living. It is in principle open to anyone encountering the ordinary challenges of parenting and family living.

**Protective family support** might include, for example, day fostering, refuges/support groups for women who are victims of domestic violence, and programmes in child behaviour management for parents encountering problems.

**Compensatory family support** might include high-quality day services for pre-schoolers from disadvantaged home circumstances or special programmes for youth in communities with high rates of truancy/ early school-leaving.

**2.2    Family support as a primary preventive measure**

In this chapter the Commission highlights the potential of community-based initiatives in developmental family support as a primary preventive measure which is capable of empowering families, through building on the capacities of local communities.

The Commission is informed in this approach by the literature, which supports the case for community-based initiatives to respond to families' needs and by the expert views it has received in relation to the future development of this aspect of family support.

Submissions to the Commission from expert agencies and from organisations that work with families were unanimous about the important contribution local community initiatives can make in promoting the well-being of families.

*"More resources for community-based projects which impact positively on family life."*

*"Time and resources to focus on developing and promoting structured programmes for families; e.g. peer led intervention and support for community groups."*

*"Self- help and non-professionally oriented mutual support networks that enhance and empower families."*

*"There is a need to rekindle neighbourliness and to rebuild and enhance its development."*

These are just some of the comments made to the Commission by professionals working in the field of family support.

1    The description in the following paragraphs is drawn from the chapter 'Family Support and Child Welfare, Realising the Promise of the Child Care Act 1991' by Robbie Gilligan in *On Behalf of the Child* Dublin: A & A Farmar, 1995.

## 2.3     Report of Task Force on Child Care Services

The potential contribution of community initiative in supporting families has been recognised in authoritative reference sources for some time now. The concept of Neighbourhood Resource Centres was first documented in the Irish context by the Task Force on Child Care Services (September 1980).[2] The Task Force saw the Neighbourhood Resource Centres as the focus of local and professional energies to serve the needs of children and their families. Its functions were described as mobilising community resources on behalf of children and their families by combining the resources of the community, voluntary organisations and statutory agencies to maximise their impact on the well-being of children and families in the area. Thus it was the Task Force's view that:

*"those who require help would receive that help in their own community without stigma and in a way which would build on, develop and reinforce family strengths and community ties, rather than undermine them."*

## 2.4

In the event, a number of local centres grew up organically in the 1980s. The majority of these centres were developed by national and local voluntary bodies, often with minimal grant aid or professional support and provision of premises by health boards or local authorities.[3] These centres[4] involve volunteers, social and community workers, childcare and youth workers, pre-school workers, Public Health Nurses and adult education providers.

## 2.5     Family and Community Services Resource Centres

In 1994, Family and Community Services Resource Centres,[5] providing community-based support programmes for families in disadvantaged areas which had developed in a number of communities, were taken into a new programme by the Department of Social, Community and Family Affairs (formerly the Department of Social Welfare). The programme consisted of 10 core projects[6] and over the 3-year period 1994 to 1996 the budget provided for support for the centres was £634,000.

A recent review[7] of the work of the centres illustrates the range of services on offer and the extent to which the centres are firmly rooted in their local communities.

---

2    Task Force on Child Care Services, Final Report to the Minister for Health, September 1980, Stationery Office, Dublin.

3    'From Prevention to Family Support' by Marian Murphy: in *Protecting Irish Children: Investigation, Protection and Welfare Administration*, Vol. 44, No. 2, Summer 1996.

4    Family Resource Centres- (health boards)

Some health boards are directly involved in running Family Resource Centres. Where these Family Resource Centres are in place, they provide a range of services, including mother and toddler groups, parenting courses, after school groups and teenage groups. They tend not to be community-based but directly run by health boards or are run under contract by voluntary organisations, such as Barnardos or the ISPCC.

5    Formerly known as Family Resource Centres.

6    See Appendix 1 to this chapter for a list of projects.

7    Family Resource Centres: A Report Commissioned by the Department of Social Welfare: June 1997: Stationery Office, Dublin.

Activities include personal development and leadership training courses, befriending courses, parenting courses, home management skills, arts and crafts and basic adult education. Centres provide limited childcare arrangements for participants using the centres and parent support. Some centres provide counselling and some have outreach programmes providing services to people who do not attend the centre. Urban centres attract 60 to 200 women to activities each week, while one rural centre attracts 400 participants a week. Centres have links with local schools and with the professional support services. Over 1,000 women and men a week attend seven of the centres.

The review found that centres are open and accessible and activities are organised in such a way that women and men feel welcome. Centres have built on local neighbourhood solidarity and support mutual care and self-help initiatives. They build on informal support networks and activities which develop spontaneously at local community level.

## 2.6 Potential of Family and Community Services Resource Centres in responding to family needs

The Commission is most impressed by the range of services provided by the centres. They are working with families in their immediate area and appear to be reaching a significant number of people in the communities they are serving. In one centre which the Commission visited, one in four mothers in the catchment area of the centre participate in activities. Support is available for families within "pram-pushing" distance. Activities affirm parents and families and their place in the community, while developing capacities for leadership in community development.

The Family and Community Services Resource Centres, while they are as yet under-developed in terms of resourcing and integration with mainstream and professional services, reflect a responsiveness to local community needs and a sense of community cohesion with an "open to all approach" which the 1980 Task Force on Child Care Services put forward as the distinguishing features of a centre of "community endeavour".

It is the Commission's view that the investment levels in the programme at £634,000 over a 3-year period supporting 10 centres have been modest and represent extraordinary value for money for state investment.

## 2.7 Recommendations of the Commission

It is the Commission's view that the approach to family support manifested by the Family and Community Services Resource Centres which is empowering of individuals, builds on family strengths, enhances self esteem and engenders a sense of being able to influence events in one's life, has significant potential as a primary preventive strategy for all families facing the ordinary challenges of day-to-day living, and has a particular relevance in communities that are coping in a stressful environment.

The Commission considers that a radical expansion of the Family and Community Services Resource Centres Programme would allow for the development of community-based projects for families throughout the country. It is the Commission's view that this is a development where state investment would be well directed to maximise the potential of this support service for families.

**The Commission recommends that the Family and Community Services Resource Centre Programme, administered by the Department of Social, Community and Family Affairs, be radically expanded to support a network of centres throughout the country. The initial target should be the establishment of 100 centres over the next 4 to 5 years.**

In pursuing the expansion of the programme, there should be maximum liaison with health boards in the light of their statutory responsibilities in relation to the provision of family support services.

### Costs

The eventual yearly cost of meeting the target of 100 centres based on current levels of support, averaging £20,000 per annum per centre would be in the region of £2 million. However, current levels of support are very modest. The Commission recommends that an allocation moving towards £4 million in year 4 or 5 for 100 centres would be more appropriate. This level of investment would allow for a mix of funding support, depending on the stage of development of the centres and the level of need in the catchment areas. It should also comprehend an amount for ongoing evaluation of the programme in the first 5 years.

An allocation of £700,000 in the 1998 budget will allow for the phasing in of the programme with 20-25 new centres coming on stream. This cost reflects the fact that centres will be at various stages of development and will require different levels of funding.

It is the Commission's view that, in the future, development of the funding allocations to fully established centres should allow for:

- a programme budget to help with the cost of activities and education programmes,

- the development of outreach programmes to reach families or groups who are isolated in communities and some local research on the needs of families

- an amount to meet the cost of overheads, such as light, heat and insurance

- an amount towards the cost of resource staff

The cost of equipment and securing facilities could be met on a "once off" basis from the allocation.

The Commission welcomes the allocation of £700,000 in the 1998 budget to expand the programme and provide new centres.

**2.8**     **The priority communities**

Priority areas for centres should be those areas where communities are contending with multiple disadvantages and where families are facing significant challenges in trying to rear their children and secure positive futures for them. These areas are mostly located in the large urban areas of Dublin, Cork, Limerick and Galway and on the edges of major towns, where there are few facilities for growing children and families generally are in poor social and economic circumstances. Rural communities, with their problems of isolation and population decline, should also be a priority.

Well-publicised initiatives in these communities to create a better environment for their children show an inner strength and sense of community cohesion which well-directed public policy can support and develop.

**2.9**     **Family support activities in the wider community**

Community-based initiatives, whether under the umbrella of the Family and Community Services Resource Centres or in other community projects, are an untapped resource in terms of the potential of local workers to provide after school provision and homework clubs, baby-sitting services and respite/recreational clubs. The development of more support groups for young mothers, parent support groups and toy libraries would provide an important source of help and guidance for families.

Many innovative schemes are emerging in the voluntary sector, such as "befriending" schemes, women's and men's networks, breastfeeding support groups and helplines for parents. The potential of such initiatives in the voluntary and community sector for integration into a comprehensive family support programme needs to be explored.

The Commission further recommends that family support activities and services within the voluntary and community sector should be regarded as an essential component of a comprehensive family support programme operated by the Department of Social, Community and Family Affairs. In this regard the Commission would like to draw attention to a need for support programmes for young men living in disadvantaged communities. Access to social networks through personal development programmes and parenting education and outreach programmes, as well as a concerted effort by services working locally to involve and support their participation in the life of the community, have an important contribution to make in enhancing the self-esteem of these young people and promoting their potential to be positive role models in their families and in the community.

**The Commission recommends that family support activities and services which are developing within the voluntary and community sector to meet specific community needs should be eligible for funding from a mainstream programme under the Family and Community Services Resource Centre Programme of the Department of Social, Community and Family Affairs.**

**The Commission would like to highlight in particular the need to prioritise new and emerging initiatives to promote the involvement and participation of young men in the life of their family and community.**

## 2.10　What works best - the importance of evaluation

The role of evaluation in this developing field is particularly important. In recent years there has been a mushrooming of community response projects. Government initiatives in support for community development projects and for women's and men's groups developmental programmes, together with the partnership approach (backed by the social partners at national level and funded through the local development programme) to tackling unemployment in areas of disadvantage, have been the catalyst for much of this development.

Policy-makers now widely acknowledge the role of community initiative and there is a considerable amount of experience among all the key players of inter-agency co-operation in support of community effort. There is much to be learned about what works best for families, for their communities and how the state services can support/facilitate and complement community effort by taking a strategic interest in the outcomes for families.

The Commission is of the view that the development of Family and Community Services Resource Centres should be informed by the results of continuous evaluations of the outcomes for families and their communities during the first 5 years of the programme. In this context, the Commission would like to highlight the importance of quantitative research to inform policy development.[8]

---

8　This point is referred to in Part 7 of the report.

# Appendix 1

**Family and Community Services Resource Centres**

Balally Family Support Centre, Dublin 16

Baldoyle Family Resource Services Centre, Baldoyle, Dublin 13

Ballyboden Family Resource Centre, Dublin 16

Ballynanty Family Resource Centre, Limerick

Boyle Family Life Centre, Boyle, Co. Roscommon

Cherry Orchard Family Resource Centre, Dublin 10

City Quay Project, Dublin 2

Killinarden Family Resource Centre, Dublin 24

St. Kevin's Family Resource Centre, Kilnamanagh, Dublin 24

St. Matthew's Centre for Families, Ballyfermot, Dublin 10

Chapter Three **Customised service for families through transformation of the local offices of the Department of Social, Community and Family Affairs**

**3.1     Introduction**

It is the Commission's view that the imaginative developments taking place at local community level in support of families should be matched by a refocusing of the delivery of state services at local level, to provide a new customised approach to meeting an individual's needs in the context of his/her family and community.

The new emphasis in the reform of the public services on the longer term effects of state policies and services on people and the commitment to excellence in services for the public suggests that this is an opportune time for a radical reappraisal of the delivery of state services to families.

**3.2     Services of the Department of Social, Community and Family Affairs**

The Commission considers that these objectives are of particular relevance in relation to the services provided by the Department of Social, Community and Family Affairs. That department has contact with people at every stage of their lifecycle through maternity payments, child benefit for almost 1 million children in 490,000 families and contact with active age adults who are working and paying PRSI, those who are employers or who are self-employed, those who are out of work or unable to work because of illness, and older retired people drawing their pensions.

Some 834,046 people, together with their families, are either wholly or largely dependent on weekly income support payments from the Department of Social, Community and Family Affairs.[1]

The Department's overriding day-to-day responsibility is to provide income supports to those who depend on its services. It is for these families that the introduction of a "customised" local service has the potential to transform the way the State responds to the needs of families.

**3.3.     A local service for families**

The Department of Social, Community and Family Affairs has a network of over 130 offices throughout the country. These include over 60 local offices and 71 offices which are run on a contract basis. All offices of the Department have information technology, allowing for ready access to up to date information about an individual's eligibility and entitlements and a speedier delivery of payments to people.

---

1     End June Statistics, 1997, Department of Social, Community and Family Affairs. This figure includes older retired people receiving pensions, families who are unemployed or unable to work because of illness or invalidity, carers of people who are unable to look after themselves because of illness or invalidity, as well as widows, widowers and lone parents raising children without the support of a partner, and parents rearing children on low pay.

## 3.4 Development towards the one-stop shops

In 1991, plans were launched for a major restructuring of the way in which social welfare services are delivered. Eight regional management centres were established by the Department to support a localisation of social welfare services and the introduction of the one-stop-shop - a move to expand the range of services available in local offices which traditionally dealt with unemployment payments - to provide a range of information and advice for pensioners, lone parents, people out of work and employers. Less frequent "signing on" for unemployed people and more flexible payment arrangements were introduced including post office drafts and payable orders. A programme was initiated to upgrade offices and information services to allow time for more individual attention and privacy for callers in their dealings with the Department.

Closer links with FÁS - the Training and Employment Authority, and local health board services and the development of new supportive relationships between local offices and voluntary and community groups were key objectives of a new customer focus and the localisation of the services.

Over recent years the Department has been making progress in relation to the one-stop-shop. Some of the larger offices now provide the main services envisaged in the restructuring plan.

The core services of the one-stop-shop are:

- **information and advice** about a range of social services.

- **income support,** with the Social Welfare Inspector (who assesses entitlements) and Deciding Officer (who decides on entitlements) on hand so that entitlements can be established with minimal delay and the Community Welfare Officer, available to assist with additional needs,

- **employment support services** (including FÁS) with Job Facilitators to help explore the options for returning to education, training or taking up a job or self-employment.

The services are underpinned by an **emphasis on information** about a range of state services, including income support, pensions, local authority and health services, revenue information and education grants.

At regional management level, supportive relationships are being developed with local community and voluntary organisations.

## 3.5 An integrated service - the next step

The next step is the development of a completely integrated service, encompassing all state services in the social service arena that is "a single local contact point for customers which would be the gateway to the full range of social services provided by the State".[2]

---

2   Interdepartmental Report on the Development of an Integrated Social Services System, Department of Social Welfare, August 1996, Government Publications Office, Dublin.

An integrated service would mean an end to the current, fragmented, benefit by benefit, department/agency approach to delivering income maintenance payments. For example, when a customer seeks unemployment benefit, his/her entitlement to all related schemes and services, a medical card, rent/mortgage assistance would be an integral part of the claim process. *The customer and his/her needs would be the focus, rather than the particular scheme.*

A properly organised and resourced information service has been identified as being critical to the establishment of the new service. Such a service would mean that customers making claims would be advised of potential entitlements to other social welfare and health board schemes, as well as any other agency's services which might be relevant. It would include direct referral to other organisations. At a minimum, customers would be given a contact name and address and the hours of opening of the service. Where possible, an appointment would be made.

Pilot schemes to test this concept have been underway in two Dublin local offices, Tallaght and Ballymun, and an Inter-departmental Committee[3] has recommended that the initiatives should be extended to other locations. The training of staff has been identified as the vital factor in the provision of a quality service.

**It is the Commission's view that the welcome decline in the numbers of unemployed people on the live register, which is still the main business of local offices of the Department, provides the opportunity for a new impetus and an acceleration of developments towards the provision of access to a complete range of services locally. The objective should be to introduce a new customised approach to meeting the needs of individuals in the context of their families and communities.**

**3.6    Transformation of local offices of the Department of Social, Community and Family Affairs**
The Commission proposes that local offices of the Department of Social, Community and Family Affairs be developed to provide a customised local service to families.

Building on the development of the one-stop-shop as a gateway to all services for families would require:

- A greatly *enhanced information service,* to provide comprehensive information to allow access for families to community and other local social services; for example, marriage counselling, family mediation,[4] parent education and local youth programmes, adult education, employment services and improved information services for older people and carers. The role of the National Social Service Board in the development of a specialised family information service would be important.

- Local offices taking on an *advocacy role* for individual customers where this is needed. Referral[5] and direction for further assistance or services would be a feature

---

3    Interdepartmental Report on the Development of an Integrated Social Services System, Department of Social Welfare, August 1996, Government Publications Office, Dublin.

4    Responsibility for support for voluntary marriage counselling services and the Family Mediation Service was transferred to the Department of Social, Community and Family Affairs in January 1998.

5    Including referral to the services provided by Family and Community Services Resource Centres.

of a "customised service".

- Close *links* between local offices and Family and Community Services Resource Centres and other agencies, including health boards providing services to families.

The objective is access to a comprehensive programme of services, including income support, employment and social and community services, in a convenient location to meet the needs of families.

### 3.7 Importance of staff training

Investment in the training of staff to provide a holistic and customised service to meet the needs of individuals and their families within their own communities is important in realising the goal of a better delivery of State services. The Commission endorses the recommendations of the National Economic and Social Forum[6] in relation to improved training for staff dealing with customers on a day-to-day basis. Training to improve the communication and interview skills of staff is an important prerequisite for the provision of comprehensive information to meet the needs of customers today.

### 3.8 Pursuing shared family and community interests

It is the Commission's view that the Family and Community Services Resource Centres have the potential to develop a unique competence in countering the *causes* of family stress and in responding to the needs of their own communities. The state welfare services, traditionally geared to respond to the *material effects* of family difficulties, have a strategic interest in building on this preventive approach by refocusing the delivery of services to provide a more integrated, customised service to meet the individual needs of families.

The key to the success of an integrated approach to the delivery of social and state income support services for families is close links between the main partners involved: the local offices of the Department of Social, Community and Family Affairs, the Family and Community Services Resource Centres and the health board services, including health board family supports, with an important role also for social work and psychiatric services. The fundamental importance of effective collaboration to the successful delivery of an integrated and holistic service to families at local level is clearly set out in a recent report of a pilot project to provide integrated services to a community in the north-east inner city of Dublin;[7] this was funded by the Department of Social, Community and Family Affairs.

The approach to collaboration suggested in the report provides a model for the relationship between the local Family and Community Services Resource Centres and the local offices of the Department of Social, Community and Family Affairs.[8]

---

6    Quality Delivery of Social Services, National Economic and Social Forum Report No. 6.

7    Common Goals, Unmet Needs: Meaningful collaboration in tackling social exclusion in Dublin's north east inner city: Integrated Services Initiative, Dublin, 1997. The report puts forward a model for a collaborative partnership between State and local community agencies, based on the findings in the north-east inner city project and research from abroad in relation to what works best.

8    Appendix 1 to this chapter sets out an illustrative model of the relationship between the partners and the range of services which might be provided to families.

- A local management committee, drawn from the Family and Community Services Resource Centres and the local offices of the Department of Social, Community and Family Affairs and other agencies providing services locally such as health board services, could promote the co-ordination of services locally; enhance community participation; identify the potential for further co-ordination or integration; and formulate a response to family and community issues which arise.

- At a policy level, the proposed Family Affairs Unit[9] would support the local committee in achieving its co-ordination and integration objectives, pursue inter-agency issues which arise, evaluate the effectiveness of the local initiatives and promote best practice by disseminating the results of local initiative and using them to promote further policy development.

It is the Commission's view that the new collaborative relationship between local community initiative and the providers of services to families on behalf of the State would bring new synergies to the pursuit of shared family and community interests.

3.9     **Realising the new vision of integrated services for families in their own community**
The Commission acknowledges that the development towards a customised service will have to be undertaken on a progressive basis. The priority of the Department of Social, Community and Family Affairs is and must continue to be the prompt and efficient payment of income supports to those who depend on this service.

The development in relation to delivering better services to people is already underway throughout the public service. The Commission's main objective in promoting this initiative is to influence the direction of development towards focusing on individuals in the context of their family and community.

It is the Commission's view that considerable progress can be made in the next few years. The infrastructure, in terms of technology and a network of offices throughout the country, is already in place, so the Department of Social, Community and Family Affairs is well placed to take the lead in developing an integrated service for families.

3.10    **A Pilot Programme**
It is in this context that the Commission puts forward its recommendation for a pilot programme.

**The Commission recommends that the Department of Social, Community and Family Affairs put forward a pilot programme for the development of local offices in a number of key areas to provide a range of services for families through the one-stop-shop. The transformation of local offices would be a first step in the provision of a programme of integrated and co-ordinated services for individuals in the context of their families and local communities and would complement the development of local Family and Community Services Resource Centres.**

---

9     See Chapter 24.

**Costs**

The Department of Social, Community and Family Affairs has indicated to the Commission that an allocation of £200,000 would initiate such a pilot programme. The Commission welcomes the allocation of £200,000 in the 1998 Budget to initiate the pilot programme in a number of local offices.

# Appendix 1

**A new approach to providing services for families**

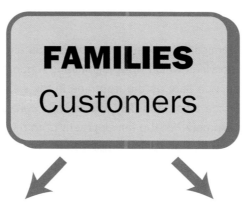

FAMILIES
Customers

Activities:
- budgeting & home management
- leadership & assertiveness
- counselling
- basic adult education
- parenting programmes

Family and Community Services Resources Centres

One-stop-shops for families

Local Offices of the Department of Social, Community and Family Affairs providing:
- customised services for individuals
- single contact point for comprehensive information
- income support
- employment and training
- access to services of other agencies

Management Committee
Local Social Welfare Offices, Family and Community Services Resource Centres, Health Board Services, Community Welfare Officers, Statutory Bodies, Voluntary Organisations

Supported by

Family Affairs Unit
Department of Social, Community and Family Affairs

**4.1**    **Introduction**

In this chapter the Commission examines some aspects of *family support* as it is being developed in the health boards. These services have a particular relevance for families coping with disadvantage.

In the course of the Commission's examination of various aspects of family support, it identified a number of services which offer significant support to families on a daily basis. While the social work service acts as the front line in the health board's response to child protection work, the service also has *a key role in child care and family support work* and is responsible, for example, for the development of the Family Support Workers scheme. Increasingly, child care workers are being employed in community settings and frequently work directly with children and families in their own home. The Commission offers some perspectives on the services provided by the Public Health Nurse, the GP and the Community Welfare Officer.

**4.2**    **The Child Care Act 1991**

The Child Care Act 1991 is the basis for the most significant changes that have taken place in the child care services since it was enacted. The focus of the Act is on the promotion of the welfare of children. It is specific in Section 3 as to the duty of the health boards to identify children, up to age eighteen, who are not receiving adequate care and protection and the promotion of their welfare, through the provision of "child care and family support services".

The Act places the child at the centre of the picture and states that, with due regard to the rights of parents, a health board shall

i)   regard the welfare of the child as the first and paramount consideration;

ii)  give due consideration, having regard to his age and understanding, to the wishes of the child and

iii) have regard to the principle that it is generally in the best interests of the child to be brought up in his own family.

These principles, set down in the legislation, underpin the basic tenet that the welfare of the child is to be paramount.

**4.3**    **Families and family support**

Family support is a term which is used to describe a range of services provided by health boards and other agencies to meet various needs of families. In more general usage, family support refers to a range of formal and informal arrangements which families draw on in managing their daily lives.

The primary source of support for most families is their own family and their friends. Relatives and neighbours are very important informal sources of support for parents. Grandparents may offer advice and guidance and may baby-sit or have their grandchildren to stay with them for a time, giving the parents a break. Studies in the north east inner city area of Dublin confirm the value that mothers attach to the support of relatives and neighbours and the practical help provided by grandmothers in advice and emotional support.[1]

### Families and support within the community

Mother and toddler groups, playgroups and formal school are important sources of contact and networking which can promote contact between parents and stimulate mutual support.

Community-based initiatives such as the health board Family Resource Centres and the development of the Department of Social, Community and Family Affairs funded Family and Community Services Resource Centres, providing basic adult education and personal development, parent support and youth programmes (which is recommended in Chapter 2) have significant potential for promoting positive support and as such are regarded as primary prevention strategies.

Family support thus has a broad meaning and is applicable to a very wide range of families. The term 'family support' is most commonly used to describe the range of initiatives which the health boards provide in complying with their statutory responsibilities under the Child Care Act 1991.

## 4.4    Implementing the Child Care Act 1991

The Child Care Act 1991 sets out the nature and scope of the powers and duties of health boards with regard to the provision of child care services. However, the Act does not specify the detail of what is required under the provision of family support. The context of the Act, however, suggests that the priority is to promote the welfare of children in vulnerable families and to minimise those circumstances in which a child might have to be removed from his/her family and placed in alternative care.

The formulation and monitoring of policy on child care and family support services by the health boards is the responsibility of the Child Care Policy Unit established in the Department of Health and Children in 1993. The Child Care Policy Unit is concerned with policy relating to the promotion of the welfare of children who are not receiving adequate care and protection, and with monitoring the implementation by health boards of the Child Care Act 1991. The Unit is also responsible for the formulation of adoption policy and legislation.

The Child Care Act 1991 provides for the establishment of a Child Care Advisory Committee (Section 7) in each health board area to advise the board on the performance of its functions under the Act. The Advisory Committee[2] is composed of persons with a special

---

1    "Common Goals, Unmet Needs", Integrated Services Initiative, 1997.

2    The main function of this committee is to:

-    advise the Board on the performance of its functions

-    consult with the providers of child care and family support services in the area.

-    report on child care and family support services in its area

-    review the needs of children in its area who are not receiving adequate care and protection.

interest or expertise in matters affecting the welfare of children, including representatives of voluntary bodies providing child care and family support services in that area.

## 4.5     Pressures on the childcare services

Over the past decade there has been an increasing awareness of and public concern about the abuse of children. Disclosure of both present-day abuse and abuse that occurred in the past has created phenomenal pressure on the health board services. This pressure has increased faster than services have been able to expand to cope. Consequently, child care developments, to date, have concentrated on the development of a child protection service to protect children who are at risk and children who have been subjected to abuse.

However, the range of children who are not receiving adequate care and protection, as set out in the Child Care Act 1991 is much wider then those who will ever come to the attention of the child protection services. Unsupported, the health and development of these children might be significantly impaired. The reports on the Kilkenny incest case, Madonna House and the Kelly Fitzgerald case have highlighted *the need for continued development of family support services and recognised prevention programmes as an intrinsic element of a comprehensive and integrated approach to the problem of child abuse.*

A short summary of some statistics from a Department of Health and Children 1996 survey of children in care underlines the extent to which the problems facing providers of child care services are much wider than reacting to incidences of child abuse. Only 45 per cent of children in care on the night of 31 December 1996 were in care under care orders. The primary reason for 46 per cent of admissions to care was that parents were unable to cope, were ill, or were addicted to alcohol or drugs. Physical, sexual and emotional abuse accounted for 17 per cent of admissions with neglect counting for another 25 per cent of admissions.

This is borne out by the recent research in one health board which found that "persons referred to the social work service, either for general reasons or specific child abuse and neglect concerns, are likely to be suffering both financial and material pressures, as well as significant family or personal difficulties. Despite the fact that both types of referrals appear to experience significant socio-economic and emotional stresses, it was found to be far more likely that clients referred in relation to child abuse and neglect would receive an ongoing service than those involved in general referrals." [3]

Recent research from the Mid-Western Health Board indicates that 45 per cent of referrals to child care services related to child welfare problems, i.e. there was no immediate threat of abuse but there was concern about the general welfare of the children. This concern arose from, inter alia, behaviour/ control problems, parenting problems and addiction/ alcohol problems. The Mid-Western Health Board research also shows that less than 50 per cent of cases investigated received any home services and that cases categorised as abuse (rather than welfare problems) were much more likely to receive services. The findings point to a shortfall in services, particularly services to provide direct assistance to families. In terms of the profile of families concerned, the research indicated that 46 per

---

3     Buckley, Skehill and O'Sullivan, *Child Protection Practices in Ireland* - A Case Study South Eastern Health Board. Oak Tree Press, Dublin, 1977.

cent of referred children lived in one-parent families and 75 per cent of families were on social welfare. This study reflects international research which links features such as poverty, unemployment and drug/ alcohol abuse with a higher risk of child abuse and points to supporting families at risk as the most effective way to prevent and reduce the risk of child abuse. The research highlights the desirability of a more holistic approach to families in need.

What this information makes clear is that there is a major child welfare issue to be tackled and one for which a child protection service can provide only short-term solutions. A key priority of the Department of Health and Children in developing childcare services is to build up the family support services so as to achieve an appropriate balance between child welfare and child protection.

A study carried out in the Eastern Health Board[4] has shown that 81 per cent of the 1996 child care budget was allocated to child protection activities The point has been made to the Commission that the intention would be that any additional resources coming on stream will be used to concentrate more and more on family support and prevention. These services would be delivered as part of an integrated and broad-based strategy to tackle social exclusion across a number of Government Departments.

**Comprehensive services - the longer term solution**
An effective, comprehensive and co-ordinated family support service is required to work towards a long-term solution.

In line with the above-mentioned reports and statistics, the health boards have been developing a broad range of family support services to meet the needs of vulnerable children.

Since 1993 there has been additional investment of some £50 million in ongoing funding for the development of services to implement the Child Care Act 1991. It is estimated that £100 million approximately is now allocated annually for the delivery of child care and family support services through the health boards. Over 900 new posts have been established in the child care and family services.

4.6     **Family Support Services - developments in the health boards to date**
All health boards have introduced programmes to meet their statutory obligations under the Child Care Act 1991. In the main, services are being developed which are aimed at preventing young people falling into the 'at risk' category and needing alternative care. Such services are targeted at parents and children and some examples of these services include the following:

• **Family Support Workers** have been introduced in a number of health board regions in recent years. The service is designed to *provide practical support and guidance to families who are having difficulties in caring for their children.* Children may range in age from toddlers to teenagers. Experienced mothers are recruited from the local community and undergo basic training before being matched to a particular family. The service is a preventive measure and is intended to support the family during difficult times to

4   Unpublished material supplied by the Department of Health and Children: EHB/ IMPACT Review Group.

31

maintain their children at home whenever possible. The service, which is home-based, is provided for a specific number of hours per week. It is co-ordinated by the health board social work department and can offer a range of possibilities from parenting skills programmes; confidence building and personal development; home care and management; diet, nutrition and healthcare to budgeting and family finance.

- The **Community Mothers programme** currently operates in some health board regions. The programme assists new parents by *offering support and guidance in their child's early days.* The children in the scheme are generally under two years of age. An experienced and sympathetic mother, who has been specifically trained for the programme, visits a family and provides advice and information on feeding, early education, health, language and child-minding. Important objectives of the programme include building up the confidence of parents and involving fathers more in the work and the life of the family and in rearing their children.

The programme has been evaluated and is proving to be highly effective. One report on the programme concludes that the success of the *Community Mothers* programme has come about because "parents have been supported to become better parents".

The programme is becoming well established in some parts of the Eastern Health Board region. There are about 150 voluntary Community Mothers involved, working with 1,200 families per year. They work under the guidance of a Public Health Nurse who is assigned as a family development nurse. Other health boards are interested in the initiative.

*Community Mothers* programmes have been introduced in the North Eastern, Southern, Midland and Western Health Board regions but the numbers of families catered for throughout the country are limited.

The *Community Mothers* programme is an example of a low cost, community-based initiative which could provide important supports to young families.

- Some health boards are directly involved in running **family resource projects**. *Family Resource Centres* tend not to be community run, but directly run by health boards or operated under contract by voluntary organisations. Where centres are in place, they provide a range of services, including mother and toddler groups, parenting courses, after school groups and teenage groups. Each centre has developed in a way that reflects the needs of the community in which it is located. Geraldstown House in Ballymun works with families and young people who are mainly referred by Eastern Health Board services. The Moyross project in Limerick works with referred families whose circumstances suggest that they require additional support.

- **Nursery Services** Annual expenditure by health boards in supporting centres which provided day care services for pre-school children is in the region of £2.7 million.[5]

5    Information from the Department of Health and Children shows that health board funding for pre-school services in 1996 was £2.7 million, with some 490 centres being involved.

Two main types of service are supported:

(a) Day **nurseries** where children are looked after for most of the day and provided with a midday meal (for historical reasons, these are mainly in the Dublin area) and

(b) **Playgroups** where children attend for a couple of hours per day once or more each week.

The policy of the health boards is to give priority to children whose parents are experiencing difficulty in caring for them or who are unable to cope because of medical or social problems. Provision is also made for children of lone parent families.

- A number of health boards are developing **community-based services for adolescents.** For example, the Western Health Board, in pursuing its approach to family support policy, has appointed a co-ordinator of adolescent and family support services. Work with adolescents is intended to strengthen their coping capacities at an age when they are vulnerable and provide practical support in addressing difficulties at home or at school. Parent support is also an important aspect of the work and helping parents to recognise and make use of their own sources of informal support provided by family and friends as well as the contribution of organised activities for teenagers in releasing parents for a time from demanding responsibilities are important aspects of developing services. The development of a "mentoring" programme for parents of adolescents has been suggested. This is a *community mothers* type scheme for the parents of teenagers.

- **Neighbourhood Youth Projects (NYPs)** work on the basis of building relationships with individual children and group activities. Parents are encouraged to be involved. To bring a resource to the community is an important objective. In Neighbourhood Youth Projects the emphasis is placed on *maintaining and supporting young people at school,* and encouraging participants to remain out of trouble and drug free. There are Neighbourhood Youth Projects in a number of health board areas.

4.7     **Moves towards a co-ordinated development of family and child services**
The significant increase in staffing in the child care service in the health boards has led to developments in the management structures. These include the establishment of the post of Regional Director of Child Care, one in each of the eight health board regions, to oversee the planned and co-ordinated development of the family and child care services. In addition, the introduction of the Child Care Manager posts at Community Care area (county) level and the planned introduction of Child Protection Committees at area level, are intended to promote a more effective and co-ordinated delivery of child care and family support services in each area.

It is proposed to establish a Social Services Inspectorate within the Department of Health and Children. The intention is that the Inspectorate would contribute to the development of national standards in good child care practice and, working in partnership with the health boards, would ensure a comprehensive national monitoring system for the child care services.

## 4.8   Prioritising Family Support Services

The Commission welcomes the health board initiatives with their emphasis on intervention and support in the early years of child rearing, with a view to strengthening families and preventing difficulties. It is the Commission's view that the approach to the development of family support initiatives must be flexible to meet the diverse needs of families at different stages in their life cycle. Some imaginative services are being developed in this context to support families that are coping with considerable disadvantage and to strengthen the coping and resilience of children and adults in relation to identified risks experienced within individual families.

**The Commission is firmly of the view that this aspect of family support work by health boards must be made a priority and a mechanism found to ring-fence resources, money and professional time for family support work at the preventive and developmental level.**

A number of issues arise in relation to the prioritising of family support work at this level.

**The allocation of resources and the optimal level of provision of family support services for those families most in need**

While all health boards have introduced family support services, the general view of those who have contributed their expertise to the Commission is that there are insufficient resources allocated to family support work at this level and consequently the level of provision of services for families is too low. With limited resources, health boards face an ongoing problem in relation to how to find the balance between their child protection responsibilities and their role in prevention.

A further difficulty arises for health boards in defining those children who are "not receiving adequate care and protection". The Child Care Act lists certain children in this category.[6] However, there are children who do not fall into these categories yet who are not receiving adequate care. Health boards find it more difficult to identify this wider group of children and therefore harder to make decisions about services and resources for them.

This dilemma is one of the major issues currently facing the health boards. It is an ongoing problem to find the balance between their child protection responsibilities and the necessity to develop family support services which will aid prevention.

**The role of other agencies**

One of the most important points which emerged from the Health Board study was the need to engage other key agencies in addressing, appropriately, the needs of children. The recognition of the importance of working together, towards a common goal, was emphasised. The Department of Health and Children through the Health Boards, and other Government Departments such as Justice, Equality and Law Reform; Education and Science; Social,

---

6   Section 8 of the Act in particular lists:

a)   children whose parents are dead or missing

b)   children whose parents have deserted or abandoned them

c)   children who are in the care of the board

d)   children who are homeless

e)   children who are at risk of being neglected or ill treated

f)   children whose parents are unable to care for them due to ill health or for any other reason.

Community and Family Affairs; and Enterprise, Trade and Employment, all have a role to play in achieving a more integrated approach to helping vulnerable families.

In this context, the Commission notes the recent decision by the Government to extend the responsibilities of the Minister of State at the Department of Health and Children, to include a co-ordinating function in relation to child care policy with two other Departments with responsibility for children: the Department of Education and Science and the Department of Justice, Equality and Law Reform.

### Evaluation of initiatives

There is a need to evaluate the effectiveness of family support initiatives for families in different circumstances. Health boards will need to build in mechanisms for the continuing evaluation of such initiatives.

Related to the issue of evaluation is the need for a greater exchange of information at each level about the effectiveness of initiatives, what works best in different situations and models of good practice. The Department of Health and Children has indicated that the proposed Social Services Inspectorate will have a role to play in assessing outcomes and disseminating information on best practice. It has been suggested to the Commission that a *newsletter produced by health boards and widely circulated among professional workers and practitioners in family support would go some way towards disseminating information and guidance about good practice.*

### Developing new initiatives

A further issue relates to the need for more innovative work in family support services. Policy in relation to the development of family support must encourage the development of new initiatives to meet the changing needs of families. A number of examples of innovative responses to different families' needs have come to the Commission's attention.

In one health board area, support services for adolescents are being developed as an intrinsic part of a family support strategy. This approach is informed by an increasing recognition by workers in this health board area of the importance of the informal support networks provided by family and extended family in young people's lives. [7]

### Commitment to prioritising the services

**It is the Commission's view that leadership and commitment to making a positive difference to the lives of vulnerable children and their families must be matched by a clear prioritising of family support work throughout the health services from policy level in the Department of Health and Children through to the health boards and their administrative offices.**

A prioritisation of this aspect of family support involves:

- the identification and establishment of clear objectives in relation to the level of provision of family support services by health boards and the allocation of resources to meet those targets

---

7    Based on an oral presentation to the Commission.

- the prioritising within the health boards of professional time and resources including financial resources for work at the level of preventive family support, so that they do not become dissipated in attaining other objectives and providing other services.

- recognition in the formulation of policy of the need for;
- **research** to prompt the development of new initiatives
- **co-ordination** in the development of services in family support, including services in other departments as well as the Department of Health and Children
- the **engagement of other key agencies** and departments in meeting the needs of children
- **evaluation of services** in terms of outcomes for families. This requires commitment to a specific budget to fund research and evaluation and to sponsor and pilot new initiatives in family support.

**Significant extra resources required for Family Support at a preventive level**

Notwithstanding the need to address these issues the Commission is firmly of the view that significant extra resources are required to develop family support services at the preventive level in the health boards. International research highlights the fact that supporting families at risk is the most effective way to prevent and reduce the risk of child abuse and is cost effective in the longer term. The point has been made to the Commission that, because of the urgency of providing an effective response to child protection concerns, to date preventive and family support services have had to take second place in the allocation of development funding.

**The Commission is of the view that an argument can be made, therefore, for significant extra resources, specifically for the expansion of family support services at a preventive level in all health board areas.**

The Department of Health and Children has indicated to the Commission that resources of the order of £50 million (i.e. £10 million a year over the next five years) would be required. The Commission suggests that the Department of Health and Children should explore the possibility of this level of investment over the next five years in the development of family support services at a preventive level in the health boards with the Department of Finance with a view to progressing this matter.

The Commission suggests that any future investment should include specific allocations for scientific evaluation of the effectiveness of family support measures in terms of outcomes for families, and for the development of new initiatives.

## 4.9 Dealing with family issues - the use of the family conference

The emerging interest in the use of the Family Conference[8] as an approach to dealing with family issues and crisis has been brought to the Commission's attention. This approach is

---

8   Family Conferencing, currently in operation in New Zealand, allows the extended family of a child at risk to become actively involved in decisions central to their lives. The process consists of meetings facilitated by a Care and Protection Co-ordinator and attended by a child/young person, his /her parents or guardians, members of the extended family and any other people the family group wishes to have present. This description is from Family Decision making, Family Group Conferences, Practitioners Views, Wilcox et al, New Zealand.

provided for in the Children Act 1997, which is concerned with reform of the juvenile justice system. In addition, a number of pilot schemes are under consideration in the health boards to incorporate the Family Conference into work with families where children are at risk and as part of an innovative approach to the placement of children with relatives in foster care arrangements. Using a Family Conference approach has the advantage of empowering the extended family (including grandparents) to protect and care for their own young people and of maintaining contact between the child and his/her family.

**It is the Commission's view that the piloting of new initiatives which incorporate the use of the Family Conference should be encouraged. It is also the Commission's view that the development of mechanisms for exchanging experiences and knowledge gained across the family support sector would assist in developing new responses to meet the needs of families.**

## 4.10 Irish research is needed

A great deal of research has been carried out abroad, particularly in the US and the UK in relation to the causes of family breakdown and the effects of social and economic dis- advantage. This work has formed an authoritative basis for initiatives abroad to secure improved outcomes in the longer term for families facing difficulties. Many such initiatives have proved to be adaptable to the needs of Irish families.

While there has been a very welcome increase in the amount of research carried out in Ireland since 1991, and this trend looks set to continue, there are still many aspects of child care which have yet to be examined.

**The Commission is of the view that those government departments concerned with family support policy should be allocated a budget to carry out innovative research in relation to the difficulties families experience in Irish circumstances and the responses required to meet their needs. The research budget would also allow for the funding of pilot projects which could be developed within a specific framework, drawn up on the basis of responding to an identified need in a community, with an emphasis on quantitative approaches.[9]**

## 4.11 The co-ordination and integration of services is important

Families themselves, experts, organisations that work with families, and professional workers in family support have all pointed out to the Commission the need to integrate the range of services available to families and to co-ordinate the delivery of those services.

The importance of addressing these issues and possible mechanisms to achieve a level of integration and co-ordination have been discussed in Chapters 2 and 3. Delivering services to families in a co-ordinated and integrated way need not be costly. It requires leadership in the management of state services at local level and in the responses of local community initiative and voluntary organisations that work with families at local level.

9    See part 7 of this report for details of the Commission's further views about the importance of research.

**37**

The Commission notes the establishment, within the health boards, of Regional Child Care Development Officers and the appointment at local area level of Child Care Managers. The aim of the appointment of these officers is to provide an integrated approach to the field of child care and family support.

## 4.12 Some specific family support initiatives to be expanded

The Commission is also making specific recommendations in relation to family support initiatives as follows:

### The Community Mothers programme

The Commission has already recommended that the *Community Mothers* programme should be introduced in all health board areas.[10] The Commission considers that to maximise the potential of the programme:

- objectives need to be set in relation to the appropriate (optimal) level of service for priority groups and

- targets should be set in relation to expanding the scheme to reach these groups.

**The Commission recommends that the *Community Mothers* programme be extended so that priority groups in all health board areas have access to the service. The Commission recommends that models of *Community Mothers* programmes used by health boards should be those programmes which have been evaluated.**

The *Community Mothers* programme is particularly focused on children's early development and nutritional needs. It is important that the model of support used is based on clear evaluated evidence of effectiveness. The Commission suggests that, in considering the introduction of an appropriate model of the scheme to suit their areas, health boards should be guided by the model of the *Community Mothers* programme which has been professionally evaluated and shown to be effective.

### Costs

The cost of the *Community Mothers* programme works out at £300 per family per year.[11] On this basis, the introduction of a programme throughout all health board areas to reach 10 per cent of children under age 2 (i.e. 9,743 children) would cost in the region of £3 million a year.

### The Family Support Workers Scheme

The Family Support Workers Scheme is designed to assist families with children, who may range in age from toddlers to teenagers, at times of crisis or in stressful situations. The scheme is well developed in the UK and Northern Ireland and its recent introduction on a limited basis into the Irish social services has proved to be a most effective family support. There is now evidence (from experience abroad ) to suggest that this scheme may be even more valuable in its preventive function and that placing family support workers with families before there is a crisis may be of more benefit in the long run.

10   *See Strengthening Families for Life*, Interim Report of the Commission on the Family, November 1996.

11   Based on information supplied by Eastern Health Board. Costs include volunteer Community Mothers' expenses, materials and the extent of the role of the Family Development Nurse in co-ordination and training.

**The Commission recommends that the Family Support Workers Scheme be extended to all areas and that its potential as a preventive measure be examined with a view to developing the service with that focus.**

In particular, the Commission recommends that special consideration be given to the funding of the further development of the Primary Health Care Project for Travellers, under which a number of women from the Travelling community have been trained as family support workers.[12]

Costs

The Department of Health and Children has indicated that the cost of developing the initiative, which would include placing the women with families as part of the family support service, would cost about £45,000 per annum.

4.13    **The Public Health Nurse Service**

There are 1,222[13] public health nurses employed in the public health service. The work of the public health nurse includes: services to mothers with a chronic illness, and to babies, infants, families with a member with a physical disability or a member who is seriously ill, to elderly people deemed to be "at risk", meaning that, without support, their health will deteriorate, and to people who are over age seventy-five.

A variety of other initiatives are also undertaken by public health nurses, including: health education in schools and in the community, parenting skills training, and pregnancy prevention with teenagers.

A much valued service

Submissions to the Commission described how the public health nurse is a much valued source of support and advice, particularly in the early weeks of parenthood, but also in relation to families with demanding caring responsibilities because of illness or disability. The importance of the Public Health Nurse in providing care to older people and supporting them in continuing to live at home was stressed in several submissions from families. Most people wanted to see more frequent visits and extra attention for these families.

Submissions from the professional services that work with families described the demands on the services of the public health nurse, spanning the spectrum through health promotion, prevention, treatment and care. It was stated that priority needs of people who require curative care impacts on the time available for family support and child health promotion.

---

12    The Primary Health Care Project is a partnership initiative between Pavee Point and the Eastern Health Board. The project was funded on an initial one year pilot basis (October 1994 - October 1995) in the Finglas/ Dunsink areas of Community Care Area 6, Dublin. Fourteen women from the Travelling community have completed their training under the initiative. The project is very much in line with the recommendations of the Task Force on the Travelling Community regarding access to health services. Specific objective of the project include:

- to increase Traveller awareness and knowledge of health issues

- to access and disseminate health information to the Traveller community

- to offer information, advice and support to Travellers to facilitate them in gaining access to health care.

- to provide skills training for Primary Health care to the Traveller women involved.

13    Statistics relate to 31 May 1996.

### Review of services

A review of the work of the public health nurse service is underway in the Department of Health and Children, in line with the strategies for improving health care set out in *Shaping a Healthier Future*. The work of the public health nurse is also under examination by the Commission on Nursing, set up in March 1997.

### Key role for the public health nurse service in family support

It is the Commission's view that the public health nurse service has a key role to play in family support. The public health nurse provides a service to children and families in prevention, health promotion, treatment and care, which includes family support and child protection.

The public health nurse has access to people's homes and is often the first point of contact for persons seeking health services. The service is provided in the family's own home, health centres, schools and other community settings. The child health service is offered free of charge to all families, irrespective of socio-economic circumstances. This contributes to the acceptability of a service which does not have the connotation of being a service which is problem related. The public health nurse is ideally placed to provide family support. In practical terms, this is a major part of her work.

The public health nurse service enjoys a well-deserved reputation for quality and excellence. It is a unique service and it is the Commission's view that the public health nurse service is a national resource. It is also the Commission's view that maximising the potential of the service in supporting families calls for an urgent and radical reappraisal of the focus of the service and how it is delivered.

### Maximising the potential of the service

The issues which need to be addressed have been identified in submissions to the Commission by professionals who work in the broader health services and by nurses themselves.

A significant issue relates to specialisation and development of a skill-mix approach to the provision of public health nurse services.

It has been suggested that it is no longer reasonable to expect any individual public health nurse to provide services for all problems and sectors of the population. Therefore, particularly in urban areas, individual nurses should be given the opportunity to develop a particular expertise, for example in family support, child healthcare, care of the elderly, or palliative and terminal care. To some extent this happens. The demography of particular populations dictates the main work of the public health nurse in that area. To acknowledge this and place it on a more formal footing would greatly enhance support for families.

The ancillary supports necessary for the public health nurse, such as home help and meals services, and community mothers services should be integrated into the service to facilitate a greater skill mix approach to services.

Further issues include:

- the need for ongoing training and development for nurses and for opportunities to enhance skills, including the observation of the parent-child relationship or opportunities to specialise in certain problems, for example sleep problems and enuresis [14]

- the need for information for families, carers of older people and professionals working in family support about the service and the role of the Public Health Nurse

- the need for clerical back-up for the service and the introduction of modern communication facilities such as mobile phones, and pager systems

- the need for flexibility in working hours and the development of 24-hour and week-end services where these are needed,

- the provision of an appointments system
  The home visiting child health service is generally provided by means of a "drop-in" service during normal working hours (9am to 5pm). With the increasing number of parents who work outside the home and of children in crèches or with childminders, it is clear that this approach is no longer an effective way of reaching parents. It has been suggested to the Commission that this calls for the introduction of an appointments system. Ineffective calls in some cases can be as high as one in three.[15] The introduction of some flexibility in working hours would facilitate mothers who work outside the home and promote greater participation by fathers.

- enhanced co-operation with other professionals working in the field.

The appropriateness of the *population basis* only criteria for the allocation of public health nurse services needs to be examined. It is suggested that criteria such as population profile, which takes account of the need in an area, would allow for a better match of resources with needs. Relevant factors might include the age profile and geographic spread, the population density, the socio-economic conditions and the community and social support available in an area.

Developments towards the introduction of a *team approach* to child health care, with a key role for the public health nurse should also be considered as part of a wider review in relation to the delivery of health services.

---

14   There are formal scientific studies showing how effective public health nurses may be in dealing with these problems.

15   In 1995, almost 1 in 3 calls by public health nurses in one Community Care Area in the Eastern Health Board area were ineffective i.e. no one was at the house when the public health nurse called. A pilot system instigated in a community care area showed that the situation could be improved, with a large reduction of ineffective calls and more effective use of nurses' time, according to *"Common Goals, Unmet Needs" Integrated Services Initiative 1997*.
According to information from the Department of Health and Children a pilot project on appointments carried out in 1995/96 in one community care area in the Eastern Health Board reduced the number of ineffective calls from 57% to 14.5% (in the Kilbarrack area) and from 44% to 11.25% in the Swords area.

The issue of *equity of service* provision to families and older people in remote rural areas also needs to be addressed. Families in remote rural areas require additional resources in terms of time and travel.

**The Commission is of the view that considerable improvements in the service could be pursued while the review under way addresses these issues. In particular, the Commission considers that improvements should be made in relation to the provision of information on the Public Health Nurse Service.**

Many mothers do not have sufficient information about the service provided by the public health nurse. The Child Health Review Group in relation to public health nursing and Child Care and Family Support Service (1995) have made a number of recommendations in relation to this area. These include:

- That public health nurses should have an *input at ante-natal classes* in maternity hospitals.

- That an *information pack* on the relevant community services should be given to the mother at the first ante-natal visit.

- That information about the public health nurse should be displayed at ante-natal clinics and classes. An *information leaflet* with details of health centres should be given to all mothers on discharge from hospital.

- Home visits should be concentrated in the first three months of a baby's life to facilitate rapport between nurse and mother and to better support first-time and breast-feeding mothers.

- To facilitate parents who work outside the home and to promote greater participation by fathers in the care of their children, *flexible working hours* for public health nurses should be explored.

**The Commission suggests that many of these recommendations could be introduced throughout the public health nurse service in the short term.** The introduction of improvements in information services would not be difficult. The average annual birth-rate is now 50,000[16] and, given the target population, it need not be costly to introduce improved information services for young mothers.

Carers of older people looking after a person with a disability also have needs for enhanced information about matters which are particularly relevant to their responsibilities, for example, other local support services, including home help and access to respite care. They also need reassurance about the caring responsibility which they are undertaking. The Commission suggests that enhanced information, for carers, about the public health nurse service should also be a priority.

16   Census 96, Principal Demographic Results, P 10, Average annual birth rate in the period 1991-1996 is 50,000.

## 4.14 The General Practitioner

There are at present 2,427 active general practitioners in Ireland of whom 1,324 participate in the General Medical Services Scheme. Each general practitioner provides an average of 130 face-to-face consultations per week.[17] Their distribution throughout the community and the comprehensiveness of the service they provide means that GPs are often the first port of call for families in times of crisis. This type of support is at present provided as part of the day-to-day work of general practitioners. Its effectiveness can be enhanced by the more formal integration of general practitioners with other family support services and in particular by improved liaison within the public health system. The GP units now functioning in each health board area would have a key role in developing this liaison and integration.

More information about the dynamics of families' behavioural problems and the impact of social problems on family life would enhance the GP's capacity to respond to the wider needs of families. The nation-wide continuing medical education network for general practitioners is attended monthly by over 70 per cent of general practitioners. It has been suggested that this would provide a suitable forum for disseminating general information on family issues. It has also been suggested to the Commission that vocational training for general practice should include studies in relation to family dynamics and behaviour to promote awareness of these issues to new graduates.

## 4.15 The Community Welfare Officer

Community welfare officers are employed in health boards on behalf of the Department of Social, Community and Family Affairs as the primary agents in the delivery of income support services. The community care service now employs over 400 community welfare officers who operate clinics at over 800 locations throughout the country.

The community welfare officers were introduced in 1977 as part of a newly conceived community welfare service. The service and its administrators, the community welfare officers, had two broad objectives.

It *first* aimed to relieve social distress and, where possible, to help prevent its recurrence by:

-   informing people of the statutory income maintenance services that were available and assisting them to avail of the services

-   where necessary, providing financial support through *supplementary welfare allowance.*

The *second* objective was to help determine eligibility for the health and welfare services administered by the health boards, which report to the Minister for Health and Children.

The community welfare officer was intended to form part of a localised community care structure with the aim of intervening in a multi-faceted way in the cycle of poverty.

---

17    Material from the National General Practice Survey, 1997, Irish College of General Practitioners.

### Supplementary welfare allowance

Supplementary welfare allowance was originally intended as a scheme of possible last resort for people - a safety net for those who had no income from any source or who had special needs. This combination of financial assistance with a community-based social service model was to distinguish the scheme from other income support services provided by the State.

The Department of Social, Community and Family Affairs is responsible for funding supplementary welfare allowance and providing overall policy direction and regulation, while the health boards are responsible for the recruitment of staff and other procedures.

The core objective of supplementary welfare allowance is to give immediate and flexible assistance to those in need who do not qualify under existing social welfare schemes. In this regard, supplementary welfare allowance is the statutory guarantee of a minimum income, below which no citizen is expected to fall. In addition to the basic supplementary welfare allowance payment, the scheme provides for: supplementary help for those whose needs are inadequately met under the main income support schemes; assistance with rent/ mortgage interest, supplements for special heating or dietary needs, back to school clothing and footwear allowances and assistance for those with exceptional or emergency needs. Exceptional needs include clothing, essential household equipment and assistance with other costs which might arise; for example, a funeral. These aspects of the scheme are administered on the basis of guidelines, and community welfare officers have discretion in relation to the assessment of the particular need and the appropriate response.

Demand for supplementary welfare allowance has grown since its introduction. The growth in demand for supplementary welfare allowance payments has severely impinged on the ability of the community welfare service to fulfil the community care role.[18]

### Some issues arising

The original vision for the role of the community welfare officer was that s/he would be community-based and could provide a flexible response to situations encountered in the community which they serve, including the provision of emergency income and material support, accommodation and referral to health specialists, such as psychologists and social workers as the need arose and was so identified by the Community Welfare Officer.

While that remains the stated role of the community welfare officer, the reality is that almost all their time is taken up with social welfare administration and assessing eligibility for medical cards to the exclusion of wider community care activity. Outside Dublin, about two thirds to three quarters of their time is taken up with the supplementary welfare allowance scheme, administered by health boards on behalf of the Department of Social, Community and Family Affairs, and much of the remainder is taken up with medical card processing. Community welfare officers in the Dublin area spend nearly all their time administering the supplementary welfare allowance.

18  In 1996 the scheme cost £136,708,000, compared to the 1987 cost of £31,920,000. During 1996, basic rate Supplementary welfare allowance was paid to 86,514 people; Rent and Mortgage Supplements to 95,224 people, while Exceptional Needs Payments were made to 91,532 people.

The social environment in which the supplementary welfare allowance scheme operates has changed radically since the scheme was initiated in the 1970s. The supplementary welfare allowance service is currently being computerised. This computerisation drive has transformed the community welfare officers'[19] working environment. Two major reviews of the supplementary welfare allowance scheme are planned for 1998. One will examine policy issues in recognition of the major social changes that have taken place since the scheme was set up. The other will examine operational issues in the light of changes which have taken place in the work environment of the community welfare officer.

### A key role for the community welfare officer in family support

**Community welfare officers are a vital resource in the wider welfare area, yet it appears that the best possible use is not made of these key people because of the burden of welfare administration work which they are obliged to carry out. It is the Commission's view that this is one of the key issues that should be examined in the forthcoming reviews.**

**In Chapters 2 and 3 the Commission has pointed to the need for a more integrated delivery of local services to families and the need for key agencies and services to adopt a collaborative approach to ensure that services are responsive to the different needs of families. The Commission suggests that its recommendations here should also inform the proposed review of the role of the community welfare officer in community care.**

### 4.16 Developmental health screening services for children

The priority given to preventive care for children is a key factor in determining their subsequent health status. The main issues to be considered are the best means of monitoring the progress of young children and identifying health problems as early as possible.[20]

The Public Health Nurse and the school medical screening examination have for many years been a key part of the health strategy to monitor the development of the child in infancy and early childhood.

The last review of child health services took place in 1967. Recommendations as to the most appropriate pre-school and school health services were made on the basis of knowledge and medical practice current at that time.

In recent years, certain elements of the services for children, such as the maternity and infant care scheme and the immunisation services, have been reviewed. A fundamental review of the other aspects of childcare services, such as pre-school and school services, was promised in the health strategy document. According to *Shaping a Healthier Future,* the aim will be to implement recommendations for the most effective service, in tune with modern thinking and practice in child health.

---

19  All Community Welfare Officers in seven of the eight health boards now operate exclusively through a common computer system, as do almost half of the Community Welfare Officers in the Eastern Health Board. Computerisation will be completed in the Eastern Health Board by the end of 1998.

20  P56 "Shaping a Healthier Future: *A Strategy for Health Care in the 1990s*

Aspects of the review underway by chief executive officers of health boards in relation to the services for schoolgoing and pre-school children include an examination of developmental screening[21] in schools and for pre-school children. This is being undertaken by a team headed by a Director of Public Health. The team has undertaken a review of published and unpublished literature, and qualitative research with parents, and has hosted a multidisciplinary workshop of child health services.

The preliminary findings of the team's examination echo many of the issues which have been brought to the Commission's attention in submissions from the public and from expert bodies and in the Commission's examination of the public health nurse service.

The main findings at this stage point to a new approach to child health screening to encompass:

- *all the key people:* parents, teachers, public health nurses, general practitioners and child health professionals

- *more targeted and selective approaches* to identifying health problems in children

- more emphasis being given to the identification of *behavioural and emotional problems* and learning disorders, such as dyslexia (i.e. not just physical conditions)

- *better co-ordination* between the child health professionals involved, including a distinct role for the G.P. and clear and *prompt referral mechanisms* when health problems are detected

- *a new relationship with the schools* and the establishment of links that ensure that referrals are followed through, i.e. by a visit to relevant health professional

- *prompt feedback* to parents, the GP and the Public Health Nurse and the person who made the referral and *improved collaboration arrangements* between these key people in family support

- ongoing *evaluation of the effectiveness of measures* to monitor children's developmental health, with an emphasis on a quantitative approach to such evaluations.

### What parents need

The concerns of parents in relation to their children's developmental health have been well expressed in submissions to the Commission and, not surprisingly, these same concerns are arising in the examination that is now underway. The concerns point to:

- The need for an *appreciation of the effectiveness of parents* in identifying difficulties or health conditions in their children.

21    Developmental screening relates to the developmental examinations of children carried out by Area Medical Officers and Public Health Nurses at specified ages in infancy and early childhood.

- The need for *information for parents about the services,* about their children's health and about medical conditions which may be detected in screening procedures.

- The need for parents to have a *single point of contact with health professionals:* sometimes parents may ring five or six people to make an appointment for their child. They should have consistent and appropriate support in their child's early weeks or if difficulties arise.

In particular, the point has been made to the Commission that parents should have consistent and continuing support when difficulties are first identified and a diagnosis made.

It has been suggested to the Commission that many professionals working in the field of child health would welcome the introduction of a *multi-disciplinary team* in each community care area and that a National Steering Group for Child Health could have an important role in ensuring the co-ordination of services, driving a new approach to the promotion of child health and ensuring follow through on evaluation and pilot programme findings.

### Addressing organisational issues

The Commission welcomes the review of services for children and endorses the work underway in this important aspect of child health. The results of the review and the recommendations arising will have a very important contribution to make to improving the effectiveness of child health services and better support for families in rearing their children.

**It is the Commission's view that many of the findings of the examination to date point to the need to address organisational issues relating to the delivery of health services to children including:**

- **Integration of services - bringing a more holistic response to the child and to his/her family**

- **Co-ordination - bringing together the different services and maximising their beneficial impact on the child and his/her family**

- **Collaboration - parents and professionals working together to achieve a common goal in relation to their child's development**

- **Availability of information for parents about the services and consistent support if difficulties arise in the child's early weeks or where there is a special need.**

These are the same issues that arise again and again throughout the Commission's examination of families' experiences of the response of the state services.

The Commission has already highlighted the widespread commitment to the provision of quality services to the public which exists at all levels throughout the public service. The Commission again points to the strategic management initiative for public service reform, which provides a unique opportunity to harness this commitment and to make responsive public services in the health sphere a source of empowerment for families needing support.

### 4.17 Schools- a setting for the delivery of health services

The Commission is of the view that consideration should be given to the concept of delivering more health and social services in the school setting. It is apparent from the Commission's preliminary examination of preventive health services that there is a wide-spread view among those working with families that the potential of the school setting for the delivery of primary preventive health services is under-utilised.

**It is the Commission's view that schools have the potential to play a major role in the comprehensive delivery of preventive health services. The school setting allows for services to be delivered to a total population of children and for the treatment of children where intervention is required, in their everyday environment.**

The concept has a particular relevance in relation to the detection and treatment of psycho-social and behavioural problems arising in children and the role of the Public Health Nurse and the Area Medical Officers in monitoring the developmental health of children. Close links between GPs and the schools is important in relation to physical problems or conditions such as asthma, diabetes and epilepsy.

The 'school population' of children presents a focal point for a much-called-for integrated approach to the early detection of problems in children and preventive action. A team approach in addressing the child's difficulties involves a close working relationship between parents, the GP, the Public Health Nurse, an Area Medical Officer, teachers and the school psychological service.

The development of services for children in the pre-school age groups presents possibilities for the clustering of pre-school settings to facilitate the delivery of health services to younger children in the future. The school setting also presents a positive environment for the delivery of parenting support programmes discussed in chapter 6. In rural communities, such an approach would have the advantage of overcoming transport and travel problems for parents who may have difficulty in bringing their children to health professionals.There are strong arguments in favour of the school setting as the base for out-of-school-hours service and these are described in chapter 12.

#### Integrated services in schools - the experience abroad

A recent report presented information about a number of models for integrating the delivery of services to improve the delivery of services for children in the USA, (Chicago and San Diego), the UK (Corby), the Netherlands and Australia (New South Wales). The basic goal of these integrated approaches is to restructure services to be more responsive to children and families in the context of their local communities, resulting in a better matching of resources and services to needs and ensuring that better educational and developmental outcomes for children are achieved. Some of the models presented the school as the focal point for the delivery of a range of services to families.

The report [22] describes how the use of the school setting as a focal point for integrated approaches to the delivery of a range of services for children and their families is well developed in the US, where local public elementary (primary) schools have tended to become the focus for developing many integrated child and family services.

New structures and programmes have been developed within schools that encourage parents to enrol for home-visiting services linked to school-based health, welfare, personal development and vocational training programmes. Underlying this approach is a view that sees the school as being capable of creating home-school partnerships and of mobilising parents, community and social services to engage in new partnerships on behalf of children and their families. In this view, leadership is provided by the school and school leaders become advocates for developing school-based social services. This comprehensive approach to such school-linked services has led to the term 'full service schools'. Full service schools have been described as follows:

The vision of the *full-service school* puts the best of school reform together with all other services that children, young people and their families need, most of which can be located in a school building. The educational mandate places responsibility on the school system to recognise and innovate. The charge to community agencies is to bring into the school: health, mental health, employment services, child care, parent education, case management, recreation, cultural events, welfare, community policing and whatever else may fit into the picture. The result is a new kind of 'seamless' institution, a community-oriented school with a joint governance structure that allows maximum responsiveness to the community as well as accessibility and continuity for those most in need of services.

An Australian model (Inter-agency School Community Centres Pilot Project) described in the report also promotes the school as community centre by providing services with activities at the school which link families with the education, health and community services available to support their children's development.

In New York, the use of local school buildings as active community centres for use after school, on weekends and during the summer is a key element of the Beacons Community Centre programme. The programme is an integrated strategy to prevent young people getting caught up in violence, drug abuse and other social problems in inner city areas. Community workers, police officers, health and education professionals and local community activists are involved in the projects.

### The potential of the school setting should be explored

**The Commission considers that the school setting presents a number of prospects for improving support for families. The Commission would like to see a further exploration of the potential of the school setting for the delivery of a number of services. Aspects the Commission would particularly like to see explored include:**

- **making the school setting a sustained contact point for working with families**

- **making school buildings available for community and family initiatives after school hours and during school holidays.**

---

22    A report for ISI (Integrated Services Initiative) on models for integrating services for young families in the Community: Barry Cullen, The Children's Centre TCD, Paper delivered, Combat Poverty Agency Seminar, Dublin Castle, May 1997.

It has been suggested to the Commission that the development of a school health and treatment service is extremely difficult because of the lack of structural facilities. There may be a lack of facilities in schools. As it is, most schools (except the most modern), lack suitable schoolrooms where a health service can be provided. In the smaller schools, the school medical examination often takes place in the principal's office, the gym or in the teachers' common room. **The Commission is of the view that if it proves feasible to use the school setting these are issues which could be looked at in the context of the school building programme for the future.**

# Summary of Recommendations in Part 2

## The policy approach

The Commission recommends

- **an approach to building strengths in families which**
- **is preventive,**
- **is empowering, building on family strengths, enhancing self steem and a sense of being able to influence events in one's life,**
- **draws on community based responses.**

### In relation to the development of family support services (Chapter 2)

- **the introduction of a network of Family and Community Services Resource Centres throughout the country**
- building on community based initiatives already in place (The Family and Community Services Resource Centre Programme of the Department of Social, Community and Family Affairs),
- providing a range of services including basic adult education, personal development, home management skills, parenting information and supports for parents, services for children, outreach programmes for families and projects to promote the involvement of young men in the life of the community,
- informed by continuous evaluation in terms of outcomes for families,
- **one hundred centres is an appropriate target over the next 4 to 5 years.**

### In relation to the development of a customised local service for families (Chapter 3)

- **a refocusing of the delivery of social welfare and other services at local level to better meet the needs of families involving,**
- transformation of local offices of the Department of Social, Community and Family Affairs building on the one-stop-shop concept to provide a gateway to all services for families, with enhanced information services, covering a range of services relevant to families, including local community initiatives,
- a customised approach to people's needs, with advice, guidance and referral to other agencies which can assist,
- close co-operative links between all local agencies, including health boards, other state agencies, and community based services, in pursuit of shared family and community objectives.

### In relation to the family support services under the health boards (Chapter 4)

- **prioritising family support work at the preventive level, involving:**
- a greater focus on family support services at a preventive level,
- greater investment in the development of family support services in the health boards,
- research on emerging needs and evaluation of what works best for Irish families,
- co-ordination of the development and delivery of services and the engagement of relevant agencies and other government departments in addressing the needs of children,
- that the Department of Health and Children explore with the Department of Finance the possibility of a significant increase in resources for family support work in the health boards at a preventive level.

- realising the potential of the public health nurse as a national resource in family support work;
- enhancing the contribution of other services which have the potential to be key players in an integrated and comprehensive programme of support for families;
  - addressing the need for specialisation in the services,
  - addressing structural and organisational issues, including a better match of public health nurse resources with the needs of different communities throughout the country,
  - ongoing training and development and a team approach to the delivery of services for families,
  - more information and education for GPs about family relationships and behaviour within families,
  - a review of the work of the community welfare officer to enhance the role of the service as part of the local community welfare structure for families.

- addressing organisational issues relating to the delivery of health services for children;
  - integration and co-ordination of services to maximise beneficial impact on children and their families,
  - collaboration - parents and professionals working together to achieve goals for their children's development,
  - better information and consistent support for parents when difficulties arise.

- exploring the potential of the school setting for the delivery of more services for children and families in the future.

## Making a start Part 2

### Recommendation 1

The Commission recommends

- the introduction of a network of Family and Community Services Resource Centres throughout the country
  **Target:** - 25 centres in 1998,- 100 centres in 4-5 years
  **Priority areas** - those areas where communities are coping with significant disadvantage
  **Costs:** £700,000 in 1998, £4m in year 5

### Recommendation 2

The Commission recommends

- a mainstream programme under the Family and Community Services Resource Centre Programme of the Department of Social, Community and Family Affairs to support the development of family support activities within the voluntary and community sector.
  Personal development and parenting education programmes to promote the involvement and participation of young men in the life of their family and community should be given special encouragement.

### Recommendation 3

The Commission recommends

- a pilot programme for the transformation of local offices of the Department of Social, Community and Family Affairs in priority communities to provide a gateway to all services for families, complementing the development of the Family and Community Services Resource Centres. **Cost:** £200,000 in 1998.

## Recommendation 4

The Commission recommends

- **Community Mothers Programmes, which offer support and guidance to parents in their child's early days, be extended so that priority groups in all health board areas have access to the service.**
  **Models of Community Mothers Programmes used by health boards should be those programmes which have been evaluated.**
  **Cost:** The introduction of Community Mothers throughout all health boards areas to reach 10 per cent of children under age 2 would cost in the region of £3 million per annum.

## Recommendation 5

The Commission recommends

- **that the Family Support Workers Scheme, which offers practical support and guidance to families who are having difficulties in caring for their children, be extended to all health board areas and that the potential of the Family Support Workers Scheme as a preventive measure be developed,**
- **that consideration be given to funding a pilot Family Support Workers programme under the primary health care project for Travellers, at a cost of £45,000 per annum.**

## Recommendation 6

The Commission recommends

- **that the provision of information on the Public Health Nurse service be improved.**
- Public Health Nurses should have an input at ante natal classes in maternity hospitals
- An information pack on relevant community services should be given to the mother at the first ante natal visit
- The introduction of flexible working hours for Public Health Nurses should be explored

## Recommendation 7

The Commission recommends

- **more information and education about the dynamics of family relationships and behaviour within families for GPs**
- **the proposed review of the Community Welfare Officer Service should be informed by the need for a more integrated delivery of services to families.**

**part 3**

**Supporting families in carrying out their functions
(the care and nurturing of children)**

**Desired outcome**

- Children receive the best care possible. Parents are affirmed by the State and the wider community as the primary carers and educators of their children.

**To be achieved through**

- The adoption of policy options in income support which would better support the choices parents may wish to make for the care of their young children.
- Recognition for caring work carried out by parents in the care of young children.
- Support programmes to enable parents to be the best they can be by giving them practical help with child-rearing and equipping them with the knowledge and skills for parenting.
- Support programmes for lone parents which strengthen their capacities to rear their children and to secure their futures.
- Facilitating and enabling parents and other workers with caring responsibilities for children or for a family member who is dependent on them to devote time and resources to their children while meeting the demands of the workplace.
- Assisting families that are unemployed to gain access to the labour market.

**In Part 3, the Commission**

- Documents current issues in relation to income support policies and families.
- Presents options for greater investment in support of the care arrangements which parents make for their young children in their first three years.
- Sets out the case for a comprehensive programme to support positive parenting, which involves access to parenting information and parent education.
- Examines the need for policies supporting lone parents in their role as primary carers for their children, while strengthening their capacities to secure positive futures for themselves and for their children.
- Explores the growing importance of initiatives to assist families to reconcile work and family life and makes proposals for a concerted effort on behalf of families who are unemployed.

# Overview of Part 3

**The Commission has put forward the principle that "the unique and essential family function is that of caring and nurturing for all its members". It is in the family context that a person's basic emotional needs for security, belonging, support and intimacy are satisfied. These are especially important for children.**

**It is the Commission's view that parents are the first educators and carers of their children. The role of the State and of the agencies of the State is to support parents in carrying out their responsibilities. Policies should support parents in their choices in relation to the care of their children, enable them to be the best parents they can be by giving them practical help with child-rearing and equipping them with knowledge and skills. Sharing caring responsibilities with families should underpin the policy approach in promoting a 'family friendly' work environment which values families' caring roles and in ensuring that families can get access to the labour market.**

In Part 3 of the report, the Commission notes the work underway in examining radical proposals which have been suggested in recent years in relation to income support policies. The proposals for a basic income for all citizens is being considered in the context of Partnership 2000. The programme for Government proposes a discussion paper on the implications of introducing basic income. The treatment of one and two parent families under the tax and social welfare codes is being examined by an expert group. The Commission notes the objectives to achieve an adequate level of weekly income support as recommended by the Commission on Social Welfare which are set out in the National Anti-Poverty Strategy.

The Commission is its examination of the issues surrounding income support has concentrated on the role of income support policies in meeting the needs of families when their childcare responsibilities are at their most demanding.

The Commission endorses the high contribution to families and society of unpaid caring work which is carried out within the home, usually by women although a growing number of men are taking on these responsibilities in the care of young children or other dependent family members. The Commission considers policy options whereby the State may recognise the value of this caring work and the cost of childcare for the increasing number of parents who work outside the home and which will better support parents in their choices in relation to the care of their children.

The effectiveness of the current tax arrangements for married persons in supporting families with the most demanding caring responsibilities for young children, or for a family member with a disability for an older family member is explored.

The Commission considers the range of parenting supports available to families and makes recommendations for a programme for positive parenting which would involve access to parenting information and parent education.

The Commission considers the particular needs of lone parent families and makes recommendations on the future direction of State policy in relation to these families. In the main, the Commission's recommendations relate to its concern to secure positive outcomes for children. The role of maintenance payments in the income arrangements for lone parents is examined. The wider issues in relation to lone parenthood, the growth in unmarried parenthood and the particular difficulties faced by very young mothers as well as the areas where public policy may support or constrain young people in relation to the choices they make are all discussed.

The Commission examines the changes in employment which have taken place in recent years and notes the increase in the number of workers with caring responsibilities. Information about the demanding working schedules with mothers and fathers are undertaking is presented and the growing importance of initiatives to assist families to reconcile work and family life is examined. The Commission examines the role of income support policies in assisting families when their family and work responsibilities are at their most demanding. In this context the case for paid parental leave is presented. The Commission highlights the importance of social protection for workers in a changing working environment. The promotion of family friendly initiatives is considered and suggestions are presented in relation to the adoption of initiatives to further meet the needs of workers with caring responsibilities for older family members and to encourage and facilitate men in availing of options to take on caring responsibilities for children or older family members. The Commission suggests that there is a role for the commercial lending sector in facilitating parents who wish to take time out of the workforce to spend time at home when their children are young. The Commission considers the situation of families who are unemployed and proposals are made for a concerted effort to address their needs.

# Chapter Five **Supporting families with their childcare responsibilities**

**5.1**    **Introduction**

The Commission's interim report[1] presented its preliminary findings of its examination of state provision in family income support. The level and structure of state support for family incomes, and the way in which support is financed, are matters of central importance in considering how families may be strengthened and supported in carrying out their functions. State policy on income support has both direct and indirect effects on the incomes, living standards, life choices and welfare of all citizens.

Many of the issues have been examined in detail over the years by the Commission on Taxation, the Commission on Social Welfare, and, more recently, by the Expert Working Group on Integration of Tax and Social Welfare systems.

Some of the key themes in this work are:
- the need to provide an adequate level of income support for those without other resources
- the need to maintain an adequate financial incentive to take up and remain in employment
- a particular need to reform the structure of child income support, to reduce or eliminate the "unemployment trap" and the "poverty trap".[2]

The Commission fully recognises the fundamental importance of these themes. In addition, it has drawn attention in its interim report to the need to take into account the financial incentives created by tax and welfare policy for family and household formation. In this regard the Commission has stated that "family incentives" such as the incentive to marry and form a stable relationship; and to provide joint parenthood to children, should be accorded a greater prominence in evaluating the outcomes of social welfare and taxation policy, similar to that at present accorded to matters such as work incentives and the other economic effects of social welfare provision.

**5.2**    A further issue arises in relation to the adequacy of income for families. In this regard, the Commission endorses the objective set out in the National Anti-Poverty Strategy that policies in relation to income support, whether these policies relate to employment, tax, social welfare, occupational pensions or otherwise, should aim to provide sufficient income for all those concerned to move out of poverty and to live in a manner compatible with human dignity.

---

1    "Strengthening Families for Life", Interim Report of the Commission on the Family to the Minister for Social Welfare, November 1996.

2    Disincentives may arise for a family where the income available from employment (i.e. take home pay) leaves them no better off or only marginally better off than if they remain on unemployment payments. Families on low pay may also face disincentives to improving their financial position for example, by taking on additional hours of work or doing overtime, if they stand to pay substantial extra tax or their income brings them over a threshold, which means that they lose valuable benefits such as a medical services card or family income supplement. These disincentives give rise to what are known as the "unemployment trap" and the "poverty trap".

The Commission further notes the commitments in the National Anti-Poverty Strategy and in Partnership 2000 that all social welfare payments will be increased to the minimum of the lower range recommended by the Commission on Social Welfare. Policy actions are proposed in the National Anti-Poverty Strategy to ensure that income adequacy is achieved through a set of consistent policies relating to social welfare, employment and labour market measures, pay rates and occupational pensions.

## 5.3 The focus on financial support directly related to children

The focus of the Commission's examination has been on financial supports directly related to children. The Commission's examination was undertaken on the premise that the State and the wider community should share with all parents the cost of rearing children.

The main elements of child income support are:

- **Child Benefit,** which is paid to all families with children, regardless of the income or employment status of the family.

- **Child dependant allowances,** which are paid with social welfare payments, such as unemployment and sickness payments, widows/widowers pensions and one-parent family payments.

- **Family Income Supplement (FIS),** which is paid to workers rearing families on low wages.

- **Child additions to tax exemption limits** for taxpayers on low incomes.

## 5.4 Complex issues involved

Recent expert reports on the subject of provision for children illustrate the complexity of the issues involved:

### Objective of child income support policy

Nolan (1993)[3] identifies the major objectives underlying child income support policy. There is a clear role in alleviating and preventing child poverty: child dependant allowances with social welfare payments can be seen as addressing this objective in a particularly direct fashion. At a more general level, the State has taken a role in sharing the costs of raising children across the community: in part, this can be seen as involving an element of redistribution of income over the life-cycle, and in part an element of redistribution as between those with and without children. A further objective is to provide child income support in a way which is most "employment friendly": it is the concern with financial work incentives which led to the setting up of the Family Income Supplement scheme and the child additions to income tax exemption limits.

---

3    B. Nolan, Reforming Child Income Support,:Combat Poverty Agency, Poverty and Policy Series, Paper No. 1 1993, Dublin.

The Expert Working Group examined in detail the different elements of child income support. In particular, it considered the way in which the different payments affect families on social welfare or in low paid jobs in relation to disincentives to take-up work or opportunities to increase their earnings.

The report confirmed that child dependant allowances with social welfare payments, Family Income Supplement paid to workers on low pay and the child additions to income tax exemption limits all have the potential to pose significant disincentives for families with children in taking up employment or opportunities to increase the family's income. The Expert Working Group went on to consider ways in which child income support could be restructured so that the mechanism used for channelling income support to families would not contribute to unemployment or poverty traps for those families.

The Expert Working Group identified various options for the future direction of the child income support. It rejected a basic income for children on the basis that it would be extremely costly, with a high proportion of the gains going to families on higher incomes. It put forward three reform options in the area of child income support which are more selective in their application. These were an *Integrated Child Benefit*, i.e. a basic income for children that would be taxed, thereby reducing the cost and clawing back a proportion of the payment from taxpayers; a *Child Benefit Supplement*, i.e. a means-tested supplement for families with children, paid to all families on lower incomes, whether unemployed or in work; and an *In-Work Benefit*, payable through extending and enhancing the current Family Income Supplement.

The Expert Working Group did not recommend any one of these options over the others.

The Commission on the Family agrees with the overall thrust of the options put forward by the Expert Working Group which point towards the need for a continuing strengthening of the role of child benefit as a mechanism for providing income support to families and a lessening of the importance of child dependant allowances with social welfare payments.

## 5.5 Basic income - a radical solution

Other radical approaches to the reform of tax and welfare policy are worthy of consideration. For instance, proposals for a basic income- a single payment to all citizens (differentiated only on the basis of age), replacing all social welfare payments and financed largely by a flat rate income tax in place of the current system have many attractions. Such schemes were considered by the Expert Working Group on the Integration of Tax and Social Welfare Systems, but were rejected largely on the grounds of the high tax rates needed to finance them. Proposals put forward by the Conference of Religious of Ireland[4] are to be considered in the context of Partnership 2000 for Inclusion, Employment and Competitiveness[5] by a special working group.

---

4    Charles M.A. Clark and John Healy, Pathways to Basic Income, Justice Commission, Conference of Religious of Ireland (April 1997).

5    Para 4.35 of Partnership 2000 for Inclusion, Employment and Competitiveness states: "A further independent appraisal of the concept of, and the full implications of introducing a basic income payment for all citizens will be undertaken, taking into account the work of the ESRI, CORI, and the Expert Group on the Integration of Tax and Social Welfare and international research. A broadly based steering group will oversee the study".

The Commission further notes the commitment in the Programme for Government to the publication of a Green Paper on the issue of basic income.

**5.6     Basic Income - Commission's preliminary views**

From the point of view of the Commission on the Family, a key consideration is that some of the advantages of the basic income scheme could be obtained at a lower cost. A more limited, less costly, but still quite radical reform, would focus purely on individualisation of social welfare payments, and, possibly on the accompanying individualisation of the income tax system. Again, the costs of such a reform are a key consideration. Individualisation of social welfare entitlements could do away with many of the concerns about obstacles to joint parenting, but would involve payments to couples which are twice the individual rate, rather than approximately 1.6 times the individual rate, as at present. The current structure recognises that there are economies of scale in living as a couple. Failure to recognise this (in an individualised system) would mean that the level of support for single individuals would have to be lower than at present, or the costs of provision (and hence the tax rates required to finance it) would be higher.

These issues, as well as the basic income proposal, require more intensive investigation than was possible in the Commission's time frame.

**5.7     Income support policies and child-rearing**

The Commission, having regard to the fact that these issues are the subject of examination by the Working Group on the Tax and Social Welfare Treatment of One and Two Parent Households and in the proposals for a Green Paper on basic income, has decided to concentrate its examination on the role of state income support policies in assisting with the cost of rearing young children and, in particular, on the role of income support policies in relation to the so far unacknowledged hidden costs of rearing children.

The hidden cost for families with a parent working full-time in the home is reflected in terms of earnings and pension rights forgone and loss of productivity to the economy as a whole. For parents who work outside the home, the costs include the cost of purchased childcare services.

The role of non-cash based supports - for example, parenting support which may be appropriate for families at different stages of their life cycle are dealt with in chapters 4 and 6.

**5.8     Submissions about childcare**

Almost one in three submissions to the Commission raised issues to do with rearing children and childcare. The consensus was that crèche/nurseries and pre-school services and after school hours services are urgently required throughout the country and not just for children whose parents work outside the home. Quality childcare was often perceived to be vital to family life in that it supports the development, education, care and welfare of the child, as well as provides support to mothers who have to undertake other commitments outside the home.

Over twenty per cent of all submissions to the Commission raised issues to do with the recognition of women's unwaged work in the home. In almost all these submissions it was suggested that there should be some form of direct payment to mothers working full-time in the home. Various suggestions were made for a weekly allowance, increased child benefit, for pension entitlements and for tax credits for the unwaged worker in his or her own right.

Many submissions expressed concern about women in low paid employment who were only marginally better off working after their childcare and going to work expenses had been taken into account. Most submissions on this issue took the view that many women, if given a choice, would prefer to take time out of the workforce to be at home with their children. The dominant view was that these parents should be assisted in that choice. In addition to the concerns about pressures on parents balancing work and family life, submissions looked for support for mothers in their important job and for rights to further education and opportunities to take on training.

### 5.9    Recognising the value of unpaid caring work

It is the Commission's view that the unpaid caring work which is carried out within the home for young children or for a family member who has a disability or for an older person who is dependent on family care and support is invaluable to society and should be recognised in the Constitution. The Commission's views in relation to how this work may be acknowledged in the Constitution are set out in its submission to the All-Party Committee on the Constitution.[6] The Commission's further deliberations in relation to Article 41.2 and, in particular, its relevance to the domestic role of women as wives and mothers are set out in Appendix 1 to this chapter.

The Commission welcomes moves to acknowledge the extent of unpaid caring work which is carried out in the home and in the community mostly by women. In this context, the Commission welcomes the commitment in Partnership 2000 for Inclusion, Employment and Competitiveness,[7] to the development of statistical methods to evaluate the full extent of the contribution of unpaid work. In 1997 the Central Statistics Office completed the fieldwork on a pilot Time Use Survey, which covered some 300 households. Work is now underway on analysis of the data collected and it is expected that the results will be available in 1998. The Commission welcomes this initiative. The project will, it is hoped shed new light on how the extent of unpaid work which is undertaken in the home and in the community could be measured and made visible.

---

6    Chapter 23 contains the Commissions submission to the All-Party Committee on the Constitution.

7    Paragraph 5.11 of Partnership 2000 for Inclusion, Employment and Competitiveness states that:

"statistical methods to evaluate the full extent of the contribution of unpaid work will be undertaken during the course of this Partnership. The Central Statistics Office will undertake a pilot study based on a time-use survey during 1997 as the first stage of this process".

Note: The initiative to evaluate unpaid work follows a number of developments at international level. The Platform for Action agreed at the United Nations Fourth World Conference in Beijing in September, 1995 includes several references to the recognition and valuing of unremunerated work.

continued over...

## 5.10    Financial support for caring responsibilities- the gap in the policy approach

It is the Commission's further view that this work can and should be given financial recognition by the State in a more direct and effective way than at present. The need for financial support is most evident in relation to family responsibilities for young children, the care of family members with a disability and the care of older people who are dependent on family care.

In this report the additional needs of families where disability is involved are highlighted by the Commission in Chapter 15, while the supports needed for the care of older people are considered in detail in Chapter 14.

In relation to childcare, the State assumes a significant element of the care responsibility for children when they are old enough to attend school, through the education system. It is in the younger age groups that childcare responsibilities are most costly. In particular, it is in the years before entry into school that the issue of parents withdrawing (fully or partly) from the paid labour force to care for children, or incurring substantial childcare costs, arises most sharply.

It is the Commission's view that there is a significant gap in the policy approach to support for families in these important years. Apart from child benefit and limited intervention programmes for some children at risk of educational or social disadvantage, there is almost no state investment in the care of children in the years before entry into primary school.

---

Paragraph 68 (b) calls on national and international statistical organisations to:

*"devise suitable statistical means to recognise and make visible the full extent of the work of women and all their contributions to the national economy, including their contribution in the unremunerated and domestic sectors, and examine the relationship of women's unremunerated work to the incidence of and their vulnerability to poverty."*

Paragraph 165 (g) calls on governments to:

*"seek to develop a more comprehensive knowledge of work and employment through, inter alia, efforts to measure and better understand the type, extent and distribution of unremunerated work, particularly work in caring for dependants and unremunerated work done for family farms or businesses, and encourage the sharing and dissemination of information on studies and experience in this field, including the development of methods for assessing its value in quantitative terms, for possible reflection in accounts that may be produced separately from, but consistent with, core national accounts;"*

Paragraph 209 calls on multilateral development institutions and bilateral donors to:

*"encourage and support the development of national capacity in developing countries and in countries with economies in transition by providing resources and technical assistance so that countries can fully measure the work done by women and men, including both remunerated and unremunerated work, and, where appropriate, use satellite or other official accounts for unremunerated work."*

A major review of national accounting methodologies undertaken under the auspices of the UN Statistical Commission culminated in the publication of a new system of national accounts in 1993. This extended the existing system to include the output of all goods produced on own account, for example, farm produce consumed by the owner of the farm. Household own account services were not included, partly because of the difficulty of valuation. Work is continuing at an international level to develop ways of valuing these services.

The tax arrangements for married persons which allow for the tax free allowance for the spouse who works full-time in the home to be transferred to the spouse who is working in the paid labour market provide some measure of financial support to families, although that support is limited to those families where the main earner comes within the tax net. It does not benefit those families who do not have sufficient earnings to be eligible to pay tax, or those (considerable number of) families where there is no earner in the household, families where the parents are not married, or families where the parent is rearing children alone. Furthermore, the tax arrangement is applicable on the basis of marital status and not whether or not there are children in the household. As such, it is a poorly directed measure in so far as it is intended to recognise any childcare or other caring responsibilities which families may have. There is no state assistance for childcare costs incurred by parents who purchase services for children in crèches/nurseries or other pre-school arrangements, or for the services of a childminder.

5.11    **Supporting the functions carried out by families in the care of young children - the wider context**
The Commission's examination of how state policy might provide practical recognition by way of financial support for the childcare responsibilities undertaken by parents has been undertaken in the context that:

- for an increasing number of women, working full-time in the home is a phase in their life and not a permanent choice

- more women are staying on in the labour force after marriage and childbirth and more married women are returning to the labour force after a period spent caring for children full-time in the home. Higher educational attainments commanding higher rates of pay and proposed reductions in income tax liability over the coming years will enhance this trend for younger married women

- there are concerns about the supply of labour in the future; studies[8] have identified in this context the labour force participation of married women as a key issue for research

- there is a growing consensus among labour market experts that effective access to employment and economic participation should be equal for both sexes and that public policy should be neutral as between the economic incentives faced by men and women in the choices they make in relation to employment participation

- participation in paid employment presents the best prospects for improving incomes and the living standards of lone parents and their children. It has further advantages because it offers choice, less isolation and more active involvement, which are particularly important for young single mothers.

- access to the labour market is equally important to two-parent low-income families which have insufficient earnings or which have no earner at all in the household.

8    Tim Callan, Brian Farrell *"Women's participation in the Irish Labour Market"*, NESC No. 91, December 1991

## 5.12 A child-centred approach

In considering all the issues the Commission is adopting a child and family-centred approach, with a focus on supporting parents with their childcare responsibilities whether their choice is to work full-time in the home or outside the home.

The Commission considers that childcare must first focus on meeting the child's needs for an optimal experience of childhood, while supporting parents' choice in relation to their children. In this context, the Commission recognises that there is a strong case for the provision of public financial support for purchased services for children in the years immediately before entry into primary school.

The Commission's conclusions in relation to the case for investment in early years opportunities for children in this age-group are set out in Chapter 12. There is clear evidence in support of the benefits to children on reaching age three of having opportunities to participate in quality early years services in nurseries, crèches and playgroups. Early education and pre-school services are important. They offer long and short-term value to children and in the long run they may have an impact on the quality of society.

The need to continue to pursue the equalisation of economic opportunities between men and women and between parents and those without childcare responsibilities and to realise the potential economic benefits, now and in the future, arising from women's increased participation in the paid labour market add to the case for state support with childcare.

**It is the Commission's view that the State has a role in providing financial support to meet the needs of children who are being cared for in their own homes and outside their homes in their early years.**

## 5.13 Tax allowances will not benefit all families with children

Much of the debate about financial support has focused on the affordability of subsidising childcare, in the context of public finance restraints; it has assumed that if a subsidy is to be provided, it should be done through the income tax system, in the form of tax allowances or tax credits.

However, the Commission is of the view that tax credits or tax allowances may not be the most suitable mechanism for the provision of support for families with this aspect of their child-rearing responsibilities. Tax credits would be of no value to those families on the lowest incomes, which are not liable to tax. Tax allowances tend to be of more benefit to those with the highest incomes and would not be of direct benefit to those who work full-time in the home.

Tax approaches may have the potential to be divisive. Submissions to the Commission expressed concern about the difficulties of hard pressed parents trying to balance the demands of working life with their childcare responsibilities. Submissions also described the need for childcare support for parents working full-time in the home and managing on a low income, often with no means of social support and no recognition of their valuable work.

Several submissions made the point that it was inappropriate for "single income" families to fund childcare tax concessions for "dual" income households.

**5.14** **A child-centred approach- provision in the years immediately preceding entry into school**

In Chapter 12, the Commission puts forward detailed recommendations for investment in children in the years immediately preceding entry into primary school through an Early Years Opportunities Subsidy. The Early Years Opportunities Subsidy is intended to secure, for all children whose parents want it, opportunities to participate in quality services in nurseries/crèches, pre-schools and playgroups on reaching age three years up to school-going age at four or five years.

It is the Commission's view that early years opportunities should be available to all children in this age-group irrespective of their parents' employment status, whether they are working full-time in the home or go out to the workplace or are unemployed. The Commission's recommendations in Chapter 12 are designed towards this end.

The survey undertaken for the Commission of the care arrangements made by parents for their children indicates that, while most children are cared for at home by a parent, there is a growing recognition of the benefits of early experiences outside the home for this age-group among families where the mother works full-time in the home, as well as families when the mother works outside the home.

The Early Years Opportunity Subsidy involves investment of some £1,000 (1998 terms) per annum per child in the important years from age three up to school entry.

**5.15** **A child centred approach- the "under threes" support for parents choice**

In this chapter the focus of the Commission's deliberations is provision for children under three years of age. The survey undertaken by the Commission shows that most children in the age group up to two years of age are cared for in their own home by a parent. Outside the home, the most commonly used service is a childminder who looks after the child in her own home, followed by a childminder in the child's own home. Services provided by nurseries/crèches become more important when children are aged two and three years. While, again, the majority of children are cared for by a parent in the home, almost 20 per cent of children in this age-group attend a nursery/crèche or other pre-school arrangement, a further 12 per cent are with a childminder.

In considering the options in relation to provision for children under three years old, the Commission's starting point is the premise that parents are the primary carers and educators of their children and that the role of public policy is to support parents in carrying out these functions and to support their choice in relation to the care of their children. It is in this context that the Commission presents for discussion some detailed options for providing financial support to assist with the costs of childcare, whether that childcare is provided by the family themselves or by purchasing services for children.

The Commission, conscious of the very considerable extra resources required to pursue any one of the policy options proposed, has also considered how the additional resources required might be identified.

**5.16**     **Direct support for the care of young children- the priority**

The Commission considers that providing direct support to parents at a time when their childcare responsibilities are at their most demanding, and initiatives to facilitate parents taking time out of the workforce, if this is their preferred choice in relation to the care of their young children, are priority considerations in formulating future policy in support of families with childcare responsibilities.

**Option A - Parent Allowance and Childcare Allowance**
***A parent allowance for the parent who works full-time in the home***
Some Commission members are of the view that the choice to work full-time in the home should be particularly facilitated by a special allowance, payable directly to the parent who works full-time in the home.

Option A proposes the payment of a weekly allowance to the parent who works full-time in the home.

- The parent allowance could take the form of a payment for the parent (either mother or father) of a child under three who works full-time in the home irrespective of the employment and income status of the other parent or the main earner in the household.

- The parent allowance initially would be set at £30 a week.

- The parent allowance would be payable until the child attains age three and becomes eligible for the Early Years Opportunities Subsidy proposed in Chapter 12 or until the parent returns to the paid workforce if this is sooner.

- The parent allowance would be paid in addition to social welfare entitlements where the family is dependent on social welfare (including lone parents).

***In support of a parent allowance for a parent who works full-time in the home***
The payment of the parent allowance would:

- underwrite the recognition of the value of the caring work undertaken by parents who work full-time in the home, which is specifically acknowledged in the Constitution (in respect of mothers).

- give the parent the opportunity to choose to work full-time at home in the care of their small child and would lessen the need to seek work outside the home.

- facilitate children in having the security, stability and comfort of being cared for at home by a parent.

### Parent allowance - the drawbacks

The main drawback to a parent allowance is the fact that it would be available only to those parents who choose to work full-time in the home. It is not intended to meet childcare costs and, as such, it does not assist those parents who work outside the home or who are engaged in training or in education and have childcare costs in respect of children under age three.

A further issue arises in relation to making provision for parents who take care of their children jointly, if both parents are job-sharing, or working part-time.

### Childcare allowance

A particular dilemma arises in relation to support for the care of children who are not catered for by the parent allowance. On equity grounds, the Commission considers that complementary measures would be required to address the needs of these families. A child care allowance providing a similar level of investment (£30 a week) in the care of children whose parents work in the paid labour market would indicate a level of resource investment of the order of £69 million a year.

The Commission notes the work of the Expert Working Group under Partnership 2000 for Inclusion, Employment and Competitiveness in drawing up a national framework for the development of the childcare sector.[9] As part of its work, the group has commissioned a study on the economics of childcare. The aim of the study is to estimate the following key aspects of childcare in Ireland: (1) the current and likely future level of need for childcare services; (2) the current and likely future level of demand for childcare services; (3) the current and likely future level of supply of childcare services; (4) the job potential of the child-care sector; (5) the economic cost of childcare provision; and (6) the benefits of childcare.

The Commission notes that the study will comment on different models for financing child-care and their appropriateness to Irish conditions. This aspect of the study is particularly relevant to the future direction of policy in supporting families with childcare responsibilities.

### Costs

An analysis of the 1995 Labour Force Survey indicated that there were at that time 94,000 wives not in the paid labour force with at least one child under age five. In addition, there were some 13,300 lone mothers.

The number of mothers with children under age three would be lower. For the purposes of this costing, it is estimated that there are some 102,500[10] parents with children under age three who would choose to work full-time in the home if an allowance was available. On this basis, a parent allowance at £30 a week for 102,500 parents would cost £159 million per annum. The childcare measures for children not catered for by the parent allowance would involve an additional £69 million. This brings the total cost of **Option A to £228 million.**

---

9    The task of the Expert Working Group is explained more fully in Chapter 12.

10   This estimate is underpinned by data which show that some 70% of children in the relevant age cohort are at home with a parent.

**Option B - Extended paid parental leave: PRSI-based parental leave and childcare allowance**
A further approach for consideration could take the form of extended parental leave,[11] with a paid parental benefit specifically targeted at parents who wish to take time out of the workforce for a period in order to be with young children.

Under Option B, the parental benefit should initially be set at a rate of £70.50, the same rate as the personal rate of disability or unemployment benefit.[12] Further development of a PRSI parental benefit may allow for the rate of benefit to move towards a higher level of income replacement for workers who take time out of the workforce. A significant level of income replacement would be important if the scheme is to provide a realistic option to low paid workers. It would also be important to encourage take-up of the option, particularly among fathers.

### *In support of option B- Sharing the cost of childcare*
This approach raises the possibility that the PRSI system could be extended to fund the cost of a paid period of parental leave for parents who take time out of the workplace. A social insurance based approach to meeting the cost has a number of advantages:

- The cost of childcare is shared across individual workers, employers and the State.

- It would introduce the concept of a rights-based approach to parental leave to support the care of young children. This may encourage the take-up of parental leave among mothers and fathers.

- A parental leave benefit would complete the continuum of social insurance protection from maternity through to pensions provision.

- It would provide new affirmation and support for the concept of social solidarity which underpins the social insurance fund.

- It would recognise the societal value attached to parenting the next generation.

Provision for caring responsibilities which may arise in the future is the contingency for which families must plan in the new century. This is increasingly being recognised in relation to caring needs which may arise on account of old age or disability. A situation may arise where a worker finds himself or herself taking on caring responsibilities for another dependent family member and in need of income support to undertake this responsibility. Provision for personal caring needs which may arise in the future is already a consideration for policy-makers. For these reasons, it is suggested that the social insurance fund could be extended to cover provision for income support arising because of time spent out of the workforce in caring for young children.

---

11  An EU Directive to be implemented by member states by June 1998 provides for 3 months parental leave for workers with children. The issues in relation to parental leave in line with the EU Directive and whether or not that leave should be paid are examined in Chapter 8 of this report.

12  Proposed rate from June 1998.

### Option B- the drawbacks

The main disadvantage to a PRSI-based parent benefit during a period of paid parental leave is that the benefits of such an approach would accrue almost entirely to those who are in insurable employment, and be of little benefit to those outside insurable employment. If it is assumed that all mothers who qualify for maternity benefit opt to take up the extended paid parental leave, the scheme would benefit about one child in five in the relevant age-group.[13]

A proposal for the extended parental leave would be a matter for negotiation with the social partners. Significant issues arise in relation to the right to return to the same employment and the longer term effects on security of employment, pensions rights and accrued employee benefits.

### Costs

The cost of parental benefit for those who take extended parental leave from the workforce would depend on a number of factors:

- take-up of the extended parental leave[14]

- duration of the period spent in the care of young children before returning to the workforce

- whether or not the full period up to three years would be paid, and

- the level of the parental benefit throughout the period of leave.

### Illustrative costs

It is assumed for the purpose of estimating the costs which might be involved in paying a parental benefit for a period of time taken out of the paid labour market that

- the extended leave will be availed of mainly by the mothers who qualify for PRSI maternity benefit. In 1996 some 17,600 mothers qualified for maternity benefit.

- in line with international experience, not all eligible mothers will take up parental leave benefit, or take the full period of entitlement, and few fathers will avail of the option.

---

13   It is possible, however, that a number of parents who are presently working full-time in the home would have PRSI cover.

14   *Likely take up of parental leave*

Take-up of paid parental leave is difficult to predict because factors such as the right to return to the same employment, and the level of income replacement of earnings forgone provided by any benefit which becomes payable, are key issues for workers with family responsibilities in considering whether or not to take time out of the workforce.

Several countries have introduced parental leave arrangements. Some provide paid leave. Others do not. Scandinavian countries have the most far-reaching and innovative schemes to enable parents to take leave. Leave arrangements in Sweden are widely recognised as the most financially generous and flexible in the world and have the highest take-up. France, Germany and Austria provide for extensive periods off work and job protection during that leave but have low, if any, levels of wage replacements. Where take-up figures are available, the information suggests that leave arrangements are largely availed of by women. Schemes in southern European countries, Spain, Greece, Portugal and Italy, in general provide for shorter periods of leave and have very low levels, if any, of financial compensation.

There is very little information available on the level of take up of parental leave arrangements across all these countries. (See also Chapter 8, in particular Appendix 2 which contains relevant details from the study "Time Out: the costs and benefits of paid parental leave" by Helen Wilkinson with Stephen Radley, Ian Christie, George Lawson and Jamie Sainsbury which is published by DEMOS, 9, Bridewell Place, London EC4V6AP, 1997).

**Year 1**

(i)   Some 17,000 mothers take up parental leave benefit for up to one year after the birth of their child following a period of maternity leave which usually ends 6 weeks after the birth of the child (46 weeks, parental leave benefit).
*Cost:* £55m in year 1.

**Year 2**

(ii)  Some 10,000 eligible parents continue paid parental leave in their child's second year.
*Cost:* additional £37 million.
*Full cost in year 2:* £92 million.

**Year 3**

(iii) Some 5,000 parents continue to take paid parental leave in their child's third year.
*Cost:* Additional £18.3 million.
*Full year cost in year 3:* £110.3 million.

**Note:** Overall costs could be lower for this cohort of parents (i.e. those with PRSI entitlements) if a reduced rate of benefit was paid after the first year. However, additional costs will arise in relation to the payroll costs of public servants who do not have cover for PRSI benefits. Nevertheless, employees who joined the public service on or after 6 April 1995 pay full PRSI and have cover for the full range of social welfare benefits and pensions, including maternity benefit. This group would therefore benefit from any future extension of PRSI benefits.

### *Childcare allowance*

The equity arguments in support of a similar level of investment in the care of children not catered for by a payment to the parent who chooses to take time out of the workforce to work full-time in the home arise also in relation to Option B. The complementary measures to address the needs for those not catered for by the PRSI paid parental leave would be required for two distinct groups:

(i)  the parents who are in the paid labour market and who have costs arising in relation to purchased childcare for children in the relevant age category.

(ii) the parents who are not in the paid labour market but who have children in the relevant age category.

Investment in complementary measures to support the care of the children of these groups would indicate resources in the region of £200 million. On the basis of the data used in costing Option A, it is assumed that the number of parents involved is in the region of 146,400. It has already been assumed for the purposes of these costings that 17,000 of these mothers are in a position to take up the PRSI extended paid parental leave. It is further estimated that a figure of 129,400 would cover the remaining parents with children under age three for whom the complementary childcare support measures involving £30 per week would be required. This brings the **total cost of Option B in year 1 to approximately £255 million.**

**Option C- Child benefit- special rate for children under three years**

In the light of these considerations, some members of the Commission see particular advantages in the unified approach based on a family income support approach which is centred on child benefit.

Option C proposes a special increased rate of child benefit for children in the youngest age-group - up to age three.

- The special rate of child benefit would apply to all children from birth up to age three when the child would become eligible for the Early Years Opportunities Subsidy proposed in Chapter 12.

- The special rate of child benefit would be paid irrespective of the parent's employment status or whether the parent providing the main care works full-time, in the home or outside the home, or is unemployed.

**Note:** The proposed level of child benefit from September, 1998 is £31.50 per month for the first two children and £42 for each subsequent child. The Commission suggests that if the rate of child benefit is to move in the direction of supporting the cost of childcare for children in the youngest age-groups, in terms of parental care full-time in the home or purchased childcare for those parents who work outside the home, a significant increase in the rate of payment for this age-group would be required to bring the rate of payment to £30 a week.

### *In support of option C*

A number of factors point towards the need for a continuing strengthening of the role of child benefit as a mechanism for providing income support to families.

Targeting State investment in support for children through the child benefit scheme is generally and for a number of reasons, put forward in the economic and social literature as a preferred policy option for supporting parents with their child-rearing responsibilities. Child benefit provides a very direct mechanism for channelling resources to children. It is universal, payable in respect of all children irrespective of their parents' employment status. It is for these reasons that child benefit as a means of channelling support to families is preferred over other mechanisms, such as tax allowances or tax credits. Tax allowances or tax credits do not provide any support to those families with children whose incomes are too low to pay tax. A switch of resources into child benefit and away from child dependant allowances, which are payable with social welfare payments, can help to improve both incentives to take up paid employment and improve the incentives for joint parenting.

Child benefit is neutral as to the choices parents make in relation to the care of their children. If the parent decides to work full-time in the home, the child benefit may be used to support the family budget. If the parent goes out to the workplace, the child benefit may assist with the cost of childcare. The approach of option C therefore, does not present either incentives or disincentives in relation to the particular choice the parent may wish to make, whether this is to take a job outside the home or to work full-time in the home, a factor which may be important for those families who are most in need of opportunities to participate in the labour market.

A special rate of child benefit for the first three years could help to address these issues in a focused and systematic way and provide the basis for development towards "basic income for children" for the youngest age-group (the first three years of life).

### Option C: the drawbacks

The main disadvantage of Option C is the converse of its major advantage: it is a uniform payment to all children. It is not specifically a recognition of "parenting" work carried out by the parent full-time in the home.

### Costs

There are come 146,439[15] children in the age-group up to three years. A rate of child benefit of £130 a month (£30 a week) per child in this age-group would cost an **additional £173m per annum.**

**5.17    Options are presented for further consideration but the policy priority in the years ahead is investment in the care of young children**

The lack of direct State investment in the care of the next generation and in support for families with childcare responsibilities at this important time in their lives is a significant gap in the policy approach to support for families in carrying out their functions.

It is the Commission's view that significant resources should be directed to meet this objective. In this context, the Commission suggests that an appropriate level of investment in children who are not yet attending school would, in equity, approach the level of per capita investment for younger children who are already in the primary school system (say £20 per week in 1998 terms). On this basis, an appropriate overall target level of invest-ment in children not yet attending school would amount to approximately £260 million per annum.

The Commission has presented some options in relation to providing financial support to assist with childcare responsibilities for young children.

Some Commission members feel that a specific payment should be available to enable parents who wish to do so to take time out of the paid workforce and to work full-time in the home when their children are very young. Options A and B present two approaches to such a payment. Each option recognises the requirement for complementary measures to invest in the care of young children who are not catered for by a parent allowance approach.

Other Commission members prefer an approach which would provide support for all children under age three and which is neutral in relation to choices that parents make whether that choice is to work full-time in the home or outside the home. Option C presents the case for this approach and proposes a special rate of child benefit for the first three years.

---

15    Census 1996, Principal Demographic Results.

At this point the Commission is not recommending one option in preference to the other. However, the Commission is strongly of the view that investment in the care of young children must be a prime objective of income support policies in the years ahead.

### 5.18    How the costs might be met

The Commission, in putting forward these options for consideration, is conscious of its responsibility to identify, in so far as this is possible, where resources of the level required to radically improve the income support arrangements for the care of young children might be found. In this context, the Commission has considered the effectiveness of the tax arrangements at present in place for married couples which to some extent support unpaid caring work where one spouse is not in the paid labour market. **The Commission questions whether the very considerable taxpayers' investment in the present arrangements could be better directed to provide more support for those with the most demanding caring responsibilities.**

The Commission's preliminary examination of this matter suggests that there is considerable potential in the restructuring of the tax arrangements for married couples over time, to better support those with the most demanding caring responsibilities, in particular those with young children under school-going age, or those caring for a family member who is ill or has a disability and needs care and attention, and those caring for elderly family members who are no longer independent in their daily lives.

Furthermore, a reorientation of the tax arrangements to better support the caring responsibilities which families are undertaking would help cohabiting couples whose less favourable treatment under the tax system gives rise to particular difficulties in relation to the incentive for one of the partners to take up employment.[16]

### 5.19    Could the present tax arrangements be better directed to support those families with the most demanding caring responsibilities?

The Commissions' examination of the effectiveness of the tax arrangements in supporting families with their caring responsibilities has been informed by an analysis of the Labour Force Survey data carried out by Dr. Tony Fahey of the ESRI. Dr. Fahey's discussion document on this issue set out in Appendix 2 to this chapter. The Commission is of the view that the cost of these present taxation arrangements represents the substantial amount of investment by the taxpayer, some £350m in 1991. [17] However, in so far as this investment is channelled through the present income tax arrangements for married couples, it could be better directed to provide more support to those spouses and parents with the most  demanding caring responsibilities for young children or other dependent family members.

---

16    In its interim report *Strengthening families for life*, the Commission drew attention to the tax treatment of cohabiting couples and the incentive and disincentive effects which not having the benefit of the tax allowance transfer arrangements available to married couples posed for low income couples in moving off social welfare and into employment. The Commission in its interim report, supported the view of the Expert Group on the Integration of Tax and Social Welfare that consideration to give to the possibility of allowing for joint taxation of cohabiting couples in cases where the couple have a child mainly resident with them.

17    Tim Callan, Brian Farrell, *Womens participation in the Irish Labour Market*, NESC No.91, December 1991.

One possibility is to phase out the arrangements in the income tax code and, using the resulting increase in tax revenues, to fund the policy options presented earlier in relation to supporting parents in their choice about the care of young children whether that policy option is to introduce a parent allowance for those who choose to work full-time in the home while the children are young, to provide a childcare allowance, or to introduce a special rate of child benefit- a move towards a basic income for the youngest age group. Resources should also be directed to the Early Years Opportunity Subsidy recommended in Chapter 12 and to improve the Carers Allowance for the care of family members who have a disability or who are elderly and dependent on family care.(Chapters 14 and 15)

**5.20**   **Review of tax arrangements**

The Commission would like to see a complete review of this aspect of tax arrangements. In particular, the review should examine the extent to which the present arrangements support families in their caring functions, particularly for young children under school-going age and for those looking after elderly people or family members with a disability and whether or not alternative arrangements could better meet this objective for those target families.

The Commission's recommendations for greater investment in children in the pre-school age-groups in this chapter and access to quality pre-school services for children (Chapter 12) are relevant to the review, as are our recommendations in relation to the needs of carers of older people (Chapter 14). The review should have regard to:

- the implications of the judgement in the *Constitutional case*[18] which gave rise to the introduction of the special tax arrangements

- the likely future trends in relation to the *labour force participation of women* who are still and are likely to remain the primary care givers in our society

- the *increase in tax revenues* arising from that participation and how these might be reinvested to support the *caring functions* traditionally carried out by women in the home and in the community

- the need to *protect the position of older women* who have retired from the labour force at a time when the expectation was that women would not continue working outside the home after marriage and children. These women are unlikely to return to the labour force. In many cases their educational attainments are not competitive with those qualifications of younger women and men who have had better educational opportunities and can command reasonable earnings in the workplace.

The Commission would like to see the outcome of the review set out a long term strategy for the reform of the income tax arrangements to better meet family objectives in relation to State support for the caring functions carried out by families.

---

18   *Murphy* v *The Attorney General* [1982] IR241 (HC, SC).

The Commission suggests that such a review could be undertaken by the Working Group which has been established to examine the tax and social welfare treatment of one and two parent households.[19] The terms of reference of the working group which include *inter alia* identifying and costing ways of ensuring consistent and equitable treatment of different households (i.e. married, cohabiting and one-parent households) under the tax and social welfare codes provide an appropriate family-focused context within which to explore this aspect of current tax arrangements.

---

19    The Working Group was established in May 1997:

   •    To examine and compare the treatment of married, cohabiting and one-parent households under the tax and social welfare codes, including an examination of the income support arrangements attached to labour market programmes, with particular emphasis on the Community Employment Programme.

   •    To carry out research as necessary, on household costs, equivalence scales.

   •    To take account of previous reports on this issue, such as the report of the Household Review Group and the Expert Group on Tax/Social Welfare Integration, as well as the forthcoming final report of the Commission on the Family.

   •    To examine approaches in other countries regarding treatment of one-parent households and spouses working in the home, and the applicability of such approaches to Ireland.

   •    To identify and cost ways of ensuring consistent and equitable treatment of the household types concerned under the tax and social welfare codes

   •    To produce a report with recommendations based on the above.

The Group is expected to complete its report in mid summer 1998. The Group is chaired by the Department of Social, Community and Family Affairs. It includes representatives of the Departments of the Taoiseach, Finance, Enterprise and Employment, Justice, Equality and Law Reform and the Revenue Commissioners, together with a representative of the Combat Poverty Agency and the National Social Service Board.

# Further comments from Commission members

**Commission member Anne Waters**

I do not agree with the statement: "On equity grounds the Commission considers that complementary measures would be required to address the needs of the families not catered for by the Parent Allowance. A Childcare Allowance providing a similar level of investment (£30 a week) in the care of children whose parents work in the paid labour market, would indicate a level of resource investment of the order of £69 million a year."

I believe that the automatic linking of a payment of £30 a week in the case of children whose parents work in the paid labour market with the Parent Allowance provided in Option A would serve to nullify the intention of said option, namely the recognition of the valuable work undertaken by a parent who chooses to remain in the home to care for his/her young children. It is my opinion that facilitating parents in their choice to work full-time in the home in the care of their young children by financially recognising the value of this unpaid caring work is quite separate to the issues to do with support for the childcare costs that parents in the paid labour market incur. Recognition for the unique contribution of a parent who makes the individual choice to forgo opportunities in the paid labour market to work full-time at home while children are young is long overdue.

The Parent Allowance has the attraction that it would be of most practical benefit to those parents on low incomes who wish to care for their young children themselves in the home or who are only marginally better off when working, after account is taken of their going to work expenses. The Childcare Allowance, as a universal measure, does not serve to target low-income households where additional support is most needed.

I consider that it would be more appropriate to allow the options for support with childcare needs for parents in the paid labour market to be dealt with by the Expert Working Group under Partnership 2000 for Inclusion, Employment and Competitiveness which is at present undertaking a study on the financing of childcare.

**Commission member Deirdre Carroll, representative of the Minister for Social, Community and Family Affairs**

Deirdre Carroll, does not agree with the statement: "On equity grounds the Commission considers that complementary measures would be required to address the needs of the families not catered for by the Parent Allowance. A Childcare Allowance providing a similar level of investment (£30 a week) in the care of children whose parents work in the paid labour market, would indicate a level of resource investment of the order of £69 million a year."

She believes that each of the Options A, B and C should be examined on their own individual merits. A Childcare Allowance, providing a similar level of investment as that proposed in Options A and B for parents in the paid labour market should not be automatically linked on "equity grounds" to these options. The incomes of parents in the paid labour market, cover a spectrum from low income to high income. If any arguments can be made on "equity grounds", it should at this stage of the analysis be confined to low-income parents whose spouses are in low paid employment and who wish to work in the paid labour market to increase household income. The many demands on Exchequer finances- a range of which have been identified in this Report- would not suggest that a universal Childcare Allowance to all parents in the paid labour market can be justified. At any rate the whole question of the economics of childcare financing is under major examination by the Expert Working Group under Partnership 2000 for Inclusion, Employment and Competitiveness established to draw up a national framework for the development of the childcare sector and which is chaired by the Department of Justice, Equality and Law Reform. The outcome of that important examination should be awaited in the context of any proposals on a Childcare Allowance specifically.

**Commission member Gemma Rowley**

Gemma Rowley concurs with the views expressed by Deirdre Carroll and Anne Waters.

She does not agree that it is necessary to have complementary childcare allowance measures as described in Options A and B.

She supports the Parent Allowance because it recognises the valuable work carried out within the home by the parent who takes on the day-to-day caring responsibility for the child.

**Commission member Marie-Therese Naismith**

Marie-Therese Naismith concurs with the views expressed by Deirdre Carroll, Anne Waters and Gemma Rowley.

# Appendix 1

## Recognition in the Constitution for work within the home

Many of the submissions received by the Commission which raised issues to do with the recognition of women's unwaged work within the home referred to the Constitution of Ireland. Article 41.2 assigns to women a domestic role as wives and mothers. Article 41.2 of the Constitution states: In particular, the State recognises that by her life within the home, woman gives to the State a support without which the common good cannot be achieved.

Article 41.2.2 states: The State shall therefore endeavour to ensure that mothers shall not be obliged by economic necessity to engage in labour to the neglect of their duties in the home.

The Review Group on the Constitution [1] suggested that the wording of the provision be updated and revised to read: The State recognises that home and family life gives a support to society without which the common good cannot be achieved. The State shall endeavour to support persons caring for others within the home.

It is the Commission's view that the revised Article 41.2 suggested is more in tune with developments in family life today. The revised wording suggested provides for recognition of the contribution within the home of both men and women in caring for children and other family members. By imposing a duty on the State to endeavour to support people carrying out these functions it presents a realistic objective for policy to give practical effect to that recognition in a way that the present, largely aspirational Article 41.2 has not done to date.

It is interesting to note the findings of the Review Group in relation to the contribution of Article 41.2 in its present format in practical terms to the lives of women who work in the home. The Review Group concludes that, notwithstanding its terms, the provision in the Constitution has not been of any particular assistance even to women who work exclusively in the home.

Their report documents the case of L v L where the Supreme Court rejected a claim by a married woman who was a mother and had worked exclusively in the home to be entitled to 50 per cent interest in the family home. The report also describes how at common law, it has been held that a married woman who makes a financial contribution directly or indirectly to the acquisition of a family home is entitled to a proportionate interest in it. However, this principle is of no help to the significant number of women who do not have a separate income from which they can make contributions to a family home, but who work within the home and in many instances relieve their husbands of domestic duties, thereby permitting them to earn money.

It is the Commission's view that the unpaid caring work which is carried out within the home, for young children or for a family member who has a disability or who is elderly and dependent on family care and support, is invaluable to society and should be recognised in the Constitution.

---

[1]  The Review Group was established by the Government on 27 April 1995 to review the Constitution and to establish those areas where constitutional change may be desirable or necessary, with a view to assisting the All-Party Committee on the Constitution in its work. The Review Group published its report in May 1996.

# Appendix 2

**Note on Labour Force and Family Status of Married Women, with reference to the implications of income tax treatment of married couples**

**by Tony Fahey, Economic and Social Research Institute**

The present treatment of married couples in the income tax code means that substantial tax expenditures are incurred in support of stay-at-home spouses among couples where one spouse is earning a taxable income. This arises because the tax free allowances and tax bands of the non-employed spouse are transferable to the employed spouse, thus greatly reducing the income tax liability of the employed spouse. At the level of the couple, the benefit involved increases with the size of the employed spouse's taxable income: the larger the taxable income, the larger the benefit. At the aggregate level, the cost of this tax expenditure to the Exchequer was estimated in 1991 at £350 million.[2]

The concern has sometimes been raised that the stay-at-home spouse may not always receive the benefit of this tax expenditure, since the employed spouse is the immediate recipient. This question of equity between spouses is not the concern of the present note. Rather, the concern is with the purpose and impact of the tax expenditures involved viewed as a family benefit. This concern arises because of the large cost of the benefit to the Exchequer, the somewhat unthinking way it was originally adopted, and the absence of any considered defence among policy-makers for continuing with it in present circumstances. The questions that arise are: What objective of family policy is this very large tax expenditure supposed to achieve? Are there better ways of achieving the same end?

The present policy was introduced in the 1980 Finance Act in response to the *Murphy* judgement in the Supreme Court in the same year. That judgement ruled that the income tax treatment of married couples up to 1980, by which a married couple could have to pay more income tax than if they were treated as two separate persons, was unconstitutional, in that it discriminated against married couples and was therefore contrary to the state's constitutional obligation to protect the institution of marriage. The Government responded to that judgement, not by equalising the tax treatment of married couples with that of two separate persons, which was the narrow implication of the court ruling, but by bestowing a considerable tax advantage on married couples compared to two separate persons. This advantage is as outlined above and is still in force.

At its introduction, this policy was justified as a 'subvention to childcare', on the assumption that the majority of stay-at-home spouses stayed out of the labour force in order to look after children. However, the tax benefits involved are not tied to the presence of children but depend solely on the non-earner being married to the earner. To what extent are the beneficiaries actually engaged in caring for children and thus to what extent is the subvention involved being received by those who were its original target?

We can get an approximate answer to this question by looking at Labour Force Survey data on the family status of married women who were not in the labour force.

---

2   Tim Callan, Brian Farrell, *Women's participation in the Irish Labour Market*, NESC No, 91, December 1991.

**Labour Force Participation Among Married Women aged under 65 by Presence of Children 1995**

| | Number | In labour force | | Not in labour force | | |
|---|---|---|---|---|---|---|
| | | No. | % | No. | % | % of wives not in labour force |
| Wives with no children in household | 127,500 | 66,500 | 52.1 | 60,800 | 47.8 | 15.2 |
| Wives with children age 15+ only in household | 149,900 * | 35,000 | 23.3 | 114,000 | 76.7 | 28.4 |
| **Sub-total** | **277,400** | **101,500** | **36.7** | **174,800** | **63.3** | **43.6** |
| Wives with at least one child aged under 15 | 372,800 | 146,700 | 39.9 | 226,100 | 60.6 | 56.4 |
| Of which: (Wives w/at least one child under 5) | 168,400 | 74,600 | 44.5 | 93,800 | 55.5 | 23.4 |
| **Total** | **650,200** | **248,200** | **38.2** | **400,900** | **61.8** | **100** |
| Memorandum item: Lone Mothers with at least one child under 5 | 18,800 | 5,500 | 29.2 | 13,300 | 70.8 | n/a |

\* Includes some married women aged 65 or over.

Source: derived from Labour Force Survey 1995, Table 43.

FINAL REPORT OF THE COMMISSION ON THE FAMILY

The data are not wholly informative for present purposes since they do not indicate how many of the husbands of these women were earning taxable incomes and thus were in a position to benefit from the double tax free allowances and tax bands. However, the data do provide some impression of the orders of magnitude involved.

The data in the table show that in 1995 400,900 married women aged under 65 were not in the labour force; they, through their husbands, were the potential beneficiaries of the tax benefits in question. Of that group, 60,800 (15 per cent of wives not in the labour force) had no children of any age in the household and so could not be engaged in the care of children in the household. A further 114,000 non-labour force wives (28.4 per cent of wives not in the labour force) had children aged 15 and over only in the household. A certain proportion of those could be counted as engaged in child-care, to the extent that 15 -16 and 17-year-olds warrant being cared for as children. However, it is likely that a large proportion had adult 'children' only in the household. Although the women in question might well have been providing large amounts of household services to those 'children', this would be as a substitute for services which those 'children' could well provide for themselves and so could not be counted as 'childcare' in the usual sense. Even in the case of, say 16 or 17-year-olds, one could argue that the 'childcare' they genuinely require is limited. While they might well generate a large housework requirement (cleaning, cooking, grocery shopping etc.), a large proportion of the housework could be and perhaps should be provided by the 16 and 17 year olds themselves. Children of that age could well be expected to make a large contribution to housework in the homes they lived in so that they provide as much housework as they receive. In any event, wives with children aged 15 and over in the household are not as tied up in 'childcare' in the strict sense as those with younger children.

If, to follow this line of reasoning, we were to assume that one-third of the wives with children aged 15 and over in the household who were not in the labour force were engaged in childcare, while the other two-thirds were not, we would arrive at an estimate of *about 75,000 wives in that category who were not engaged in childcare.* If we added these to the 60,800 non-labour force wives who have no children of any age in the household, we would get a total of 135,800 non-labour force wives who were not engaged in childcare. This amounts to 33 per cent of all wives who are not in the labour force. From this we can conclude that of those wives who are not in the labour force and therefore (through their husbands) are potential beneficiaries of the favourable income tax treatment of couples with only one employed spouse, *one in three are not engaged in childcare.*

At the other end of the spectrum were those wives who were not in the labour force and who had at least one child aged under 5 in the household. These could be considered unambiguously as providing childcare, and in most cases were likely to have remained outside the labour force for that purpose. They could therefore be considered as the prime targets of the benefit represented by the favourable tax treatment of couples with only one partner in paid employment. However, there were only 93,800 wives in that category. They represented less than a quarter (23.4 per cent) of wives not in the labour force and amounted to only 55.5 per cent of wives with children aged under 5.[3]

---

3    It is striking to note that the rate of labour force participation among married women with children aged under 5 (38.2 per cent) is relatively high. For example, it is quite similar to the rate for married women who have no children aged under 15, which is 36.7 per cent. This similarity in labour force participation rates between groups of women in very different family circumstances undoubtedly reflects a greater tendency towards labour force participation among younger married women than among older married women, which in turn may be strongly influenced by their differing educational profiles. Among younger married women, as far as labour force participation rates are concerned, the heavier demands represented by young children are outweighed by the labour force advantages of higher levels of education.

*These prime candidates for favourable income tax treatment, therefore accounted for only a minority of those actually receiving that favourable treatment, and a little over half of all mothers of young children.*

It is clear from this analysis that in so far as the present income tax treatment of married couples is designed to provide a subvention for wives who devote themselves full-time to childcare, it is poorly directed to that end. Many who receive the subvention are not engaged in childcare and many of those with young children who have a heavy childcare burden do not receive the subvention.

Given that this is so, the present tax treatment of married couples needs to be reviewed, especially in view of the large tax expenditures it entails. Either a better justification for it needs to be found, or, as seems more rational, a better means to achieve its present ostensible purpose needs to be devised. A range of such means are readily available. The purposes of family policy could be achieved by introducing tax allowances for children in conjunction with the treatment of spouses as two separate persons for income tax purposes, or by abolishing all family-related provisions in the income tax code and using the resulting increase in tax revenues to fund a greatly improved Child Benefit system, or by introducing an allowance of some kind specifically targeted at the childcare costs of families with young children. There would be arguments for and against each of these approaches, but any of them would seem to serve the purposes of family policy a great deal more effectively and efficiently than does the present approach, as far as income tax and married couples are concerned.

## Chapter Six Positive Parenting through Family Support and Parent Education

**6.1    Introduction**

In this chapter the Commission examines the need for help and support for parents in rearing their children.[1]

Support with and for parenting was a significant topic in submissions to the Commission. Overall, those who made submissions felt that parenting is a challenging task and that sharing the responsibility was important. Some people wrote that not enough attention or support was given to the importance of the role of fathers in parenting and that mothers often need access to support and help. Parents were concerned to do their best for their children and to rear them as responsible caring adults. There was a focus on the needs of new parents, on supports for young people who become parents at an early age, and on the needs of mothers and fathers who parent alone. It was suggested that there should be a public information campaign on responsible and positive parenting. A national free phone facility for parents to obtain information and to deal with problems was also suggested. Specialised information for parents whose child has a disability and programmes relevant to Irish families and to the communities in which they live were considered necessary.

**6.2    Parenting - support can help[2]**

Most parents rear their families without difficulty, but all need extra help at some time or another. Some families need support more than others; for example, families coping with considerable pressures. In its interim report to the Minister for Social Welfare, November 1996, the Commission identified some of the important stages in life when families need extra support, including:

- the birth of a first baby

- when children are under school-going age, and child care demands are at their most intensive.

There are vulnerable points in the lives of many parents when they need assistance to help them bring up children and this is usually provided by family, friends or State services. Some families will not seek help, fearing this to be an acknowledgement of failure, or that they will be judged as an inadequate parent. The prevailing attitude in the community towards being a good and coping parent often  makes it difficult to admit to problems or to seek help before a crisis occurs.

---

1    In October 1996, the Minister of State at the Departments of Health, Education and Justice, requested the Commission on the Family to consider the role of parenting programmes in supporting families and to recommend how the development of suitable services might be advanced.

2    This chapter draws on information about parenting support contained in Robbie Gilligan: *Family Support and Child Welfare* from *On behalf of the Child* edited by Harry Ferguson and Pat Kenny, Farmar, Dublin (1994) and *Parents as Teachers*, a report of a conference 12/13 Oct, Bryson House, Belfast, 1995 and material from South Australia "Parenting SA", The Office for Families and Children (April 1996).

Parents hold the key to their children's welfare. Experiences in family relationships from the earliest years onwards shape the individual's development through childhood, adolescence and adulthood. "Parenting" has been described as being about the care, nurture, protection, love and guidance of children and young people. It is about the transmission of values and culture. It is also about teaching aspects of citizenship, such as respect for laws, social responsibility, tolerance and personal contribution to the greater good.

The birth of a child has a major impact on most people's lives and the gulf between the expectations and experiences of parenthood is often great. Most parents learn as they go, influenced by the way they were brought up or by what they have read and watched others do. Being a competent parent requires knowledge, confidence and skills and having the support of other family members. *Parenting information* and *support* at different stages of a child's development and at times of family transition, stress and change may help parents and their children to make the most of new developments in their lives.

## 6.3     The case for a comprehensive programme to support positive parenting

In research findings and in recent policy developments, there has been a growing recognition, at home and abroad, about the important role of parents. For example, the U.N. Convention on the Rights of the Child (1990) and the Council of Ministers (EU) Recommendation on Child Care (1993) have drawn attention to the rights of children, the responsibilities of parents and the importance of their involvement in the care and protection arrangements for their children. The involvement of parents in the Early Start programme and the Home School Community Liaison Scheme highlights the value and effectiveness of working with parents in support of children. The Department of Health and Children funded two studies on parenting programmes currently available in Ireland, one in 1995 and a follow-up survey in 1997. These studies were carried out by the National Children's Resource Centre, Barnardos.

A study carried out in Australia which examined parent education services found that parent education groups enhanced the mothers' sense of competence and the benefits were immediately felt by mothers[3] Improvements as regards the mothers' sense of isolation came about later after participation in the programme, and there was more satisfaction in the relationship between parent and child. The researchers concluded that parent education groups provide a vehicle for the promotion of self-confidence and the erosion of social isolation in vulnerable families.

Studies abroad have pointed to the important preventive role of parenting education. Programmes to enhance parenting skills of new mothers and fathers have been identified as having a role in reducing the risk where a child might be at risk of abusive behaviour.[4] A major study into the causes of young offenders in North America identified parent education as one of the important preventive measures. Poor parental supervision, lack of positive communication and harsh discipline were significant precursors of criminal behaviour in adolescence.[5]

---

3   James G. Barber: *Evaluating Parent Education Groups: Effects on sense of Competence and Social Isolation*, *Research on Social Work Practice, Vol. 2*, No. 1 Jan. 1992.

4   R. Kim Oates, M.D. Brunner: *The Spectrum of child abuse*: assessment, treatment prevention, Mazel Publishers, New York, 1996.

5   Wilson and Loury, 1987, referenced in Discussion Paper 1996 published by "Parenting SA" Office of Children and Families.

## 6.4 Parents - the first educators and carers of their children

It is the Commission's view that parents are the first educators and carers of their children. The role of the State and the agencies of the State is to support parents in carrying out these responsibilities. Empowering families and strengthening them for life is an important objective of a programme for positive parenting as a primary preventive strategy in providing support for families.

The Commission's approach is underpinned by a belief that children are generally best looked after within the family, with both parents playing as full a part as possible in the lives of their children. The welfare of the child must, however, remain the paramount consideration.

## 6.5 Comprehensive programme to support positive parenting

Having examined the case for parent support and having discussed with a number of expert agencies the needs of families for parent support, the Commission concludes that *there is a need for a comprehensive programme* to support positive parenting. This programme should be a *core feature* of family policy and should include:

- access to information for parents and

- formal parent education by way of structured parenting programmes.

The programme should be *developmental* and should strengthen the social supports and coping capacities of all families with children. It should be *affirmative* of parents. It should develop parents' skills and it should be *available* to anyone encountering the ordinary challenges of parenting and family living.

### Principles to underpin a programme to support positive parenting

The Commission has identified the following principles which should underpin a programme to support positive parenting:

- parents are the *prime carers* and *educators* of their children and should be given the best information and support available

- recognition of the importance of the *role of parents and the level of competence and knowledge they have* of their own children

- equal emphasis should be placed on *the parental responsibilities of both fathers and mothers.* Special attention should be focused on the *role of fathers in parenting*

- recognition of the important role of *extended families,* the *local community, services for children* and schools

- the programme should be *affirmative*, identifying parents' skills and strengths and building on their confidence

- there should be *partnership* between the State services, professionals, parents and the community

- parent education should be available to all families that wish to avail of it.

## Families with particular needs

The Commission further considers that the parenting programme should recognise that there is a need for *additional support* for families with special requirements and at certain times. These include:

- lone parent families and families without strong family networks or community links

- Traveller families

- teenagers who are parents

- families going through separation or divorce

- families facing traumatic situations including serious illness, domestic violence, bereavement or very demanding caring responsibilities for a dependent family member

- families with a child or a parent with a disability

- families with a child who has behavioural problems.

## Families with a child with a disability

Parents of children with disabilities have special needs which may continue beyond childhood into adolescence and adulthood.

*Having a disabled child can have profound effects for a family. Parents often feel they don't know how to parent a disabled child. They may become lenient or too strict, pay too much attention or too little to the child. Siblings may also feel that they have to take on parenting responsibilities and may resent the attention their disabled brother or sister receives.[6]*

The Commission is of the view that a comprehensive programme should provide for the special needs of families with a child or a parent with a disability. The need for programmes to meet special parenting needs has been brought to the Commission's attention. The indications are that participation in parenting skills programmes can be of great benefit to parents and their children in these situations. The effectiveness of an existing parenting course, which was offered by the Eastern Health Board to parents of children with a disability, in decreasing parental stress and reducing child related problems, were documented in a scientific journal.[7] The indications are that parenting programmes are particularly beneficial to these families.

---

6 Submission to the Commission on the Family from the Eastern Health Board Parenting Skills Unit, May 1997.

7 Eileen Mullin, Keith Oulton and Trevor James: *International Journal of Rehabilitation Research 18, 142-145 (1995), Skills Training with Parents of Physically Disabled Persons.*

*continued over...*

The need for further work in developing specialised parenting programmes to suit Irish families who have a child with a conduct disorder, has been brought to the Commission's attention. The longer term outcomes for children with such a disorder, if left untreated, are poor. They can encounter many problems in later life.[8]

## 6.6 A national programme of information for parents

It is the Commission's view that a comprehensive parenting programme should address in particular the need for research to support and develop parent education programmes for Irish families who are coping with parenting difficulties. Funding to support innovative work in the research and development of programmes relevant to families in Ireland should be a central feature of State provision for parenting education.

Accessible information about parenting and child development, which strengthens the capacity of families in carrying out their essential functions of caring for children, is the first step in a comprehensive programme to support positive parenting.

### Recommendation of the Commission on the Family

**The Commission recommends the introduction of a national, readily accessible programme of information for parents. The programme should be a permanent feature of family health and welfare promotion. It should include dissemination of leaflets (including parenting guides), media campaigns and a telephone helpline.**

The programme should focus on the importance of parenting and good parenting practice and providing parents with relevant information at a broad level about the resources available both within themselves and their families and the outside support services available to assist when required. The core of the programme would be the production and dissemination of guidance leaflets for parents which would provide simple advice in relation to the developmental needs of their children at different ages and how parents can meet those needs. Special attention should be focused on the role of fathers in parenting their children.

---

*...continued from previous page*

7    The results of the study indicate that participation in the parenting skills course has been of great benefit to parents and their children. The results indicate a reduction in stress in mothers from a mean level considerably above the suggested threshold for identifying borderline psychiatric illness to one which is more acceptable. The results alone are justification for the provision of the course to parents, as the reduction in parental stress would be expected to lead to an improvement in family life and therefore an improvement in the children's environment. The main focus of the programme was on increasing the parents' ability to identify and modify undesirable behaviours in their children. In this, the programme has also been clearly effective, with substantial reductions in problem behaviours being reported. The benefit of the course is not confined to the targeted children. The skills the parents have learned generalise so the problems caused by non-targeted children are also reduced.

Interestingly only two of the targeted children were disabled, suggesting that it was the behaviour of the siblings that was causing most worry to parents.

Since the parents were previously meeting regularly as a group, it is a reasonable to suppose that the benefits obtained were as a direct result of the course rather than through the sharing of experiences.

8    The Commission acknowledges the contribution of Dr. Carol Fitzpatrick, Our Lady's Hospital for Sick Children, who has undertaken work in this field.

**Components of a national information programme for parents**

Components of a national information programme for parents could include:

- widespread *dissemination* of information (leaflets and guides), about everyday parenting experiences

- *media campaigns*, including the use of new technology focusing on
- availability of information, access to help
- promoting the positives of parenting and family life

- a *telephone* helpline - this is particularly important to provide access to information for families who are housebound

- a *promotional video* would provide much needed information for first-time parents and could be used to provide informal networks of support for parents, particularly for parents who are isolated in rural and urban areas

- access to specialist help where this is needed.

**Costs**

The Commission suggests that an amount of £300,000 could initiate the programme. The full cost would need to be determined on the basis of a national programme to reach all parents following an evaluation of the pilot phase.

This cost would include the following elements:

- commissioning a pilot series of information guides

- printing and distribution of guides

- a telephone helpline

- piloting a national programme of information. The pilot programme might target new mothers claiming child benefit, parents of 2-year-olds and parents of children who are starting school

- an information campaign to promote the initiative

- evaluation of the pilot phase of the programme.

The Commission suggests that the commissioning and implementation of this information programme could be undertaken by the proposed Family Affairs Unit in the Department of Social, Community and Family Affairs, in pursuit of its responsibilities to raise awareness and promote information about family issues in consultation with the Health Promotion Unit of the Department of Health and Children.

The Commission welcomes the allocation in 1998 to the Department of Social, Community and Family Affairs to initiate a pilot programme of parent information.

### Experience abroad

A programme introduced in South Australia is proving to be highly successful and could provide a useful model for a similar development in Ireland.[9] Parenting SA (South Australia) is a Government initiative to support parents with their demanding and important role. The programme is showing that providing information to parents to improve their knowledge, skills and confidence promotes the status of parents and allows them to acknowledge that being a parent doesn't mean that you have to have all the answers all the time.

## 6.7    Parent education - structured parenting programmes

The Commission has highlighted in its Interim Report[10] the need to adopt a lifecycle approach to parent education, as suggested by the findings of expert studies.[11] The availability of and access to structured parenting programmes are essential features of the lifecycle approach to parent education and have a key role to play as part of a comprehensive programme to support positive parenting. Well-organised and accessible programmes can provide lasting benefits to families. They can be the catalyst for support networks for families in local communities which are of benefit to them throughout their lifecycle. The importance of community-based work with parents who are coping with disadvantage, in particular the work of the Family and Community Services Resource Centres described in Chapter 2 and local schools, is also relevant to the promotion of parent education. Personal development courses and leadership and assertiveness programmes can promote interest and enthusiasm for parent education, building on the strengths within local communities. The Commission notes the increasing demand for structured parenting skills programmes.[12] It is the Commission's view that the relevance and importance of such programmes for all families who want them cannot be overemphasised.

### Recommendation of the Commission on the Family
**The Commission recommends that**

- **the demand for structured parenting skills programmes be facilitated and supported**

- **a national co-ordinating group should be established and the development and provision of parent education should be co-ordinated at regional level also through a system of regional co-ordinators**

- **the benefits of participating in parenting skills programmes should be promoted. In this context, the Commission considers that the potential should be recognised of State and voluntary services as key agents in promoting the benefits of parent education.**

---

9    See Appendix 1 to this chapter for some details of the programme.

10    "Strengthening Families for Life", Interim Report of the Commission on the Family to the Minister for Social Welfare, November 1996, Chapter 3.

11    "If education for parenthood is to adopt a lifecycle approach it needs to introduce appropriate support and learning opportunities at each stage of the life cycle." Pugh G. and D'Ath 1984, *The Needs of Parents: Practice and Policy in Parent Education*, National Childrens Bureau, Macmillan, Dublin.

12    According to a study undertaken by Barnardo's and the Department of Health, in a 12-month period between June 1993 and June 1994, over 8,000 people attended more than 400 parenting courses throughout the country.

**Co-ordination of the development of parent education programmes is needed**

The Commission, in consultation with some providers of parent education, has considered the development of programmes in Ireland. There is a wide range of parenting courses already available and many more are becoming available with the development of policy and legis- lation in relation to the welfare of children. While some programmes are excellent, they are not always appropriate to the Irish context or to different socio-economic groups. Many programmes are not readily accessible for those interested. Access may be restricted because of copyright or programme requirements in relation to qualification or training of the facilitators. Where parenting courses are available, there may not be a choice of programme. Courses differ to some extent in their aims, their ethos and their design and content.

The need for co-ordination was highlighted in a 1995 study.[13] A follow-up study in 1997[14] confirmed the wide variation in availability and in the content of programmes. The later study referred to several new parenting programmes being piloted; very few parenting programmes having been externally evaluated; the fact that very few programmes are specifically oriented towards disadvantaged communities; and that there was wide variation in the level of training for facilitators of programmes.

It is the Commission's view that there is a need to co-ordinate the development of structured parenting programmes. Agencies working in parent education should co-ordinate their approach to the delivery and content of programmes.

**A National Co-ordinating Group**

A National Co-ordinating Group, drawn from the agencies involved in the provision of parenting courses, could take on the responsibility of

- developing *standards* (a quality mark) for parent education programmes. This could include the core content of programmes, the approach to delivery of the courses and the training and back up support for facilitators

- developing a *library and information service* to include all available materials, guidance and resources, including grant aid, available for parent education

- promoting the *benefits of parent education*.

The National Co-ordinating Group could draw on the work of a *regional support team*. Regional co-ordinators from within the voluntary sector could take on responsibility for:

- an audit of programmes available in the region,

---

13   Parenting Programmes in Ireland, Health Promotion Unit of the Department of Health and Children and Barnardo's. 1995.

14   The study, Parenting Programmes in Ireland 1997 (Draft report), Barnardo's (funded by the Department of Health), covers some 31 parenting programmes in Ireland. The aims of the study were:
-   to detail the current provision of parenting programmes nation-wide
-   identification of the aims and objectives of each programme so that facilitators can more readily choose programmes suitable for participants
-   identification of the key elements common to those programmes which are considered to be working well by the groups using them.

- being an access point (contact-person) for information about parent education,

- organising training and support for facilitators.

The Commission suggests that the co-ordination of parenting programmes could be initiated by the proposed Family Affairs Unit in the Department of Social, Community and Family Affairs, in consultation with the Health Promotion Unit of the Department of Health and Children.

### Promoting parent education - some key agents

The Commission has identified a number of services which could take the lead in promoting the benefits of parent information and parenting education programmes:

- Department of Health and Children and the health boards, through the public health nurse and G.P. services and through the family support services, including Community Mothers and Family Support Workers, whose roles are described in Chapter 4.

- Department of Social, Community and Family Affairs, through the grants schemes for voluntary and community services.

- Department of Education and Science, through Home/School/Community Liaison and Early Start co-ordinators.

- Family Mediation Service, through promoting the benefits of specialised parent education programmes for families who are separating.

- Local development programmes and Area Partnerships, through acknowledging and supporting the role of parent education programmes in enhancing family networks and in building communities.

- Voluntary organisations and support groups for people with disabilities, through developing and organising programmes and providing information for parents.

- The social partners, through promoting opportunities in the workplace to enhance parenting skills and better manage work and family commitments.

### 6.8    Ante-natal services

The Commission considers that the further development of the ante-natal support services is an important preventive measure for parenting and family difficulties. Such a development should include basic information on parenting and provide support to parents, in particular first-time parents. Most maternity hospitals provide parentcraft programmes. It is the Commission's view that these services provide an opportunity to raise awareness about parenting issues and to promote information about assistance available and access to parent education.

## 6.9 Specialised parenting programmes - marital separation

The Commission considers that there should be a recognition of the benefits of specialised programmes at known stress points for families. For example, a special parenting skills programme which is available in some states in the US for couples who are separating is proving to be highly successful in educating parents to the needs of their children and in developing agreements about parenting responsibilities.[15]

The Commission is of the view that access to appropriate parent support programmes, through the Family Mediation Service would provide valuable support to families at a crucial time, focusing on the vulnerability of children and their special needs in separation situations.

### Recommendation of the Commission on the Family

**The Commission recommends that specialised parent information programmes for parents who are separating and their children should be promoted and should be accessible through the services provided by the Family Mediation Service.**

---

15    See Appendix 2 to this chapter for further details of the parenting programmes.

# Appendix 1

## South Australia Programme

### 1. Main features
- **Parent Information Centres** to provide information, resources and advice about caring for children and adolescents.
- **Government Information Kiosks**\* to dispense advice and information in libraries, chemists, large shopping malls and petrol stations.

### 2. Content
- A **television commercial** to promote the status of parents and provide them with **a one-stop shop help line number.**

- **Grants** to 154 community groups throughout the State to provide programmes to support parents, including a **Best Practice** grant for an agency to develop a programme of excellence for single parents.

- 24-hour, 7 day a week **helpline,** providing information support and referral service to parents.

- A **Parent Directory**\* to provide information about what services are available, where they are located and how to make contact.

- A **first parent package** of information\* for every first-time parent.

- **Home visitation for all new parents,** with a follow up visit, to provide education and support.

- Development of **home based parent programmes.**

- The distribution, through family and resource centres and other centres, of one million information sheets to assist parents. **Parent Easy Guides** cover 48 issues with which parents are often faced from their child's early weeks and months through to adolescence, in a practical, encouraging and easy to read form.

- Features on the **Internet.**

- **Evaluation** of the programme.

- **Education in the workplace** to help in a practical way workers who are dealing with work and family responsibilities.

### 3. Costs
In 1997, Aus.$500,000 (£250,000) was allocated to the Parenting SA Programme for 12 months.

---

\*    In development at the time of writing.

**Second baby**
Parent Easy Guide # 8

**Teenagers and drugs**
Parent Easy Guide # 15

**Being a Parent**
Parent Easy Guide # 1

Becoming a parent does not come with an instruction manual for all the things you will face. It is one of the most important and difficult things you can do as well as one of the most rewarding. To raise a child is an enormous responsibility which is usually taken for granted and for which there is little training. Most parents learn as they go, influenced by the way they were brought up or by what they have read and watched others do. Parenting styles may be different but we all share a common goal — we want our children to turn into .......healthy, happy, well adjusted, caring, responsible adults who will be respectful of others, be able to get along with others and be able to co...... Your children and your community

**Your feelings**
One of the most important things in par... is your own attitude to it. Do you like f... you feel scared about it or are you the... enjoying it?

As a parent you will experience a ... emotions which are all normal and ... can make you feel like you are o... counter ride. You will feel love, ... but also more frightening emoti... be very strong, such as anger, ... hatred. Often parents feel tha... appreciated by their children ... others. Such emotions can m... guilty as well as thinking y... parent. It is important to ... not expected to be perfe... parents feel that they ha... at some stage. Most pa... tired and upset and qu...

**Things that m...**
Find out what y...
• Be aware of h...
• Be wise en... things diff... strong... to...

**6 Ways to be a Better Dad!**

Dad, your kids need you!

Dads from all walks of life have found these tips make a positive difference — have and find out for yourself.

**Discipline with Love**
(Children 0-12 years)
Parent Easy Guide # 2

Many parents these days feel that they are not allowed to discipline their children. Parents need to feel confident that discipline is an important part of a child's upbringing. Children need discipline. They need it to feel safe and secure while learning to get along with others and to live in society. The best discipline leads to children learning self-discipline. Often there is confusion for parents when "discipline" and "punishment" are talked about. They are used to mean the same thing, when in fact they are quite different.

**What is Discipline?**
Discipline is about teaching and learning.
As parents we discipline our children when they are able to understand what we want to teach them, so that they will learn how to discipline themselves. We should use less limits as our children are able to make responsible decisions for themselves.
Discipline should not be harsh or unfair.
It should be positive and used to encourage good behaviour as well as to stop behaviour that you don't want your child to be doing.
Discipline can be given without the use of physical punishment. Discipline is given with rules followed by consequences.
Discipline, which builds on your child's wish to please you, is more likely to produce a well-behaved, contented child and a less stressed parent.
Discipline is about understand... (of the home, the school... understanding school... broken. It is about h...

**What parents ca...**
The methods you use are ... child's age, abilities and ... mean you will use differe... child within your family ... change them as your child ... as you talk to your chi... see as to whether or n... child. Discipline usually...

careful thought and methods which include:
• planning
• teaching
• explaining
• showing
• distracting
• making rules
• giving consequences

**Making the Rules**
When telling your child what you want him to do make sure you:
• are clear e.g. "no" to your toddl... out explanation of why it... little to him and h... again. If you...

parents b...

**Feeling Sick?**
Parent Easy Guide # 11

When you or I are not well, what we mostly want is someone to look after us, to give us food and sympathy, peace to be able to rest, and something to keep us amused when we are feeling better. When children are sick, they need all of this and more. When they are unwell, and especially if they are in pain, children often feel frightened or worried. They need to be cared for by the people they feel closest to.

**What about child care or school?**
Child care workers or family day care workers can be loved by and trusted by children, but usually they are so busy that it is difficult to give the time and attention that a sick child needs. It really is not fair to send a sick child to child care or school. Rest is usually not possible in a busy child care or school room. Also your child can pass on infections to other children and to the care givers or teachers.

**What parents can do**
Here are some of the things that you can do to help your children when they are sick.

**Rest**
Unless they are very sick most young children will not stay in bed.
• Sick children want to be near you, or to be where the 'action' is.
• Being able to lie on a soft chair where they can watch you is more restful than being alone in a bedroom.
• Watching TV may not be best for a child who has a headache, but it can be relaxing for a child who is not well enough to play. It also gives you a break.
• Many sick children just want to lie in your arms for a while.
• Gentle massage of the tummy, head, legs, etc. may be very soothing to them.

**Drinking and eating**
• Most children who are unwell do not want to eat much.
• Not eating for a few days will not do them any harm.
• It is important for them to drink extra fluids, especially if they have tummy upsets or diarrhoea or asthma.

• Try giving small drinks often; such as milk, water, diluted fruit juice, or fruit juice ice blocks. (If your child has gastro, ask your doctor about what he should drink).

**Behaviour**
When a young child is sick, she is likely to act in a more baby-like way for a while. Your child may:
• cry or whinge more.
• want you to be near all the time.
• want lots of holding and cuddles.
• speak in a more babylike way.
• need a dummy again (even if she has given it up).
• wet the bed or her pants.

Some sick children, especially those under 3 years, refuse to be with anyone except mum or their main caregiver. They may get very distressed if left with even a close family member like dad. This is a sign of being ill and worried and does not mean the child does not like the other person.

These behaviours are all normal for a child who is sick, and they are signs that your child needs more care and attention for a while. It may be hard not to be irritated by clinging and whinging, but it will stop when your child is feeling better. If you are able to give this extra attention, usually your children will begin to 'act their age' quicker when they get better.

**Sleep**
Sick children usually need extra sleep, but the sleep can be restless and broken. If children are in pain from an ear ache for example, it is hard to sleep and they may be quite frightened by the pain. They can also have nightmares. Stay near by, so that your child can see you or hear you during the night. This may help your child relax and go back to sleep. You

helping parents be their best

Produced by: Parenting SA - an initiative of the Government of South Australia

Written by: Child and Youth Health and The Office for Families and Children

# Appendix 2

## PEACE Programme (Parent Education and Custody Effectiveness)*

1.  **Main features**

    PEACE is an interdisciplinary programme for separating and divorcing parents. The programme provides education on three topics:
    - the **legal process** for making child-related decisions
    - the **adult experience** of separation and divorce and how parents can help their children to cope with this transition
    - the **child's experience** of separation and divorce and how parents can help their children to cope with this transition.

2.  **Content**

    Local programmes are organised by volunteer Local Advisory Committees of judges, court administrators, lawyers and mental health professionals. Each local advisory committee is provided with curriculum materials, training, consulting and evaluation support from the PEACE programme at Hofstra University, School of Law, Hempsted, New York.

    Materials include:
    - a **manual** describing programme organisation and curriculum
    - a forty-five-minute documentary **videotape** which informs parents about how they can help their children to cope with the stresses of parental separation and divorce. The videotape is based on extensive interviews with children of separated and divorced parents.
    - a **Parents Handbook** designed to give divorcing or separating parents helpful information about legal and emotional processes associated with separation and divorce.

3.  **Benefits of the programme include**
    - parents learn how to focus on the **best interest** of their children during the reorganisation of their family
    - parents receive valuable **information** that will help their children to cope with these difficult transitions
    - by encouraging **communication** between parents, parents may voluntarily develop a workable post-divorce or separation plan for their children
    - participation in PEACE **reduces parental isolation** and encourages their reintegration into the community.

* Source: *Hofstra Law Review*, Volume 23, No.4, Summer 1995: School of Law, Hofstra University, Hempsted, New York.

## Chapter Seven **Parents rearing children without the support of a partner**

**7.1**    **Introduction**

In this chapter the Commission considers lone parent families and how State services and policies strengthen and assist them in carrying out their caring responsibilities and in building secure futures for their children. The Commission's recommendations on these matters are confined to the areas where there is a valid role for public policy to intervene in family life. In the main, the Commission's concern is to focus on the needs of children and how family life may be strengthened to secure positive outcomes for them. The Commission has stated that the fundamental human activity of care, intimacy and belongingness can take place in a variety of family forms and that family policy should recognise this diversity.[1]

One of the most important and dramatic changes which has occurred in families in recent years has been the increase in lone parent families. These families comprise widowed parents, those who are separated from their spouse, and families where the parent is unmarried. According to the 1996 census of population, over one in six families are headed by a lone parent: 130,000 out of 806,800 families.[2] In a substantial number of these families the children are grown up. The figures indicate that somewhere in the region of 72,500 families, headed by a lone parent, have children under age twenty.

**7.2**    The increase in marital breakdown is a concern. It is almost always traumatic for the family members involved, particularly children, and it can present many new challenges to the parent, who takes the main responsibility for the children in building secure futures for them.

The increasing percentage of births to unmarried parents and the growing numbers of unmarried parents within the total lone parent group is a frequent topic of debate among policy-makers, the media and the general public. The topic is further complicated by concerns about teenage sexual activity, premarital sex and contraception.[3]

In addition, one of the major difficulties for policy-makers in analysing the issue is the lack of research on the outcome for unmarried parents and their children over time. The dearth of research in this area is an issue that the Commission highlights in this report.

It is worth remembering that Ireland is not unique in experiencing these changes in family forms. The numbers of lone parent families are growing across all industrialised societies. In this context the point has been made that lone parent families are not a new phenomenon. It is only during the 20th century that the death of a parent/spouse at a young age has ceased to be a common event.

---

1    See also Chapter 23, Submission of the Commission on the Family to the All-Party Oireachtas Committee on the Constitution, March 1997.

2    Census 1996, Principal Demographic Results, Central Statistics Office, Dublin. The actual figure for lone parents may be higher, since the Census is unlikely to contain figures of lone parents who are not heads of households in their own right; for example, younger lone parents who are living with their parents.

3    A number of these issues have been documented in a review of the literature in relation to unmarried lone parents for the Commission by Valerie Richardson and Gabriel Kiely of the Family Studies Centre UCD. Appendix 1 to this chapter contains an extract from the review.

## 7.3 The growth in lone parenthood

Two main reasons have been identified for the increase in lone parent families.

The *first* is the growth in marital breakdown. The 1996 Census shows that the number of separated people has grown from 37,200 in 1986 to 87,800 in 1996. The changes which have taken place in marriage and in society and the many pressures on families in today's fast-moving world are some of the reasons that social commentators and researchers cite for the increase in marital breakdown and consequent rise in the number of families headed by a lone parent. These changes and their effects on families are described further in Chapter 10.

The *second* reason is the rise in the numbers of unmarried mothers who are rearing children on their own, without the support of the child's father. In 1996, unmarried parents, the vast majority of whom are unmarried mothers, accounted for 15.3 per cent of all lone parent families.[4]

The last 30 years have seen a major growth in the proportion of births by single mothers. Between 1961 and 1981 there was a slow rise in births to single mothers from under 2 per cent to just over 5 per cent.[5] Since 1981 the situation has changed radically so that by 1996, 25 per cent of all births (12,484 per annum) were to unmarried mothers.[6]

Not all non-marital births will result in the formation of a new lone parent family. Many parents marry following the birth of their child, although the marriage rate of these is not known. The child may be born to a cohabiting unmarried couple. The child may be a second or subsequent child in an existing lone parent family or the child may be placed for adoption.[7]

## 7.4 Lone parent families- a mix of groups

A 1997 study[8] contains an analysis of lone parent families. The study shows that lone parent families cover a range of different family situations. They are a mix of groups. They differ in age, family life cycle, marital status and economic status. Table 1 from the study provides a breakdown of lone parents by marital status and age.

---

4   Census 1996: Principal Demographic Results and Volume 3, Household Composition and Family Units, Central Statistics Office, Dublin.

5   Welfare Implications of Demographic Trends, Tony Fahey and John Fitz Gerald, Combat Poverty Agency, Dublin 1997.

6   Vital Statistics, 1996, Department of Health and Children.

7   In 1995, 490 adoption orders were made, of which 297 were family adoptions.

8   Anthony McCashin: *Employment Aspects of Young Lone Parenthood in Ireland*, National Youth Federation and TREOIR, Dublin 1997.

**Table 1**

Percentage Distribution of Lone parents in Different Marital Statuses, by Age, 1995

| Age | Marital Status | | | | |
| --- | --- | --- | --- | --- | --- |
| | Single | Married[9] | Separated | Widowed | All |
| 15-24 | 39.4 | 0.6 | 0.6 | 0.0 | 6.8 |
| 25-44 | 60.6 | 35.5 | 61.1 | 6.3 | 32.4 |
| 45 and over | 0.5 | 64.4 | 38.3 | 93.7 | 61.1 |
| Total | 100% | 100% | 100% | 100% | 100% |
| LFS estimated total (000s) | 20.3 | 4.5 | 33.2 | 57.3 | 115.2 |
| LFS subtotal: 15-44 (000s) | 19.3 | 1.6 | 20.5 | 3.6 | 45.1 |

Source: Labour Force Survey 1995, Special Tabulation.

Note: Totals may not add up, due to rounding.

Unmarried lone parents are by and large in the younger age-groups, with 40 per cent under age 25 in 1995. Unmarried lone parents tend to be at an early stage in the life cycle. Separated parents are mostly in the over 25 years category. Over 60 per cent are in the age-group 25 to 44 years. They have both younger and older families. Widows, by contrast, are almost all (94 per cent) over age 45.

A key characteristic of young lone parents is low educational attainment. The study notes that about 25 per cent of younger lone parents have primary level education or less and a further 37 per cent have intermediate level. Therefore, about 60 per cent have a level of education which would bring them to minimum school-leaving age. The study reveals that the broad educational profile of all lone parents parallels to a remarkable degree that of the long -term unemployed.

A further characteristic revealed in the study relates to housing tenure. Younger lone parents tend to rely on rented accommodation: in almost equal proportions they rent from local authorities and from private landlords, with evidence of a growing reliance for assistance with rent on the Supplementary Welfare Allowance Scheme. Older lone parent families tend to be owner-occupiers.

There are some other characteristics that are particularly applicable to lone parent families. The majority of lone parent families, more than 4 in 5 families, are headed by women.[10]

---

9    The small figure for 'married' could be regarded as "separated" since these are lone parents who use the term married to describe their current status.

10   Census 1996, Principle Demographic Results, CSO Dublin.

Lone parent families face a greater risk of poverty than other families.[11] They have low rates of participation in employment. In 1995 under 30 per cent of lone parents, across all phases of the life cycle, were at work.

The majority of lone parents depend on social welfare as their main or only source of income. Maintenance payments from husbands and fathers are not a significant source of financial support for lone parents.

## 7.5    Income support arrangements for lone parents

In December 1996 there were almost 70,000[12] lone parent families receiving weekly income support payments from the Department of Social, Community and Family Affairs. This figure includes:

- 9,257 widowed parents receiving contributory widows'/widowers pensions

- 10,060 deserted wives with children receiving deserted wives' benefit,

- 50,557 lone parents receiving the means-tested lone parents' allowance.[13]

A lone parent receiving the One-Parent Family Payment receives £85.70 for herself and her child. An amount of £15.20 is paid in respect of each subsequent child.[14] Policy objectives to facilitate as far as possible lone parents who wish to take up employment have led to the introduction in recent years of relatively generous "disregards" in the way in which "means" are calculated in determining entitlement to the weekly One-Parent Family Payment. Thus, for example, a lone parent can earn up to £12,000 a year and retain entitlement to some weekly payment. Earnings up to £6,000 a year will not affect entitlement to the full weekly payment.

The rate of widows'/widowers' contributory pension and deserted wives' benefit which are not means-tested and are payable irrespective of earnings is £74.10 (personal rate), plus £17 for each dependent child.[15]

Social welfare expenditure on the means-tested lone parent allowance (now One-Parent Family Payment) in 1996 was £218 million, representing 5 per cent of the social welfare total of £4.38 billion.

## 7.6    Payments to one-parent families and incentives to marry and provide joint parenthood to children

There is evidence that lone parents' employment decisions are more responsive than many other groups to financial incentives formed by tax and social welfare policies. Long periods

---

11    Poverty in the 1990s Tim Callan, Brian Nolan, Brendan J. Whelan, Christopher T. Whelan, James Williams, Department of Social Welfare, Economic and Social Research Institute, Combat Poverty Agency, Oak Tree Press, 1996.

12    Statistical information on Social Welfare Services, 1996; Government of Ireland.

13    Now One-Parent Family Payment.

14    Rates from June 1998.

15    Rates from June 1998.

spent out of the labour market by lone parents can create difficulties for them re-entering the labour market, so that policy in Ireland, as in many other countries, has been shaped by a particular concern to facilitate the labour market participation of lone parents. As a result, the means-testing facing those entitled to One-Parent Family Payments contains elements which are more favourable to labour market participation than the means-test facing couples depending on Unemployment Assistance. This has given rise to concerns that the tax/transfer system may be putting obstacles in the way of joint parenthood. For example, it has been suggested that the One-Parent Family Payment and accompanying benefits may provide an incentive to remain a lone parent rather than to marry a partner who is depending on an unemployment payment.

The Commission is concerned that the tax/social policies should contain no unnecessary obstacles to couples in establishing a stable relationship and providing joint parenthood to children, but recognises that no system which has a support conditional on lone parenthood can avoid some financial incentive to lone parenthood and an obstacle to the formation of a stable relationship. It recommends that these issues be kept under review and notes in particular that the Working Group which has been established to examine the tax and social welfare treatment of one and two parent households[16] has a remit which will include consideration of this.

## 7.7    Payments to one-parent families and the growth in lone parenthood

The Commission has considered the concerns which have been expressed about State policies improving the financial situation of lone parents relative to that of couples and that this might be a factor in contributing to the growth in lone parenthood.

Concerns about the impact of welfare programmes on family structure have been particularly to the fore in the US, where, in many states, welfare payments have been highest for lone-parent families with children, and much lower (or in some circumstances, non-existent) for two-parent families. A recent study[17] found "no evidence that welfare raises the propensity to form female-headed households for either whites and blacks....suggesting that previous studies may have overstated the effect of welfare programs on family structure". A key difference from earlier studies was that this study used panel data - with repeated observations on the same individuals over time, including inter-state migration - allowing the identification of individual, state and welfare effects. Previous studies[18] found effects which were statistically significant, but so small that they did not suggest that a great deal of the growth in numbers of lone parents could be attributed to welfare effects.

---

16    The Working Group which was established in May 1997 is expected to complete its report in mid- summer 1998. The Group is chaired by the Department of Social, Community and Family Affairs. It includes representatives of the Departments of the Taoiseach, Finance, Enterprise, Trade and Employment, Justice, Equality and Law Reform, and the Revenue Commissioners, together with a representative of the Combat Poverty Agency and the National Social Service Board (see Chapter 5 for further details).

17    Hoynes, H. (1997) "Does welfare play any role in female headship decisions?", *Journal of Public Economics*, Vol. 65, No. 2, pp. 89-118.

18    Reviewed by Moffit, R. "Incentive effects of the US welfare system: A review", *Journal of Economic Literature*, Vol. 30, pp.1-61

Similar concerns have been evident in the UK debate on these topics. The number of detailed empirical studies is more limited than in the US, with much of the work based on data gathered in a special 1980 Women in Employment Survey. One such study[19] found results which contradict the assertion that higher welfare payments prolong single parenthood; another[20] finds no evidence that higher welfare benefits encourage marital dissolution.

### 7.8     Income support is essential for lone-parent families

It is the Commission's view that while empirical studies of the Irish situation are needed, the fact that the stronger incentive in the US system towards lone parenthood seems to play a limited role in the growth of numbers of lone parents is relevant to the discussion. Nonetheless the Commission believes that research should be carried out in Ireland in this area.

The financial security afforded by the One-Parent Family Payment is very important to lone-parent families. Their options, in terms of improving their financial situation, can be severely limited because there is only one parent to carry the childcare responsibility, as well as being the main breadwinner for the family, and because young lone parents often have low educational attainments and find it difficult to get a place in the highly competitive jobs market. The One-Parent Family Payment provides a degree of security to families when they are at their most vulnerable. Women (mainly) are not constrained to remain in relationships which may be unhealthy for themselves and their children.

**It is the Commission's view that income support for lone-parent families is and must continue to be an essential priority for State policy in relation to families.**

### 7.9     Improving the prospects for children - the priority

Of immediate concern to the Commission is the fact that children in lone-parent families face a higher risk of poverty than children in two-parent families.

International comparisons suggest that lone-parent families in many countries experience poverty. They do best in countries where State support is relatively generous to all families with children and worst where they have to rely on social assistance.

Participation in employment represents the best prospect for improving income and hence the living standards of lone parents and their children. In this regard, there is now a considerable body of research at home and abroad which shows the clear material advantage of an employment-led support policy for lone-parent families. Employment has further advantages in offering choice and dignity, less isolation and more active involvement to lone parents. This is particularly important to young single mothers.

Comparative research shows that lone parents in Denmark or Sweden, where there is considerable degree of gender equality, more individualised tax and social welfare systems

19   J. Ermisch and R. Wright "The duration of lone parenthood in Great Britain", *European Journal of population*, 1991, Vol. 7., No. 2, pp.129-158.

20   J. Ermisch and R. Wright, "Entry to lone parenthood: analysis of marital dissolution", Birbeck College Discussion Papers in Economics, December 1989.

and higher levels of labour force participation by women and women with children, *are more likely to be in paid employment and less likely to be financially poor* or dependent on State payments.[21] Lone parents are able to secure a higher income in countries where they are supported in finding employment.

**7.10    Employment-led support policy approach**
Essentially, an employment-led support policy approach would build on policy initiatives adopted in recent years to facilitate the participation in employment of lone parents. It would involve a focus on:

• access to education, training and employment opportunities

• access to childcare

• information, guidance and support for lone parents in their efforts to secure a place in the labour market

• income support arrangements to ensure that these do not present barriers for lone parents in seeking access to the paid labour market.

**Changes introduced in recent years**
In recent years there have been substantial adjustments to the One-Parent Family Payment to facilitate lone parents to take up paid employment. In the main, these adjustments mean that a reasonable amount of weekly earnings will not affect the one-parent family weekly payment. These adjustments in the means test have greatly reduced the financial barriers which lone parents face in re-entering the paid labour market.

**Options for improvements in income support arrangements**
In Chapter 5, the Commission has drawn attention to the case for a restructuring of child income support provision, with an increased role for child benefit and a less important role for child-dependent additions to social welfare payments, including payments to lone parents. In this way a greater proportion of the family income support is centred on the child. Since child benefit is paid whether the parent is working or not, this approach affords the parent maximum potential to increase family income by taking up employment in the knowledge that the child benefit is secure. The overall restructuring of child income support, which the Commission argues for in Chapter 5, should further reduce financial disincentives that arise for families on social welfare in considering opportunities to take up paid employment.

**The rent allowances - removing the disincentive**
For the group of lone parents who rely on rent supplements under the supplementary welfare allowance scheme, a significant barrier still exists to improving their income position. The rent allowance is reduced directly in relation to earnings, so while lone parents

---

21    A recent study compared the employment situation of lone parents across several countries. Details of "Policy and the Employment of Lone Parents in 20 countries", Jonathan Bradshaw, Steven Kennedy, Majella Kilkey, Sandra Hutton, Anne Cordon, Tony Eardley, Hilary Holmes, Joanne Neale, European Observatory on Family Policies, August 1996 are set out in Appendix 2 to this chapter.

are encouraged to take-up work with the introduction of incentives into One-Parent Family Payment, the value is clawed back through the supplementary welfare allowance rent supplement scheme. A further issue arises in that the rent supplement is withdrawn completely if the person works more than 30 hours a week. The Expert Group on the Integration of Tax and Social Welfare[22] suggested that this might be addressed by a tapered withdrawal of rent allowance. The Government has undertaken to consider the issue in consultation with the social partners.[23] **The Commission recommends that the suggestion be explored further with a view to removing this disincentive.**

## 7.11     Information, guidance and support is important

There is a need to develop **an integrated package of support for lone parents** to include information and advice about access to education, training and employment schemes and job opportunities. Elements of the package might include:

- A comprehensive approach to information about different programmes available and the effects of the various options on family income and advice and guidance in assessing the financial gain to the family of opportunities which arise.

- Practical help in finding a suitable job opportunity and help in finding out about local childcare services and about support available to help meet childcare needs.

The Commission is of the view that there is a distinct role for the *customised service*, as proposed for the local offices of the Department of Social, Community and Family Affairs in Chapter 3, in providing enhanced information services to lone parents in their own community. One to one advice and guidance is a feature of personalised services being developed in a number of countries, for lone parents and other people who have difficulty in getting access to opportunities in the labour market. Job facilitators, introduced in recent years as the key workers in the Employment Support Services of the Department of Social, Community and Family Affairs, are proving to be highly effective. The Employment Support Service could provide the model for a customised service to meet the needs of lone parents with the possible extension of the role of jobs facilitators with appropriate training and closer links with services in the community to meet the needs of lone parents.

A further issue arises in relation to encouraging lone parents to use the services of local offices of the Department of Social, Community and Family Affairs. Lone parents (even if they are not registered as unemployed) can qualify for many work/ training opportunities.[24]

22    Report of the Expert Working Group on the Integration of Tax and Social Welfare systems, 1996 Department of Social Welfare, Dublin.

23    Partnership 2000, for Inclusion, Employment and Competitiveness states:

Para 4.20 Under the Supplementary Welfare Allowance Scheme, a weekly supplement may be paid in respect of rent or the interest element of a mortgage repayment, provided a person is not working for more than 30 hours per week. The withdrawal of this allowance can constitute a severe unemployment trap.

Para 4.21. Specific consideration will be given to alleviating this unemployment trap, through the introduction of an appropriate tapering arrangement. The Government will consider this issue within the first year of this Partnership, in consultation with the Social Partners.

24    See paragraph 7.14 for details.

However, the One-Parent Family Payment is paid by a book of payable orders which is cashed weekly at the post office. Thus lone parents do not as a rule have reason to visit local offices of the Department, although some lone parents use the local office information service if they have an enquiry from time to time about their claim. Since the local office is the main source of information about schemes and programmes, lone parents can miss out on opportunities to explore education and training options which might be available to them.

The welcome decline in the numbers of unemployed calling to local offices of the Department to sign on the Live Register of Unemployed affords an opportunity to provide services to a wider group of people who are seeking employment. The transformation of local offices of the Department of Social, Community and Family Affairs to provide a range of services, building on the one-stop-shop concept, to families in their own community, as proposed in Chapter 3, will open up possibilities for the delivery of enhanced information and employment advice services.

The proposal for close collaborative links between the new style local offices and the Family and Community Services Resource Centres and more exchange of information about services, including community-based support services as recommended in Chapter 2 and Chapter 3, will provide a solid basis for the development of a responsive service to meet the needs of lone-parent families.

**7.12  Promoting opportunities to participate in education, training and employment when childcare responsibilities have eased**

For most lone parents, their child's entry into primary school at age four or five brings with it a considerable easing of childcare responsibilities. The Commission suggests that this important transition time in the family's lifecycle presents an opportunity to engage lone parents as active participants in planning secure and positive futures for themselves and their children. A proactive information policy designed to meet the needs of lone parents in terms of the options for education, training and employment with an emphasis on support and guidance has the potential to be particularly effective at this time. It is recommended that the relevant departments and agencies consider an approach to such a policy and bring forward proposals in this area.

**7.13  Access to childcare**

Lack of access to affordable childcare is a significant obstacle for lone parents in looking for training or employment or opportunities to return to education. Parents need reassurance about the care of their children in their absence. Access to affordable quality services for children is a prerequisite for real parental choice in relation to participation in employment, education or training.

It is the Commission's view that the investment in children under school-going age, as recommended in Chapter 12 to secure for children, on reaching age three, opportunities to participate in quality services in crèches/nurseries and in pre-school playgroups, would contribute to the development of quality services for this age- group, thereby increasing the number of places available. The Commission also suggests there is a distinct role for public policy in partnership with local communities in the development of services for children. Community - based facilities to meet the needs of different groups, including lone - parent families and children with special needs, should be a core feature of a national strategy on childcare.

The Commission, in Chapter 5, has presented options for greater financial support in respect of younger children under age three to recognise the additional childcare costs arising for this group. The measures proposed in Chapter 5 and Chapter 12, if implemented, would provide significant assistance to all families, including lone -parent families, in meeting the cost of childcare for children who are not yet attending primary school.

**7.14**    **Employment and training programmes which are available to lone parents**

The introduction of a more employment friendly ethos in social welfare provision for lone parents in recent years has been paralleled by greater access to training programmes, which were traditionally targeted towards long term unemployed people who were on the Live Register.

The main schemes in which places are available for lone parents are:

**Community Employment Scheme:** Lone parents may retain One-Parent Family Payment while participating in community employment. In 1995 about 4,000 lone parents participated in the programme.

**Vocational Training Opportunities Scheme (VTOS):** Ten per cent of places are reserved for some groups, including lone parents and people receiving disability allowance. Lone parents may retain One-Parent Family Payment while participating in the scheme. There were 4,753 participants in October 1997. Information is not available about lone-parent participation in Vocational Training Opportunities Scheme.

Lone parents may also avail of the **Back to Work Allowance Scheme** which allows participants to take up job opportunities in employment or self-employment while retaining seventy-five per cent of weekly One-Parent Family Payment in the first year, fifty per cent in the second year and twenty-five per cent in the third year, as well as secondary benefits such as a medical card, butter vouchers, back to school payments, a Christmas bonus, and differential rent or rent supplement if these are in payment. Secondary benefits may be retained while income is under £250 a week. Lone parents may also return to **second or third-level education** and retain their One-Parent Family Payment.

There were over 21,000 participants in the Back to Work Allowance scheme in December 1997, of whom 180 were recipients of One-Parent Family Payment. In relation to participation in second and third-level education: of the 330 people attending second-level education, 17 were receiving One-Parent Family Payments, while 114 of the 3,760 participants in the Third-Level Education initiative were receiving One-Parent Family Payments. Young lone parents may also secure places in **Youthreach**, which is designed for 15 to 18-

year-olds who leave school without qualifications, and in other locally based projects such as those funded under the INTEGRA and NOW programmes for disadvantaged communities. Some of these projects are designed specifically to focus on employment and training issues for women. Community-based projects to meet the needs of lone parents are also emerging in the community sector.

## 7.15 Suggestions to improve participation in programmes

The issues for lone parents in relation to participation in these programmes have been comprehensively examined in a recent report.[25] In the course of the examination the author identifies a number of features of provision which have a particular relevance to the extent to which the schemes and programmes recognise the particular needs of lone parents.

The first issue relates to the age requirement for participation in schemes. For most schemes - Community Employment Scheme, Vocational Training Opportunities Scheme, Back to Work Allowance, Third-Level Education initiatives - the participant must be 21 years or older. The age requirement has the effect of excluding a very distinct group of lone parents: the very young unmarried mothers who are most likely to have left school early but whose familiarity with the school system is most recent. In relation to the education-focused initiatives, there is a case to be made for reviewing the age requirements so that younger lone parents may gain access to programmes.

Further suggestions have been put forward in relation to enhancing the potential of VTOS to offer lone parents with poor educational qualifications an opportunity to bring their educational standards up to Leaving Certificate level. Improvements suggested include crèche facilities, pre-VTOS provision and stronger linkages post-VTOS with employment and further educational opportunities.

The programme structure of Youthreach, which operates on a full week/full day basis, and the absence of childcare are barriers to participation for lone parents. The structure of Youthreach needs to be examined to see if adjustments can be made to better meet the needs of lone parents with childcare responsibilities.

**The Commission is of the view that many of the improvements suggested could be introduced into the employment and training programmes to enhance the opportunities for lone parents, particularly young lone parents, to participate.**

## 7.16 In support of an approach to policy based on encouraging employment

It is the Commission's view that an employment-led support policy for lone-parent families should not undermine the core objective of the One-Parent Family Payment which is to provide secure income support for lone parents in caring for their children.

Throughout this report, the Commission has emphasised that parents are the primary carers and educators of their children and that policy should facilitate and support parents in the choices they make in relation to the care of their children. This approach is evident in

---

25    Anthony McCashin; *Employment aspects of young lone parenthood in Ireland* National Youth Federation and TREOIR, Dublin 1997.

the Commission's recommendations for improved support for parents with their childcare responsibilities, presented in Chapter 5 and in Chapter 12. These recommendations are underpinned by an objective to provide practical support to all parents with their childcare responsibilities and affirmation of their role as the primary carers of their children. This objective has a particular relevance to an employment-led policy approach for lone parents.

**7.17**   There are two very significant factors in relation to lone parents in support of a policy approach which facilitates and encourages participation in training and education programmes and employment.

The *first* relates to the considerable amount of evidence which points to participation in paid employment as representing the best prospects for improving income and living standards for lone parents and their children.

The *second* factor relates to the significantly lower levels of participation in employment of lone parents compared to mothers with young children in general. Special tabulations drawn from the Labour Force Survey 1996 show that in almost half of all families with children under age 15 the mother works outside the home either on a part-time (14 per cent) or a full-time (28 per cent) basis. By comparison, a recent analysis[26] of the principal economic status of lone parents based on the Labour Force Survey 1995, shows that under 30 per cent of lone parents, across all phases of the lifecycle, are at work.[27]

**7.18**   **Teenage mothers**
There is some misunderstanding about the "rising" incidence of births to teenage mothers. In fact, the rate of teenage pregnancy has been rising less sharply than the rate for other age-groups and has fallen in some recent years. The total number of births to teenage mothers in 1996 was lower than in 1980.[28] What has happened is that there has been a change in the marital status of these teenage mothers. For teenage mothers, the great majority of births (almost 95 per cent) now take place outside of marriage.

Statistics from the Department of Social, Community and Family Affairs show that 2,375 teenage girls were receiving One-Parent Family Payments at the end of 1996.[29] The number of teenage mothers receiving the payment at the end of December 1995 was 2,400.

26   Anthony McCashin: *Employment aspects of young lone parenthood in Ireland*; National Youth Federation and TREOIR, Dublin 1997.

27   A recent study is of interest in this context. The study found that lone parents in the study were positively disposed to taking up employment at some stage. Anthony McCashin, 1996, *Lone Mothers in Ireland, a local study* Combat Poverty Agency; Oaktree Press, 1996.

28   Vital Statistics for 1980 show that there were 3,580 births to mothers under age 20, of which 1,431 were births outside marriage. In 1996 there were 2,700 births to mothers under age 20, of which 2,560 were births outside marriage.

29   The statistics show that 15 teenage males were also receiving the allowance.

## 7.19    Young lone mothers - some characteristics

Many young lone parents have huge family support and indeed research shows that social support offered by families is a significant determinant of the well-being of young people faced with challenging situations. A study in the UK which tracked some 700 lone mothers from 1991 found that families were socially and materially better off if they had grand-parents available to support the family.[30] However, research[31] also shows that lone parent-hood is firmly concentrated among the most disadvantaged young women, those with few educational attainments and those who are unemployed.

## 7.20    Young lone mothers- the difficulties

A recent review of young mothers groups,[32] an initiative introduced by Foróige, the National Youth Development Organisation, describes the very specific problems which young lone mothers encounter in society. The need to bring up their babies is all-consuming with most of the young mothers. They were either living by themselves with the baby or with their parents - an older generation. The young mothers are often tied to the house and cannot afford to go out because it might take money from the baby. Friends call less frequently and have little in common with the young mothers. The net result for the young mother is spending long periods in the house without adult company, becoming more and more isolated and feeling depressed. These young women often have no outlet or opportunity to meet and talk with young women of their own age.

In all life situations they are first and foremost seen as young mothers, inseparable from their child. The second dimension of their young life experience, the fact that they have been catapulted into adulthood and are often early school-leavers and have little time to focus or concentrate on their own development is often overlooked.

## 7.21    The policy response to premature parenthood

The Commission has a particular concern to address the policy response to teenage parenthood because of the difficulties premature parenthood predicts for these young people and their children. The path to adulthood is interrupted, opportunities for completing education are restricted and it is difficult in the longer term for these young people to get a foothold in the labour market.

The Commission recommends the development of a comprehensive policy response to teenage parenthood involving:

- a prioritisation of *support services for teenage mothers*

- an approach which covers two main objectives
- encouraging young people to defer parenthood by *improving life's chances and choices*

---

30    *Young Single Mothers: Barriers to independent living*, Suzanne Speak, Stuart Cameron, Roberta Woods, Rose Gilroy; Rowntree Foundation Study of various supports of lone parents. July 1995.

31    D.F. Hannan, S. O' Riain, *Pathways to Adulthood in Ireland*, ESRI, Dublin, 1993.

32    *The First Step*: Review of work carried out by Foroige with Young Mothers Groups, Written and compiled by Stephen Rourke, Foroige, National Youth Development Organisation, Dublin, 1998.

for young women through training and education and offering these young people a realistic hope that they may succeed in education and in securing employment

- *information for young people* through education programmes which seek to influence their behaviour and their choices in relation to their future.

### 7.22    Support programmes for young mothers - the priorities

Support services should address a number of needs for young mothers. These needs include:

- support with parenting and childcare responsibilities and programmes which recognise the need for these young mothers to complete their own transition to adulthood
- improving the future prospects for completing their education and obtaining access to employment and training programmes.

The experience of the youth organisations that work with young lone mothers is that there is a need for personal support on a one-to-one basis for these women, particularly at the ante-natal and post-natal stage and in the first year with their new baby.

**It is the Commission's view that young lone mothers should be a priority for family support work, as described in Chapter 4. Extra attention and support from the Public Health Nurse, Community Mothers programmes and mentoring schemes are of particular importance to these young mothers in their parenting role. In this regard, the Commission recommends that the 2,400 young lone mothers under age 20 who are dependent on One-Parent Family Payment should be a priority group for family support programmes.**

Support groups and peer programmes become important in the post- natal stage. The youth services sector, largely through Foróige - The National Youth Development Organisation, and the National Youth Federation, have introduced a number of initiatives to respond to the needs of young mothers.[33]

### Young mothers groups

Young mothers groups, which have been introduced by Foróige, provide an important and effective support for these young women and an opportunity to build up their self-esteem and confidence. The young women themselves are involved in the planning, implementation and evaluation of the programme. Most of the activities are low cost and cover a range of interests; for example, information on women's health, social welfare entitlements, first aid training and education opportunities, sport and recreation, arts and crafts, childcare and development, parenting skills, child health, personal care, nutrition and diet, and trips and outings. Childcare facilities are provided for the young mothers in the group. Through participation, the young women build up their skills in decision making, organisation, budgeting, team work and leadership and show positive benefits in terms of self-esteem, happiness and belief in themselves, gaining the confidence to progress onto various courses, programmes and jobs. There are now eight young mothers groups in four different areas in Ireland.[34]

33    The various initiatives are designed for all young mothers. There is no age restriction, young married mothers also participate.

34    There are currently three groups in Blanchardstown (Dublin), two in Tallaght (Dublin), two in Ballymun (Dublin) and one in Cork City (The Glen)

**Moving on programme**

A variety of options for education and training and clear progression routes for young lone parents are features of the 'Moving on' vocational training project introduced by TREOIR and the National Youth Federation under INTEGRA.[35] This programme, aimed at overcoming the barriers to further the education and employment of young mothers, was developed by a consortium of national and local agencies. The programme operates in two areas, Dundalk (urban) and Carlow (rural). Self-development and peer support are important features of this programme. Moving on has identified the need for a co-ordinated delivery of support services to lone parents, involving the Departments of Health and Children, Education and Science, FÁS and the community sector.

**7.23**    **Essential supports for young mothers**

The youth services have identified a number of features which are central to the provision of services for young mothers. These include:

- the provision of appropriate *childcare services* to facilitate the participation in support, training and education programmes

- the importance of *peer support programmes.* Many young lone mothers depend on the mutual support which they obtain from other young women in a similar situation to themselves. It is difficult for them to maintain a commitment to a programme where they have little in common with other participants who do not have childcare responsibilities

- the importance of *outreach services* to reach those women who are most isolated

- the importance of *one-to-one support and personal action plans* to enable them to measure progress and to achieve realistic objectives

- the importance of *transport*, particularly in bad weather, to assist in maintaining commitment to participation

- the need for *programmes to be developmental and challenging:* while support is important, women want to learn and develop new skills.

In line with this experience, recommendations have been made to the Commission for a comprehensive approach to the provision of support services for young mothers.

**7.24**    **Strengthening the role of youth services**

**The Commission recommends that the role of the youth services in the provision of support programmes for young lone parents should be strengthened and a specific budget allocated to these services to expand provision for young lone parents.** It is suggested that the allocation should comprehend the additional needs which young lone mothers may have over and above the needs of other young people, such as childcare, transport and one-to-one support.

---

35    Formerly the Horizon programme (EU).

It is further suggested that the initial target level of provision should be funding for support programmes in the youth services sector to reach 2,400 young lone mothers under age 20 who are dependent on the One-Parent Family Payment.

**7.25** **Improving prospects for completing education and gaining access to employment and training programmes**

A further strand of the policy in relation to young lone parents relates to improving prospects for completing education and gaining access to employment and training programmes. The Commission has proposed earlier in this chapter that the age criteria for education programmes such as VTOS and the Third-Level Education Scheme should be reviewed in relation to lone parents.

A further suggestion relates to the development of school re-integration projects in specific areas and communities.[36] The suggestion has been presented in the context that many young lone mothers can be thought of as early school-leavers since they left school during pregnancy or after their child was born.

A community-based initiative in the south east has been brought to the Commission's attention; it supports pregnant young women who are completing their education. The programme involves Saturday morning support group meetings in which the young women participate in parenting skills, self-esteem programmes and time management programmes. Four local schools are involved in the programme.

**The Commission considers that these initiatives should be explored further, with a view to developing a programme for young lone mothers to keep them in the school system, or reintegrate them into the school system as part of the range of initiatives to address early school leaving which are described in Chapter 13.**

**7.26** **Health Promotion Initiatives for teenagers are important**

The Commission in Chapter 13 has highlighted the role of social, personal and health education in informing young people about responsibility in relationships and sexuality and in influencing their choices in relation to their futures. The relationship between lack of educational attainment and early school-leaving and premature parenthood is documented and the Commission points to the need to prevent early school-leaving so that young people may reasonably expect to succeed in educational attainment and may look forward to securing a place in the labour market. The Commission would like to highlight in this context the particular importance of social, personal and health programmes for those young people who are at risk of early school-leaving or who are outside the formal school system.

---

36  This suggestion has been put forward in the report *Employment Aspects of Young Lone Parenthood in Ireland* by Anthony McCashin, National Youth Federation and TREOIR, Dublin 1997.

In the course of his examination, the author draws attention to the level of early school-leaving and its possible link with lone parenthood. There is an annual average of 4,000 early school-leavers per annum (LFS 1996). If half these are girls, the potential arithmetical overlap between the young single mother population is highlighted. The number of births to girls aged 15 to 18 years (inclusive) in 1995 was 1,414 and while there is no empirical evidence of the number of early school-leavers who are pregnant or already mothers, it is highly likely that a very significant portion of the female school leavers are in the young single mother category.

**A role for the youth service in teenage health promotion**

The need to address teenage parenthood was a significant issue raised in the Consultative Process on Women's Health in 1995. The consultative process prioritised the identification of ways of reaching the most vulnerable sections of young people and targeting them with special education programmes. As part of its response, the Eastern Health Board has introduced a Teenage Health Promotion Initiative. The initiative is a primary prevention programme to develop and enhance the competencies and self-esteem of young people and to inform them of sexual health matters. The programme centres on the training of youth leaders and other key people who work with young people and who have their confidence to deliver the Health Promotion Initiative. To date some 40 workers have been trained to deliver the programme. Initiatives are also underway in some schools for young people who are continuing in school.

The Commission welcomes the introduction of a Teenage Health Promotion Initiative, which in many respects parallels the opportunities presented to young people in schools by social, personal and health education with relationships and sexuality education. The Commission suggests that the introduction of these programmes for early school-leavers should be viewed as an equity measure to afford those young people who are out of the school system the opportunity to participate in a social and personal health education type programmes. On this basis, the Commission suggests that such education programmes to reach the 3,000[37] or so young people, both young men and young women, who leave school early would be an appropriate target.

The Commission would like to draw attention to the need for programmes which deal with sexuality and relationships for young men.[38] These might include peer education programmes dealing with relationship and sexuality and preparation for parenthood for young men. There is also a need to develop young fathers' support groups for those who have some involvement with their children.

**Experience abroad**

A strategy for prevention which concentrates on the two main objectives, improving young people's prospects of reasonable education achievement and future employment and education about relationships and sexual health is a feature of programmes which have been introduced abroad.

One such programme is promoted through the Office of Child Development in the University of Pittsburgh.[39] The programme includes the following elements: *Education* - to educate young people about sexuality, how to adjust their own behaviour and that of their partners

---

37   *Early School Leavers and Youth Unemployment*, NESF Report No. 11, January 1997. The report shows that 3,200 young people left school without completing the Junior Certificate in 1995.

38   A report, Teenage parents - issues of policy and practice, Magee C., Irish Youthwork Press, Dublin 1994, pointed out the importance of such programmes for young men..

39   The University of Pittsburgh Office of Child Development was established in 1986. The office promotes interdisciplinary research and educational programs within the University that pertain to children, youth, and families; manages interdisciplinary and multi-institutional research and demonstration programs involving University faculty and community service professionals; conducts programme evaluations, needs assessments, and policy studies; and disseminates research and professional information on children, youth, and families to policymakers, service professionals, parents, and citizens.

in sexual situations, and family planning, and *Life Options* - to provide teenagers at highest general risk with reasonable life options, principally a hope for a personal future of competence and self-sufficiency, to motivate these adolescents to delay sexual activity and defer pregnancy. The Office has reported that results from their work show that:

- effective prevention programmes must start early and

- a comprehensive integrated approach is required:
- education pertaining to responsible heterosexual relations, resisting the pressure to have sex, and reproductive health and behaviour
- access to reproductive health services
- motivation to delay sexual activity by providing realistic hope for current educational success and future psychological and financial self-sufficiency.

It is suggested that any future development of policies in this area should take account of such programmes abroad where there has been a longer lead in time.

### 7.27    Maintenance as a source of income for lone parents
The Commission has considered the role of maintenance as a source of income for lone parents.

#### Present maintenance arrangements
When couples separate, some reach an informal, agreed arrangement regarding financial support, while others draw up a formal separation agreement and incorporate maintenance in the agreement. There is no way of knowing the numbers of families involved in these out of court arrangements. While some fathers undoubtedly continue to contribute to the support of their children after marital separation, the evidence is that maintenance from former partners is rarely a significant source of income for lone parents in Ireland.

The setting of maintenance in Ireland is a judicial function. The courts are responsible for setting and enforcing maintenance obligations. A recent study shows that maintenance payments, where they are set, are quite low and can be inadequate for the support of a family.[40] Against that background, the social welfare system guarantees a regular weekly payment for lone parents through the One-Parent Family Payment.

---

40    The study found that 60 per cent of legal cases and one-third of private cases concluded without a maintenance arrangement and the presence of such arrangement was strongly influenced by the employment status of the partners. In cases with a maintenance arrangement, the median payment was £100 per week for private cases and £60 per week for legal aid cases. The median payment for District Court cases was £48 per week and in the Circuit Court it was £110 per week. For cases settled out of court it was £120 per week. There is no up to date evidence of the rate of default of payments: *Marital Breakdown and Family Law in Ireland:* Tony Fahey, Maureen Lyons, ESRI, Oaktree Press, Dublin, 1995. Single parents may obtain an order for maintenance for the child under the Family Law (Maintenance of Spouses and Children) Act 1976 as amended primarily by the Status of Children Act 1987 and also for lump sum payment orders. According to the Department of Justice, Equality and Law Reform, a total of 854 Family Law Maintenance Applications were made by unmarried mothers in the district courts in the period 1.8.96 to 31.7.97.

## 7.28 Liability to maintain spouse and dependent children

The Social Welfare Acts of 1989 and 1990 introduced a provision whereby family members have a liability to maintain their spouse and children. Under the legislation, a spouse is liable to maintain his or her dependent spouse and children and the Department of Social, Community and Family Affairs can require any liable relative to repay some or all of the amount of a social welfare payment made to a claimant. This requirement initially applied to separated lone parents.

In 1990 the Department set up a Liable Relatives Unit. This Unit traces non-resident spouses and decides if they are liable for maintenance.

Out of 22,142 parents investigated by the Liable Relatives Unit, 46 per cent were living on social welfare payments and so were not in a position to pay; a further group (25 per cent) were untraceable with the majority believed to be living abroad. Only about 28 per cent were in employment or self-employed, with a potential capacity for making payments to the Department. Up to the end of 1997 the Department of Social, Community and Family Affairs had recovered almost £1.9 million from 479 fathers. It is interesting to note that almost £700,000 of this amount was recouped in 1997, reflecting a growing acceptance of financial responsibility by absent parents.[41]

A particular development in this area is that under recent regulations, unmarried parents will now be required to seek maintenance in respect of their child from the other parent when applying for social welfare payments. The requirement has been introduced for equity reasons because of the requirement which applies to separated lone parents. The Department has stressed that it will adopt a reasonable approach in pursuing this maintenance.

## 7.29 Commission's view- some options for improvement

**It is the Commission's view that there should be a stronger link between social welfare policy and the legal maintenance system. There should be more co-ordination in the policy approach adopted in the two systems in relation to securing maintenance for families. Lone parents are legally obliged to attempt to obtain maintenance but now that the maintenance offsets the One-Parent Family Payment, there is no clear incentive for fathers/parents to top-up the family's social welfare income. The systems should be co-ordinated and mechanisms developed to ensure that partners have an incentive to pay maintenance.**

The Commission considers that realising the potential of improving income for lone parents through adequate maintenance arrangements for children, has to be part of a longer term strategy involving the promotion of responsible joint parenting by young women and men which is desirable in their child's interest.

Given the available evidence which suggests that almost half the non-resident parents are not in a position to pay, tackling unemployment and achieving entry into the labour market for long- term unemployed parents would also mean that separated parents would be in a better position to contribute to their child's upbringing.

---

41   Information supplied by the Department of Social, Community and Family Affairs, as at end December 1997.

FINAL REPORT OF THE COMMISSION ON THE FAMILY

115

### 7.30 Family mediation and the pursuit of maintenance

The Department's responsibility for the development of the Family Mediation Service is of relevance in relation to policy objectives to enhance lone parent access to maintenance contributions. The benefits of family mediation as a non-adversarial approach to the resolution of issues, such as custody and access and financial provision for children on the break-up of marriage, are documented in Chapter 11. Studies have shown that agreements reached through mediation are more likely to be adhered to by the partners involved. It has also been shown that parties to mediated agreements are more likely to remain in contact with their children after the separation. Thus family mediation can facilitate ongoing joint parenting for children.

The promotion of the benefits of family mediation as recommended by the Commission in Chapter 11, and a greater awareness about the ongoing role of mediation in resolving post-settlement disputes where these arise, would in the longer term support policy objectives in relation to enhancing lone parents' access to maintenance.

### 7.31 Making reasonable efforts to obtain maintenance

The benefits of family mediation have a particular relevance to the requirement on lone parents receiving the One-Parent Family Payment to make reasonable efforts to obtain maintenance from their separated spouse, partner or the father of their child. Family mediation presents mothers and fathers with an opportunity to discuss, in a non-adversarial way, the financial support arrangements for their children. It provides an opportunity to engage fathers in the parenting of their children and presents a positive context for them to take on their family responsibilities.

It is the Commission's view that family mediation should be promoted as the preferred route to the resolution of maintenance issues in the policy and procedures of the Department of Social, Community and Family Affairs in relation to the maintenance requirements on lone parents.

The role of family mediation has a particular relevance in relation to the policy approach to encouraging unmarried lone mothers to pursue maintenance contributions from their child's father. It is particularly important to safeguard any future possibilities for the joint parenting of children that these (usually) young families are presented with an alternative to the adversarial court procedures for resolving the parenting issues in relation to their children.

### 7.32 Maintenance payments from unmarried fathers

The Commission welcomes the acknowledgement in policy that there is an obligation on fathers, including unmarried fathers to contribute towards the maintenance of their child. The Commission urges that implementation of the new requirement is carried out sensitively and having regard at all times to the Commission's recommendation that family policy should promote joint parenting for children where this is in the child's interest. In this context, the Commission draws attention to a number of considerations which arise in relation to pursuit of maintenance from unwilling fathers at this time.

One consideration is the legal position of unmarried fathers in relation to their children. A natural father has no constitutionally protected rights in relation to his child.[42] Furthermore, an unmarried father does not have a right of guardianship in relation to his child. Up to 1987 an unmarried father had to go through a court procedure to establish that right.[43] Under the Children Act 1997, an unmarried father may acquire guardianship rights by agreement with the mother by making a joint statutory declaration without having to go to court.

Another consideration relates to the procedures for the registration of births. The position in practical terms is that there is an obligation to register the birth of a child but there is no obligation to register the father's name in the case of children born outside marriage. If a couple decides to register the father's name, it is necessary to do so at the Registrar's Office. It cannot be done in hospital. The view has been put to the Commission that all parents should have the option to register their children either at the hospital where the child is born or at the Registrar's Office. **The Commission agrees with this suggestion and recommends that the procedures should allow for registration of the father's name at the hospital where the child is born or at the Registrar's Office.**

Changes in these procedures could facilitate the promotion of joint parenting and joint responsibility for the care and nurturing of children and set a more positive context for the imposition of maintenance liabilities on unmarried fathers.

A further consideration relates to recommendations for the strengthening of the constitutional rights of children, which have been made in recent times.

The Constitution Review Group[44] recommended that a child ought to have a right, as far as is practicable, to his or her own identity, which includes a knowledge and history of his or her own birth parents. The child ought to be entitled to this information not only for genetic and health reasons but also for psychological reasons. This recommendation is supported by a considerable number of non-governmental organisations that are concerned with the rights and welfare of children. The Commission agrees with the views of the Constitution Review Group and supports their recommendation for an express constitutional guarantee of certain rights of children. Again, it is the Commission's view that the child's right to know his/her father presents a positive context for encouraging unmarried fathers to accept their legal and financial responsibilities towards their child.

---

42   See, for example, Report of the Constitution Review Group, May 1996.

43   The Guardianship of Infants Act, 1964 provides that the married parents of a child are the guardians of that child jointly. In the case of unmarried parents, the mother is sole guardian of the child. Until the Status of Children Act, 1987 there was no way by which an unmarried father could establish guardianship rights other than by subsequently marrying the mother of the child. The 1987 Act amended the 1964 Act by empowering the court, on the application of an unmarried father, to appoint him to be a guardian of his child jointly with the mother. It also provides for a special informal court procedure to be used where the mother consents to the appointment of the father as a guardian and the father's name is registered as such on the births register. At present some 700 applications are made to the court each year by unmarried fathers who wish to become guardians of their children jointly with the mother. Of these some 400 are by agreement. The Children Act 1997 introduces new provisions whereby a father can become joint guardian of his child by agreement with the mother upon the making of a statutory declaration without having to go to court.

44   Report of the Constitution Review Group, May 1996.

### 7.33 The cohabitation rule[45] and family stability

One of the requirements for receiving the One-Parent Family Payment is that the recipient is not cohabiting with a partner as husband and wife. The rationale for the cohabitation rule is linked to the need to ensure the one-parent allowance is directly targeted to lone parents who are rearing children on their own without the support of a partner. Any change in the rule would undermine the premise on which One-Parent Family Payment is made.

In the context of income support for lone parents, the cohabitation rule which debars eligibility for the One-Parent Family Payment remains controversial. It has been argued that where reasonable prospects of joint parenting and joint responsibility for children exist, the cohabitation rule is a particular obstacle to the promotion of continuity and stability for children in family life. At its worst the rule interferes with the child's right to be brought up by both parents. It prevents the consolidation of relationships between a child's father and mother and militates against reconciliation where relationships might be re-established. The other parent (usually the father) cannot be acknowledged, becomes marginal to his child's life and remains marginal to the family's life and role in the community.

The point has also been made to the Commission that the existence of the rule reinforces women's economic dependence on men.

Individualisation of social welfare payments, that is, a move towards a system of social security of individual entitlements could do away with many of the concerns about obstacles to joint parenting and would reduce the relevance of the cohabitation rule in determining entitlement to the One-Parent Family Payment but, as pointed out in Chapter 5, the costs of such a move are a key consideration. Individualisation of social welfare entitlements would involve payments to couples which are twice the individual personal rate. Hence it is costly. The present system, which is based on payment of a personal rate with an additional amount which equates to 0.6 of the personal rate for the second adult, recognises that there are economies of scale in living as a couple.

**The Commission recommends that the relevance of the cohabitation rule in determining eligibility for family income support for lone parents should be kept under review in the light of the developments in social welfare provision in the years ahead. In this context, the outcome of the deliberations of the working group[46] which has been established to examine the tax and social welfare treatment of one and two-parent families and which has a specific brief to identify and cost ways of ensuring consistent and equitable treatment of these households under the tax and social codes; and the work underway in relation to an independent appraisal of basic income proposals and a Green Paper on Basic Income[47] are particularly relevant.**

---

45  The rule means that the One-Parent Family Payment is removed if the parents marry or cohabit as husband and wife.

46  See earlier reference in this chapter.

47  Para 4.35 of Partnership 2000 for Inclusion, Employment and Competitiveness commits the partners to an independent appraisal of the concept of and the implications of introducing a basic income payment. The programme for Government (Action Programme for the Millennium) contains a commitment to the publication of a Green Paper on Basic Income

## 7.34 The need for research into lone parenthood

The Commission has found in its examination of lone parenthood that there is a dearth of information in relation to the trends underlying this important development in family life. The main demographic features in relation to lone parents have been analysed, the growth in lone parenthood has been documented and important studies have been carried out which add greatly to our knowledge about lone-parent families and their characteristics in terms of age, family composition, financial circumstances, educational attainment and labour force participation. However, there is little information available on how many families leave lone parenthood through marriage, remarriage or new partnerships or for how long families remain lone-parent families during their life cycle.

**The Commission recommends that lone parenthood should be singled out as a priority for research so that we may learn more about this important development in family life in Ireland. The Commission's recommendations for a longitudinal study on children[48] will provide a further opportunity to examine issues relating to lone parenthood.**

## 7.35 Support for bereaved families

Families that experience the death of one of the parents can face huge changes in their lives. Submissions to the Commission from families who have been bereaved explain the great difficulties widowed parents have to face in taking on sole responsibility for parenting, the running of the family home and in many cases making the transition to being the main breadwinner, on whom the family depends. Expense arises on the death of a partner and there are changes in the family finances on account of changes in tax liabilities and entitlements to income support. There may also be legal matters to be sorted out.

Access to information and advice in relation to state and community services which may be of assistance to families is important to families at this time. In 1996, the Department of Social, Community and Family Affairs received in the region of 10,000 claims for widows'/ widowers' pension.[49] The Department is the first point of contact for most families when a husband or wife dies and as such it is uniquely positioned to provide a service to assist families at this difficult time.[50] **The Commission recommends that a comprehensive service for families to meet their needs for information about entitlements and other support on widowhood should form part of the customised local service to better meet the needs of families recommended in Chapter 3.**

If the death of the parent is unexpected or occurs in distressing circumstances, it is particularly hard for all concerned. There is a need in these circumstances for a great deal of support and specialist help. Several national organisations have developed support services to assist bereaved families. In this context, the Commission would like to acknowledge the role of the National Association of Widows in Ireland in pursuing, over the years, the interests of widows and their families, and in developing counselling and support

---

48  See Chapter 20.

49  Information for the Department of Social, Community and Family Affairs showed that in almost 20 per cent of pensions awarded, the widowed person had a dependent child. Of 7,163 claims awarded in 1996, 5,897 had no dependants: 1,266 had dependants

50  PRSI now provides cover for widows' pension to all major sectors of the population; employed workers including public servants, the self-employed and part-time workers, except those earning less than £30 a week.

programmes for newly bereaved widows. More services are needed and the Commission considers that further development should be promoted and encouraged. **It is the Commission's view that such services in the voluntary and community sector are an important component of family support and should be eligible for grant aid under the mainstream family support programme, as recommended in Chapter 2.**

# Appendix 1

**Extract from a review of literature in relation to lone parent issues carried out by Family Studies Centre, University College Dublin on behalf of the Commission on the Family**

**1.** **Unmarried Lone parents**

The increasing percentage of births to unmarried parents - now almost 25 per cent of all births *(Department of Health Vital Statistics 1996)* and the increasing numbers of unmarried parents within the total lone parent group is regularly highlighted by policy-makers, the media and the general public. While the causation of pregnancies outside marriage has been hypothesised by many, it is unlikely that any one theory could explain adequately the complex interaction of a number of affecting variables. As Dockery and Powell (1984) pointed out: the causation... by its nature is complex and is made up of multifactorial elements which include psychological, environmental, social, educational in its broadest sense and financial. The subject becomes further complicated by the number of emotion-laden issues involved, such as pre-marital intercourse, contraception and abortion.

**2.** Unmarried lone parents are not a homogeneous group. In any discussion of unmarried pregnancy a distinction must be made between planned and unplanned pregnancies. For some women the pregnancy is planned either within or outside a stable cohabiting relationship, while for others pregnancy is an unintended outcome of sexual activity. There is frequently, however, a blurred line between planned and unplanned pregnancies. For example, although a conscious decision may not be made to conceive, conception may nonetheless be welcomed. The distinction must, however, be borne in mind when discussing the rising numbers of non-marital births.

It appears that a large number of factors are at play in the changing rates of pre-marital conceptions. These include changes in societal expectations of young women, changing rates of physical development, ignorance, contraceptive usage, media pressure, the nature of courtship relationships, financial issues, status- seeking and changes in the perception of and access to marriage (Flanagan and Richardson, 1992, 11-15). Several reports have suggested that young women who become pregnant outside marriage do so because they have poor or inadequate information on their fertility and contraception (Rynne and Lacey 1983, Dockery and Powell 1984, Richardson 1991, Eastern Health Board 1991).

**3.** The Eastern Health Board report (1991) also dealt with the popular perception that teenage girls become pregnant to enhance their financial or housing entitlements. This criticism is possibly the one that is made most frequently against unmarried mothers, particularly in times of economic stringency. It is the level of social welfare dependency and cost to the State of maintaining unmarried mothers which seems to engender so much negative feeling. Although often related to so-called 'financial incentives' the element of status-seeking or role-seeking in pre-marital pregnancies is a distinct concern. The Irish Family Planning Clinic pinpointed this element in a report in which it was stated that 'having a baby for some teenagers, appears to be their most viable career choice' (The Irish Times 26 July 1990). TREOIR - the

Federation of Services for Unmarried Parents and their Children has also stated that the crux of the problem is that many young women have little else to look forward to. (The Irish Times 26 July 1990). Furthermore, Richardson (1993) found that teenagers in her samples were not future orientated and perceived having a baby as having certain immediate advantages with little regard for the long-term prospects.

However, Richardson (1993) found that the financial or role incentives were less related to conception and more related to the decision-making process in that they were more likely to influence the decision to keep the baby than to lead to a decision to become pregnant. Decisions made by unmarried mothers have changed over the past decade partly because of changing societal attitudes and increasing liberalisation of Irish society, leading to a greater acceptance of unmarried parenthood. Marriage is no longer seen as a solution to unmarried pregnancy and the Catholic Church's position has been to discourage a couple from marrying when the woman is pregnant, stating that there is a real danger that the existence of pregnancy may cause pressure to be put on the couple, either by their families or by one another so that the decision to marry may not be entirely free and mature (Irish Bishops' Pastoral 1985, 24). The number of women choosing to place their child for adoption has dropped dramatically. In 1994 there were 424 adoption orders made compared to 1,195 in 1984. In addition, of the 424 orders made 43.4 per cent were made in favour of the child's birth mother and her husband (Report of An Bord Uchtala 1995).

4.  There has been an upward trend in the number of women choosing to terminate their unplanned pregnancies (Flanagan and Richardson 1992, p. 62).[1]

---

1   Note: A study on women and crisis pregnancies was commissioned from the Department of Sociology of Trinity College, Dublin in 1995 by the then Minister for Health as part of a comprehensive approach to the abortion issue. This followed the passing of the Regulation of Information (Services outside State for Termination of Pregnancies) Act, 1995. The objective of the study was to assist the Department of Health and Children in understanding the factors which contribute to unwanted pregnancy and in particular those factors which lead to women seeking abortions. The report was published in March 1998. In December 1997, the Government established a Cabinet Committee to oversee the work of an Interdepartmental Working Group whose task it is to prepare a Green Paper having considered the constitutional, legal, medical, moral, social and ethical issues which arise regarding abortion and having invited views from interested parties on these issues. The detailed work on the preparation of the Green Paper by the Interdepartmental Working Group which involves officials  from the Department of Health and Children and other government departments has commenced. The Cabinet Committee is chaired by the Minister for Health and Children, Brian Cowen, T.D. and also comprises Ms. Mary O' Rourke T.D., Minister for Public Enterprise, Mr. John O' Donoghue T.D., Minister for Justice, Equality and Law Reform, Ms. Liz O' Donnell T.D., Minister of State at the Department of Foreign Affairs and Mr. David Byrne S.C. Attorney General. The Terms of Reference of the Interdepartmental Working Group are as follows; "Having regard to: Section 58 of the Offences against the Person Act, 1861; Section 59 of the Offences against the Person Act, 1861; Article 40.3.3 of the Bunreacht na hEireann; The decision of the Supreme Court on 5 March 1992 on the Attorney General v X and Others [1992] 1 L.R. 1; Protocol No. 17 to the Maastricht Treaty on European Union signed in February 1992 and the Solemn Declaration of 1 May 1992 on that protocol; The decision of the people in the Referendum of 25 November 1992 to reject the proposed Twelfth Amendment of the Constitution. The decision of the High Court on 28 November 1997in A & B v Eastern Health Board, Judge Mary Fahy, C and the Attorney General (Notice Party): and having considered the constitutional,legal, medical, moral, social and ethical issues which arise regarding abortion and having invited views from interested parties on these issues to prepare a Green Paper on the options available in the matter.

Richardson (1991) has argued that being an unmarried mother is in fact a total decision process and the decision-making begins far earlier than when the pregnancy occurs. Prior decisions involve a decision to become sexually active, and a decision to use or not to use contraception (Flanagan and Richardson 1992, 59). It is at all these points in the decision process that interventions need to be considered, not just at the post-conception period. Policies need to be geared towards the introduction of prevention programmes. Such programmes are particularly relevant to the prevention of adolescent pregnancy.

5.    One of the major difficulties for policy-makers in Ireland is the lack of research on the outcome for unmarried mothers over a period of time. A longitudinal study on unmarried mothers carried out in the National Maternity Hospital does provide some data (Richardson 1992). When comparing single-parent families with married family units, the report showed that there were differences across a number of selected criteria; accommodation, income and expenditure, parenting and health status but concluded that, for that particular group of unmarried mothers, the results did not indicate that these differences combine to put the single-parent family, at one year in the family life cycle, at a disadvantage, in comparison with the marital family unit. Indeed, in some circumstances the single mothers who returned to live in their family home with their own parents were doing better than the marital family units. However, it is important to stress that this was after one year, during which time the support services for young mothers is at its greatest. Other research on children in care (Richardson 1985, O' Higgins 1993) has shown that children of single parents are particularly liable to be admitted to the care of health boards between the ages of two and five years. It raises the question, therefore, of what the long-term effects for single mothers and their children are over time and how long they remain in single family units. O' Grady (1991), in an analysis of unmarried mothers allowance over time, found that recourse to the allowance was a short to medium term measure and the major reason for ceasing to claim allowance was marriage, with 56 per cent of claims discontinued for this reason. Only 13 per cent ceased to claim because their means exceeded the limit.

# Bibliography

Dockery, C.J. and Powell, B.
**Psychological Aspects of Adolescent Pregnancies in Ireland**
Dublin: St. James Hospital, Unpublished Paper, 1984

Eastern Health Board **Interim Report of the Committee on Single Parent Births and Families**
Dublin: EHB, 1991

Flanagan, N. and Richardson, V.
**Unmarried Mothers: A Social Profile**
National Maternity Hospital/ UCD, Dublin: 1992

O'Grady, T.
**Married to the State: A Study of Unmarried Mother's Allowance Applicants**
Unpublished Thesis, University of Dublin, 1991

O'Higgins, K.
**Family Problems - Substitute Care**
Dublin: Economic and Social Research Institute, 1993

Richardson, V.
**Decision Making by Unmarried Mothers', The Irish Journal of Psychology**
Vol. 12, No. 2 pp. 165-181, 1991

Richardson V.
**The Family Life Styles of Some Single Parents In Ireland**
in G. Kiely (ed.) *In and Out of Marriage*, Dublin: Family Studies Centre, Dublin, 1992

Richardson V.
**Mothers Too Soon? A study of the decision making process of unmarried pregnant adolescents**
Unpublished PhD Thesis, National University of Ireland, 1993

Rynne A., and Lacey L.
**A Survey of 249 Irish Women Interviewed While Pregnant and Out of Wedlock**
Dublin: Unpublished Report, 1983

# Appendix 2
**Summary of comparative information relating to the policy framework in various countries as it affects the employment participation of lone parents[2]**

**1.   Lessons from abroad**

There is now a substantial body of comparative research on lone parents and on the wider social policy framework as it affects women generally. This research has generally identified some countries as being more 'gender equal' than others, across a wide panoply of public policies which include childcare, social security, family provisions for employees, training opportunities, and so on. In this research, Ireland is not identified as such a country. More significantly, studies show that the circumstances of lone parents in various countries are strongly associated with countries' policies affecting women in general. Thus, lone parents in countries (such as Denmark or Sweden) with some degree of gender equality, more individualised social security and tax systems, and higher levels of labour force participation among married women and women with children, are more likely to be in paid employment and less likely to be financially poor or dependent on State social security payments.

**2.** With the aid of a very detailed and recent comparative study, it is possible to briefly compare the Irish situation with that in other countries and to report on possible explanations for cross-national differences. The following table reproduces in very condensed form some of the details of the analysis. As the table indicates, the approach is to distil the intricate details of countries' policies and practices into summary scores of High, Medium and Low. The most striking aspect of this analysis, as the researchers point out, is that no one single explanatory factor or cluster of factors seems to be strongly correlated with cross-national employment variations: there are patterns, but no quantifiable, strong determinant of employment variations.

2   Information reproduced from *Policy and the Employment of Lone Parents in 20 countries*, Jonathan Bradshaw, Steven Kennedy, Majella Kilkey, Sandra Hutton, Anne Cordon, Tony Eardley, Hilary Holmes, Joanne Neale, European Observatory on National Family Policies, August 1996.

## 3.    Lone Mothers in Selected Countries: Employment Rates and Summary Measures of Selected Employment Related Policy Provisions

| Country | Per cent of Lone mothers employed | Level of female earnings | Childcare costs | Replacement rates | Marginal tax rates | Public or subsidised childcare | Quality of training education services | Employment/ maternity leave package |
|---|---|---|---|---|---|---|---|---|
| Belgium | High | Middle | Low | High | High | High | High | High |
| Denmark | Middle | High | Middle | High | High | High | Medium | High |
| Germany | Low | Middle | Middle | Medium | High | Low | Low | Medium |
| Greece | Middle | High | Low | Low | Low | Low | Low | Medium |
| Spain | High | Low | High | Low | Low | Low | Low | Medium |
| France | High | Low | Low | Medium | Low | High | Medium | Medium |
| Ireland | Low | Low | High | Medium | High | Low | Low | Low |
| Italy | High | Middle | Low | Low | Middle | Low | Low | High |
| Luxembourg | High | Low | Middle | High | High | Medium | Low | Low |
| The Netherlands | Low | High | High | High | Middle | Medium | Medium | Medium |
| Austria | Middle | High | High | High | Middle | Medium | Low | High |
| Portugal | Middle | Low | Middle | High | High | Medium | Low | Medium |
| Finland | Middle | Low | Middle | High | High | High | High | High |
| Sweden | High | Middle | Middle | Medium | Low | High | High | High |
| United Kingdom | Low | Middle | High | Low | Middle | Low | Low | Low |
| Australia | Low | High | Middle | Low | High | Medium | High | Low |
| Japan | High | Low | Low | Medium | Low | Medium | Low | Low |
| New Zealand | Low | Middle | High | Medium | Middle | Low | Medium | Low |
| Norway | Middle | Middle | Middle | Medium | High | High | High | High |
| United States | Middle | High | High | Medium | High | Low | Low | Low |

Source: Bradshaw et al., 1996, Table 6.6

4.    Some countries have specific programmes targeted at lone mothers, particularly in relation
      to employment, education, training and childcare. While most countries provide voluntary
      public training programmes for which non-employed lone mothers are eligible, three
      countries (France - Stage FNE Femme Isole, Australia - Jobs, Education and Training
      Programme (JET), and the UK *(New Deal for Lone parents)*[3] have schemes which are
      exclusively for lone mothers.

5.    In countries where there are no specific training provisions for lone mothers, the study
      suggests that this may be a reflection of the already high rate of employment among this
      group. However, this is not the case in the United Kingdom, Ireland, New Zealand, Germany
      or the Netherlands. The authors suggest that the absence of programmes designed
      exclusively for lone mothers may represent a weakness in the training policies of these
      countries. Moreover, this weakness may be exacerbated since lone mothers are generally
      not required to register with an unemployment benefit office or its equivalent, although such
      offices are the main source of information on the availability of training schemes.

6.    The provision of childcare and assistance with the costs of childcare are likely to be
      important elements for lone mothers within any training scheme. No such support is
      provided in Germany, Greece, Luxembourg or Portugal and in Ireland provision is available
      on only some schemes. In Denmark, Sweden, Finland, Belgium, the Netherlands, Australia
      and the United States, lone mothers participating in training schemes have access to free
      childcare. In Norway and New Zealand, lone mothers are paid an allowance to assist with
      the cost of substitute care. In the United Kingdom, a childcare allowance is available.

7.    Children from lone-parent families are awarded priority in access to childcare across only
      seven countries (Denmark, Greece, France, the Netherlands, Sweden, Finland and Norway).
      In a further seven, including the United Kingdom, there is a complete absence of such a
      priority. Furthermore, in the case of public provision in the United Kingdom, and indeed in
      Ireland, places are generally not available to children of employed lone mothers since they
      are targeted at children deemed to be 'at risk'.

8.    Looking at childcare generally, the study shows that the UK, Ireland and New Zealand score
      poorly in the context of leave and childcare arrangements. In all three of these countries,
      measures to support mothers' employment after childbirth are poor, the provision of
      statutory childcare is limited and private childcare is expensive. The availability of leave and

---

3    The UK scheme was announced in the UK Budget of June 1997:

     "Lone parents whose youngest child is aged five or over will be offered an individualised case-managed assistance; job
     search help and advice; training and re-skilling; and help with childcare. The programme will be demonstrated in eight
     pilot areas from 21 July 1997 and be fully implemented nationally from October 1998. Childcare is a key issue for lone
     parents. Three new measures will increase the supply of high quality, affordable childcare and improve the help with
     childcare given to working parents on low incomes. The childcare disregard in Family Credit and other in-work benefits will
     be extended, lottery money will be made available to develop after-school clubs, and the New Deal for young unemployed
     people will include 50,000 places for trainee childcarers. The Budget provides 200 million pounds over the lifetime of the
     Parliament for the cost of the New Deal for lone parents and the extension of the childcare disregard."

childcare is equally poor in the United States, where employment rate among lone mothers is ranked as middle. The picture is also unclear among countries with low rates of employment for lone mothers. In the Netherlands, leave provisions, the availability of statutory childcare and childcare costs all rank as medium. In Germany, while the availability of public and private/subsidised childcare is limited, the cost of childcare is medium and leave provisions are medium. The quality of the leave and child-care package is also quite diverse among those countries where lone mothers have a high overall rate of employment. To varying degrees, in Belgium, France and Sweden, a high ranking for lone mothers' employment appears consistent with a highly supportive system of leave and childcare. However, this is not the case in Spain, Italy, Luxembourg and Japan, where weaknesses are found in either leave provisions or childcare. It may be that these countries are making a choice in the way mothers' labour market participation is supported. For example, Spain and Italy provide leave until the child is aged three, as opposed to providing childcare for this age-group.

## Chapter Eight **Families and Work**

### 8.1      Introduction

In this chapter the Commission explores the difficulties men and women face

- in coping with the demands of work and earning while carrying out their parenting responsibilities and devoting time to their children

- in getting access to the jobs market when they are unemployed

- in undertaking the care of dependent family members while working outside the home.

### 8.2      An overview of changes in employment

There have been substantial changes in the Irish labour market in recent years. The most significant and the most welcome change has been the growth in employment. There have also been changes in the structure of the labour market. These changes have a significant impact on families and how they organise their family lives. They include:

- changes in the organisation of jobs and working time and in the type and location of work.

- the continued decline in agricultural and manufacturing employment and the growth in services sector jobs with more contracting out of jobs in service-type operations.

- increasing participation by women, particularly married women, in the labour force and the resultant rise in the number of dual income households.

The demand for workers to be more flexible in their approach to work is very much a feature of the 1990s, with businesses facing increased competition and a new emphasis on customer service, sometimes outside traditional hours of work. The *organisation of working time* is changing with the growth in shift work, contract work, night work, weekend work and part-time work.

The *type and location* of work is also changing. The numbers employed in the services industry are on the increase, with a total of 818,000 employed in this sector in 1997. The numbers employed in the agricultural sector, however, continue to decline - from 154,000 in 1992 to 134,200 in 1997.[1]

The increasing use of information technology and the possibility of teleworking in a variety of forms, including home-based telework, present new possibilities for the performance of work in other than the traditional workplace. Teleworking is a feature of the labour market which is expected to grow in the years ahead. It has a number of advantages for those who want to work from home and it has significant potential in relation to providing work opportunities to rural homes and in isolated areas of the country. A number of issues in relation to telework from home will need to be addressed by the social partners in the years ahead as the sector grows. These include the status of workers (employed or self-

---

1    Labour Force Survey 1997.

employed), health and safety issues, including isolation from co-workers and the social implications to do with the home as workplace and the employer's access to it.

The *numbers of self-employed have increased* from 237,000 in 1981 to 258,000 in 1995. In the non-agricultural sector the numbers of self-employed persons rose from just under 90,000 in 1981 to nearly 149,000 in 1995- an increase of 65 per cent. This was attributable to a number of factors: the growing practice for companies to purchase services from firms which operate on a self-employed basis and the tendency for governments to promote an enterprise culture by means of schemes and grants. Some 80 per cent of those who are self-employed are male.[2]

There has been a *significant growth in the number of part-time workers in recent years* - from 5 per cent of the workforce in 1983 to over 10 per cent in 1995 or in absolute terms from 56,000 to 124,000 workers. This number had grown to 169,000 part-time workers by 1997.[3] For males, the proportion of part-timers rose from 2 per cent to 4.5 per cent, while for females the increase was from 11.5 per cent to 20 per cent. Nearly all this increase has occurred in the services sector.[2]

Detailed analysis[4] based on an International Labour Office (ILO) classification in the Labour Force Survey 1997 facilitates a comparison of the approach to part-time working between men and women. Some *114,000 women* working part-time are not underemployed, that is they *are not available for full-time work*. The figure for *men* is almost 34,000. The figures in relation to part-time workers who are underemployed and available for full-time work are 11,600 men and 10,200 women.

*More women are working* now than in earlier years and more married women are staying on at work or re-entering the workplace after a period spent caring for young children. A 1997 study[5] documents the extent of the change between 1988 and 1994. In this period the participation of women reached about 40 per cent.[6] (According to the 1997 Labour Force Survey, it is now 43 per cent). The study suggests that by 2011 the labour force participation of women in the working age-groups will have risen to around 55 per cent.

In particular, the participation rate for married women has risen rapidly in the past ten years as younger women remain in the labour force and women in their forties return to it. The study pointed out that in the past marriage played an important part in determining whether or not a woman remained in the labour force. In 1981 single women *with* children were more likely to be in the labour force than married women *without* children. However, between 1981 and the early 1990s this pattern changed radically in that the presence of children, rather than marriage, became the crucial factor affecting women's participation.

---

2   Labour Market Studies Ireland, Sexton et al, December 1996, European Commission, Directorate General for Employment, Industrial Relations and Social Affairs and Labour Force Survey 1997.

3   Labour Force Survey 1997.

4   Labour Force Survey 1997.

5   *Welfare Implications of Demographic Trends*, Tony Fahey, John Fitz Gerald, Combat Poverty Agency, Oak Tree Press, Dublin, 1997.

6   In 1988 the total participation rate for women was 31.3 per cent PES (Principal Economic Status) classification (35 per cent ILO classification)

By 1992 women without children had much the same participation rates in the labour force, irrespective of whether they were married or single, while the participation rate for single women with children (30 per cent) had fallen below that of married women with children (40 per cent).

As women's educational attainment has risen, so too have their financial gains from participation in the labour force. Higher levels of education have also helped produce a cultural change where women are more disposed to continue on in the labour force after marriage or to return to it as their children grow older. The study found that a range of other factors, including the economic environment, have contributed to the change in participation rates since 1971.

## 8.3 Changing work patterns and families

Special tabulations carried out for the Commission on the Labour Force Survey 1996[7] present information in relation to changes in the labour force as they are reflected in the pattern of employment and working practices within families. Some of the principal findings from the analysis are:

*The traditional arrangement of men as the exclusive breadwinners and women as the exclusive carers (within the home) is now changing.*

- Fathers are the exclusive breadwinners in half of all families in Ireland. In three out of ten families, the parents are dual earners, while almost two out of ten families have no earner and depend on social welfare because they are unemployed or a lone-parent family.

*Employment among parents tends to be at a maximum when child care duties are at their most demanding.*

- 42 per cent of *younger* mothers,[8] that is mothers with children under 15 years, are in employment (28 per cent full-time and 14 per cent part-time). This compares with *older* mothers, that is mothers with children older than 15 years, 24 per cent of whom are in employment (15 per cent full-time and 9 per cent part-time).

- 84 per cent of *younger* fathers were in employment (81 per cent in full-time and 3 per cent in part-time).

- 62 per cent of *older* fathers were in employment (60 per cent full-time and 2 per cent part-time).

---

7   The analysis of the Labour Force Survey was carried out by Dr. Anthony Murphy of UCD. The detailed findings of the analysis are contained in an abstract of the report *Fathers: Irish experience in an international context* by Kieran McKeown, Dermot Rooney, Harry Ferguson; see Chapter 18.

8   For the purpose of analysis, a younger mother was defined as a woman over age 20 who has any child under 15 years old living with her. An older mother was defined similarly but all of her children are over age 15. On the basis of this definition, there were approximately 412,000 younger mothers and 203,000 older mothers. On the basis of a similar definition for fathers, there were approximately 373,000 younger fathers and 166,000 older fathers in Ireland in 1996.

- Mothers, where they are employed, work an average of 31-32 hours per week outside the home. Fathers work an average of 46 hours per week and a significant minority (33 per cent) work 50 hours or more per week.[9]

- The data reveal that a small proportion of fathers do shift work, nearly half do evening work, a quarter do night work, two-thirds do Saturday work and two-fifths do Sunday work, with very little difference between younger fathers and older fathers. Mothers are much less likely to work anti-social hours.

- A significant minority, 15 per cent of younger fathers, usually or sometimes work at home. This rises to 19 per cent for older fathers. Men are twice as likely as women to work from home.

The report contains some interesting comparisons between Irish parents and their EU counterparts, with Irish fathers and mothers in several cases working longer hours.

## 8.4 Carrying out family functions and the demands of work

The ability to secure an adequate income and to provide for family members by participating in employment is fundamental to a family's capacity to successfully carry out its functions in relation to caring and nurturing for family members.

There have been many welcome changes in the Irish labour market in recent years. Employment has risen and the employment prospects for young people on leaving education are today very good. The growth in part-time jobs has provided workers who have family responsibilities with new opportunities to participate in the paid labour market and improve the family income and at the same time to spend time with their children while they are young.

However, the changes in the organisation of the labour market have also brought about many new insecurities for families. Concern about their livelihood or the security of their jobs may drive people to work longer and harder and have less time for their families. For many families today, it takes more than one income to meet their needs and the lack of longer term security in many jobs can cause people to maximise their attachment to work in their peak earning years.

There have been changes in the culture of many workplaces. While there are some excellent examples of family-friendly employments, an emphasis on the number of hours worked and achieving targets, accompanied by expectations about a rigid separation between work and family life, workaholism and an organisational culture which expects employees to devote time to social or business events after working hours or at weekends, are not uncommon features in the world of work today.

---

9   The report highlights the significance of this in view of the fact that, under the Organisation of Working Time Act, 1997, the maximum working week is 48 hours. The report also points out that Irish fathers work longer hours than some of their EU counterparts. In Denmark, for example, where the maximum working week is 37 hours, fathers of young children work an average of 41 hours per week, five hours less than Irish fathers. Irish fathers also work longer hours than British fathers: 27 per cent of fathers in Britain but 33 per cent of fathers in Ireland work 50 hours a week or more.

8.5    **A better balance between work and family life**
**It is the Commission's view that bringing about a suitable balance between work and family life is a key issue for Government and the social partners as we approach the new century.**

Having regard to the national objective of the continued development of an efficient and modern economy, capable of high and sustainable economic and employment growth, which is essential to the future well-being of all families, and the importance to the achievement of this objective of competitiveness issues: the Commission is of the view that a better balance between work and family life may best be brought about through a range of approaches to policy in relevant areas. These policy areas include:

- the role of **income support** in meeting the needs of families when their responsibilities are at their most demanding

- a policy approach which supports and promotes the introduction of **family-friendly initiatives** in the workplace

- **protection for workers and their families** in a changing work environment.

8.6    **Income support policies must take account of the needs of families when responsibilities are demanding**
The policy approach must primarily continue to provide adequate income support for families in times of need, in old age or retirement, and when contingencies arise which involve loss of earnings to the family such as: unemployment, disability, maternity and in the longer term cover for pensions on retirement.

However, income support policies must also take account of the needs of families when their responsibilities are at their most demanding. In this report, the Commission presents the case for greater investment in the care of young children. Chapter 5 examines the options in relation to how this might be channelled in relation to children under three years of age. These options include a weekly parent allowance to facilitate the parent who wishes to work full-time in the home, (Option A) or a paid parental leave benefit for working parents who wish to withdraw from the workforce for a time,(Option B) or a special rate of child benefit for all children in this age-group (Option C). Both options A and B include provision for a childcare allowance to meet the needs of families not catered for by the parent allowance approach. In Chapter 12, recommendations are put forward for an Early Years Opportunities Subsidy to secure for children at three years of age, having regard to their parents' wishes opportunities to participate in quality services for children in crèches/ nurseries, pre-schools and playgroups. This recommendation is presented in the context of a range of suggestions for the development of quality services for pre-school children.

## 8.7 The EU directive on parental leave

The Commission has considered the introduction of a statutory right to parental leave in line with the recent EU directive, which is due to be implemented by June 1998. Under the terms of the Directive, each parent will be entitled to a minimum of three months' parental leave on the birth or adoption of their child. The Directive provides that parental leave should in principle be non-transferable between parents. This means that if one parent does not take up his or her three month's leave, it is a lost opportunity to the family. The leave has to be taken before the child reaches a given age, which may be up to eight years. The Directive also provides for entitlements to time off work for urgent family reasons.[10]

It is up to individual states to bring forward the detailed proposals to give effect to the Directive.

The Directive is based on proposals produced by the social partners under the social protocol to the Maastricht Treaty. The proposals were jointly developed by the representatives of employers and employees at European level. Significant contributions were made by national employer and employee organisations including the Irish Business and Employers Confederation and the Irish Congress of Trade Unions. The proposals are the first instance of a document developed by the social partners under the Maastricht Treaty being accorded the legally binding status of a Directive. The Directive leaves states free to decide whether or not the leave will be paid, to decide all matters relating to social security and for how long after the birth of the child the leave can be taken.

The availability of three months' parental leave (six months if both parents avail of the leave) will greatly enhance the opportunities for parents to spend time with their children in those important first few months and years. **The Commission welcomes the parental leave initiative and recommends that Government bring forward proposals for the implementation of the parental leave Directive soon. The Commission urges all parties to the proposals - employers, employees and Government to ensure that the proposals for the implementation of parental leave provide for the maximum flexibility for workers in relation to availing of this leave.**

### Paid parental leave

The Commission considers that if parental leave, in line with the EU Directive, is to provide practical assistance to parents who wish to have the opportunity to spend time with their young child, the issue of paid leave or compensation for loss of earnings must be examined. The Commission has stated in Chapter 5 that providing direct support to parents at a time when the childcare responsibilities are at their most demanding are priority considerations in formulating future policy in support of families with childcare responsibilities.

Furthermore, the Commission agrees with the view put forward to it in a submission that, unless the period of parental leave is paid it will not fully realise key family objectives, which include providing real opportunities to mothers and fathers in balancing their work and family responsibilities, promoting equality for working parents in the workplace and in the home in the sharing of childcare responsibilities.

10   This may be limited to a certain amount of time per year and/or per case.

It is the Commission's view that the introduction of a statutory right to paid parental leave would be an important first step towards these family objectives.

The Commission urges that consideration be given to an extension of the PRSI maternity benefit scheme[11] to cover parental leave with the payment of a weekly benefit to the parent availing of parental leave. This would meet the need for basic income security during the period of leave for parents who are likely to avail of the option.

### Costs

The cost of paid parental leave depends on its duration and on how it is paid. The likely take-up of the scheme is difficult to predict. As shown in Chapter 5, international experience suggests that, even when paid, parental leave is not fully taken up by mothers and the rate of take up by fathers is insignificant. A tentative costing of a parental benefit payment on the lines of the present maternity benefit payments suggests that an extension of the maternity benefit scheme to cover parental leave could cost in the region of £40m per annum.[12]

**The Commission recommends that the Government bring forward proposals for the introduction of 3 months, parental leave for workers with children, in line with the terms of the EU Directive; and that the PRSI maternity benefit scheme should be extended to cover parental leave and to provide a weekly payment on the lines of maternity benefit to workers availing of the parental leave under the Directive.**

## 8.8    Parental leave- initiatives abroad

The recent adoption of EU parental leave Directive has brought about a new focus on parental leave initiatives.

---

11    Maternity protection legislation provides for 14 weeks paid leave on the birth of a child. Health and safety legislation provides for additional rights for women working in jobs where there are health and safety concerns in relation to pregnant women and women who have recently given birth or who are breastfeeding. Legislation also provides for leave for mothers on the adoption of a child. Maternity benefit (PRSI) is normally paid for 14 weeks to mothers in employment with 39 weeks PRSI contributions paid. Maternity benefit is paid at 70 per cent of the woman's average reckonable weekly earnings. The minimum payment is £82.50 and the maximum weekly payment is £162.80.

12    The estimated cost of the 14 weeks maternity benefit for 21,500 women was £39.3m in 1998. This figure does not include many public service employees (civil servants, teachers etc..) who do not pay full PRSI or part-time employees who earn less than £30 per week. There are no figures available on the number of public servants who do not pay full PRSI and who take maternity leave- it is probably about 5,000 people. If it is assumed that parental leave lasts for 12 weeks and it is availed of by some 21,000 women who work outside the home and by a small percentage of men, the cost would be about the same as the cost of the maternity benefit scheme. i.e. £40m per annum. This would not include the payroll costs of public servants who opt to take parental leave. However, employees who joined the public service on or after 6 April 1995 pay full PRSI and have cover for the full range of social welfare benefits and pensions, including maternity benefit. These could therefore benefit from any future extension of the PRSI-based maternity leave scheme.

13    Helen Wilkinson with Stephen Radley, Ian Christie, George Lawson and Jamie Sainsbury Time Out - the costs and benefits of paid parental leave published by DEMOS, 9, Bridewell Place, London, EC4V 6AP, 1997. The research makes the case for a universal right to parental leave for UK workers funded by a small premium on national insurance. The report calls for a UK policy initiative involving a right to paid parental leave of up to 36 months, some of which would be paid in some form which should be non-transferable between parents. An overview of the parental leave arrangements in several European States and further afield as described in the report is contained in Appendix 1 to this chapter.

A recent UK Report[13] contains a detailed analyses of the costs and benefits of parental leave. The research draws on UK data, on a MORI poll and a survey of employers, as well as detailed analyses of the parental leave experience abroad. The report contains some useful insights into the factors which make parental leave arrangements successful in terms of take-up by working parents.

The report highlights features of the most child-centred schemes and features which promote take-up by fathers. The report states that the most successful schemes are universal, offering opportunities to all employees and to the self-employed. Successful schemes need to offer a significant level of wage replacement with job protection if they are to benefit low paid workers and attract men as well as women. Conversely, the costs of parental leave to the employer, individuals and the State need to be contained if they are to be viable in the long term.

Some of the most innovative schemes abroad have been used as part of a strategy to reduce unemployment, to facilitate workplace training and to promote voluntary reductions in working time over the lifecycle. The Commission suggests that the lessons from abroad identified in the report are particularly relevant in the consideration of policy initiatives to develop a framework for extended parental leave for Irish workers.

**8.9    Supporting the introduction of family-friendly initiatives in the workplace**

The Government has stated its support for the introduction of family friendly initiatives in Partnership 2000[14] for Inclusion, Employment and Competitiveness. In this context, the Commission recommends the early adoption of the Action Plan for the development of family friendly workplaces as put forward in the Employment Equality Agency policy document.[15] The Action Plan requires the participation and commitment of employers, and their representative organisations, trade unions, employees, voluntary community groups and the support of Government.

Essentially, the introduction of family-friendly initiatives means a greater investment by employers in their employees' well-being. Preliminary indications are that such initiatives provide benefits for employers in terms of the retention of skilled and experienced workers, a more highly motivated workforce, improved productivity, reduced employee stress and an improved company image.[16]

14   Para 5.9 of Partnership 2000 states: " In tandem with the development of a childcare strategy, the Government will seek to support the growth of family friendly policies in employment, in line with the recommendations contained in the policy document issued by the Employment Equality Agency in 1996, and having regard to competitive requirements. The expertise of the Employment Equality Agency in this regard will be utilised".

15   The Action Plan from *Introducing Family Friendly Initiatives in the Workplace*, Employment Equality Agency 1996, is set out in Appendix 2 to this chapter.

16   *Introducing Family Friendly Initiatives in the Workplace*: Employment Equality Agency, 1996.

## 8.10 Protecting workers and their families in a changing employment environment

A number of legislative changes have been introduced in recent years to protect the rights of workers in the changing employment environment. These improvements include better health and safety legislation, adoptive and maternity leave protection, PRSI pension cover for self-employed people and PRSI income support for part-time workers. Part-time workers now have PRSI cover for pensions, for maternity leave and for periods of unemployment and disability. They also have cover for holidays, unfair dismissals, worker participation schemes and insolvency situations.

The Organisation of Working Time Act, 1997 sets out maximum working times. A new average working time of 48 hours a week for workers will be phased in by the year 2000 (60 hours in 1998, 55 hours in 1999). The Act provides for minimum holidays for full-time workers and part-time workers. From April 1999 full-time workers will be entitled to a minimum of 20 days' holiday a year. Part-time workers will be entitled to holidays amounting to 8 per cent of the hours which they work.

**It is the Commission's view that protective legislation and the social welfare system must be kept under review to see that it is responsive to the changing needs of workers. Income protection for vulnerable families is a particular priority.**

In this context, the Commission would like to raise the issue of cover for occupational injuries for certain categories of self-employed people.

Workers who have moved from employee status to self-employment no longer have income support protection for occupational injuries benefits. Typical examples are tradesmen and construction workers who have moved from employee to self-employed status in recent years. Other examples are the significant number of people who are moving from social welfare into self-employment under the Back to Work Allowance scheme. The change in employment status means that these workers, in the event of an occupational accident or illness, have no cover for an insurance based benefit.[17] Instead, they must depend on a means-tested payment if they become incapable of work because of an accident or occupational disease.[18]

**It is the Commission's view that the question of cover for incapacity arising from an occupational accident, injury or illness should be examined with a view to enhancing the protection of the social insurance system for these workers and their families.**

## 8.11 Developments in the workplace to assist in the reconciling of work and family responsibilities

A number of initiatives to assist workers in reconciling their work and family responsibilities have been introduced into the workplace in recent years. These include initiatives such as flexitime, job sharing, career/employment break and extended leave. Term time working with

---

17   Self-employed participants on the Back to Work Allowance are liable for PRSI contributions at the self employed rate and have cover for pensions only.

18   A widow's or widower's contributory pension would be payable on the death of a the worker if the self-employed worker or the surviving spouse had an up to date PRSI record.

unpaid leave during school holidays, flexi-place- the option to work from home for agreed periods of time, and paternity leave are further examples of initiatives which facilitate working parents. The development of flexible work practices is, however, still at an early stage and is to a large extent confined to the State and semi-State sectors and to a relatively small number of private sector companies.

In Ireland the take-up of *job sharing* has not been widespread. A 1996 study[19] found that over 30 per cent of private sector employees work in organisations with job-sharing options, while 90 per cent of public sector employees have access to these options. The number of employees in the private sector who availed of such schemes was only 5,300 - less than 1 per cent of total private sector employment. In the public sector, the estimated figure for job-sharing was 8,000, or between 3 or 4 per cent of total employment.

Extended leave options or *career breaks* are available in 82 per cent of enterprises in the public sector, and 12 per cent of public sector employees sampled had taken a career break at some stage. Less than 10 per cent of private sector employers provide a facility for extended leave and only 2 per cent actually had an employee on extended leave during the survey. Career breaks were most popular with female employees, especially those in the managerial and professional grades.

### Some issues arising in relation to flexible working arrangements

There is limited data available on the views of employers' organisations and trade unions on flexible working arrangements, the benefits of such practices to employers and employees or the evaluation of existing schemes in meeting employer/employee needs.

However, a number of issues arising in relation to the development of flexible working practices have been brought to the Commission's attention.

### Participation in flexible working arrangements

Although take-up rates are low, it is significant that women have overwhelmingly responded to initiatives such as job-sharing, part-time work and career breaks. There is no doubt that these initiatives are of great value to women with family responsibilities. For these women, the availability of job-sharing, career breaks and extended leave options reduces the pressures associated with trying to balance child care with work and a career. Indeed, the initiatives afford many women the opportunity to stay on in the Labour Force when they might otherwise have had to leave. In addition, it affords them the opportunity to spend more time with their children and to have a positive experience as a parent for the few short years that their childcare demands are at their highest.

### Over-representation of women

Limited studies[20] to date are, however, suggesting over-representation of women and under-representation of men in these employment options. This development poses questions for women's own career prospects and the future development of family-friendly initiatives to facilitate both parents in caring for their children.

19  B. Fynes, T. Morrissey, W.K. Roche, B.J. Whelan and J. Williams, *Working Lives: The Changing Nature of Working Time Arrangements in Ireland*: Dublin, Oak Tree Press., in Labour Market Studies, Ireland, edited by J.J. Sexton, P.J. O' Connell, Employment and Social Affairs, European Commission 1996.

20  This section draws on material presented to the Commission by Dr. Eileen Drew, Department of Statistics/ Centre for Women's Studies, Trinity College Dublin.

**Distinct career paths for men and women**

Research findings involving EU comparisons of family-friendly work practices confirm the emergence of two distinct career paths for men and women:

- **Fast Track**

  Men, including fathers, retain the primary breadwinner role, display stronger and continuous attachment to the labour market, in a full-time capacity. This may increase rather diminish when children are born.

- **Slow Track**

  Women, particularly mothers, face the dilemma of juggling with the dual burden and the stress associated with being workers and taking on the main caring responsibilities for children.

**A dual role - the personal costs**

A picture is emerging that, while family-friendly policies have undoubtedly enabled many women who would not otherwise have been able to do so to combine career and family responsibilities, this has been at a high cost in terms of stress and adverse effects on careers associated with the dual role for many women.

It has also been suggested that job sharers are sometimes viewed as less committed than full-time workers and job sharing is not availed of by managerial grades to any significant extent in comparison with its acceptability at lower grades. Men who opt for career breaks usually do so for career, education or travel reasons. Women, on the other hand, usually opt for career breaks for family reasons.

**The Gerster judgement**

Of particular interest in this context is the recent judgement of the European Court of Justice on how the service of a part-time worker in the German public service, Ms. Helen Gerster, should be reckoned for promotion purposes. The essence of the judgement is that in a situation where the vast majority of part-time workers in an employment are female, it is discriminatory to reckon the service of such staff for promotion purposes as less than full-time service. At present, a job-sharer (working part-time) receives only six months credits for each year of service when seniority is being calculated.

At the time of writing, the full implications of the judgement are not known. However, the judgment appears to have a major significance in addressing some of the adverse consequences for parents opting to job share for family reasons.

**8.12    Changing the culture surrounding work and family life**

The indications in relation to the work patterns of many families today are that there must be considerable conflict between the time and energy available for caring and family relationships and the time and energy required to meet work commitments. Families, pressured as they are by demanding work schedules, have too little time for themselves, for their wider family and for their friends - and these are crucially important supports in today's society.

The conflict is exacerbated by the fact that in today's society family and work are increasingly segregated. This conflict was described by Dr. Kathleen Lynch of UCD in a paper appended to the Report of the Constitution Review Group (May 1996). She makes the point that what many people feel is not sufficiently protected in contemporary society is the right to have time for a family or personal life. Although there is great debate as to what constitutes a family life, there is little disagreement about the need to protect people's time to have a family life.

**It is the Commission's view that change can be brought about only over time by a major change in our thinking and in the culture surrounding work and family life.**

One key issue for consideration in this context relates to the roles and tasks which are undertaken by men and women in society, and by fathers and mothers in the workplace and in the home.

Despite the existence of legislation on equal pay and equal opportunities at work, employment practices in many organisations still reflect a view that workers are male employees whose family responsibilities are confined to the traditional breadwinner role. There is now more open debate about the roles of men and women and about the different and complementary contributions made by men and women to society and to family life. Men have begun to explore and discuss the roles traditionally assigned to them. Many of the issues are discussed in the Commission's report on fathers.[21] There is clear scientific evidence to support a greater involvement of fathers with their children for their mutual well-being. This requires recognition in society and a fundamental change in our expectations about the level of commitment to their work that fathers and workers with caring responsibilities are expected to demonstrate.

8.13    **Sharing the care - Fathers need more time with their children**
With the increasing participation of women in the labour market the issue of sharing the care must be addressed by Government and social partners. Policies in relation to more support for children and childcare, the care of older people and family members with a disability, as well as employment and working conditions, have a role to play in bringing about an environment which facilitates men and women in meeting their family and work commitments.

However, the fundamental issue to be examined relates to how fathers are to be encouraged and facilitated in taking on a significant role in carrying out the childcare and caring functions which traditionally have been the domain of women. Taking on a more significant role means spending more time in carrying out these functions, and this has implications for the amount of time that fathers are spending in the workplace and for the financial situation of families. Even in situations where fathers have a partner who is working in paid employment, the evidence from the special tabulations on the Labour Force survey 1996[22] is that the number of hours worked by fathers is still higher than men who are not fathers.

FINAL REPORT OF THE COMMISSION ON THE FAMILY

21    *Fathers: Irish Experience in an International Context:* Kieran McKeown, Harry Ferguson, Dermot Rooney. An abstract of the report is contained in Chapter 18.

22    See Chapter 18.

The Commission's recommendations in relation to income support policy are particularly relevant to this issue.

**Promoting options for fathers**
The Commission considers that it is important to ensure that the new flexibility in employment has broad application and does not serve to reinforce existing segregation in the labour force and in relation to caring work carried out within the home by:

- isolating women into atypical and part-time low-paid work

- containing fathers' opportunities to spend more time with their children against all the evidence about the benefits to both parents and child of the greater involvement of fathers in their children's lives.

To date, almost all of the arguments in favour of family-friendly measures in the workplace are presented as having benefits for mothers; unless the corresponding benefits for fathers are also highlighted, these measures will continue to be taken up disproportionately by mothers.

The report on fathers undertaken for the Commission argues that the manner in which family-friendly measures are implemented and promoted can be just as important as the initiatives themselves. The introduction of family-friendly measures in the workplace does not automatically mean that these measures will be taken up by fathers. The reasons suggested for this are many, but include loss of earnings, which can have a negative effect on the entire family, increased workload from taking time off, and the fear that taking leave for family reasons may have a negative impact on one's career. In addition, the culture of the workplace can discourage men from availing of family-friendly measures because it does not expect men who are fathers to behave any differently from men who are not fathers.

**The Commission considers that a concerted effort should be made by the social partners to promote flexible work arrangements to fathers and to promote their introduction in all sectors of the labour market, but particularly in sectors where traditionally these facilities have not been available.**

A fundamentally important part of this development should be the **identification of ways and means of bringing about societal and cultural change to promote men's role within the family** and with their children. In this regard, the Commission points to a recommend-ation made in the report on fathers that the language used to promote family-friendly measures should be less gender-neutral and use terms like father and mother to indicate that it is precisely for parents and their children that the measures are being introduced. A further suggestion made to the Commission relates to provision of parent education programmes in the workplace which would be relevant and supportive to workers who are fathers and mothers. Positive advertising, promoting greater awareness of the benefits to children of more engagement by fathers in their rearing is also recommended.

### 8.14 Easing financial pressures- a role for the commercial sector

One of the most pressing reasons why both parents remain in the workforce when their childcare responsibilities are at their most demanding is the financial commitment they have undertaken because of their mortgage. In recent years, housing prices have soared and many young couples have no choice but to work demanding schedules to pay for their housing costs.

With increasing competition among the lending agencies, banks, building societies and other mortgage providers are developing mortgage packages to attract customers. It is the Commission's view that these developments could focus more on meeting the needs of young families who may wish to take time out of the workforce to care for their children at home. From a commercial perspective, the increasing participation of married women in the workforce and the rate of return to the labour force of women after time spent rearing children in the home provides a solid basis for continuity in relation to family incomes in the future.

The availability of mortgage holidays could facilitate young families who wish to spend more time with their children when they are young. Alternatively, longer term mortgages, for example for 30 years, might also suit the circumstances of some families. Borrowers however, should be made fully aware of all the implications of different mortgage options and lending institutions should ensure that they are given all necessary information, advice and guidance in this regard, including variations in repayments over the life of the loan and possible implications in the events of changes in circumstances, such as changes in interest rates or in income or employment status or increased financial commitment in the future. **It is the Commission's view that there is a role for the commercial lending sector, in facilitating families' to take time out of the workforce to undertake family caring responsibilities.**

At a wider-level, the Commission is concerned about the work demands being imposed on young people today by the high costs associated with trying to establish a family home. The Commission welcomes the publication of the Government study of the housing market and Action on House Prices, the Government's response to the consultants' study.[23] From the Commission's perspective, the key issue in the study relates to the affordability of a home for young families. The Commission urges that the important obligation on the State to support families in carrying out their functions, principally in relation to the care and nurturing of children and the care of dependent family members, should inform future policy development in relation to making a home affordable for families today.

---

23  The package of measures to tackle the issue of house prices in response to the report of the Study on House Prices by Peter Bacon & Associates, Economic Consultants is set out in the Government's " Action on House Prices". The package involves a range of measures to increase the supply of housing, reduce overheating in the market and assist first-time house buyers. It is designed to help restore balance to the housing market, dampen down house price increases and help lower-income households into home ownership. Measures to assist first-time buyers form a key element of the package, including the increase in the income limit for the local authority shared ownership scheme to £20,000 for single income households, with corresponding increase joint income households. Other measures include the removal of fiscal incentives to investors who were pricing low income buyers out of the market and reductions in stamp duty rates, particularly at the lower house price levels.

**8.15 Research**

**The Commission is of the view that research should be undertaken on the effects on workers and on employers of balancing the demands of work and family life, and on the effects on employment of initiatives introduced to assist workers. Of particular interest is the possible development of a dual labour market structure.**

Research might examine how family-friendly policies can facilitate women's involvement in family life but restrict their progress in the workplace, while the same policies support male partners in their commitment to the workplace, but restrict their opportunities to devote more time to their role in family life.

A number of agencies have an interest in these developments; for example, the Department of Social, Community and Family Affairs and the pensions sector, in relation to the long-term effects on women's earnings, which interruptions in their labour market attachment might indicate. The Employment Equality Agency, while its statutory role is confined to equality in the workplace, already has an interest in promoting equality of opportunity in terms of both men and women having access to such initiatives as are available to assist workers with their family responsibilities. Employers and their representative organisations and the trade unions also have an interest in the effects on workers, and on productivity, of the work arrangements parents have to adopt to try to balance their commitments to family life and to work.

**8.16 Workers with caring responsibilities for older relatives or people with disabilities**

The changes in the nature of employment, in the organisation of work, the increasing participation of women in the workforce and the more demanding work schedules which are being undertaken by many families today all have implications for the care of older people and other family members who may be dependent on support with day-to-day living. The family is the main source of care and support for older family members and for family members with a disability who are dependent.

As we move towards a new century, the care of the elderly is a subject of serious social and economic concern for all member states of the European Union. All EU countries are experiencing similar demographic changes. Families are getting smaller. Family structures are changing. The numbers and proportion of elderly people in the European Union are increasing, and will continue to increase in the next 20 years. Improved lifestyles and better health provision mean that older retired people will go on to live active healthy, independent lives but increasingly Europe is concerned about who will care for those who become frail and dependent in old age.

While the aging of the Irish population is not as advanced as that of some of our European partners, here, too, there is a growing awareness of the need to address the future caring needs of an elderly population.

Projections[24] of the population show that:

---

24   Actuarial Review of Social Welfare Pensions, Department of Social, Community and Family Affairs, September 1997.

- the number of persons over age 65 is projected to grow from 414,000 (11 per cent of the population) in 1996 to 1,018,000 (27 per cent of the population) in 2056 and

- the number of persons over age 80 is projected to grow from 90,000 (2 per cent of the population) in 1996 to 317,000 (8 per cent of the population) in 2056.

Women, as daughters and, to a smaller extent, as daughters-in-law, traditionally have been the carers of older family members. Women, also, are the mainstay of many community-based services for older people. The contribution of men to the care of family members (mainly as spouses) is also very considerable and generally unacknowledged. Caring responsibilities may vary from incidental care a couple of times a week to full dependence on the carer for physical care and emotional support.

Most carers are outside the workforce. Their caring responsibilities can be demanding and they have needs for support, often financial support, access to respite care and information, and advice about the very important responsibilities which they are undertaking. In Chapter 14, the Commission examines the needs of carers for support at different levels. In this chapter the Commission considers the particular needs of carers who are working outside the home.

The nuclear family today is small. Its capacity and resources to undertake all its caring functions is often limited. Caring responsibilities for older people, for an adult family member who needs additional support or for the spouse who is ill can present intense demands on families in managing their caring and work responsibilities.

8.17    **Caring responsibilities and the workplace**
It has been pointed out to the Commission that the care of elderly parents and of other dependent family members is assuming a growing significance for families with the demanding work schedules they are undertaking. A number of studies give details of the participation in employment of carers. A 1988[25] study showed that 16 per cent of carers were in paid employment. The majority of carers, 77 per cent who were outside the workforce had, however, been in employment at one time: twenty per cent of those who had a job left specifically to become carers. Men were more likely than women to have given up work for this reason.

A 1993 study[26] suggests that 42 per cent of male carers and 16 per cent of female carers are in paid employment.

To date, the issue of workers with caring responsibilities has not received a lot of attention. There is very little information available about the effects on workers of trying to meet their care and work commitments, or the effects on the work situation of caring demands on a worker. However, it has been suggested to the Commission that it is only a matter of time before eldercare becomes an issue in the workplace.

25    *Caring for the Elderly Part II, The Caring process: A Study of Carers in the Home*: National Council for the Aged, 1988. See also Caring without Limits ? Sufferers of Dementia/Alzheimer's Disease, A Study of their Carers; H. Ruddle and J. O' Connor, Policy Research Centre/Alzheimer Society of Ireland, Dublin 1993.

26    *Women: Working and Caring for their Elderly Parents.* J. Hannelore, 1993

Where workers cannot balance the conflicting demands on their time, they may choose or be forced by circumstances to leave their jobs. Studies from abroad show that carers have great difficulty in re-entering the labour market when their period of care is ended, and that their caring responsibilities can affect work opportunities over the carers' lifetime. It is also known that caring over a long  period causes financial disadvantage; for example, the accumulation of pension rights can be affected and subsequently the carer receives a lower income on retirement than might have been anticipated.

### 8.18    The effects of caring responsibilities on workers

Studies from the US[27] and the UK give an indication of the effects of caring responsibilities on the work situation of carers. These include: losing time from work or coming in late, having to take leave of absence, moving from full-time to part-time work, taking early retirement and, in some cases, having to give up work entirely. Other effects mentioned include reduced promotion prospects, loss of pension and loss of other benefits.

It seems evident that the personal work experiences of workers with caring responsibilities revealed in the American study are likely to be the experiences of most workers with demanding caring responsibilities. Thus, the effects of combining work and care demands on employees will be reflected for most employers in the workplace in terms of loss of productivity, absence from work and in some cases, the loss of an experienced worker and consequent increase in recruitment and training costs.

The availability of part-time work or job-sharing and extended leave arrangements, although limited to certain sectors of the labour market as described earlier, provides some facility to workers who are in a position to take up these options.

There is very little information available on the benefits to employers of these initiatives. The information that is available tends to focus on the benefit to carers. Carers welcome developments to support them. They report lower levels of stress, higher levels of job satisfaction and less work family conflict.

### 8.19    The case for improving the situation of workers with caring responsibilities

In today's competitive environment, the value of the commitment and loyalty of skilled employees and their well-being are increasingly being acknowledged as important factors for success. Support for employees who for a time in their working lives must balance the demands of family and work will contribute to a work environment which makes it easier for employees to give of their best in both situations.

The State, for its part, has an interest in supporting workers with caring responsibilities. They have an important responsibility within their family as well as contributing to economic growth through their participation in the workforce. Initiatives in the workplace should be matched by greater State support for community-based services, such as respite care, community support groups and community services, to assist with the care of older people, as recommended by the Commission in Chapter 14. These services can provide significant back-up supports for worker/carers. It is important that community based services are

---

27    See for example: *Working Carers: International Perspectives on Working and Caring for Older People, edited by Judith Phillips, Averbury Studies of Care in the Community,* Avery,1995; *Managing Work and Family Life,* Viola M. Lechner, Michael A. Creedon, Springer Publishing Company, New York, 1994.

accessible and flexible enough for worker/carers so that the carer can maximise the potential for assistance that workplace initiatives can provide.

**8.20    According a priority to workers with caring responsibilities**

It is the Commission's view that improving the situation of carers and assisting them in the reconciliation of their caring demands with work should be a major issue for the social partners in the years ahead. **The Commission's main recommendation is that there should be a specific recognition in employment and social policies for workers who are looking after a family member with a disability or an elderly relative who is dependent on family care. This issue should be accorded as much priority on the agenda of employers, trade unions, and the Government as childcare issues.**

The Commission welcomes the commitment in Partnership 2000 for Inclusion, Employment and Competitiveness to Government support for the growth of family-friendly policies in employment.

In relation to the needs of workers with caring responsibilities for an older family member or a family member with a disability, the Commission would like to offer some suggestions in relation to the adaptation of existing initiatives to better meet the needs of these workers. In this context the Commission would like to draw attention to a recent study[28] which provides an overview of eldercare initiatives in the European Union and in the United States. The Commission in making its suggestions in this area is conscious of the costs that even modest initiatives can have for small organisations. Over 95 per cent of Irish businesses employ fewer than 50 people. The Commission suggests that the social partners could make a start by building on existing initiatives in place to facilitate workers with childcare responsibilities.

It is suggested that;

(i)    **Existing practices** such as flexitime, job sharing and part-time work **should be reviewed** to see to what extent they could be further adapted to meet the kinds of flexibility required by workers with caring responsibilities. Extended lunch breaks, opportunities for evening work and home working can provide different types of flexible working hours to meet carers' needs.

(ii)    Consideration should be given to providing **leave for adult care on the lines of the proposed parental leave arrangements.** The leave may be either paid or unpaid but if it is unpaid, pension and social security entitlements should be protected for the period of the leave.

---

28    From *Eldercare and Employment: Workplace Policies and Initiatives to support workers who are carers, European Foundation for the Improvement of Living and Working Conditions:* Working Paper WP/94/32/EN. The study showed that the incidence of employer supported eldercare initiatives in the EU member states is low. However, in the United States, with its limited social service network, employers are increasingly aware of the problems and provide a variety of facilities to help family carers. A summary of the main eldercare initiatives set out in the report is contained in Appendix 3 to this chapter.

(iii) The possibility of introducing **phased retirement** for older workers ( particularly spouses) with caring responsibilities should be examined further. This might be undertaken in the context of the response to the National Pensions Policy Initiative.

(iv) Special consideration should be given to **worker carers** who have the responsibility **of caring for a dependent relative who is seriously ill** or dying, particularly when the carer is the spouse. A pilot scheme to provide leave of absence for worker carers facing this situation in Denmark is proving to be very successful, with significant benefits for the patient, the carer who wants to take on this role and the State.

The development of a similar scheme in Ireland to provide the opportunity to workers to take leave while caring for a very close relative at home, in their last months, might include the following features:

- The worker/carers should be able to avail of full or part-time leave for the period, which may be between two and six months.

- The employer must be agreeable to the leave.

- Where the leave is unpaid, the possibility of a PRSI carers benefit could be explored.

- Pension and PRSI cover should be protected for workers who take up the leave.

(v) Consideration should be given to **expanding employee assistance programmes** to include **counselling, information and advice** for those with caring responsibilities. Many larger companies and the public service have well-developed employee assistance programmes. The Commission is of the view that these programmes could better support those with responsibilities for caring for older people in a practical way by providing information and advice to worker/carers.

(vi) **Other workplace initiatives** could be developed at a little cost. For example, workplace catering might provide takeaway meals. Company-sponsored social and retirement clubs for former employees could focus on the caring demands made on retired employees and develop supports such as carer/worker networks, company-organised respite evenings, and patient-sitting arrangements, as well as practical information about access to help.

**8.21**     **Assisting families who are unemployed in getting access to the jobs market.**
In the first section of this chapter the Commission has considered the situation of families who are trying to balance the demands of the workplace with family life. In this section the Commission examines the policy response to families who are at the other end of the spectrum. These are the families who are unemployed or who have insufficient work.

**Unemployment - an overview**
Despite strong economic growth over recent years and the increase in employment, Ireland continues to experience a significant unemployment problem. Between 1975 and 1980,

Irish unemployment remained unchanged at about 7 per cent of the labour force. Between 1979 and 1986 unemployment, as measured by the Labour Force Survey (PES measure) increased from 6.8 per cent (85,000 people) to 17.3 per cent (227,000 people). By 1990 this had fallen to 13.4 per cent. It rose again, to a peak of 16.7 per cent in 1993 and has since fallen to an estimated 10.3 per cent (179,000 people) in 1997.

### Long-term unemployment - a particular concern

Long-term unemployment that is, unemployment for one year or more is a particular concern because of its association with low levels of education, low skill levels and a declining chance of finding a job as the duration of unemployment increases.

The rate of long term unemployment has fallen from a high of almost 10 per cent (135,000) in 1993 to 5.6 per cent (86,000 people) in 1997. This has been possible because of a concerted programme of direct interventions to provide work opportunities for long-term unemployed people in the social economy (mainly the Community Employment scheme) and various programmes to subsidise the return to employment or self-employment. The numbers of people involved in these programmes are equivalent to 75 per cent of the numbers recorded as long-term unemployed (ILO basis) in April 1997.[29]

### Income support for unemployed people

People who are unemployed in the main depend on social welfare payments. Unemployment payments consist of unemployment benefit, which is based on PRSI contributions paid in recent years. Unemployment benefit is paid for up to 390 days. The means-tested unemployment assistance is paid after entitlement to unemployment benefit is exhausted or if the unemployed person has no recent record of PRSI or has not enough social insurance contributions. This is the case, for example, if the unemployed person has been abroad or if he or she has never worked or has been away from the workforce in recent years.

The rates of unemployment payments are £70.50 for unemployment benefit and unemployment assistance (long term) and £68.40[30] for unemployment assistance (short-term), with additions for qualified adults and dependent children. People receiving these payments sign on the Live Register.[31]

Information from the Department of Social, Community and Family Affairs shows that 84 per cent of people receiving unemployment payments get less than £100 a week, 13 per cent get between £100 and £150 and 3 per cent get over £150.[32]

### Unemployed families

Most people on the Live Register (63 per cent) do not qualify for additions for dependents. Nearly 40 per cent of people have families, i.e. qualified adults or dependent children.

29   Special European Council on Employment: An Irish Perspective 1997.

30   Proposed rates from June 1998.

31   The Live Register is an administrative count of people who are signing for Unemployment Benefit and Unemployment Assistance and for credited PRSI contributions. It includes seasonal and part-time and casual workers who are entitled to payments, and people who are not entitled to payments but who are available for work and entitled to PRSI credited contributions.

32   Information supplied by Department of Social, Community and Family Affairs, based on the Live Register for November 1997.

- 22 per cent of those on the Live Register are under 25 years of age and over half of these people are young men.

- 52 per cent are between 25 and 45 years of age.

- 17 per cent of people are between 45 years and 55 years of age.

## 8.22 Unemployment and social exclusion[33]

Families with children headed by an unemployed person face a particularly high risk of poverty. At present 15 per cent of Irish households containing children under 15 have no person employed. It has been shown that there is a clear link between unemployment, poverty and ill-health and psychological distress.[34] In addition to the financial and economic challenges facing families in this situation there is also the link between unemployment, especially long term unemployment, and social exclusion. This is especially the case when unemployment is transmitted across the generations and is reinforced by being concentrated in particular areas.

Unemployment has been identified as the biggest single contributor to social exclusion and poverty and the main reason for the high level of child poverty.[35] The strategy for achieving greater social inclusion has been clearly identified for policy-makers. It involves an **integrated approach across several fronts in increasing employment and reducing unemployment.**[36]

### Partnership 2000

Partnership 2000 for Inclusion, Employment and Competitiveness pinpoints the objectives to tackle unemployment through enterprise, promotion and job growth, employment incentives and the reduction of unemployment traps, active labour market measures and direct targeting of the priority groups of unemployed people who find it most difficult to get a placement in training or in a job. These priority groups include: long-term unemployed people depending on means-tested payments, young unemployed people under age 18, lone parents, the spouses of people on means-tested payments and persons receiving disability allowances.

## 8.23 Social inclusion - the policy approach to include unemployed people in social and economic progress

The success of the macro-economic policies which have contributed to significant increases in employment in recent years have been well documented.[37]

---

33  Social exclusion has been described as a condition or process whereby a person is cut off from access to normal expectations or standards considered to be acceptable in society.

34  Christopher T. Whelan: Damian F. Hannan and Sean Creighton *Unemployment Poverty and Psychological distress:* ESRI, 1991.

35  T. Callan, B. Nolan, B.J. Whelan and J. Williams: *Poverty in the 1990s:,* ESRI, Combat Poverty Agency, Department of Social Welfare, Oak Tree Press, Dublin 19, 1996.

36  See for example, *Strategy into the 21st Century* NESC no. 99 November 1991. *Sharing in Progress National Anti-Poverty Strategy, Partnership 2000: for Inclusion, Employment and Competitiveness*

37  See, for example, ESRI Medium-Term Review, May 1997

Specific policy objectives to ensure that unemployed people share in progress include

- access to training, skills enhancement and education for long-term unemployed people

- ensuring that it is worthwhile for unemployed families to take up work and increase their earnings by assisting workers on low earnings and improving child income support

- ensuring that people and their families have adequate incomes while they are unemployed

- facilitating the transfer from welfare payments to work.

### Reducing unemployment

The targets to substantially reduce unemployment are set out in the National Anti-Poverty Strategy. These are:

- to reduce the rate of unemployment to 6 per cent by 2007

- to reduce the rate of long-term unemployment to 3.5 per cent, with a particular focus on reducing the number of very long-term unemployed, who are especially at risk of being consistently poor

- to eliminate early school-leaving before Junior Certificate and to reduce early school-leaving, such that the percentage of those completing senior cycle will increase to at least 90 per cent by the year 2000 and 98 per cent by the year 2007.

The broad strategy to achieve the targets involves enhancing policies to increase employment opportunities and opportunities to acquire skills and training, improving access to work for unemployed people by means of a public employment service, reducing disincentives in income support policies, and easing the transition to work.[38]

### Preventing unemployment

At a level to prevent unemployment, the strategy involves:

- preventing early school-leaving through programmes such as the Early Start pilot pre-school programme and Breaking the Cycle, and increased resources at primary school level, particularly for those children at risk of educational disadvantage

- compensatory education, training and skills-enhancing programmes such as Youthreach for those who leave school early without educational attainments or qualifications.

### 8.24    The commitment to tackling unemployment

The Commission welcomes the comprehensive commitment across all sectors- the social partners, trade unions, employers, farmers and Government- to tackling unemployment[39]

---

38    Details of labour market measures and income support initiatives are set out in Appendix 4 to this chapter.

39    The Government programme *An Action Programme for the Millennium* recognises the need to tackle unemployment via a range of measures in the areas of tax reform, investment in education and programmes for the long-term unemployed.

and ensuring that families who are unemployed share in the unprecedented economic progress which Ireland is now experiencing. The Commission also welcomes the renewed commitment at EU level to reduce unemployment[40] and the recent Government announcement of a £1 billion action plan as part of its response to the EU guidelines.

## 8.25 An opportunity to make rapid progress

The recent fall in unemployment is directly attributable to the strong performance of the Irish economy in recent years. Economic growth has averaged 7.5 over the past 3 years bringing increased employment. This growth is set to continue over the coming few years.[41]

The number of people at work increased by 41,000 in the year to April 1997[42] and is expected to increase by a further 50,000 in 1998. In 1997 the labour force exceeded 1,500,000 for the first time. The ESRI, looking ahead, has suggested that the unfamiliar situation is beginning to arise where economic growth could be limited by labour supply constraints and concludes that if the number at work is to continue to increase to sustain growth, the obvious source of extra employed is from the still high numbers of unemployed.

**The Commission considers that the favourable outlook for continued growth in jobs presents an unprecedented opportunity for a concerted effort to make rapid progress in achieving the employment objectives so comprehensively identified for long-term unemployed men and women and their families.**

## 8.26 More support for people in taking up employment- tackling some incentive issues

In particular, the Commission would like to single out the following areas for action.

### The transition from social welfare to work

In addition to specific schemes and programmes to help unemployed people to get back to work, the recommended policy approach to income support generally is to minimise, and where possible to counteract, the effects of disincentives which arise for unemployed people and people on low incomes in improving their financial situation.

Disincentives may arise for a family where the income available from employment (i.e. take home pay) leaves them no better off or only marginally better off than if they remain on un-employment payments. Families on low pay may also face disincentives to improving their financial position; for example, by taking on additional hours of work or doing overtime, if they stand to pay substantial extra tax or if their income brings them over a threshold, which means that they lose valuable benefits such as a medical services card or the family income supplement.

---

40  The special EU Summit on Employment (November 1997) adopted a common strategy to combat unemployment. (There are some 18 million unemployed in the EU). EU member states have agreed to draft national plans for implementation of the guidelines in their countries. The measures covered in the guidelines include: improving employability, developing entrepreneurship, fostering adaptability and strengthening policies for equal opportunities.

41  Quarterly Economic Commentary, ESRI October 1997.

42  Labour Force Survey 1997, Selected Results, October, 1997.

These disincentives give rise to what is known as the "unemployment trap" and the "poverty trap" respectively. The Expert Working Group on the Integration of the Tax and Social Welfare Systems[43] noted that such traps arise, particularly for families with children, owing to the structure of family income support in the social welfare system, and also made the point that on social grounds, a measure to tackle unemployment among families with children is important.

The Expert Group therefore examined a number of ways in which income support for children could be made more neutral vis-á-vis the labour force status of parents. While the Group did not reach agreement on recommending one of the options identified over the others, it did conclude that some form of child income support should be included in any package of reforms aimed at addressing unemployment and poverty traps.

The Commission, in Chapter 5 refers to the benefits of an approach to income support which involves a strengthening of the role of child benefit as a mechanism for providing income support to families and a lessening of the importance of child dependent allowances with social welfare payments. This approach is suggested for a number of reasons:

- It would help to minimise disincentives to parents in relation to taking up employment or improving income, which is in the interest of the family.

- It would facilitate parents' choice in relation to the care and education of their children.

- It would facilitate family incentives, such as the incentive to form stable relationships and to marry and to provide joint parenting to children.

It is the Commission's view that a concentration of resources into child benefit and away from the child dependent allowance, payable with social welfare payments, has very measurable advantages in relation to the future direction of family income support policy to achieve "family objectives".

### Minimum hourly wage

The earnings that unemployed people can command on taking up a job is the main factor which determines the extent that the incentives described earlier affect low-income families. It is therefore important that employment and training programmes for unemployed people which are designed to assist with re-entry into the labour market also encourage ongoing training and skills acquisition and provide progression routes for people so that they have reasonable prospects for increasing earnings in the future.

The proposed introduction, after consultation with the social partners, of a national minimum hourly wage[44] is relevant also. An effective national minimum wage has the potential to be an important policy instrument, along with the income tax and PRSI systems, child benefit and family income supplement, in improving the incomes of those most at risk of poverty because they are on low wages and in improving incentives to take-up or stay in employment.

---

43   Expert Working Group on Integrating Tax and Social Welfare, Department of Social Welfare, June 1996. (para 4.1)

44   See Government Programme- *Action Programme for the Millennium*

The absence of a minimum hourly wage may be relevant to the number of hours which younger fathers are working, as was illustrated earlier in this chapter. A minimum wage may also introduce greater equity for fathers and mothers who are on low pay.

The critical issue in relation to a national minimum wage is the impact of the measure on employment levels and the creation of new jobs. This is an issue which requires in-depth examination. In this context, the Commission welcomes the publication by the Government of the report of the Minimum Wage Commission to advise on the best way to introduce a national minimum wage.[45]

**Family Income Supplement (FIS)**

The Family Income Supplement is paid to workers who are rearing families on low pay. Entitlement to the supplement is calculated as 60 per cent of the difference between gross pay and a ceiling which is related to the number of children in the workers' family. Some 13,000 are now receiving the supplement.

In 1989, five years after the introduction of FIS, two independent reports, one of which was commissioned by the Department of Social, Community and Family Affairs, estimated that only about 25 per cent of 20,000 eligible families were in receipt of the supplement and forty six per cent of potential expenditure on the scheme was in payment. Improvements to the scheme, combined with intensive promotion, have resulted in the number of recipients increasing to almost 13,000 at present. However, the policy of progressively increasing the income limits has also increased the number of families that are eligible for the payment. Consequently, the increase in the rate of take-up has not been as significant as the increase in the number of recipients appears to suggest. Data from the ESRI 1994 *Living in Ireland* study suggest that FIS take-up is in the region of 20 per cent to 45 per cent (depending on the particular definition used). Various reasons for the poor take-up have been put forward, including lack of knowledge about FIS, workers' reluctance to claim the allowance and a reluctance to involve their employers.

The fact that entitlement has been calculated on gross wages rather than net wages may also be a factor in discouraging workers from claiming. **The Commission welcomes the announcement in the 1998 Budget that assessment of FIS on the basis of net income will be phased in from October 1998.**

---

45   The Minimum Wage Commission published its report in April 1998. The Commission's fundamental recommendation was the introduction of a single national minimum hourly wage for all adults in the economy. The rate recommended by the Commission was about two-thirds of media earnings (£4.40 per hour currently). In relation to young people the Commission recommended that

-   there should be a separate rate for under 18s set at 70 per cent of the full rate and

-   a separate training rate should apply to job entrants without experience, regardless of age.

This reduced training rate should operate on the basis of a sliding scale: first year employees should be paid 75 per cent of the full rate, with 80 per cent and 90 per cent of the full rate in the second and third year respectively. The Commission also recommended that a statutory Minimum Wage Commission be established, with representatives from unions, employers, government and independent members, chaired by an independent person appointed by the Minister, to review the rate at one to two-year intervals, taking into account the trend in prices, overall economic conditions, employment and competitiveness, and make recommendations to the Minister.

### FIS and the self-employed

It is the Commission's view that consideration should be given to extending Family Income Supplement to self-employed people and to farmers on low incomes. Self-employed people do not come within the scope of the scheme at present. Given the increased numbers of workers who are becoming self employed because of changes in the labour market or because they are being facilitated to set up on their own as evidenced by the fact that 50 per cent of the 21,000 people on the Back to Work Allowance scheme are self-employed, the Commission considers that the potential of the scheme to assist families depending on low earnings from self-employment should be explored. It is also the Commission's view that an expanded FIS would be of considerable assistance to low income farm families and to those depending on traditional sectors of the economy who have in recent years found themselves outside the employer/employee relationship; for example, self-employed low-skilled workers in the building industry and in the services sector. **The Commission recommends that the possibility of FIS for the self-employed should be explored.**

### Assistance with rent and mortgage payments

At present, under the supplementary allowance scheme, assistance with rent or mortgage interest is withdrawn where the person takes up employment of more than 30 hours a week. In Chapter 7, the Commission has highlighted the effect of the withdrawal on lone parents who have an opportunity to take-up employment. It has been suggested by the Working Group on the Integration of the Tax and Social Welfare Systems that a tapering arrangement, rather than the sharp withdrawal of all assistance, may help alleviate the effects of this disincentive for families to take up a full-time job.

**The Commission recommends that the introduction of a tapering arrangement in the withdrawal of rent and mortgage assistance be examined to see how the disincentive effects of the withdrawal of the assistance could be mitigated for families where they have the opportunity to take on full-time work and they depend on supplementary welfare allowance assistance to help with their housing costs.**

### Back to Work Allowance

A recent evaluation of the Back to Work Allowance scheme has acknowledged effectiveness in affording thousands of unemployed people opportunities to try out employment or self-employment while retaining the security of a social welfare payment for the first few years while they consolidate their place in the jobs market. In December 1997, some 21,000 people were participating in the scheme.

The evaluation report put forward a number of recommendations for improvements in the scheme including:

- More aftercare for workers.

- Better recognition in the structure of the scheme for the different needs of employees and self-employed people to improve job survival rates.

- A code of practice in relation to employment conditions.

- Enhanced information about non-financial supports, such as access to training, financial management and budgeting courses.

- Improved support for jobs facilitators who market the scheme and provide services to participants.

**The Commission recommends that these findings of the report be pursued to maximise the potential of this very worthwhile scheme to help families get back into employment or self-employment.**

### 8.27 Close co-operation in pursuing shared objectives

There is now a range of programmes and services to assist unemployed families. In the main, these programmes are administered by the Department of Social, Community and Family Affairs through its local offices and by the Department of Enterprise, Trade and Employment through FÁS and the Local Employment Service.[46] In addition, there are a number of support programmes operating under the County Enterprise Boards and under the Partnership companies which have been established throughout the country. Many of these supports would be firmly focused on promoting entrepreneurial skills and on identifying new opportunities for jobs in both the commercial and the social sectors of the economy. On the education side there are many initiatives underway to encourage second chance education; these are supported by the Vocational Education Committees, by adult education providers and by the Department of Education and Science.

**The Commission is of the view that there is a need to strengthen the links at local level between agencies who are the providers of programmes for unemployed people, including the local offices of the Department of Social, Community and Family Affairs, FÁS, the Local Employment Service, County Enterprise Boards, Partnership Companies, VECs and adult education providers to improve the all round service for unemployed people seeking a path back to the world of work.**

The importance of an integrated approach to the delivery of services to families has been discussed in Chapter 3. It is suggested that the models for providing an integrated service and for the development of close collaborative links at local level in the interests of delivering an excellent service to families are also relevant to the provision of a comprehensive programme of support for employment for families.

### 8.28 Priority groups for support

The Commission notes and welcomes the specific and detailed initiatives set out in Partnership 2000 and in the Programme for Government to assist priority groups of unemployed people:

- Long-term unemployed or those on means tested schemes - through extra places on Community Employment schemes and the local employment service and a targeting of access to places for those who are longest unemployed.

---

46    See Appendix 4 to this chapter for details about the Local Employment Service.

- Unemployed young people under age 18.

- Lone parents - through places being earmarked in Community Employment and in other schemes, including education and through improved income disregards, so that entitlements to the one-parent family payment may be retained.

- Persons in receipt of Disability Allowance and unemployed people registered with the National Rehabilitation Board - through access to Community Employment and Jobstart, and the workplace experience programme.

- Dependent spouses of people on long-term unemployment and other means tested payments.

**8.29    Dependent spouses in low income families**

The particular difficulties facing dependent spouses in low income families have been brought to the Commission's attention.

These families depend either on social welfare payments or on low wages. The dependent spouse, who is usually the mother working in the home and the main caregiver, is locked into a dependency status which ties her to home and children irrespective of their ages and whether or not there are substantial childcare demands on the family. She faces significant barriers in participating in the workforce even on a part-time basis.

It has been suggested that these women are among the most disadvantaged in terms of their access to employment and training opportunities.

**Unemployed families**

If the husband is on social welfare and on the Live Register of Unemployed, the only way for the wife to get access to the Live Register is for her to separately claim an unemployment payment[47] on the basis that she is available and looking for work. However, there is no material advantage to the family. The rate of social welfare payment is capped at the rate that would be payable in any event, to an unemployed person with a qualified adult dependent and dependent children.

If this wife gets a job, she may earn up to £60 per week and the qualified adult allowance continues to be paid to her husband; earnings between £60 and £90 mean that the allowance is reduced.  Earnings over £90 means that the qualified adult allowance is no longer payable and half the child dependent additions are also lost to the family. In effect, unless significant earnings are available to substantially outweigh the loss of social welfare income to the households, the family is locked into a situation where there is no earner in the household.

It is estimated, that out of approximately 90,000 people on social welfare payments, about 10,000 spouses are working outside the home.

FINAL REPORT OF THE COMMISSION ON THE FAMILY

47   There are arrangements in place in relation to places on some schemes, principally Community Employment, for husband and wife to swap their social welfare status. Thus the wife could go on the Live Register and the husband would become the adult dependant. The family would be no better off financially.

**Low-earner families**

If one of the couple is working, half the earnings, after allowances for travel and other going to work expenses, are assessed against the spouse who claims the unemployment payment. This is a further disincentive for the spouse, usually the wife who wants to work. If she succeeds in getting employment, she faces high effective tax rates. The expense of going to work, together with the cost of childcare, effectively debars her from taking up an employment opportunity unless significant earnings are available.

This situation is particularly frustrating for families when access to paid employment outside the home would provide significant benefits to the mother, parents and children and improve the prospects for the family's future financial well-being.

**Access to training and employment opportunities through the Live Register**

The difficulty experienced by spouses which are described above is part of a wider issue which relates to women's access to the labour market and training opportunities in general and the fact that access to many of these programmes is tied to a Live Register attachment. The Commission notes that this issue is the subject of consideration by a working group established under Partnership 2000[48] for Inclusion, Employment and Competitiveness; the report of the working group is due to completed in mid 1998.

---

48   The working group includes representatives of the relevant Government Departments and agencies, the National Women's Council of Ireland, Irish Congress of Trade Unions, Irish National Organisation of the Unemployed, AONTAS; the National Association of Adult Education, Irish Business and Employers Confederation and the Irish Farm Families Association.

## Appendix 1
**Parental leave in some European States and further afield.**

(Note: the information in this Table has been taken from *Time Out: the costs and benefits of paid parental leave* by Helen Wilkinson with Stephen Radley, Ian Christie, George Lawson and Jamie Sainsbury published by DEMOS, 9 Bridewell Place, London, EC4V 6 AP; 1997.

| | Duration | Individual/Family right | Payment | Funding | Take-up |
|---|---|---|---|---|---|
| **Sweden** | Up to 36 months | Combination of individual and family right to parental leave. Each parent has a right to 18 months, parental leave. 360 days of leave is paid. During the 360 days, each parent is allotted 30 days non-transferable leave. The remaining 300 days are transferable to either parent. | 85% wage compensation for the two 30-day periods. 75% for the next 210 days. Low fixed rate for last 90 days. | Through Social Insurance. Over 80% of revenue is through a payroll tax, 15% from general taxation. | 90% of women 78% of men |
| **Norway** | 42-52 weeks | Combination of individual and family right to parental leave. Father has a four-week quota, which cannot be shared with mother. The remaining time is a family right. | 100% of wages for 42 weeks. Extra 10 weeks available at 80% of wages. Time account periods are paid pro rata. | Through Social Insurance. | 94% of women 33% of men |
| **Finland** | Up to 36 months | Combination of individual and family right to parental leave. The first 105 days are non-transferable maternity leave. Fathers have 6 days' additional paid paternity leave' which can be taken at any time within the parental leave period. The rest of leave is a family right. | Parenting allowance equal 66% of recipient's earnings for 158 working days. Low fixed rate for remaining period. | Through Social Insurance. | 99% of women 2% of men |

| | Duration | Individual/Family right | Payment | Funding | Take-up |
|---|---|---|---|---|---|
| **Denmark** | Up to 2 years | Combination of individual and family right to parental leave. Parents are entitled to between 13 and 52 weeks' parental leave taken as single blocks. For children under 1, parents are entitled to 26 weeks' leave. Additional periods must be agreed with employers. | Leave-takers receive benefits of up to 60% of the maximum rate of unemployment benefit. | Through Social Insurance. | 93% of women 3% of men |
| **France** | 3 years | The entire leave is a family right. | None, except for second child and after. | General taxation (family allowances fund) | NA[1] |
| **Germany** | 3 years | The entire leave is a family right. | 600DM per month is provided on a means-tested basis until the child is 2. | General taxation | 95% of women 1% of men |
| **Austria** | 2 years full-time or 4 years part-time[2] | The entire leave is a family right. However, the mother must forego her right to all or part of it if the father takes leave. | Allowance available for working people, amount depends on age. Monthly allowance for couples equivalent to c. stg £280.[3] | Through Social Insurance | 90% of women 1% of men |
| **Netherlands** | 12 months | 6 months' individual part-time non-transferable leave is reserved for each parent. | None, except if reduced hours take lone parent below social assistance level. | None | 40% of women 9% of men |
| **Italy** | 6 months | The entire leave is a family right. | Parent receives 30% of normal earnings. | Through Social Insurance | NA |
| **Spain** | 3 years | The entire leave is a family right. | None | None | NA |

---

1  NA = No figures available.

2  The father must take six months' leave for the leave period to last this long. Otherwise leave lasts only until a child is eighteen months old.

3  A subsidy of approximately stg£125 per month is available to a single parent. This must be paid work.

|  | Duration | Individual/Family right | Payment | Funding | Take-up |
|---|---|---|---|---|---|
| **Portugal** | Between 6 and 24 months | Combination of individual and family right to parental leave. The first 98 days are paid maternity leave. The remainder of leave is a family right. | None | None | NA |
| **Greece** | 6 months | 3 months' individual non-transferable leave reserved for each parent. | None | Employees on leave pay social security contributions during their absence. | NA |
| **USA** | 24 weeks | 12 weeks' individual non-transferable leave for each parent. | None | None | Between 2% and 3.6% |
| **New Zealand** | 12 months | The entire leave is a family right. | None | None | NA |
| **Canada** | 10 weeks basic right under unemployment insurance. Duration of additional leave varies between provinces (12 to 34 weeks) | The entire leave is a family right. | 10 weeks | Unemployment insurance | NA |
| **Australia** | 12 months | The entire leave is a family right. | None | None | NA |

# Appendix 2

**Extract from Introducing Family-Friendly Initiatives in the Workplace, Employment Equality Agency, 1996.**

## Action Plan

The development of family-friendly workplaces in Ireland requires action by individuals, employers and their representative organisations, trade unions, and government. A comprehensive action plan is required.

## Employer Representative Organisations

- Lobby government to implement a national childcare strategy.

- Encourage individual employers to promote family-friendly initiatives.

- Liaise with community and voluntary groups in relation to the provision of care for dependent relatives.

- Produce and publicise examples of 'good practice'.

## Employers

- Recognise that employees need support in balancing work and family responsibilities.

- Make an organisational commitment to become a family-friendly employer.

- Conduct a survey of employee needs in relation to flexible working, childcare, eldercare and care for family members with disabilities.

- Ensure that family-friendly initiatives are developed and implemented for the benefit of both the organisation and employees.

- Develop an organisational culture that supports employees who take up family-friendly initiatives.

- Ensure that employees working flexible or reduced hours are given pro rata pay and benefits.

- Liaise with other local employers to explore possibilities for shared childcare and eldercare facilities.

- Liaise with community and voluntary groups in relation to childcare and eldercare provision.

- Monitor the 'take-up' of training opportunities to ensure a gender balance.

- Develop initiatives such as Employee Assistance Programmes, family days.

- Ensure that job applicants and employees returning to the workplace are not treated less favourably on grounds of age, gender or parental status.

**Trade Unions**

- Identify employee needs in relation to family-friendly initiatives.

- Highlight the issue of family-friendly initiatives within the workplace and ensure that it is placed on the agenda in negotiations.

- Negotiate flexible work arrangements which allow workers to combine work and family responsibilities.

- Work to ensure the successful implementation of family-friendly initiatives.

- Assist in monitoring the take-up and success rates of policies.

- Develop the union's policy in family-friendly initiatives.

**Employees**

- Encourage employers and trade unions to address the issue of family-friendly initiatives.

- Contribute to developing a family-friendly culture within the organisation.

- Co-operate with the development of family-friendly work practices.

**Voluntary/Community Groups**

- Liaise with local employers to provide support with childcare, eldercare and the care of dependent relatives.

# Appendix 3

**An overview of some employer supported eldercare initiatives in the US and in Europe**[4]

1.  **United States**

    Traditionally, most of the care needs of older dependants in the United States are provided not by Government but by family carers. Since many people in the prime (labour) age-groups are the main carers and the main source of labour, US employers are taking an increasingly active role in eldercare by developing initiatives to assist employees. In the United States, a lot of literature about eldercare has appeared and a range of concrete eldercare support initiatives provided by companies can now be seen.

    **Types of eldercare support**

    In general, the support initiatives offered in the United States can be divided into 4 categories:

    *   financial aid/benefits

    *   counselling/support

    *   information/referral

    *   flexible work arrangements/leave of absence.

    **Financial aid/ benefits**

    This includes continuing health and life insurance benefits during leave of absence. There are also dependent care reimbursements that can be used for care of both parents and children, permitting employees to reduce their salaries to cover eligible dependent care expenses on a pre-tax basis, and cafeteria benefits schemes that make it possible to choose from salary and eldercare benefits as one's personal needs require.

    **Counselling/support**, including activities such as Employee Assistance Programmes, support groups, lunch-time fora, individual consultation with care managers, education programmes.

    **Information/referral**, including information programmes and materials, referral services to private and public support facilities, care-givers exhibitions. Organisations such as the American Association of Retired Persons (AARP) offer a low-cost eldercare guide for employers to help them set up eldercare facilities. Included in this guide is a survey designed to elucidate the need for care facilities.

    **Flexible work arrangements/ leave of absence**

    A number of corporations in the United States offer leave of absence - the longest period of 3 years being offered by IBM. Some companies also offer flexible work schedules. According to Creedon (1991),[5] only about 15 per cent of US companies offer flexible work schedules.

---

4   From Eldercare and Employment: Workplace Policies and Initiatives to Support Workers who are Carers, European
    Foundation for the Improvement of Living and Working Conditions, Working Paper WP/94/32/En.

5   Creedon M.A. *Employers and the care of older Americans*, Vienna, VA 1991.

## Other developments

Studies in the United States reveal that short-term carers need, first and foremost, information while long-term carers need home-care services, adult day-care and respite arrangements. A study conducted by the International Foundation of Employee Benefit Plan in 1990 stated that by the year 2000 some 10 per cent of the company respondents expected to offer adult day-care, while 28 per cent said that they would offer on or near-site child care facilities (Creedon 1991).

An increasing number of companies are joining forces to provide care arrangements and to establish community links.

## 2.    Europe

The information in relation to Europe is derived from a limited survey about the extent of employer initiatives to support workers who are carers of older people.

In the survey, nine companies were identified (all sited in Germany or the United Kingdom) which had established some formal eldercare policy. Another five organisations that were providing some kind of eldercare facilities for workers who are carers were also identified.

### Eldercare Initiatives identified in the survey

Of the companies offering support to employees who were carers, two had conducted a survey to estimate the extent of eldercare obligations.

- All the companies offered (unpaid) career-breaks/ leaves of absence - the longest period being two years, with the majority of firms offering leave for a one year period.

- Six companies offered flexible working hours, while five offered job-sharing and four also had the option of part-time employment.

- Six companies offered some kind of information service and/ or referral system.

- Three of the nine companies offered in some cases financial support and one offered an insurance scheme.

- One company offered adult day-care provision to the employees.

# Appendix 4

**1.** **Labour Market Measures**

These include training schemes and programmes. In 1996 over 84,000 people received places in training or employment schemes run by FÁS.

### Community Employment

This programme enables a range of projects to be undertaken by sponsor organisations in communities and provides work and training opportunities for those experiencing difficulty rejoining the workforce.

Community Employment (C.E.) includes:
Integration option- a year long programme for people over 21 who are on the Live Register (or lone parents) for 12 months or more. Work option- a programme of up to three years for the over 35-year olds who have been unemployed for more than three years.

At the end of 1996 there were 41,000 people employed on over 3,000 CE projects. 89 per cent of those who participated had previously been classified as long-term unemployed. Following the scheme, 36 per cent went on to secure, industrial or service work. A further 30 per cent moved to other FÁS programmes or returned to education.

### Job initiative programme

This provides full-time work at going rates of pay, with local sponsors for people who are over 35 and who are unemployed or receiving the one-parent family payment for more than five years.

### Training

A further 29,700 people participated in FÁS training programmes. Of these, 12,500 people took part in specific skills training and almost 2,000 participated in Youthreach.

### Jobstart

Jobstart provides a recruitment subsidy of £80 a week for a year to employers who take on people who are unemployed or receiving the one-parent family payment for at least three years or registered with the National Rehabilitation Board. In 1996, 700 people commenced employment under the programme.

### Workplace

Workplace is a work experience programme providing up to 5 weeks placement with employers. Unemployed persons or lone parents in receipt of payment for at least 6 months are eligible. Persons registered with the National Rehabilitation Board are also eligible. In 1996, 541 persons participated in the programme.

**2.** **The Local Employment Service**

The Local Employment Service (LES) was established in October 1996 under the aegis of the Department of Enterprise, Trade and Employment.

The service provides a gateway or access point to the full range of options to assist long-term unemployed people who have the most difficulty in getting access to training and jobs. It offers guidance and a personal progression path to training, education and employment supports.

The service is available in twelve areas throughout the country and the services in two further areas will be introduced shortly. Partnership 2000 gives commitment that the LES will be extended on a phased basis to all designated disadvantaged areas. The core feature of the service is confidential, individual counselling and guidance and assistance in drawing up a career path for the long-term unemployed person. A special education and training fund meets the costs of compensatory, preparatory or foundation skills/training not available from mainstream training programmes and is used to fund job clubs. Clients are placed in jobs, community employment or work experience, education or training programmes. A co-ordinator in each local area manages a team of mediators, guidance counsellors and employment liaison officers.

3. **Income Support Programmes**
The Department of Social, Community and Family Affairs has developed a proactive approach to assisting unemployed people who are depending on social welfare payments and who wish to return to the active labour force as soon as possible. The supports include:

*Employment Support Service*
The Employment Support Service through jobs facilitators offers a range of supports to unemployed people. The cornerstone of the service is the Back to Work Allowance, which affords unemployed people the opportunity to test employment options while retaining a degree of financial security during the early years of employment and self-employment. Under the scheme people may retain 75 per cent of their unemployment payments in the first year and 50 per cent in the second year as well as secondary benefits, such as medical card and rent or mortgage assistance, while income remains under £250 a week.

The scheme has been particularly successful with 21,000 unemployed people (in 1997) who were formerly dependent on social welfare taking up the scheme. Around half have opted for self employment in a wide range of innovative projects in the manufacturing and services sectors.

The jobs facilitators market the scheme, provide information to potential customers, canvass employers for vacancies which might suit the scheme, provide unemployed people with access and advice on the full range of options and choices open to them, including what is available from other agencies.

**Other measures**
The Department of Social, Community and Family Affairs has also introduced changes in various aspects of social welfare schemes to facilitate people going back to work. These include reductions in PRSI for employers and a PRSI exemption scheme allowing exemption to employers from PRSI liability for up to two years in respect of employees taken on from

the Live Register. For lone parents, earning disregards have been introduced to recognise work-related expenses such as child-minding. The Family Income Supplement provides a weekly cash supplement for workers rearing families on low wages.

### Part-time job incentive scheme

Unemployed people receiving the long-term rate payment or having first completed community employment may take up a part-time job and receive a flat rate payment instead of unemployment payment.

### Income support while participating in second chance education

Unemployed people who are over age 21 or who are lone parents who wish to return to education have a number of options open to them.

### Vocational Training Opportunities Scheme (VTOS)

The VTOS is for those who are over age 21 and who are 6 months unemployed, for spouses of unemployed people and for those receiving disabled persons maintenance allowance. Participants work towards a Leaving Certificate. A weekly allowance at the same rate as social welfare entitlements is payable. Participants retain their secondary benefits. A lunch allowance is payable and in some cases a travel allowance. At the end of October 1996 there were 4,753 people on the programme.

### Second-Level Certificate

Unemployed people may attend second-level education at any community, comprehensive, secondary or vocational institution while retaining their payment. In December 1997 there were 328 people participating in the programme.

### Third-level education

In December 1997 there were 3,760 people participating in third level education while retaining their social welfare payments.

# Summary of Recommendations in Part 3

## The policy approach

The Commission recommends

- **an approach to supporting families in carrying out their functions which**
- prioritises investment in the care of young children
- supports parents' choices in the care and education of their children
- provides practical support and recognition to those who undertake the main caring responsibilities for children, whether their choice is to work full-time in the home or to participate in the paid labour market
- facilitates families in balancing work commitments and family life
- supports unemployed families in getting access to the labour market.


*In relation to recognising the value of caring work carried out by parents in the care of their children (Chapter 5)*

The Commission highlights the gap in policy in relation to support for the care of young children who are not yet attending school. Apart from child benefit and limited interventions for children at risk of social or educational disadvantage, there is virtually no state investment in the care of children in the years before entry into primary school.

The Commission identifies options for investing in the care of young children who are under three years of age. The options in relation to children under three years are presented in the context that the Commission, in Chapter 12 recommends direct financial investment in children on reaching three years of age by way of an Early Years Opportunities Subsidy, to secure for these children, having regard to their parents' wishes, opportunities to participate in quality services for children in nurseries/crèches and pre-school playgroups. The Commission notes the study underway by the Expert Working Group under Partnership 2000 in relation to the economics of childcare.

The Commission suggests direct investment in support for the care of young children rather than tax concessions. Tax concessions tend to be of more benefit to high earners and though they are of help to those paying tax they do not provide any benefit for those who do not come within the tax net, for example mothers working full-time in the home and families on low incomes.

The main features of the options put forward by the Commission for investment in the care of children under three years of age are;

- **Option A:** proposes a parent allowance of £30 a week, to be paid directly to the parent who works full-time in the home. The parent allowance is intended to recognise the value of the unpaid work that is carried out in the care of young children in the home.

- **Option B:** proposes a PRSI funded extended period of parental leave for up to three years with the payment of a weekly parental benefit which may initially be paid at the same rate as social welfare benefit i.e. £70.50 in 1998 but may vary over the full period of the leave. The paid parental benefit would address the situation of the parent who wishes to take time out of the workforce to care for their young children full-time in the home.

Both options A and B acknowledge the need for a complementary measure to support the care arrangements of children whose support needs would not be addressed by the parent allowance approach. A childcare allowance of £30 a week is suggested.

- **Option C** proposes a special rate of child benefit of £30 a week to be paid to all children under three years of age irrespective of their parents' employment status. Child benefit is neutral as to the choices parents make in relation to the care of their children. If the parent decides to work full-time in the home, the child benefit may be used to support the family budget. If the parent goes out to the workplace the child benefit may assist with the cost of childcare.

## Costs

Option A (parent allowance and childcare allowance) would cost £228 million per annum (in 1998 terms).

The cost of Option B - PRSI paid parental leave - would depend on take up and whether or not the full period of leave would be paid and rate of payment applicable. An illustrative cost including a complementary childcare allowance to address the situation of families not covered by paid parental leave approach suggests an amount of £255 million per annum in 1998 terms.

Option C would cost an additional £173 million (in child benefit) per annum in 1998 terms.

The advantages and the drawbacks to each option are discussed and the reservations of some Commission members to different aspects of the options are documented. These Commission members while supporting a parent allowance approach have reservations about a complementary measure taking the form of a childcare allowance. The reservations relate to two issues; whether with the many calls on Exchequer finances, a universal childcare allowance to all parents in the paid labour market with children under age 3 can be justified; and whether such a childcare allowance undermines a parent allowance approach which is intended to recognise the value of unpaid caring work and facilitate the parent who chooses to work full-time in the home when their child is very young.

**The Commission does not recommend one option over the other.** All options are presented for consideration. However, the Commission is strongly of the view that significant financial investment in the care of the youngest citizens not yet attending school should be a policy priority in the years ahead.

An investment target is suggested of the order of **£260 million** in 1998 terms to include the Early Years Opportunities Subsidy (proposed in Chapter 12), and the payments for children under three years of age.

### In relation to meeting the cost of a significant investment in supporting the caring responsibilities which families undertake (Chapter 5)

The Commission considers the present tax arrangements in place for married persons. The Commission is of the view that the cost of these present arrangements represents a substantial amount of investment by the taxpayer, some £350 million in 1991. However in so far as this investment is channelled through the present income tax arrangements for married couples it could be better directed to provide more support for families when their caring responsibilities are at their most demanding, for example, when children are very young or when a family is providing full-time care for a family member with a disability.

The Commission suggests that a review of the present tax arrangements should be undertaken. The review should have regard to:

- the constitutional case which gave rise to the introduction of the present tax arrangements,

- the likely future trends in labour force participation of women who are and are likely to remain the primary care givers in our society,

- the need for investment in support of the caring functions traditionally carried out by women in the home and in the community;

- the need to protect the position of older women who retired from the labour force at a time when the expectation was that women would not continue working outside the home after marriage and children.

The review might be undertaken by the Expert Group on the Treatment of One and Two-parent families under the Tax and Social Welfare Codes.

### In relation to support for parents with their parenting function (Chapter 6).
- **the introduction of a national readily accessible programme of information for parents;**
- **the demand for parenting skills programmes should be facilitated and supported and a National Co-ordinating Group should be established.**

The programme should focus on the importance of good parenting practice and on providing parents with relevant information at a broad level about the resources available within themselves and their families, and outside support services that are available to assist. It should be affirmative of parents. It should be available to anyone encountering the ordinary challenges of parenting and family living. The need for additional supports for families with special requirements and at certain times, for example lone parent families, families with a family member with a disability, teenagers who are parents, families without strong family networks or community links should be recognised.

- **specialised parent education programmes for families who are separating should be accessible through the Family Mediation Service.**

### In relation to parents rearing children without the support of a partner (Chapter 7).
- **that income support for lone parent families is and must continue to be an essential priority for State policy.**

The opportunities for lone parent families to improve their financial situation are severely limited because there is only one parent to carry the childcare responsibility, as well as being the main breadwinner, and because lone parents often have low educational attainments and find it difficult to get a place in the jobs market. The policy priority is to secure positive outcomes for children. Of immediate concern is the fact that lone parent families face a higher risk of poverty than children in two-parent families.

- **an employment-led policy approach to support lone parents, building on developments in this direction in recent years.**

Participation in employment presents the best prospects for improving income and hence the living standards of lone parents and their children. Lone parents are able to secure a higher income in countries where they are supported in finding employment. There is now a considerable body of research at home and abroad which shows the clear material advantage of an employment-led support policy for lone parents. Employment has further advantages in offering choice and promoting self esteem, less isolation and more active involvement in society, which is particularly important for young single mothers. An employment-led policy approach would build on developments in this direction in recent years and would entail:

- *a focus on income support arrangements to ensure that these do not present barriers for lone parents who are seeking access to the paid labour market.* A restructuring of child income support would help to address disincentives. A tapered withdrawal of rent supplement instead of the present sharp cut off of payment when a lone parent works over 30 hours a week should also be considered.

- *information, guidance and support for lone parents in securing a place in the labour market.* An integrated package of support is recommended including one-to-one advice and guidance, practical help in finding a suitable job opportunity and help in finding out about local childcare.

- *access to education, training and employment opportunities.* Improvements in employment and training programmes are suggested, to enhance the opportunities for lone parents, particularly young lone parents, to participate.

- *access to childcare.* The Commission's recommendations in Chapters 5 and 12 in relation to investment in children under school-going age and the development of services to respond to families with additional needs in Chapter 12 are particularly relevant in addressing the childcare needs of lone parents.

- **A pro-active approach to information and support for lone parents in returning to education, training or in taking up an employment place when their childcare responsibilities have eased.**

For most lone parents their child's entry into primary school at age four or five years brings with it a considerable lessening of childcare responsibilities. This represents an opportunity for lone parents to avail of a proactive information and support programme, providing assistance for those lone parents who are seeking out training or education opportunities in order to secure a place in the labour market.

### In relation to teenage parenthood

- **a comprehensive policy response to teenage parenthood involving**
  - a prioritisation of support services for teenage mothers, and more initiatives to keep them in the school system
  - a strategy which encourages young people to defer parenthood by improving life chances and choices for young women through training, education and offering young people a realistic hope that they may succeed in education and in securing employment
  - information for young people through education which seeks to influence their behaviour and their choices in relation to their futures
  - strengthening the role of youth services and a specific budget to expand services in this area.

Support services should target the 2,400 young mothers who are under age twenty and who are dependent on the one-parent-family payment. Greater resources are recommended for social and personal health education type programmes to reach the 3,000 young people who leave school early each year. Programmes for young men about sexuality and parenthood are important. The youth sector has an important role to play. Greater resources are recommended for the work of the youth services in this area.

### In relation to maintenance payments

- **a stronger link between social welfare policy and the legal maintenance system.**

  There should be more co-ordination in the policy approach adopted in the two systems in relation to securing maintenance for families.

- **the procedures for the registration of births should allow for the registration of the father's name at the hospital where the child is born as well as at the Registrar's Office.**

### In relation to families and work (Chapter 8)

- **that bringing about a suitable balance between work and family responsibilities is the major issue for the social partners in the years ahead.**

  Having regard to the national objectives for the continued development of an efficient economy capable of continued and sustainable economic growth, securing a better balance between work and family life involves a range of policies.

- *Income support* is the safety net for families. Policies must primarily continue to provide adequate support for families in retirement and in time of need and when unexpected 'contingencies' arise, such as unemployment or illness. Child support and income protection for vulnerable families is a particular priority.

  In order to provide practical assistance to those parents who wish to take time out of the work-force to care for their young children, the Commission is of the view that the proposals for 3 months parental leave in line with the EU Directive should provide for the period of leave to be paid.

- **Protective and social legislation** must be kept under review to see if it is responsive to the needs of workers in today's changing work environment.

- **Social partnership objectives** should support and promote the introduction of 'family friendly' flexibility in work arrangements to meet parents' needs - job-sharing, extended leave arrangements, career breaks, term-time working and parental leave.

- Government and the social partners must address the issue of **sharing the care**. This involves:

- More State support for children and childcare and for the care of family members with a disability and those who are older and depend on family care.

- Ensuring that new flexibility in employment has broad application and does not reinforce existing segregation in the labour force and in work carried out in the home.

- Facilitating fathers in taking on a significant role in carrying out childcare and caring responsibilities, and addressing the implications this has for the fathers' attachment to work and for the family finances.

- Promoting flexible work arrangements for fathers and introducing family friendly work arrangements in sectors where they have traditionally not been available.

- Identifying ways of bringing about societal and cultural change in thinking about the roles of men and women in family life, with children, in the workplace, and using language which is not gender neutral and which is appropriate to family roles in promoting family initiatives, for example, "father" and "mother".

- Research and monitoring of developments by interested agencies, Department of Social, Community and Family Affairs, the pensions sector, the Employment Equality Agency, employer representative organisations and trade unions.

### In relation to facilitating parents taking time out of the workforce
- **There is a role for the commercial lending sector in facilitating families who wish to take time out of the workforce to undertake family caring responsibilities.**

Mortgage holidays and extended repayment periods could facilitate families who wish to spend more time at home while their children are young.

### In relation to workers with responsibility for dependent elderly family member or for an adult or spouse who is ill and depends on family care
- **A specific recognition in employment and social policy for workers who are looking after a family member with a disability or an elderly relative who is dependent on family care,**

- **Elder-care should be accorded as much priority on the social partner's agenda as childcare.**

If workers cannot balance conflicting demands on their time they may choose or be forced to leave their jobs. Experience shows that they have real difficulty re-entering the labour market when their period of care is over. Caring over a long time causes financial hardship, loss of promotion opportunities, reduced earnings or loss of pension rights because of early retirement. With an ageing population and the greater participation of women in the workplace it is only a matter of time before eldercare emerges as an issue in the workplace. Employers have an interest in retaining experienced, skilled workers. The State has an interest too. These workers have an important caring responsibility within the family and they are contributing to economic growth through participation in the workforce.

- **The social partners could make a start by building on existing initiatives to facilitate childcare responsibilities.**

Existing practices could be adapted to better meet the needs of carer workers, for example;

- leave for adult care on the lines of the proposed parental leave arrangements,

- phased retirement to suit those workers with caring responsibilities,

- a leave of absence arrangement for workers who are caring for a seriously ill dependent family member,

- expanding employee assistance programmes to provide information, advice and support. Low cost suggestions to provide more support include: workplace catering providing take away meals, company sponsored social and retirement clubs for former employees, respite evenings and practical information about access to help.

*In relation to unemployed families*
- **A concerted effort to achieve employment objectives so comprehensively identified in recent reports for long-term unemployed men and women and their families.**

- Income support policy should pursue a strengthening of the role of child benefit together with a lessening of the role of child dependent additions with social welfare payments as recommended for lone parent families who also encounter disincentives in taking up work.

- An effective *hourly minimum wage* has the potential to be an important policy instrument, together with the income tax and PRSI systems and child benefit and family income supplement, in improving incentives to take up or stay in employment, and in improving the incomes of those most at risk of poverty because they are on low wages. The Commission welcomes the publication by the Government of the report of the Minimum Wage Commission.

- Family Income Supplement for self employed people should be considered given the increasing number of workers who are becoming self employed because of changing work arrangements or because they are being helped to leave the live register and set up their own business through various schemes.

- The introduction of a *tapering arrangement* in the withdrawal of rent and mortgage assistance is recommended.

- **close co-operation in pursuing shared objectives.**
  There is a need to strengthen the links at local level between the providers of programmes for unemployed persons, including local offices of the Department of Social, Community and Family Affairs, FÁS, the Local Employment Service, County Enterprise Boards, partnership companies, VECs and adult education providers.

## Making a start Part 3

### Recommendation 8

The Commission recommends

- **the introduction of a comprehensive programme to support positive parenting, to include access to parent information and parent education programmes. Components of a national parent information programme could include dissemination of leaflets, an awareness campaign in the media, a telephone helpline, access to specialist help. The programme should be a permanent feature of family welfare promotion.**
  **Cost:** £300,000 (in 1998 terms) to initiate the programme

### Recommendation 9

The Commission recommends

- **specialised parent information programmes for families that are separating should be promoted and should be accessible through the services provided by the Family Mediation Service.**

### Recommendation 10

The Commission recommends

- **the development of an integrated package of support for lone parents to include**
- **a comprehensive approach to information about education, training and employment programmes that are available and the effects of the various options on family income and advice and guidance in assessing the overall financial gain to the family of opportunities which arise**
- **practical help in finding a job opportunity and help in finding out about local childcare and about support available in meeting childcare needs. The Employment Support Service of the Department of Social, Community and Family Affairs could be developed to meet the needs of lone parents for this type of support.**

- **a review of the age requirement for participation in Community Employment, the Vocational Training Opportunities Scheme, Back to Work and second chance education programmes so that younger lone parents may gain access to the programmes**

- **a review of Youthreach to see if the programme may be adjusted to accommodate the childcare responsibilities of young lone parents.**

## Recommendation 11

- the possibility should be explored of developing programmes to support young girls who are pregnant in completing their education and to reintegrate young lone mothers back into the school system.

## Recommendation 12

- more programmes to develop and enhance the competencies and self-esteem of young people and to inform them of sexual health matters should be developed to reach the 3,000 or so young men and women who leave school early each year. Programmes for young men are important.

## Recommendation 13

- the role of the youth organisations in working with young mothers and with early school leavers should be strengthened and a specific budget allocated to expand provision for this group of young people
- the initial target level of provision should be funding for support services to reach 2,400 young lone mothers under age twenty who are dependent on the one-parent-family payment.

## Recommendation 14

- the development of stronger links and more co-ordination between the legal maintenance system and the Department of Social, Community and Family Affairs in pursuing overall policy objectives in relation to securing maintenance from former partners for families.

## Recommendation 15

- family mediation should be promoted as the preferred route to the resolution of maintenance issues in the policy and procedures of the Department of Social, Community and Family Affairs in relation to the requirements on lone parents and their former partners.

## Recommendation 16

- more research into lone parenthood, how long they remain lone parent families, how many families leave lone parenthood through marriage, and the outcomes for children over time.

## Recommendation 17

- the introduction of a comprehensive information service for bereaved families - with access to information, advice and specialist help where this is needed. The Department of Social, Community and Family Affairs as the first point of contact for families on the death of a parent is well placed to develop this service.

- the further development of services to assist bereaved families through grant aid for the voluntary and community sector.

## Recommendation 18

The Commission recommends

- that the Government bring forward proposals for the introduction of 3 months parental leave, in line with the terms of the EU directive and
- that the PRSI Maternity Benefit Scheme be extended to provide a weekly payment on the lines of maternity benefit to workers availing of the parental leave under the directive.
  **Costs:** £40 million in 1998 terms

## Recommendation 19

The Commission recommends

- Family Income Supplement for the self-employed should be considered.

## Recommendation 20

The Commission recommends

- a tapering arrangement in the withdrawal of rent and mortgage subsidies for lone parents and unemployed people who take up full-time employment.

## Recommendation 21

The Commission recommends

- the commercial lending sector could consider 'mortgage holidays' and longer term mortgages to facilitate families who wish to spend more time at home when their children are very young. Borrowers should, however, be made fully aware of all the implications of different options and they should be given all necessary information, advice and guidance.

part 4

**promoting continuity and stability in family life**

**Desired outcome**

- Continuity and stability in family relationships are recognised as having a major value for individual well-being and social stability, especially as far as children are concerned. Commitment to long-term continuity and stability, as expressed by most people through their commitment to marriage, is supported and affirmed in public policy.

**To be achieved through**

- Support for marriage in public policy
- The availability of accessible services to promote, support and maintain stable relationships in the interest of children, and, as far as possible, to prevent marital breakdown
- In the event of marital breakdown, assistance to facilitate the transition of families at this very difficult time and to protect and promote the interests of children.

**In Part 4 the Commission considers**

- The place of marriage in our society and the role of public policy in supporting the continuity and stability which marriage represents for the majority of families.
- The role of the marriage and relationship counselling services in assisting couples who are experiencing marital difficulties, and the potential of these services in promoting better preparation for marriage and maintaining commitment in relationships.
- The promotion of family mediation in the interests of children, as a non-adversarial approach to resolving issues on the breakdown of marriage.

## Overview of Part 4

**The Commission has suggested that family policy must have regard to the principle that continuity and stability are major requirements in family relationships. Continuity and stability should be recognised as having a major value for individual well-being and social stability especially as far as children are concerned. Joint parenting should be encouraged with a view to ensuring that, as far as possible, children have the opportunity of developing close relationships with both parents. In cases where joint parenting is in the child's best interest public policy has a key role in promoting that interest.**

**For many people marriage represents their commitment to long term continuity and stability. In this context the Commission considers that marriage should be supported in public policy.**

In Part 4 of the report the Commission sets out its views in relation to the valid role of public policy in supporting marriage and the continuity and stability it represents in society, the need for better preparation for marriage, for promotion of the benefits of marriage counselling and for the greater use of family mediation as a non-adversarial approach which is in the interests of children, to the resolution of issues on the breakdown of marriage.

The Commission considers the changes taking place in society and in family life and the changes that are taking place in the institution of marriage. Marriage is under pressure as a private lifelong relationship between two people and as an institution which has a valued role in society. Society looks to the State to support marriage. Marriage as a visible public institution underpinned by contractual obligations presents clear advantages from a public policy perspective in promoting security and stability in family life. The Commission sets out the basis for its conclusion that marriage should be supported in public policy and points to the areas where greater priority should be accorded to this objective. The Constitutional protection for marriage contained in Article 41.2. is examined and the significance for families of the rights, duties and legal safeguards which marriage as a legal contract brings into a relationship are discussed. The Commission considers the situation of families who are outside the legal framework of marriage.

The 1996 Census data shows that there were 31,298 family units consisting of cohabiting couples in 1996. Of this 18,640 (60 per cent) were couples without children. Of the remaining 12,658 family units, 52 per cent had one child while a further 28 per cent had two children. Cohabiting couples accounted for 3.9 per cent of all families in Ireland in 1996.

The Commission considers the many pressures on families in today's fast-moving world and the numbers of families experiencing breakdown. The figures show there were more than twice as many separated persons in 1996 as there were ten years previously (87,800 in 1996, compared to 37,200 in 1986). The Commission states that there is a need for a greater emphasis on building strong relationships and a better preparation for marriage is needed. Recommendations are put forward in relation to how this might be achieved through the education system and through greater promotion of marriage preparation programmes.

Marriage counselling is described and the emerging scientific evidence is presented in support of the effectiveness of marriage counselling in helping couples through the complexities of modern "companionate" marriage and in helping them with relationship problems. The Commission makes recommendations for greater investment in support for and promotion of the marriage counselling services and sets out a suggested policy approach to the future development of these services to take on a preventive role.

The Commission considers the research in relation to the distressing effects of separation and the events leading up to it in the life of a family - for parents but particularly for children. The competitive, adversarial approach of litigation and adjudication which requires the parents to take opposing stances has negative consequences for children. The process and outcome of family mediation, with its collaborative approaches to decision-making, improved communication between parents, reduced misunderstanding and conflict and with parents retaining control over the context of their own agreements, has recognised advantages for children.

The Commission documents the mechanisms of family mediation and what participation in family mediation entails for the couple in working out constructively an agreement to settle the various issues arising from the marital breakdown. The Commission makes recommendations in relation to the expansion of the Family Mediation Service to provide an accessible service throughout the country and identifies those facets of family conflict where family mediation might take on a new role.

## Chapter Nine The place of marriage in our society and the role of public policy in supporting the continuity and stability which marriage represents for the majority of families

### 9.1 Introduction

In various chapters of this report the Commission documents the considerable changes which are taking place in society and in family life in Ireland today. Marital breakdown, the fall in the rate of marriage and in the birth rate, and the continuous rise in births outside marriage have brought into sharp focus the changes taking place in the institution of marriage. Against this background it is worth setting a wider context within which to consider the place of marriage in Irish society today.

- Marriage is the experience of the majority of people. The 1996 Census indicated that 1,356,600 people described themselves as married and another 272,200 who have been married and now are either widowed or separated.

- In 1996 there were some 16,255 marriages.[1]

- Over 85 per cent of the population who are single are under age 35. Most will probably marry in the future.

It is also worth remembering that research, although limited, shows that the most usual reason for unmarried mothers to stop claiming the one-parent family payment from the Department of Social, Community and Family Affairs is because they marry.[2]

Dr. Kiely, in his article as a foreword to Chapter 10, documents the changes which have taken place in the institution of marriage as a private affair. He describes how marriage is becoming more and more a social and companionate relationship. Changing roles of men and women, the demands of the workplace and increased expectations for emotional and personal fulfilment make high demands of partners. It is certainly the case that marriage is under pressure both as a relationship for life and as an institution which has a valued role in society in promoting continuity and stability in family life. It is also the case that society looks to the State to support this valued institution.

### Submissions to the Commission

Concern about what is happening to marriage and the impact that these changes might have on family life was a prominent issue in the submissions to the Commission. Most of these submissions focused on marriage as a life-long commitment and as providing a stable basis for family life and for children. Submissions unanimously looked to State support for marriage as a unique social institution which has substantial internal and familial benefits. Many of these submissions expressed concern that the constitutional protection for marriage should be safeguarded. There was also concern in submissions for the legal position of unmarried parents. There were suggestions in relation to constitutional and other legislative changes for children of unmarried parents to ensure their rights and their protection.

1 Appendix 1 to this chapter provides some recent statistics in relation to marriage.

2 Tony O' Grady, *Married to the State*, unpublished research.

## 9.2 Supporting the institution of marriage

The Commission, in its interim report, has stated that: Public policy has a fundamental role in expressing and affirming society's values and ideals concerning family life at symbolic as well as practical levels.

It is evident that, for most people, marriage represents the expression of their commitment to long-term continuity and stability in their relationship. In this context, there is a valid role for public policy in affirming this public expression of their family life.

This is not to say that marriage always represents the ideal for family life or that marriage should be supported in all situations. A bad marriage is clearly not in the interests of the individual family members, particularly children, whose needs at all times must be a paramount consideration in public policy. The fundamental human activity of care, intimacy and belonging can take place in a variety of family forms; policy must recognise this diversity and provide appropriate supports where necessary.

Rather, it is to say that marriage as a visible public institution, underpinned by contractual obligations, presents clear advantages from a public policy perspective, in promoting security and stability in family life and in providing a continuity in society.

## 9.3 Changes in perceptions about the role of marriage in society

While supporting the institution of marriage, the Commission acknowledges that there are issues which many people consider are impinging on our perceptions of the role of marriage in society.

At the economic level, marriage has, in the past, been an institution in which there were clear-cut roles for males and females. With men as the wage-earners and women as the (non-paid) workers in the home, income and expenditure was by and large determined by the employment of one-half of the couple. Today, there are many more dual incomes within marriages and some families have no income from employment at all. What are the economic implications of this? How does this affect our view of marriage?

At the sociological level, there have been several changes. Equal rights for women have brought an equality of access to employment and the removal of the marriage bar; greater knowledge about family planning has enabled couples to plan their families; changing attitudes to equality between men and women has meant that roles within marriages have changed considerably; the development of individualism away from community has brought about a change in social values so that there is more emphasis on the rights and needs of individuals.

Television, films and other aspects of the media often reflect an unrealistic picture of marriage - either idealising marriage or dismissing it. The introduction of divorce in Ireland will affect society's view of marriage in both positive and negative ways. Many people can now get married who were previously unable to do so. Second marriages mean that some families have very different structures from those where there has been only one marriage.

Blended families (a term given to families where the adults have had previous relationships and children who may or may not be living in the new family) may have different needs requiring a particular response. These needs may be financial, psychological or social.

At the psychological level, people's fundamental needs to belong, to be loved and to have a secure base from which to operate have not changed. Spirituality is very important in people's lives but changes are taking place whereby religion is becoming a more private matter. These factors influence people's behaviour and the way they seek to have their psychological needs met.

9.4    **Supporting marriage - the policy approach**

The Commission's recommendations throughout this report relate to the role of public policy in strengthening families and preventing family breakdown. Key issues for families and for *marriage* in the new century are supporting families with their parenting responsibilities; getting the balance right between employment and family life for men and women who now have too little time to themselves and their families; strengthening the role of fathers in family life, more sharing of household responsibilities; minimising the adverse effects of unemployment on families.

**Promoting family incentives**

There are in-built characteristics within the present structure of some social welfare schemes (for example, the one-parent family payment and payments for families who rely on unemployment payments) which restrict the choices of parents who depend on these payments in relation to developing long-lasting and stable relationships for themselves and their children.

In Chapter 7 the Commission sets out its findings in relation to the different aspects of the policy approach to support for lone parents, including the effects of present policies on family incentives.

The Commission recommends that these issues be kept under review so that income support policy does not present any unnecessary obstacles to children obtaining the advantages of the stability and security which a loving two-parent family can provide for them. The Commission has also made the point that family incentives, such as the incentive to marry, to form stable relationships and to provide joint parenting for children, where this is in the child's best interest, should be accorded more prominence in evaluating the outcome of income support policies.

**Greater equity in support for married families**

There is a need to introduce greater equity in support measures for low income married families so that these families are not treated less favourably in public policy as a result of their married status. In Chapter 8 the Commission describes the pressures facing low income married families who are unemployed or at work on low pay. Their situation is much the same as that of lone parents in similar financial circumstances. The Commission's recommendations in relation to the approach to income support for children are intended to assist all families in improving their income and to support parents' choices in relation to the care of their children and thus provide greater equity in support for married families.

### Better preparation for marriage

Better and more effective preparation for marriage and education, from an early age, about relationships and good communications have been identified as key areas where public policy can support marriage. In Chapter 10 the Commission suggests the future policy direction for State support for marriage counselling services, with a greater emphasis on marriage preparation, marriage care and on early intervention as soon as difficulties in the family are identified. The Commission's recommendations for education for family life to be included as part of the school curriculum at second level (Chapter 13) are intended to encourage young people to explore and appreciate the many aspects of family life and to equip them with the knowledge and skills to help to sustain commitment in a relationship.

## 9.5  The legal position of marriage

Marriage has been legally defined as the voluntary and permanent union of one man and one woman, to the exclusion of all others, for life.[3]

Marriage establishes legal rights and responsibilities under the Constitution and in legislation, including:

### Property

- Favoured treatment is accorded a spouse who claims an equitable interest in property arising from direct or indirect contributions towards its purchase.

- A non-owner spouse is given a number of protections in respect of the matrimonial home and its contents.

- On separation or divorce, the court has wide discretionary powers to reallocate property between the spouses.

- A surviving spouse has a statutory right to a share in the estate of a deceased spouse.

### Financial obligations

- Under family law legislation, a spouse or an ex-spouse may apply for a maintenance order for his/her own support or for the support of a dependent child. Social welfare legislation imposes on spouses an obligation to maintain each other and dependent children.

### Children and parental responsibility

- Married parents have equal guardianship rights and duties in respect of their dependent children. They are automatically joint guardians of their children.

---

3    By Mr. Justice Costello, President of the High Court in the case of *B* v *R* [1995] 1ILRM 491 (HC); [1995] 1 Fam LJ 27 (HC)

- Either or both parents may be obliged to maintain a dependent child.[4]

In addition, there are a number of formalities which apply or need to be undertaken in relation to getting married, which in effect reinforce the significance both legally and personally of the major step being taken by the couple.[5]

## 9.6    Couples outside the legal framework of marriage

The legal significance of marriage is perhaps best understood when it is contrasted with the situation of cohabiting couples. The legal situation in these cases has been described comprehensively in the White Paper on Marital Breakdown published in 1992, and in a recent publication about family law.[6]

Neither party to the relationship enjoys the same legal protection available to the parties to a marriage. They are in the same legal relationship as any two people who choose to live together (unlike the law of some other countries, Irish law does not provide for contracting a "common-law" marriage). The father is not a guardian of any children of the union unless the court has so ordered under section 6A (1) (inserted by the Children Act 1997) of the Guardianship of Infants Act 1964[7] or both parents have agreed to the appointment of the father as guardian and have made a statutory declaration to that effect in the form set out in the Schedule to the Guardianship of Children (Statutory Declaration) Regulations 1998, which came into operation on 1 February 1998.

---

4    Parents' duty to maintain their children is not dependent on marriage or the acquisition of guardianship rights.

5    The Family Law Act 1995 introduced certain new requirements in relation to marriage. The minimum age of marriage is 18 years. The age was raised from 16 to 18 years in the Family Law Act 1995, following a recommendation by the Second Commission on the Status of Women and others. Couples are required to give three months notice in writing to the Registrar of Marriages for the district concerned of their intention to marry. Couples may apply to the Circuit or High Court for an exemption to the requirements. However, the Act provides that such exemption shall not be granted unless the applicant shows that its grant is justified by serious reasons and is in the interests of the parties to the intended marriage. The large majority of marriages in Ireland are celebrated in a church. In 1995 14,529 marriages out of a total of 15,623 marriages in Ireland were celebrated in accordance with the rites and ceremonies of the Roman Catholic Church. In the law, provision has been made so that these marriages are also civil marriages and various provisions are made for their registration. The Second Commission on the Status of Women has pointed out that this procedure can give rise to confusion in people's minds about the legal significance of marriage and its religious significance. A similar opinion was expressed earlier by the Joint Oireachtas Committee on Marriage Breakdown which proposed that the law should require that a specific reference to the civil contract of marriage be made in a separate part of the marriage ceremony before the exchange of vows in a religious ceremony. The Second Commission on the Status of Women recommended that a form of civil marriage should be introduced and that a civil registrar should attend all marriages.

6    William R. Duncan, *Family Law in the Republic of Ireland in Family Law in Europe,* Carolyn Hamilton and Kate Stanley, (eds) Butterworths: 1995 and *Marital Breakdown: A Review and proposed changes,* Minister for Justice 1992.

7    The Guardianship of Infants Act, 1964 provides that the married parents of a child are the guardians of that child jointly. In the case of unmarried parents, the mother is sole guardian of the child. Until the Status of Children Act 1987 there was no way by which an unmarried father could establish guardianship rights other than by subsequently marrying the mother of the child. The 1987 Act amended the 1964 Act by empowering the court, on the application of an unmarried father, to appoint him to be a guardian of his child jointly with the mother. At present some 700 applications are made to the court each year by unmarried fathers who wish to become guardians of their children jointly with the mother. Of these some 400 are by agreement. The Children Act 1997 introduces new provisions whereby a father can become joint guardian of his child by agreement with the mother upon the making of a statutory declaration without having to go to court.

There are no proceedings by which one cohabitee may obtain from the other maintenance or any other form of financial provision for his/her own support. A cohabitee has no guaranteed rights in respect of the estate of a deceased partner nor any right to apply for provision out of that estate. Subject to the rights of any child or spouse of a deceased, there is nothing to prevent specific provision by will for the benefit of a cohabitee. However, because he or she is not treated as a member of the deceased's family, the cohabitee is subject to tax on such a legacy at a low threshold. The Family Home Protection Act 1976, which contains provisions to prevent a spouse from disposing of the family home without the consent of the other spouse, does not apply to cohabitees. The principles by which a non-owner spouse may acquire an interest in the matrimonial home or other family property, proportionate to the value of the contributions to purchase made by that spouse, apply also in the case of cohabitees.

The Status of Children Act 1987 removed discrimination in the law as between children born within or outside marriage. The matters covered by the Act include maintenance, property and succession rights.

The Domestic Violence Act 1996 extended to cohabitees certain rights in relation to barring, protection and safety orders.

The White Paper sums up the situation thus: since the remedies available in family law were introduced on the basis that the ordinary rules of law did not give sufficient protection to spouses, parties to a (second) union outside marriage - who must rely on the ordinary rules - do not have as high a level of safeguards and entitlements as spouses have.

9.7     **Information is important for parents in non-marital relationships**
Recent changes in the formalities in relation to getting married - for example, the require-ment on couples to give three months notice of their intention to marry - may help to give a new prominence to the significance of marriage as a legal contract which brings with it rights, duties and responsibilities. This is a welcome development since traditionally many couples did not realise the legal significance of marriage until difficulties arose in the relationship.

As indicated, it is evident that families which remain outside the legal framework of marriage do not have the same legal supports and protection. This may not be apparent to them. The Commission considers that, where children are involved, information should be available from the relevant authorities to non-marital parents about the legal situation in relation to their relationship and their parenting rights and responsibilities. In particular, there is a need to draw parents' attention to the legal situation of fathers in relation to guardianship and the procedural differences which arise for unmarried fathers in the registration of their child's birth. Information is important so that parents who are not married may make informed decisions in relation to parenting responsibilities and provision for the future.

## 9.8 The growth in cohabitation outside the legal framework of marriage

The 1996 Census[8] was the first census in which information on cohabiting couples was explicitly sought. Table 1 provides information on the number of cohabiting couples in 1996, classified by size of family unit.

### Table 1

Cohabiting couples with and without children by size of family unit, 1996.

| Number of Children | Total '000s | No children | All children <15 '000s | All children 15+ | Remainder* |
|---|---|---|---|---|---|
| None | 18.6 | 18.6 | - | - | - |
| One | 6.6 | - | 6.0 | 0.6 | - |
| Two | 3.5 | - | 2.9 | 0.2 | 0.4 |
| Three | 1.5 | - | 1.0 | 0.1 | 0.4 |
| Four or more | 1.1 | - | 0.5 | 0.0 | 0.5 |
| Total family units | 31.3 | 18.6 | 10.4 | 0.9 | 1.4 |
| Total children in family units | 23.0 | - | 17.0 | 1.4 | 4.7 |
| Average number of children per family | 0.7 | - | 1.6 | 1.5 | 3.4 |

\* Family units with children both under and over 15 years of age.

There were 31,298 family units consisting of cohabiting couples in 1996. Of these, 18,640 (60 per cent) comprised couples without children. Of the remaining 12,658 family units, 52 per cent had one child, while a further 28 per cent had two children.

Cohabiting couples accounted for 3.9 per cent of all family units in 1996. Those without children accounted for 10.7 per cent of all childless couples in 1996, while those with children represented 2.5 per cent of all couples with children.

The commentary on the data in the Census states that: A more in-depth analysis of the data in Table 1 reveals that just over three-quarters of cohabiting couples without children were unions in which both partners were single, while in a further 5 per cent of cases both partners were separated. The corresponding proportions for cohabiting couples with children were 51 per cent and 13 per cent, respectively. Furthermore, 43 per cent of women and 55 per cent of men in cohabiting unions were aged 30 years or over and thus it would appear that cohabitation is not just a precursor to marriage but a more permanent form of union in many cases.

FINAL REPORT OF THE COMMISSION ON THE FAMILY

**188**    8    Census 1996, Principal Demographic Results, Central Statistics Office, Dublin.

Information is beginning to emerge in relation to the extent of cohabitation, including the numbers of couples who appear to be choosing to remain outside the legal framework of marriage, and the number of couples where one or both partners are in fact in a second union.

## 9.9 The trend toward cohabitation - the issues for public policy and the need for research

There are substantive policy implications arising in relation to an increasing trend towards cohabitation and away from marriage. These issues include the legal implications of cohabitation breakdown, not least when there are children of the union, the implications for parental rights, the division of property, pension entitlements and the care of older family members.

The Commission is of the view that cohabitation is an important subject for social research in Ireland. It is important that underlying factors in relation to the decision to cohabit are fully understood and that this development in family formation is monitored and researched given the significant policy issues which arise in relation to non-marital families.

## 9.10 Experience abroad

The growth in cohabitation where couples choose to live together without getting married is one of the fundamental ways in which  family life is changing across Europe and in western industrialised  countries. This phenomenon is increasingly the subject of research and studies to try to determine the factors which underlie the trend and what this development means for society.

A number of recent studies in the UK have presented interesting perspectives in relation to cohabitation.

### (i) European experience

One study,[9] which tracked the rise in cohabitation and extra-marital childbearing in Britain and Europe, provided an overview of the development in a number of European countries. There have been increases in cohabitation and extra-marital childbearing in many northern and western European countries.

- Cohabitation is most popular in Nordic countries- Sweden, Denmark, Finland and Norway. In Western Europe, it is more common in the Netherlands, France and Germany than in Britain and Austria. Cohabitation is rarer in Southern and Eastern European countries. The evidence suggests that cohabitation is a relatively youthful practice and that there is no permanent wide-scale rejection of marriage. Even in countries where the practice is more long-standing, such as Sweden and Denmark, 75 per cent or more of women in their thirties who are living with partners are married.

- Across Europe there is a marked variation in the extent of extra-marital childbearing. At one extreme are Iceland and Sweden, where over 50 per cent of children are born out of wedlock; at the other are counties such as Switzerland, Italy and Poland on 6 per cent and Greece on 2 per cent. In the Nordic countries, and in Britain and France, couples are

9    Kathleen Kiernan and Valerie Estaugh, *Cohabitation. extra-martial childbearing and social policy,* Family Policies Studies Centre, 9 Tavistock Place, London WCI H9SN (1993).

increasingly having children within cohabiting unions, whereas in countries such as Germany, Switzerland and the Netherlands cohabiting unions are more likely to be childless, with children continuing to be born pre-eminently within marriages.

- Generally those countries with longer experiences of the cohabitation issue have opted for legislative solutions that compensate cohabitees for the most significant drawbacks arising from being outside the legal framework of marriage, but mainly on an *ad hoc* basis. In Sweden, where cohabitation has been long-standing, there is still a reluctance to accord the same rights to cohabitees as to married couples.

### (ii) Attitudes and motivation

Another report,[10] based on a comparative study of mothers with at least one child who were either married or cohabiting at the time of the birth of the baby, presents a number of useful insights into the attitudes and motivations which may underlie the decisions people make in relation to cohabitation. The study found that cohabitation in Britain usually lasts a short time, preceding marriage rather than replacing it, but a growing number of women are continuing to cohabit long after their children are born. Findings in relation to attitudes included the following:

- There is a steady flow of cohabiting mothers into marriage. This remains true even when women have continued to cohabit for a number of years after the birth of a child.

- The three main reasons that long-term cohabiting mothers give for not marrying their partners are: fear of divorce, the high cost of weddings and objections to the institution of marriage.

- Few unmarried parents understand the legal implications of cohabitation for their children, including the father's lack of automatic rights as a parent.

- Parents who have been cohabiting for a long time appear to be no more egalitarian in their way of life than their married counterparts.

The Commission suggests that many of the responses elicited may be relevant to couples in Ireland who choose not to marry. The findings from studies undertaken abroad point to the need for similar studies in the Irish context.

### 9.11 The Constitution of Ireland

The family recognised and supported in Articles 41 and 42 of the Irish Constitution is the family based on marriage.

Article 41.3.1 states: The State pledges itself to guard with special care the institution of marriage, on which the family is founded and to protect it against attack.

The effect of this Article is that the State may not penalise marriage or the married state. The Article has been relied on successfully to challenge a number of provisions which had

10    Dr. Susan McRae, *Cohabiting mothers: Changing marriage and motherhood ?*; Policy Studies Institute, 100 Park Village East, London NW 1 3SR.(1993)

the effect of penalising the married state, for example, *Murphy v Attorney General* [11] which challenged the prejudicial taxation of married couples.[12] The Review Group on the Constitution[13] considered in detail the effects of Article 41.3.1 on the married family and on families not based on marriage and what would be involved in an amendment of this article to afford constitutional protection of the rights of families other than the family based on marriage.

**9.12**    **Submission to the All-Party Committee on the Constitution**

In its submission[14] to the All-Party Committee on the Constitution, the Commission supported the retention of Article 41.3.1 in the Constitution by which the state pledges to guard with special care the institution of marriage and to protect it against attack. The Commission also agreed with the Review Group that the pledge by the State on marriage should not prevent the Oireachtas from legislating for the benefit of family units not based on marriage and that a clear constitutional basis for this should be provided in Article 41.

In its approach to the submission to the All-Party Committee, the Commission was guided by the views of the Constitution Review Group. The Review Group expressed the opinion that significant difficulties arise in relation to a definition that goes beyond the family based on marriage.

The first difficulty arises in relation to the multiplicity of differing units which may be capable of being considered as families. Questions arise such as the duration of cohabitation which should qualify for treatment as a family. Furthermore, some persons living together may be choosing deliberately not to have a legal basis for their relationship.

The Review Group considered provisions in relation to family and marriage in other constitutions and in international instruments. None appears to attempt a definition of a family in terms other than one based on marriage. On consideration of all the issues, the Review Group considered that there were significant uncertainties in extending the definition beyond the family based on marriage. The preferred approach of the Review Group was to retain in the Constitution a pledge by the State to protect the family based on marriage but also to guarantee to all individuals a right to respect for their family life, whether that family life is, or is not, based on marriage.

---

11    [1982] IR241 (HC,SC).

12    The effect of this judgement and the subsequent change in the tax arrangements for married couples are described in Chapter 5.

13    The Review Group was established by the Government of Ireland on 27 April 1995 to review the Constitution, and in the light of this review, to establish those areas where constitutional change may be desirable or necessary, with a view to assisting the All-Party Committee on the Constitution, to be established by the Oireachtas, in its work. The report of the Constitution Review Group was published in May 1996.

14    See Chapter 23.

# Appendix 1

## Some Statistics[15]

**1.**　　**Marriage**

For most of this century, Ireland was unique among western countries with its low marriage rate and high marital fertility.

In 1974 the marriage rate reached a high of 7.4 per 1,000 people. It has been steadily declining since then to a rate of 4.4 in 1993 - the lowest in 100 years, with the actual number getting married (15,728) the lowest since the 1950s. In 1996, the marriage rate was 4.5 per 1,000 people (men, women and children). In the 1970s and 1980s the increase in the marriage rate was accompanied by a decline in the age at time of marriage for both men and women, although there has been a slight upward turn in recent years.

The average age for brides and grooms has risen from 24 and 25 years respectively in 1977 to 26 and 28 years in 1993. Details of the annual number of marriages over the past 11 years are given in Table 1.

## Table 1
Annual Marriage Rates 1986-1996

| Year | No. of marriages | Year | No. of marriages |
|------|------------------|------|------------------|
| 1986 | 18,573 | 1992 | 16,636 |
| 1987 | 18,309 | 1993 | 16,824 |
| 1988 | 18,382 | 1994 | 16,297 |
| 1989 | 18,174 | 1995 | 15,623 |
| 1990 | 17,838 | 1996 | 16,255 |
| 1991 | 17,441 | | |

FINAL REPORT OF THE COMMISSION ON THE FAMILY

15　Imelda Colgan McCarthy (ed.), Irish Family Studies: Selected Papers, published by the Family Studies Centre, UCD 1995.

# Marriage and relationship counselling in a changing society

As a foreword to Chapter 10 the Commission is pleased to reproduce a paper prepared by Gabriel Kiely which describes the importance that marriage counselling has assumed in the context of the changing society today.

**Dr. Kiely is a lecturer in Social Science at University College Dublin. He has practised as a marriage and family counsellor. He is the Director of the Family Studies Centre at UCD and he is a member of the Steering Committee of the Family Mediation Service.**

Marriage and relationship counselling in a changing society
**Gabriel Kiely**

Marriage is both a private affair and a public concern. How people conduct their private lives is for the most part a personal matter. However, the private and public domains are interlinked. What happens in the family has consequences for society just as what happens in society affects the family. They are interdependent social systems. Society, therefore, both through the institutions of the State and through other collective responses, such as voluntary action, has a role to play in supporting families and responding to family needs. This includes the provision of assistance to couples in the form of relationship counselling at both a preventive and remedial level.

Recent changes in family behaviour, such as the reported rise in marital breakdown, in cohabitation, and in non-marital births, illustrate the interdependence of families and society. These trends reflect changes in people's private lives and changes in society. For example, changes in society, such as increased awareness of gender equality, changing attitudes to sex, availability of information about family planning, the rise in the labour force participation of mothers, the development of economic prosperity, and the growth in urbanisation, also impact on how people live their private lives.

In the context of marriage, changes in Irish society in recent decades have had a profound influence not only on how people live their lives in intimate relationships but in the very nature of marriage itself. If we as a society are committed to the belief that stability in relationships is a desirable goal, then we must seek to understand what contributes to stability. Where stability is at risk, we must respond with appropriate services and supports.

There are no easy answers to this quest nor is there a single causative factor. In one sense there are as many causes as there are couples in relationships. Each couple develops a unique relationship which is influenced by what they bring to the relationship as individuals and by how they separately and together interact with the wider society. The stability of a relationship depends, then, not only on what each individual brings to it but also on how their relationship is affected by what is happening outside their relationship in the rest of society.

One of the most significant factors influencing marriage in recent decades is the radical transformation of Irish society, which began with the process of industrialisation in the 1960s. In a relatively short period of time, Irish society was changed from dependence on a rural agrarian economy to an urban industrial society. The economic and social changes that resulted were both extensive and rapid and influenced most aspects of Irish life, including marriage and the family.

Reliance on the family as a basic economic unit of society diminished as prosperity increased, while the related importance of marriage as a social institution was simultaneously giving way to marriage as a social relationship.

This shift in emphasis to marriage as a social relationship has significant consequences for the stability of marriage. Relationships based primarily on feelings are more fragile than relationships that have an institutional base. There are two main reasons for this. First, people's feelings are open to change over time and can change as a result of new experiences. This requires couples to be able to adapt to change. Second, if the relationship does not continue to generate mutual feelings of satisfaction, the relationship is less likely to endure. Relationships with an institutional base, on the other hand, are less dependent on how the individuals experience their relationship. In the case of marriage, relationships with an institutional base rely more on bonds of duty and mutual obligation with these bonds taking precedence over personal fulfilment. Therefore, if a couple are united around bonds of affection more than bonds of duty, the stability of their relationship will be significantly influenced by their success in meeting each other's needs for affection.

Changes in society have also influenced people's expectations of marriage. The emphasis in society on the pursuit of personal satisfaction, whether arising from increased prosperity, the media or social pressures, has also raised people's expectations of fulfilment in marriage. People entering marital relationships have expectations of emotional intimacy, sexual satisfaction and personal fulfilment. These expectations place a high demand on the partners and, if they are left unfulfilled, they can become a source of major tension, irrespective of how realistic the expectations might be.

The risk of tension in relationships is further compounded by the problems of individual and societal adaptation to new norms and values which arise in any society experiencing rapid social change. Take, for example, the changing roles of men and women both in and out of marriage. For an individual couple this tension can be seen where one partner continues to adopt a traditional breadwinner/housewife relationship model while the other partner does not. On a societal level, this same tension is manifested when increasing numbers of mothers join the paid labour force while community attitudes press for their return to the home. These tensions arise when there are differences both between partners and in society on the nature of couple relationships and the norms and values that govern them.

For most couples marriage also brings with it parenthood. If Ireland is to follow the trend in other European countries with a rise in cohabitation before marriage, then parenthood will lead to marriage for many couples rather than coming after marriage. Balancing the demands of both these roles, partner and parent, can pose new difficulties in modern society where children hold a different position in families than they did in more traditional times. Couples now tend to have children for more child-centred reasons than they did in the past. Now children tend to be planned, as is evidenced by the dramatic decline in the birth rate, and parents have become increasingly concerned with trying to create the optimum opportunities for their children's full development. In traditional society the child was often seen as an economic asset to the family, either as an extra pair of hands or as someone who would provide care for parents in their old age. This shift in the position of children has added a new dimension to partnership: the need to also be a good parent.

It can be argued that the family, traditionally conceived of as the basic unit of society is not in fact one unit but several units, which include the spousal unit and the parent-child unit. The rewards and demands of parenthood are quite distinct from those of partnership. This distinction is particularly evident where there is marital conflict whether or not the conflict eventually results in marital separation. The needs of children and the needs of adults do not always coincide. Likewise, the ability to maintain an intimate parent-child relationship is quite independent of maintaining an intimate partnership relationship.

Marriage and the family have changed just as our society has changed. These changes have brought new challenges to couples. They have also brought new opportunities. For example, with increased life expectancy, fewer children and younger age at the time of marriage, most couples can now expect to have no dependent children living at home for almost half their married life. This opens up new possibilities for couples to experience life on their own, following the years spent in child-rearing. This same opportunity, however, also creates a new challenge as the couple seek to find ways of building a new type of relationship free from the responsibilities of parenthood.

The demands on couples in today's society are different to the demands made on couples in the past. Previously economic security was a major function of families. This is no longer the case since economic survival whether in reality or illusion, is now seen to be secure. Couples now need more than ever to have skills in interpersonal relations and conflict management. They need to be adaptable, flexible and able to assume multiple roles. But, above all, they need to be able to maintain an intimate relationship while meeting the caring needs of family members. The success of this caring function will determine to a large extent the stability of individual relationships. It is within this context that services to couples in the form of relationship counselling is crucial to the welfare of marriage in our society.

These services, while helping couples to resolve difficulties in their own relationship, also influence the environment of their children. The roles of partner and parent are not easily separated by children and for many children they are indistinguishable. Services need, therefore, to take account of the outcomes of relationship counselling on children. In the midst of change, these services play a crucial role for all family members in promoting and maintaining stability in relationships.

## Chapter Ten **Supporting marriage: the role of marriage and relationship counselling**

**10.1.** **Introduction**

Marriage is going through a process of change just like society itself. During the twentieth century the nature of the marital relationship has undergone dramatic change. As Dr. Kiely has described, personal fulfilment and emotional considerations have assumed much more importance for individuals within marriage. The effect of these changes is that marriage is becoming a highly specialised social system based on bonds of love and affection. In it, men and women have a great potential for personal fulfilment and affirmation.

There are many pressures on individuals and on families in today's fast-moving world. These may be linked to economic conditions, such as low income or unemployment, or they may result from stress arising from demanding jobs and long working hours, or with trying to balance the demands of caring for children or elderly relatives with the need to work or trying to manage a home in today's work -and consumer-oriented society.

All these changes have significant consequences for the stability of marriage and its place as an institution in society.

In this chapter, the Commission acknowledges the valuable work of marriage counselling services[1] and suggests a framework within which the services might be developed in the future. The services available and the role of the State in supporting marriage counselling agencies are discussed. The Commission makes recommendations for a new partnership approach between State and voluntary marriage counselling services to ensure the future development of those services. The Commission sets out the case for the development of services to take on a preventive approach and as an early intervention to support families in dealing with marital and relationship difficulties. The importance of timely access to information and advice is discussed and the role of voluntary and community groups in providing social supports to families in transition is acknowledged.

**Submissions to the Commission**

Submissions to the Commission identified a range of counselling services as a preventive measure to assist families in times of crisis or family difficulty. It was felt that the absence of the extended family has left many families without the support and back-up that was available to earlier generations.

Specific services were highlighted as being particularly important in supporting families. These are:

- **Pre-marriage courses.** Some people were keen to see attendance at pre-marriage courses made mandatory.

- **Marriage and relationships counselling.** The importance of facilitating people to resolve their difficulties if possible and to stay together was stressed in many of the submissions.

FINAL REPORT OF THE COMMISSION ON THE FAMILY

1    In the context of this chapter, 'marriage counselling' refers to marriage and relationship counselling services provided for couples and individuals.

Contributors wanted to see *wider availability* of and earlier access to counselling support services for families and to marriage counselling for couples. More *funding* was urged to improve and extend existing services.

## 10.2 The role of marriage counselling in assisting couples

There has been an increase in the numbers of families experiencing marital breakdown and separation, and in lone parenthood. The 1996 Census shows that there were more than twice as many separated persons[2] in 1996 (87,800 people) as ten years previously (37,200 people).

However, marriage is still the popular choice for the vast majority of young people. Most couples bring to their marriage mutual love and affection, commitment to their relationship and determination to succeed. They overcome the challenges which life and parenthood bring and succeed in finding fulfilment and affirmation within stable marital relationships.

Social commentators point to the changes in society and in the expectations about marriage as an explanation for the increase in marital breakdown and separation. Very little research, however, has been carried out into the causes of marital breakdown or, indeed into why most marriages succeed. We do not know very much about how couples successfully overcome difficulties in their relationship, whatever their cause - financial problems, unemployment or great emotional stress, such as that resulting from one of the partners being unfaithful.

There is now solid evidence beginning to emerge about the value of marriage counselling when relationships are in difficulty. Marriage counselling provides couples with the support and assistance they need at this time and equips them with the skills and knowledge to build better relationships. It also teaches couples the value of thinking in terms of prevention of difficulty.

## 10.3 Building strong relationships

The Commission's examination of the difficulties families face presents a convincing case for better preparation for marriage, with greater emphasis on building strong and stable relationships. Where marriages are in difficulty, an early response system is needed which can provide assistance, at a point where the potential to save the marriage still exists. The goal of intervention must be a reduction of conflict between parents so that children's well-being remains centre-stage. Where couples have decided to separate, ongoing parenting relationships and continuing relationships with other family members where this is in the children's best interest need to be encouraged and the transition of the couple to a positive future for themselves and their children needs to be facilitated.

## 10.4 A focus on the relationship between two people

Marriage counselling focuses on the relationship between the two adults in the family. Whether one or both partners seek help, the key element is the relationship. Through exploring the

---

2    Includes deserted, marriage annulled, separated and divorced people.

feelings which have developed and providing a safe place for these feelings to be expressed and acknowledged, counselling can help the couple or individual to understand the dynamics of their relationship. Through this understanding, an awareness of what change is needed can be negotiated and implemented. The counsellor facilitates this process and supports the individuals involved in agreeing a course of action and achieving their chosen goals.

Couples/individuals who have a specific sexual difficulty which is affecting their relationship may avail of psychosexual therapy. A psychosexual therapist is a trained relationship counsellor with further expertise in sexual health.

Couples who have decided to take the difficult decision to end their relationship need support while coping with the emotional impact of change. In these situations a counsellor with specialised training can help the couple or individual to come to terms with the loss and facilitate them in coping in this transitional period with less acrimony and more understanding of what went wrong.

Counselling for children and teenagers in marital breakdown situations is a more recent development by the marriage counselling services and other services. It involves working with children, and guidance for parents about their children's needs when the parents part. The counsellors may see children ranging in age from 3 to 18 years old, with the parents' agreement.

## 10.5 The voluntary marriage counselling services

The first service of its kind in Ireland, the Marriage Counselling Service, was set up by a church initiative in the early 1960s. The organisation was affiliated to the Church of Ireland until 1977, then to the wider sphere of the Council of Churches and finally evolved to become a non-denominational service. Recently changing its name to Marriage and Relationship Counselling Services, it provides counselling from several Dublin locations by trained counsellors. Training and education programmes are also run for professionals in related fields.

The Catholic Marriage Advisory Council was set up in Dublin in 1968 and became an independent national body in 1975. From an initial 6 centres, it now has over 57 centres throughout the country with some 1,100 trained counsellors. The Council changed its name to ACCORD in 1995 to reflect the range of services provided, which include marriage preparation and relationship counselling. Services are available to anyone seeking assistance irrespective of financial situation, religious affiliation or marital status.

There is now a network of over 90 centres providing marriage counselling services throughout Ireland, with over 1,000 trained counsellors, most of whom are volunteers.[3] Many services are provided through church or community centres. Agencies recruit and train their own workers and support staff. They are dedicated, professional volunteers who bring enthusiasm and commitment to their work. The voluntary agencies depend on income from the State and from voluntary contributions for services to fund their activities. They organise their own activities to promote the work of marriage counselling.

3   *Services for Marriages in Difficulty,* a booklet published by the former Department of Equality and Law Reform, lists some 90 counselling services throughout the country funded or supported by the Government. These organisations generally provide their services to the client free of charge, or at a small cost.

In recent years there has also been a growth in local and community organisations providing services to families with marital difficulties.

## 10.6 State support for the marriage counselling services

The marriage counselling services run by the voluntary organisations are largely dependent on State assistance to fund their services. State support to date has taken the form of grant-aiding organisations on a year-to-year basis.

Up to the 1990s, the grants were channelled mainly through the health boards. In the early 1990s specific organisations received grants through the annual budget. Some organisations were also eligible for grants under the Department of Social, Community and Family Affairs scheme of grants for voluntary and community groups. These grants were in the main for 'once off' capital projects. In 1994 the (then) Department of Equality and Law Reform[4] assumed responsibility for grant-aiding the marriage counselling services and introduced a scheme of grants for voluntary organisations providing marriage counselling services.

In 1994 and again in 1995, £750,000 was allocated for voluntary marriage counselling services. In 1996, the amount was increased to £900,000 and the scheme was extended to cover the counselling of children whose parents have separated. In 1997, £900,000 was again allocated. Responsibility for support for the marriage counselling services was transferred to the Department of Social, Community and Family Affairs in January 1998.

Following recommendations from the Commission for a substantial increase in funding, the Government has allocated an additional £600,000 for Marriage Counselling Services bringing the total allocation in 1998 to £1.5 million. The Commission has welcomed the increase in funding.

## 10.7 The case for greater promotion of the benefits of marriage counselling

There has been a growing appreciation of the role of marriage counselling services in offering professional assistance to couples where difficulties arise in their relationships.

Recent research[5] carried out in the UK, based on an evaluation of marriage counselling provided by RELATE Marriage Guidance[6] suggests counselling can help couples renegotiate their relationships and help them through the personal anxieties connected with relationship problems. It clearly has a role to play in helping people through the complexities of modern "companionate" marriage, although it does not work for everyone and many couples who start counselling do not complete the process.

---

4   Now the Department of Justice, Equality and Law Reform.

5   *Mediating Modern Marriage: a role for marriage counselling*, Peter McCarthy: Centre for Family Studies, University of Newcastle upon Tyne, Newcastle UK: *Sexual and Marital Therapy*, Vol. 17. No. 3 1997

6   RELATE is a voluntary agency founded some 50 years ago. It provides a counselling service at 130 centres throughout England, Wales and Northern Ireland, where more than 2,200 counsellors work with some 76,000 people per annum. The study was based on 2,000 clients using RELATE counselling services in Northern Ireland and 4 centres in the midlands region of England.

The findings of the study were summarised as follows:

Clients who went beyond an initial interview tended to develop more sharing relationships and to show more affection towards their partner than they had before counselling and six months after counselling 56 per cent felt that their relationship had improved. Those who were married and living together at the time they first went to RELATE were more likely to continue to do so if they went beyond a single interview and fully participated in the counselling process. Eighty per cent of clients who were married and living with their spouse when they first went to RELATE and who went beyond the first appointment, were still co-resident with that partner when they completed counselling. This compares with 74 per cent of those who attended just a single appointment.

Of those clients who were initially separated, 18 per cent of those who completed the counselling process got back together with their partner either during counselling or shortly after completion. The proportion of those who did not complete the process but who got back with their partner was higher (25 per cent), perhaps implying that re-establishing a relationship can be a reason for ending counselling early. Indeed, 16 per cent of separated clients who attended only a single interview had reconciled with their partner.

In some cases counselling helps clients to decide if their relationship is worth saving. Moreover, the evidence suggests that when the relationships are not saved, counselling can enable couples to end them without the kind of acrimony which sours the ongoing relationships of many couples who separate and can leave clients who separate from partners in a more positive state of mind.

Thus counselling can alleviate many of the anxieties which arise when individuals recognise they are not getting satisfaction from their relationship. Clients who went beyond a first interview made significant improvements in their psychological well-being and several described how counselling had helped them to feel better about themselves and more positive about the future.

The findings of the study in relation to the benefits of marriage counselling echo the experience of the voluntary agencies that provide marriage counselling in Ireland. Other findings of the study have direct parallels with the Irish experience: for example, the main reasons clients sought counselling were that they wanted help with communication problems and to preserve their relationship.

### 10.8 Developing and promoting marriage counselling services

It is the Commission's view that there is a need for greater investment in support for and promotion of the marriage counselling services. The evidence is that marriage counselling can be effective in assisting couples who are encountering difficulties in their relationship. The services can minimise conflict and address in a positive way the effects of marital disharmony. In the event of couples taking the painful decision to separate, evidence suggests that counselling can help them to come to terms with their new family situation and assist them in making the transition to a positive future. Marriage and relationship counselling services have the potential to play an important role in promoting stability in family life. Studies show that children have fewer problems in low conflict, stable families.[7]

**10.9**    **Acknowledging in the policy approach the importance of reconciliation and the potential of marriage counselling to assist couples**

Over the past ten years there has been a comprehensive programme of family law reform[8] to deal with the consequences of marital breakdown. The potential contribution of marriage counselling in supporting families is acknowledged by the Oireachtas and Government in the legislative and administrative systems.

Both the Judicial Separation and Family Law Reform Act 1989 and the Family Law (Divorce) Act 1996 contain specific provisions so that couples are made aware of the alternatives to separation proceedings.[9] In effect, there is a requirement in these Acts on all legal advisers to advise clients commencing litigation about reconciliation or non-adversarial approaches to reaching agreement on the terms of a settlement. Where the proceedings come before the court, an adjournment will be possible either to assist reconciliation or to assist agreement on the terms of a settlement. A similar provision is contained in the Children Act 1997. A solicitor is required before instituting custody, access or guardianship proceedings to discuss with the applicant the possibility of engaging in counselling or mediation to resolve the dispute. This provision is intended to facilitate as far as possible a non-adversarial approach to disputes in relation to children and to provide an alternative disputes resolution mechanism.[10]

Increasingly it is being recognised that the law cannot stand alone in dealing with the intensely painful and private matters to do with marital breakdown in families. The Commission has pointed out in its interim report, that support services, such as marriage counselling, need to be *developed in tandem* with the formulation of family law. It is important for families that development of the support services, including marriage counselling, is accorded a high priority.

---

7    Cockett and Tripp: *The Exeter Family Study: Family breakdown and its impact on children*; University of Exeter, 1994.

8    See Appendix 1 to this chapter for a list of legislative changes.

9    Judicial Separation and Family Law Reform Act, 1989.

     Section 5-(1) A solicitor, if any, acting for an applicant for a decree of judicial separation shall, prior to the making of an application for a decree of judicial separation-

     (a) discuss with the applicant the possibility of reconciliation and give to him the names and addresses of persons qualified to help effect a reconciliation between spouses who have become estranged, and

     (b) discuss with the applicant the possibility of engaging in mediation to help effect a separation on an agreed basis with an estranged spouse and to give to him the names and addresses of persons and organisations qualified to provide a mediation service, and

     (c) discuss with the applicant the possibility of effecting a separation by the negotiation and conclusion of a separation deed or written separation agreement.

     Section 6-(1) A solicitor, if any, acting for a respondent in an application for a decree of judicial separation shall, as soon as possible after receiving instructions from the respondent - (a) - (c) as above.

     Family Law (Divorce) Act, 1996, Section 6(2) (a)-(c) and Section 7(2) (a) - (c) contain similar provisions

10    Children Act, 1997, Part IV, Section 20(2) (a) - (c) contains provisions similar to the above in relation to mediation.

While there has been a growing appreciation of the role of marriage and relationship counselling in providing assistance to couples, no *explicit policy* has been developed to date in relation to:

- the *future development of the marriage counselling services* to meet new demands

- *ongoing financial support* for the voluntary sector in providing the services

- the *need for research* in relation to the causes of marital breakdown and the role of the marriage counselling services in assisting families.

The Commission welcomes the commitment in the Government Programme, *An Action Programme for the Millennium*, to address the effects of divorce on families. The Commission hopes that the recommendations set out in the following paragraphs for the future develop- ment of services, to prevent, as far as possible, marital disharmony and promote early intervention to sustain commitment to marriage will help to realise the Government's objective of a country-wide counselling service, making the protection of marriage and the continuity and stability which it represents for children a primary policy goal.

**10.10    Consultation with providers of marriage counselling services**

In framing its recommendation for the future development of marriage counselling services, the Commission has taken account of the issues and priorities identified in consultation with key providers of marriage and relationship counselling. The consultation took the form of an expert workshop, held on UN International Day of Families, 15 May 1997, in which the directors of the leading providers of marriage and relationship counselling services participated.[11]

**10.11    Some features of the provision of marriage counselling services which should inform the policy approach**

The Commission has identified a number of features in relation to marriage counselling services which distinguish the service within the voluntary sector. It is important that these features inform policy development in relation to State support for marriage counselling.

- The State is wholly reliant on the voluntary sector to meet the need for support for marriages and relationships in difficulty.

- Marriage and relationship counselling involves the provision of a highly professional service by trained counsellors within an environment which is largely dependent on voluntary commitment to meeting the needs of society for marriage and relationship counselling.

- Fund-raising, always a problem for the voluntary sector, can present particular difficulties for the marriage counselling services. The sector is largely dependent on income from the State, and on voluntary contributions for services. Fund-raising is not a significant feature of the sector.

11    See Appendix 2 to this chapter for an account of the expert workshop.

## 10.12 The immediate priority is more funding for marriage counselling

Uncertainty about the level and continuity of State funding and commitment in the future is perhaps the most significant restriction on the development of marriage counselling services in the short term. The present arrangement, whereby State grants are allocated on a year-to-year basis, sometimes with staggered payments, make development planning impossible. Delays in payments and the need to pursue promised payments are disruptive of valuable management time in a sector which, although highly professional, depends on voluntary commitment and is hard pressed to meet the growing demands on services.

As an immediate priority, the Commission considers that there is a need for a substantial increase in the level of funding provided for marriage counselling services.

The Commission is of the view that there needs to be a better balance between the resources allocated to dealing with the legal consequences of marital breakdown[12] and the resources allocated to preventive and other social supports, particularly marriage counselling, which are needed to support marriage and secure continuing stable relationships for children.

**The Commission recommends that the level of State funding provided for marriage counselling should be further increased to £3 million over the next two years.**

## 10.13 A partnership approach to the future development of services

The State is fortunate in having highly committed, professional voluntary agencies which have taken the lead in responding to families experiencing marital difficulties. Services are provided in an environment which reflects the needs and the values of clients. Flexibility in the delivery of services, for example, opening hours which are more suited to families is a feature of the voluntary services which would be difficult to replicate within a State-run service.

The Commission considers that the continuing role of the voluntary sector in the provision of marriage counselling should be acknowledged by a partnership approach with the State in developing policy for the future of marriage counselling services.

## 10.14 A new policy framework for the development of services

The Commission suggests that there is a need for a clear policy framework within which marriage counselling as a social support for families may be developed.

**The Commission recommends that the State, in partnership with the voluntary agencies, should draw up and publish within the next two years, a clear policy framework to govern the future development of marriage counselling services.**

---

12   The provision for support for the marriage counselling services and the Family Mediation Service together is £2.4 million in 1998. In 1997, £9.495m was allocated to the Legal Aid Board. Ninety-six per cent of the legal aid clients were aided with family law matters. The State-funded Family Mediation Service offers couples a non-adversarial and non-legal way of negotiating separation agreements, including arrangements for children. See Chapter 11.

The framework should set out clearly:

- the *objective* ( a mission statement) of accessible marriage counselling services, available on a nation-wide basis, as a key support to continuity and stability in family life,

- the objectives underpinning State support in relation to the *development of the services* under each of the headings:
- educational and preventive
- support for families undergoing separation and transition to a new family life
- research data

- objectives in relation to the *delivery of a timely quality service to families*

- *clear criteria* in relation to the State's provision of *financial support* for the services.

These objectives should be based on realistic expectations of what the voluntary marriage counselling services can achieve in these areas.

### Funding criteria
The funding criteria should be clear in relation to:

- *the aspects of services to be funded* and the appropriate level of funding which the providers may expect for:
- the number of counselling hours provided by professional counsellors in the service
- the expansion of services to provide more hours of service or to provide a service in a new area
- the development of counselling services at a preventive level including marriage preparation programmes and programmes to prevent marital problems arising
- research projects
- the back-up support and the administration of the service

- *priorities.* Priority groups and the appropriate level of service for them should be identified: for example, work with children, work with families with specific problems. The funding of services for priority groups/services should be on the basis of an agreed budget adequate to meet the costs of the service,

- *special projects including research and evaluation.* Projects relating to research and evaluations should be funded on the basis of an agreed financial commitment over an appropriate time period.

### 10.15    Special responsibilities for the State
The Commission is of the view that the State is well placed to promote the benefits of marriage counselling and to assist with compiling information arising from the use of the services.

The State is in a position to promote the benefits of marriage counselling and the need for early action through promotional campaigns, parent information programmes and information and advice centres, and through the work of the Family Affairs Unit of the Department of Social, Community and Family Affairs which is recommended in Chapter 24.

The State is in a position to share technological knowledge and provide assistance to providers of services in compiling data on marital breakdown. Marriage counselling organisations have a wealth of information in relation to calls on their services. Three of the main organisations which provide services advised the Commission about statistical data which could be made available for research purposes. A coherent approach to compiling data across all the organisations would facilitate research into the difficulties for which people seek help and the factors involved in marital difficulty. This is an area in which the taxpayer's investment in technology could be used to develop model systems for compiling data for use by the organisations.

### 10.16 Some important issues for the providers of marriage counselling services

The Commission considers that the development of the marriage counselling services over the next few years will require the partners to tackle:

- the fundamental structural issue of co-ordination between the organisations involved in marriage counselling[13]

- The need to develop within the services a focus on early intervention and support in sustaining commitment to marriage.

The Commission suggests that these aspects of the work of the marriage counselling services have the potential to be developed further.

#### Co-ordination between the services

Co-ordination between the agencies providing counselling services requires work in relation to training, accreditation and certification, and supervision, the development of a complaints procedures for clients and improved linkages between the agencies. It also requires co-ordination of the advocacy efforts and one voice in support of the contribution of marriage counselling to stability and continuity in family life.

There is no formal organisation which represents the voluntary organisations that provide marriage counselling services. Umbrella bodies or networks have been developed in various sectors of voluntary activity; they have an important role to play in the context of the overall development of the voluntary sector. They provide support, training, information and other developmental services for the affiliated organisations. The role of umbrella groups and networks is important in reconciling the inherent tension between the autonomy of individual organisations and the need for planning for the pursuit of common sectoral interests. They

---

13   This is an issue which the Commission highlighted in an interim report to the Minister for Social Welfare in November 1996. In that report, the Commission recommended the establishment of a committee to examine and report on the extent of counselling provision and the gaps in provision. This recommendation has taken on a new significance in the light of the enthusiastic response of the key providers of services to the Commission's examination of this question and the willingness within the marriage counselling services to identify the challenges facing the marriage and relationship counselling sector for the future.

can help to develop internal cohesion in the sector.[14] Umbrella groups can be important in influencing policy at national level, at EU level and in other international fora, for example the UN. The Commission suggests that this is an issue in which the voluntary agencies have a mutual interest.

Liaising with Government and undertaking a co-ordinating role for the sector is time-consuming, and resources are required for this task. The Commission recommends that the policy framework should acknowledge the important role of umbrella and advocacy groups.

### 10.17 Prevention begins in the earliest years of family life

The Commission considers that there is a need for a greater emphasis on preparation for marriage and parenthood.

The Commission's recommendations in Chapter 13 in relation to education for family living as part of the formal school curriculum and for equipping young people to make informed choices about their futures are part of a lifecycle approach to supporting family life and preventing breakdown. As individuals, we develop our expectations of family life from what we experience as children. The model for prevention of difficulties must therefore begin in our earliest experiences of family life. The Commission's recommendations throughout this report are centred on strengthening the capacities of families to provide continuity and stability for their children. Parent education and information in the early years of child-rearing are key supports for families.

### 10.18 Better preparation for marriage and support in the early years of married life are important

The main churches advocate and promote the benefits of marriage preparation programmes for engaged couples. Courses provided by the agencies cover the different aspects of the marriage relationship - what holds two people together and what can separate them. The programmes include communication, sexuality, fertility, family planning, conflict resolution and marital support, as well as the practicalities of managing a home and rearing a family. Marriage maintenance courses and personal enrichment programmes for men and women offer couples the opportunity to look at their relationship and take time to reflect on what is valuable and what needs attending to, in order to keep the relationship in good working order.

**Promotion of emotional well-being through prevention of difficulty in relationships and more practical support**

Concern to prevent marital break-up in other countries, and in the US in particular, is leading to the development of a variety of approaches to teach couples the skills, behaviours and attitudes for good relationships before they encounter difficulties. The rationale for these prevention approaches is simple: provide couples with basic skills and concepts for handling disagreements and the problems of married life *before* these arise.

FINAL REPORT OF THE COMMISSION ON THE FAMILY

14   Draws on Supporting Voluntary Activity, Green Paper on the Community and Voluntary Sector and its relationship with the State, Department of Social Welfare, National Anti-Poverty Strategy, 1997.

A recent study of one particular approach provides evidence that couples can benefit a great deal from prevention programmes.[15]

Evidence in relation to the effectiveness of marriage preparation comes mostly from studies undertaken in the US. The evidence indicates that relationship skills can be taught and have more measurable effects than information-giving. However, it is still not clear how lasting the effects might be, or how successful skills training might be for people who are less motivated. It has been suggested that there might be a role for booster programmes throughout marriage. Preparation programmes which include sessions after the wedding can provide an opportunity to redress early problems and encourage couples to develop skills to sustain their marriage[16].

These are areas which the marriage counselling services in Ireland have started to develop. **The Commission is of the view that the marriage counselling services should consider the future development of their services towards earlier intervention to prevent difficulties and towards support programmes for couples to sustain and enhance their commitment to marriage.** The importance of preventive services should be acknowledged in the development of the policy framework for the services of the future.

**10.19    Information and advice- the first step in resolving difficulties**

The marriage counselling agencies' experience is that too many couples seek help only after significant heartache and damage to their relationship has occurred. The Commission has made the point that timely information and advice is an important first step in providing access to marriage counselling services and help with relationship difficulties. The need for family information and advice has been highlighted by the National Social Service Board[17] and the Law Reform Commission.[18]

The Commission has expressed the view that access to information is a fundamental social support. Families in difficulties are not always aware of the range and type of services available to help them. The Commission's recommendations about the State's role in promoting public awareness about services and for the development of Family and Community Services Resource Centres (Chapter 2) are particularly relevant to this issue.

Also relevant in this context is the Commission's recommendations in its interim report to the Minister for Social Welfare (November 1996). The Commission recommended that funding be allocated to the NSSB to develop a pilot Family Information Service to:

- give information and advice on the range of services available to families

---

15    Peter Fraenkel, Howard Markman and Scott Stanley; *The Prevention Approach to Relationship Problems*, The study covered the research findings about the outcome for couples who had participated in various PREP programmes in the US and also in Germany and Australia. Overall couples show benefits in terms of improved communication, conflict management and satisfaction over time. Initial findings suggest that couples who had undergone the programme have lower levels of pre-marital break-up and post-marital divorce.

16    From a report by Fiona McAllister of a seminar on Marriage and Divorce held in March 1997 in Family Policy Bulletin, Summer 1997, Family Policy Studies Centre, 9 Tavistock Place, London, WCI 9SN.

17    *Family Matters - A Social Policy Report*, National Social Services Board, 1994.

18    Report on the Family Courts - Law Reform Commission, 1996.

- have available trained personnel with counselling/listening skills to advise and refer the individual/family to the service appropriate to their needs

The pilot scheme could be developed as part of the customised local service for families described in Chapter 3.

**10.20** **Specialised information and advice services in the voluntary and community sector**

Several voluntary and community groups have developed highly specialised information and advice services for families in recent years. Some services provide referral for marriage counselling and mediation.

A number of support organisations have been formed to respond to the needs of separated and lone-parent families. These groups have largely developed to represent the interests of families who are without the support of a partner and to highlight the financial and legal difficulties these families can encounter. They also aim to build friendship and support among members.

Specialised work of this nature, in assisting couples who are going through marital break-down and in helping families at an important time of transition in their lives, meets an important need for information and for social support for families.

The Commission considers that the importance of this work should be appropriately recognised in the provision of State support for the development of services in the future.

**10.21** **Support for children**

The sense of loss and grief which children may experience on the separation of their parents is an aspect of bereavement which is often overlooked in the distressing circumstances surrounding marital breakdown.

A number of innovative support programmes for children have been brought to the Commission's attention. One such programme, Rainbows Bereavement Group, aims to teach children that they are special, that they are not responsible for other people's pain and that it is alright to be angry. The objective is to bring children through their anger to a certain acceptance of the situation and a willingness to be positive about the possibilities in their own lives going into the future.[19]

The programme has been described to the Commission as a peer support group where children can learn that they are not alone in their grief and can also increase their self-esteem and inner contentment. It is not counselling or therapy. The programme, is led by parents and teachers who volunteer to train as facilitators. Initial response to the programme from children, parents and teachers is very positive.

**The Commission considers that the potential of this type of programme in supporting children should be explored further and evaluated.**

19    Extract from a submission to the Commission on the Family.

# Appendix 1

## Schedule of Family Law Legislation since 1989

1.  **Judicial Separation and Family Law Reform Act 1989**

    The Act extended the grounds for obtaining a judicial separation. The courts can order a distribution of the property of the spouses on separation. The courts also have power to order maintenance (including lump sums) for dependent spouses and children. The Act specifically recognises a person's work in the home, or in looking after children, as a contribution to be taken into account in making such orders.

2.  **Children Act 1989**

    This Act makes provision for the care of children in certain cases.

3.  **Criminal Law (Rape) (Amendment) Act 1990**

    The Act extended the offence of rape to include marital rape.

4.  **Child Abduction and Enforcement of Custody Orders 1991**

    The legislation provided for international co-operation in enforcing child custody.

5.  **Adoption Act 1991**

    The Act provided for the recognition of foreign adoption orders.

6.  **Child Care Act 1991**

    The Child Care Act, 1991 sets out a comprehensive code on welfare, care and the protection of children.

7.  **Courts Act 1991**

    The Act extended the jurisdiction of the Circuit and District Courts in family cases and provided for additional judges.

8.  **Jurisdiction of Courts and Enforcement of Judgements Act 1993**

    That Act provides for the enforcement of civil orders, including maintenance orders in other European jurisdictions.

9.  **Maintenance Act 1994**

    The Act deals with international enforcement of maintenance orders.

10. **Social Welfare (No. 2) Act 1995**

    The provisions in the Act ensure that divorced people will not be disadvantaged in their social welfare entitlements.

11. **Family Law Act 1995**

The legislation strengthens the powers of courts in relation to maintenance and pensions; raises the age of marriage to 18; provides for a three month notice period for marriage; for new procedures for declarations as to status of a marriage; and for a role for the welfare service in family cases.

12. **Civil Legal Aid Act 1995**

The Act puts the legal aid service on a statutory basis.

13. **Domestic Violence Act 1996**

The Act repeals and re-enacts, with substantial amendments, the scope of the law on barring and protection orders.

14. **Family Law (Divorce) Act 1997**

The legislation allows domestic divorce in Ireland in certain circumstances.

15. **Family Law (Miscellaneous Provisions) Act 1997**

The main purpose of this Act is to provide for the validation of marriages where the three-months notification of marriage requirement, under the Family Law Act 1995, was given by some couples to the wrong Registrar of Marriages.

16. **Children Act 1997**

The Act updates the law on guardianship, custody and access by allowing a father who has not married the mother of his child to be appointed guardian by agreement with the mother without the need to go to court; it introduces a comprehensive range of measures to safe-guard the interests of the child by encouraging alternative dispute resolution mechanisms in guardianship, custody and access disputes and providing for the appointment of a guardian ad litem and separate legal representation. The Act also makes provision for matters to do with the evidence of children in civil cases.

# Appendix 2

**UN International Day of Families 1997**

**Consultation with providers of counselling services**

1.  The consultation took the form of an expert workshop hosted by the Commission on the Family. The workshop was held on UN International Day of Families, 15 May 1997. The directors of the leading marriage and relationship counselling services participated.

2.  The objective of the day was to hear the opinions of the experts in relation to what is required to facilitate an environment for the development of marriage and relationship counselling over the next ten years, including:

    - the priorities which should drive the development of policy in relation to marriage and relationship counselling services,

    - the fundamental issues to be addressed over the next three and ten years.

3.  There was a consensus among the providers that the objectives which should drive policy development are:

    - *accessible counselling services*, available on a nation-wide basis to all

    - the development of a *clear status* and *recognition* within the community and at State level for the contribution of the counselling services in promoting emotional and relationship healthcare

    - *research into marital breakdown* and evaluation of the effectiveness of marriage and relationship counselling

    - the need to develop services toward *earlier intervention.*

4.  The priority objectives to secure the development of the services over the next few years to meet new demands were identified as follows:

    - the development of *partnership* between the State and voluntary agencies

    - a better *co-ordination* of services

    - a *quality* service, with *common standards* in relation to training, certification, code of practice, accountability, and a complaints procedure for customers

    - *continuity* of funding.

Chapter Eleven **The role of family mediation in helping couples who have decided to separate**

## 11.1 Introduction

In this chapter the Commission endorses the greater use of mediation as a non-adversarial approach which is in the interests of the children to resolving issues where a marriage has broken down and a couple has decided to separate.

Separation and the events leading up to it are a great stress in the life of a family, for children and for parents. The pattern of research findings is now well established. Parental separation is almost always very distressing for children; they may feel angry, sad, powerless and abandoned. Reactions are varied in both their intensity and kind. The effects are most marked where the conflict is intense, frequent and involves violence.[1] Ongoing conflict is associated with low self-esteem in children and this can be a factor in reduced educational attainment and can lead to relationship problems with others.

Research suggests that at a time when parents move apart, a majority of children have not had a clear explanation of what is happening from either parent.[2] Anxiety may grow and self-esteem may be further depressed by a lack of direct communication with either parent.

Parents engaged in the emotional turmoil of marriage break-up have been shown to have poorer psychological and physical health.[3]

Teenagers, especially girls, tend to leave home earlier if there has been parental separation, especially if this is followed by remarriage or a new relationship. This may lead to young people being removed from the direct influence of parents.[4]

Thus social and economic ties can be lessened with less support from their children for elderly parents and less support for young people from a separated parent.

Research also suggests that it is the background to the separation which will influence how well the child will recover from it. Factors such as how parents manage the separation, how conflict is managed, whether children are exposed to it, how change is managed and how the continuity of a relationship with both parents is made possible for the child are important in striving to avoid difficult outcomes for children.

## 11.2 Family mediation has recognised advantages for children

The competitive, adversarial approach of litigation and adjudication, which requires the parents to take opposing stances, has negative consequences for children. Family mediation is a process which helps couples negotiate their own separation agreement away from the adversarial legal system. This process, involving collaborative approaches to

1    Grych and Finchan, 1990,- *Marital Conflict and Children's Adjustment- A Cognitive- Contextual flavour*, Psychological Bulletin 108. Cockett and Tripp, 1994, The *Exeter Family study: Family Breakdown and Impact on Children*, Exeter.

2    Mitchell A, *Children in the Middle*, London, Tavistock, 1985.

3    Amato P.R., *Children's Adjustment to Divorce: Theories, Hypothesis and Empirical support, Journal of Marriage and the Family* 55, pp 22-38, 1993.

4    Kiernan,1992,- The Impact of Family Disruption in Childhood on Transitions made in Young Adult life, Population Studies 46.

decision-making, improved communication between parents, reduced misunderstanding and conflict and parents retaining control over the context of their own agreements, has recognised advantages for children.[5]

Mediation can be an important tool in enabling couples to negotiate their separation without unnecessary acrimony. It is a distinct service: it is not marriage counselling and it is not a legal advice service. Mediation encourages the couple to co-operate. Decisions taken jointly at mediation are more likely to be honoured than those imposed by law.

## 11.3 The case for greater promotion of family mediation

Increasingly the role of mediation as a non-adversarial approach to dispute resolution on the breakdown of a marriage is being adopted in Australia, New Zealand, England, Canada and the United States. In the US several states are actively promoting mediation, particularly in relation to parenting issues. Five states now mandate mediation as a first step in attempting to resolve custody or access disputes.[6]

There is a growing body of opinion that the common interest and mutual collaborative effort centred on children in the mediation process offers the best setting for the needs of the child to be met.

Research shows that positive features of mediation can be enduring for families.

A follow-up study in 1995, in the UK, on couples who had engaged in mediation in 1990 showed that:

- Couples were more likely to feel that mediation had helped them to end the marital relationship amicably, to reduce conflict and carry less bitterness into their post-divorce lives.

- They were more satisfied with the agreed upon childcare arrangements and less likely to have disagreements about contact with their children.

- They were able to reach agreements which had stood the test of time.

- They were glad that they had used mediation.[7]

Another study in 1996 of couples nine years after they had settled at mediation, showed that the non-custodial parents currently had more frequent contact and were more involved in decisions about the children. Mediation parents had also communicated about the child on a more frequent basis in the time since the dispute had been resolved.[8]

---

5   Cockett and Tripp, 1994, *The Exeter Family Study: Family Breakdown and Impact on Children*, Exeter.

6   Kelly J. (1994) *The Determination of Child Custody, Children and Divorce 4.1* Spring 1994.

7   Janet Walker; Mediation: *The making and remaking of co-operative relationships*, RELATE Centre for Family Studies: Newcastle University, 1994.

8   Dillon and Emery, 1996, *Long-Term Effects of Divorce Mediation, a field study of child custody dispute resolution: American Journal of Othopsychiatry.*

The Law Reform Commission, in its report on the Family Courts, drew attention to the fact that research into, and assessment of, the mediation process is still at an early stage. However, it was the Law Reform Commission's view that there is enough evidence to indicate that many families benefit from a non-adversarial approach to dispute resolution. The Law Reform Commission then went on to advocate a shift in emphasis away from the adversarial process and towards mediation.[9]

## 11.4    Family mediation - a summary of the benefits

At an individual family level, the benefits of mediation can be summed up as follows:

- It encourages co-operation and reduces bitterness and distress.

- It enables each party to recognise and understand the position/interests of the other person.

- It enables couples to clarify their own goals, resources, options and preferences in order to make informed decisions.

- It promotes co-operation in developing thoughtful parenting plans that address the needs and interests of the children.[10]

- It encourages couples to own their decisions and introduces them to a decision-making process that can be used in future communication between them.

- It enables couples to remain in control of decisions about their lives.

- It is less costly than the adversarial route.

- It is focused on priority issues.
- **Property** - Where is each person going to live ? How are two homes to be set up?
- **Finance** - How much does each person need to live and to support their children? How can income be shared and divided between each person?
- **Parenting** - How can each parent be fully involved with their child ? How can children be assured of a close relationship with each parent ?

---

9    Report on the Family Courts, Law Reform Commission, 1996.

10    A recent very limited survey (100 cases) on mediated agreements carried out in 1996 and 1997 in the Family Mediation Service illustrates the potential of mediation to facilitate ongoing parenting relationships in the interest of their children:
- 39 per cent of parenting plans showed that children reside with their fathers at weekends and may stay overnight in the middle of the week
- 26 per cent of parents had more or less equal parenting time with their children
- 66 per cent of parenting plans showed that the children would reside with their mothers during the week
- 62 per cent of parents' agreements reflected that both parents would be involved in special family occasions such as Christmas and birthdays.
- 18 per cent of mediation agreements had no parenting plans either because the couple had no children or their children were adults.

In mediation the couple assume responsibility for reaching a workable settlement tailored to meet their own specific needs and those of their children. Thus, mediation can provide practical help to a family in reaching agreement about parenting the children, maintenance and property.

## 11.5 How mediation works - a practical and positive approach to separation

In mediation, the separating couple use a professional mediator to help them work out an agreement to settle the various issues arising from the marital separation. The approach to the process is highly constructive. The couple are seen together by their mediator in a suitable, private environment. The mediator takes the couple through the various stages of mediation.

The various stages of mediation might include the following:[11]

- **Introduction:** The mediator explains what is involved and the couple contract to take a co-operative approach in the search for the options open to them.

- **Exploration of issues and development of options:** Each issue is taken and dealt with; for example, finance, property, children. All the options are explored fully. Where positions or stances are taken in relation to an issue, the task of the mediator, having confirmed the facts of the situation, is to steer the couple away from these positions to a discussion of the needs, fears or interests that lie behind the position being taken. In relation to children, this approach encourages an awareness of the couple's common interest in their children's welfare and focuses on the needs of children. This leaves the way open for thoughtful parenting plans.

  Financial issues are dealt with by focusing on personal budget data and the financial needs of the individuals and their children and how to bridge the gap between the needs and the financial means available.

- **Negotiation and decision-making:** In this stage, the options identified are chosen and a final agreement is reached on all relevant issues.

- **Writing up the agreement:** The agreement document is written up in a way that reflects the co-operative process that underlies it. The document can be taken to solicitors who will draw up a legal agreement.

  The couple might then be invited to bring in their children to a joint session. The purpose of this session is for the couple to tell the children that, while they are separating as husband and wife, they are going to continue to be parents to them. The parenting plan is shared with the children in a hopeful and positive way.

  It takes anything from two to six working sessions to complete these stages. Where it is needed in the course of mediation, couples are encouraged to seek legal advice.

---

11   This section draws on *Stages in the Mediation Process* by Anna Connolly: .in *Mediation- A Positive Approach to Marital Separation*, Family Mediation Service, 1988

Some cases will inevitably end up in court because no agreement will be forthcoming. Equally importantly, there are certain types of cases which may not be appropriately resolved by mediation.[12] Many couples will still want to go to court to settle their differences. However, the legal system need not always be totally adversarial. Mediation can work in harmony with a sympathetic family law system to enable a couple to achieve a less difficult separation and to minimise the risk of adverse consequences for their children. Mediation should be viewed as only one of a number of methods employed in the resolution of marital disputes.

## 11.6    Access to family mediation services

Family mediation is a relatively new and developing service in this country.

The State-funded Family Mediation Service was established on a pilot basis in 1986. The service is independent of the courts. Comprehensive family mediation, which covers all issues arising from marital separation, parenting the children, financial matters, the family home and property, is offered as a free confidential service by professionals, who are trained in mediation. The service is based in Dublin. In recent years the Family Mediation Service has expanded and a second centre was opened in 1996 in Limerick. The Family Mediation Service deals with approximately 350 cases a year.

From January 1998, the Family Mediation Service comes under the aegis of the Department of Social, Community and Family Affairs.[13]

Funding for the service was increased from £120,000 in 1992 to £300,000 in 1994. Funding continued at the level of £300,000 up to 1997. The allocation for the Family Mediation Service in 1998 has been increased to £900,000.

The Commission welcomes the allocation of an additional £600,000 in 1998 to expand the Family Mediation Service.

## 11.7    The need to expand the service

It is generally agreed that there is an urgent need to expand the service. There is a requirement in the Judicial Separation and Family Law Reform Act 1989, the Family Law (Divorce) Act 1996 and in the Children Act 1997 on all legal advisers to advise clients about reconciliation, mediation and separation agreements in advance of commencing litigation. This poses problems for lawyers outside the Dublin and Limerick areas since there is no free mediation service available to couples who are experiencing marriage difficulties. Even in the Dublin and Limerick areas, there have been significant delays for couples awaiting mediation.

The Law Reform Commission[14] has highlighted the need for an accessible, professional mediation service with adequate numbers of trained mediators, proper consultation facilities and a supporting administrative framework.

---

12    Consultation Paper on Family Courts, Law Reform Commission, March 1994.

13    Up to December 1997, the Department of Justice, Equality and Law Reform (formerly the Department of Equality and Law Reform) had responsibility for the service.

14    Report on the Family Courts, Law Reform Commission 1996.

Outside the State-funded Family Mediation Service, *private practitioners* offer mediation services. According to the Mediators Institute of Ireland, the umbrella body for mediators, there are currently 23 *accredited mediators* in private practice. Fees charged for services are a private matter between mediators and their clients. However, it is estimated that the costs for mediation services are in the region of £30 to £35 an hour.

A small number of *voluntary organisations* working in the field of support for families experiencing marital breakdown offer mediation services. These organisations do not receive State funding for these services.

## 11.8 A professional national family mediation service is the priority

The Commission has stated that there is a need for the promotion, where possible, of the greater use of mediation as a non-adversarial approach, to the resolution of family matters when couples have decided to separate.[15] A non-adversarial approach has recognised advantages for children. Family mediation can facilitate an ongoing parenting relationship with both parents for a child, where this is in the child's interest.

**It is the Commission's view that access to family mediation services should be an integral part of the legislative and administrative framework to minimise the trauma of marital conflict for families.** The Commission supports the view that there is a need for an accessible, professional mediation service available countrywide and welcomes the commitment in the Programme for Government, *An Action Programme for the Millennium,* to the establishment of a National Mediation Service.

**The Commission considers that the development of policy in relation to family mediation should be centred on the Family Mediation Service.** The immediate priority, having regard to the constraints which arise because of the fact that the profession is only at a developmental stage, with the implications this has for the availability of trained mediators, should be the establishment of a service to meet the requirements of family law legislation which imposes an obligation on legal advisers to advise clients about mediation.

**The Commission recommends the adoption of a priority development plan[16] for an extension of the Family Mediation Service over the period to 1999 to provide a network of regional centres for the provision of family mediation throughout Ireland.**

### Costs

The proposal envisages a substantial increase in the State's allocation to the Family Mediation Service over the next few years. The cost in 1997 terms of the Family Mediation Service when a network of regional centres is in place, would be £1.6 million per annum. It is understood that the additional allocation to the Family Mediation Service in 1998 will provide for the setting up of some new centres and for an expansion of the service.

---

15   Interim Report of the Commission on the Family to Minister for Social Welfare, November 1996.

16   The plan was formulated following discussions with the Family Mediation Service. It draws on preliminary developmental work undertaken by the former Department of Equality and Law Reform which had responsibility for the Family Mediation Service up to 1998. The Family Mediation Service from 1998 comes under the Department of Social, Community and Family Affairs.

**11.9    Some principles to guide policy on family mediation - Council of Europe Recommendation**

In framing recommendations for the future development of family mediation, the Commission has taken account of the suggested principles of family mediation and the provision of family mediation services, as set out by the Council of Europe in a recommendation on family mediation adopted by the Committee of Ministers of Member States in January 1998.

The suggested approach to the various issues to do with family mediation outlined in Recommendation No. R (98)1 is very much in line with the views of experts who are working in family mediation and who have contributed their expertise to the Commission.

In particular, the Commission is guided by the suggestions in the recommendation that:

- Mediation *should not in principle be mandatory.*

- States should endeavour to take the necessary measures to *allow access to family mediation, including international mediation,* in order to contribute to the development of this consensual way of resolving family disputes.

- States should *promote the development of family mediation* through information programmes for the public.

- States should see to it that there are procedures for
  - the selection, *training and qualification* of mediators
  - *standards* to be achieved and maintained by mediators.

**The Commission is of the view that policy formulation over the next few years must comprehend these objectives. Policy must encourage training, qualification and accreditation and facilitate the development of standards in this new and developing profession in Ireland in the interests of providing high quality professional services to families.**

**11.10    Training and accreditation for mediators are important**

The Commission notes the focus in the recommendation on the State's responsibilities in relation to promoting standards in family mediation services. Considerable work on this has been undertaken in Ireland.

In this context, the Commission considers that the role of the Mediators Institute of Ireland, as the umbrella body for mediators and as the main body for the development of training and the provision of accreditation, must be acknowledged. The Commission commends the work of the Mediators Institute of Ireland in relation to the training and accreditation of mediators in Ireland.

This issue is of further relevance in that the expansion of the Family Mediation Service is contingent on adequate numbers of trained mediators becoming available over the next few years. In acknowledgement of the State's responsibility, the Family Mediation Service is providing six training places in 1998 to enable students to complete their studies and to meet the supervision requirements for their qualification.

The Commission considers that the initiative of the Family Mediation Service in providing training places at this crucial stage in the development of the mediation profession is making an important contribution to furthering the interests of families which have recourse to mediation services. The contribution of the Family Mediation Service to the training and qualification of up-and coming mediators should be taken into account in the formulation of policy for the development of the services over the next few years.


**11.11    Future development of the Family Mediation Service**
The Commission considers that development of the Family Mediation Service should include the following areas:

- The introduction of preliminary information sessions before legal proceedings are advanced for all couples who have decided to separate.

- Development of awareness programmes to promote the benefits of family mediation for lawyers and judges and for those providing family information services and those who work with families that are experiencing marital difficulties.

- The introduction of parent education programmes as an ancillary service.

- Engagement of children in the family mediation process where parents have different opinions about their children's needs.

- The development of appropriate responses by mediation to meet the requirements of families where domestic violence is involved.

- The development of the role of the mediation services in relation to post-settlement disputes, particularly in relation to the parenting of children. There may also be a role for the Family Mediation Service in the resolution of custody disputes where one parent is abroad.

- Evaluation of practice and procedures used in mediation.

- Research into the outcomes for families who use family mediation.

- The development, under the Strategic Management Initiative, of mechanisms for inter agency co-operation. This is an important prerequisite to the development of a comprehensive support service for couples who are separating and their children. Other agencies involved in responding to families experiencing these difficulties include: marriage counselling services, the Legal Aid Board and the National Social Service Board.

In particular, the Commission would like to draw attention to a recommendation made earlier in this report in relation to access through the Family Mediation Service to a specialised parenting information programme for families that are going through the separation process; (Chapter 6) and the promotion of family mediation as the preferred route to the resolution of maintenance issues in the policy and procedures of the Department of Social, Community and Family Affairs in relation to maintenance requirements for lone parents (Chapter 7).

**11.12    Some pilot programmes for new family mediation initiatives**
The Commission considers that it would be appropriate to explore and assess the full implications of some of these developments by introducing the initiatives on a pilot basis.

It is suggested that resources should be allocated as a priority to the Family Mediation Service for pilot programmes for preliminary information sessions for couples before they commence legal proceedings; children attending mediation in certain circumstances and for the development of appropriate procedures, including screening procedures for couples where domestic violence is involved.

- **Preliminary information sessions** provide an opportunity for couples who have made up their minds to separate to consider the benefits to themselves and to their children of the non-adversarial route to agreement which family mediation can offer. Couples who have decided to separate are invited to attend an information session about mediation. These sessions could be organised on an individual or on a group basis. A trained mediator provides comprehensive information about the process of mediation, about issues relating to separation and divorce and about the impact of separation and divorce on couples and children.

  The Commission considers that the information session might also draw attention, to supports available to aid reconciliation if this is at all possible and if it is in the interests of children. Information in relation to parenting support could also be provided.

- **Children attending mediation sessions:** In mediation, parents are facilitated to represent their children's needs and views when deciding on a parenting plan. Where this cannot be adequately achieved or where parents have different opinions about their children's needs, a separate session for children may need to be included in the mediation process. Children need more time and it is important to bring all parties to a satisfactory agreement. There are different models of engaging children in mediation and these need to be explored.

- **Domestic violence in families:** There is a need to devise appropriate procedures, including screening procedures, for couples where domestic violence might be involved and to evaluate the appropriateness of mediation in these situations.

**The Commission recommends that resources be allocated to the Family Mediation Service to undertake pilot projects in relation to:**
- **the introduction of information sessions about mediation for couples who have decided to separate**
- **the engagement of children in mediation sessions in certain circumstances**
- **the development of appropriate procedures, including screening procedures, for couples where domestic violence is involved**
- **the evaluation of the appropriateness of mediation in all these circumstances.**


## 11.13    Some family mediation issues for the future

Two further issues arise in relation to the future direction of policy regarding the provision of family mediation services, which the Commission would like to see kept under review.

### Provision of family mediation free of charge

The first issue relates to the provision of mediation services through the Family Mediation Service free of charge to clients.

A view has been expressed to the Commission that the existence of a free State-run service can inhibit the growth of mediation as a profession in Ireland. It has been suggested that private practitioners are discouraged from entering the field and that the lack of competition prevents the improvement of standards, skill enhancement, diversity of thinking and approach among mediators and a wider choice for clients.

The Commission has considered the issues in relation to the provision of a free service. There is considerable merit in providing access on a "no charge" basis at this stage, when the State is promoting the use of mediation as a non-adversarial approach to the resolution of family disputes. However, the facts are that the lack of availability of trained mediators and the consequent restrictions on the expansion of the Family Mediation Service has in the past caused waiting lists to build up. In the absence of *timely* access to services, clients will either go elsewhere or move on to legal proceedings. The Commission is of the view that this situation will continue until there are an adequate number of trained mediators available. In that time the situation will be exacerbated if demand for mediation services grows rapidly, as might be expected if mediation is widely promoted.

The Commission considers that a vibrant private sector of mediation practitioners has a significant contribution to make alongside the Family Mediation Service in increasing access to family mediation.

The Commission considers that the issue of providing mediation services free of charge must be kept under review in the light of:
- the demands on the Family Mediation Service and the cost involved
- the availability of services on a commercial basis and the willingness of clients to have recourse to them.

The Commission considers that any review of the issue should have regard to:

- the continuing need to promote the use of mediation
  - as a non-adversarial approach in the interests of children and
  - as an alternative to more costly legal proceedings

- the need to ensure that those who are not in a position to pay have ready and timely access to family mediation services.

**A statutory basis for the Family Mediation Service**

The second issue relates to the establishment of the Family Mediation Service on a statutory basis. The Commission agrees with the recommendation of the Second Commission on the Status of Women that the State-funded Family Mediation Service should be established on a statutory basis. The establishment in law of the Family Mediation Service would mark a major step forward in giving expression to the widespread political commitment to supporting families that are going through marital breakdown and providing a forum where they can conduct their negotiating in a non-adversarial way. It would also provide a degree of certainty and continuity to underpin the development of the service in the future.

**The Commission recommends that proposals to provide for the establishment of the Family Mediation Service on a statutory basis should be brought forward as soon as the network of regional centres is in place.**

# Summary of Recommendations in Part 4

## The policy approach

**The Commission recommends**

*In relation to support for marriage in public policy (Chapter 9)*

- **family incentives such as the incentive to marry and to form long term stable relationships and to provide joint parenting to children should be accorded a greater prominence in evaluating the outcomes of income support policies**

  There are inbuilt characteristics within the present structure of some social welfare schemes, for example the one-parent-family payment and the payment schemes for families who rely on unemployment payments which may restrict the choices of parents who depend on these payments in developing long lasting and stable relationships for themselves and their children. The Commission recommends that these issues be kept under review, so that there are no unnecessary obstacles to children having the advantages of the stability and security which a loving two parent family can provide for them.

- **Greater equity in support measures for low income married families so that these are not treated less favourable in public policy as a result of their married status.**

- **State support for better and more effective preparation for marriage and relationships and more support for marriage counselling services**
  - through education, from an early age, about relationships and good communication
  - more State support for marriage counselling services and development of the role of these services in marriage preparation, marriage care (helping to sustain commitment to marriage) and in early intervention when difficulties arise in families.

*In relation to the situation of parents who are outside the legal framework of marriage*

- **Information should be available to unmarried parents about the legal situation in relation to their relationship and their parenting rights and responsibilities.**

  In particular, there is a need to draw parents' attention to the legal situation of fathers in relation to guardianship and the procedural differences which arise for fathers in the registration of their child's birth so that couples can make informed decisions about parenting responsibilities and provision for the future.

- **Cohabitation is an important subject for social research.**

  There are substantial policy implications arising in relation to an increasing trend towards cohabitation and away from marriage. Cohabiting couples who are outside the legal framework of marriage do not have as high a level of safeguards and entitlements as spouses have. From a policy perspective, substantive issues arise if the relationship breaks down. Matters such as parental rights, the division of property, pension entitlements and the care of dependent family members are a particular concern.

*In relation to the constitutional protection for marriage*

- **The Commission supports the retention of Article 41.3.1 in the Constitution by which the State pledges to guard with special care the institution of marriage and to protect it against attack.**
  This should require the State to specifically support marriage in public policy. This recommendation is made in the submission of the Commission to the All-Party Committee on the Constitution. The Commission also agrees with the Constitution Review Group that the pledge by the State on marriage should not prevent the Oireachtas from legislating for the benefit of families not based on marriage and that a clear constitutional basis for this should be provided in Article 41.

*In relation to the role of the voluntary marriage counselling services (Chapter 10)*

- **Support services, including marriage counselling services, need to be developed in tandem with the formulation of family law.**
  There should to be a better balance between the resources allocated to dealing with the legal consequences of marital breakdown and the resources allocated to preventive supports such as marriage counselling services, which are needed to support marriage and secure continuing stable relationships for children. Support services such as marriage counselling need to be developed in tandem with the formulation of family law.

- **Greater investment in the support and promotion of marriage counselling services and their role in promoting continuity and stability in family life.**
  The evidence is that marriage counselling can be effective in assisting couples who are encountering difficulties in their relationship.

- **The continuing role of the voluntary sector in the provision of marriage counselling should be acknowledged by the State in a partnership approach to the development of policy for the future of marriage counselling services.**

- **The State, in partnership with the voluntary marriage counselling agencies, should draw up a clear policy framework for the development of marriage counselling services in the years ahead.**
  The framework should set out clearly:
  - the *objective* ( a mission statement) of accessible marriage counselling services, available on a nation-wide basis, as a key support to continuity and stability in family life,
  - the objectives underpinning State support in relation to the *development of the services* under each of the headings:
    - educational and preventive
    - support for families undergoing separation and the transition to a new family life,
    - research data,
  - objectives in relation to the *delivery of a timely quality service to families,*
  - *clear criteria* governing the State's *provision of financial support* for the services.

- **The policy framework should look towards:**
- **Early prevention programmes to support families in dealing with relationship difficulties.**
- **Support programmes for couples to sustain and enhance their commitment to marriage and more support programmes for parents in the early years of marriage.**
- **Better preparation for marriage and parenthood to be achieved through the education system**

and through greater promotion of the benefits of marriage counselling.

*In relation to the role of family mediation in helping families who have decided to separate (Chapter 11)*

- the promotion of family mediation as a non-adversarial approach in the interests of children to the resolution of issues arising on marital breakdown

- access to family mediation services should be an integral part of the legislative and administrative framework to minimise the trauma of marital conflict

- policy in relation to the future development of family mediation services be centred on the State funded Family Mediation Service.

The immediate priority is the expansion of the service to provide an accessible, professional family mediation service throughout the country.

- future development of the Family Mediation Service to include:
- preliminary information sessions about family mediation before legal proceedings have begun for couples who have decided to separate
- promotion of awareness about the benefits of family mediation
- specialised parent education programmes as an ancillary service
- the engagement of children in the family mediation process in certain circumstances
- ongoing evaluation of family mediation procedures and research into the outcomes of family mediation for families.

Some of these developments should be introduced on a pilot basis.

Future policy development should have regard to the role of a vibrant private sector of family mediation practitioners alongside the State funded service in overall provision to meet the needs of families and the need to encourage ongoing training and development of standards and support the development of the profession of family mediation.

# Making a start Part 4

## Recommendation 22

**The Commission recommends**

- that the level of State funding provided for marriage counselling be increased to £3 million, over the next 2 years.
- Cost: £3 million per annum in 1998 terms.

## Recommendation 23

- that the State, in partnership with the voluntary agencies should draw up and publish within the next 2 years, a clear policy framework to govern the future development of marriage counselling services. The policy framework should include clear criteria in relation to funding to meet policy objectives.

## Recommendation 24

- that the State promote the benefits of marriage counselling and the need for early action through promotional campaigns, parent information programmes and information and advice centres.

## Recommendation 25

- that the potential of support programmes for children experiencing the loss of a parent through separation or bereavement should be explored further and evaluated.

## Recommendation 26

- the adoption of a priority development plan for an extension of the Family Mediation Service over the period to 1999, to include an extension of the service in Dublin and a network of regional centres to provide services throughout the country,
- Cost: £1.6 million per annum in 1997 terms.

## Recommendation 27

- resources be allocated to the Family Mediation Service to undertake pilot projects in relation to:
- the introduction of information sessions about mediation for couples who have decided to separate
- the engagement of children in mediation sessions in certain circumstances
- the development of appropriate procedures including screening procedures for couples where domestic violence is involved and
- evaluation of the appropriateness of mediation in all of these circumstances.

## Recommendation 28

- proposals to provide for the establishment of the Family Mediation Service on a statutory basis should be brought forward as soon as the network of regional centres is in place.

part 5

protecting and enhancing the position of
children and vulnerable family members

**Desired outcome:**

- Children are recognised as individuals within a family and in the wider community with rights to adequate support, care and promotion of their well being.
- Young people are equipped and prepared for family and community life.
- The contribution of older people to family life and to society is affirmed by State and community support.

**To be achieved through:**

- The State and wider community sharing with parents the cost of care and education for children.
- Pre-school children have the opportunity to participate in quality services in crèches/nurseries and pre-school playgroups if this is their parents' choice.
- The education system and families working together to improve the options for young people and to prepare them for family life.
- Older people today and future generations of retired people may look forward to an adequate income in retirement. Families and local communities are well supported in taking on caring responsibilities.

**In Part 5, the Commission**

- examines in particular, the position of pre-school children, with rights to recognition of their developmental needs, and sets out a policy approach to support for parents in the arrangements they make for their children's care, education and development,
- documents the different arrangements which families make for the care and education of their children and the role of services for children in family life, the extent to which services are used by families, and how the development of services needs to be supported,
- discusses the role of the education service which complements the efforts of parents, in equipping young people for family life,
- acknowledges the contribution of older people to family life, to society and in their community and identifies the main issues to be addressed to secure their continued active participation in family life and in their local communities.

# Overview of Part 5

**The Commission has made the point that family policy must have a particular concern with protecting the vulnerable members in families. This concern points to the role of public policy in protecting and enhancing the position of children in families and in their community and promoting their well-being as well as that of older dependent family members, or a family member with a disability.**

In Part 5, the Commission undertakes a comprehensive examination of the issues in relation to supporting the care of young children under school-going age. The Commission is adopting a child and family-centred approach to this issue with a focus on meeting the child's need for an optimal experience of childhood as well as supporting parents in the arrangements they wish to make for the care of their children.

The Commission examines the role of services for children in family life. Services for children cover a wide range of services including; nurseries/crèches, pre-schools, playgroups and naoinraí (playgroups which foster the acquisition of the Irish language) and family day-care by childminders, either in the childminder's home or in the child's home. Publicly funded services and services available on a commercial basis are described. The largest provider of pre-school services to children is the Department of Education and Science through the primary school system.[1]

The case for greater investment in children who are not yet attending primary school is presented. Reference is made to Chapter 5, where options are put forward for payments in respect of children under three years of age. In Chapter 12, an Early Years Opportunities Subsidy is proposed for children in the age group from 3 years up until the time they start school. The Early Years Opportunities Subsidy is intended to secure for children, having regard to the wishes of their parents, opportunities to participate in quality services for children in crèches/nurseries and pre-school playgroups. The Commission presents information about the social, recreational and educational benefits of opportunities for children to participate in these services in the years immediately preceding entry into primary school. Increasingly, parents are seeking out these opportunities for their young children.

Recommendations are made about the State's role in facilitating the future development of services for children. The need for greater co-ordination of the development of service across government departments and their agencies and the voluntary and community sector, parents, and the private sector is highlighted.

The Commission examines the role of the State in partnership with the community and voluntary sector in provision for children in less well off communities and in provision for children with additional needs. The potential of the Equal Opportunities Childcare Programme for an expanded programme to support community responses to a broad range of childcare needs is highlighted. The Commission makes suggestions in relation to the development of "out of school hours" services. The regulation of services is discussed. The Commission makes recommendations to enhance the capacities of local childminders to carry out their important work and to encourage the formation of support networks and the promotion of good practice for them.

The Commission's examination has been informed by the findings of a major survey of the arrangements families make in relation to the care of their children. The national survey was carried out by the Economic and Social Research Institute. Information has been collected about families

---

1    In line with most European countries the compulsory school age is 6 years in Ireland. In practice most children start school on 1 September following their fourth birthday and consequently half of all 4 year olds and most 5 year olds are attending primary schools.

with a parent working full-time in the home and families where the parent works outside the home; the care arrangements families make from relatives to créches/nurseries or local childminders; and the alternative care arrangements families depend on during school holidays, periods of illness or other family upset. The survey[2] shows that 1 in 3 children (77,000 children out of 244,700 children who are not yet attending primary school) experience periods of care outside their own home and away from their parents for some part of the week.

The Commission presents a profile of the education system at each level and notes the contribution of investment in education to Ireland's present economic well-being. The Commission states that the case for continued investment in education in terms of continued economic well-being is most persuasive. The importance of education attainment in determining the life chances of people today is discussed. The majority, 90 per cent, of young people successfully make the transition to adulthood, independence and parenthood. There is a need for special interventions to meet the needs of 10 per cent of children who are at risk of leaving school early without any qualifications. Truancy and early school leaving are particular concerns because of the damaging employment and social consequences they present for young people.

The Commission puts forward the view that there is a need to prioritise investment in education in favour of the pre-school early years and throughout primary level. In this context the work of a National Forum on Early Childhood Education and the proposed White Paper on this topic is welcomed. The Commission calls for a broad approach to what should constitute a quality early years curriculum for young children. The Commission examines the role of the education system in preparing young people for family life and for parenthood.

The Commission considers the place of older people in Irish society today. The demographic profile of an ageing population is considered. Information about family networks, the level of contact older people have with their families and their continuing contribution to their families is presented.

The Commission considers and makes recommendations about income support arrangements for older people and the options for ensuring future generations have adequate income in retirement. The Commission puts forward a number of recommendations for consideration in the context of the policy response to the National Pensions Policy Initiative. In its examination of the income position of older people, the Commission concludes that the value of state pension in comparison to average earnings has been falling in recent years. The Commission recommends that the policy priority in the years ahead must be to continue to increase social welfare pensions and that the future objective should be to relate increases in social welfare pensions to movements in average earnings. The Commission considers the growing significance of occupational pensions in provision for the future.

The Commission goes on to consider how best to secure the position of older people with their families in the context of the changing social environment. The Commission presents recommendations in relation to the policy approaches to be adopted to support families with their caring responsibilities and to improve community supports. Aspects of the support for older people examined include the role of the public health nurse and the future of the home help and meals services. The Commission suggests further development of the potential of community based initiatives in the social economy to respond to future needs. The need for co-ordination of care services to maximise their effectiveness is also raised. Recommendations are made in relation to tackling housing and accommodation issues for vulnerable older people and to continue initiatives to enhance the security of those who are living independently in the community.

2    For full details of the survey findings see Chapter 19.

## Chapter Twelve **Services for Children- State support for children in the pre-school age group**

### 12.1    Introduction

Services for children cover a wide range of services including: nurseries/crèches, pre-schools, play groups and naoinraí and family day-care by childminders either in the child-minder's home or in the child's own home. Some services: - for example, nurseries/crèches and childminder services- are traditionally associated with the task of providing care for children of employed parents. They are usually what people have in mind when they refer to childcare. There is a growing recognition that quality early years' experiences are valuable and important to all children and increasingly parents are seeking out opportunities for learning, socialisation and recreation for their pre-school children. In recent years, there has been a growth in services to meet the childcare needs of employed parents and also to meet the common needs of all parents for social support and for quality early experiences for their young children.

#### Submissions to the Commission

Childcare and the provision of services for young children was a significant topic in submissions to the Commission. One in three of all submissions raised the issue. Quality childcare was seen as important, not just for parents who work outside the home but also for mothers who work full-time in the home. The consensus was that crèches/nurseries and other pre-school services and after school hours childcare are needed throughout the country to support parents with their child-rearing responsibilities.

The Commission's examination covers the broad range of services for the general population of children who are not yet attending primary school, i.e. services which provide care for babies through to services which provide care, protection and early years' educational experiences for children up to the time they are eligible to enter primary school. After school hours services for older children are examined.

### 12.2    Previous reports about childcare

In recent years expert groups have examined childcare provisions from several different perspectives. For example, childcare facilities are frequently raised in the context of affording women equal access to the labour market as their male counterparts or assisting parents on low incomes to gain access to education and training. The potential of childcare arrangements for the creation of jobs is yet another context within which the provision of childcare facilities has been discussed. Issues in relation to the provision of services to meet these various objectives have been thoroughly examined and the Commission is pleased to have the benefit of the expert reports[1] to inform its thinking.

---

1    Previous reports include:

Working Party on Child Care Facilities for Working Parents, Report to the Minister for Labour, 1983.

*Irish Women: Agenda For Practical Action,* Report of the Working Party on Women's Affairs and Family Law Reform, 1985.

Childcare and Equal Opportunities Policies and Services for Children in Ireland: Anne McKenna; Employment Equality Agency, 1988.

*Womens Participation in the Irish Labour Market:* National Economic and Social Council, 1991.

Second Commission on the Status of Women, Report to Government,1993.

Working Group on Childcare Facilities for Working Parents: Report to the Minister for Equality and Law Reform, 1994.

Jobs Potential of the Services Sector: National Economic and Social Forum, April 1995.

## 12.3    The Role of the State in the development of services to date

To date, the role of the State in relation to the development of pre-school services in Ireland has been concentrated on provision for children of families who may be at risk of social, economic and educational disadvantage. There is a growing recognition of the significance of services for all children as a number of policy developments illustrate.

### Partnership 2000 for Inclusion, Employment and Competitiveness

Under Partnership 2000 - the national agreement between Government and social partners - an Expert Working Group on childcare has been established. Its task is to develop a national framework for the development of the childcare sector. The expert working group is broadly representative of a wide range of interests, and expert bodies that work with children, including parents, health boards, government departments, national women's organisations, trade union and employer organisations, experts working in early years' education and with children with special needs and those with an interest in childcare training. The report of the expert working group is expected to be ready in 1998.[2]

### Part VII Child Care Act 1991

The Child Care Act 1991 places a statutory duty on health boards to identify and promote the welfare of children who are not receiving adequate care and protection and to provide a range of childcare and family support services. The practical application of the Act is largely to be seen in the field of child welfare and the protection for children who are at risk of neglect or abuse and the preventive family support services which health boards have introduced.[3] Part VII of the Act has a wider application in relation to the general population of children. Section 50 enables the Minister for Health and Children, in consultation with the Minister for Education and Science and the Minister for the Environment and Rural Development, to make regulations for the safety of children and for promoting the development of children attending pre-school services.

Regulations which came into effect in January 1997 cover in the main centre-based services for young children, pre-schools, playgroups, day nurseries and crèches. The regulations set down standards in relation to health, welfare, safety and the physical environment. Providers of services must notify the regional health board and they will be inspected. Care provided by relatives is exempt. The regulations do not apply to childminders who take care of not more than three pre-school children of different families, excluding their own children.

---

2    The Expert Working Group was established in July 1997. It will consider the following issues:

- needs and rights of children in relation to a national framework

- maximising the job potential within the childcare sector

- national systems for registration, training and qualifications

- resourcing and sustaining childcare in disadvantaged urban areas

- resourcing and sustaining childcare in rural areas

- standards and regulations

- equality of access and participation in relation to a national framework.

Childcare, for the working group's examination, covers children aged from birth to twelve years old. The group is being chaired by the Department of Justice, Equality and Law Reform.

3    See Chapter 4 for further details of health board family support services.

**Eight Government Departments with a remit in childcare**

There are some eight government departments which have a remit directly or indirectly in the provision of services for children under school-going age.[4] This includes responsibility for the training of some childcare workers which is undertaken by FÁS and funding measures by departments which include aspects of childcare provision.

**12.4    Survey of the arrangements which families make for the care of their children**

The Commission has undertaken a major survey of the arrangements families make in relation to the care of their children. The national survey was carried out by the Economic and Social Research Institute. Information has been collected about families with a parent working full-time in the home and families where the parent works outside the home; the care arrangements families make, from relatives to crèches/nurseries or local childminders; and the alternative arrangements they depend on during school holidays, periods of illness or other family upset.

The survey collected data in relation to the arrangements for children up to and including twelve years of age in some 1,300 households throughout the country. The report of the survey prepared by the ESRI presents for the first time comprehensive information about the care arrangements which children experience and the services used by families in Ireland today. The report makes a significant contribution to knowledge about this issue and will be of use to researchers, analysts and policy-makers. The Commission is very pleased to include the full report of the ESRI in Chapter 19 of this report.

The survey shows that one in three children (77,000 children out of 244,700 children who are not yet attending primary school) experience periods of care outside their own home and away from their parents for some part of the week. The findings of the survey illustrate the compelling case for a comprehensive approach to the development of services for children in support of parents with their childcare responsibilities.

**12.5    Primary school- the largest provider of early education services to young children**

The largest provider of pre-school services to children is the Department of Education and Science through the primary school system.

Compulsory school age is six years in Ireland. In practice, most children start primary school on 1 September following their fourth birthday and, consequently half of all four-year-olds and almost all five-year-olds attend primary school, where quality early education is provided by trained teachers in infant classes free of charge. The ESRI survey estimated that some 28,900 four year olds and 59,900 five-year-olds were attending primary school when the survey was being carried out at the end of 1996 and the beginning of 1997. Indeed primary school provision for children under six years could be regarded as the only publicly funded universal service for children in this age-group.

In addition to the provision for children in the infant classes in primary school, the Department of Education and Science funds some specific pre-school services. These are:

4    Details of the remit of the different Departments are set out in Appendix 1 to this chapter.

- the Early Start programme, a pilot pre-school education initiative for children who are most at risk of not succeeding in education. The pilot programme caters for some 1,500 children in 40 centres in eight locations around the country

- a programme in the inner city community of Rutland Street, Dublin, The Rutland Street Project

- special programmes for children of Traveller families. There are 56 programmes catering for approximately 700 children.

The Commission notes the work undertaken by the recent National Forum on Early Childhood Education, which was convened by the Minister for Education and Science. The Forum was representative of all interests in the childcare area. It considered current and future provision in early childhood education. A report on the Forum is being prepared. The Commission further notes the proposal of the Minister for Education and Science to develop a White Paper on Early Childhood Education.

## 12.6    Publicly funded and private services for children

Outside of the provision within the publicly funded school system services for the general population of children who are not yet attending primary school have developed along two distinct strands: *publicly funded or subsidised childcare and private non-subsidised* care.

## 12.7    Publicly funded and subsidised childcare

Publicly funded and subsidised childcare includes:

(i) a small number of *nurseries* operated by or administered on behalf of the health boards. In the main these services cater for children on referral by the welfare services. These nurseries are predominantly in the greater Dublin area and up to 90 per cent of the running costs are funded by the Eastern Health Board. The majority of children are between two and four years but some children may be five or six depending on the child's readiness for school.

(ii) the subsidisation of fees by health boards for children from birth to six years in community-based facilities in areas of disadvantage. In 1993, there were about 9,000 children whose fees were subsidised in this way, representing under 3 per cent of the population of children in this age-group. About 25 per cent of these children attended *nurseries* on a full-time full day basis; the rest attended *community playgroups* on a part-time basis.[5]

In 1996 the health boards allocated some £2.6m[6] for pre-school services.

(iii) A number of the larger voluntary organisations working with people with disabilities provide *special pre-school services for children with disabilities*. The Early Intervention programme funded by the Department of Health and Children and the health boards

5    A Review of Services for Young Children in the European Union 1990-1995: European Commission

6    See Appendix 2 to this chapter for details of health board allocations in 1996.

includes provision for special pre-school services.

(iv) *Pilot childcare initiatives for the provision of childcare facilities in disadvantaged communities.* The Pilot Childcare Initiative introduced by the Department of Justice, Equality and Law Reform[7] in 1993 was designed to afford mothers or fathers in disadvantaged communities opportunities to take up employment, training and development and education. Grants were made available to improve existing services or for significant renovations or building work to set up or to expand services. Grants were not available to assist with running costs. In the years 1994 to 1996, the Pilot Childcare Initiative catered for 3,650 children in 73 projects in Dublin (36 projects) and other urban areas (27 projects) and rural areas (10 projects). Up to the end of 1997, 153 projects have been funded, at a cost of £2.6 million.

The pilot childcare initiative is to be replaced by the Equal Opportunities Childcare programme, which was recently announced by the Minister for Justice, Equality and Law Reform. Funding of £2.65 million[8] has been allocated to the new programme.

(v) *NOW (New Opportunities for Women).* The programme is concerned with the promotion of employment and training measures for women. Some 13 pilot projects on childcare have been included in the programme to date. Between 1992 and 1999 approximately £4 million will be spent on pilot childcare projects.

(vi) *Family and Community Services Resource Centres.* This programme, funded by the Department of Social, Community and Family Affairs, is concerned with addressing disadvantage by providing support programmes for families. The work of the centres includes adult education and training and provision of child care while parents attend programmes. There were twelve projects in the programme in 1997 and about 100 childcare places were available. The allocation for the activities of the family resource centres, including childcare, for 1997, was £165,000. In 1998, it is almost £1,000,000.[9]

(vii) The *scheme of grants for locally based women's groups and the scheme of grants for lone parents* to encourage participation in second chance education and return to work opportunities. The schemes are funded by the Department of Social, Community and Family Affairs, and provision of childcare is also assisted.

---

7    Formerly the Department of Equality and Law Reform.

8    The Equal Opportunities Childcare Programme provides:

• A fund of **£800,000** for the development/enhancement of community childcare projects.

• A fund of **£1 million** to provide support to meet the expenditure required for full-time senior childcare workers in up to 25 community childcare projects with a focus on equal opportunities and disadvantage.

• An **employer demonstration childcare initiative**, with £650,000 funding to be developed with the employer's, representatives organisation, IBEC, to stimulate employer interest and involvement in childcare facilities.

• An amount of £200,000 for the development of a **national childcare framework** by the Expert Working Group under Partnership 2000 for Inclusion, Employment and Competitiveness.

9    See Chapter 2 for further information about the Family and Community Services Resource Centres and the Commission's recommendations in relation to realising the potential of the centres in family support.

## 12.8    Private non-subsidised childcare services

Private non-subsidised care for young children is offered in nurseries/créches, pre-schools and playgroups and by childminders.

(i) *Nurseries/crèches* usually offer care on a full or part-time basis for babies and children up to school-going age. Some nurseries offer after-school services. They are usually open on a full-day, all-year basis. Within this category there is a small number of work-based nurseries, providing services for the children of staff.[10]

(ii) *Childminders* are self-employed family day carers (almost always women) who mind children, typically from three months upwards in their own home, often along with their own children. Childminders who provide care to children in the child's own home are also available. Parents who work outside the home particularly rely on childminders when their children are too young to attend nurseries/crèches or when these facilities are not available to them. These families often rely on a childminder for out of school hours care for older children.

(iii) *Private playgroups* for children aged two-and-a-half to six years usually open in term time for a 3-4 hour session each day between two to five days a week. They are usually provided in private houses or sometimes in specially adapted premises.

(iv) *Community playgroups* run on a not for profit basis are increasingly becoming available. They cater for children aged two and a half to six years. They are often based in the local community hall or school premises and are managed by a parent committee. They are generally open for 4-5 sessions a week. Some receive public funding.

Playgroups have been described as providing children with the opportunity to explore, discover and mix socially through play under the guidance of responsible adults who are aware of the needs of pre-school children.[11] *Naoinraí* have similar aims to playgroups but with the added objective of fostering the acquisition of the Irish language. In Gaeltacht areas, the *Naoinraí* provide a significant support for parents whose first language is Irish.

### No assistance with costs for parents

Parents pay fees for all these services. There is no system of tax deduction or cash grants to assist parents with the costs of these services.[12] The Minister for Finance announced in his Budget 1998 that he will review the question of tax relief on childcare in the light of the reports of the Commission on the Family, the Expert Working Group on Childcare set up under Partnership 2000, and the Working Group which has been established to examine the tax and social welfare treatment of one and two parent households (report due in 1998). In this context the Commission's recommendations in relation to support for parents with their childcare responsibilities in Chapter 5 and in this Chapter are particularly relevant.

---

10   *Introducing Family Friendly Initiatives in the Workplace* published by the Employment Equality Agency in 1996 shows some 16 work-based nurseries established by a range of organisations including UCD, the Electricity Supply Board, Aer Rianta and other organisations.

11   Based on a definition of the Irish Pre-School Playgroups Association.

12   The income support system recognises the cost of childcare for one-parent families where the parent is trying to secure a place in the labour market. Some earnings are disregarded in the calculation of entitlement to payment to comprehend the additional costs lone parents face in participating in paid employment.

### 12.9 Use of services for children by families

The Commission has had an analysis carried out of the survey findings on the use of services for children provided by nurseries/crèches, childminders and in other settings by families with children who are not yet attending school.

Table 1 provides a breakdown of the survey findings of the care arrangements which children aged 0 to 5 years experience.

## Table 1
Based on the use of services from 9am to 1pm[13]

| Total Population | 0-1 | 2-3 | 4 | 5 | Total |
|---|---|---|---|---|---|
| | 106,000 | 108,800 | 58,900 | 60,300 | 334,000 |
| At school | 0 (0%) | 300 (0.3%) | 28,900 (49.1%) | 59,900 (99.3%) | 89,100 |
| Mother and Toddler Group | 0 (0%) | 800 (0.7%) | 0 (0%) | 0 (0%) | 800 |
| Nursery/crèche etc | 3,300 (3.1%) | 21,600 (19.9%) | 15,100 (25.6%) | 0 (0%) | 40,000 |
| Childminder's home | 13,200 (12.5%) | 11,000 (10.1%) | 2,500 (4.2%) | 0 (0%) | 26,700 |
| At home with non-relative | 5,400 (5.1%) | 2,100 (1.9%) | 900 (1.5%) | 0 (0%) | 8,400 |
| Relative's home | 5,000 (4.7%) | 3,400 (3.1%) | 1,200 (2%) | 0 (0%) | 9,600 |
| At home with parent/relative | 79,000 (74.7%) | 69,600 (64%) | 10,400 (17.6%) | 400 (0.7%) | 159,400 |

All figures rounded to nearest hundred.

The survey findings were further analysed in relation to the use of services by households. Since almost all five year-olds are at school, the focus in the analysis of the use of crèche/nursery services is on those families with children who are aged four years or less. There are 179,000 households (16 per cent of all households in the population) with children aged four years or less. In relation to childminding services, data on the use of these services by families with children up to twelve years of age were analysed.

#### Crèches/Nurseries, Preschool Playgroups - Children age four years or less
The survey shows one in five households (38,100 approximately) with young children in this age-group use the services of a crèche/nursery. In 41 per cent of these 38,100 households, both parents work outside the home (the mother on a full-time or a part-time basis)

FINAL REPORT OF THE COMMISSION ON THE FAMILY

---

13   Based on the activity pattern on the Monday morning preceding the survey.

representing 15,600 households. In a further 46 per cent of households (17,500 house-holds), the mother is on home duties, suggesting a primary motivation to provide children with the opportunity to socialise and to have some educational experience.

**Childminder services - children age twelve years or less**
In relation to childminding services, the survey shows that 31,900 households of the 382,600 households in the State with children aged 12 years or less use the services of a childminder in the childminder's home. Childminder services are used almost exclusively by families where the mother works outside the home. The survey findings indicate that in over 70 per cent of families using childminder services the mother worked full-time outside the home and in a further 26 per cent of families the mother worked on a part-time basis outside the home. Some 14,800 households with children aged 12 years or less use the services of a childminder in the child's own home.

In all, almost 85,000 households are using nurseries/crèches or childminder services.

**12.10    EU Policy on Services for children**
The European Union over a number of years has been promoting the case for greater access to services for children. In particular, the EU's competence in relation to equality of treatment and opportunity for men and women in the labour market and the need for measures to combine family responsibilities and occupational ambitions, has led the various institutions of the EU, including the EU Parliament and the Council of Ministers, to take up the call for quality services for young children.

The 1992 Council of Ministers' recommendation on childcare, *inter alia*, urges member states to take and/or encourage initiatives in relation to provision of services to provide care for children while parents are working or pursuing education or training in order to obtain employment.

The recommendation is specific in relation to member states endeavouring to ensure that services:
- are **affordable** to parents
- combine **reliable care** with a **pedagogical** approach
- take into account the **needs of parents and children** when access to service is determined
- are **available** in both urban and rural areas and
- are **accessible** to children with special needs.

The recommendation also looks to member states to:
- encourage flexibility and diversity in childcare services to increase the choice for parents and their children
- ensure that the training of workers in childcare services is appropriate to the importance and the social and educative value of their work
- encourage childcare services to work closely with local communities and to be responsive to parents' needs and local circumstances.

**12.11    Services for children- some development trends in the EU**

The European Union's interest in promoting the case for childcare and the adoption of the recommendation by the Council of Ministers has led to several reviews and comparisons of the services for children available in member states.

In the European Union states, most countries have achieved or are moving towards *comprehensive publicly-funded services for children age 3-6 years* in either pre-primary schooling or kindergarten.

Levels of provision of *services under age three* vary more between the different member states and are generally far lower than provision for three to six year olds. As in Ireland, there are different views about the care of young children up to age three. In several countries the objective is to actively promote choice between employment and caring for children at home through public measures supporting both options. Other countries have policies supporting parents in employment after 12 to 15 months' leave. In some countries parents are facilitated to remain at home until children are three years old.

In most countries services for children below compulsory school age are divided between the education and welfare systems. The main exceptions are the Scandinavian countries and Spain where services have been integrated within one system- welfare (Scandinavia) or education (Spain).[14]

**12.12    Ireland/ EU - Some comparisons**

There are few official statistics available about the level of services provided, whether private or publicly funded for pre-school children. Thus, it is difficult to make comparisons between the level of provision in Ireland and the level of provision for children in the other member states. In the next few years a clearer picture should emerge of the level of services being provided as the notification requirements on pre-school services introduced in 1997 take effect.[15]

The survey findings, however, illustrate the extent to which the pattern of use of services by parents with children in the different age categories resembles the experience in the other member states of the EU.

The findings show that for babies and very young children up to age two the most common arrangement is for the child to be cared for at home by a parent (75 per cent of children). The most commonly used service for this age group is a childminder in the childminder's home, (about 13,200 or 13 per cent of children) followed by a childminder in the child's home. Crèches and nurseries become more important for parents with children aged two to three years. While almost two-thirds of children (69,600) in this age-group are at home with a parent, almost 20 per cent of children (21,600) attend a nursery/crèche, or other pre-school service. About 13,100 children in this age-group (12 per cent) are with a childminder either in the childminder's home or in their own home.

---

14    *A Review of Services for Young Children in the European Union 1990-1995*: European Commission Network on Childcare and other Measures to Reconcile Employment and Family Responsibilities (January 1996).

15    Under Part VII of the Child Care Act 1991 providers of services with the exception of most childminders, for inspection purposes, must notify the health boards about their services.

## 12.13 The case for a comprehensive policy on services for children in Ireland

The findings of the ESRI Survey illustrate a discerning pattern of use of services by families with different needs. The use of services for children reflects trends in the labour market which have been well documented elsewhere in this report and which are set to continue.

The world of work is making huge demands on many families: fathers are working longer hours and mothers are increasingly participating in the workforce on both a full-time and a part-time basis. For most of these families, the period requiring their maximum attachment to the workforce coincides with the most demanding period of parenting responsibilities. They need access to secure high quality care for their children in their absence.

Access to affordable childcare is essential for lone-parent families to improve their financial prospects and those of their children in the long-term. Participation in the workplace or in training or education is not possible for these families unless they have access to reliable childcare services. Parenting alone is very demanding and for parents and children in these situations access to childcare arrangements can be an important source of social and recreational support. The same restrictions apply to mothers and fathers on low incomes. Whether they are seeking employment outside the home or not, parenting is a demanding task for these families and access to childcare can also be a vital social support.

Services for children have a role in promoting community development at all levels in rural areas. Rural children are entitled to the same opportunities as their urban counterparts. Services for children have a role in supporting the language, values and identities of rural communities. Rural women are frequently significant contributors to the family income. They are often partners in farming and traditional enterprise, and access to services is important in facilitating rural parents to effectively participate in the economic, political and social life of rural communities.[16]

The pattern of use of services, as illustrated in the survey reflects a growing recognition by families of the role that high quality services can play in meeting children's needs for socialisation, recreation and new experiences outside the home. For young children care and education are inseparable. At home and within the family children learn independence, personal autonomy, self care and skills for social and group life, but, increasingly, families are looking to nurseries/crèches, playgroups and naíonraí to enhance their children's attainment of these skills and their opportunities for development.

Having regard to these factors, the Commission is of the view that there is a compelling case for action in relation to services for children.

Children are important in their own right. Their needs are paramount. Their needs for care, nurturing and protection are primarily met by their parents within their home and family life. The ESRI survey shows that for children under age three this continues to be the situation for the majority of families. For children aged three and upwards there is a growing recognition of the benefits of early education and participation in quality services outside the home. Access to services in crèches/nurseries and in playgroups, provides an important support for parents in the work of parenting, whether their choice or need is to

---

16    Draws on material in *Supporting Children and Families in Rural Areas* - a Cross Border Action Research programme proposal.

work in the home or in the workplace.

**12.14**   **The role of public policy in services for children**

Meeting the demands for childcare in all these contexts involves several key interests: the State, parents, employers, the private sector, and the community and voluntary sector. The Commission in this report is focusing on the role of the State and on how public policy can support parents with their childcare responsibilities. The Commission has identified four main responsibilities which public policy must assume in relation to services for children. These are:

- sharing with parents the cost of childcare through **investment in children**
- **co-ordination of developments in childcare provision and direct assistance for the development of services**, in partnership with the community and voluntary sector for
  (i)  children in communities which need additional assistance because they are less well off and
  (ii) children with special or additional needs; for example, because of disability
- **facilitating** the development of services in partnership with the community, voluntary and the private sector for the general population of children
- encouraging and **promoting standards** in all services for children.

The Commission sets out in the following paragraphs its views in relation to the role of public policy in each of these.

**12.15**   **Investing in the youngest age-group**

The Commission in Chapter 5 has pointed out that there is a significant gap in policy provision for children who are not yet attending school. The Commission has further stated that significant financial investment in support of the care of these youngest citizens should be a priority policy objective in the years ahead. The Commission suggests that an investment target in these, the youngest age groups of the order of £260 million.

It is the Commission's view that the approach to policy in this sphere must be childcentred focusing on children's rights to an optimal experience of being a child and supporting parents in their choices in relation to the care and education of their young children. Key considerations are support for families when their child-rearing responsibilities are at their most demanding by way of financial assistance and initiatives to facilitate parents in taking time out of the workplace to care for their young children full-time in the home, if this is their preferred choice.

Children under age three

In relation to younger children up to three years, the Commission, in Chapter 5, has set out various options which address these considerations. The options involve a substantial increase in State investment in the care of young children.

**Option A** proposes a parent allowance for the parent who wishes to work full-time in the home for the period when their children are very young. **Option B** proposes the development of the PRSI system to provide for paid parental leave for those parents who wish to take time away from the paid labour market. Both options recognise the need for complementary measures to support the care of those children who are not catered for by the parent allowance approach. **Option C** proposes a special rate of child benefit for children under age three, to be paid to all children in the age-group irrespective of parents' employment status, i.e. whether the parent works full-time in the home, in the paid labour market or is unemployed and dependent on social welfare.

### Children age three and over who are not yet attending school

The consensus about the benefits of participation in quality services for children in nurseries/crèches and pre-school playgroups, for children in the immediate years preceding compulsory school attendance (in the scientific literature and in the findings of the survey) suggests a policy response for children in the age-group from three years to school-going age which would support all parents, irrespective of their employment status and whether their choice is to work full-time in the home or outside the home.

Children have needs for socialisation, for recreation and for opportunities for exploration irrespective of their parents' employment status. Quality services for children in nurseries/crèches and playgroups can meet these needs while supporting parents with their childcare needs, whether their choice is to work in the home or outside the home.

The research evidence in support of pre-school education services for children aged three to school-going age is clear-cut. Early education fosters learning and social and emotional development. The role of good quality early education in compensating for social and background disadvantage and in improving educational achievement and life chances is well documented. There is a growing recognition that these services are valuable and important to all children.[17]

Opportunities to participate in quality services are particularly important in the immediate years preceding compulsory school attendance, that is, from three to six years. The reality is that most four year olds and almost all five year olds are attending primary school. This is confirmed by the ESRI Survey which shows that half of all four year olds and practically all five year olds were at school. **It is the Commission's view that the level of investment in children in infant classes in primary school should be matched by a similar level of investment in children in the earlier age -group from age three years until they start primary school.**

**The Commission recommends that the importance of the years immediately preceding entry into primary school should be reflected in the level of public investment in children in this age- group i.e. from three years up to the age the child starts primary school at four, four-and-a-half or five years old. The target level of investment should be £1,000 per child per annum (in 1998 terms), in line with investment levels for children in the infant classes in primary school.**

The Commission considers that the financial support that is recommended should apply to all children from three years to school-going age, whatever their parents' employment status.

---

17      See for example, *The Case for a National Policy on Early Education*- Noirin Hayes, Poverty and Policy Discussion Paper No. 2, Combat Poverty Agency, Dublin.

## 12.16 An Early Years Opportunities Subsidy

The Commission considers that the recommended financial support should be directed to securing opportunities for children in the relevant age-group to avail of quality early services in crèches/nurseries, pre-schools and playgroups, which meet the standards required by Part VII of the Child Care Act 1991.

The Commission has considered the various ways in which the level of investment might be employed to secure these opportunities for individual children. It is the Commission's view that the investment **should be centred on the child** and directly related to the purchase of quality services. In this context, an **Early Years Opportunities Subsidy**, to be redeemed against the purchase of services for children, has a number of advantages.[18] It would:

- make quality **services accessible**, to children irrespective of social or economic background or their parents' employment status

- **expand the range of options** for all parents, including lone parents and families on low incomes, while respecting their choices in relation to the care of children

---

18   In examining the issues in relation to a subsidy directly related to the purchase of services for children, the Commission has taken account of developments in the UK with regard to the pilot Nursery Education Voucher Scheme which it has been decided to discontinue. The UK scheme was announced in July 1995. Parents of all four-year-olds would be given a voucher worth around £1,100 which they could exchange for three terms of good quality pre-school education. The vouchers could be exchanged for a part-time place- five half days a week- in any of a number of settings providing nursery education or a full-time place in a reception class in a State school or a full-time place in a playgroup. The scheme was introduced on a pilot basis from April 1996 in four areas. Phase 2 was to include the rest of England and Wales. All the indications from press reports and from comments of UK agencies who work in childcare were that the scheme was beset with difficulties from the start. Many of the issues which caused the difficulties are described in the evidence given to the House of Commons Education and Employment Committee in its report, *the operation of the nursery education voucher scheme (March 1997)*. Without in any way attempting to prejudge an evaluation of the pilot scheme, a reading of the House of Commons report suggests that the main difficulty in relation to the unsatisfactory outcome of the UK scheme was that participating State-funded primary schools, having had their budgets for the under fives reduced, set out to maximise their take-up of voucher children. This led to a lowering of the age of entry to full-time school for these children and gave rise to concerns about the appropriateness of reception classes and full-time school for the youngest four- year-olds. The move of four-year-olds towards full-time school had a knock-on effect on playgroups and nurseries which were left in many cases with mostly three year olds and very few four olds. This proved to be particularly difficult for the voluntary and community sector which, providing only part-time services, were attractive now only for three-year-olds and felt "squeezed out".

**It is important to point out that the proposals of the Commission on the Family relate to early years services in nurseries/crèches, pre-schools and playgroups, including community playgroups, prior to entry to primary school.**

The UK scheme was considered to be bureaucratic with many parents formerly availing of free places in the reception classes of schools, or local authority free nursery places, not understanding the importance of tendering their voucher under the new arrangements. Voluntary and community groups and small-scale private operators complained of the administrative burden. There were also difficulties with the inspection process which was designed to ensure quality in services, although many providers were glad of the affirmation inspection brought to their services.

The new Government in the UK, on taking office in May 1997, announced arrangements for abolishing the nursery education vouchers. The new plans are for a programme providing for a good quality place, free of charge, for all four-year-olds whose parents want it, the extension of the programme over time to three-year-olds, and the promotion of partnership between voluntary and private providers and employers.

- encourage **extra places** in a variety of services for children in the **private** sector and in **community**-based initiatives

- be particularly **helpful to community based nurseries/crèches and playgroups** which often have difficulties in meeting running costs and which are trying to provide affordable services to children who are from less well-off backgrounds

- allow for the recognition of the **additional needs** of some children (for example, by the allocation of an additional subsidy)

- facilitate a **social mix** within services
- encourage and promote the development of **standards** in the care and education of young children.

Further enhancement of the Early Years Opportunities Subsidy would allow for the subsidy to be redeemed against the purchase of the services of certain childminders and against costs of local community initiatives which are centred on children's development. A degree of flexibility would facilitate imaginative, community-based responses to the needs of children in rural areas.

### Costs

The cost of the Early Years Opportunities Scheme would depend on take-up and on the availability of places for families that wish to avail of services. This in turn depends on the development of provision in the community and in the private sector. A number of scenarios are presented to illustrate costs.

> Cost in 1998 terms, based on present use of services as per survey findings.
> Three-year-olds and four-year-olds who are not at school
> 25,000 (approx.) children = £25 million

> Cost assuming an increase in use of services and that extra places are available.
> 50,000 children = £50 million

> Cost in 1998 terms, based on eventual provision for all three-year-olds and all four year-olds who are not at school.
> 85,000 (approx.) children = £85 million

*Note: The target level of investment suggested by the Commission in children not yet attending school - the Early Years Opportunities Subsidy and payments in respect of children under age three, for which various options are set out in Chapter 5 - is of the order of £260 million per annum.*

### Early Years Opportunities Subsidy - part of overall strategy to develop provision for children

The Commission envisages that the Early Years Opportunities Subsidy would be an important part of the overall income support policy for children.

### 12.17 The need for co-ordination in the approach to developing childcare provision

It is evident from the range of aspects of childcare, as set out in Appendix 1 to this chapter, which are the legitimate concern of the various departments involved, that no one government department can satisfactorily deal with all the issues. No one government department can satisfactorily meet the care, socialisation, educational and equality requirements of a positive childcare service for children from 0-12 years. A comprehensive approach to the planning and development of childcare provision to meet the needs of children and their parents requires greater co-ordination between all participants, the Government departments with a remit in childcare; their agencies; the voluntary and community sector interests; and the private sector.

The strategy in relation to the provision of services will require all Departments and agencies to work with the community, voluntary sector and the private sector. The health boards and the Department of Education and Science have a key role in relation to the development of promotion of standards in services and an appropriate curriculum.

There is a need for a mechanism at national level to promote co-ordination of effort and the pursuit of shared objectives in relation to childcare provision, among the state sector, parents, the voluntary sector and the private sector. The Strategic Management Initiative presents an opportunity to introduce new working arrangements with a focus on the co-ordination of effort to maximise the impact of state, voluntary and private initiative in childcare provision.

There is a clear need for one department to lead a co-ordinating effort across all interests in childcare provision. However, any department designated to play such a role can be effective only if it leads as the first among equals. The co-ordinating mechanism at national level must reflect the partnership approach which is more and more evident at local and regional level. In this context, the Commission notes that the Government has requested the Minister for Justice, Equality and Law Reform to consider the feasibility of preparing a co-ordinated national approach in relation to childcare, in consultation with other ministers. The Commission further notes that the Department of Justice, Equality and Law Reform has been designated by the EU and the Government to take a lead role in co-ordinating EU-funded childcare and that that Department chairs the Expert Working Group under Partnership 2000 which is representative of a wide range of interests in childcare. The Commission further notes the initiatives underway in the Department of Education and Science, the work of the recent National Forum on Early Childhood Education and the proposal for a White Paper on the subject.

**The Commission suggests that the need for a *co-ordinating mechanism* at national level should be a priority in relation to the national framework for the development of the childcare sector being prepared by the Expert Working Group.**

### 12.18 A variety of services - the State's role in partnership with the community, voluntary and private sector in the provision of services for children

The Commission considers that there is a distinct role for public policy in the development of services for children with disabilities and in services for children from less well off backgrounds and in the regulatory and quality aspects of all childcare.

There is a need for a variety of services in different settings to meet children's and parent's needs in different communities. These may include community playgroups and *naoinraí*, nurseries/crèches providing part-time sessional care as well as full-time services and out of school hours services. Promoting a variety of services to meet diverse needs must be an important policy objective. The contribution of the community, voluntary and private sector is an essential element in ensuring that services are responsive to the different needs of children and parents.

It is the Commission's view that the development of services in these circumstances can best be achieved through a programme of support for the community and voluntary sector in developing appropriate services to meet the needs of these children and their families.

### Community initiatives in childcare - responding to local needs

The State's remit in relation to services for children has been expanded significantly with the growth of community and voluntary initiatives which have sought to respond to their own local community needs for services. The pilot childcare initiative funded by the Department of Justice, Equality and Law Reform and supported by Area Development Management Ltd. was one model where local community interests with State support have developed childcare services to meet the needs of local parents. The pilot phase of the project was found to be highly effective in the financial return on investment and in expanding the services available in less well off communities. Some 150 local projects have been assisted. The pilot childcare initiative is now being replaced by the Equal Opportunities Childcare Programme. The Commission welcomes the introduction of the programme and notes that it is being evaluated by the ESF Evaluation Unit of the Department of Enterprise, Trade and Employment because it will be assisted by EU funds. The programme involves the provision of core funding for up to twenty-five community childcare projects, and a partnership approach with the Irish Business and Employers Confederation (IBEC) in promoting employer interest in childcare. The criteria for core funding will emphasise quality, and innovation in childcare projects.

**The Commission suggests that the Equal Opportunities Childcare Programme may provide the model for the development of an expanded programme to support community responses to a broad range of childcare needs.**

The Commission suggests that the priority areas for programmes to support the development of community based responses to childcare needs should be those areas where communities are coping with considerable economic and social disadvantage, including rural areas. The Commission is further of the view that programmes should also cover support for initiatives in the voluntary sector to meet the additional needs of children with a disability and Traveller children.

### Promoting the role of the community sector in services for children

Further development of a proactive State policy to encourage and promote the role of community responses in services for children might include:

- the development of State-supported, community-based services for children as models of excellence to encourage high standards in the wider childcare sector
- providing access to schools outside school hours for use by community-based interests in developing services for children
- the development of pre-school services attached to primary schools in rural areas,[19] based on the cluster concept where resources are shared.

**12.19    Out of school hours provision of services for children**

Out of school hours provision for children to date has not received a great deal of attention in public policy. The Commission considers that there is a significant potential in the promotion of community initiatives, through state support, for the development of out of school hours services for older children.

At one level, out of school hours provision is very important to parents who are working outside the home and whose children are at an age where they prefer to be involved in structured activities with their peers, rather than with a childminder or a relative, in their parents' absence.

At another level, the development of out of school hours provision presents an opportunity to enhance support for children who may not have many opportunities for learning and recreation and may be unoccupied outside of school hours. There are several initiatives underway throughout the country to support children who may be at risk of early school-leaving; for example, homework clubs and mentoring schemes i.e. where an older student who has successfully completed second-level mentors a younger student. In communities where there are few facilities and children have little pocket money, there is often a need for recreation programmes and activities to keep young people engaged in school life and to develop an interest in community activity. It has been pointed out to the Commission that development of homework clubs and out of school hours services is essential to support Traveller children and their families in continued participation in education. Traveller children, who are not living in permanent accommodation, do not have the basic facilities to enable them to pursue their studies, which are taken for granted in the settled community. An out of school hours service presents many possibilities for extra support for these children and for children who are experiencing difficulty in school.

A number of developments have taken place in recent years in relation to after school provision. Some second-level schools provide supervised study periods after classes. Parents usually pay fees for this service. Homework clubs have also been developed in the community sector in some areas of the country. Many individual schools organise summer holiday programmes for sport, recreation and play and local authorities sponsor several summer projects in different communities around the country.

FINAL REPORT OF THE COMMISSION ON THE FAMILY

19   The National Economic and Social Forum made this suggestion in the context of combating social exclusion in rural areas. See Rural Renewal and Combating Social Exclusion, Forum Report No.12 March 1997.

The potential of the school setting[20] for the development of out of school hours services adds to the compelling case for opening up school premises for greater use by community interests. It has been suggested that the non-emergence of commercially provided after school services may result from the fact that, if buildings were to be used only for this purpose, rental costs could be prohibitively expensive. In this context it has been suggested that school premises may be the most suitable and efficient locations for out of school hours services.[21]

The Commission appreciates that there are a number of practical difficulties associated with opening up school premises for community use. However, this is an area where, as suggested by the Commission on the Status of Women, initiatives might usefully be proposed.

**The Commission recommends that the provision of out of school hours services, with its emphasis on community participation, should be supported by way of a specific initiative within the community development programme administered by the Department of Social, Community and Family Affairs. The Commission on the Family further suggests that the Department of Education and Science has a role to play in encouraging and facilitating the development of out of school hours services as part of a comprehensive approach to address educational disadvantage.**

Out of school hours provision- An example from abroad

Recent developments in New Zealand could provide a model for developments in Ireland. Under OSCAR (Out of School Care and Recreation Programme), grants are provided to community projects to start up before school and after school services.[22] Communities or groups of parents may apply under the programme for a start up grant to initiate a local service. Community interests/parents then negotiate with the local school for the use of facilities before and after school hours (for example, from 8 am to 8.30 am and from 4 pm to 5.30 pm). The community group/parents employ a local person, often a local mother, as a resource worker, who then takes on the task of supervising the children's activities for the number of hours involved. The resource worker may also have the assistance of a local student. Parents pay for the service according to use.

The initial response suggests that the scheme is working well. Costs to parents would appear to be working out at under 50 pence an hour. After-school clubs vary. Some concentrate on supervising homework; others provide a range of structured activities for the children. The intention is to encourage high quality in all services and to particularly invest in the community services for children who would benefit from additional assistance to maintain their interest in school.

Moves to develop out-of-school services are also underway in the United Kingdom. It has been announced that funding from the National Lottery will be allocated to support after-school services.

20  See also Chapter 4 where the Commission draws attention to the potential of the school setting for the delivery of family support and other services relating to children.

21  T. Callan and Brian Farrell, *Women's Participation in the Irish Labour Market*, NESC No.91, December 1991.

22  In 1995 $2.04m was allocated for the development of 5,000 OSCAR places for the 18 months from July 1996.

## 12.20 Encouraging and promoting standards in services for children

The Commission has considered some of the issues in relation to quality and standards in services for children.

In Chapter 13, the Commission highlights the need for a broad approach to what constitutes quality care and education which is developmentally appropriate to young children and the need for recognition of a wide range of qualifications. The Commission welcomes the establishment of a National Forum on Early Childhood Education and the proposed publication of a White Paper on future provision of early education services which would draw on the views of parents, expert groups and community interests. The educational and care philosophy which should underpin provision of educational services for children will be considered in this context.

Training and qualifications are key issues in relation to 'quality' in services for children. Standards in relation to staff /child ratios, the suitability of the settings in which services are provided, the protection of health and welfare, and measures to ensure the safety of children are fundamental to the provision of a quality service.

### Promoting and monitoring standards of services

The Commission acknowledges that a considerable amount of progress has been made with the introduction of the new regulations under Part VII of the Child Care Act. Under the Act, health boards have a statutory duty to promote the development, and secure the health, safety and welfare, of pre-school children attending services. Providers of services are required to notify health boards of their services and are liable to inspection by health boards. The regulations set out the measures which must be in place to meet the requirements of the Child Care Act. They cover:

- the adult/child ratios and the number of children who may be catered for
- the premises and facilities, including the ventilation and sanitary requirements and facilities for rest and play
- the provision of food
- measures for the children's health, safety and welfare.

It appears that the new regulations are having effect. Up to the end of July 1997, the health boards had been notified of 1,500 facilities for pre-school children.

The Commission welcomes this development and calls for **the continued publicising and promoting of the regulations** so that parents can start to look for the application of high standards in the care of their children.

### Inspection - A Supportive Approach

The Commission is of the view that inspection alone will not secure high standards. It would like to see the adoption of a supportive approach by the health boards alongside the inspection procedures. Some health boards have contracted outside agencies, mainly voluntary organisations which work with pre-school children, to provide advice and guidance to providers of services in relation to good practice and procedures and the requirements under the new regulations.

**The Commission endorses this approach and recommends that each health board should be resourced to establish an advisory and support service for those engaged in the provision of services for children.** The development of agreed guidelines and a co-ordinated approach to inspection are important. In this context, the suggestion made earlier is relevant: that certain community-based services for children should be developed to provide models of excellence. The models of excellence would facilitate the compilation of codes of practice and the exchange of information about the most desirable features in services for children.

In Chapter 13 the Commission offers suggestions in relation to training and a broad approach to a curricular framework in services for young children. The Commission would like to see future development of the regulation and inspection of services to cover broader quality objectives in the services provided for children.

**12.21   Childminders**

A significant number of families where the parents work outside the home make private arrangements with childminders, who are usually local women, for the care of their children. The ESRI Survey illustrates the extent to which working parents rely on the services of childminders. About 31,900 households which have a child aged twelve years or less use the services of a childminder, who minds the children in her own home.

The survey data shows that households which used the services of a childminder in the childminder's home did so for an average of 1.57 children. The average number of hours which each child spends in the childminder's home is 23.5 hours per week.

Some 14,800 households use the services of a childminder who comes to the family home.

**Childminders and the Child Care (Pre-school Services) Regulations 1996**
The childcare regulations, designed to ensure the health, welfare and safety of young children, do not apply to childminders who are looking after not more than three pre-school children of different families excluding the childminders own family. Thus, the vast majority of childminders, who are in the main caring for one or two children along with their own children, are not covered by the regulations.

There is no doubt that there are examples of excellent day care being provided by childminders. Childminders provide flexible services at prices that families can afford. They can be an important source of assistance and social support to families that have demanding work commitments. Strong supportive relationships often develop between families and their childminder, and children are looked after in their own community environment. However, childminders operate on the basis of a one woman enterprise. They are not in a position to provide back-up cover in the event of their being unable to carry out their childminding commitments and, as the ESRI survey shows, dependent families must fall back on their own resources in the event of a breakdown in their usual arrangements.

### Childminders and Low Pay

The point has been made to the Commission that most childminders who care for children in the childminder's own home work in the informal economy. Thus payment rates are low. The ESRI survey data[23] indicate that in circumstances where only one child is involved the cost per hour to the household using the service of a childminder in the childminder's home is of the order of £1.77. In circumstances in which two children are being looked after, this falls to £1.32 per child per hour. If, as is widely assumed, most childminders are looking after one or two children along with their own, these costs suggest an hourly rate of pay for the childminder of between £1.77 and £2.64 depending on whether one or two children are involved. In this context, the recently published recommendations of the National Minimum Wage Commission for a single national hourly minimum wage of £4.40 is of particular relevance to the work of the childminder.

Childminders working in the informal economy have no rights in regard to hours of work, paid holidays, sick leave or pension cover.[24] There is no doubt that many childminders are interested in the support and benefits which organisation would bring to their sector. Attempts to organise the sector over the years have not been successful mainly because of the lack of incentives to childminders to make themselves visible. The National Childminders Association, a voluntary association established to promote high standards in family day care and to promote the interests of childminders, initiated a voluntary registration system for childminders. Out of 1,500 registration forms which were issued, only 100 completed applications were received.

The vast majority of childminders are conscientious in their approach to the job and committed to the responsibilities they have taken on for other people's children but, as was pointed out in a report on childcare published in 1988,[25] all that is on offer to them publicly is the possibility of taxation.

The Commission strongly supports the valuable work of childminders in the provision of services for children. The Commission would like to see the services become visible with explicit standards in relation to the care of children, with formal and informal support networks for those providing the services and for parents, and proper conditions in relation to pay and conditions for childminders.

Many of our European counterparts have registration arrangements in place for family day carers. Registration or approval by local authorities can involve inspection, sometimes initial training is required, and often the family day carers work under an organised scheme whereby they are either attached to a nursery or creche or work independently and on a self-employed basis, but are subject to supervision on the basis of one authority supervisor to 20 or 30 family day carers.

---

23  The ESRI report is somewhat cautious about presenting information in relation to the cost of childminders services for a number of reasons. The survey data do not capture the full picture in relation to the pricing arrangements which are agreed between household and childminder and there is a wide variation in the number of hours involved for children. Details of the calculations and the assumptions underlying the hourly costs information are set out in section 4 of the ESRI Report. See chapter 19 of this report.

24  Where an employer pays PRSI, the childminder has PRSI cover for pensions and for disability, unemployment and maternity payments.

25  *Childcare and Equal Opportunities* by Anne McKenna, Employment Equality Agency 1988

## A supportive environment for childminders

The Commission has considered what might be involved in the formal registration of childminders and their inclusion in the childcare regulations. The Commission is of the view that the priority objective for the immediate future is that parents are reassured about the care of their children in their absence and that the important job undertaken by childminders in caring for our youngest citizens receives practical support and is accorded a status in the community. It is the Commission's view that it is in the interest of parents and children and childminders to enhance the supportive network within the community for childminders and to encourage standards in relation to the care of children.

The Commission considers that the main policy objectives in relation to the childminding sector over the next few years should be the creation of an environment for high standards by:

- **Promoting awareness among parents and childminders** about what families might expect in relation to the care of their children in their absence.

  In this context, the Commission would like to draw attention to Recommendation 4.3.5. of the Second Commission on the Status of Women on a code of conduct for childminders and an information guide for parents choosing a childminder.

  The Commission on the Family suggests that information guides might examine matters such as the role of the childminder in the life of the family, the tasks involved in undertaking childminding, the responsibilities involved for both parties, including legal obligations and a duty of care, and some basic guidelines in relation to child safety, protection and health and hygiene.

- **Supporting directly through financial assistance** (that is grant schemes) umbrella organisations and childcare organisations which promote and encourage standards in childminding through education and training services for affiliated members.

- **Encouraging the establishment of networks** to support childminders in the community. The networks could provide the channel for information and advice to childminders and access to training. This objective might be achieved through special grant schemes for the community and voluntary sector to develop support networks. This type of initiative might be of interest to Family and Community Services Resource Centres (recommended in Chapter 2) and to community-based childcare projects. Future development within a well-formalised childcare sector might promote direct links between childminders and community-based services for children, facilitating additional support for childminders and the exchange of good practice and information. This would help community and other resource centres to build up full information on the childcare services in the locality.

There are several examples across the European Union member states of supportive arrangements for childminders. Networks and linking in with other local facilities can greatly enhance the capacities of childminders in their important work. Ideas from the European experience include: clustering arrangements for childminders within local communities, with access to shared facilities such as laundry facilities, a toy library service, and the requisite household and safety equipment needed for young children.

**The Commission recommends that a framework for the future development of services for children should include a package of measures to support the work of local childminders and promote standards and good practices in the sector. Elements of such a package of measures might include:**

- **information guides about the role of the childminder in the life of the family**

- **financial assistance by way of grant aid to encourage affiliation to standard setting organisations to promote the establishment of local networks to support childminders in the community.**

12.22    **Expanding the provision of services for children.**

Apart from specific programmes to support the development of community-based services and to meet specific needs of families (detailed earlier), the Commission on the Family considers that there are several areas of public policy where the State can facilitate and encourage provision of additional services for the general population of children.

Some of these have been highlighted in the reports of various groups which considered childcare issues:

- The Second Commission on the Status of Women has highlighted the significance for **employers of tax allowances for capital costs** incurred in constructing or altering a building to provide a childcare facility and has suggested that tax law should provide special allowances for investment in childcare facilities. Employers already receive allowances in relation to the running costs of facilities which they provide.

- The Working Group on Childcare Facilities for Working Parents (February 1994) made a number of recommendations:
- Planning approval for new shopping and housing developments should be made conditional on the provision of a site and building for a nursery or a children's centre.
- The Government should take a more proactive role in increasing the numbers of places in existing facilities supported through public funds. The Working Group envisaged that in partnership facilities such as public sector nurseries or nurseries financed by health boards, the capital costs and overheads would be met by the public sector interests involved. Thus, for example, the health board could take up a fixed proportion of places available, with the balance of places being taken up by public and private sector employers or other users.

The Commission on the Family further suggests:

- Additional **capital grants and tax allowances** should be made available for the establishment of services to cater for children with special needs or for the adaptation of services to accommodate children with special needs.

- The development of **workplace children's facilities** in feasible locations should be pursued on the social partner agenda.

- Potential providers of services should be eligible for **technical assistance**, support, employment and capital grants similar to those which are available for small businesses.

# Appendix 1

**Government Departments with a remit, directly or indirectly, in the Provision of Childcare Facilities in Ireland 1997**

| Name of Department | Agencies and programmes which directly or indirectly affect provision of childcare facilities |
|---|---|
| **Health and Children** | (i) Department is responsible for the Child Care Act 1991 and has introduced statutory guidelines for childcare facilities.<br>(ii) Department funds health boards to provide a number of childcare facilities. |
| **Enterprise, Trade and Employment** | (i) Department is the National Authority for the EU New Opportunities for Women (NOW) Programme.<br>(ii) Department is responsible for Operational Programme for Human Resource Development (1994-99) which contains provision for childcare training.<br>(iii) Department is responsible for FÁS under which the Community Enterprise programme has helped to provide staff for some childcare facilities and has helped to set up some childcare facilities. |
| **Education and Science** | (i) Department subsidises childcare facilities in some third-level and VEC colleges<br>(ii) Department is responsible for the Early Start Pre-School Pilot Scheme, pre-school programmes for Traveller children and the Rutland Street project. |
| **Taoiseach** | (i) Department is responsible for the Operational Programme for Local Urban and Rural Development (1994-99) which contains provision for childcare facilities.<br>(ii) Department chairs the Central Review Committee on Implementation of Partnership 2000 which contains commitments on a childcare strategy. |
| **Social, Community and Family Affairs** | (i) Department funds the Community Development Programme which includes projects with an involvement in childcare facilities.<br>(ii) Department co-funded projects in the Pilot Childcare Initiative (1994-95)<br>(iii) Department funds Family and Community Services Resources Centres which provide some childcare services. |
| **Justice, Equality and Law Reform** | (i) Department funded the Pilot Childcare Initiative and now funds the Equal Opportunities Childcare Programme.<br>(ii) Department chairs and services the Expert Working Group on Childcare under Partnership 2000, with the objective of developing a national framework for the co-ordination and further development of childcare.<br>(iii) Department is responsible for overseeing the implementation of the 1993 report of the Second Commission on the Status of Women.<br>(iv) Department is responsible for ensuring co-ordination between various departments and agencies in receipt of EU funding for childcare measures. |
| **Environment and Rural Development** | (i) Department funds Local Authorities, some of which, in turn, fund Community Playgroups. |
| **Agriculture and Food** | (i) Department is the National Authority responsible for LEADER 1 (1991-94) and LEADER 11 (1995-99) which encompass measures for women, some of which, in turn, include a childcare element. |

# Appendix 2

**Health Board Funding for Pre-School Services- 1996 allocations***

| Health Board | Number of Centres | Funding in 1996 |
|---|---|---|
| Eastern | 41 | £1,568,000 |
| Midland | 28 | £ 122,676 |
| Mid-Western | 67 | £ 164,920 |
| North-Eastern | 12 | £ 74,000 |
| North-Western | 71 | £ 95,000 |
| South Eastern | 93 | £ 180,000 |
| Southern | 90 | £ 233,766 |
| Western | 82 | £ 191,170 |
| TOTAL | | £ 2,629,532 |

* Source: Department of Health, Child Care Policy Unit.

The above figures represents the funding allocated for pre-school services by the eight Health Boards in the year 1996. Some boards have included in their figure block grants to organisations such as Barnardo's, and the Irish Pre-School Playgroup Association for provision of pre-school support.

### 13.1    Introduction

Education was the most frequently mentioned topic in submissions to the Commission. People saw education as fundamental to the equipping of the next generation to meet the challenges of a changing society. They expressed great confidence in the potential of education to redress inequalities in society and improve life's prospects for children. The partnership role of parents in educating their children and in the ethos of the school were considered important. There were strong views about education promoting children's self-esteem, about pressures on students and about overcoming the inequalities faced by children from disadvantaged backgrounds.

The contribution of the education services and their role in the economic and social well-being of society is immense, as the submissions to the Commission illustrate. For the purposes of this report the Commission is concentrating on a number of specific topics. These are:

- The need for a new focus on provision of services for children in the pre-school age-group and the need for greater investment in services at primary school level.
- The contribution of education services in relation to
- equipping young people to reach their potential as adults, family members and contributing members of society,
- improving life choices for young people.

## AN OVERVIEW OF EDUCATION PROVISION

### 13.2    Primary level education

The primary sector comprises national schools, special schools and non-aided private primary schools. There are approximately 458,000 children aged between four and twelve in primary schools throughout the country. The national schools, which account for the education of 98 per cent of children in the primary sector, are staffed by more than 20,000 teachers. More than half the schools have four or fewer teachers. The pupil-teacher ratio for 1997/98 is less than 22:1.

The primary school curriculum is based on child-centred principles, which include the full, harmonious and individual development of the child, the central importance of activity and guided discovery learning and teaching methods, and teaching and learning in an integrated way, which is related to the child's environment.

**Studies at primary level**

Children follow a curriculum which is arranged in the following categories: Religion, Language (comprising Irish and English),Mathematics, Social and Environmental Studies, Art and Craft Studies, Music, and Physical Education. According to the *Primary School Curriculum Teachers Handbook 1971*, curricula allow for flexibility in selecting the programmes most suitable and feasible for each school and for each pupil. The school and its environment, its facilities, and the particular aptitudes and interests of pupils and teachers, are the relevant considerations when making the selection.

Work is well advanced within the National Council for Curriculum and Assessment[1] and the Department of Education and Science on a wide-ranging revision of the primary level curriculum. According to *Charting our Education Future*[2] greater emphasis will be placed on speech, reading, writing, basic numeracy and problem solving skills. The development of personal and social creativity and technological skills will be fostered through arts education and a new science programme.

## 13.3    Second-level education

There are approximately 368,000 students in second level. There are 768 publicly aided schools: 445 of them are secondary, 246 are vocational and 77 are community or comprehensive. [3]

Sixty-one per cent of students are attending secondary schools. These are privately owned and managed. The majority are conducted by religious communities. Over 95 per cent of the cost of teachers' salaries is met by the State. In addition, allowances and capitation grants are paid to 95 per cent of secondary schools which participate in the free education scheme.

Vocational schools cater for 26 per cent of students. Vocational schools receive 93 per cent of their costs from the State. The remaining funds are raised locally.

Community and comprehensive schools are allocated individual budgets by the State. Thirteen per cent of second-level students are attending these schools.

### Two cycles at second level

There are two cycles of second-level education. A three year junior cycle leads to the Junior Certificate. The aim at junior cycle is for pupils to complete a broad, balanced and coherent course of studies in a variety of disciplines. The approved course for the junior cycle must include the following subjects : Irish, English, Mathematics, History and Geography (not compulsory in community, comprehensive or vocational schools), Civic, Social and Political Education, and not less than two other subjects from the approved list of examination subjects.

This is followed by a Transition Year programme which is available as an option in most schools. There is a choice of three two year Leaving Certificate programmes: the established Leaving Certificate, the Leaving Certificate Applied and the Leaving Certificate Vocational programme, which provide a range of programmes appropriate to the students' needs and are designed to develop each student's potential to the full and equip him/her for work or further education.

---

1    The NCCA advise the Minister for Education on all matters relating to curriculum development and their work is overseen by a Council composed of 22 members, eighteen of whom are appointed on a representational basis, which includes representatives of management authorities of schools, Teacher Unions, Parents Representative Organisations, Third-Level Institutions, Industry and Trade Union interests.  Amongst the nominating bodies are the National Parents Council, both Primary, and Post-Primary.

2    The publication of the Green Paper, *Education for a Changing World,* was followed by a long consultative process, which included the National Education Convention of 1993, involving all  the partners in education, and culminated with the publication of  the White Paper in Education, Charting Our Education Future (1995), which set out a framework for the future development of education into the next century.

3    Statistics for 1995/96 supplied by the Department of Education and Science.

**Leaving Certificate Programmes**

In the case of the established Leaving Certificate, the approved course for students must include not less than five of the subjects from the following five groups, of which one shall be Irish: language group, science group, business studies group, applied science group and the social studies group.

The Leaving Certificate Vocational programme is aimed at strengthening the vocational, technical, language and entrepreneurial dimensions of senior cycle curricula. Students choose at least two related technical/ vocational subjects, or a technical/vocational subject linked with business skills, allied with new technology skills, a continental language, enterprise training and a work experience programme. They follow three Link Modules on Enterprise Education, Preparation for Work and Work Experience, and take at least five Leaving Certificate subjects, one of which must be Irish. Subjects can be taken at either higher or ordinary level and students can progress from the programme to Post Leaving Certificate courses, or directly to Regional Technical College/ Dublin Institute of Technology or degree programmes. The Link Modules are recognised for points purposes by the Regional Technical Colleges' and Institutes of Technology. This programme is now being followed by approximately 23,000 pupils in 440 schools.

The Leaving Certificate Applied is an approved course for senior cycle students. The Leaving Certificate Applied is intended to meet the needs of those students who are not adequately catered for by other Leaving Certificate programmes or who choose not to opt for such programmes. It is an innovative programme, in the way students learn, in what they learn, and in the way their achievements are assessed. All Leaving Certificate Applied courses are organised in modules (periods of study of approximately 40 hours). Students take a total of 40 modules over the two-year programme. The modular approach allows for the setting of short-term goals for students, provides them with a wide range of course material, and familiarises them with an approach to learning which they will encounter in later study/work. The Leaving Certificate Applied programme is followed by over 7,000 pupils at present and is scheduled to expand further in the coming years.

**13.4    Promoting recognition of a wide range of abilities**

The Commission welcomes the move towards recognition for and assessment of, a wider range of abilities and recent initiatives to promote public awareness of new programmes. These include briefing sessions for parents and funding to schools for initiatives involving the social partners in the programmes. Discussions have also taken place with government departments, public bodies and  employer bodies regarding the suitability of the programmes to a range of employments and further education.

While there is not direct access from the Leaving Certificate Applied to third-level education, there is access to most Post Leaving Certificate courses and thereby to higher education in accordance with the pathways of progression devised by the National Council for Vocational Awards in consultation with the various institutes of technology.

These moves towards recognition of a wider range of abilities are particularly welcome in relation to providing for those children who may be at risk of dropping out of school because the system does not place a value on or recognise their individual abilities and competencies. **The Commission is of the view that if the value of education is to be reinforced for these young people and their families, then it is important that all forms of State certification have a value in terms of training and employment prospects and progression to third-level education. In this context, it is important that the qualification criteria for access to apprenticeship and training programmes and for further education are kept under review and that employers are fully informed about new developments in the Junior and Leaving Certificate programmes.**

## 13.5    Early school leaving

The National Economic and Social Forum, in its report on early school leavers[4] and youth unemployment, has set out details which illustrate the extent of early school-leaving and educational disadvantage.

The details, which refer to the period 1993-95, show annual averages :
- up to 1,000 children did not progress to second level school
- 3,000 of which 1,970 were boys and 1,030 were girls left second-level school with no qualification
- 7,600 (4,900 boys and 2,700 girls) left school having completed Junior Certificate only , of which 2,400 failed to achieve at least five grade Ds in the Junior Certificate
- 2,600 young people (1,400 boys and 1,200 girls) left school having completed the Junior Certificate and a Vocational Preparatory Training course only
- around 7,000 (some 4,000 boys and 3,000 girls) did not achieve five passes in the Leaving Certificate examination.

The rate of drop-out of those who leave school without junior cycle qualifications has decreased from 4,600, or 7.5 per cent, in 1983/84 to 2,700, or 4 per cent, in 1994/95. Completion rates to Leaving Certificate have increased from 70 per cent in 1986 to 81 per cent in 1994/95. The National Anti-Poverty Strategy sets a target that the percentage of those completing senior cycle should increase to at least 90 per cent by the year 2000 and 98 per cent by the year 2007. [5]

Early school-leaving is a particular concern because of the damaging employment and social consequences which young people face if they have low educational attainments.

### Increasing provision for early school-leavers

As part of the Mid-Term Review of the Structural Funds, 1994-99, new initiatives have been agreed for implementation in 1998 and 1999, under which :
- funding will be provided for an additional 1,000 places for early school-leavers in the Youthreach and Traveller training programmes
- £1.97 million will be provided for bridging and progression options for early school leavers through the FÁS Training System, and 725 places within the FÁS system will be re-deployed to progression options for Youthreach and Traveller trainees in 1998. This will increase provision for early school-leavers from 4,525 places to 6,250, with a further 440 places per annum available under the FÁS bridging measures.

---

4    National Economic and Social Forum, *Early School Leavers and Youth Unemployment*, Report No. 11. January 1997.

5    *Sharing in Progress*, National Anti-Poverty Strategy, April 1997, Stationery Office, Dublin.

In addition, £2.96 million will be provided over 1998 and 1999 for pilot projects in urban and rural areas to cater for young people aged 8-15 at risk of early school-leaving. A Department of Education and Science Working Group has been established to advance the initiative, with a view to implementation in early 1998.

The White paper *Charting Our Education Future* proposed to raise the minimum school-leaving age from fifteen years to sixteen years or the completion of three years of junior cycle education, whichever is later. It is proposed that this change should be included in the new school attendance legislation, to be formulated in 1998.

### 13.6    Third-Level and other Post-Leaving Certificate courses

Numbers in third-level education have grown rapidly in recent years - to more than 105,000 in 1997/98. In 1980, 20 per cent of young people of the relevant age cohort went on to third-level education. In 1995, this figure had increased to 48 per cent, of which about half take degree level programmes. Third-level education institutions comprise: seven universities, twelve institutions designated under the Regional Technical Colleges Act 1992, the Dublin Institute of Technology, Colleges of Education and privately funded institutions.

The free fees initiative was introduced from the beginning of 1995 and, from the 1996/97 academic year, the State met the full tuition fees of eligible students attending full-time undergraduate courses. A total of over 95,000 students at present benefit from the initiative.

### 13.7    Maintenance grants for students

Means-tested grants are available to eligible students who are pursuing approved university courses, in general full-time undergraduate courses of not less than two years' duration. Students eligible for grants under the scheme include those entering approved courses for the first time, mature students who are entering an approved course at postgraduate level for the first time or are re-entering to complete an approved course at undergraduate level, and second chance students (those who are returning to pursue approved courses following a break from study of five years). In general, a student must be seventeen years of age, be an EU national, be ordinarily resident in the administrative area of the local authority, obtain a place on an approved course and satisfy the means test.

Maintenance grants will be introduced for participants on post-Leaving Certificate courses with effect from September 1998. The rates of grant and means-testing criteria will be on a par with the existing third-level schemes.

Expenditure on the Higher Education Grants Scheme in 1996 was almost £66 million; over 27,000 students received grants in that year.

There is a widely held view that the level of maintenance grant is too low, particularly in comparison with the level of unemployment payments. The view has been expressed to the Commission that the fact that rates of unemployment payments or supplementary welfare allowance are higher than rates of maintenance grants is an incentive to young people to leave the education system as soon as they become eligible for such payments, with consequent adverse implications for their further educational development.

**With this in mind, the Commission recommends that an analysis be undertaken of the rates of maintenance grants for students with a view to ensuring that future levels reflect the importance of encouraging young people to remain in the education system until they have obtained a qualification which can contribute to their future economic and social development. As an interim measure, the Commission recommends that the maintenance grants should be increased to assist students in low income families.**

## 13.8 Alternative educational programmes

A range of alternative educational programmes has been developed in recent years, including post-Leaving Certificate courses (21,263 students in 1997/98) and apprenticeship courses, where the target annual intake into 24 existing statutory recognised trades is 3,500 young people.

## 13.9 Continuing Education

There are also extensive adult education programmes and informal and continuing education programmes. These are provided by the Vocational Education Committees (VECs) and other educational institutions. They play an increasingly significant role in widening access to education and in providing opportunities for skills development for people.

In this context, the Commission notes the appointment of a Minister of State with a brief which specifically includes adult education and it welcomes the commitment to adult education in the Government's programme.

In recent years there has been a growth in second chance education, providing opportunities for unemployed people and early school-leavers to pursue qualifications. Second chance programmes include the Vocational Training Opportunities Scheme of the Department of Education and Science (about 5,000 places). In addition, some 4,525 places are provided on programmes for early school-leavers and Travellers by FÁS and the VECs. The Department of Social, Community and Family Affairs also enables educational opportunities to be taken up by long-term social welfare recipients through their second and third-level allowance schemes.

The problem of illiteracy among adults has recently been shown to be of much greater proportions than had been realised. A survey carried out by the OECD, published in October 1997, revealed that 25 per cent of the adult population, some 500,000 people, were at the lowest literacy level. Resources made available to VECs to tackle the adult literacy problem have been significantly increased.

## 13.10 The constitutional right of families to educate their children

Article 42 of the Constitution sets out the framework within which the education system has developed. The constitutional provisions acknowledge the family as the primary and natural educator of the child and set out the roles of parents and the State in providing for the education of children.

Article 42.1 states: The State acknowledges that the primary and natural educator of the child is the family and guarantees to respect the inalienable right and duty of parents to provide, according to their means, for the religious and moral, intellectual, physical and social education of their children.

In their purest form, these provisions support the right of parents to educate their children privately, at home or in schools, with minimum involvement by the State.

Although most parents choose to avail of formal schooling for their children, the role of the family in the child's development remains central up to and into adulthood. Parents bring to their children's education the unique expertise derived from intimate knowledge of their child's development, of their child's particular needs and interests and of circumstances outside the school.

The parental role confers on parents the right to active participation in their child's education. This entails parents' rights as individuals to be consulted and informed on all aspects of the child's education and their rights as a group to be active participants in the education system at local level (in the school) and at national level (in planning and consultation). They also have responsibilities. Parents are expected to nurture a learning environment, to co-operate with and support the school and other educational partners, and to fulfil their special role in the development of the child.[6] The NCCA provides a specific role for parents in the development of new curricula at first and second level.

### 13.11 Legislation

There has been no substantive legislation enacted in relation to first and second-level education since the Vocational Education Act, 1930. In regard to third level, the National University of Ireland legislation was enacted in 1908 and the University of Dublin charters date from 1591. Legislation in relation to the University of Limerick, Dublin City University, the Dublin Institute of Technology and Regional Technical Colleges is of very recent origin. The Universities Act 1997, restructures the National University of Ireland (NUI) through the reconstitution of the three former constituent colleges, at Dublin, Cork and Galway, as constituent universities of the NUI and the establishment of the former NUI Recognised College at St. Patrick's College, Maynooth as a constituent university of the NUI. [7]

The Education (No. 2) Bill, published in December 1997 provides for specific legislative provision to underpin the administration of the education system, and for the fundamental rights and duties of parents, patrons/owners, students, teachers and the State in the education system. According to the Department of Education and Science a central objective of the Bill is to provide a statutory framework within which the education system can function in a spirit of partnership between the various parties involved, in the interests of ensuring the provision of a high quality education to each individual, including those with special educational needs.

---

6    Draws on *Charting Our Education Future*.

7    The Act provides for revised governance structures for the universities generally. It provides for a framework for interaction between the institutional autonomy of the universities and central government. The Act recognises the centrality of academic freedom and institutional autonomy to the mission of the universities and makes the provision for the obligations of the institutions in relation to equality of opportunity and access, quality assurance, the effective and efficient use of resources and the requirements of public accountability. The Higher Education Authority is given key functions in respect of these aspects of the operation of the universities.

## INVESTING IN PRE-SCHOOL SERVICES

### 13.17  Pre-school Early education

The Commission is of the view that there is a need for a new focus on provision for children under school-going age.

The role of good quality early education in compensating for social and background disadvantage and in improving educational achievement and life chances is well documented. More generally, good quality programmes have an impact on children's aspirations, motivation and school commitment, [15] as well as long-term positive effects on the quality of life of the adult.[16]

The Department of Education and Science programmes for pre- school children are directed at compensating for background disadvantage. The Rutland Street Project, the pre-school services for Traveller children and Early Start have been introduced to meet this objective.

However, there is a growing recognition that quality early education experiences are valuable and important to *all children*. Our greater knowledge about child development, and emerging findings in relation to the competencies and capabilities of young children, is leading more and more parents to seek out quality learning experiences for their young children. This is an important priority for parents who depend on day-care outside the home for their children. It is also being recognised as important by those parents who choose to rear their children full-time in the home.[17]

The rationale for the provision of services for young children[18] is entirely centred on the beneficial effects for all children, in terms of educational and social development. However, the issue cannot be divorced from the growing demand for childcare services in Ireland as parents struggle to balance their need to work outside the home with their child-rearing responsibilities. Lack of such services also poses a major barrier to those who are seeking to re-enter education and training and can result in continued poverty and marginalisation for families, given the proven inter-generational effects of educational disadvantage. The pressures which parents are under and the very real difficulties they face in securing quality childcare places has to some extent distracted attention from the case for a *national policy on early years services* centred on the child's educational and social development.

---

15   Sylva, K, OP Cit P11; Tobin, J.J. Wu, D. Y. Davidson, D.H. (1989) *"Pre-school in Three Cultures"* London: Yale University Press.

16   Berruti-Clement et al (1984) Changed Lives: *The Effects of the Perry Pre-school Programme on Youth Through Age 19*, Ypsilanti, Michigan: The High Scope Press: Kellaghan, T and Greaney, B (1997) *The Educational Development of Students following participation in a pre-school programme in a disadvantaged area'*, Dublin : ERC Research paper: Osborn A.F. & Millbank J.E.

17   According to the survey undertaken by the Commission, a significant number of children under school-going age with a parent working full-time in the home are attending crèches or nurseries. In almost half the households (46% or 17,300 households) which use the services of a creche/ nursery, the mother works full-time in the home.

18   As pointed out in  Chapter 12 services for children cover "childcare" and "pre-school". They include a whole range of services for young children provided outside the home, including childminding, nurseries/ crĒches, pre-schools and playgroups. In Ireland, these services range from a predominantly childminding focus to those which are designed to foster learning and the emotional and social development of the child. Fees are usually paid for these services.

In chapter 12 the Commission sets out its views on the role of public policy in supporting parents with their childcare needs and the future development of services for children. In this chapter, the Commission considers the educational aspects of pre-school provision.[19] The Commission's approach to the issues involved is rooted in its conviction that provision for children must be centred on the child's need for a positive experience of childhood and support for parents and their choices in relation to rearing and educating their children.

### 13.18 Development of a policy on early years services for children

There is no explicit State policy in relation to early years services. There has been a huge growth in family day-care, nurseries, crèches, pre-school and playgroups to meet the demand for childcare and, to some extent, the demand for social development for children, but outside the role of pre-school provision in compensating for social disadvantage, little attention has been given by policy-makers to the wider benefits of early education for the general population of children.

The Commission in Chapter 12 has highlighted the increasing attention now being paid to this topic.

The Commission has recommended in Chapter 12 that the importance of the years immediately preceding school entry for opportunities to participate in quality services for children should be acknowledged by *public investment*, on a par with the investment in children in the infant classes in primary school.

It is recommended in Chapter 12 that, in today's terms, the target level of investment should be £1,000 per child per annum. The Commission further recommends that the investment should be centred on the child and, having regard to parents' choice in relation to the care of their children, the investment should be directed through an Early Years Opportunities Subsidy to secure opportunities to avail of quality services for children in crèches/ nurseries, pre-schools and playgroups which meet the standards set out in Part VII of the Child Care Act 1991.

### 13.19 National Forum on Early Education

The Commission welcomes the commitment in the programme for Government for a specific budget for pre-school education and the recent National Forum on Early Childhood Education, representative of all interests in this area. The Commission welcomes the commitment by the Minister for Education and Science to prepare a White Paper, setting out policy in relation to early childhood education.

The Commission recommends a child-centred approach in the exploration of the issues surrounding early years education and, in this context, the Commission would like to offer the following comments:

A quality early years curriculum

The Commission considers that the formulation of the curricular framework for early education is fundamental to the development of early years services for young children.

---

19   All services for this age-group include an element of care and protection as well as education. There are issues about promoting good practices and high standards in the care of children and the Commission's views on these issues and in relation to the State's role in ensuring adequacy, quality and accessibility in the services for young children are set out in Chapter 12.

There is a need for a broad approach to what should constitute a quality early years curriculum. It is generally accepted that early years services must meet all the needs of children - physical, emotional and cognitive - and not just focus on the academic.

The Commission would like to draw attention to the report of the EC Network on Childcare, *Quality Targets in Services for Young Children*.[20] Education in the context of pre-school children is described as a broader concept than schooling. The report says : It is about beginning to understand the significance of a print-rich and numerate environment, but also about the need for personal autonomy, self-sufficiency and self-care and the need to acquire skills for social and group life. While accepting that all young children acquire some of these skills, whatever their circumstances, the report puts forward a number of targets in relation to the education aspects of services for children to enhance such development and enable young children to be autonomous, to enjoy their lives and to relish learning.[21]

### Training and qualifications

It is the Commission's view that there should be recognition of *a wide range of qualifications* in relation to the provision of early year's services for children. The availability of different approaches to early years' education provides more choice for parents in meeting their children's needs, as well as increasing the opportunities for more people to take up work in providing services for children.

The Commission would like to see a broad assessment  of the potential contribution to quality early education of training and accreditation increasingly being made available through community and 2nd chance educational initiatives. The Commission considers that these initiatives may provide a role for experienced women from the community in the provision of pre-school education and care.

The Commission would like to recognise the work of both FÁS and the National Council for Vocational Awards in developing national certification for childcare qualifications. The Commission further considers that initiatives such as the DIT NOW[22] childcare project, which is attempting to address the situation by seeking mutual agreement on a co-ordinated system of accreditation for training in early childhood care and education and the setting up of a system for the accreditation of experience, achievement and learning, can provide valuable assistance in promoting recognition of qualifications.

*Early Start has the potential to make an important contribution* to *the development of national policy on early education.* The National Economic and Social Forum[23] has highlighted the potential of Early Start for providing a model of excellence in relation to the provision of early education. The Commission concurs with the view expressed by the National Economic and Social Forum that the experience and the evaluation findings of Early Start should be made available to all those interested in early education and childcare.

---

20    The report offers ideas, examples and guidance, drawing on Europe-wide experience in relation to criteria for quality in relation to services for children.

21    *Quality Targets in Services for Young Children*, European Commission Network on Childcare and other Measures to Reconcile Employment and Family Responsibilities.

22    Dublin Institute of  Technology/New Opportunities for Women: Childcare Project.

23    *Early School Leavers and Youth Unemployment,* Forum Report No. 11., January, 1997.

### 13.20 Prioritising investment in primary-level education

The Commission is further of the view that there is a need to balance investment at different levels of education in favour of the early years of school and throughout primary level. On equity grounds alone, there is a case for comparable investment in these early years. Moreover, research shows the value of early intervention and investment to offset the risk of lack of attainment in education.

The projected falling enrolments, owing to the decline in the birth rate, and the favourable forecasts for continued improvement in Ireland's economic well-being provide a unique opportunity for increasing investment in education, particularly in primary-level education.

Declining enrolments in the primary system in recent years have meant that hundreds of teaching posts which became surplus were retained to effect improvements to the staffing schedule and to provide additional teaching posts for the special education/ educational disadvantage areas.

The Commission considers that the savings arising from the demographic changes should continue to be used to meet the special needs of pupils including the need for more resource materials and equipment for schools, and to further improve pupil teacher ratios, particularly in the early years of primary school, the priority being those schools catering for children who live in communities that are coping with multiple disadvantage.

**The Commission recommends**

- increased resources be invested in primary education
- continued reductions in the pupil teacher ratios, particularly in the earlier years of primary school, the priority being those schools catering for children who live in communities coping with multiple disadvantage.

The Commission notes the commitment in *An Action Programme for the Millennium* to give primary education a clear priority in allocating resources.

## EQUIPPING YOUNG PEOPLE TO REACH THEIR POTENTIAL AS CITIZENS, FAMILY MEMBERS AND CONTRIBUTING MEMBERS OF SOCIETY.

### 13.21 Curriculum undergoing change

*"Living a full life requires both knowledge and skills appropriate to age, environment, and social and economic roles as well as the ability to function in a world of increasing complexity and to adapt to continuously changing circumstances without sacrificing personal integrity".* [24]

Education plays an important role in preparation for life. In recent years the importance of equipping young people with the knowledge and skills they need to reach their potential as citizens, family members and members of society has taken on a new prominence.

24    "Charting our Education Future", Part 1

The educational system in Ireland is now undergoing changes at all levels. As part of this change the National Council for Curriculum and Assessment is undertaking reform of the curriculum for first and second-level pupils. Reference has been made earlier to the review of the curriculum at primary level. Some of the changes which have been introduced for students at second level include :

### Civic, Social and Political Education
The introduction of a new course in Civic, Social and Political Education replacing Civics.

### Junior Cycle Schools Programme
In September 1996 a new Junior Certificate Elementary Programme (now called the junior cycle schools programme) was introduced to cater for students whose learning needs are not being adequately met by the junior certificate. The programme was introduced into 45 centres in the 1996/97 school year; it was extended to an additional 16 in 1997/98 and it is intended to extend it to a further 20 in 1998/99.

### Transition Year
The Transition Year - between the end of the Junior Certificate and the beginning of the Leaving Certificate - is intended to promote the personal, social, educational and vocational development of students and to prepare them to participate as responsible members of society. Each school designs its own programme, to meet the particular needs of its students within guidelines set by the Department of Education and Science.[25]

In the 1996/97 school year, 501 schools provided Transition Year to approx.24,000 students.

The Commission particularly welcomes the introduction of the Transition Year Programme (TYP). The Commission is of the view that the basic rationale of the TYP, based on the development of personal skills, curriculum flexibility, an emphasis on preparation for life, and negotiated, self-directed learning without examination pressures, has the potential to make a significant contribution to young people in equipping them for the world of adulthood.

**It is the Commission's view that the year-long programme should be widely available in all second-level schools and that it should be the norm for students to avail of this option before embarking on senior cycle studies.**

## 13.22 Family awareness studies
In pursuance of its terms of reference which *inter alia* required the Commission to raise awareness and improve understanding of family issues, the Commission has developed a module of studies on family matters, which is offered as an option to students in Transition Year.

---

25  The support services to assist schools to introduce the new programmes are in place. Fourteen teachers have been seconded to the Transition Year Support Team in the Blackrock Education Centre to assist schools to develop and implement their Transition Year programmes.

The Family Awareness module of studies was formally launched in March 1997. It is now available to 26,000 students.

The family awareness module presents students with an opportunity to explore in a classroom setting, the complexities of family life, through studying topics such as:
- roles and responsibilities within the family
- communication and understanding between the generations,
- the management of family finances
- the media and its influence on family life.

### A National competition

A national competition on family themes which was also developed by the Commission for Transition Year students attracted the participation of over 2,000 students in 1997. The projects submitted by the students covered a wide range of family topics.

*Social studies projects* in Irish and English, investigated a mosaic of family situations and experiences.

*Short stories* and *one-act plays* written by students explored the feelings of young adults and their peers and relationships within families.

*The Art category* attracted entries which displayed the talent and creativity of young people.

The winning entry in the art category was exhibited by the National Gallery of Ireland to celebrate UN International Day of Families 1997. The Commission was most impressed by the enthusiasm, commitment and talent of all the students who participated in the competition and their ability to undertake and explore, social developments within Irish society.

**The Commission suggests that the possibility of an annual competition on family themes which would promote awareness among students about families and their importance to society should be explored further by the proposed Family Affairs Unit in the Department of Social, Community and Family Affairs.**

**13.23    Health promotion and Social, Personal and Health Education**

The general aim of education is to contribute towards the development of all aspects of the individual, including the creative, cultural, intellectual, moral, political, religious, social and spiritual development for personal and family life, for living in the community and for leisure.[26]

Two initiatives have been introduced into the education system which provide a framework within which the need for "all round" development of the individual can be examined. These are Health Promoting Schools and Social, Personal and Health Education.

---

26    Relationships and Sexuality Education, Interim Curriculum and Guidelines for post-primary schools, Department of Education.

**Health Promoting Schools**[27]

A project entitled the Health Promoting School is underway in a number of primary and second-level schools. The basic aim of the project is to develop a whole school approach to health promotion with links to parents and the community and an emphasis on social and personal development. The Health Promoting School sets out to create the means for all who live and work within the school to take control over and improve their physical and emotional health. Schools are encouraged to adopt an integrated, holistic approach to health promotion and the curriculum is structured to present pupils with opportunities to study aspects of health education throughout their school careers.

Essential elements of the Health Promoting School concept are :
- a health promoting environment - physical and psycho-social
- a timetabled co-ordinated programme for social, personal and health education
- links with families and community- promoting involvement in all aspects of school life
- the development of supporting policies for the implementation of good practice and procedures.

There are now 20 primary and 20 second-level schools involved in the Health Promoting School Network. The Commission has been advised that the intention is to expand the network gradually.

**The Health Promoting School provides the framework for Social, Personal and Health Education**

It is the Commission's view that the introduction of the Health Promoting School concept is a very valuable and positive development in Irish schools. **The Commission recommends that the Health Promoting School concept to be extended to all schools. Furthermore it is the Commission's view that the objectives of a Social, Personal and Health Education programme can best be realised within the supportive framework of the Health Promoting School.**

**13.24    Social, Personal and Health Education (SPHE)**

The curriculum in primary and post-primary schools is undergoing adaptations relating to education for life and personal development.

Providing young people with opportunities to acquire basic personal and social skills which will foster integrity, self-confidence and self esteem and nurture sensitivity towards others is an essential component of Social, Personal and Health Education. A young person who has a high degree of self-worth, a sense of security and a positive self-image will be more predisposed to participate in school life and in the variety of learning situations it offers. This is increasingly being recognised within the education system and schools at all levels are developing Social, Personal and Health Education programmes.

---

27    Draws from conference resolution of First Conference of the EU Network of Health Promoting Schools, May 1997.

Several initiatives of health and personal development come within the framework of Social, Personal and Health Education.

### Stay Safe programme

The Stay Safe programme aims to prevent child abuse by equipping parents and teachers with the knowledge and skills to protect the children in their care so that they are aware of the difficulties children can encounter and know how to respond to them. Children are taught personal safety skills as part of a broad safety curriculum which aims to prevent various types of victimisation and enhance self-esteem. Stay Safe is being taught in 80 per cent of primary level schools (1996-97) and is being extended to second-level schools in the context of the Relationships and Sexuality Education (RSE) programme.

### Substance Misuse Programme (primary level)

In 1996/97 a major anti-drugs awareness campaign was introduced for young people. The campaign focused initially on areas where the drug problem is particularly acute. As part of the campaign, a Substance Misuse programme was introduced in primary schools. The programme consists of :

- awareness and information initiatives for the school management, teachers and parents in co-operation with the local community
- the preparation and dissemination of educational resource materials for schools
- a particular focus on areas where drugs, especially heroin, are known to be seriously abused.

An important part of the programme is the development of a range of educational resource materials for use with primary pupils. The materials have been tested on a pilot basis in twenty-six primary schools. They are being introduced to primary schools on a phased basis, first to schools in the priority areas identified in the Government's strategy for tackling drug misuse. These areas are mainly parts of Dublin city and Cork city, and thereafter in primary schools throughout the country. A programme of in-service training for teachers is also being put in place. Training has commenced for teachers in the pilot schools and this training will continue as the programme is expanded to include all the country's primary schools.

### Substance Abuse Prevention Programme (Second level)

"On My Own Two Feet" is the educational initiative against drugs misuse at second level. Development of personal and social skills is an integral part of the programmes and the Health Promoting Schools Network plays a significant role in prevention programmes at second level.

### Youthreach

"On My Own Two Feet" has also been introduced in Youthreach centres. A new Copping On crime awareness programme is also being implemented on a phased basis in Youthreach centres; part of the programme is designed to foster assertiveness, self-esteem and the decision making skills needed to challenge attitudes to crime and to substance abuse.

### Healthy living initiatives

Health boards have introduced several initiatives for schools in their own localities for example, nutrition, education, growing up in health and projects to promote awareness about skin cancer.

**13.25** **Relationships and Sexuality Education**
Submissions to the Commission on health and welfare aspects of education generally welcomed the introduction of social, personal and health education and spoke positively about the contribution that relationships and sexuality education, taught in a sensitive atmosphere, could make to enhancing the life skills of young people. Some people were concerned to ensure that the context within which relationships and sexuality education was taught reinforced the primary values which the young person learns at home.

There is growing consensus about the importance to young people of social, personal and health education programmes including relationships and sexuality education. An ESRI School-Leavers Survey of 1991 showed that only one-fifth of young people expressed satisfaction with their preparation in school for adult life roles and relationships with friends of the opposite sex.[28]

*A Relationships and Sexuality Education (RSE) programme,* [29] prepared by the NCCA, is being introduced as part of the primary and post-primary curriculum. The content of the programme has been developed to suit the age and maturity of the student. The RSE programme is designed to equip children and young people with knowledge and understanding of human sexuality and relationships in a way that will enable them to form values and establish behaviours within a moral, spiritual and social framework.

Parents are involved in the development of the RSE programme at two levels:
- nationally, as members of the NCCA, and also as members of the National Implementation Group, they have helped to develop the programme,
- at school level, the implementation strategy for the RSE programme provides for the establishment of a committee, to include representatives of parents, to draft an RSE policy statement for each individual school. The draft statement will be disseminated to all parents and their views sought.

In the meantime, some schools had already developed policies and programmes in this field. It has been suggested to the Commission, however, that availability of relationships and sexuality education to date has been uneven, fragmented and often delivered in a way which is unconnected to the school curriculum. The introduction of the new RSE programme will redress this difficulty.

---

28   D.F. Hannan, S. Shortall, *The quality of their education* ESRI 1991

29   See Appendix 1 to this chapter for details of the framework for the development of the programme.

The involvement of parents is a key feature of the policy approach to introducing RSE at school level. It is the Commission's view that parents are the primary educators of their children in this sensitive matter and as such have a partnership role to play in the development and implementation of an appropriate school policy for the delivery of an RSE programme. [30]

The Commission notes the widespread interest and general approval in submissions which it has received for the Relationships and Sexuality Education programme. The Commission also notes the concern that this programme should be taught in accordance with the values expressed in students' own homes. **The Commission welcomes the partnership approach adopted by the Department of Education and Science in both developing and introducing this programme. The Commission considers it crucial that this approach be maintained and where possible further developed.**

### 13.26    A broad approach to studies relevant to family life

The Social, Personal and Health Education Programme, incorporating the Stay Safe programme, the Substance Misuse programme and the Relationship and Sexuality Education programme, are particularly welcome in that they provide young people with knowledge and skills which will enhance their ability to make informed judgements about their relationships and the way they lead their lives. However, outside these specific programmes, it is the Commission's view that other opportunities to take on studies relevant to health and personal development and family life are somewhat diffuse and peripheral to the core curriculum.

Opportunities to explore and learn about personal and health development and relationships and family issues arise elsewhere in the curriculum, for example through work in English and Irish literature, Religious Education, Home Economics - Social and Scientific, through the Civic, Social and Political Education programme at junior cycle level, and through the Transition Year programme and the Leaving Certificate Applied, which provide students with the opportunity to pursue specific modules on parenting, care of older people and education for family life.

The Commission notes that the National Council for Curriculum and Assessment was requested to provide guidelines for the introduction of SPHE as part of the core curriculum of all schools at both levels. It further notes that the NCCA's committee dealing with the primary curriculum has produced its report and that SPHE will be a part of the revised primary curriculum. At second level, the report is expected before recommendations are made along the same lines.

---

30    This view underpins the approach of the Expert Advisory Group set up by the Minister for Education to advise on RSE. The principles put forward by the Expert Group in relation to a framework for the development of RSE in schools are based on the premise that "parents are in law and in fact, the primary educators, that home is the natural environment in which Relationship and Sexuality Education should take place and that the school has a role to play in supporting and complementing the work of home in this task." See Appendix 1 to this chapter for further details.

**13.27    Family life education - throughout school years**

The Commission believes that a far more fundamental response to the requirements of young people today is needed, together with a radical approach to the introduction of family life education throughout the school curriculum, from early school years through to completion of formal education. **This could be achieved through the introduction of an expanded Social, Personal and Health Education programme which is fully integrated in the school curriculum. The programme could be introduced within the framework of the Health Promoting School.**

An expanded Social, Personal and Health Education programme might include:

- **Healthy life styles**
  including personal care, nutrition, the importance of a balanced diet and exercise, information about eating disorders, illness and disease, and the effects of smoking, alcohol and substance abuse. Studies should be informed by the health promotion and disease prevention objectives set out in the Health Strategy for the 1990s. [31] Co-operation between the Department of Education and Science and the Health Promotion Unit is a feature of working towards the achievement of many of the targets in the health strategy. The Commission considers that making nutrition and health and personal welfare studies a central part of the curriculum would contribute to the achievement of the targets of the strategy.

  In this context, the Commission would like to draw attention to the importance of Home Economics, a subject which has been on the second-level curriculum for many years. At present one in three students take Home Economics at their Leaving Certificate. The subject is still taken up largely by young women. In other countries, in the UK in particular, there is a growing appreciation of the relevance of home economics subjects in improving health and nutrition in a young population where lifestyles are rapidly changing.

  **The Commission recommends that Home Economics - Social and Scientific should be promoted among students both male and female. The Commission suggests that part of the promotion might include a more appropriate title for the subject to reflect the fundamental importance of the syllabus content.**

- **Personal growth and development**
  This should include growing up, adolescence, friendships, relationships and sexuality, personal responsibility and decision-making, self-esteem and the development of coping strategies to deal with difficulties in life.

  "Young people need to grow up in an environment in which they can love and be loved, respect and be respected; trust and be trusted; develop self -confidence; establish good personal relationships both within the family and with their peers and make balanced decisions about how they wish to lead their lives."[32]

---

31    *Shaping a Healthier Future,* Department of Health

32    *Education for Parenthood and Family Life,* National Children's Bureau, No. 130

Self-esteem programmes undertaken in schools in other countries have proved to be particularly successful in increasing young people's self-confidence, self-respect and understanding of themselves.

- **Family and parenting skills**

  Experts are agreed on the need to adopt a lifecycle approach to education for parenthood. This approach involves the introduction of appropriate learning opportunities during the school years. Programmes need to present young people with a realistic picture of parenthood, including the difficulties which arise because of premature parenthood. Information about the responsibilities parenthood brings, the difficulties premature parenthood poses in meeting those responsibilities, the demanding needs of a baby and the care and development needs of children must be realistically presented to young people.

  The aim should be to improve knowledge about child development and children's needs and to challenge traditional gender stereotypes about parenthood and responsibilities. The Second Commission on the Status of Women has pointed out that it is important to develop emphasis within such a programme which would educate girls about the costs - in terms of missed opportunities - of early unplanned pregnancy. The Commission also points out that innovative programmes to present young people with practical examples of the demands of parenthood have been tried out abroad and could provide models for adaptation in the Irish context.

  The interdependence of family members and the rights, duties and responsibilities of families towards each other and the wider community could be explored as part of the programme. It is also important that family studies cover issues such as household budgets, consumer issues and the effective management of family resources.

- **Social awareness** studies could include issues to do with the wider community, social issues, disadvantage and an inclusive society, an appreciation of the role of older people and the contribution of all individuals to community and family life, the role of the statutory, public and voluntary services, and the importance of making a contribution by undertaking work of social and community value.

**13.28**   **Family and life education: some issues**

The Commission considers that an approach to the introduction of family and life education should reinforce the high status of the subjects related to family and life education in the school curriculum. The issue of status is essential to the successful implementation of such a programme throughout the school curriculum.

It has been suggested to the Commission that core subjects which are assessed at Junior and Leaving Certificate level and are relevant to third-level education are accorded a high status by students because of their potential to provide a structured career path for those who are considering further education. Other subjects which are considered by students as not being relevant to their chosen careers will not be accorded such a status.

**The Commission considers that in order to enhance the status of family and life education for students, their parents and teachers.**

- **relevant aspects of family and life education should be developed for assessment at junior and senior cycles**
- **relevant studies undertaken which are pertinent to family and life education should be accredited in assessing entrants for colleges of education, and perhaps other careers, such as careers in public health and childcare,**
- **there should be ongoing inservice training for teachers and the development of support services for schools in the provision of family and life education.**

### 13.29 Improving life chances and choices

In the earlier part of this chapter, the Commission made recommendations in relation to investment in primary level to provide more individual attention for children and improve resources, materials and equipment for schools. The Commission further considers that better access to support services for children with additional needs and their parents is particularly important at primary level so that children have access to help at an early age.

Education initiatives, such as Early Start, Breaking the Cycle, the Home/School/Community Liaison scheme, and the recently announced programme for eight to fifteen year olds to prevent early school leaving, have the potential to have a significant impact in redressing the implications of education disadvantage, preventing early school-leaving and improving the life choices of adults. Together with the effective management of attendance issues by schools, these initiatives are important components of a strategy to encourage and support young people at risk of early school leaving to stay on in the education system. Enhancing the attractiveness of staying in the education system must also be part of that strategy.

In this section the Commission makes a number of recommendations in relation to
- the education support services
- special education initiatives to prevent educational disadvantage and encourage young people to complete their education,
- provision for those who have left school without qualifications.

## EDUCATIONAL SUPPORT SERVICES

### 13.30 School psychological service

The school psychological service and the remedial teaching services have been identified in submissions to the Commission as key services which need to be expanded. The report on the National Education Convention concluded that the psychological service ought to be developed as an integrated one for both primary and post-primary schools. [33] The report acknowledged that, while the nature of the psychologist's role varies at primary and second levels, there is a need for more emphasis on educational guidance at both levels and a greater integration of the work of psychologists and teachers.

---

33   *Charting Our Education Future*, White Paper on Education, p.66.

The White Paper *Charting Our Education Future* states the case for early identification of a child's learning difficulties in the context of the objective that having regard to the assessment of their intrinsic abilities there are no students with serious literacy and numeracy problems in early primary education within the next 5 years.

The White Paper refers to classroom teachers carrying out the main responsibility for identifying and responding to learning difficulties. The expansion of the school psychological service to support teachers in this task and to ensure that every child with learning or behavioural difficulties has access to help at the earliest possible stage, are part of the strategy proposed to meet the needs of these children.

The National Economic and Social Forum has drawn attention to the inadequacies in the school psychological service with fewer than 40 psychologists in the service.

The Commission welcomes the commitment in the Programme for Government to the setting up of a national psychological service to address learning difficulties. The Commission notes also that a planning group, representative of the appropriate partners in education, and the Departments of Education and Science, Health and Children, and Finance, has been established by the Minister for Education and Science to produce proposals for a national educational psychological service. The report of the Group is expected in 1998. In the meantime, 15 additional educational psychologists are being employed to expand the service in primary schools.

**The Commission welcomes the prioritisation of proposals for the expansion and development of the school psychological service to meet the needs of all students at both primary and second level.**

13.31   **Remedial teachers service**
Remedial teachers are allocated to schools to enable them to meet the needs of pupils who might have difficulty in acquiring literacy skills and mathematical skills and to support schools in teaching those who experience serious problems in acquiring these skills. Research, for example the IEA[34] English Reading Survey 1993, indicates that between 6.5 per cent and 9 per cent of pupils at eleven years of age (or 5th class) and at fourteen years of age have serious learning problems with literacy and learning mathematics. The focus of the remedial teachers' work should be on those pupils who have the greatest needs, both in terms of prevention and remediation.

The Department of Education and Science is currently conducting a review of the remedial education services in primary schools. This review will inform further developments in remedial provision.

The Commission endorses the work of the remedial teachers service and welcomes the review currently underway. The Commission suggests that the review might also consider new models of prevention of learning difficulties which are being developed. For example, reading recovery programmes, involving very early intervention by the classroom teacher

34   International Association for the Evaluation of Educational Achievement

with a child experiencing difficulty, may prevent the need for the child to have recourse to remedial teaching.

**13.32 Education initiatives for those at risk of not succeeding in education**

The Commission's recommendations in relation to tackling educational disadvantage have been developed in the context of the priorities identified in the National Anti-Poverty Strategy[35] and the need for ongoing evaluations of educational programmes and their outcomes in tackling low educational attainments and early school-leaving.

The Early Start pilot pre-school programme referred to earlier is targeted at young children who, because of socio-economic disadvantage, are most at risk of not succeeding in education. The programme caters for children aged three and four years. An important aspect of the programme is that it brings parents into the education process. In September 1996, some 1,566 children were enrolled in the pilot phase of the programme in 40 centres in eight locations around the country. The pilot phase of the programme is currently being evaluated. The results of the evaluation will inform further developments in pre-school educational provision.

Breaking the Cycle provides a targeted programme of supports, including reduced pupil-teacher ratio and additional financial supports, at primary level for some of the most disadvantaged schools. In September 1996 some 156 schools with 12,824 children were in the pilot phase of the programme. The pilot phase of the programme is currently being evaluated. The results of the evaluation will inform future developments in educational disadvantage.

**The Commission recommends:**
- **the extension of pre-school education to all areas of disadvantage**
- **subject to the current review of the pilot phase, the extension of the Breaking the Cycle initiative, or other initiatives to prevent educational disadvantage on a phased basis. Initially the extension should be within the existing programme, i.e. to include schools with lower levels of disadvantage. Later the scheme might be extended to other areas of the country, with the possibility of clustering schools which might otherwise not come within the description of being disadvantaged but might have significant pockets of disadvantage**

---

35    *"Sharing in Progress"*, the National Anti-Poverty Strategy sets out a target of eliminating early school leaving before the Junior Certificate; reducing early school-leaving so that, by the year 2000, the percentage of young people completing the senior cycle will reach 90 per cent and 98 per cent by the year 2007, and tackling literacy and numeracy problems so that, having regard to the assessment of their intrinsic abilities, there are no students with serious problems in these areas in early primary education within the next five years.

The report identified a number of strategies as necessary in order to achieve this target, including :

- increased pre-school services, with consideration to be given to a phased extension of the pilot Early Start Programme

- preventing educational disadvantage and early school leaving through increased resources at primary level and in the early years of post-primary schooling. This should encourage active parental involvement at the earliest possible age and include consideration of an expansion of the pilot Breaking the Cycle initiative, consideration of an enhancement of the Home/School/Community Liaison Scheme, remedial guidance and psychological services and a targeted reduction in class sizes in the early years of education.

- subject to the current review of the pilot phase at primary level, the potential for a similar initiative to Breaking the Cycle, or other disadvantage initiatives at second level should be explored.

**13.33**   **Home/School/Community Liaison**
The Commission is of the view that the participation of parents in their children's education has huge potential for making a significant difference, not only to their children's chances of success in education, but also in terms of enhancing the capabilities and skills within local communities.

In Home/School/Community Liaison, the focus is on the adults, parents and teachers in the interests of children's learning. Schools provide a wide range of courses for parents, including self -development, parenting and leisure courses, and parents become involved in school activities. Home/School/Community Liaison is operating in some 181 primary and 84 second-level schools, supported by 105 co-ordinators.

The Commission is convinced of the potential of the scheme to provide important supports to children throughout their school years, but particularly when they are moving from one level of education to another. Children can be particularly vulnerable when starting school or moving from pre-school to primary or from the integrated pupil-centred approach at primary level to subject-centred second-level school. The second year in second level may also be a vulnerable time for some youngsters as they approach the minimum school-leaving age. [36]

**13.34**   The Commission considers that the Home/School/Community Liaison scheme should be ultimately developed in all areas but, as a priority, it should be extended to all designated areas of disadvantage.

The Commission considers that links between local Home/School/Community Liaison schemes and community education initiatives would enhance the benefits of the scheme to parents, while building up capabilities and competencies in local communities. It is also important that the scheme be developed to reach those families who are most alienated from the education system. Research and development of new mechanisms to involve these families would be helpful. The Commission considers that increased participation of parents in the scheme should be a target objective of the further development of Home/School/Community Liaison.

**The Commission recommends:**
- **the extension of the Home/School/Community Liaison scheme to cover all schools in designated areas of disadvantage within the next three years**
- **that the importance of continuity in relation to the transitions which children make from pre-school to infant classes to primary education to second level be asserted within the scheme**
- **that resources be allocated to research and the development of appropriate mechanisms, including outreach programmes, to reach those parents and families who are most at risk of disadvantage and who are at present outside the scheme**

36   Information in an oral submission to the Commission.

- **that new links be developed with other community and local development initiatives, such as "second chance" education programmes with the objectives of providing progression opportunities for parents who develop an interest in pursuing education and self-development.**

**13.35** The Home School Preparatory Work programme in operation for some final year primary children and their parents is an innovative way to further enhance the potential of parents to be a resource in their children's education. The Commission agrees with the National Economic and Social Forum that this scheme should be extended to all primary schools in disadvantaged communities and should be developed for the first year of second level.

## MANAGING ATTENDANCE AT SCHOOL

**13.36 Non-attendance and truancy**

The issue of truancy was examined by a Department of Education Working Group (1994) and by the National Economic and Social Forum (1997).

The findings of the Department's Working Group comprehensively cover the action which the Group considers needs to be taken at legislative, administrative and local level (in the schools) to address truancy and non-attendance and to empower key players to better manage the difficulties associated with non-attendance in the interests of the children. The Group highlighted the importance of individual schools pursuing vigorous policies in relation to attendance issues. The Working Group concludes that its recommendations for revised structures and programmes must be key elements of the Government's strategy for promoting equity in the school system and that, accordingly, the changes recommended should be funded as part of the policy to tackle educational disadvantage.

The National Economic and Social Forum has endorsed the approach taken by the Working Group, while highlighting the need to address a number of specific issues contributing to the complex difficulties associated with truancy and non-attendance.

The Commission is aware that studies have shown that serious non-attendance at school is usually linked to disadvantage. [37] Tackling educational disadvantage is therefore a key element of the strategy to prevent non-attendance at school. The Commission's recommendations made earlier in this chapter are therefore of particular relevance.

The Commission agrees with the expert reports on the need for urgent action in relation to :
- the introduction by school principals of procedures for monitoring and enforcing attendance
- the introduction of a tracking mechanism
  - to ensure that children transfer into second-level school
  - to track school dropouts and ensure that schools are encouraged to report dropouts to the appropriate school attendance officer or to FÁS
- the introduction of record-keeping and notification and appeal procedures in relation to suspensions and expulsions
- the introduction of proposals to remedy deficiencies in the structure of school attendance areas.

37    School Attendance/Truancy Report issued by the Minister for Education, April 1994.

The Commission welcomes the proposed new initiative aimed at 8-15 year olds at risk of early school-leaving.

**The Commission urges the Government to bring forward soon proposals in response to the recommendations of the Working Group on Truancy.**

The Commission notes that legislation in regard to school attendance is currently in preparation in the Department of Education and Science.

## ENHANCING THE ATTRACTIVENESS OF STAYING IN EDUCATION

**13.37    Additional costs of education for families**

The additional costs associated with education were a major issue for the families who wrote to the Commission. Families gave lengthy lists of school costs, including voluntary contributions, school transport, examination fees, lockers, photocopies, books, uniforms, materials, outings, games, extra-curricular activities and school books. Research from a study in Waterford shows that difficulties arise for families because costs are often hidden and therefore unexpected and demands in relation to payment methods can place additional burdens on parents.[38] The National Economic and Social Forum has highlighted these costs and suggested that they may be a factor contributing to truancy.[39]

It is evident that it is a continuous struggle to meet education expenses for a significant number of families, particularly those who are unemployed or on a low income. The added disadvantage posed by these costs for children living in areas of disadvantage is a major concern for the Commission.

### Meeting the running costs of schools

It is the Commission's view that the imposition of these costs on parents is largely to do with inadequate investment in the infrastructure, resource materials and equipment for schools. The Commission's recommendations in relation to increased investment in primary level are particularly relevant in this regard. The Commission is of the view that the contribution to school maintenance/running costs should be reviewed. At present the State pays the full cost of teachers' salaries and the bulk of the cost of providing and maintaining schools. At primary level, the State pays a capitation grant of £45 per pupil per year while the local community pays £10; in the case of schools designated as disadvantaged, the State pays £75, while the local community pays £9.50. At second level, the capitation grant currently stands at £177 per pupil with an additional £30 per pupil in schools designated as disadvantaged.

Despite the additional funding made available to disadvantaged schools, these schools are often much less well-equipped and less well-resourced than schools in better off areas, mainly because the local communities cannot supplement the funds available to schools, through, for example, local fund-raising. In recent years, the State has sought to redress this situation by introducing the Disadvantaged Areas Scheme and the Breaking the Cycle Scheme. Schools benefiting under these schemes all receive the special capitation rates mentioned above.

38    *"In a class of their own"*, a report into the factors influencing participation in secondary school education as experienced in Ballybeg Community, Waterford found that "cost" was perceived by parents to be the greatest obstacle to their children remaining in school.

39    *Early School Leavers and Youth Unemployment,* National Economic and Social Forum Report No. 11., January, 1997.

Adequate resourcing is required for the basic materials and equipment for schools. **The Commission is of the view that there is an urgent need to realistically assess the costs of running schools on a daily basis and to plan for the funding of these costs.** Caretaking and administrative support for schools, particularly for those in disadvantaged communities, should also be taken account of in assessing running costs. While the Commission acknowledges the funding currently provided by the Department of Education and Science to defray the cost of caretakers and secretarial services for schools, **the Commission considers that extra resources should be allocated to schools in disadvantaged communities to meet these costs in full for children.**

### Examination Fees

Examination fees have been highlighted by the National Economic and Social Forum as a critical issue for families on low incomes. [40]

The Commission welcomes the announcement by the Minister for Education and Science (November 1997) that fees would no longer be payable by students who hold a medical card or are dependent on a parent or guardian who is the holder of a medical card. It is expected that about 40,000 students will benefit from this initiative.

### School books

A scheme for the provision of assistance in the supply of school books to needy pupils[41] is administered locally by the principal teachers of the participating schools. The means by which such assistance is to be provided, whether by direct financial subsidy or by presentation of books to pupils, or whether the books are supplied on loan or as personal property of the pupils, is a matter for decision for the school authorities and may vary from school to school. Subject to the amount of money made available each year by the Department, principal teachers have discretion in the selection of pupils to be assisted and in the degree of assistance to be given to each one.

The Commission is of the view that further initiatives need to be taken to reduce the cost of purchasing school books.

A report to the Department of Education in May 1993 recommended that rental schemes should be introduced in schools where they do not already exist to reduce the cost of book bills to parents.

---

40  At present (1998) the exam fees are £45 for Junior Certfiicate and £48 for Leaving Certificate. Revenues generated by the fees amount to £6 million a year.

41  A needy pupil, for the purpose of the scheme, is defined as a child from a home in which genuine hardship exists because of unemployment, prolonged illness of parents, large family with inadequate means, mother a widow, single parent or other circumstances which indicate a similar degree of financial hardship.

According to the report, book rental schemes are not a new concept. Dozens of schools are operating schemes and have succeeded in reducing the cost of books to the parent from over £100 to as little as £15 per annum. Schools surveyed indicated that in secondary schools the mean rental worked out at £10.31 per annum at Junior Certificate level and £18.13 per annum at Leaving Certificate Level. This compares with average bills for new book purchases at Junior and Leaving Certificate of £148 and £147 respectively. In primary schools the rental charge ranged from £1 to £25, excluding the cost of workbooks. (The cost of purchasing new books at primary level ranged from £11.19 at junior infants to £38.32 at sixth class). The report estimated the costs to the State of providing core books to be £17.4 million per year for three years and £10.9 million thereafter (1993 costs).

Since 1994 the Department of Education and Science has provided seed capital for book rental schemes in disadvantaged schools. Schools which were officially designated as being disadvantaged, which did not already operate a book rental scheme and which committed themselves to setting up a scheme, were grant-aided.

**The Commission recommends that the Department of Education and Science should continue to promote the introduction of book rental schemes throughout the school system and should continue to increase resources for funding them where possible.**

*Note: The Commission would like to draw attention to the importance of a sensitive approach being adopted by schools in their administration of programmes to alleviate expense for individual pupils. While the majority of schools adopt a sensitive and caring approach to the handling of these situations, unfortunately instances of insensitivity in the manner of dealing with pupils who are entitled to assistance have been brought to the Commission's attention. The Commission considers that it is intolerable that any young student should be singled out or made to feel embarrassed because of his/her family circumstances. It is suggested that the Department of Education and Science continue to emphasise for schools the child's right and his family's right to confidentiality and discretion in the handling of personal matters and the importance of dealing sensitively with these situations.*

### 13.38 Sport in Education

Extra-curricular activities, providing an interest outside the timetabled school programme, can also provide motivation and an outlet for young people. A study from the US illustrates the importance of extra-curricular activities in keeping young people engaged in education. It has been found that extra-curricular involvement has a stronger association with school completion than a variety of other factors, including academic intelligence. Statistics from the US show that 60 per cent of high-school dropouts were not involved in any extra-curricular activities during their high-school years.[42]

The Commission would like to draw attention to the need for greater emphasis on the development of sport in education. A recent survey of 365 second-level schools carried out by the Association of Secondary Teachers of Ireland showed that 67 per cent had no sports coaches, while 98 per cent provided sport as an extra-curricular activity only.[43]

42 *"Early School Leaving - Lessons from other Countries".* in *Poverty Today*, No.30 December/January 1996.

43 Survey on staffing, funding and facilities in Irish second level schools, ASTI November, 1996.

The National Economic and Social Forum has recommended that the Department of Education and Science[44] bring forward proposals for the development and resourcing of the role of sport in education. *Targeting Sporting Change in Ireland*, the national sports strategy published in February 1997, endorses sport as an essential part of life-long learning. The strategy document identifies some of the important issues in relation to promoting sport in education. These include training facilities in schools, school and community links, and new links with local sports structures.

The Commission concurs with the view in the strategy that physical education and sport are essential and complementary elements which need to be further developed within the education system at primary, secondary, further and tertiary levels of education. The sense of achievement, lifeskills, confidence, self esteem and team work arising from participation in physical activity should be a central part of the education of every child in Ireland.

**The Commission urges implementation of the strategy to introduce sports in education.**

The Commission notes the announcement by the Minister for Education and Science of his intention to introduce physical education as a subject at senior cycle and to request the NCCA to begin work on a new syllabus.

## 13.39 The potential of youthwork in helping young school-leavers

The Commission would like to highlight the contribution of youth work in meeting the needs of young people at risk of leaving school early.

Youth work promotes the personal and social development of young people, through ensuring the provision of high quality, effective and efficient youth work services outside of, but complementary to, the formal education system.

### Support for youth organisations

The Youth Affairs Section of the Department of Education and Science supports, by way of financial assistance, a range of national voluntary youth organisations which meet educational and other criteria, including voluntary adult involvement and the active participation of young people in the running of their organisations. The allocation for 1997 was £12.72 million.

Support for youth work is channelled through the following schemes:

- The *youth service grant scheme,* which is a scheme of annual grants to national and major regional voluntary youth work organisations.
- The *grant scheme for projects to assist disadvantaged youth,* which supports out-of-school youth work programmes and services for disadvantaged young people.
- The *national network of youth information centres*, the *Youth Resource Unit* and *the National Youth Health Programme;*
- *Gaisce* (The President's Award Scheme) and *Leargas* (The Exchange Bureau).

---

44    Since June 1997, sport has been the responsibility of the Department of Tourism, Sport and Recreation.

- A range of other agencies, programmes and activities, including the Voluntary Youth Councils, National Youth Arts Programme, and various education and training programmes.
- The *Youth Services Development Fund,* which is aimed at helping young people to deal with the challenges of the use of drugs in society.

### Support for special projects

In 1997, £6.1 million funding was given to special projects/ schemes for disadvantaged youth. Priority is given in the scheme of grants to out-of-school youth work projects that seek to assist in the personal and social development of young people who are disadvantaged. Up to 150 projects are grant-aided under the scheme.

The point has been made to the Commission that major significant extra investment is required to keep pace with the demand for schemes and to include new projects. Since 1988, few new projects have been added to the list.

Special initiatives, together with the major contribution made by the national voluntary youth organisations, have highlighted the contribution that youth work can make to the lives of young people in disadvantaged communities. Very often these young people's experience of the formal education or training systems is negative. An important objective of youthwork is to facilitate the return of these young people to the formal education or training systems. Youthwork can help to counteract the experience of alienation, to restore a sense of self-esteem and to support positive action, which will in turn develop potential.

### Helping young people to stay in school

The Commission is most impressed with the work of the youth organisations in relation to helping young people to stay in the school system and also their work with early school-leavers and lone parents, for example the Moving On programme referred to in Chapter 7.

The strategy, adopted by the youth services, such as Foróige - the National Youth Development Organisation and the National Youth Federation, the Catholic Youth Council and others in helping early school-leavers to remain in and participate more fully in school, is indicative of the approach taken by the youth services to prevent early school leaving. The approach is based on programmes of:
- training  potential school-leavers to improve personal effectiveness skills, develop self-esteem and become self empowered
- developing special curricula with potential early school-leavers based on their particular needs, interests and suggestions,
- involving the young people in their community so that they can benefit from its support and
- the active support and co-operation of the school principal, teachers and Home/School/ Community liaison officers.

Programmes for those who have left school early are designed to develop the social and personal skills of the young people. For young people under age fifteen who cannot return to school, these programmes are often the only option.

Close collaboration and co-operation with schools and with the Home/School/Community Liaison officer and working within the school structure are also features of the Neighbourhood Youth Projects which have been brought to the Commission's attention. Contracts between the schools and the project in relation to the work with early school-leavers help to provide and encourage commitment and stability for all the parties.

### Greater investment in youth services

The point has been made to the Commission that youthwork is underfunded and this limits the expansion of youth initiatives in areas where they are most needed.

The Commission is of the view that the strategy to redress early school-leaving should include the youthwork sector in its role as the provider of services to young people coping with disadvantage. In addition:

- the development of new initiatives which would operate *within the education structure* should be encouraged.
- *collaboration and co-operation* between local schools and the youth organisations and community groups should be promoted, in the interests of providing an integrated response to young people who are potential early school-leavers.
- information, evaluation findings and models of *good practice should be shared* and disseminated among all those working with young people who are faced with the prospect of early school-leaving.

**The Commission recommends that additional resources be made available to the youth sector.**

## 13.40 Youthreach

Young people who drop out of school early or who leave school without attaining any qualification have few options in relation to further training. The main programmes for them are Youthreach, provided in out of school centres by VECs and by FÁS in Community Training Workshops, and a similar programme for Travellers in a network of Senior Traveller Training Centres. There are currently 4,525 places in the programmes.

Youthreach provides two years' integrated education, training and work experience for young people in the 15-18- year age-group who are at least six months in the labour market and who have left school early without any qualifications or vocational training. The programme is structured around two distinct years: *a Foundation Year* to help overcome learning difficulties, develop self-confidence and a range of competencies essential for further learning, and a *Progression Year*, which provides for more specific development through a range of education, training and work experience options. Basic skills training, practical work training and general education are features of the programme, and the application of new technology is integrated into all aspects of programme content. Courses are full-time, of 35 hours duration per week, and are available on a year-round basis. A training allowance is paid to participants, this ranges from £27 to £64 per week, depending on age.

The programme emphasises the development of literacy, numeracy and communication skills along with work experience. There is a choice of vocational options, such as Catering,

Hairdressing, Computers, Woodwork, Photography, Video, Sports, Art and Craft. National Certification at Foundation Level is available from FÁS and the NCVA.

The programme in Senior Traveller Training Centres, which has been extended to two years, is similar to that in Youthreach, except that (a) there is no upper age limit and increasingly adults are being encouraged to participate and (b) there is also a key emphasis on meeting the needs of the Traveller community in a culturally supportive environment.

The National Economic and Social Forum has acknowledged the good work which is being done on behalf of early school-leavers by Youthreach. Both the European Social Fund Evaluation Unit Report on Provision for Early School Leavers and the report of the National Economic and Social Forum on Early School Leavers and Youth Unemployment recommend a number of reforms, including:

- a substantial increase in places on the programme; the NESF recommended 1,000 extra places
- a more flexible range of options, which, together with the increase in places, would encourage more participants to complete the Progression Phase of the programme
- an increased focus in promoting pathways to mainstream education and training provision
- development of national certification for the programme and the marketing of this with employers.

The Commission welcomes the steps taken by the Government to implement these recommendations, including:
- planned expenditure in 1998 and 1999 of £19.733 million to provide a minimum of 1,000 additional places for early school -leavers in the Youthreach and Traveller training programmes. Arrangements are underway to establish 750 Youthreach places and 250 Traveller places with a view to having them operational in 1998 by FÁS and the VECs
- provision of £0.987 million for the strengthening of counselling, guidance and psychological services for participants in these programmes. A Task Force is being established to define and quantify the needs in this field in collaboration with the National Centres for Guidance in Education and in FÁS, with a view to implementation in 1998
- the introduction of childcare provision for VTOS, Youthreach and Traveller programmes.

Extensive consultation is taking place with the key interests including the Area-Based Partnerships and youth, community and Traveller organisations in order to respond to local needs in an integrated way.

The strategic objectives underpinning the provision of these places is that :
- All unqualified early school-leavers in the 15-18-year age-group will have access to an appropriate programme with an integrated Foundation and Progression Phase, designed to provide a bridge to mainstream education/training or employment.
- The progression phase can be extended as necessary to facilitate access to Leaving Certificate qualifications or equivalent (either in school or in Youthreach or other

training centres).

- The range of progression options can be widened to ensure a range of choices in the education or training sectors. An expansion of the FÁS Linked Work Experience programme and the new bridging and progression measures will be an important feature in this approach.
- Travellers are treated equally in the initiatives for early school-leavers.
- The ongoing training of trainers, the networking of centres and the dissemination of good practice and learning from new developments are also features of the developments.

## EQUALITY AND EQUITY

The Commission would like to highlight the important findings of two recent reports in relation to equality of access and opportunity in education for all children.

**13.41    Equality and equity in education for young people with disabilities and their families.**[45]
"If one is to measure the status of people with disabilities by their rate of participation and success in education, equality is still a long way off. Participation by people with disabilities in education at all levels is significantly below that of the population in general."[46]

According to the report of the Commission on the Status of People with Disabilities, the number of people with disabilities in education is estimated to be at least 4 per cent of the school-going population. Approximately 8,000 pupils with disabilities are enrolled in 114 special schools and some 3,800 pupils with various disabilities are in special classes in primary schools. There are also about 8,000 pupils with "specific disabilities" in ordinary classes in primary schools. A further 2,300 pupils are enrolled in 48 special classes at post-primary level, while 100 pupils with disabilities are enrolled in the five designated post-primary schools.

The most recent figures for those attending third-level education indicate that there are approximately 1,000 students with disabilities. Unfortunately, no comprehensive figures are available for the number of children with disabilities in pre-school or the numbers of adults with disabilities attending local adult education centres. The report has pointed out that a minimum of 4 per cent of all pupils and students have special education needs, because of disability, in both special and mainstream schools, in third-level colleges and in adult education centres of learning.

The Commission on the Status of People with Disabilities set out a comprehensive strategy to redress the difficulties in relation to the participation in education of children and adults with disabilities. The recommendations include :
-    An Education Act to
- assert the rights of students to education appropriate to their needs
- set out the rights and entitlements of students and their parents
- provide for individual assessments of need and the development of individual education plans.

---

45    This section draws on the findings of the Commission on the Status of People with Disabilities. The Commission, following widespread consultation and participation by people with disabilities, their families and experts, has presented a comprehensive strategy to remove the barriers which stand in the way of people with disabilities who want to live full and fulfilled lives.

46    Report of the Commission on the Status of  People with Disabilities, November 1996.

It is recommended that the legislation would provide for Community Education Plans to meet the needs of students with disabilities on a regional basis. Services specifically mentioned include :
- speech and occupational therapy
- physical education
- support and counselling for parents
- psychological support
- technical aids and supports
- communication support
- school transport
- classroom assistants
- resource and remedial teaching
- personal assistants.

The report also contains recommendations in relation to :
- support services, including remedial, resource and visiting teachers
- reviewing the curricular needs of pupils in specialist settings and greater flexibility in assessment and examination arrangements
- reclassifying special schools as primary and post-primary schools so that education up to age eighteen years can attract facilities such as the improved pupil-teacher ratios, posts of responsibility and additional capitation grants that apply to mainstream schools,
- actions to bridge the gap between special and mainstream schools
- full integration and better access for students with disabilities at third level
- provision of high quality pre-schools to children with disabilities,
- improvements in teacher training (including in-service training) to promote awareness of disability issues
- more opportunities for people with disabilities to become teachers.

The report recommends that a figure of 1 per cent of the education budget of additional expenditure be allocated annually to meet the educational needs of students with disabilities.

### 13.42 Submissions to the Commission on the Family

The issues identified in the report of the Commission on the Status of People with Disabilities arose in submissions to the Commission on the Family. The consensus of submissions dealing with the issue of education for children with disabilities was that most children benefit from and are entitled to mainstream education in the ordinary classroom, with suitable personal and educational support. Some children were identified as needing special schools, often as part of an evolving response to learning disability. The prevalent view was that each child with a disability should have an educational training programme tailored to his or her individual needs and that support programmes were needed for the families of these children, to help them cope with the additional needs of the child, with emphasis on the involvement of the father. Many submissions deplored the fact that, when education is completed, there is nothing for many of these children but to remain with elderly parents, or with siblings who have their own family commitments, or to live in institutional care.

**The Commission on the Family concurs with the view expressed in the report, that meeting the needs of people with disabilities can and must be regarded as an investment, and not a burden on society. The Commission endorses the recommendations of the Commission on the Status of People with Disabilities on access to and participation in education for people with disabilities. The Commission endorses the principles set out in the strategy to underpin education, legislation and policy and administrative practice.**

The case for equity and equality for people with disability in relation to participation in education is captured in the text of the principles set out by the Commission on the Status of People with Disabilities: "Every child is educable. All children, including those with disabilities, have a right to free and appropriate education in the least restrictive environment."

" It is the responsibility of the State to provide sufficient resources to ensure that pre-school children, children of school-going age and adults with disabilities have an education appropriate to their needs in the best possible environment."[47]

There has been widespread acceptance of the report of the Commission on the Status of People with Disabilities. Commitments to implement the strategy are contained in Partnership 2000 and in the programme for Government, *An Action Programme for the New Millennium*. Recent legislation in relation to education makes specific reference to pupils with special needs. The Commission on the Family welcomes these commitments and urges that progress towards implementation of the report of the Commission on the Status of People with Disabilities in relation to education should remain a priority commitment for Government and the social partners.

## 13.43    Access to education for children of Traveller families [48]

Despite considerable progress[49] in provision of education for the children of the Travelling Community in recent years, access to education continues to present major problems for large numbers of Traveller children. A significant amount of work still needs to be undertaken to achieve participation levels for these children on a par with the general population of children.

Approximately 4,200 Traveller children attend *primary schools*. About 1,800 of these children are full-time in ordinary classes while the remaining 2,400 children attend special classes for Travellers.

Only a *small minority* of Traveller children have successfully transferred to second-level schools and very few of those have completed a full second-level education. Third-level education is not a possibility for the vast majority of Travellers.

---

47   For a complete text of the principles set out by the Commission on the Status of People with Disabilities, see Appendix 2 to this chapter.

48   This section draws on the work of the *Task Force on the Travelling Community*, Department of Equality and Law reform July 1995.

49   The Commission notes that the number of Special Teachers has risen steadily in recent years. There are now 296 resource teachers for Travellers at primary school. The number of visiting teachers for Travellers has been increased to 15. In 1997/98 school year, this figure will be increased to 20. This service will operate at both primary and post-primary levels.

Apart from the provision for early school-leavers with the network of Senior Traveller Training Centres, access to mainstream adult education and training for Travellers is a problem. Lack of resources, difficult entry requirements, lack of childcare facilities, lack of funds for books, materials and transport and illiteracy are all major barriers to participation in adult education for Travellers.

The report of the Task Force on the Travelling Community identified a range of measures and initiatives to better respond to the education needs of Traveller families and to bring about more co-ordinated structures and a comprehensive approach to education for the Travelling community. The 167 recommendations of the Task Force in relation to education alone illustrate the extent of work to be undertaken to respond to the education needs of this community.

A Traveller Education Co-ordinating Committee, comprised of representatives from all the sections in the Department of Education and Science dealing with Travellers, including the Schools Inspectorate and the National Education Officer for Travellers, has been established by the Department of Education and Science to advance the recommendations of the Task Force.

In a complementary development, which is aided by the European Social Fund under the Local Urban and Rural Development Programme, a research study[50] has been commissioned on the future role of the Senior Traveller Training Centres in the light of emerging needs.

A separate action under the EU Community Initiative INTEGRA, focuses on the development and piloting of methodological tools to overcome barriers for Travellers in mainstream education and training programmes.

The Commission's recommendations in this chapter for improving access to and participation in education have a particular relevance for one of the most disadvantaged communities within Irish society. The Commission's recommendations in relation to greater investment in primary level education, tackling educational disadvantage and preventing early school-leaving are particularly important in relation to developing a better response to the difficulties experienced by Traveller children.

The Commission further recommends that the findings of the Task Force on the Travelling Community should inform policy development in relation to the future provision of education services for Traveller children. In particular, the Commission supports the views of the Task Force in relation to the need for :
- additional support and resources for the visiting teacher service,
- pre-school provision for Traveller children
- greater involvement of Traveller parents in schools and in the education system
- the development of an intercultural and anti-racist curriculum for all pupils and a pilot programme to implement such a curriculum and the inclusion of intercultural education in the training programmes for all students

---

50    The project has been commissioned by Pavee Point and is overseen by a committee representing FÁS, the Department of Education and Science, National Association of Traveller Training Centres, Pavee Point and Traveller organisations networked to the Irish Traveller Movement.

- greater integration of Traveller children in mainstream schools
- new supports to help Traveller children make the transition to second-level schools
- a greater role for youthwork in assisting young Travellers in second-level age groups
- more resources and innovative programmes to tackle adult illiteracy
- more research and a compilation statistics in relation to Travellers' participation and their achievements in education.

# Appendix 1

**Extract from the Report of the Expert Advisory Group on Relationship and Sexuality Education[1]**

**"A Framework for the Development of Relationships and Sexuality Education in Schools"**

**1.**      Taking into account the general aim of education, and with due regard for the primary responsibility of parents and their key role in influencing the growth and development of their children, each school, at both primary and post-primary level, should formulate and make known its policy on Relationships and Sexuality Education.

**2.**      The following principles provide a framework for the development and implementation of such a policy.

     (i) Parents are in law and in fact the primary educators, and home is the natural environment in which Relationships and Sexuality Education should take place.

     (ii) The school has a role to play in supporting and complementing the work of the home in this task. This requires the management of each school, after consultation within the school community, to develop a clear policy on Relationships and Sexuality Education which is made known to all parties within the school. This policy will make provision for the rights of parents who hold conscientious or moral objections to the inclusion of such programmes on the curriculum and will state how the school intends to redress the situation. This would include the situation where children are being educated in schools whose dominant ethos is not of their faith or beliefs. In upholding the rights of these individual parents, the rights of the majority to have the programme implemented in the school must be upheld.

     (iii) There should be a collaborative, whole-school approach to the development of the school programme with the Principal having a key leadership role in facilitating consultation within the school community.

     (iv) The values inherent in the programme should be consistent with the core values and ethos of the school and with its policy statement, bearing in mind the existence of schools managed by the different religious authorities and ... other ethically or culturally motivated groups.

     (v) Education for Relationships and Sexuality should be an integral part of the Social, Personal and Health Education (SPHE) programme, which should be a required part of the school curriculum for all children, including children with special needs.

     (vi) SPHE needs to be supported by a positive climate and culture within the school and by meaningful home-school relationships.

---

1     The Expert Advisory Group was drawn from representatives of the partners in education, including parents, teachers and school managers.

(vii)At primary and post-primary level, the SPHE programme, of which Relationships and Sexuality Education is a part, should be delivered through one or two time-tabled core periods per week. Cross-curricular links should be identified and co-ordinated across the class/subject timetables.

(viii)Parent and teacher education training should be developed as part of the school programme.

(ix) Adequate resources need to be allocated to the programme, within the framework of resources available to schools.

3.    Developing a school policy and programme on Relationships and Sexuality Education, within the context of Social, Personal and Health Education, requires the collaboration and goodwill of all the partners for the benefit of the pupils.

# Appendix 2

## Education Charter of Rights for people with disabilities

### Principles of a strategy to provide equality in education for people with disabilities.[2]

The Commission on the Status of People with Disabilities asserts the following principles in regard to the education of every citizen with a disability. The Commission further asserts that the rights explicit and implicit in these principles should be incorporated in all education policy, and should be enshrined in any legislation.

- Every child is educable. All children, including those with disabilities, have a right to a free and appropriate education in the least restrictive environment. Appropriate education for all children with disabilities should be provided in mainstream schools, except where it is clear that the child involved will not benefit through being placed in a mainstream environment, or that other children would be unduly and unfairly disadvantaged.

- Every individual has an equal right to educational provision, which will enable him or her to participate in all aspects of economic, social, cultural and political life to the fullest extent of his or her potential.

- The unique needs of the individual person must be the paramount consideration when decisions are being made concerning the appropriate provision of education for that person. In so far as is practical a continuum of services must be available to meet those needs close to the person's home and family.

- It is the responsibility of the State to provide sufficient resources to ensure that pre-school children, children of school-going age and adults with disabilities have an education appropriate to their needs in the best possible environment.

- Parents have primacy in the decision-making process as soon as their disabled child has been identified as having particular educational needs. They (and the child whenever appropriate) must be entitled to make an informed choice on the educational placement of their child.

- There shall be an accessible appeals procedure on educational enrolment recommendations. This will have due regard for the rights of the child, the rights of the parents and the educational rights of other children.

- All schools have a responsibility to serve children with disabilities in the least restrictive environment. Each school plan must strive to make schools inclusive institutions to facilitate inclusive education due recognition must be given to the rights and needs of teachers for resources, initial education and continuing professional development.

---

2    Reproduced from *A Strategy for Equality*, report of the Commission on the Status of People with Disabilities.

- Flexibility and formal linkages should be built into educational provision at local level. It must be a statutory duty of all existing or new management structures to secure access to high quality and appropriate education for all children and adults with disabilities.

- Priority should be given to the needs of people with disabilities, within the broad framework of educational provision and this should be reflected in the allocation of resources.

**14.1**  **Introduction**

The contribution of people now retiring to the present generation is enormous. This generation have funded the country's education, health and infrastructure systems, the benefits of which will be reaped for decades to come.  Many of today's older people left school with little education, have experienced urban migration and  high emigration levels in the 1940s and 1950s and, having contributed to the country's rapid economic expansion in the 1960s and 1970s, many of them saw their own well-educated children emigrate in the 1980s, seeking better opportunities abroad.

For many of the women of this generation, marriage and motherhood meant leaving paid employment. The marriage bar, unequal pay, often uneconomic, discriminatory tax arrangements, unheard of childcare arrangements, contrived to ensure that for most women, options on marriage and motherhood were clear-cut. Many of them, once married, had to cease employment, and thus forgo earnings and pension rights. For those who continued working and for widows with dependent families who out of economic necessity had to work outside the home, wage and tax rates were structured in favour of the male breadwinner. Wages were often low and many employment sectors were closed to women.

Men bore the economic responsibility of the family (as sole breadwinners) and were expected to shoulder complete responsibility for the financial well-being of their dependants.

Most older people are completely independent in activities of daily living and do not rely on their family for care or financial support. In fact, the reverse often applies: many people well into retirement are working voluntarily in parish and community work - for example, in literacy schemes, caring for children and people older than themselves, advising industry and passing on skills. Every community can give examples of older people involved in voluntary work in the community

**Family links are important**

Irish families benefit greatly from their links with older relatives. Many new mothers would be lost without the support and advice of an experienced grandparent. Older people contribute in many ways to Irish family life : through caring for ill and dependent relatives, care for grandchildren, shopping and errands for relatives, housework, household repairs and everyday emotional support and advice. Grandparents keep the family history alive, and help grandchildren to know where they fit into the family. They also build their self-esteem by taking a personal interest in them. They represent an important store of local, historic, economic and social knowledge.

**Older people are a valuable asset to community life and our society**

In an increasing consumer- and technologically-driven age, it is important that society recognises the continuing contribution of older people to community life and to continuity and stability in family life.

## Some facts about older people in the community

### Changing Age Profile [1]

- The population aged over 65 is projected to increase from 414,000 in 1996 to over 759,000 in 2026, an increase of over 83 per cent, and to over 1 million by 2046.
- The population aged over 80 is expected to increase from 90,000 in 1996 to 167,000 in 2026 and to 290,000 by 2046, an increase of 222 per cent.

### Marital Status [2]

- In 1996, 77 per cent of older men (65 years +) are or have been married, 16 per cent are now widowed
- 82 per cent of older women are or have been married, 48 per cent are now widowed
- In 1996, 23 per cent of males and 18 per cent of females aged over 65 were unmarried.
- Most other countries in Western Europe have less than one in ten older people who never married.

### Life Expectancy [3]

- In 1996, life expectancy for the average Irish man is 73.1 years and for the average Irish woman it is 78.7 years. It is projected that this will increase to 77.2 and 83.2 years respectively by 2026.

### Living Arrangements [4]

- Most older people live in private family households
- Among older people, the most common household type is the two-person household of husband and wife (33 per cent), followed by the lone-person household (26 per cent), married couples with unmarried children (12 per cent) and widows or widowers with unmarried children (10 per cent)
- One in four older people in Ireland lives alone - an increase from one in ten in 1961.
- 90 per cent of older Irish people live in owner-occupied housing (i.e. they or their immediate families own the house or are repaying mortgages).

### Family networks are important [4]

- Older people in Ireland, with the exception of those who have never married, have a large extended family. On average, they have 3.4 children, 6.5 grandchildren and 2.6 siblings.
- Most old people have high levels of contact with their families. The vast majority have at least weekly contact with relatives living outside their households. Even the single elderly still maintain contact with other family members - over half have at least weekly contact with relatives living outside their households.
- There is, however, a small minority of older people who have little or no contact with relatives. About 3 or 4 per cent have less than yearly contact.

1  Actuarial Review of Social Welfare Pensions, undertaken by the Irish Pensions Trust Ltd. on behalf of the Department of Social, Community and Family Affairs, Stationery Office, Dublin, September 1997.

2  Census 1996, Principal Demographic Results, Central Statistics Office, Stationery Office, Dublin

3  Census 1996, Principal Demographic Results, Central Statistics Office, Stationery Office, Dublin

- T. Fahey and P. Murray, *Health and Autonomy Among the Over 65s in Ireland.* Dublin National Council for the Elderly, 1994

- *The Elderly, the Family and the State in Ireland:* report prepared by Tony Fahey, ESRI for the Interim Report of the Joint Committee on the Family, Jan 1997.

4  T. Fahey and P. Murray, *Health and Autonomy Among the Over 65s in Ireland.* Dublin National Council for the Elderly, 1994

As set out in the *Actuarial Review of Social Welfare Pensions*, the percentage of the population aged over 65 is projected to increase from 11 per cent in 1996 to 19 per cent in 2026 and to 27 per cent in 2056. Ireland's population is therefore ageing, but at a slower rate than other European countries. This places Ireland in a unique and favourable position among western countries as far as population ageing is concerned. The pace of our demographic changes and the favourable economic outlook into the early years of the next century present a unique opportunity to put in place social and financial supports to ease the transition for an ageing population.

## 14.2    Recent reports

In recent years several important policy documents in relation to provision for older people have been presented[5]. These reports have drawn on considerable expertise, including that of older people themselves. They have set out clearly the framework within which provision for retired and older people should be planned for the future. In particular, the Commission would like to highlight the Report of the Joint Committee on the Family, *The Elderly, the Family and the State in Ireland.* The report and the background study provide a comprehensive and wide-ranging examination of the issues affecting older people currently and in the future. The report of the Pensions Board on the National Pensions Policy Initiative - *Securing Retirement Income*[6] identifies the key issues and the questions which need to be addressed in developing a national pensions system for the years ahead. Targets are recommended in relation to the level and coverage of pensions and proposals are made in relation to funding future pensions provision.

The issues identified in the various reports are broadly reflected in the concerns of the families and organisations who wrote to the Commission on the Family and have been comprehensively set out for the Commission by expert agencies such as the National Council on Ageing and Older People. The Commission endorses the work of these expert groups and urges that their expertise continue to inform policy formulation in the years ahead.

## 14.3    The priority concerns

The Commission in this report is proposing to single out for attention two broad concerns to older people and their families. These relate to:
-   adequate income support for older people today and for future generations of retiring people
-   securing the role of retired people in the community and with their families, as they grow older and need additional supports.

In this chapter, the Commission offers views in relation to the direction State policy might take on a number of areas, to attain these objectives.

---

5   *The Years Ahead : A Policy for the Elderly,* was published in 1988. *Developing the National Pensions System :* The Final Report of the National Pensions Board : 1993 examines the question of the future development of the pensions system to cover all employees. The National Anti-Poverty Strategy, 1997  sets out the direction and objectives across all Government departments to place the needs of the poor and the socially excluded at the top of the national agenda.

6   The Report of the Pensions Board on the National Pensions Policy Initiative - *Securing Retirement Income,* published by the Pensions Board, May 1998

## 14.4    State policy in relation to pensions

There is a growing consensus among policy-makers and experts in pension provision that the way forward in relation to pension  provision on retirement should be built around:

- the further development of the State pension scheme to provide a guaranteed income that provides for essential needs on retirement
- the further development of occupational and private pension cover to supplement the State pension and to maintain established standards of living for people in retirement.

Both at home and abroad, the question of pensions provision for the future is under scrutiny. Issues of particular relevance include:

- the projected growth in the number of older people in the coming decades
- how best to plan for the steady rise in the cost of pension provision
- how provision can meet the new and emerging needs of older people, for example: medical needs, dietary needs, caring and security.

## 14.5    National Pensions Policy Initiative - *Securing Retirement Income*

These issues lie behind many of the submissions to the Commission on the Family. Under the recently completed National Pensions Policy Initiative wide-ranging consultations have taken place with employers, trade unions, pensions and financial experts, pensioners and the public generally. A survey of pension coverage of the population was undertaken and an actuarial review to help estimate the cost of future social welfare pension liabilities over the next 60 years was completed. This review analysed the value for money provided by the contributory social welfare system from the contributors' perspective. The actuarial review makes an important contribution to the debate about striking an appropriate balance between adequate pension provision and affordability and between the responsibility of the State, employers and the individuals themselves.

The Commission notes the publication of *Securing Retirement Income,* the report of the Pensions Board on the pensions initiative, and sees it as providing a clear, convincing and evolutionary approach to future pensions policy development. It also notes the immediate response of the Minister for Social, Community and Family Affairs in *Action on Pensions* (May 1998) and looks forward to the outcome of the deliberations of the working groups which it is proposed to establish to pursue the recommendations in the report on occupational pensions

The Commission proposes to contribute to this major policy debate by singling out for attention a number of issues which it would like to see addressed.

## 14.6    Income sources for older people

The majority of elderly people rely on social welfare provision for their income on retirement. An ESRI report[7] presented details about the incomes and income sources of older people in Ireland.

The report shows that the average income per week of people aged over 65 in nominal terms increased from £23.67 in 1977 to £95.3 in 1995. State pensions were by far the most important source of income and the percentage of people receiving pensions had

---

7    *Occupational and Personal Pension Coverage, 1995* G. Hughes, B. Whelan: ESRI, Department of Social Welfare and Pensions Board, 1996

increased from 79.1 per cent in 1977 to 83.2 per cent in 1995.

Farming continued to decline as a source of income, while occupational pensions as a source of income had increased. In 1977 about 15 per cent of older people had occupational pensions. By 1995 this had increased to 23 per cent. Only £3 per week, on average, was earned from interest on savings and dividends by older Irish people. Table 1 gives a detailed breakdown of income sources.

## Table 1
Income sources of people aged 65 and over, 1977 and 1995[8]

| Source | Data for 1977 | | | Data for 1995 | | |
|---|---|---|---|---|---|---|
| | % with income from this source | Average weekly income | | % with income from this source | Average weekly income | |
| | | £ | % of total income | | £ | % of total income |
| State pension or allowance | 79.1 | 12.12 | 51.4 | 83.2 | 52.58 | 55.2 |
| Pension from previous employer | 15.2 | 2.87 | 12.2 | 22.7 | 22.05 | 23.1 |
| Farming | 11.8 | 6.49 | 27.5 | 6.9 | 8.17 | 8.6 |
| Non-farm self-employment | 1.4 | 0.23 | 1.0 | 1.1 | 2.54 | 2.7 |
| Employment | 2.2 | 0.59 | 2.5 | 2.1 | 4.74 | 5.0 |
| Interest, dividends | 15.8 | 0.88 | 3.7 | 23.5 | 2.96 | 3.1 |
| Other sources | 5.5 | 0.39 | 1.7 | 4.6 | 2.25 | 2.4 |
| All sources | - | 23.57 | 100 | - | 95.29 | 100 |

### Social welfare provision
Social welfare pensions comprise contributory social insurance payments for those who have paid PRSI during their working life and social assistance means-tested payments for those who have not been covered by PRSI in their working life, or who do not have sufficient

8    *Occupational and Personal Pension Coverage,* 1995. Dublin, G. Hughes, B. Whelan: ESRI, Department of Social Welfare and Pensions Board, 1996  Based on reports of the Department of Social Welfare 1977 and 1995, Labour Force Surveys 1979 and 1995, Living In Ireland Survey 1995, B. Whelan and R. Vaughan (1982).

PRSI contributions to qualify for a pension and who do not have a reasonable income from another source.

The payments are made up of a personal rate of payment and, if applicable, an allowance for qualified adult and child dependants.

Table 2

Rates of Social Welfare Payment from June 1998

| Pension Type | Personal over age 66 £ | Qualified adult under age 66 £ | Child Dependant £ |
|---|---|---|---|
| Old Age (Contributory) and Retirement Pension[9] | 83.00 | 52.50 | 15.20 |
| Old Age (Non-contributory) Pension | 72.50 | 41.20 | 13.20 |
| Widows/Widowers (Contributory) Pension | 76.10 | - | 17.00 |
| Invalidity Pension (over age 65) | 83.00 | 46.50 | 15.20 |

Additional allowances of £6 and £5 respectively are also paid to pensioners living alone and to those aged over 80 years. In addition, pensioners may be eligible for allowances for electricity, telephone rental, TV licences and fuel in the winter months. In the main, these allowances are for social welfare pensioners who live alone. All those aged 66 years or over are entitled to free travel on public transport. The weekly value of the free schemes to individual recipients has been estimated at £10.22 per week, or £13.60 in the case of an elderly couple.[10]

Total social welfare pensions payments (including free schemes) amounted to £1.7 billion in 1996.

Coverage of the population for pensions

Currently about 83 per cent of the population aged over 66 are receiving social welfare pensions. When account is taken of the derived entitlements of dependent spouses (who are usually wives), pension coverage rises to almost 90 per cent.

---

9    Retirement pension is payable at age 65 years.

10   ESRI, *A Review of the Commission of Social Welfare's Minimum Adequate Income*. Policy Research Series, Paper No. 29, December 1996, P.83

Over the years there has been a shift from non-contributory means- tested pensions to contributory pensions as a result of the extension of PRSI cover to different sections of the working population. For example, the percentage of pensioners in receipt of old-age contributory pension rose from 47 per cent in 1986 to 58 per cent in 1996. This shift is expected to continue as more and more workers on retirement qualify for PRSI contributory pensions and is projected to increase to 86 per cent by 2016.

In 1988 social insurance cover for pensions was extended to self-employed people (including farmers) and about 164,000 are now covered[11]. Part-time workers and new entrants in the public service were subsequently brought into PRSI cover in 1991 and 1995 respectively. As a result, workers can now look forward to a basic pension on retirement, the level of which will not be reduced by any other source of income.

Recent initiatives which will improve access to contributory pensions for people in the future include the homemaker regulations, which allow for gaps in a person's PRSI record arising on account of time spent in the home caring for young children (up to age twelve) or for another family member who requires full-time care because of old age, illness or disability, to be disregarded in the calculation of entitlement to pension - a total gap of 20 years can be disregarded .

The recent reduction in the yearly average test for old age contributory pension from 20 to 10 years makes it easier for people to meet PRSI criteria to qualify for a contributory pension. This initiative will be of particular benefit to women.

### 14.7    The level of pension payment and adequacy of pensions

As a result of the improvement in social welfare pension coverage and rates of payment since the late 1970s, and increased coverage under occupational pension schemes, material living standards among older people have greatly improved and the levels of poverty among the elderly have declined. Older people have a high reliance on social welfare pensions and, while the increase in elderly incomes is sufficient to keep pace with inflation, it has fallen behind the rate of growth of the economy. Average replacement ratios (ratio of current earnings compared to income they would receive if they were still working) for pensioners dependent solely on social welfare payments are modest and have been falling in most cases over time. The relationship between the rate of increase in the old age contributory pensions and (i) prices and (ii) earnings is set out in Table 3.

11    Actuarial Review of Social Welfare Pensions, undertaken by the Irish Pensions Trust Ltd. on behalf of the Department of Social, Community and Family Affairs, Stationery Office, Dublin, September 1997.

Table 3

Social Welfare Increases in Old Age (Contributory) Pension vis-à-vis Earnings and Prices

| Period over | Real Increase Relative to Earnings | Real Increase Relative to Prices |
|---|---|---|
| Last 5 years | - 3% | + 7% |
| Last 10 Years | - 8% | + 10% |
| Last 20 years | +18% | +59% |

It can be seen that over the last 20 years the pension rate has increased by more than earnings. While this has not been the case in the last 10 years, the increases have been well in excess of price inflation. The significant real rates increases in the past have occurred in an ad hoc way, partly in response to the income position and demands of older people. In more recent years, priority was given to raising the lowest rates of social welfare for unemployed families and for those depending on illness payments, in line with the recommendation of the Commission on Social Welfare. As the income position of elderly people in real terms was improved more modestly, the risk of relative poverty for households headed by an elderly person increased, as illustrated in Table 4.

Research [12] by the ESRI indicates that there was an increase in the number of households headed by persons in receipt of an old age pension with incomes below 50 per cent of the national average over the 1987-94 period. This is a much lower level of poverty than prevailed in the 1970s, but still means that many elderly people are living at unacceptably low standards of living. The growth in poverty among older people has been particularly high in households that rely on non-contributory pensions. Within this group, older widows, usually living alone, are at the greatest risk of all.

Table 4

Risks of Relative Poverty for Households Headed by an Elderly Person

| Relative Poverty Line[13] | Household Budget Survey | | 1987 ESRI % | 1994 ESRI % |
|---|---|---|---|---|
| | 1973 % | 1980 % | | |
| 40 | 12.9 | 7.1 | 3.6 | 3.2 |
| 50 | 30.9 | 24.4 | 7.2 | 9.8 |
| 60 | 44.0 | 46.6 | 20.9 | 41.5 |

Source : *ESRI (1996), Poverty in the 1990s*, p. 93

12   *Poverty in the 1990s*, Tim Callan, Brian Nolan, Brendan J. Whelan, Christopher T. Whelan, James Williams, Department of  Social Welfare, ESRI, Combat Poverty Agency, Dublin 1996.

13   Income poverty standards or lines are based on the view that poverty should be examined in relative (not absolute) terms and this relates to the standard of living of the society in question. In this discussion, these standards are based on the 1987 and 1994 ESRI surveys of some 4,000 households. Average household disposable income is estimated from the sample and then converted to average disposable income per adult equivalent. The relative income poverty line/ standard is then derived at 40 per cent, 50 per cent and 60 per cent of this income - the choice of standard is arbitrary.

### The level of pension payments

**14.8.** It is evident that, despite a real increase of around 10 per cent in the rates of payment over the last 10 years, the real value of pension payment in comparison to average industrial earnings has been falling over that period. It is also evident that there has been an increase in the numbers of households headed by pensioners with incomes below 50 per cent of the national average.

It is the Commission's view that budgetary policy over the next few years must be redress this situation. In this context, the Commission welcomes the increase of £5 per week in the personal rate of pension announced in the 1998 Budget and the specific commitment to and prioritising of older people in the programme for Government *An Action Programme for the Millennium.*[14]

**The Commission agrees with the recommendations in the report on the National Pensions Policy Initiative - *Securing Retirement Income* - that at a general level the future policy priorities should be:**

- **To continue to increase social welfare pensions payments and to support the extension of occupational pensions coverage to achieve a reasonable standard of income in retirement for all people.**
- **To have as a target that older people do not lose out in terms of economic growth over time. Ideally, the Commission considers that the target should be to relate increases in social welfare pensions to movements in average earnings in future years.**

#### Qualified adult allowance

The Commission suggests, in the context of the adequacy of income in households relying on social welfare pensions, that consideration be given to moving towards a greater degree of individualisation of payments for retired couples, that is where both persons of a couple get a payment in their own right. In this context, it is of interest that the old age non-contributory pension has always been on an individual basis because of the means test. If a couple are both over age 66 and qualify for a non-contributory pension, each will receive the same rate of pension.

The Commission has already questioned the structure of social welfare payment with its emphasis on the dependency role of one partner in the family. The Commission is of the view that the concept is particularly inappropriate in relation to couples who have completed their time in the active labour force and as homemakers and who, on retirement, should be able to look forward to a new recognition of the contribution they have made within the home and in the workforce. This recognition is particularly relevant to retired women who have worked full-time in the home.

At present 'derived dependency' payments vary from 56 per cent to 69 per cent of the personal rate of pension which is paid to the former breadwinner. The Commission considers that there is no justification for this variation and that policy should move towards standardising these rates.

14   The proposal is to increase the old age pension to £100 over a 5-year period, i.e. by 2002.

Younger women, as the Commission has documented in this report, are continuing in the workforce, or returning after a period spent rearing children. A greater proportion of women in the future will thus have pension cover in their own right. Recently initiatives have been introduced to ensure that women who have taken time out of the workforce for family care reasons are not disadvantaged by resultant gaps in their PRSI records on retirement. Thus the pool of dependants who must fall back on derived entitlements in the future will get smaller. There are 25,500 women over age 66 in this situation at present. **The Commission would like to see the feasibility of substantially increased payments to qualified adults explored in the Government response to the National Pensions Policy Initiative, and in the context of the Working Group on the Tax and Social Welfare Treatment of One- And Two-Parent Households.**

## 14.9 Sharing the cost of pensions - an important expression of social solidarity

The Commission strongly supports the contributory principle underlying the PRSI system. The sharing of the costs of protection between employers and workers and the wider community and the funding by the workers of today of the pensions for the older retired generation are important expressions of social solidarity and solidarity between the generations. The Commission, in Chapter 5 has cited the social solidarity underpinning the social insurance fund in support of policy options presented in relation to meeting the cost of caring for young children for workers with family responsibilities.

## 14.10 Occupational Pensions are of growing significance for the future

Pensions from former employment are significant for a growing number of people. Occupational pension schemes are essentially voluntary private arrangements between employers and their workers. Over 501,000 people in Ireland are members of occupational pension schemes. A recent study [15] shows that 46 per cent of those at work in 1995 were covered by an occupational pension scheme. Within these figures there is a wide variety of coverage for different groups of workers in different sectors of the economy, ranging from 83 per cent of public sector employees having cover to 35 per cent of private sector employees. Less than 10 per cent of part-time and temporary workers have cover for occupational pensions.

The State promotes and encourages these private arrangements through the tax system. Pension contributions are not subject to tax and the returns on the investments of the pension funds are not taxed. The tax allowances for pension schemes have provided strong incentives for workers to join pension schemes. The State, through the Pensions Board, has also taken on the regulatory and supervisory responsibilities for the protection of pension funds to ensure that pensions promised are there for workers on retirement.

Pension funds are a very successful vehicle for savings for workers who are providing for themselves and their families. With assets of some £21 billion, these workers' savings are also making a very important contribution to the economy.

---

15  *Occupational and Personal Pension Coverage 1995*, Gerard Hughes and Brendan J. Whelan ESRI, Department of Social Welfare and Pensions Board. 1996.

### 14.11 Increasing coverage of occupational pension schemes is important

The Commission shares the concerns about the fact that more than half of all workers are not covered by occupational pension schemes. This means that a significant segment of the workforce is at risk of a sharp drop in living standards on retirement. The Commission notes that those working in temporary or part-time jobs and those working in small companies (who are mainly female employees) have the lowest rates of participation in schemes.

According to the National Pensions Policy Initiative Consultation Document[16], the reasons for non-coverage have not been adequately researched. Some employers may pay above average salaries and expect staff to make their own arrangements. Many small employers say that there is no demand or that they cannot afford it. The reasons why individuals do not make their own plans are equally unknown. Some people may already feel that they have adequate provision in their spouse's pension plan or regard other assets, such as their business, as sufficient provision. Others simply may not be able to afford to pay.

The Commission considers that many of the reasons suggested may be particularly relevant to families who are struggling to balance work commitments with childcare responsibilities. In Chapter 8 the Commission has described how part-time and temporary work and long working hours, in order to improve income, are features of life for many young families. **The Commission would like to see this issue explored in greater detail in the policy response to the National Pensions Policy Initiative to identify the supports that families in this situation need now and to identify how they can be better facilitated to provide for their retirement.**

### 14.12 Assessing occupational pensions for eligibility for medical services

**The Commission would also like to see a broad review of current policy and practice in relation to the way in which occupational pensions are assessed on retirement for the purposes of eligibility for secondary benefits, particularly for health services.** Many pensioners who are on the margins of eligibility for pension services feel penalised because during their working life they provided for additional income on retirement. In many cases it is suggested that the benefits of eligibility for particular services, such as medical services, can far outweigh the value of the occupational pension. The Commission is of the view that some aspects of current policy in this field is penalising thrift and providence and is not congruent with the basic approach to promotion of personal pension provision for retirement.

### 14.13 Securing the Role of Older People in the Community and with their Families

The social support experienced within family networks is recognised as an important contribution to physical and mental well-being. This is particularly true of the relationship between husband and wife.

When asked to nominate the things that most affected their quality of life, *family and health* were the most commonly mentioned issues by a sample of older Irish people living in the community[17]. Irish older people enjoy large networks of close kin living locally (i.e., within ten

---

16    National Pensions Policy Initiative, Consultation Document, Department of Social Welfare and the Pensions Board, 1997

17    J.P. Browne, C.A. O' Boyle, H.M., McGee, C.R.B. Joyce, N.J. McDonald, K. O' Malley, and B. Hiltbrunner. *Individual quality of life in the healthy elderly. Quality of Life Research*, 3, 235-144.1994.

miles). A national survey found that married or widowed older persons had on average two or three children, four to five grandchildren and one sibling living locally. Older people in urban areas, and from skilled or semi-skilled working-class backgrounds were the most likely to have children living locally.[18]

Social isolation is a minority experience for single older people, since the majority maintain regular contact with friends, neighbours, and, to a lesser extent, relatives. Indeed no consistent links have yet been reported between subjective well-being and levels of family contact in older Irish people living in communities. This is despite relatively high admission rates to psychiatric facilities among single older Irish people[19] and international evidence suggesting that married older people enjoy a higher life expectancy and better health[20].

Contrary to the perception that older people are dependent on their families, the evidence suggests that older people contribute greatly to Irish family life. In terms of within-family financial transfers, older people are more likely to give than receive occasional gifts of large monetary value (exceeding £200) and are as likely to give routine financial support as they are to receive it.[18] It is fair to say that Irish families generally benefit from their links with older relatives: most older people are completely independent in activities of daily living and do not rely on their family for care or financial support.

## 14.14    Family Support for Older People

For a minority of older people, the family is an important source of care and support. Studies report that between 18 and 21 per cent of older people living in the community need some informal care at home[21]. It was found that some 17.5 per cent of the elderly population (66,000 persons) were receiving substantial informal care of some kind. The care was mostly provided by daughters, daughters-in-law or wives, living with the older person. Spouses were the main carers in one out of four cases.

A report [22] on older people makes the point that public policy for older people has evolved in such a way that there are now many aspects of life where public provision is the norm and family provision is not significant. The report cites the example of income provision by way of State pensions, which is now widely regarded as a matter for public, rather than private, responsibility. According to the report, the one area where adult children as well as spouses have provided unambiguous and extensive support to older people is in connection with informal care in cases of illness or increasing frailty. The report goes on to say that public policy has tended to take the availability of family support for granted. While health policy acknowledges the role of informal family care as a key element of community care, the bias

18    T. Fahey and P. Murray, *Health and Autonomy Among the Over 65s in Ireland.* Dublin National Council for the Elderly, 1994

19    F. Keogh and A. Roche, *Mental Disorders in Older Irish People : Incidence, Prevalence and Treatment Dublin,* National Council for the Elderly, 1996.

20,    G.C. Myers, *Marital Status Dynamics at Older Ages,*in, United Nations Ageing And The Family, New York: United Nations, 1994.

21    T. Fahey and P. Murray, *Health and Autonomy among the over 65s in Ireland, Dublin,* National Council for the Elderly, 1994 , J. O'Connor, E. Smyth and B. Whelan, Caring for the Elderly, Part 1: A Study of Carers at Home and in the Community, Dublin, National Council for the Aged 1988

22    *The Elderly, the Family and the State in Ireland:* report prepared by  Tony Fahey, ESRI for the Interim Report of the Joint Committee on the Family, Houses of the Oireachtas, Jan 1997.

in actual public provision is towards institutional care for frail older people.

The report draws attention to the upheaval which becoming dependent causes for many older people. The transition from active independent lives to illness and dependency is normally the most traumatic transition in an older person's life. Many older people worry about becoming a burden on their families and are often concerned about not being able to return help as much as they would like. Families are committed to caring for their older family members and caring in these circumstances has its reward. Nevertheless, caring responsibilities can be demanding and at times stressful. Extra supports, in the form of respite care and training and information for the carer, are recommended in the report and it is suggested that the policy approach should focus on improving the quality and experience of care for both carer and recipient.

The report also points out that there is a significant minority of people who, never having married, have no immediate family and who are very dependent on formal State support services. Improvements in marriage rates in more recent years will alter this situation for future generations. Nevertheless, there will continue to be a substantial minority of older people who are "family less" in the years ahead.

### 14.15 Priorities in supporting the care of elderly people

The health strategy document sets out clear priorities in relation to care for older people[23]. Over the next few years priority will be given to strengthening home, community and hospital services to provide much-needed support to older people who are ill or dependent and to assist those who care for them.

Support for families in carrying out their caring functions and enhanced community support services are the main areas which the Commission considers needs to be addressed to realise the widely supported policy objective to maintain older people in dignity and independence at home in accordance with their wishes, as expressed in many research studies. The Commission considers that there is a need for a strong shift in the policy approach if this priority is to be realised. Moreover, the Commission considers that caring for elderly people is a matter where public policy needs to be sensitive to both the needs of family carers and the needs of the dependent older people.

### 14.16 The incidence of people needing full-time care from a family member

It is difficult to estimate the number of people who are providing a significant level of care to elderly people and to other dependent family members. Two reports commissioned by the National Council for the Elderly and referred to already, estimate the incidence of care needed among older people. The estimates suggest that between 77,000 and 86,000 older people require some level of care, with about 31,000 requiring a lot of care. Much less detailed information is available in relation to people with disabilities and in relation to the incidence of care among children with disabilities. A recent report[24] suggested that somewhere in the region of 58,000 adults and 9,000 children with disabilities require a significant level of care.

---

23   *Shaping a Healthier Future*, A Strategy for Effective Healthcare in the 1990s, Department of Health, Dublin.

24   *A Long Term Support Framework for Female Carers of Older People and People with Disabilities* 1995-2011, Fifth report of the Fourth Joint Committee on Women's Rights: 1996.

The extent of the responsibilities of carers varies: some may be required to provide a few hours support a day, or a week; others try to balance their caring responsibilities with participation in a paid job on a full or part-time basis; and some carers have heavy demanding responsibilities and provide full-time care on a round the clock basis. For some carers, caregiving is not confined to just one person; some look after more than one person. For example, some 25 per cent of the 10,000 people receiving the carer's allowance look after more than one person.

The contribution of family carers is enormous, both socially and economically.

**The cost of caring**

Submissions to the Commission have pointed out that there are often extra expenses involved in caring for a dependent older member of a family or a family member with a disability. Not the least of these costs is the financial cost of caring. Many families have to make some (often fairly substantial) adaptation to the house to facilitate care for the dependent relative. There are also extra expenses involved in caring, such as heating, travel, diet and other costs, including loss of income for those who leave employment or for those who can work only part-time.[25]

---

25 In Chapter 8, the Commission examines the situation of workers with caring responsibilities and makes a number of recommendations in relation to improving arrangements for them to carry out their caring responsibilities while remaining in the workforce.

## Some facts about carers [26]

### Those who are cared for by members of their own household

- The vast majority of older people receiving care (92 per cent) are cared for by a relative.
- Daughters are most likely to provide care, (30 per cent of older people receiving care) followed by a spouse (24 per cent), son (16 per cent) and daughter-in-law (14 per cent). Some 14 per cent of older people were cared for by other relatives.
- The majority of carers are aged between 20 and 54 years of age, with a large group aged between 40 and 54 years. However, one-quarter of the carers are over 65 years of age.
- Help is most commonly given with domestic tasks such as shopping (80 per cent of older people receiving care), laundry and ironing (76 per cent), transport (69 per cent).
- Over 18 per cent of elderly people receiving care receive help with all aspects of living (personal care, mobility around the house), thus enabling the older person to live within a family in the community

### Those who are cared for by people who are not living with them

- While care is provided mostly by relatives it is worth noting that 40 per cent of those needing help receive help from non-relatives, showing the extent of informal care in the community.
- The tasks undertaken by these carers emphasise the importance of social contacts. Some 86 per cent of carers provide company and offer help with routine daily activities (57 per cent undertake shopping and collection of pensions; one-quarter provide help with cooking, laundry etc.)

Note :

*More recent studies generally concur with the findings of this 1988 study, in that they show that relatives, especially female relatives, remain by far the most important source of care for older people living at home. However, a recent study [27] shows that smaller numbers of carers live with the cared-for person. Some of this difference may be the result of sampling variability in the two surveys, but it may also reflect a slight move away from relatives as providers of care.*

26  *Caring for the Elderly Part I; The Caring Process: A study of Carers in the Home and in the Community,* J. O' Connor, E. Smyth. B. Whelan, National Council for the Aged (1988), Report No. 18.

27  T. Fahey and P. Murray, *Health and Autonomy among the over 65s in Ireland,* Dublin National Council for the Elderly, 1994.

Many carers spend long hours providing care - one study showed the most spent an average of 47 hours per week engaged in caring activities, a figure which rises considerably as dependency increases[28]. As a result, some carers report a strain on health- both mental and physical, - tiredness and a restriction of social life. Caring has also been found to have effects on family life, including changes in the family routine and a deterioration in relationships with other members of the family[29].

Despite the stress and strain experienced by many carers, most derive an immense amount of satisfaction from the care they provide. They do not want to give up caring; they just want some assistance to help them carry out their role more effectively.

## 14.17 Support for families with their caring responsibilities

The principal forms of support with caring responsibilities for which elderly people and their carers look to public provision are: financial support, either for the dependent person or the carer, information and advice about services and entitlements, training and guidance for the carer in looking after the older person, and respite care[30].

The main income support payments are :
- the means-tested carer's allowance (payable by the Department of Social, Community and Family Affairs). The allowance is payable to carers of persons requiring full-time care and attention. The current full rate of payment is £73.50[31] and just over 10,000 persons, most of whom are women, are in receipt of the payment,
- A person who is totally incapacitated or whose spouse is totally incapacitated may claim a tax allowance of up to £8,500 towards the employment of a person to provide care and attention. About 300 people avail of this allowance. There are also general tax allowances in respect of incapacitated children (up to £700 a year) and in respect of dependent adult relatives (£110 a year). About 9,000 claim the incapacitated child allowance and about 22,000 people claim the dependent relative allowance.

## 14.18 Financial support for caring needs

The Commission notes the review of the carer's allowance underway in the Department of Social, Community and Family Affairs and that part of that review will involve examining various options in relation to making provision for meeting caring needs in the future. In this context, the role of PRSI and the private sector is being explored.

The Commission further notes the establishment of a working group by the Minister for Finance to consider how to devise a targeted relief at a reasonable cost which will complement health and social welfare policy objectives for those in the home looking after a family member in need of care.

---

28   *Care provision and cost measurement : Dependent Elderly People at home and in Geriatric hospitals :* J. Blackwell, E. O' Shea, G. Moane, P. Murray : Dublin ESRI 1992.

29   National Council for the Aged, 1988, *Caring for the Elderly Part II, The Caring Process: A study of carers in the home,* J. O' Connor, H. Ruddle.

30   *The Economics and Financing of Long Term care of the Elderly in Ireland,* Eamon O' Shea, Jenny Hughes, 1994 , National Council for the Elderly

31   Rate for carers under age 66 from June 1998.

In Chapter 5 the Commission considers the present tax arrangements in place for married persons and whether the considerable amount of investment involved in these arrangements, some £350 million in 1991, could be better directed to provide more support for families with the most demanding caring responsibilities. The Commission's suggestion for a review having regard to, *inter alia*, the need for investment in support for the caring functions carried out traditionally by women in the home and in the community, is particularly relevant to the issue of greater financial support for carers.

14.19    **Advice, information and training, support networks and respite care**

Most carers take on the job of caring with no specialist knowledge or training. They have to learn as they go along, frequently at considerable cost to their physical and psychological health and often at considerable economic expense.

In order to be able to give the best possible care, the carer needs advice, information and training so that she/he may be properly prepared for the tasks involved. Carers also wish to know about the long-term prognosis and treatment and caring options related to the medical condition of the person they are caring for. Information is a very effective and relatively low cost method of providing support for carers.

In recent years a number of carers' support groups have grown up around the country. Most of the groups have carers among their members. They meet regularly and provide a range of supports including information, emotional support, recreation and entertainment activities. Practical help, by way of training and health educational programmes, a shopping service, organising respite breaks and a sitting service as well as organising holidays and outings, are examples of some of the initiatives developed by carers' groups. A recent study[32] found that such services were vital to maintaining carers in good health and are critical to their well-being. According to the study, these groups receive minimum funding; in fact the study showed that the maximum received by any group was £10,000 per annum. Many groups in the study expressed the view that they could and would greatly enhance services if they had more resources.

The Carers Association is one such organisation. It is a national voluntary organisation with a small number of offices around the country. Their services include a helpline, the production of education and information packs and teaching materials. The Association helps carers to organise carers' groups and pursues carers' interests at national level.

Soroptimists International, Republic of Ireland, as part of its national project 'Caring for Carers' has introduced a Carers Charter[33] The Carer's Charter in Action pilot programme in the Mid Western Health Board area involves a range of activities, education, training and caring for the sick, personal development programmes for carers and advocacy services.

It is the Commission's view that the voluntary support services have a significant contribution to make to providing support to carers. **The Commission considers that investment in the work of voluntary carers' organisations is highly cost-effective.**

---

32    *Support Services for Carers of Elderly People Living at Home* : P. Finucane, J. Tiernan, G. Moane National Council for the Elderly, Dublin :1994.

33    See Appendix 1 to this chapter.

**Substantial State support for the voluntary sector should be a key feature of policy in relation to meeting the caring needs in the future.**

### Respite care

Respite care can take many forms, including day centres, temporary residential care, holiday stays for dependent people, short-term relief care and domiciliary relief care. The availability of regular respite can reduce the number of people seeking residential care in the longer term. Services, such as home help and community day care services, are essential forms of non-residential respite. Informal respite evenings and activities for older people organised at local and community level on a voluntary basis can provide significant help to carers. It is the Commission's view that the voluntary sector can make an important contribution here and should be supported financially by way of grant aid.

## 14.20    Home and Community Care Services

The key support services for older people and their carers as identified in the 1988 *Years Ahead* report are domiciliary nursing, Home Help[34], day care centres and meals services, with occupational therapy, physiotherapy, chiropody, speech therapy and social work services additional as appropriate.

### Public Health Nurse

The public health nurse provides a valuable service to older people and their carers, as evidenced in submissions to the Commission. The Commission has suggested in Chapter 4 that a broader nursing skill mix within the community nursing service should be developed and that specialisation is required so that the different needs of older people and their carers might be better met. It is suggested that certain services might be more appropriately provided by trained skilled carers to assist public health nurses. In this regard, the Commission notes the development of the position of Home Care Assistant to focus on personal care as an extension of the public health nursing service. The point has been made to the Commission that some of this work overlaps with work undertaken by the Home Help service and that this is an issue which will need to be examined as the new service is developed. Submissions to the Commission have highlighted the need for a 24-hour community nursing service to respond to the needs of older people and their carers, as well as families with demanding caring responsibilities.

### Home Help

Home help includes various forms of help with everyday household tasks, such as cleaning, cooking, shopping, help with personal care and companionship. The service is designed to help elderly, sick or infirm individuals and their dependants to continue to live in their own homes. According to submissions received by the Commission, this service is highly important in maintaining the independence of older people. The home help service is essential for the continued independence of many older people living at home.

---

34    Section 61 of the Health Act 1970 empowers, without obliging, health boards to provide support services, such as home help, laundry and meals.

There are 11,215 part-time and 126 full-time home helps employed throughout the eight health boards. In practice, about half the home helps are employed directly by the health boards[35]. The rest are from voluntary organisations who receive funding from the health boards.

Health boards have different methods for determining eligibility for the service. In 1993 approximately 3.5 per cent of older people nationally were able to avail of this service. It has been suggested to the Commission that in many cases where the elderly person has a full-time carer resident with them, the elderly person was not eligible to avail of the service. In addition, the average number of hours per week home help received varies from health board to health board. The average number of hours per week received by home help clients varied from 14.8 hours in the Midland Health Board, to 5.8 hours in the North Western Health Board[36].

### Meals service

The meals service involves the provision of meals to elderly persons in their own homes, at day centres, day clubs and sheltered housing schemes. Meals are either prepared in the local hospitals or provided by voluntary organisations grant-aided by the health boards. (The Eastern Health Board provides approximately 1,000,000 meals per annum.)

The meals service is highly effective in a number of ways. It provides food and comfort for older people, enhances their social networks and their sense of security, strengthens the sense of neighbourly obligation towards older people and provides a cost-effective watchdog for the community on the situation of vulnerable older people.

**14.21    Adequate resources and standard guidelines for services**

It has been suggested to the Commission that services such as home help and meals, community health care services and day-care services should be regarded as core services for older people who are unable to cope with daily living independently and that appropriate funding should be provided to secure the provision of these services[37].

The Commission agrees that there is a need for increased investment in these services.

**As an immediate priority, the Commission recommends that standard guidelines for eligibility for home care services and meals should be adopted by all health boards. The eligibility criteria should admit older people who need the service, irrespective of whether they have a carer resident with them. Health boards should be adequately resourced to provide these services.**

**14.22    Local communities and the provision of services to older people**

Services such as the meals service are largely dependent on the contribution of voluntary workers, mainly women who, while working full-time in the home, contribute a number of

---

35    data supplied by the Department of Health and Children.

36    Lundstrom, F. and McKeown, K., *Home Help Services for Elderly People in Ireland,* Dublin, National Council for the Elderly, 1994 and information from the *National Council on Ageing and Older People*

37    Submission to the Commission from the *National Council on Ageing and Older People.*

hours per week to community work. The greater participation of women, particularly married women, in the workforce, as documented elsewhere in this report, has significant implications for the future of this and other services and points to the need for a concerted effort to maintain these vital services.

The development of core services, including home helps and meals, has enormous potential for the quality of life for older people and at the same time for the creation of new sustainable jobs in local communities.

In this context, the Commission notes the establishment under Partnership 2000 of a working group to undertake a detailed examination of the potential of the social economy[38]. The potential for increasing employment in the social, economy in, for example, home services, particularly in home help and childcare, has been well documented by the National Economic and Social Forum.[39] The Forum's report has cited a Conference of Religious of Ireland initiative[40] in this area and the increase in the number of community employment places as evidence of the considerable employment potential in the activities of the social economy.

**The Commission considers that the potential of the social economy in responding to the need for support services in the community should be explored further and that the area-based partnerships and County Enterprise Boards should be encouraged to develop initiatives responding to the needs of the community** (including meals services and care initiatives for older people). The Commission draws attention to the recommendations in the National Economic and Social Forum's Report for the full range of official support and programmes, particularly training and seed capital, management skills, and start-up assistance, i.e. support packages appropriate to the social economy, to be made available for initiatives designed to respond to social needs.

The Commission is of the view that the development of the social economy to provide services to older people has enormous potential for:

(i) improving the quality of life of older people
(ii) the creation of jobs through the provision of necessary social services
(iii) the development of a community dynamic to support a dependent older population.

## 14.23 Community health care services

A comprehensive system of community health care services, such as physiotherapy, occupational therapy and chiropody, was a key recommendation of *The Years Ahead* to underpin the strategy of caring for older people at home.

---

38  Para 4.39 of Partnership 2000 for Inclusion, Employment and Competitiveness states: A Working Group will be established immediately to undertake a detailed examination of the potential of the social economy, both in terms of employment and also the supply of services, such as childcare, eldercare and services improving the quality of life in disadvantaged areas, The Working Group will comprise representatives from relevant Government Departments and the Social Partners. Appropriate support mechanisms to facilitate the achievement of the full potential of the social economy will be established in the light of the recommendations of the Working Group.

39  National Economic and Social Forum, Report No. 7, *Jobs Potential of the Services Sector,* April 1995,

40  The Conference of Religious of Ireland created, over a 12-month period, 1,000 jobs in a wide range of fields, including tourism, adult education, the arts, sports, child care and caring for older people.

A conference to review progress since the publication of *The Years Ahead* [41] noted that this was one area where almost no progress had been made and that the plan for a comprehensive system of domicilary services has not been implemented. It appears from discussions at the expert conference that the appropriateness and cost-effectiveness of the delivery of these services in the home setting seem to have called into question the feasibility of the provision of these services in the way that was envisaged by the working party which drew up *The Years Ahead*.

The inadequacies in community health care services was a significant topic in submissions to the Commission. It is the Commission's view that access to these services is an important feature of support for older people and their carers. The Commission recommends that a review should be carried out of the way in which these services (physiotherapy, speech therapy, chiropody and social work services) are delivered to older people. **The objective of the review should be the development of an action plan for the delivery of services in a cost-effective way, which is feasible to implement and which meets the needs of elderly people and their carers.**

### 14.24    Co-ordination of Services is important

It has been suggested to the Commission that the multiplicity of public and private agencies involved in providing health and social care to older people leads to a fragmentation of services and a lack of co-ordination between services. It may also lead to confusion for older people and their families and may restrict the take-up of services.

The National Council on Ageing and Older People has highlighted the need to develop an approach to co-ordination at the level of the individual. The Council has indicated how this could be achieved by the provision of a package of services to those older people identified as being on the margins of institutional care but who might benefit from such a case management approach. A 'care co-ordinator' could draw together the elements of the caring network - statutory, family, neighbourhood and voluntary - and supervise the implementation of an agreed package of care for an individual and his/her family. A 'care co-ordinator' would contribute much to the quality and consistency of care for an individual older person. He/she would ensure appropriate use of statutory services and support the caring network of family and neighbours.

Research[42] carried out in the UK showed that the introduction of a case management approach to the care of elderly people resulted in a reduction in the use of institutional care facilities. The quality of life of older people and their caregivers improved significantly. The study showed that these gains were achieved at no greater cost than for providing existing services over the same time period and could thus bring about greater efficiency in care provision for older people.

---

41   National Council on Ageing and Older People, Conference: Review of the Implementation of the Recommendations of *The Years Ahead.... A Policy for the Elderly* and Implications for Future Policy on Older People in Ireland, Held in Dublin on 11 and 12 September, 1997.

42   Challis, *Case Management in Social and Health Care* - Lessons from a United Kingdom Program, Journal of Care Management, Volume 2, Number 3, Fall 1993

**The Commission is of the view that a case management approach to health care should be further explored with a view to developing this approach as a basis for co-ordinated care in the community.**

### Risk register

The introduction of a case management approach in local areas which draws on all of the elderly person's support network would provide a very sound basis to underpin the maintenance by health boards of 'risk registers' of vulnerable elderly people in particular locations.

### 14.25 Safe and secure living for older people

A safe and security living environment for the small numbers of very vulnerable older people has to be a priority objective for community care policy in the years ahead. In this context, the Commission draws the attention of policy-makers to a report prepared for the Joint Committee on the Family[43]. The report contains a comprehensive analysis of the housing issues affecting older people and highlights some significant deficiencies in provision for especially vulnerable older people. The policy priorities identified include :

- A concerted drive to address the need for basic facilities (such as indoor toilets, running water, bathrooms and damp-free dwellings) in the households of 5 to 10 per cent of older people,
- The development of community supports and special housing to meet the needs of the 'hidden homelessness' that is, those who are on the margins of independent living and lack social supports and appropriate housing in the community.

It is the Commission's view that the target within the next five years should be the development of community supports and special housing to meet the needs of this group.

The Commission further suggests that, as well as enhancing the provision of sheltered housing by local authorities and some voluntary agencies, the possibility of private sector involvement (as a counterpart to the senior citizens' housing schemes provided by many local authorities and voluntary housing agencies) should be explored, as suggested by the researcher in his report.

### 14.26

The Commission welcomes initiatives in recent years to enhance the security of older people who are living independently in the community. These initiatives include the provision of financial assistance to voluntary groups towards meeting the costs of installing security devices for those older people who may feel vulnerable and insecure in today's society.

43   *The Elderly , the Family and the State in Ireland,* Joint Committee on the Family, Houses of the Oireachtas, January 1997.

# Appendix 1

## Soroptimists International, Republic of Ireland

### Carers' Charter

1.   Carers have the right to be recognised for the central role which they play in community care and in creating a community of caring.
2.   Carers have the right to acknowledge and address their own needs for personal fulfilment.
3.   Carers have the right to acknowledge and address their own needs in relation to their contribution to their family and community.
4.   Carers have the right to practical help in carrying out the tasks of caregiving, including domestic help, home adaptations, appliances, incontinence services and help with transport.
5.   Carers have the right to support services, e.g. public health nurses, day centres and home helps in providing medical, personal and domestic care.
6.   Carers have the right to respite care both for short spells as in day hospitals and for longer periods to enable them to have time for themselves.
7.   Carers have the right to emotional and moral support.
8.   Carers have the right to financial support and recompense which does not preclude carers taking employment or sharing care with other people.
9.   Carers have the right to regular assessment and review of their needs and those of the people for whom they care.
10.  Carers have the right to easily accessible information and advice.
11.  Carers have the right to expect involvement of all family members.
12.  Carers have the right to have counselling made available to them at different stages of the caring process, including bereavement counselling.
13.  Carers have the right to skills' training and development of their potential.
14.  Carers have the right to expect their families, public authorities and community members to provide a plan for services and support for carers, taking into account the unique demographic developments up to and beyond the year 2000.
15.  Carers have the right to involvement at all levels of policy planning, to participate and contribute to the planning of an integrated and co-ordinated service for carers.
16.  Carers have the right to have an infrastructure of care, a supportive network to which they can relate when the need arises.

### The context:
### Creating a Caring Community - The role of the Carer

A community of caring implies that the carer does not find her or himself caring for a person in isolation. A central element in a community of caring is the provision of services from formal, informal and voluntary sources which will address the different needs of the carer and the people for whom they care at each stage of the caring process. A CARERS' CHARTER recognises and acknowledges the value of the role of the carer. It sets out the support required to enable the carer to continue to care in a way that ensures a high quality of life.

The CARERS' CHARTER was compiled by Professor Joyce O' Connor, Director National College of Industrial Relations, in association with Soroptimist International, Republic of Ireland National Project Caring for the Carers and with the help and support of carers and groups working with carers.

# Summary of Recommendations in Part 5

## The Policy Approach

**The Commission recommends**

### In relation to services for children (Chapter 12)

- **the importance of the years immediately preceding entry into primary school for opportunities to participate in quality services for children should be reflected in the level of overall public investment in children in this age group (i.e. from three years up to the age the child starts school at four, four and a half or five years old.),**
- **the target level of investment should be £1,000 per child per annum (in 1998 terms) in line with the investment levels for children in the infant classes in primary school,**
- **the investment should be centred on the child and directly related to the purchase of quality services- an Early Years Opportunities Subsidy (EYOS).**

The Commission considers that the EYOS should apply to all children from 3 years to schoolgoing age whatever their parents' employment status.

The Commission refers to the policy options put forward in Chapter 5 in relation to investment in the care of young children under 3 years old. In support of the recommendation for direct investment in children in the years immediately prior to primary school attendance, the Commission cites the consensus in the scientific literature about the benefits of participation in quality services to children in this age group. Children have needs for socialisation, for recreation and for exploration and new experiences. In this context early education and pre-school services are important. They offer short and long term value to children and in the long term they may have an impact on the quality of society. Quality early education fosters learning and social and emotional development.

The recommendation for an Early Years Opportunities Subsidy is intended to secure for children in this age group, while respecting parents choices in relation to the care of children, opportunities to avail of quality services for children in crèches/nurseries pre-schools or playgroups which meet the notification requirements under the Child Care Act, 1991.

It is envisaged that the Early Years Opportunities Subsidy would;
- provide access to quality services to children irrespective of social or economic background or parents employment status
- expand the range of options for all parents, including lone parents and families on low incomes
- encourage extra places in the private and in the community sector
- be particularly helpful for community-based nurseries and playgroups in meeting running costs
- allow for recognition of additional needs of some children ( for example by way of extra subsidies)
- facilitate a social mix in services
- encourage and promote standards in services.

The Early Years Opportunities Subsidy could be developed further to facilitate imaginative community-based responses to local needs; for example, in rural communities.

**Costs:** £25 million per annum in 1998 terms based on present levels of participation in services.

£50 million per annum in 1998 terms assuming an increase in take-up and that extra places are available.

£85 million per annum (approx.) in 1998 terms based on eventual provision for all 3 year olds and half of all 4 year olds who are not at school.

### In relation to the State's further role in the development of services for children
The Commission suggests

- **That the need for a co-ordinating mechanism at national level should be a priority consideration in the national framework for the development of the childcare sector which is being examined by the Expert Working Group under Partnership 2000.**

### In relation to community initiative in the provision of services for children
The Commission suggests

- **That the Equal Opportunities Childcare Programme with its emphasis on parent, community and employer involvement may provide the model for the development of an expanded programme to support community responses to a broad range of childcare needs.**

There is a distinct role for public policy in partnership with local communities in the development of services for children. There is a need for a variety of services to meet the needs of different communities and children with special needs. These may include community playgroups and naoinraí, nurseries/crèches providing part-time sessional care as well as full-time services and "out of school hours" services. Promoting a variety of services to meet diverse needs must be an important policy objective.

Further suggestions in relation to the development of community childcare initiatives include:

- selection of State-supported community-based services for development as *models of excellence* to encourage high standards and quality across all services
- *opening up schools* for greater use by community-based initiatives for services for children
- the development of *pre-school services attached to primary schools* in rural areas, based on a cluster concept where resources are shared.

### In relation to encouraging and promoting standards

- **Each health board should be resourced to establish an advisory and support service for those engaged in the provision of services for children.**
- **Future development of the regulation and inspection of services should cover broader quality objectives in relation to the standards in services provided for children.**

The regulations under Part VII of the Child Care Act, 1991 require providers of services to notify health boards of their service. Services are liable to inspection by health boards. The regulations cover the adult/child ratios and the number of children who may be catered for, the premises and facilities, the provision of food and safety measures. The regulations do not apply to childminders who are looking after not more than three pre-school children of different families along with their own children. The Commission would like to see the adoption of a supportive approach by health boards alongside inspection procedures. The Commission would like to see further development of the inspection procedures to cover broader developmental and appropriate educational objectives in relation to quality in services for children.

### In relation to childminders

- **The priority objective for the immediate future is that parents are reassured about the care of their children in their absence and that the important job undertaken by childminders in caring for our youngest citizens receives practical support and is accorded a status in the community.**

The Commission considers that the main policy objectives may be achieved through:
- *promoting awareness among parents and childminders* about what families might expect in relation to the care of their children
- supporting directly through financial assistance *umbrella organisations and childcare organisations* which promote standards through affiliation to their organisation and education and training services for members
- encouraging the establishment of *networks to support* childminders in the community.

Suggestions are put forward as to how these policy objectives might be pursued.

### In relation to expanding provision of services for children

- **Tax arrangements might provide for allowances for investment in childcare facilities by employers.**
- **Planning approval for new shopping and housing developments should be made conditional on provision for a site for a children's service.**
- **Public sector interests should be more proactive in increasing the number of places in existing facilities.**
- **Additional grants and tax allowances should be available for the establishment of services for children with special needs or the adaptation of services to accommodate children with special needs.**
- **Workplace facilities should be pursued on the social partner's agenda.**
- **Potential providers of services should be eligible for technical assistance and employment support similar to that which is available to small businesses.**

### In relation to education (Chapter 13)

**The policy priorities in the immediate years ahead should be**
- **investment in children who are not yet attending primary school as recommended in Chapters 5 and 12,**
- **greater investment in primary level education.**

*In welcoming the establishment of a National Forum on Early Education and the proposal for a White Paper*

The Commission urges

- **a child centred approach to the exploration of issues in relation to early years education :**

A quality early years curriculum should meet all the needs of children- physical, emotional and cognitive - and not just focus on the academic. There should be recognition of a wide range of qualifications in relation to early years services for children to provide more choice for parents and increase opportunities for people to take up work in services for children.

*In relation to greater investment in primary education*

The Commission considers

- **on equity grounds that there is a case for greater investment in primary level education. Spending is considerably less at primary level than at second and third level.**

The policy priorities may be achieved by:

- increased investment in primary level education,
- the continued use of the savings arising from demographic changes to address the special needs of pupils and to improve pupil-teacher ratios, particularly in the earlier years of primary school, the priority being those schools catering for children who live in communities coping with multiple disadvantage.

*In relation to changes in the curriculum at second level to recognise a wider range of abilities*

- **All forms of State certification should have a value in terms of training and employment prospects and progression to third level.**
- **Qualification criteria for access to apprenticeship and training programmes and for further education should be kept under review and employers should be kept fully informed about new developments in the Junior and Leaving Certificate and Leaving Certificate Vocational Programme.**
- **Progression routes into third-level education should be further expanded for young people who take the Leaving Certificate Applied Programme.**

*In relation to equipping young people to reach their potential as adults, family members and contributing members of society*

- **The objectives of a social, personal and health education programme may best be achieved within the supportive framework of the Health Promoting School.**
- **The partnership approach with parents adopted by the Department of Education and Science in the delivery of relationship and sexuality education in schools should be developed further.**
- **A radical approach to the introduction of family life education throughout the school curriculum from early school years through to the completion of formal education.**

The Health Promoting Schools concept focuses on a health promoting environment, physical and psycho-social with a timetabled co-ordinated programme for social, personal and health education, and links with families and local communities. An expanded social, personal, and health education programme might include:

- *healthy lifestyles,* including personal care and nutrition, the importance of a balanced diet and exercise, and the effects of smoking, alcohol and substance abuse
- *personal growth and development,* including growing up, friendships, relationships, sexuality, personal responsibility and decision-making, and self-esteem and coping strategies
- *family and parenting skills* which present young people (both boys and girls) with a realistic picture of parenthood including the difficulties which arise because of premature parenthood, and the care and development needs of young children
- t*he interdependence of family members* and the rights, duties and responsibilities of family members towards each other and the wider community, including household budgets, consumer issues and the effective management of family resources
- *social awareness issues,* including studies about the wider community and the important contribution all individuals make to society, the problems of disadvantage and the promotion of an inclusive society.

### In relation to the introduction of family and life education and according a high status to family and life studies
The Commission suggests

- **Relevant aspects of family and life education be developed for assessment at junior and senior cycles.**
- **The accreditation of relevant studies undertaken which are pertinent to family and life education in assessing entrants for colleges of education, and perhaps other careers, such as careers in public health and childcare.**
- **Ongoing in-service training for teachers and the development of support services for schools in the provision of family and life education.**

### In relation to improving life's chances and choices
The Commission

- welcomes the prioritisation of proposals for the expansion and development of the schools' psychological service
- endorses the work of the remedial service and welcomes the review currently underway
- endorses the strategies set out in the National Anti-Poverty Strategy in relation to tackling education disadvantage and early school leaving.
- is of the view that additional resources should be made available to the youth sector for work with those at risk of early school leaving.

### In relation to managing attendance at school and truancy issues
The Commission

- urges the Government to bring forward proposals in response to the report of the working group on truancy
- notes the proposals for legislation in relation to school attendance.

### In relation to enhancing the attractiveness of staying in education
**The Commission**

- considers that extra resources should be allocated to schools in disadvantaged communities to meet the full costs of running the schools on a daily basis and the caretaking and administrative support needed in these schools
- welcomes the initiative to remove examination fees from pupils in low income households
- urges implementation of the national sports strategy in relation to sports in education
- welcomes recent initiatives to enhance the role of Youthreach in provision for early school leavers
- endorses the recommendations of the Commission on the Status of People with Disabilities on access to and participation in education
- identifies a number of priorities in relation to additional supports and resources to assist children in Traveller families.

### In relation to older people in family life and in society (Chapter 14)
**The Commission identifies the issues as follows:**

- **adequate income support for older people today and for future generations of retiring people**
- **securing the role of retired people in their families and in the community as they grow older and are in need of additional supports.**

### In relation to adequate income support
**The Policy priorities are**

- **to continue to increase social welfare pensions payments and to support the extension of occupational pensions coverage to achieve a reasonable standard of income in retirement for all people,**
- **to have as a target that older people do not lose out in terms of economic growth over time. Ideally the Commission considers that the target should be to relate increases in social welfare pensions to movements in average earnings in future years.**

### In relation to pension payments for qualified adults
- **The policy approach should move towards standardising the rates of payment for qualified adults.**

At present, derived dependency rates vary from 56 per cent to 69 per cent of the personal rate of pension. The Commission considers that policy should move towards standardising these rates.

The Commission suggests that the feasibility of substantially increased payments to qualified adults should be explored in the response to the National Pensions Policy Initiative and in the context of the review of the Tax and Social Welfare treatment of One and Two Parent households. The Commission is of the view that the dependency role is particularly inappropriate in relation to spouses who have completed their time in the active labour force and as homemakers. These qualified adults, who are mostly dependent wives, should be able to look forward, on retirement, to a new recognition of the contribution they have made within the home.

### *In relation to the growing significance of occupational pensions...*
**The Commission**

- shares the concern about the fact that half of all workers are not covered by occupational pension schemes. The Commission considers that many of the reasons for non-coverage are particularly relevant to families that are struggling to balance work commitments with childcare responsibilities.

- looks for a broad review of current policy and practice in relation to the way occupational pensions are assessed on retirement for eligibility for secondary benefits, such as health services.

### *In relation to support in the care of older people*
**The Commission suggests that**

- substantial state support for voluntary and community groups and the services they provide to carers should a key feature of policy in relation to supporting carers,
- care services for older people such as home help, community health care services, day care services and meals on wheels should be regarded as core services for people and should be appropriately funded,
- the potential of the social economy in responding to the need for support services should be explored further,
- financial support for the voluntary sector to assist them in the provision of respite care should be improved,
- a case management approach to healthcare for older people, which would draw together the elements of the caring network- statutory, family, neighbourhood and voluntary- thereby providing a 'package of care'- should be further explored with a view to providing a basis for co-ordinated care for older people in the community,
- a concerted drive to address the need for basic facilities (running water, bathrooms, indoor toilets) in households experienced by 5 to 10 per cent of older people should be a priority,
- the development of community supports and special housing to meet the needs of the 'hidden homeless' i.e. those who are on the margins of independent living and lack social supports and appropriate housing in the community is important,
- the provision of sheltered housing by local authorities should be enhanced and a role for the private sector in providing sheltered housing should be explored.

# Making a start Part 5

### Recommendation 29
**The Commission recommends**

- **the introduction of a specific initiative within the community development programme of the Department of Social, Community and Family Affairs to assist local communities in developing out of school hours services.**

### Recommendation 30

- the continued publicising and promotion of the Childcare (Pre-school services) Regulations 1996, so that parents can start to look for the application of high standards in the care of their children.

### Recommendation 31

- that the framework for the future development of services for children should include a series of measures to support the work of local childminders and to promote standards and good practice in the sector. Elements of the package might include:
- information about the role of the childminder in the life of the family
- financial assistance by way of grant aid to encourage affiliation to standard setting organisations and to promote the establishment of local networks to support childminders in the community.

### Recommendation 32

- that an analysis be undertaken of the rates of maintenance grant for students with a view to ensuring that future levels reflect the importance of encouraging young people to remain in the education system until they have obtained a qualification which can contribute to their future economic and social development. As an interim measure the Commission recommends that grants should be increased to assist students in low income families.

### Recommendation 33

- that the Transition Year programme should be widely available to all second level schools and that it should be the norm for students for avail of this option before embarking on senior cycle.

### Recommendation 34

- that the Health Promoting School concept be extended to all schools.

### Recommendation 35

- that Home Economics, Social and Scientific should be promoted among students, both male and female. The Commission suggests that part of the promotion might include a more appropriate title for the subject to reflect the fundamental importance of the syllabus content.

### Recommendation 36

- the *extension of pre-school education* to all areas of disadvantage,
- subject to the current review of the pilot phase, the extension of the *Breaking the Cycle* initiative or other disadvantage initiatives on a phased basis.

- the *potential for a similar initiative to Breaking the Cycle* at *second level* should be explored.

### Recommendation 37

- the *extension of the Home/School/Community Liaison scheme* to cover all schools in areas of disadvantage within the next three years,
- that the importance of *continuity in relation to the transitions* which children make from pre-school to infant classes to primary education to second level be asserted within the scheme,
- that resources *be allocated to research* and the development of appropriate mechanisms including *outreach programmes* to reach those parents and families who are most at risk of disadvantage and who are outside the scheme at present,
- that *new links* be developed with other community and local development initiatives such as those providing second-chance education and those providing community support groups to provide progression opportunities for parents who develop an interest in pursuing education and self-development,
- The *Home School Preparatory Work Programme* be extended to all primary schools in disadvantaged communities and should be developed for the first year of second level.

### Recommendation 38

The Commission recommends that

- the Department of Education and Science should continue to promote the introduction of book rental schemes throughout the school system and should continue to increase resources for funding in this field.

### Recommendation 39

The Commission recommends that

- the adoption by all health boards of standard guidelines for eligibility for home care services and meals. These eligibility criteria should admit older people who need the service, irrespective of whether they have a carer resident with them.

### Recommendation 40

The Commission recommends

- increased financial support for the voluntary sector to assist them in the provision of respite care.

### Recommendation 41

The Commission recommends

- a review of the way in which community health care services (physiotherapy, speech therapy, chiropody and social work services) are delivered to older people.

FINAL REPORT OF THE COMMISSION ON THE FAMILY

## part 6

**Family concerns/the wider family**

**In Part 6, the Commission**

- identifies for further action some issues raised in the submissions.
- presents some perspectives in relation to strengthening kin networks for families with relatives abroad.

# Overview of Part 6

In parts 1 to 5 of the report the Commission has examined in a comprehensive way those aspects of public policy which have a significant impact on families and on how they carry out their functions. In the main, the thrust of the Commission's approach has been to examine those issues where the policy approach adopted can have maximum impact in strengthening and supporting families in a changing social and economic environment.

In Part 6 of the report the Commission considers the further concerns in relation to families which were raised in submissions. The range of issues and concerns which arose in submissions to the Commission is extensive. The Commission acknowledges the views expressed in submissions in relation to very specific topics and presents information on recent policy initiatives which are relevant to the response to people's concerns.

The Commission considers the issues in relation to families and the law which were raised in submissions. Recent policy developments are noted and the recommendations of the Law Reform Commission in relation to the court facilities at the family courts and access to legal remedies on marital breakdown are endorsed. Matters to do with community, housing and the environment were a central concern in submissions. The Commission points to the need for greater local involvement and participation in the planning and development of communities. The important role of community development in the mobilisation of communities in disadvantaged areas is discussed. The Commission welcomes the commitment in Partnership 2000 for Inclusion, Employment and Competitiveness to strengthen the programme. The development of locally based voluntary and day-time education is noted. The Commission highlights issues concerning the affordability of housing for young people trying to set up home, and suitable accommodation for vulnerable people who need support to live independently in the community. The concern about alcohol and drug problems which arose in submissions is examined and the major policy initiatives which are underway to tackle these issues are welcomed. The Commission welcomes the development of a comprehensive and co-ordinated response for families in relation to domestic violence.

The Commission notes the preparation of a Green Paper by an Inter-departmental Working Group, having considered the constitutional, legal, medical and ethical issues which arise regarding abortion and the fact that a considerable number of organisations and individuals have responded to the invitation to submit their views to the Working Group.

The difficulties faced by families living in rural areas in gaining access to services and the problems of rural isolation as expressed in submissions are described. The Commission acknowledges the work of Rural Resettlement and the Government commitment to a comprehensive programme of rural development. Suggestions put to the Commission by Bord na Gaeilge to improve state services for Irish-speaking families and Gaeltacht communities are described.

The Commission notes the work of the Task Force on the Travelling Community and endorses the policy objectives in relation to supporting Traveller children in staying on in education and improved youth work services for Travellers. The widespread commitment to providing a strategy for equality for people with disabilities is endorsed. The Commission discusses in particular the role of income support, employment and the importance of access to suitable housing and accommodation in providing independence and choice for people with a disability. Information, advice and consistent support are highlighted as being crucially important for families when a child is diagnosed and difficulties are first identified. The Commission examines the issues to do with access to respite care.

The Commission endorses the recommendations of the Task Force on Suicide in relation to the services and the strategies needed to prevent these tragic deaths. A pilot Family Information Service is proposed to provide access to a range of services.

The Commission considers aspects of emigration and its effects on family networks. Emigration has been a strong theme throughout Irish history. While the trend in emigration has been steadily downward over recent years (preliminary figures for 1997 show that there were 44,000 immigrants in that year and 29,000 emigrants - a net inflow of 15,000 people), emigration is still significant for a number of Irish families.

The Commission considers the concerns expressed by Irish communities abroad. While in recent years, Irish emigrants to the UK have been better educated and more qualified than earlier generations and are more successful in employment, emigrants without qualifications still form a substantial proportion of those going to the UK. If these young people cannot establish themselves in employment, their problems are compounded by lack of family supports and kin networks. The Commission expresses the view that ongoing financial support for the voluntary agencies that work with Irish emigrants must continue to be an important policy priority. Realistic and practical information and advice is essential for potential emigrants. The Commission welcomes initiatives to meet this objective underway in FÁS and through Youthreach and by the Department of Social, Community and Family Affairs. The Commission recommends a new approach to providing more complete information, involving government departments and their agencies working together to support young people who are potential emigrants.

The Commission endorses initiatives to strengthen the connections with the Irish community abroad, whether at business, economic or social levels. A role for the Family Affairs Unit with the Inter-Departmental Committee on Emigration is suggested to ensure that the family dimension (both at home and abroad) of emigration is reflected in proposals. The Commission recommends that proposals should be developed for visitors to Ireland to make available information in simple format, about family names, their history, where the names can be found, relevant local history and the significance of the major events in Irish history. The proposal would complement the work of the Irish Genealogical Project, which is developing a computerised data and information system relevant to family history research.

## Chapter 15 **Family concerns- some further issues which arose in submissions to the Commission on the Family**

**15.1**     **Introduction**

In this chapter the Commission acknowledges the views and concerns expressed on some specific topics which arose in submissions. Information is presented about the policy responses which are relevant to the issues raised, and the Commission welcomes the major policy initiatives which have been introduced recently.

**15.2**     **Families and the law**

Almost one in three submission to the Commission raised issues to do with the law and families. Most submissions in this category were concerned about the legal issues which arise on the breakdown of marriage. People wrote about the adversarial nature of the legal procedures surrounding marital breakdown, and their dissatisfaction and disappointment with the outcome of procedures. Delays in court lists and inadequate court facilities were common complaints. There was great concern about the effects on children of the drawn-out adversarial proceedings and the distress that families experience.

### A non-adversarial approach

It is the Commission's view that family mediation where this is possible for a couple represents the best prospects for minimising the trauma of marital separation for families. The Commission has highlighted the importance of family mediation as a non-adversarial approach to the resolution of issues on marital separation (see Chapter 11). The Commission also urges the promotion of joint parenting for children, where this is in the child's best interest. Thoughtful parenting plans arrived at through family mediation provide continuity for children in their relationship with each parent and a structure within which supportive family relationships including relationships with grandparents, aunts, uncles, cousins and the wider family network, may be encouraged and developed. The sense of loss and grief felt by relatives of a separated family (particularly grandparents) was raised in submissions. In this context the Commission welcomes the provision in the recently introduced Children Act 1997 which allows a person who is related to the child, for example a grandparent, to apply to the court for access to the child.

It is the Commission's view that the implementation of the recommendations in Chapter 11 in relation to greater promotion of the benefits of family mediation and the development of an accessible, professional family mediation service would go a significant way towards mitigating some of the more distressing aspects of marital breakdown experienced by families.

### The Court facilities

The Commission, in its interim report,[1] drew attention to concerns which had been expressed by those who made submissions, and by practitioners and organisations experienced in family law, about delay in court procedures, inadequacies in facilities and in the court support services. The Commission recommended that the upgrading of the courts and the support services to them be considered as a matter of urgency.

1     *Strengthening Families for Life*, Interim Report to Minister for Social Welfare, Commission on the Family, November 1996.

The case for the major restructuring of the family courts system and legal reforms has been comprehensively set out in the report of the Law Reform Commission. [2]

## Recent policy developments

Since the publication of the Law Reform Commission's report and the interim report of the Commission on the Family, several developments have taken place.

The Government has stated its commitment to the development of regional family courts. [3] The issue of family courts is being considered by a Working Group on a Courts Commission which was established to review the operation of the courts. The Commission on the Family has learned that the provision of proper facilities for the hearing of family law cases is a matter of priority in all courthouse refurbishment projects. The court's building programme provides for a family law suite consisting of a courtroom, two consultation rooms and two waiting areas in major towns throughout the country. These facilities have already been provided in Dublin, Galway, Cork, Clonmel, Ballina, Ballinasloe, Naas and Carrick-on-Shannon.

The provision of modern accommodation has also been allied with increased numbers of judges and court staff in order to expedite access to the Courts and delays in the hearing of family law cases have been greatly reduced and have been eliminated entirely in a number of areas. Training programmes for court managers and staff on family law legislation have been introduced to assist staff in processing family law applications as effectively as possible.

The Commission welcomes these developments and urges that the upgrading of services and facilities for families at the courts should continue to be a priority objective.

## Access to legal remedies on marital breakdown

Concerns about the development of a two-tier system of family justice are apparent in the submissions to the Commission. This dualism has been highlighted in a recent study[4] and in the report of the Law Reform Commission. That Commission has referred to the development of an unhealthy two-tier system of family justice in which poorer, often unrepresented, litigants seek summary justice in the District Court, while their wealthier neighbours apply for the more sophisticated Circuit Court remedies. Essentially the barring order is typically used to achieve a separation at District Court level, often without the benefit of legal representation, while in the Circuit Court the central remedy is the judicial separation.

---

2   *Report on the Family Courts* : Law Reform Commission, 1996. Recommendations in the report cover the establishment of a system of regional courts in 15 centres around the country, the provision of impartial information in relation to the family law proceedings and the alternatives to litigation, new case management systems to improve efficiency, a shift in emphasis towards mediation, independent representation of a child's interests where this is necessary, family assessment services, training for lawyers, and more emphasis on gathering statistical data and on research.

3   Programme for Government - *An Action Programme for the Millennium*.

4   *Marital Breakdown and Family Law in Ireland: a sociological study*, Tony Fahey and Maureen Lyons, ESRI Oak Tree Press, Dublin, 1995.

A combination of structural and legal reforms, together with a major injection of resources, has been recommended by the Law Reform Commission to address these various difficulties.

It is the Commission's view that the recommendations of the Law Reform Commission in relation to access to speedy and effective resolution procedures for all families who have recourse to family law should be a basic principle underpinning future policy developments. In this regard, the Commission would like to draw attention to the hallmarks of a good family courts system as identified in the Law Reform Commission's report.

- A family justice system should provide speedy and effective access to legal remedies and services.
- The system should as far as possible avoid the use of procedures which may have a further damaging effect on family relationships, or which may cause harm or unnecessary distress to family members and especially children. Its procedures should be geared towards the avoidance of court proceedings, except where inevitable or necessary in the interests of justice.
- The system should respect and, as far as possible, support and strengthen existing family ties, and should avoid the use of rules and procedures which unreasonably hinder or deter efforts at reconciliation.
- The system should promote the resolution by agreement of the problems consequent on the breakdown of a family relationship. It should be organised in such a way as to encourage members of a disharmonious family themselves to control the issues arising from breakdown, and should promote co-operation between them in managing any of the continuing problems, especially those connected with child-rearing.
- The system should operate with respect for the dignity and fundamental rights of all affected family members. It should give prominence at all stages to the interests and welfare of dependent children where they are affected.
- The system should be capable of addressing any problems of injustice which may arise following the breakdown of a family relationship, especially those deriving from inequalities between the parties.
- There should be appropriate linkages between the system of family courts and a range of other family services that include information, family support and welfare, mediation, health and the child protection service.
- The system should make the most effective use of the finite resources of the State, and should keep to a minimum the costs involved for the parties.

### *In camera* rule
The Commission on the Family agrees with the Law Reform Commission that *bona fide* researchers should be permitted to attend family proceedings to facilitate research into the Irish family law system.

### 15.3    Families, their communities and the local environment
The issues of community, housing and the environment were central concerns of submissions to the Commission. In all, some 123 submissions (25 per cent of the total) gave views on community life, 102 submissions (21 per cent of total) raised issues to do

with housing and 35 (17 per cent of total) discussed issues relating to the environment.

These broad headings in fact cover a wide range of issues. They include: community involvement, volunteering, local family support services, facilities for recreation and sport, access to public facilities for people with disabilities, mothers with young children and older people, facilities and services for teenagers, adult education, housing, issues to do with local authority tenancies and private rented accommodation, and the need for life-time adaptable housing, as well as a wide range of concerns to do with the environment.

Many of these issues have been considered by the Commission in the course of its examination of how policies, programmes and services could be improved to better promote family well-being. The Commission has made recommendations in relation to the setting up of Family and Community Services Resource Centres (Chapter 2) and a customised local service for families, through the one-stop shop model from local offices of the Department of Social, Community and Family Affairs (Chapter 3) and for a collaborative approach between state and local community-based services in pursuing family interests. These recommendations have a strong focus on local community involvement and the delivery of local services. The difficulties of establishing a home and the impact which this has on the working lives of young families are raised in Chapter 8. The need for suitable housing and for appropriate support in their own community for vulnerable elderly people who are on the margins of independent living are highlighted in Chapter 14. A recommendation that new housing developments take account of the need for facilities for services for children is contained in Chapter 12.

**Policy developments that are underway and that make a significant contribution in meeting concerns expressed to the Commission.**
The Commission is further of the view that a number of policy developments which are underway have a significant contribution to make in meeting many of the concerns raised in submissions. Fundamental to the concerns expressed in submissions are local involvement and local participation in the planning and development of communities and greater co-ordination between local government services and local development initiatives.

The key objectives of a new strategic policy approach to local government renewal with improved local government services which is underway at present are: enhancing local democracy and widening participation; serving the customer better; developing efficiency in local government and providing better resources to allow local government to fulfil the role assigned to it.

The approach is underpinned by the commitment of councillors, managers and staff in local authorities to play a full part in the process of change.

**Enhancing local participation in the issues which affect families and their communities.**
Better co-ordination and a bringing together of local government and the local development systems are key objectives of the policy approach which are of particular relevance to greater participation by local communities.

Local development systems include : county enterprise boards, which work to create viable local businesses building on local strengths and resources; partnership companies, which work to counter disadvantage in their areas; county tourism committees; and the LEADER community initiative, which pursues rural enterprise. The partnership and local participation approach of the local development systems will remain central features in the integration process.

### Improved access to information on a wide range of public services

A commitment to improved access to information about a range of public services, the introduction of indicators for measuring quality in delivery of local authority services which, *inter alia*, involve consultation with consumers together with more structured mechanisms for interaction between local authorities and other state agencies will enhance awareness among local communities about the ways in which they may contribute to and participate in local community development.

### Community Development Programme

The Commission would like to acknowledge the specific role of the Community Development Programme in the mobilisation of communities in disadvantaged areas in the process of regeneration. The Community Development Programme is underway in some 80 communities throughout the country. The objective of the Community Development Programme is to enable and facilitate leadership for positive change in disadvantaged areas by building up the capacities of local communities to address their own needs.

The Commission welcomes the commitment in Partnership 2000 for Inclusion, Employment and Competitiveness to strengthening and expanding the programme.

### Partnership in the management of local housing

At a local community and individual level, the commitment in Partnership 2000 for Inclusion, Employment and Competitiveness to more participative and more effective arrangements for the management of the local authority housing estates, will provide an important mechanism for communities to pursue community and family objectives at local environment level in partnership with local authorities.

### Promoting family and community living priorities

At the wider level, the considerable amount of public participation and local community involvement, which forms an integral part of the Irish planning system, presents an opportunity for promoting family and community living priorities. The point has been made to the Commission that it should be possible, through the development plan which is the main instrument for the regulation and control of physical planning, to assist in the creation of the type of physical conditions in our towns and cities which would lead to a more family-friendly environment. [5]

---

5. A wide range of family friendly objectives may be included in development plans such as:
   - regulating the layout of roads and open spaces, determining the siting of schools, churches, meeting halls, community and recreational facilities
   - reserving lands as open spaces
   - reserving lands as public park or recreation space
   - providing facilities such as seating, playing facilities, tennis courts, toilets, shelters, playgrounds

The Commission's recommendation in Chapter 24 for the development of mechanisms to promote awareness about the effects of proposals for families in all services at national and local level may have a particular relevance to the development plan process.

## Adult education

The Commission would like to highlight the importance of adult education in the community development process. There is an increasing realisation of the role of adult education in enhancing the quality of life, increasing employment opportunities providing access to further education and training and in combating social exclusion.

In disadvantaged communities, adult education is a means of effecting social change. Submissions to the Commission have drawn attention to the impact that local adult education initiatives are having in community building and in the empowerment of individuals.

It has been suggested to the Commission[6] that Adult Education should be considered in the wider context of lifelong learning. Learning is a lifelong process which does not end with the completion of primary, secondary or third-level education. Lifelong learning includes a range of activities such as further vocational and professional continuing education, which are very much features of today's changing work environment and adult education. It has been suggested to the Commission that adult education is of equal importance to first-, second- and third-level education.

## Recent initiatives to support Adult Education

The Commission endorses this approach and welcomes recent initiatives to provide improved support for Adult Education. These include:
- The commitments in Partnership 2000 for Inclusion, Employment and Competitiveness, the Government programme,[7] and the National Anti-Poverty Strategy to support lifelong learning, second-chance education and community-based education.
- The appointment of a Minister of State with specific responsibility for Adult Education.
- The allocation of £600,000 with assistance from the European Social Fund for women's voluntary education groups in 1998 and 1999.
- The provision of an additional £2m in 1998 to tackle the problem of adult illiteracy, which is estimated to affect about 250,000 adults to at least some degree.
- The preparation of a Green Paper on the rationalisation and development of the adult education services.

The additional allocation for women's voluntary education groups and community education recognises the increasingly important role of education in community life. According to AONTAS, the National Association of Adult Education, one of the most exciting and ground-breaking developments in Irish Adult Education over the last decade has been the mushrooming of locally based voluntary and day-time education groups through the towns, cities and rural areas of Ireland.

---

6.  By AONTAS, the National Association of Adult Education, AONTAS promotes learning and education throughout life, particularly for those who are educationally or economically disadvantaged. It is a voluntary organisation and registered charity. It was established in 1969 and receives core funding from the Department of Education and Science. It is an umbrella organisation whose members include providers of courses, organisations, tutors, learners and anyone interested in adult education.

7.  *People before Politics*: Fianna Fail Manifesto 1997.

These groups are typically initiated by one or two key individuals, sometimes with the support of local statutory or church officials, sometimes alone. They are small, usually made up of ten to twenty members and rely on local fund-raising or small once-off grants. Many, though not all, are women's groups in the sense that their voluntary management groups are made up of women and it is mostly women who use the services they provide.

The structures, programmes and activities of these groups are rooted in the day-to-day experiences, interests and needs of Irish adults, particularly those disadvantaged economically, socially and educationally.

AONTAS, in its submission to the Commission, has pointed to the need for more support for the development of local day-time education. There are issues in relation to ongoing secure funding so that groups may plan, develop and evaluate their activities: Secure tenure would enhance the status of their day-time education groups and allow them to develop and provide facilities such as a crèche. As more groups spring up around the country there is an ever-increasing demand for higher levels of skills in organisation and administration, management, group facilitation, tutoring, marketing and public relations.

### Some housing issues
The issues in relation housing raised in submissions broadly covered two main concerns. The first relates to access to affordable housing for young families; the second relates to concerns about homelessness and those who have special accommodation needs, for example, people who are homeless or out of their family home because of family break-up, or other family difficulty or because they have special needs.

### Accommodation for vulnerable people
Submissions to the Commission from the expert voluntary organisations who have a considerable experience in assisting those who are homeless or who have difficulty in securing suitable accommodation are most informative about the nature of the problems which vulnerable people experience. Specific groups of people have been singled out as in need of a particular policy response.

Among the most vulnerable are those who have recently been discharged from hospital, prison or another form of institutional care. These people rent privately because they have no other choice. They are vulnerable because they are not capable of independent living. They cannot manage their money and end up in arrears of rent. They keep odd hours and can upset other tenants. They cannot stand up for themselves and are exploited by landlords who are unscrupulous enough to do so. [8]

### Older people and accommodation
In Chapter 14, the Commission has drawn attention to some significant deficiencies in provision for particularly vulnerable people. The Commission looked for a concerted drive to meet the needs for basic facilities in households experienced by 5 to 10 per cent of older people; and for a policy response for the hidden homeless, that is, those who are on the margins of independent living and lack support.

8    Threshold, *Tackling the Problems* , *Removing the causes*, Report 1995.

### Young adults leaving home

The absence of good quality and affordable housing for young adults leaving home is another significant gap in housing provision which was brought to the Commission's attention by Focus Ireland. According to a report, [9] some young people who have left home because of family problems fail to establish themselves independently. Many need extra supports; they find it difficult to cope in rented accommodation. They have little money and their daily existence is lonely, with much of their time spent in their own bedsit. New services and new kinds of housing specially designed to give that helping hand to independence are needed. The difficulties of young adults in securing accommodation have been described thus "Leaving the family home and becoming independent are part of growing up. For young adults, who have a job or a place in college, enough money to get by on and the support of their families, this transition from family home to a more independent way of life is fairly painless. For many young adults though, life is just not that easy. Accommodation is expensive, which means that a young adult wanting to set up home really needs to have a good income to be able to afford a place to live. But well-paid jobs are scarce, and most of the jobs on offer to young adults offer very low rates of pay, which means that many young adults do not have the funds to support a move away from home. Many young adults need help to make this crucial transition in their lives so that they do not end up on the streets, sleeping rough, homeless." [10]

It has also been pointed out to the Commission that many young people who are unemployed and in this situation then find that they must rely on the Supplementary Welfare Allowance Scheme for assistance with their rents.

### Assessing the housing need - changes in society

The situations described are indicative of the changes which are taking place in our society and the impact some of these changes are having on some of the most vulnerable groups in the community. New needs are now emerging in relation to assistance with accommodation. These emerging needs are described in a 1995 study. [11] The focus of the study was on the nature of need for social housing in Ireland and the means by which housing administrators define and measure that need.

The assessments of housing need carried out by the local authorities in March 1993 provided the basis for the study, and while there have been many developments over the past five years, the study presents a useful picture of the way housing needs are changing and, the new issues which arise in developing housing policy into the new century.

The study found that the overwhelming demand among those applying for housing is for conventional local authority housing. However, the size of the units needed is, in many cases, smaller than the traditional three-bedroomed house. Just under half of the applicant

---

9    *Stepping Out* : Focus Ireland.

10   *Focus Ireland*, November 1997 from a press release promoting the establishment of "Foyers" in Ireland. "Foyers" projects provide an alternative form of housing for young people leaving home with support services such as training, help with finding a job and a supportive environment in which they can take those first important steps towards independence.

11   *An analysis of social housing needs*, Tony Fahey, Dorothy Watson, ESRI, December 1995.

households required a three - or four-bedroom house, while one-third required a two-bedroom housing unit. One in six of the household heads is over the age of 65. The study suggests that with the increase in lone parenthood and marital breakdown and the rise in the proportion of elderly persons in the population, there is likely to be an increased need for smaller local authority dwellings.

According to the study, the contribution of family conflict, especially marital breakdown, to homelessness was very marked, and there is likely to be a greater need for short-term emergency accommodation in the future. The requirement for supported or transitional accommodation for those with medical or psychiatric problems that are severe enough to interfere with their ability to maintain a tenancy independently also emerged in the study.

The study considered the role of the different sectors involved in social housing provision, including the private sector and the voluntary housing associations which provide accommodation with local authority assistance for some of the most vulnerable people. The report examined the effects of the policies in the housing environment at that time.

### A comprehensive approach to assessing housing need

The Commission agrees with the view put forward in the study that there is a need for a more comprehensive approach to the assessment of housing need in the light of the changes which are taking place in society and in the economic environment. In particular, the Commission suggests that a broader assessment of housing need would cover the situation of those who are not traditionally catered for by the local authority housing programme. The needs of people who are single or who are alone because of widowhood or marital breakdown, and the needs of those who are young and inexperienced and without a job, and those who are older and unable to cope in the community without support, are a particular priority. The role of voluntary and not-for-profit housing associations has become increasingly important in provision for these groups in recent years. The Commission endorses the work of this sector, and urges continued support and enhancement of the role of voluntary housing provision for those with special needs.

### Young people trying to get into the housing market

The Commission has a particular concern about those young people who are trying to get a foothold in the housing market. That concern relates to those young people, including couples, who are no longer able to buy a house because house prices have risen substantially in recent years and a home of their own is now beyond their reach. They find themselves renting from private landlords and paying high rents. Their rents are funding the cost of the house for the landlord/investor, instead of paying for a home of their own. It is the Commission's view that the strong tradition of home ownership has a positive role in Irish society. There is a case to be made for more support for those who are trying to establish a home of their own.

### Study on house prices

In Chapter 8, the Commission has highlighted the difficulties of young families who are trying to establish themselves and set up home. The Commission welcomes the publication of the Study of the Housing Market and Government's Action on House Prices and urges that the particular needs of young families should be a priority consideration in the future development of policy in this area.

## 15.4    Family concerns about addiction

In the 76 submissions (16 per cent of the total) that discussed addiction there was concern that abuse of alcohol and drugs was a growing problem, with enormous repercussions for families and society.

Abuse of substances, including alcohol, was described as the root cause of many family problems. There were calls for education programmes and for protection of young people and restriction of their access to alcohol. There was a concern that the drug problem was becoming part of the youth culture and affecting whole families and their communities and not just the addict. Strategies for the treatment of addicts and the control of this social problem were recommended.

### Some Recent Initiatives - The National Alcohol Policy

The National Alcohol Policy[12] sets out the strategic approach to be adopted by a number of state agencies in partnership with commercial interests, community interests (parents, teachers, employers) and professional health care workers to encourage moderation for those who choose to drink, and to reduce the prevalence of alcohol-related problems in Ireland.

An ambitious plan of action aims to influence people's attitudes and habits so that, for those who choose to drink, moderate drinking becomes personally and socially acceptable and favoured in Irish culture. Measures targeting the whole population, as well as specific risk groups, are envisaged. Pricing structures, the availability of alcohol and accessible and effective treatment services are all part of the comprehensive policy approach proposed. A multi-sectoral commitment to the alcohol policy at national level and a strong local ownership through health board and local communities are considered to be the key factors for success in implementing the policy.

The actions required of the different parties in implementing the National Alcohol Policy include:
- The Department of Health and Children taking the lead role in increasing awareness about the health effects of alcohol, moderate drinking and a role for the drinks industry in promoting awareness about sensible drinking.
- Professional training for teachers and health professionals, the Gardaí and others in promoting awareness and understanding about alcohol-related issues, with a role for the drinks industry in ensuring provision of responsible server training.
- Youth, parents and students will be targeted through health -promoting schools, clear school policies on substance use, education for health as part of the core curriculum, and development of personal and social skills. Parents will be encouraged to reinforce school policies and help their children to adopt responsible attitudes in relation to alcohol. Universities and colleges will be encouraged to develop a Campus Alcohol Policy and at risk groups such as pregnant women, and children of substance abusers will receive special attention.

12 National Alcohol Policy: Department of Health: Stationery Office, Dublin, 1996

The plan of action will promote community initiatives, peer-led education and outreach programmes for high-risk groups and discourage alcohol industry sponsorship of underage sports and activities. Employers and trade unions will be encouraged to adopt alcohol policies in the workplace.

The plan also covers alcohol pricing and advertising, drink driving and the treatment services for alcohol-related disorders. Research is also envisaged to evaluate the effectiveness of the national alcohol policy and to underpin policy development in future.

### Wholehearted commitment to the strategy

The Commission on the Family endorses the National Alcohol Policy and urges all partners to wholehearted commitment to the strategy. Furthermore, the Commission notes the progress in relation to the introduction of Social, Personal and Health Education in schools which aims to inform young people about the hazards of alcohol misuse. The Commission considers that the principles and goals set out in the European Charter on Alcohol, which was endorsed by the Irish Government in December 1995, capture the aspirations of those individuals and families who expressed their concerns about alcohol misuse and its effects on families.

The European Charter on Alcohol called on all member states to give expression to five ethical principles and goals.

1. All people have the right to a family, community and working life protected from accidents, violence and other negative consequences of alcohol consumption.
2. All people have the right to valid impartial information and education, starting early in life, on the consequences of alcohol consumption on health, the family and society.
3. All children and adolescents have the right to grow up in an environment protected from the negative consequences of alcohol consumption and, to the extent possible, from the promotion of alcohol beverages.
4. All people with hazardous or harmful alcohol consumptions and members of their families have the right to accessible treatment and care.
5. All people who do not wish to consume alcohol, or who cannot do so for health or other reasons, have the right to be safeguarded from pressures to drink and be supported in their non-drinking behaviour.
   (European Charter on Alcohol, Paris, December 1995).

### Drugs

In recent years there has been a series of reports[13] which have documented the extent of the drugs problem and which have put forward recommendations in relation to policies and measures which need to be adopted. The findings and recommendations in the reports, together with the commitments in Partnership 2000 for Inclusion, Employment and Competitiveness, the National Anti-Poverty Strategy[14] and in the Programme for Government[15] have informed a comprehensive policy approach to tackle the drugs problem.

---

13   These reports include : *Government Strategy to Prevent Drug Misuse,* May 1991, The First and Second Reports of the Ministerial Task Force on *Measures to Reduce the Demand for Drugs,* October 1997 and May 1997, Stationery Office, Dublin

14   *National Anti-Poverty Strategy,* Stationery Office, Dublin, April 1997.

15   Programme for Government - *An Action Programme for the Millennium.*

### The policy approach

The policy approach covers two strands, the supply reduction policy, which involves the promotion of a high level of co-operation and co-ordination at international level to control the criminal business of illegal drug production; trafficking and distribution; and national action on several fronts, including the seizure of assets to tackle distribution, the pushing of drugs and money laundering. The demand reduction policy measures to discourage drug-taking, which comprise the second strand of the policy approach, include education about drugs, investment in improving the socio-economic and environmental factors which contribute to the demand for drugs, and measures to cope with the consequences of addiction, which include treatment and rehabilitation.

### Substantial resources allocated - initiatives underway

Following the first Report of the Ministerial Task Force, [16] which recommended a range of measures, an amount of £14 million was approved to implement the recommendations. Twelve local task forces have been established in the priority areas in Dublin and a further local Task Force has been set up in north Cork city. A National Drugs Strategy Team, comprised of several government departments, was established at two levels, at policy level to address the policy issues which arise in implementing the strategy and at operational level, including representatives of the local Gardaí, the Eastern Health Board, FÁS and experienced community workers to ensure effective co-ordination between government departments and statutory agencies and to oversee the establishment of local drugs task forces. A sum of £1 million of the £14 million was allocated to health boards outside the priority areas in order to implement the report's recommendations. Three million pounds was assigned to establish estate management schemes in the areas worst affected by the drug problem. The Commission notes the recent allocation of £30 million for further measures to help tackle the problem.

### Views of the Commission on the Family

The Commission welcomes the comprehensive approach to policy and the commitment to co-ordination of effort across Government departments in tackling the drugs problem, which has such devastating consequences for families and for local communities. The Commission endorses the commitment by the Government to preventive measures through education and awareness programmes for young people inside and outside the school system and an enhanced role for youth work.

The Commission, in Chapter 13, has set out its views in relation to the importance of social, personal and health education programmes including self-esteem programmes and studies to develop skills in young people to help them to cope in difficult situations as well as personal health information. These recommendations are particularly relevant to the strategy to prevent young people becoming involved in drugs. The Commission's recommendation for a network of Family and Community Services Resource Centres

---

16    The Ministerial Task Force Report (October 1996) concluded that drug abuse was more prevalent in twelve districts in greater Dublin and in north Cork city and that these should be priority areas for action. The Ministerial Task Force's second report dealt with drugs other than heroin and found that the misuse of other drugs is a nationwide phenomenon, the misuse of ecstasy and cannabis being most common. The Report's recommendations included the establishment of a Youth Services Development Fund to develop youth services in disadvantaged areas, a prioritisation of the needs of young people in these communities and the training and employment of youth leaders.

(Chapter 2) is also of importance, intended as it is as a primary preventive measure which is empowering of families and draws on the strengths and capacities of local communities in meeting their own needs.

## 15.5 Families and the problem of domestic violence

About 13 per cent of the 536 submissions to the Commission referred to domestic violence and its impact on families. The main voluntary organisations which assist families in dealing with domestic violence put forward wide-ranging proposals on all aspects of society's response to domestic violence. For many people who wrote to the Commission, education is the key to confronting and beginning to overcome domestic violence. Submissions suggested a national information and advice service, a national freephone helpline. There was concern about women and children remaining in violent situations because they had no-one to turn to for help and nowhere to go. In rural areas, in particular, women may feel that there is no confidential source to turn to for assistance.

A number of important Irish reports were prepared in the last few years on the subject of violence against women. These reports include : *The Policy Document for Women's Refuges* (1994) from the Federation of Refuges. *Making the Links* (1995) by Women's Aid and the *Report of the Working Party on the Legal and Judicial Process for Victims of Sexual and Other Crimes of Violence against Women and Children* (1996) by the National Women's Council.

The most recent report is that of the Task Force on Violence Against Women (April 1997). The Task Force was established by the Government to develop a co-ordinated response and strategy on the problem of mental, physical and sexual violence against women. The report contains a series of recommendations on how legislation, services and supports for women could be improved and made more effective.

### Task Force on Violence against Women

The Report of the Task Force revealed a disturbing picture of the extent and prevalence of violence against women.

The Task Force pinpointed the need for women to have ready access to information and advice and recommended a National Freephone Helpline available on a 24-hours, 7-days a week basis, as well as the identification of appropriate local access points for information and advice for women.

The Task Force made a number of recommendations in relation to Garda policy covering monitoring of policy, the establishment of Garda domestic violence and sexual assault units in major urban areas and improved links between the Gardaí and voluntary and community agencies dealing with families that experience domestic violence. Recommendations were also made in relation to the legal system, covering a pilot legal advice service, the appointment and training of the judiciary and the operation of the courts.

The Task Force strongly advocated that women and children should be facilitated to remain in their home, whenever it is safe and practical to do so. However, the reality is that there will be situations where this is not possible.

The Task Force :
- identified the need to increase the level of refuge accommodation and to put the financing of the refuges on a more secure footing.
- recommended the development of transitional or second stage housing for families
- recommended the development of outreach services for women who have left refuge accommodation or who cannot or do not wish to go to a refuge

Recommendations in relation to health and social services dealt with improving training so that professional staff who come into contact with women may detect when domestic violence is an issue. Other findings covered the need for access to counselling services for women and children, further research into the effectiveness of intervention programmes for violent men and recommendations as to preventive strategies aimed at young people to equip them with the knowledge, skills and attitudes to prevent domestic violence in the future.

### National Steering Committee
The establishment of a National Steering Committee on Violence Against Women was one of the main recommendations contained in the Report of the Task Force on Violence against Women.

The Government has established a National Steering Committee.[17]

The task of the Committee is to :
- develop a publicly funded public awareness campaign
- co-ordinate and advise on the distribution of the resources among the 8 health board regions
- co-ordinate and advise on the development of policies
- oversee and monitor individual agencies' written policies and guidelines
- ensure that regional and local structures are established
- undertake research and needs assessments nationally
- promote inter-agency training
- ensure maximum value for money from available resources
- develop codes of practice for collecting statistics and monitoring responses, and
- publish periodical reports.

### Views of the Commission on the Family
The Commission endorses the recommendations of the Task Force on Violence against Women which has so comprehensively examined the issues surrounding this tragic crime, which an unacceptable number of families experience.

---

17   The Committee comprises representatives of the Departments of Education and Science, Environment and Local Government, Health and Children, Social, Community and Family Affairs, and Justice, Equality and Law Reform, the Gardaí, the Probation and Welfare Service, general practitioners, clergy, the legal profession, State agencies, i.e. the health boards, and the non-governmental organisations working in this field. The Committee is chaired by Mary Wallace T.D., Minister of State at the Department of Justice, Equality and Law Reform. An Inter-departmental Committee, which comprises representatives of the relevant departments, was also established to run in tandem with the National Steering Committee. The purpose of the Committee is to examine issues in advance of the National Steering Committee and examine the recommendations of the Task Force and advise on their implementation and, where possible, identify timescales.

(i) The Commission recommends that the priority issue to be considered in the immediate future should be the provision of secure funding for the voluntary agencies that provide refuge accommodation.

(ii) The Commission recommends the extension of the national helpline to assist families in difficulty and provide access to information locally for families. The Commission draws attention to its own recommendations in Chapters 2 and 3 of this report for the development of local Family and Community Services Resource Centres and an enhanced information service at local offices of the Department of Social, Community and Family Affairs. The Commission considers that there is a role for these services in providing an access point to information for vulnerable families that experience domestic violence.

(iii) The Commission agrees that access to counselling services is essential for women and children who experience domestic violence.

(iv) The Commission, in particular, endorses the view of the Task Force that, as far as possible, women and children should be facilitated to remain safe and secure in their own home. For children, this means that a level of security and continuity may be maintained through their attendance at school and through remaining in their own community with their friends. In this context, the Commission considers that the development of an outreach service for these families has a particular priority. Access to immediate assistance and counselling is important in these situations. Programmes to support children are particularly important and community-based responses should be financially supported in the policy approach to respond to the needs of families.

(v) At the prevention level, the Commission agrees that more research is needed in relation to working with violent men. The Commission notes the work underway in this field, such as the initiatives by the Cork Domestic Violence Project, established in 1993, and Men Overcoming Violence (MOVE), set up in 1989.

Prevention initiatives which are aimed at adolescents who have themselves been victims of domestic violence may have a particular value and should be supported. At another level the Commission fully agrees with the Task Force about the need for education to build up self-esteem and confidence in young people and to equip them with the knowledge, the skills and the strategies to ensure that they do not become either victims or perpetrators of violence in the future.

The Commission welcomes the establishment of the National Steering Committee. The Committee has given priority to the development of regional structures to facilitate improved co-ordination and the sharing of information to maximise the resources available locally to assist families in difficulty. It is envisaged that the regional structures will be developed on a partnership basis between State agencies, voluntary organisations and women's groups and local community interests. A campaign to raise public awareness about domestic violence is also a priority for the National Steering Committee.

The Commission notes the developments within the school system in relation to Social, Personal and Health Education and Stay Safe and the objectives to equip children with skills and coping strategies and to feel valued and loved.

## 15.6    Unplanned and crisis pregnancies

The possible distress of an unplanned pregnancy was raised in some submissions to the Commission. Submissions highlighted the importance of positive help through professional counselling and community support to help pregnant women and their families with the pregnancy and make positive decisions for their child. Ongoing support and help for mothers who keep their babies and for young mothers who live with their families was recommended.

A study on women and crisis pregnancy was commissioned from the Department of Sociology of Trinity College, Dublin in 1995 by the then Minister for Health as part of a comprehensive approach to the abortion issue. This followed the passing of the Regulation of Information (Services outside State for Termination of Pregnancies) Act 1995. The objective of the study was to assist the Department of Health and Children in understanding the factors which contribute to unwanted pregnancy and, in particular, those factors which lead to women seeking abortions.

The study involved extensive field work, involving interviews with women with crisis pregnancies, some of whom had opted to keep their child, some of whom planned to have the baby adopted, and others who had chosen abortion. The report was published in March 1998.

In December 1997, the Government established a Cabinet Committee[18] to oversee the work of an Interdepartmental Working Group whose task it is to prepare a Green Paper having considered the constitutional, legal, medical, moral, social and ethical issues which arise regarding abortion and having invited views from interested parties on these issues.

The detailed work on the preparation of the Green Paper by the Interdepartmental Working Group has commenced; it involves officials from the Department of Health and Children and other government departments.

---

18    The Cabinet Committee is chaired by the Minister for Health and Children, Brian Cowen, T.D., and also comprises Ms. Mary O' Rourke, T.D., Minister for Public Enterprise, Mr. John O' Donoghue T.D., Minister for Justice, Equality and Law Reform, Ms. Liz O' Donnell T.D., Minister of State at the Department of Foreign Affairs, and Mr. David Byrne S.C., Attorney General . The Terms of Reference of the Interdepartmental Working Group are as follows:

"Having regard to :

Section 58 of the Offences against the Person Act, 1861;

Section 59 of the Offences against the Person Act, 1861;

Article 40.3.3 of Bunreacht na hEireann;

The decision of the Supreme Court on 5 March 1992 in the *Attorney General* v *X* and *Others* [1992] 1 L.R. 1;

Protocol No. 17 to the Maastricht Treaty on European Union signed in February 1992 and the Solemn Declaration of 1 May 1992 on that Protocol;

The decision of the people in the Referendum of 25 November 1992 to reject the proposed Twelfth Amendment of the Constitution;

The decision of the High Court on 28 November 1997 in *A & B v Eastern Health Board, Judge Mary Fahy, C* and the *Attorney General (Notice Party);*

and having considered the constitutional, legal, medical, moral, social, and ethical issues which arise regarding abortion and having invited views from interested parties on these issues, to prepare a Green Paper on the options available in the matter."

A considerable number of organisations and individuals responded to the invitation to submit their views to the working group and the submissions are now being analysed. The target date for completion of the Green Paper is Summer 1998.

The Commission notes the concern of the Government that strategies be developed which will aim to reduce the incidence of unwanted pregnancy and that comprehensive counselling and healthcare for women with crisis pregnancies should be available. The Commission welcomes the preparation of the Green Paper and comprehensive approach being taken in considering the sensitive and distressing issues which a crisis pregnancy can give rise to for individuals and their families.

## 15.7    Families living in rural areas

Access to services for families in rural communities was a common theme in submissions to the Commission. While the benefits for families rearing children of living in small close-knit communities were highlighted, these were counterbalanced by concerns about access to services, transport, employment and training, and educational and childcare services in rural areas.

The major changes which have taken place in Irish society in the twentieth century and, in particular, the decline in the small farm economy and in agricultural employment, are well described in the work which Tony Fahey has undertaken for the Commission.[19] These changes have had a profound effect on rural communities and on rural families.

The difficulties which families in rural areas experience, as described in submissions, are among the key factors which give rise to social exclusion and marginalisation for those families who are most vulnerable.

The point has been made to the Commission that there is a lack of awareness about the extent of the difficulties faced by rural families. Poverty in rural areas is often hidden because it is dispersed over a wide area. Ownership of land may disguise a disadvantaged farm structure with a family living on a very low income. Elderly people living in the open countryside may be isolated and are vulnerable. Those families on low incomes living in towns have few prospects of improving their economic situation through participation in training.

### Report of the National Economic and Social Forum

The National Economic and Social Forum, in its contribution to the development of the National Anti-Poverty Strategy,[20] has detailed many of the difficulties facing rural communities and has set out a series of detailed recommendations to secure for people living in rural areas a more equitable share in the benefits of economic and social progress.

The NESF points out that, of an estimated 1.25 million people who live in rural areas, two out of three are not directly dependent on farming. Thirty five per cent are employed in the services sector, 15 per cent in industry and 10 per cent are unemployed.

---

19    See Chapter 17 for an abstract of Dr. Fahey's work.

20    *Rural Renewal - Combating Social Exclusion*, Forum Report No. 12 - March 1997.

The problems of rural isolation also affect those engaged in the fishing industry. This traditional livelihood now involves an often times precarious existence for families with low incomes and insecure futures. Increasingly the partner left on shore is carrying the additional burden of supplementing family income where this is possible through employment as well as carrying the day-to-day responsibility for family care.

The recommendations of the NESF cover measures to halt population decline in rural areas, continuing support for small farmers and more on farm and off farm opportunities for them and a range of strategies to enable local communities to participate in decision making, and contribute to the policy development in important areas of relevance to their survival.

### A comprehensive programme for rural development

The Commission welcomes the specific objectives in the National Anti-Poverty Strategy to tackle poverty and social exclusion in rural areas in a comprehensive and sustained manner. The policy actions proposed in the strategy relate to a renewed local Government system, access to a variety of public services, particularly transport, improved information on programmes, schemes and assistance, promoting rural development and community development for the rejuvenation of local communities and the development of a viable rural economy. The Commission further notes the commitment in the Programme for Government to a comprehensive programme of rural development. The Commission welcomes the establishment of an Inter-departmental Committee to focus on the physical and social conditions of people living in rural areas. Promoting economic diversification and development, facilitating the capacity of rural communities to participate in and contribute to their own development and addressing the issues of rural poverty and social exclusion are important objectives of the task of the Inter-departmental Committee. A White Paper is expected to be completed in mid-1998.

### The role of community development in rural life

It is the Commission's view that locally based community development has a significant contribution to make to enhance the social and economic environment for rural families. The very specific role of the community sector in the development of services for children as described in Chapter 12 has a particular relevance to rural communities. The level of investment proposed by the Commission, for opportunities for children to participate in quality services, and the flexibility in administrative procedures recommended are intended to facilitate imaginative responses from local communities to meet their childcare needs.

The potential of the social economy in addressing childcare needs and in meeting the need for services for the elderly while creating employment opportunities has been highlighted in Chapter 14 of this report. It is the Commission's view that the fact that the commercial viability of initiatives may be restricted by the characteristics of rural communities should not be a limiting factor where state support for rural community initiatives in these areas is concerned.

### Rural resettlement

The Commission acknowledges the work of Rural Resettlement and the role of this type of initiative in halting the decline of rural communities.

A clean and safe environment for rearing their children and small classes in country schools are some of the benefits which are cited by families who make the move from large urban housing estates to rural communities. The benefits to rural communities are evident. [21] Each family whatever their employment situation brings new money into the local economy. Houses that have been empty, some for a long time are again using electricity and water. Post offices and small shops and local schools all benefit. Some families bring in new skills. They get involved in community life and bring new life and new ideas to local sporting clubs and organisations.

### Gaeltacht families

The Commission would also like to mention in particular Gaeltacht Communities. Families in Gaeltacht areas have difficulties in gaining access to many services through Irish. The NESF has pointed out that this applies particularly to support services such as educational psychologists, speech therapists and training opportunities. It is the Commission's view that addressing the inadequacies in services for Gaeltacht families should be a priority issue in the development of improved customer service under the strategic management initiative.

In this context, the Commission's attention has been drawn to Services from the State Sector to the Gaeltacht Community, Directives for Action Programmes and Expanding Bilingualism in Irish Society in which the Government has set down guidelines for action programmes in the State Sector that all the public services should be available and on offer through Irish as well as English.

Bord Na Gaeilge[22] in its submission to the Commission made the point that one of the biggest problems is the fact that organisations very often fail to explicitly advertise or publicise the availability of a service through Irish. The Commission agrees with the recommendation of the Bord that the guidelines in this area need to be implemented throughout the public services.

In a wider context, relating to the Irish language and families the Commission would like to draw attention to further recommendations which have been suggested to the Commission by Bord na Gaeilge.

The Bord, in its submission to the Commission points to evidence from recent surveys that support for Irish medium education is increasing. The Bord recommends that the Department of Education and Science and others involved in adult education should provide Irish classes for parents whether their children are attending all-Irish or other types of schools.

Further issues raised by the Bord in its submission relate to the availability of services such as speech therapy and childcare for Irish speaking families and more choice and access in

---

21    Material about rural resettlement from a submission made to the Commission.

22    Bord na Gaeilge's function is the promotion of Irish as an everyday means of communication. The Bord works closely with the state sector on the development and implementation of policies for Irish. Other work includes community development projects and book distribution. The Bord is in receipt of annual grant-in-aid from the Department of Arts, Heritage, Gaeltacht and the Islands.

relation to training and employment programmes to suit those who wish to speak Irish in the workplace. The Bord also makes the case that any family wishing to deal with the courts through the medium of Irish should be able to do so.

## 15.8. Family concerns about suicide.

Some submissions to the Commission expressed concern about the growth in suicide. In particular people were concerned about suicide and attempted suicide among young people.

### Report of the National Task Force on Suicide

The recently published report of the National Task Force on Suicide[23] documents the extent of suicide and attempted suicide in Ireland. The rate of suicide between 1945 and 1995 rose from 2.38 per 100,000 population to 10.69 per 100,000. Suicide is the second most common cause of death among 15 to 24 year old males in Ireland equal to a rate of 19.5 per 100,000 population compared to 2.1 per 100,000 among 15 to 24 year old women. During the period, 1991 to 1993 young male suicide deaths increased from a position where they were as frequent as cancer deaths in 1976 to greatly exceeding cancer deaths by 1993.

In the case of older people, men aged 65 years and over have shown a significant increase in their rate of suicide from 9.4 per 100,000 population to 17.9 per 100,000 population between 1976 and 1993. The increase in suicide in recent decades has been primarily a male phenomenon. The overall rate of suicide among men in 1995 was 17.17 compared with 4.32 among women per 100,000 population.

### Recommendations of the Task Force

The report of the National Task Force puts forward a strategy for a clear systematic approach aimed at the prevention of suicide and suicidal behaviour. The recommendations of the National Task Force cover ;

- The provision of services relating to suicide and to attempted suicide with recommendations as to training for GPs, health care teams and other professionals in medical services and awareness programmes for people involved in a range of public services.
- The prevention of suicide and early intervention with people who attempt suicide including : tackling addiction, education for young people, a code of good practice in relation to reporting of suicide deaths by the media, access to appropriate support, psychological and counselling services for young people and for older people, with health boards putting in place programmes to improve coping strategies among older people and greater control of and information about commonly used drugs and medicines.
- Intervention with people who attempt suicide, to include procedures in relation to ensuring support and follow-up after care for people and for their families.
- Special training and support for professionals in dealing with traumatic situations and distraught relatives; and research into the causes of suicide and how this tragedy may be prevented.

---

23   Published by the Department of Health and Children, January 1998. The report was compiled with the assistance of the Suicide Research Foundation.

The report identifies the various authorities with jurisdiction in suicide prevention strategies and their respective responsibilities.

### Views of the Commission on the Family

The Commission considers that the report of the National Task Force contains a very comprehensive approach to the tragedy of suicide. Many of the recommendations made by the Task Force have a particular significance for the Commission in that, they reflect the Commission's own concerns to strengthen families in carrying out their functions. In particular the Commission would like to draw attention to the role of Social, Personal and Health Education in equipping young people with self esteem and in developing strategies which will assist them in coping with the difficulties they may encounter in life.

The Commission endorses the recommendations of the National Task Force and urges that the recommendations be acted upon and implemented.

## 15.9. Access to information - A Family Information Service

In the Commission's interim report[24] the Commission referred to the provision of information and advice as a fundamental social support for families when faced with difficulty.

### The need for a broad based Family Information Service

Families in difficulty are not always aware of the range and type of services available to them. There is a need to promote public awareness about services so that families can decide which service is most appropriate to their own need. Early contact with the appropriate service can frequently lessen the emotional trauma of difficult family situations.

A range of helplines are provided by the voluntary sector, for example, the helplines operated by Childline, Parentline and women's refuges are well known.

The National Social Service Board, (NSSB) in their report entitled *Family Matters- A Social Policy Report*, 1994, recommended the establishment of a family information service to provide free, impartial information on the range of services for families in distress. The report suggested that the service could provide information about social welfare, housing, counselling, joint parenting and access issues, child custody, maintenance, mediation, barring orders and legal aspects of separation. While the main priority of the service would be to provide advice and information, it could act as an referral agency for families in need of the various professional services.

In Chapter 3, the Commission proposes that local offices of the Department of Social, Community and Family Affairs be developed to provide a customised local service to families. Building on the concept of the "one-stop-shop" as a gateway to all services, development towards the new service would require a greatly enhanced service to provide comprehensive information to allow access for families to community and other local services.

---

24    *Strengthening Families for Life*, Interim Report to the Minister for Social Welfare from the Commission on the Family, November 1996.

It is envisaged that the customised service while initially focusing on the range of state services available would also provide information about access to community and other local services, for example, marriage counselling, family mediation, parent education and local youth programmes, adult education and services for older people. Referral and direction for further assistance would be a feature of a customised service and close links between local offices and other agencies providing services would underpin the development of enhanced information services. The role of the National Social Services Board in the development of a specialised family information service would be important.

### Law Reform Commission report on family courts

The need for  specialised family information was also recognised in the Law Reform Commission Report on Family Courts (1996) which stated that: Each Regional Family Court, should have attached to it a Family Court Information Centre. The Law Reform Commission envisaged that the Family Court Information Centre would be responsible for providing to those who have begun or who are considering the institution of family law proceedings impartial objectively presented information relating to available alternatives to litigation and information on available support services. Any legal information received should be information only, and not advice.

### Views of the Commission on the Family

It is the Commission's view that there is a need to develop an integrated family information service with a range of access points. These access points could include State offices providing information and national and voluntary organisations providing similar services.

The Family Courts Information Centres recommended by the Law Reform Commission may also be a part of such an integrated service.

### Pilot Information service

Access to a wide range of information is currently available from the network of Citizens Information Centres under the NSSB and other independent information givers. However, having regard to the complex and at times distressing nature of family related queries there is  a need for a more comprehensive family information service. Specialist training to enable providers of the service to acquire the skills of listening, supporting and referring clients on to the most appropriate professional agent would be very important to the development of this specialised service.

The NSSB, in the report referred to earlier, envisaged that the  family information service would;
- give information and advice on the range of services available to families
- have available trained personnel with relevant counselling/listening skills to advise and refer the individual/family to the service appropriate to their needs.

The Commission considers that the family information service recommended by the NSSB has the potential to be an important first step in developing a comprehensive information service for families.

The Commission recommends that funding be allocated to the NSSB to develop a pilot Family Information Service to assess the extent to which families needs for information may be met.

## 15.10. Families in the Travelling Community

The Commission on the Family has a particular concern with the welfare of families of the Travelling Community.

The Report of the Task Force on the Travelling Community[25] contains an in-depth analysis of the situation in which Travellers find themselves today in Irish society. The report documents the high levels of social exclusion and disadvantage which Travellers experience. It contains recommendations in relation to key policy areas including accommodation, health, education and training, the Traveller economy, labour force participation and the co-ordination of policy approaches by statutory agencies and relationships between Travellers and the settled community. The report also considers the role, needs and concerns of Traveller women and Travellers with disabilities and, from a Travellers perspective, sport, recreational pursuits, culture and the arts.

### Views of the Commission on the Family

The Commission endorses the work of the Task Force which has so comprehensively identified the strategies needed to tackle the issues facing Traveller families.

In Chapter 13, the Commission has noted the education initiatives to assist Traveller children to overcome difficulties in participating in education. Pre-school education services and extra teachers are essential to meet the additional needs of Traveller children. Only a small minority of Traveller children have successfully transferred to second level schools and very few of those have completed a full second-level education.

The Commission endorses the approach by the National Anti-Poverty Strategy which calls for improved measures for Traveller children to ensure that all children of primary school age will be enrolled and will participate fully in primary education within the next five years. Within ten years, the objective is that all Traveller children of second-level school-going age will complete junior cycle and 50 per cent will complete senior cycle.

The Commission acknowledges the work of the Interim Committee of Traveller Youth which aims to develop policy and principles on youth work with Travellers and to develop and implement an effective delivery of a Traveller youthwork service. The provision of an informal youth services for young Travellers aims at self-development and the development of self-esteem and respect for Traveller culture. The service also aims at youth Traveller participation in the community and at overcoming discrimination.

The Commission welcomes the commitments in Partnership 2000 for Inclusion, Employment and Competitiveness to continue to implement the Government strategy in response to the report of the Task Force on the Travelling Community.

25   *Report of the Task Force on the Travelling Community*, July 1995, Stationery Office, Dublin.

The Commission further welcomes the commitment in the programme for Government[26] for a new deal for the Travelling Community and the recent announcement by the Minister for Justice, Equality and Law Reform of his intention to establish a monitoring committee to co-ordinate and monitor the implementation of the Task Force's report.

The Commission would like to draw attention to the comments of the Task Force on the need to improve relationships between Travellers and settled people through the development of mutual understanding and respect. This requires an adjustment in attitudes towards one another and an acceptance of each other's culture. The Task Force called for increased levels of contact, particularly at local community level to bring about a better understanding on the part of the settled population of the general needs of Travellers and to enable Travellers to understand more about the anxieties of the settled community.

## 15.11    People with Disabilities and their Families

In all, some 12 per cent of submissions (60 submissions) discussed the issue of family members with a disability. The overwhelming sense from these submissions was the need for immediate action to improve the quality of life for people with disabilities and their families. Access, transport and the provision of information were identified as major factors in the isolation and marginalisation experienced by many people with disabilities.

Families were identified as the main source of support and care for people with disabilities and the State was seen to have a crucial role to play in planning and resourcing appropriate services to support the individual family. While the presence of any disability in a family causes additional stress and difficulties, it was pointed out that lack of information, specialised services and access to genetic counselling services, add to the difficulties of a family which has member with a learning disability.

Services identified for people with disabilities and their families include financial support, information and emotional support services, multi-disciplinary clinical supports, including social workers, psychologists, speech therapists, occupational therapists, physiotherapists and doctors, special and integrated educational facilities, vocational training, sheltered employment and supported and open employment services.  Respite and residential care services were seen as an urgent priority.

### A strategy for equality

The Report of the Commission on the Status of People with Disabilities (November, 1996) sets out a strategy for equality for people with disabilities. The implementation of the report is a key priority in the Programme for Government.[27] The programme contains commitments in relation to overhauling the means by which the State supports the incomes of people with disabilities, adequate resources for respite care, access to transport, adequate residential facilities for those with a mental disability and autism and more support for carers. The findings of the Commission on the Status of People with Disabilities have informed the negotiations in the lead up to Partnership 2000 for Inclusion, Employment and Competitiveness. The social partners agreement includes measures in relation to institutional issues, employment and training, transport and services for people with disabilities. Issues with a poverty and social exclusion dimension will be given consideration under the National Anti-Poverty Strategy.

---

26    Programme for Government- an *Action Programme for the Millennium*.

27 Programme for Government - an *Action Programme for the Millennium*

### A comprehensive policy response to people with disabilities and their families

The Commission on the Family endorses the recommendations of the Commission on the Status of People with Disabilities and urges continued priority to afford real equality to people with disabilities and their families to enable them to fully participate in society and in community life, to support the caring responsibilities carried out by families and to eliminate the large number of obstacles which prevent families enjoying truly equal status.

In the following paragraphs, the Commission on the Family offers further comment in relation to significant issues that were raised in submissions. It is the Commission's intention in highlighting these concerns to further reinforce the importance of the recommendations of the Commission on the Status of People with Disabilities for the prioritisation of a comprehensive policy response to address the needs of people with disabilities and their families.

### Independent living and choice

Supporting and promoting independent living is an important goal for the policy approach in relation to people with disabilities who may, with appropriate support, take control of their own lives, exert choice and take on responsibilities and live a life of their own choosing. Exercising a measure of independence and choice requires appropriate support by way of income support, access to transport, access to employment and suitable accommodation.

### Income support

People with disabilities have been identified as being at high risk of poverty. [28] According to the Commission on the Status of People with Disabilities, "many people with disabilities live close to the poverty line, because they are prevented from working and/or on account of the additional costs associated with disability. There are a bewildering array of schemes, matched by an equally bewildering set of eligibility and assessment procedures".

As pointed out in the National Anti-Poverty Strategy, there is a dearth of research data and basic information about people with disabilities in Ireland. However, it is known that in 1995, 85,000 adults who had disabilities were in receipt of a state payment. This included 42,000 people on Invalidity Pension, some of whom may have other sources of income. However, the 33,000 people on Disabled Persons Maintenance Allowance (DPMA) a means-tested benefit, are unlikely to have any other sources of income, and thus to be dependent on state income support.

There are disability-related costs, for example the costs of aids, adaptations, higher insurance premia, additional costs for transport, diet or heating. A study[29] on the economic circumstances of adults with multiple sclerosis in Cork and Kerry found that 80 per cent of people asked reported extra costs. For the majority of respondents the extra costs were approximately £85 per month. Some extra needs are met by the various authorities through the provision of aids and tax relief on cars.

The National Anti-Poverty Strategy makes the point that people with disabilities may also find it relatively difficult to obtain employment, if they choose to do so. Unemployment rates

---

28    *Sharing in Progress*: National Anti-Poverty Strategy, 1996 Stationery Office.

29    Multiple Sclerosis Society of Ireland and Nexus Research, 1996.

among people with disabilities have been estimated to be much higher than for other groups in society. An National Rehabilitation Board case study (1993) indicated that 70% of people with disabilities are unemployed, 70% were unable to pay for the necessary equipment which would make life easier for them and 70% were unable to make plans for the future as they did not have any money. [30]

The National Anti-Poverty Strategy points out that in recent years there have been no substantial increases in the level of payments for people with disabilities. Recommendations made by the Commission on the Status of People with Disabilities in relation to income and the costs of disability cover a legal right to payment, a national standard of payment and an appeals system, a cost of disability payment to meet the everyday costs associated with disability and improved benefits for carers.

### Transport and access to goods and services

The Commission on the Family notes the commitment in the Programme for Government to introduce a co-ordinated and comprehensive approach to promoting access by people with disabilities to the use of public spaces and facilities and to the whole of the transport chain.

### Employment

The Commission on the Family concurs with the view that people with disabilities should have full access to the training opportunities available to people on the live register. The Commission notes the commitments[31] in Partnership 2000 for Inclusion, Employment and Competitiveness that 1,000 training places be reserved for people with disabilities on existing mainstream courses and an additional 500 sheltered work places over the period of the agreement and that people in receipt of disability allowance are a priority target group for the expansion of active labour market measures for employment[32].

While the Civil Service meets the 3 per cent employment target for people with disabilities, progress towards meeting the target is much slower in the broader public service. According to the Partnership 2000 Agreement, this quota should be met during the period of the agreement. It has been suggested to the Commission on the Family that consideration should be given to extending the requirement, on a phased basis, to contractors applying for state business contracts and to private sector companies.

### Suitable housing

Central to the achievement of independent living is the availability of suitable and appropriate housing for people with disabilities. The Commission supports the proposal made by the Commission on the Status of People with Disabilities that a policy on housing for people with disabilities should have as its aim the right of people with disabilities to live as independently as possible, if they so choose.

---

30   Combat Poverty Agency, Forum for People with Disabilities and the National Rehabilitation Board (1994), *Disability, Exclusion and Poverty*. Papers from the National Conference "Disability, Exclusion and Poverty: A Policy Conference" organised by the Combat Poverty Agency, the Forum of People with Disabilities and the National Rehabilitation Board.

31   paragraphs 5.23, 5.25 of Partnership 2000 for Inclusion, Employment and Competitiveness.

32   paragraph 4.22 of Partnership 2000 for Inclusion, Employment and Competitiveness

The Commission on the Family also suggests that there should be a greater emphasis on lifetime housing, designed and built to be easily adaptable as the needs of a family or family members change. By including certain features, (such as downstairs toilets or wider doors) at the construction stage, homes can be adapted easily and more cheaply later on.

There are a number of programmes in operation to enable people with disabilities to achieve independent living. One such initiative which has been brought to the Commission's attention is the Centre for Independent Living. The centre has been set up by people with disabilities who originally came together to lobby in the area of housing, but through research, changed their starting point to personal assistance. The INCARE pilot programme operated by the centre trains people with disabilities (Leaders) and personal assistants (PAs). Each personal assistant is trained for one year to achieve City and Guilds certification and to graduate as a qualified personal assistant. The programme has enabled leaders to take up employment, a place in training or a place in college. The centre has a further programme which involves providing independent accommodation, personal assistance and back up support on all aspects of transition to independent living for people moving from institutional care.

The Centre for Independent Living has established its own housing company, INHOUSE, to actively promote the provision and availability of accessible housing for people with disabilities. INHOUSE proposes to commence its first housing programme by developing a number of housing units which will be fully accessible for a person with a disability.

The Commission on the Family recommends that initiatives to support independent living should be supported in the policy approach to meeting the needs of people with a disability.

## 15.12 Supports for families with a member with a disability

Submissions to the Commission on the Family paint a picture of families supporting a member with a disability in a relentless struggle to identify and access supports and services appropriate to his/ her needs. This applies to assessment, early intervention, schooling, training, employment, healthcare and geriatric services. This constant battle puts an intolerable strain on family members.

### The need for information

A family's need for information, advice and support are greatest when a child is first diagnosed. It is at this point that information and access to support is of crucial importance. From the moment parents are informed that their child has a disability, whether this is at birth or at a later stage in his/ her development, there is a need for information and supports for both parents and other members of the family. Every parent whose child is diagnosed as having a disability goes through an initial period of adjustment. In Chapter 4, the Commission has put forward a number of recommendations for support for families, including the need for better information and consistent support for families when difficulties arise. These recommendations have a particular relevance to families at this time. The development of the 'one-stop-shop' family information service as recommended in Chapter 3 would also assist with the provision of information on health and welfare entitlements, on support services for carers and on counselling services for families with a member with a disability.

The importance of a partnership approach between families and health professionals was highlighted in Chapter 4. The Commission has recommended a collaborative approach to the delivery of health services for children, with parents and professionals working together to achieve goals for their child's development. A multi-disciplinary clinical support team, including social workers, psychologists, speech therapists, occupational therapists, as suggested in Chapter 4 is also particularly relevant.

### Education

Submissions pointed out that with the right care and specialised education and training, children and adults with disabilities can be helped to make the best use of their potential.

An inter-departmental committee was established in late 1995 on the recommendation of the Review Group on Special Education. The role of the committee, which is representative of both the Departments of Health and Children and Education and Science, is to identify and make recommendations in respect of existing and anticipated areas of service delivery to children with special educational needs. The Commission notes that in line with the Report of the Special Education Review Committee, the Department of Education and Science has introduced a range of programmes and resources - including additional teaching resources, financial resources and special equipment to address the educational need of children with disabilities. The Commission on the Family looks forward to the report continuing to make a substantial contribution to the policy response to children with special needs.

In this report, the Commission, in Chapter 12, has pointed to the need for support for the development of appropriate pre-school services for children with special needs. The Commission further suggests that the needs of children with disabilities for pre-school services should be considered in the proposed White Paper on Early Childhood Education.

### Residential/respite care

The difficulties experienced by families who find that it is not possible to care for their child with a disability in their own home were highlighted in submissions to the Commission on the Family. Many elderly parents are no longer able to cope and spend much of their time worrying about their adult child's future. Where it is not possible for the family to provide full-time care, the residential services needed range from respite care to 5 and 7 day care in either a residential centre or a community residence.

Data[33] from the Department of Health and Children shows that an estimated 604 people have no access to services and require either a residential (including day) or day service only; others are in receipt of either a day or a residential service but require additional services. It is estimated therefore, that approximately 2,500 people will require a major element of service over the next five years. Additional residential/ respite and day places will be required to meet this need, as follows:

---

33    Services to Persons with a Mental Handicap/ Intellectual Disability: An Assessment of Need 1997 - 2001, Department of Heath and Children,

| Intellectual Disability Database: Number of places required to meet need | |
| --- | --- |
| Residential/ Respite Places | 1,439 |
| Day Places | 1,036 |

The estimated cost of putting the new services in place is £63.5 million. In 1997 some £12 million was provided towards the new service. The Commission recommends that funding for the provision of adequate services should continue to receive priority over the coming years.

## Chapter Sixteen **Family Networks - the Irish Diaspora**

### 16.1    Introduction

Emigration and its effects on family networks are strong themes throughout Irish history. While the trend in emigration has been steadily downward over the past five years, the figures show that emigration is still significant for a number of Irish families. Preliminary figures for 1997 show that some 29,000 people  emigrated. It is estimated by the Department of  Foreign Affairs that in excess of 1.2 million of the 3 million or so Irish citizens living abroad were born in Ireland. These people are members of the wider family, most of them have strong kin networks and keep in regular contact with their families back home. Their families for their part are concerned about the well-being of their relatives abroad. In this chapter, the Commission presents some perspectives in relation to acknowledging the contribution of the Irish Diaspora and strengthening kin networks and links between emigrants and their families at home, better preparation for young people who wish to move abroad, and improved support for voluntary organisations who assist Irish people in settling in their host country.

### 16.2    An emigrating population

A fundamental image running through Irish history, particularly during the last and the current century, is that of an emigrating population. Mass emigration predates the famine, when the outflow was considerable by European standards. However, the "Great Famine" (1845-1850) set off a population decline unmatched in any other European country, which lasted until well into this century. The economic and social consequences of emigration remain an abiding issue for Ireland.

Irish emigration was distinctive in several respects[1]. First, the outflow of people - about 4 million between 1850 and 1914 - was enormous by international standards. Between the Famine and the 1890s Irish overseas emigration exceeded that recorded for any other country. Second, Irish emigration was more female than any other major outflow from nineteenth century Europe, due to a complex range of factors including the division of labour in Irish farming culture. Third, a particular feature was the small proportion of returning migrants - although recent demographic data shows that this is changing due to increased prosperity in Ireland[2].

The powerful psychological effect of emigration is noted by many authors. For instance, Roy Foster states (in "Modern Ireland 1600-1972") that "both at home and abroad, the extraordinary exodus of Irish people created the sense of being part of an international community, centred on a small island that still claimed a fiercely and unrealistically obsessive identification from its emigrants. In its way, the process was one of the most influential developments in the Irish mentality over the period dealt with in this book". He notes how vital was the sense of an "Irish community", which reflected the tightly bound community ethos and strong kinship claims.

---

1    Draws on "Ireland, a New Economic History 1780-1939", Cormac O' Gráda.

2    Preliminary figures for 1997 show some 44,000 immigrants and some 29,000 emigrants, a net migration figure of 15,000 people.(although it is not clear how many of these are returned emigrants).

Ever since the nineteenth century, families in Ireland have been structured by the employment needs of core areas of the world economy[3]. The Irish family has long been loaded with a double burden as a result of emigration. On the one hand, it has acted as the social terrain of personal life, a private space where mother, father and children are expected to share a healthy emotional and material life. On the other hand, families in Ireland were not only social arenas where the inner emotional life of the family met with the full force of the external economy - they were also places where the structuring forces of national and international capitalism intersected and helped to push young adults onto the emigrant trail. Thus, in Ireland the twin forces of capitalism and emigration have had a powerful structuring effect upon the social composition of Irish families, and upon rural, working-class and middle-class communities.

### Emigration in recent years

Today, as stated earlier, it is estimated that in excess of 1.2 million of the three million or so Irish citizens living abroad were born in Ireland. The following is a breakdown of that figure based on estimates received from Embassies:-

| | |
|---|---|
| Britain | 837,464 |
| U.S. | 220,000 |
| Canada | 72,000 |
| Australia | 51,469 |
| South Africa | 20,000 |
| France | 16,000 |
| Germany | 16,000 |
| Belgium | 10,000 |
| Spain | 8,000 |
| Netherlands | 4,040 |
| Italy | 3,000 |
| Saudi Arabia | 3,000 |
| Sweden | 1,200 |
| Israel | 1,200 |
| Denmark | 1,020 |
| Luxembourg | 1,000 |
| United Arab Emirates. | 1,000 |
| Austria | 600 |
| Greece | 600 |
| Portugal | 250 |
| Finland | 144 |

Total: 1.27 million

There are also sizeable Irish communities in some African countries (e.g. Kenya, Nigeria) comprising mainly religious and lay aid missionaries and workers.

---

3    *Location and Dislocation in Contemporary Irish Society: Emigration and Irish Identities,* edited by Jim Mac Laughlin, pages 151,152.

Today while net migration is contributing to an increase in population, the main features of emigration follow much the same pattern as previous generations.

An analysis of the country of destination of emigrants shows that Britain was the destination for 44 per cent (12,900) of emigrants from Ireland in 1997[4]. After the UK the next most popular destinations were another EU State (4,100 people), the US (4,100 people) and countries further abroad (7,900 people).

The majority of emigrants, 62 per cent, were aged between 15 and 24.

**16.3**    **Some concerns of the Irish Communities abroad (as identified by the Inter-Departmental Committee on Emigration)[5]**

The many issues of concern to Irish emigrants include cultural and practical difficulties encountered by (particularly young) new arrivals many of whom leave Ireland unprepared for their new life. In the U.S. both "green card" holders and those who are "undocumented" are encountering problems resulting from changes in 1996 in U.S. immigration and welfare legislation. Many non-U.S. citizens no longer have access to basic welfare benefits. Restrictions now in force mean that "undocumented" people can no longer regularise their status without leaving the U.S. while other new rules prevent them from re-entering the U.S. for periods of three or ten years depending on the length of time they originally overstayed. There is some concern that the level of Irish Government funding for immigrant organisations has not been increased. There is also an increasing demand for information about returning to Ireland[6].

Although their numbers are relatively small, Irish people living illegally in Australia are disadvantaged from the point of view of medical care and quality of employment and face deportation if identified by immigration officials. Concerns expressed to the Embassy in Ottawa by Irish people living in Canada relate to the restrictive nature of Canada's immigration policy.

Among the concerns of some members of the Irish communities in the other E.U. countries are difficulties encountered by what they perceive as baffling bureaucracy and red tape, particularly with regard to taking up residence or employment or obtaining welfare assistance, the need for more structured Irish community networks, lack of knowledge of the local language, poor quality employment, cultural difficulties, lack of information about Ireland (e.g. education, welfare entitlements), inability to vote in Irish elections, difficulties experienced by women married to nationals in those countries, and their children (including custody issues where marriages fail), difficulties in having Irish professional and educational qualifications recognised and the necessity to have these legalised by the Irish authorities, and difficulties in transferring pension and health care entitlements.

---

4    Preliminary figures: Population and Migration Estimates, April 1997 Central Statistics Office, October 1997.

5    This information was obtained from the relevant Irish Embassies.

6    In response to this demand, the Department of Social, Community and Family Affairs recently produced a booklet entitled "Returning to Ireland", which contains information for those now living abroad contemplating a return to Ireland.

### Experiences of emigrants to the UK

The contrasting experiences of Irish emigrants to the UK has received a considerable amount of publicity in recent years.

Since the end of the 1970s the numbers of young Irish emigrants with third level or equivalent qualifications has increased and the percentage of those without qualifications has decreased[7]. With this has come movement into administrative/management, professional and managerial sectors in the case of those who have emigrated over the past 12 years and a strong representation of young Irish people (18 to 29) in managerial and professional occupations[8].

There has been a growth in the number of students pursuing third level education. However, emigrants without qualifications still formed a substantial proportion of those going to Britain. Research based on the UK Labour Force Survey 1988, indicated that 34 per cent of males and 32 per cent of females in the post 1984 Irish migrant cohorts were unqualified. The problems that these young unqualified people face at home are well documented elsewhere in this report. Abroad, if they cannot establish themselves in employment their problems can be compounded by lack of family support and kinship networks.

A worrying catalogue of concerns about those who have not succeeded in building secure lives for themselves is being raised by the support organisations who work with emigrants in Britain. These concerns include mortality and health. Irish people in Britain would appear to have higher rates of long-term illness and are more likely to be admitted to hospital with mental illness than other communities. They also have a higher incidence of cancer and coronary heart disease, and homelessness and poor housing. Various studies have shown that the Irish are over represented among those who are homeless and those in temporary and hostel accommodation.

### 16.4    Supports for Irish emigrants

There are a number of support programmes in place to assist emigrants. Examples of the range of supports for emigrants and potential emigrants in terms of practical advice and assistance, provided both by the voluntary and statutory sectors are set out in Appendix 1.

The most well known support programme for emigrants is the Díon. Through the Díon [The title is the Irish word for "shelter"] the Government provides financial support to voluntary organisations providing advisory and welfare services for Irish emigrants in Britain. The grants support the employment of professional workers to provide advice and practical assistance to disadvantaged members of the Irish community. Some funding is provided to support research in aspects of emigrant welfare. Díon grant assistance to agencies working with emigrants has increased from £500,000 in 1995 to £613,000 in 1998. Díon funding is allocated by the Minister for Enterprise, Trade and Employment on the basis of recommendations from Díon Committee[9].

---

7    E. Hazelkorn Irish Immigrants Today: A Socio economic Profile of Contemporary Irish Emigrants and Immigrants in the UK (University of North London: Occasional Papers Series, 1990).

8    Mary Hickman, Bronwen Walter, Discrimination and the Irish Community in Britain (Commission for Racial Equality, 1997).

9    The Díon Committee (1997) comprises Leo Sheedy, First Secretary (Enterprise, Trade and Employment), Irish Embassy, London (Chair); Christine McElwaine, Third Secretary, Irish Embassy, London (Secretary); Cllr George Meehan, Harringey Council; Vicki Somers, Eastern Heath Board, Dublin; Dr. Therese Joyce, Ms. Breda Gray; Mr. Jim O' Hara.

There is concern to promote the welfare of emigrants at political level. In relation to the Irish in Britain, the UK Government on taking office in 1997 has made clear its commitment to ending excluding experiences for people. In a joint statement of intent on co-operation between the Irish Government and the UK Government (May 1997) the Taoiseach and the Prime Minister highlighted homelessness among the Irish in Britain as an issue on which options for co-operation would be considered.

Since 1990, there has also been provision for grants to voluntary groups in the U.S. and Australia (since 1996) working with Irish immigrants. The provision in 1998 is £169,000. Assistance has been provided to groups in Boston, Chicago, Los Angeles, New York, Philadelphia, San Francisco and Washington and Melbourne, Sydney and Wollongong. An additional sum of £20,000 (bringing the total to £170,000) was given to the organisations in 1997 to compensate for exchange rate losses.

## 16.5.    Better preparation for people moving abroad

It is clear from the experience of State Departments, agencies and voluntary groups who work with emigrants, that the need for accessible information on a range of issues is never fully met. A significant number of emigrants depart at short notice and are ill-prepared.

Of particular importance is realistic and practical advice for young people who without qualifications are likely to go abroad to seek opportunities. Emigrant advice organisations in the voluntary sector do not consider it good enough that information simply be available from statutory or non-statutory organisations and feel that a pro-active campaign is necessary to educate potential emigrants to the point where they know where information can be got and the wisdom of preparing in advance. This means getting to potential emigrants at an early stage through the education system and Youthreach programmes. In this context the Commission welcomes the Migration Information Pack developed by FÁS and EURES[10].

## 16.6    Views of the Commission on the Family

The Commission suggests that there is a need to build on such information initiatives. A new approach to providing more complete information and guidance for those who are likely to emigrate would involve the various Government departments and agencies joining forces in the development of a programme to target those vulnerable young people, at school, in FÁS training or in Youthreach or involved in out of school initiatives in youth groups. **It is suggested that a fund of approximately £100,000 be provided towards such an initiative. This would meet the initial costs for research and compiling of information for the programme and for the design and printing costs and the delivery of a pilot programme.**

In this context, the Commission welcomes the commitment in the Government's programme[11] to enhancing the relationship with Irish people living abroad: extending pre-emigration advice and counselling and closer liaison with emigrants and their representatives.

---

10    European Employment Services of the EU.

11    "People before politics" Fianna Fail - 1997

**It is the Commission's view that ongoing financial support for the voluntary agencies who work with Irish emigrants abroad and their families must continue to be a key objective of the policy approach in strengthening the wider kin works of families both at home and abroad.**

**16.7    The Irish Diaspora - Strengthening the links**

Some 70 million people living abroad claim Irish descent. A conference in September 1997 "The Scattering Conference on Migration" held at University College, Cork, highlighted the potential of the Irish Diaspora in strengthening community and business links both at home and abroad. The conference inaugurated the Centre for Migration Studies in UCC, which will organise continuing research and be a focus for continued interest in the Irish Diaspora. More than 100 papers were presented at the Conference. They covered topics such as the need to create more effective networks between Irish people and emigrant groups in other countries, the need to confront discrimination against returned emigrants, the lack of a comprehensive policy on emigration which would deal with the fact that there are over one million native born Irish people living abroad, the issue of funding for the helping agencies in this area and the harnessing of the network of Irish people abroad (such as in the case of Israel).

It was observed at the Conference that the Irish Diaspora should be seen as a major resource going into the 21st century, providing a bridge between the local and the global, multiplying international influence and opening up channels of communication and economic contacts.

It is clear from the literature that Irish emigration and its significance for Irish family life cannot be overlooked when it comes to developing future economic and social policies which impact on families. As stated by the former President, Mary Robinson, in her speech in 1995 to the Houses of the Oireachtas,

> "Our relation with the Diaspora beyond our shores is one which can instruct our society in the values of diversity, tolerance, and fair-mindedness ..... The men and women of our Diaspora represent not simply a series of departures and loss. They remain even while absent, a precious reflection of our growth and change, a precious reminder of the many strands of identity which compose our story ... We need to accept that in their new perspectives may well be a critique of our old ones".

The term Diaspora has an implication of mutual interaction and a networking of relationships in which those who remain in Ireland are engaged in contacts with those outside Ireland. Improvements in programmes and services for Irish emigrants would serve to sustain their families back home while acknowledging that they are still very much a part of the Irish community at home.

It is the Commission's view that the strengthening of the connection with the Irish Community abroad whether at economic, business or social policy level, would have positive results for those left behind. While to date, this positive connection for business and trade may have been understood and fostered, the connection with the more private world of family life has perhaps not been so fully understood and nurtured.  The Commission's recommendation for a Family Impact Statement (Chapter 24) whereby policies, proposals and administration procedures are family audited to measure their effects on families and the extent to which proposals promote family interests, represents one possibility for highlighting the family dimension of emigration issues. **In this context, the Commission suggests that the proposed Family Affairs Unit (Chapter 24) should interact as appropriate with the Inter-Departmental Committee on Emigration to ensure that the family dimension (both at home and abroad) of emigration is reflected in proposals.**

## 16.8   Access to Family History

A key area of interest to the Irish community abroad is that relating to genealogical research. In this context the Irish Genealogical Project has been brought to the Commission's attention. The project commenced in 1988 with the aim of developing a computerised database of information relevant to family history research in Ireland. Six major genealogical sources were to be fed into computers: church records, civil records of births, deaths and marriages, the 1901 and 1911 censuses, Griffith's 'Valuation' and the tithe applotment books. It was planned that, once the database was completed, a comprehensive family history research service would be provided, based on a country-wide network of centres and independent professional genealogists. The data compiled would be stored locally on computer systems linked to a common central system maintained by a central co-ordinating agency. The hope was that this would  stimulate "genealogy tourism" which could emphasise familial connections with Ireland.

The project has been dogged by many difficulties from the start and has been the subject of many reports over the years. A report from the Comptroller and Auditor-General focuses on the value for money aspect of the IGP, particularly on the extent to which the project has succeeded in creating the computer database and in putting in place a system for delivering a family history research service. The report estimates that funding by Irish public sector agencies for the project between 1988 and July 1996 amounted to £15 million[12].  Business levels for centres participating in the IGP, according to the report, did not, on average, increase significantly between 1989 and 1995. It was estimated that 6,800 commissions for family history were undertaken by local centres (including those in Northern Ireland) in 1989. These generated revenue estimated at £122,000 or approximately £18 per commission. Approximately 6,700 commissions were serviced in 1995, with total research revenue amounting to an estimated £140,000, an average of almost £21 each. There are very considerable differences in prices charged by the local centres participating in the IGP, with prices ranging from £15 to £75 for preliminary reports and from £50 to £170 for full family history reports, although it was planned that the IGP would offer a standardised product at a uniform price. The prices charged for searches and reports on individual family events such as a birth or a marriage were also found to vary greatly.

Where centres offer a full service, the delivery time from enquiry to producing a research report can be considerable. An overseas visitor calling to a local centre cannot usually

---

12   Of this, £12.5 million was provided by FÁS, the national training agency. The rest of the funding was provided by the Department of the Taoiseach (£250,000), Bord Fáilte (£680,000), the Shannon Free Airport Development Company (£410,000) and the International Fund for Ireland (£1,130,000).

receive research findings immediately unless what is sought is confirmation or elaboration of family details which are already known. Some customers thought that the family history research could be carried out during their trip to Ireland and that they would receive relevant local information and orientation. This was impossible given the state of development of the project and led to frustrated expectation and complaints by customers. In the event, research commissioned was sent on to the tourists some time after they had left the country.

The Report of the Comptroller and Auditor General concluded that the monitoring of progress in implementing the IGP project has been ineffective. No budget or reasonable targets were set and the gathering of relevant management information was sporadic and generally incomplete. It recommends that the IGP needs to establish clear targets and periodically to assess progress relative to the targets. It notes, in conclusion that the likely effectiveness of the project in meeting its objectives cannot currently be established.

The fact that more than 4,500 young people have received computer training and that there is a cross border aspect to the project, have been put forward in support of the project.

16.9    **Accessible information needed for family research**

The point has been made to the Commission that while many people of Irish ancestry abroad are interested in their roots and may be prepared to fund the necessary research, what many seek is a simple explanation about their family name, its history, locations in which the name is found, relevant local history, the significance of the big events in Irish history, e.g. the various plantations and the Famine. While much of this material can be established through a study of the literature, there must be scope for accessible information in simple format through the normal tourist information channels. **The Commission suggests that Departments and agencies in this area should develop proposals which could be relevant not only in terms of the desirability of encouraging family research but also from a tourist and heritage point of view.**

These proposals should build on and complement the work being carried out in the IGP project. Progress in relation to the implementation of that project should be monitored in the light of the concerns expressed in the report of the Comptroller and Auditor General.

# Appendix 1

**Some support agencies for Irish emigrants and people working abroad.**

**(1)** **Díon** Through the Díon [The title is the Irish word for "shelter"] the Government provides financial support to voluntary organisations providing advisory and welfare services for Irish emigrants in Britain. The Díon aims to "promote the continued contribution of Irish residents in Great Britain to British society by supporting those voluntary agencies who facilitate access to employment or welfare services". The terms of reference of the Díon Committee, set by the Minister for Labour at the establishment of the Committee are as follows:

- to advise and report on emigrant welfare services;
- to make recommendations on the provision of financial assistance towards the employment of professional workers dealing with the welfare problems of Irish workers; and
- to consider and make recommendations on specific questions at the request of the Minister for Enterprise, Trade and Employment.

**(2)** **The EURES - European Employment Services** The EURES is the system for the exchange of information on employment opportunities in Member States of the European Union (EU) and European Economic Area (EEA). This system was established by the EU Commission to assist the free movement of workers between the Member States. Since the 1st of January 1994, the EURES system can be used by people who travel to work within the EU and certain other European countries.

The EURES system has two main components:

### 1. Euroadvisers
A European wide network of over 400 specially trained Placement Officers who operate the system and are capable of advising job seekers and employers on aspects of living and working conditions in the various states of the EURES system.

### 2. A Telecommunications System
This system provides access to three services:

- A central database of job vacancies available in each Member State.

- A central database of general information on living and working conditions in each Member State.

- An electronic mail system allowing for rapid and easy communication among the network of Euroadvisers.

In Ireland, EURES is based in FÁS employment services offices.

**(3)** **Voluntary Organisations** such as the Irish Support and Advice Service, which is a registered charity in the UK. In 1995/96, this service provided advice to 11,000 callers, 94 per cent of whom are first or second generation Irish. Advice covers such areas as housing and benefit queries, and issues relating to repatriation, identification, discrimination and harassment.

**(4)** **The Department of Social, Community and Family Affairs**. The department has prepared a number of booklets which aim to provide relevant and succinct information which would help people in preparing to emigrate and in establishing themselves when they get to their destination. The information covers areas such as housing, social welfare, health, employment, taxes, education. The booklets appear to have met a very real need and were quickly out of stock. There is considerable demand for a reprint.

**(5)** **Embassies abroad:** The embassies provide a range of basic information on such issues as need for visas, and citizenship issues. Embassies also provide limited information and advice services.

**(6)** **Irish Groups** in host countries such as the UK, the United States and Australia provide information, advice and support to emigrants. The Irish Government supports these groups.

**(7)** **Agency for Personal Service Overseas (APSO)**. APSO is the national agency which enables Irish men and women to share their skills with people in the developing world. It is part of Irish Aid - the Government's overseas aid programme. Every year APSO supports about 1,400 overseas assignments. Assignees work all over sub-Saharan Africa, Central America and South-East Asia (primarily Cambodia) - in education, health, social sciences and administration.

**(8)** Newspapers, Alumni associations and other social groups also play an important part in maintaining links with emigrants and are an informal source of support for those away from home.

# Summary of Recommendations in Part 6

### The policy approach

*In relation to the wide-ranging topics raised in over 530 submissions to the Commission on the Family ( Chapter 15)*
The Commission
- acknowledges the views and concerns expressed on a number of specific topics which arose in submissions.
- welcomes the major policy initiatives which have been introduced in recent years which address many of the issues which are of significant importance to families
- recommends that funding be allocated to the National Social Service Board to develop a pilot Family Information Service to assess the extent to which families' needs for information may be met, as a first step in developing a comprehensive information service for families.

*In relation to better preparation for young people moving abroad (Chapter 16)*
The Commission recommends
- a proactive campaign to educate potential emigrants so that they know where to get information, advice and help and so that they are well prepared in advance of going abroad

*In relation to strengthening kin networks for families with relatives abroad*
The Commission recommends
- ongoing financial support for the voluntary agencies who work with Irish emigrants abroad and their families to be a key objective of the policy approach in strengthening the wider kin networks of families - both at home and abroad
- The Family Affairs Unit of the Department of Social, Community and Family Affairs should interact with the Inter-Departmental Committee on Emigration to ensure that the 'family' dimension (both at home and abroad) of emigration is reflected in policy proposals

## Making a start Part 6

### Recommendation 42
The Commission recommends
- the establishment of a fund of £100,000 to develop an initiative to provide more complete information and advice for those who are likely to emigrate

- The information and advice initiative would target young people at school, in FÁS training, in Youthreach or in 'out of school' initiatives who are most likely to be potential emigrants

**Cost:** £100,000 in 1998.

## Recommendation 43

The Commission suggests

- that departments and agencies with an interest in Irish heritage, Irish history and promoting family research should develop proposals in relation to making simple information available through the normal tourist channels to encourage family history research.

part 7
Undertaking research

In **Part 7** the Commission presents
- Family Policy in Ireland - A Strategic Overview- An abstract of a report to the Commission on the Family, by Tony Fahey, Economic and Social Research Institute.

- Fathers: Irish Experience in an International Context - An abstract of a report to the Commission on the Family, by Kieran McKeown, Harry Ferguson and Dermot Rooney.

- Childcare arrangements in Ireland- A report to the Commission on the Family by James Williams and Claire Collins, Economic and Social Research Institute.

- The Case for a Child Development Study.

# Overview of Part 7

**In pursuance of its terms of reference " to analyse recent economic and social change affecting the position of families", the Commission has undertaken a limited number of research projects.**

In recent years there have been several ground-breaking reports which have presented new perspectives on the major important issues facing Irish society today. The report of the Second Commission on the Status of Women, under the chairmanship of the Hon Miss Justice Mella Carroll has highlighted the changes which are taking place in the role of women in family life, in the workplace and in the cultural and economic life of the country. The work of the Law Reform Commission under President, the Hon Anthony J. Hederman, former Judge of the Supreme Court in the areas of family law and the family courts documents the reforms which are needed in legal practice and procedures in the sensitive area of marital breakdown. The Constitution Review Group under the chairmanship of Dr. T K Whitaker, has presented new perspectives on the relevance today of the provisions in the Constitution on the family and on the functions carried out within the home. The work of the ESRI, the Conference of Religious of Ireland and the Combat Poverty Agency contributes greatly to our knowledge about the income support requirements of families, the dynamics of the social welfare and taxation systems as they impact on families and the effectiveness of present policies in addressing disadvantage.

A Strategy for Equality, the Report of the Commission on the Status of People with Disabilities chaired by the Hon Mr. Justice Feargus Flood sets out an agenda for future action to remove the barriers which stand in the way of people with disabilities who want to live full and fulfilled lives. The Commission on the Family for its part has drawn on these reports and on several other expert findings in specialist areas which are pertinent to families in developing its recommendations in this report. While these many reports have been most useful and have made a substantial contribution to the Commission's thinking on many issues it has been the Commission's experience that there is a dearth of original research in many of the key areas which are of interest to Irish families. Throughout this report the Commission has highlighted the importance of research to underpin the development of policy in different areas as well as the need for ongoing evaluation of the effects of policy and programmes in the longer term on the well-being of families. It was in this context that the Commission undertook a small number of innovative research projects in areas of significant importance to Irish families today.

The reports of the researchers have been of considerable assistance to the Commission in developing this report.

### Family Policy in Ireland - A Strategic Overview

Tony Fahey's report documents significant changes in Irish society in recent decades, and changes in families. It examines demographic, economic and social changes and assesses the impact these have brought about in the functioning of families and in the role of families in society. The report traces the development of State provision for families and identifies the issues which are pertinent to the future direction of family policy.

**Fathers : Irish Experience in an International Context** is a literature review of the recent work on the role of fathers in family life. The review was carried out by Kieran McKeown, Harry Ferguson and Dermot Rooney. The report presents a range of perspectives on the growing literature on fathers, particularly in the areas of psychology and sociology but also in psychoanalysis, social policy and some areas of the law as it affects fathers. The report presents information about some of the experiences of fathers as highlighted in submissions to the Commission.

## Childcare Arrangements in Ireland

The ESRI report contains the findings of a national survey of over 1,300 families with children aged 12 years or less. The survey collected information about the different care arrangements that children experience throughout the day, the services used by parents working full-time in the home as well as those who work outside the home. Information about the back-up childcare arrangements that parents use in the event of their usual arrangement not being available was collected. This includes the arrangements made during school holidays by parents who had commitments outside the home.

*The Commission would like to acknowledge in particular Anne McKenna, Psychologist and former statutory lecturer in the Department of Psychology, University College Dublin, Nóirín Hayes, Dublin Institute of Technology, Eilis Hennessy, University College Dublin and Margret Fine-Davis, Centre for Women's Studies, Trinity College Dublin for their assistance with the development of the survey. In particular the Commission would like to thank James Williams and Claire Collins of the ESRI who carried out the survey and compiled the report for the Commission.*

## Issues in Family Policy

The report[1] of Gabriel Kiely and Valerie Richardson of the Family Studies Centre, University College Dublin draws together information about current provision in different areas including family income support, labour market policies, education and family life, and health policy for families. The work covers recent policy developments in relation to families with caring responsibilities for an older member or a member with a disability, marital separation and lone parent families and families under stress. The report has been used as resource material throughout the Commission's report.

In **Part 7** the Commission is pleased to present abstracts of the overview of family policy (Chapter 17) and the report on fathers (Chapter 18) as well as the full report of the ESRI survey on childcare arrangements in Ireland (Chapter 19).

In Chapter 20 the Commission presents the case for a national longitudinal study on children. The study proposes to follow through a group of children from birth to later life cycles. The study would enable the effects on children of experiences such as marital separation to be explored and the outcomes of children in different family situations to be researched. Such a study would facilitate monitoring of the effects of policies and practices and the need for change to be highlighted. A study carried out over a number of years would be of interest in all areas of social policy, to analysts and to policy makers.

In relation to the need for more research in matters of interest to families, the Commission would like to take the opportunity to highlight the importance of high quality quantitative scientific research in contributing to knowledge about the longer-term effectiveness of programmes. In recent years there has been a growing emphasis in public service management on the evaluation of programmes. This new emphasis is welcome and the availability of evaluation reports on various programmes and schemes which describe their impact on the consumer/customer is most informative about the innovative responses which are being developed to meet different needs. In this context, it has been suggested to the Commission, that there is a need for a greater emphasis on high quality quantitative scientific research to underpin the development of appropriate policy responses which will be effective in securing the desired outcomes for families.

1    The researcher was Sarah Grattan, B. Soc. Sc., M. Soc. Sc. (family policy)

**To assist the Commission on the Family with its work, Dr. Tony Fahey compiled background research material on various aspects of the family and family policy in Ireland. Much of this material had been prepared for other purposes by Dr. Fahey and will be published independently of the Commission in due course. At the Commission's request, Dr. Fahey prepared the present overview which summarises the main points of the material he provided to the Commission.**

### 1.  Introduction

The aim of this abstract is to provide an overview of the nature and development of family policy in Ireland, as reflected both in family law and in various aspects of social policy. The focus is less on a detailed inventory of family policy measures than on the underlying models of family life and strategic objectives of state family relations on which family policy has been based.

The rationale behind the analysis is that present debates and conflicts about family policy in Ireland are as much about ends, value systems and symbols as about means. They turn on basic questions about the kind of family life the state should be trying to promote and the symbolic meaning such models of family life have for us, as well as on more instrumental questions about the best means to achieve particular ends. If family policy is to develop in a coherent way in the future, it is necessary to consider the broad framework of ideas and assumptions within which present debates about the ends of family policy are taking place. It is unlikely, and perhaps even undesirable, that a strong consensus on these questions can easily be created (the near unanimity which existed in these areas in the past could be said to have done more harm than good by smothering debate and making it difficult to highlight defects in the existing order). However, it should be possible to clarify the terms of the debate so that it is productive and illuminating rather than circular and sterile.

It is in this spirit that the present overview attempts to sketch out the fundamental principles on which family policy has been based up to now and to outline some of the dilemmas and conflicts in thinking which shape its present evolution. A more complete analysis would require that the development of family policy be located in its social and historical context. Within the space available here, all that is attempted in that direction is a broad outline of the developments in family patterns as revealed by demographic trends. The overview concludes by commenting on some of the key issues which family policy must deal with in choosing its strategic objectives for the future.

### 2.  What is 'family policy'?

Family policy has never properly come into being in Ireland as a formal, separately identified segment of public policy - Ireland has never had a government department or office of the family and the term 'family policy' itself has only recently begun to be used in this country.

A change in designation of what formerly was the Department of Social Welfare to the Department of Social, Community and Family Affairs occurred with the change in government in June 1997. The insertion of' family affairs' into the department's title in this way marked a novel step for Ireland towards the formal identification of the family as a distinct area of responsibility in public administration, though the practical significance of that step is yet to emerge.

Though family policy traditionally has not existed in formal terms in Ireland, it may be identified in a less formal but nevertheless loosely structured way as an assortment of policy items drawn from a range of areas. These comprise both *distributive* measures, which provide supports to families in the form of income maintenance or services of various kinds (e.g. Child Benefit, One-parent family payments, housing supports, certain kinds of health services, etc.) and *regulatory* measures, which consist of laws that define what the family is and how family members can or should behave towards each other (as in the law on marriage, marital breakdown, family property, parents obligations to children, children's rights, along with constitutional provisions on the family, etc). The issues these measures touch on include not just 'family' in a general sense but also its component parts such as marriage, parenthood, childhood, reproductive matters, sexuality, housing, work in the home, family property, inheritance and so on.

### Policy paradigms

In the absence of institutional integration, these diverse areas are held together not just by their common, though uncoordinated, relevance to family issues but also by virtue of unifying assumptions, ideals, and images both about the family and state-family relations which underlie them. The concept of 'policy paradigm' can be used to refer to these broader, often half-hidden dimensions of family policy (O'Sullivan 1993). This concept refers not only to explicit ideas about policy (such as format statements of principles or objectives) but also to unspoken assumptions and values which shape the way issues are viewed, types of language which are available to talk about those issues, and the implicit identification of the groups, sources of information and types of discourse which are to be regarded as authoritative in defining what should be counted as problematic and in proposing what should be considered as solutions in the policy area in question.

The nature and importance of the paradigmatic underpinnings of policy suggest that the central principles of family policy are not to be found solely, or even primarily, on the surface, in the shape either of individual policy measures or explicit statements of what family policy is about. They are to be found in addition in largely unarticulated form in the paradigms on which policies are implicitly founded and within which they acquire consistency and meaning. In order to examine the strategic dimensions of family policy, therefore, it is necessary to explore these paradigmatic foundations and examine their logic.

### Two paradigms

An organising theme of the present analysis is that the development of family policy in Ireland in recent years has been shaped by a tension between two contrasting policy paradigms. These can be labelled *patriarchal familism* and *egalitarian individualism*. These paradigms arrived in historical succession-patriarchal familism emerging first and dominating family policy in the early part of the present century, egalitarian individualism emerging largely in the post-1960s era. Today they exist side by side. Though egalitarian individualism is in the ascendant in most areas, many aspects of patriarchal familism retain considerable popular appeal and remain a potent influence in key areas of family policy. We will now look at each of these paradigms in turn.

### 3. Patriarchal familism

*Patriarchal familism* rests on a cultural ideal of the family as a solidaristic, altruistic mini-community, where values of stability, loyalty and commitment to the family are paramount and where individual welfare is deemed to depend on the individual's inclusion into a cohesive family unit. The cohesiveness of the family in turn is deemed to require a clear internal structure of well-defined roles for its members (the roles of 'husband', 'wife', 'father', 'mother', 'adult child', 'dependent child', etc.). These roles are differentiated (there is little overlap between them) and complementary (the roles are thought of as fitting together, supporting each other and adding up to a well functioning whole). They are also hierachically structured along lines both of gender (male roles have precedence over female roles) and of generation (senior roles have precedence over junior roles). Gender and generational hierarchies combine to define the male household head as the dominant figure in the family household.

The family which is constituted on this basis is considered a primary social institution, essential as a foundation both of social order and individual welfare. This in turn entails a tendency to define the legal status and social standing of persons by reference to their family status as much as by reference to broader principles of citizenship or community membership.

The version of this approach which is of most relevance to family policy in Ireland today was at its peak in the early decades of the present century, though it had a long prior history. While it belonged firmly within wider European traditions of family culture, it acquired a particular cast in Ireland by virtue of its particular linkages within the classes of small property owners (especially family farmers) who dominated the social structure in the first half of the present century.

### Patriarchal familism and the state

The linkages between patriarchal familism as a public policy paradigm and the classes of small property owners were forged against the background of separatist politics in late nineteenth and early twentieth century Ireland. The social and economic demands of tenant farmers provided much of the motor power of separatist politics. The British state's response to that movement, which was designed to ease the grievances giving rise to the demand for home rule, was conciliatory in many ways and led to major developments in the state's role in Irish life. As a result, the kind of patriarchal familism found in rural Ireland was quite statist in important respects and led to a highly interventionist approach by the state in the social realm, especially in rural areas and including certain aspects of family life. In other respects, however, nationalist sentiment resisted the intrusion of what it saw as alien modes of life through the medium of certain kinds of state action. This was manifested in a strong anti-statist strand in patriarchal familism, particularly in connection with forms of state intervention identified with urban-industrial social organisation and with certain aspects of social welfare provision and family law then emerging in industrialised countries, especially Britain.

### The agrarian dimension

The statist dimensions of patriarchal familism had a strong rural and agrarian basis. They focused most of all on support by the state for the goal of widespread distribution of small-scale agrarian property and for the kind of patriarchal family organisation associated with small property. This focus reflected a widespread social and political view in Ireland of the 'peasant model' of community and family life as a social ideal and as a bulwark against what were seen as the corrosive effects on society of both urban-industrial capitalism and state socialism. This view was central to nationalist ideology emerging in the final decades of British rule and through that channel shaped much of British government action in this area in Ireland. It was also central to government thinking in the two decades immediately after independence. It acquired an additional popular appeal because it was highly consistent with Catholic social thought and was identified strongly with the economic and political interests of large Catholic segments of the population.

The massive land reform programme represented by the Land Acts and the work of the Land Commission from the 1880s to the 1930s (and, up to independence, by the Congested Districts Board), a variety of other supports for small-scale farming and the provision of housing in rural areas were the principal policy expressions of this approach in the material realm. Together these activities entailed a degree of state intervention in social and economic organisation in rural areas which was without parallel elsewhere in Europe in its time. They amounted not so much to a 'family policy' in a narrow sense as to a broad social, economic and political project in which an arcadian vision of society, with the small-farm family at its centre, became the framework for emerging definitions of nationhood and policy formation. The central effect of this project was to promote a family-based production system both as an achieved fact and as a social ideal in the countryside and to displace alternative, market-based mechanisms for the organisation of rural economic life. This 'familisation' of the rural economy was evident especially in relation to land and labour. Intra-family transfer and inheritance came to overshadow market mechanisms in the disposition of land, and family labour went a long way to displacing paid labour in the organisation of farm work.

This merging of the economic order with the family order in the small-farm economy profoundly shaped the nature of rural family life. Complex arrangements involving property inheritance, marriage settlements, household structure, the work commitments of children and entitlements of various family members to support out of the patrimony became key organising mechanisms in family structure.[1] While it would be excessive to suggest that state action was responsible for bringing this family system into being, or that it was entirely novel to the late nineteenth century, public policy can be considered as a major influence in elevating it to the position of actual and ideological dominance it came to occupy in early twentieth century Ireland.

## The Catholic dimension

A large part of the cultural framework of this newly dominant family system was provided by Catholic social and moral teaching . In the aftermath of independence, public policy accepted, even welcomed, this fact and this provided a further basis for state intervention in family issues.  Alongside material interventions in support of family farming, law and social policy in the 1920s and 1930s promoted Catholic teaching in the areas of family, sexuality and parental authority over children. This was so especially through legislation on contraception, public morality, censorship and women's social role.  The 1937 Constitution represented the peak of these trends. It strongly echoed Catholic teaching in its provision on marriage, the family and the authority of parents, while it reflected a distinctive approach to property and rural society in its articles on private property (Article 43) and on 'directive principles of social policy' (in Article 45, which among other things commits the state to 'establishing on the land in economic security as many families as in the circumstances shall be practicable').

## The anti-statist dimension

The anti-statist strand of patriarchal familism is as notable as its interventionist elements. This strand reflected ambivalent attitudes towards capitalist industrialisation and the social policy developments which went with it, particularly as exemplified by developments in Britain. Under British rule, some developments in social provision which originated in Britain were welcomed in Ireland, such as the Old Age Pensions Act of 1908, others were tolerated, such as the Children's Act of 1908, while others were rejected, such as health insurance in the period 1912-18. After independence, the reluctance to move towards British-type social welfare principles of social provision lingered.

A range of individual measures from the 1930s to the 1950s (such as the slum clearance programmes of the 1930s and the Social Welfare Act of 1952) showed that resistance to social welfare-type measures was by no means total. Yet the degree of controversy which could surround modest measures in fields such as vocational education and mother and child health showed how insecure the level of support for such departures was, particularly where they could be construed as a threat to the integrity of the patriarchal, property-based model of family life which was favoured by public policy and public opinion (the tortuous development of the Health Act in the period 1948 to 1953, of which the notorious Mother and Child Scheme controversy was but a part, is a case in point - see Barrington 1987).

---

1    The resulting system was classically described by the American anthropologists Arensberg and Kimball in their accoints
      of the 'stem family' in Co. Clare in the 1930s. Since the 1970s, there has been considerable debate among researchers
      about the precise nature and extent of the stem family in rural Ireland at that time and the degree of regional variation it
      exhibited.

# 4.     Egalitarian individualism

By the 1950s, Irish society, especially rural Ireland, was in crisis, as evidenced by falling population and a stagnant economy. The sense of crisis rubbed off on inherited models of family organisation and state-family relations. Despite extensive state support, the 'peasant' family system had failed to generate the economic vitality necessary for economic progress Ireland.[2] In the context of the broad international movement away from family-centred production systems towards the wage-based, urban-industrial forms of the industrial era, the inward-looking, rural and small-farm bias of social and economic policy was judged to have been a cul-de-sac.

These broad social developments began to be reflected in a shift away from patriarchal familism towards a new emerging paradigm of social policy in Ireland which was influenced by principles of *individualism* and *equality* and which thus can be labelled 'egalitarian individualism'. As far as family issues are concerned, this paradigm reduces the significance accorded to family roles as principles of social organisation and gives greater significance to the needs, rights and obligations of individuals. It regards a large proportion of individual rights as basically undifferentiated - they are common to all persons, in principle at least, and are not contingent on whether one is male or female, husband or wife, parent or child (it is outside the scope of the present paper to document the many ways in which practice fell short of principle in this kind of policy approach). Egalitarian individualism points to individual welfare as the principal measure of quality in family life, and expects that family organisation should conform to the requirements of individual welfare rather than vice versa.

The ideological underpinnings of egalitarian individualism comprise a mix of liberalism, secularism, humanism and feminism. In Ireland, opposition to traditional conservative Catholicism tended to unify these approaches and gave them a common focus they might otherwise have lacked, even though manifestations of the new outlook could also be found within strands of Catholicism itself.

## The libertarian dimension

The individualistic dimension of egalitarian individualism is often regarded as quintessentially libertarian. It focuses on the individual as the basic unit and limits the extent to which the requirements of social stability can be used to justify constraints on the rights and freedoms of the individual. It assigns a great deal of importance to individual decision as a guide to personal behaviour and to negotiation and voluntary agreement between persons rather than direction from above or adherence to externally prescribed rules as the basis of social interaction. As a result, it tends to promote diversity and change as against tradition and authority, self-fulfillment as opposed to group cohesion.

In keeping with this libertarian aspect, the 'de-regulation' of personal behaviour is often identified as a central consequence of the rise of individualistic principles in family policy. Various measures to liberalise the laws relating to sexuality, such as the legalising of artificial contraceptives, the easing of censorship and the de-criminalisation of homosexuality, are instances of this trend. So too is the improvement in the legal status of

---

2     See Hannan (1979) where the post-war decline of the 'peasant family model' is described.

non-marital children brought about by the Status of Children Act 1987. In the field of social provision, the introduction of the Unmarried Mother's Allowance in 1973 (more recently merged into the One-Parent Family Payment) and the emergence of a less punitive, more therapeutic approach to disruptive children in the social services also reflect the same underlying themes of openness to choice in personal behaviour and concern for the rights of individuals in preference to traditional preoccupation with the preservation of cohesive social institutions. The recent introduction of divorce might be seen in the same light.

### The regulatory dimension

However, while this libertarian strand is real and important, egalitarian individualism also has strong regulatory and disciplinary dimensions. At the informal cultural level, these dimensions are expressed in part by reference to principles of *reciprocity* and *mutuality*. These principles amount to an obligation on family members to recognise and serve each other's interests as well as their own. The right to self fulfillment and self expression is thus constrained by a corresponding obligation to facilitate self fulfillment and self expression for others. This implies an insistence on *negotiation* as the basis on which family relations are ordered (for an empirical study of the emergence of negotiated as opposed to prescribed family roles in rural Ireland in the 1970s, see Hannan and Katsiaouni 1977). It also points to a requirement for flexibility and effective communication as a means to genuine accommodation and adjustment between different interests within the family. To the extent that those requirements are met, they impose an other-orientation on individual behaviour within the family and limit its egotistical nature.

These disciplinary aspects of the egalitarian individualist approach in informal culture have fed through into family law and social provision. These have added important new regulatory dimensions to the state's approach to family issues which counterbalance the libertarian aspects already mentioned. Much of the thrust of these new dimensions is directed at creating a framework in which equitable and effective negotiation between different interests within the family can be supported. This framework is at its most overt and directive in the form of the body of law and the associated protective or enforcement mechanisms which have been developed to prevent abuse of weaker family members by the stronger - sexual or physical abuse within families in this instance being thought of as the polar opposite of reciprocity and mutuality. Examples of such regulatory mechanisms include the recent growth of child protection legislation and practice, especially as reflected in the 1991 Child Care Act and the more intervenionist approach to children at risk within families which effective child protection requires. Legislation to protect women from sexual or other physical violence within the home provides a parallel instance of a protective impulse, in this case on behalf of vulnerable adults. This could be seen as part of a broader movement to identify and highlight gross infringements of women's rights which previously were accepted as normal or unavoidable but which now have become the targets of more stringent regulation (as in the case of the law on rape, sexual assault and sexual harassment).

### The 'self' in egalitarian individualism

In addition to these overt disciplinary constraints on behaviour within families, the culture of individualism has deeper and more subtle regulatory effects through the concept of the 'self' which it defines and institutionalises. No concept of the self refers to a pre-social, natural entity. Rather each variety of individualism proposes a cultural construct of the self which defines what the model individual is. Thus Protestant individualism portrayed the individual as moulded in God's image and possessing an inescapable duty to live by his word, democratic individualism focuses on the individual as a member of the polity with certain political rights and obligations, and classical capitalist individualism posits an individual who is self-willed, acquisitive and materially minded but who is also sober, rational and disciplined in the pursuit of economic gain. These concepts of the individual are less statements of fact than of value: they are less intended to describe real people than to portray ideal personalities to which real people are called to aspire.

Present-day family-oriented individualism similarly constructs an ideal-typical self through the distinctive view of the underlying nature of the human personality which it embodies. At one level, this view proposes not one but a range of selves within the family and argues for the need for the family to accommodate that diversity. Thus, for example, child psychology and associated cultural movements have emphasised the distinctiveness of childhood and has transformed our ideas of what children need and what is required to form them into capable, well-adjusted adults. This has led to greater demands on parents and other adults to adjust their own behaviour and expectations so as to respond to what are seen as children's real needs. New conceptions of childhood, based on individualistic principles, have thus acted as a source of discipline and constraint on the behaviour of adults.

Feminism has similarly revolutionised popular understanding of the nature and social role of women. It has proposed new definitions of women's true nature and has striven to raise that nature to the same plane of value as men's. It has powerfully affected the negotiation of needs and interests between men and women in the family as a result.

Underneath this diversity, however, conceptions of the self in egalitarian individualism have a uniform quality in the emphasis they lay on love, emotional closeness and personal intimacy as basic requirements of the human person and thus as essentials of family life rather than as optional extras to be catered for after material necessities are provided. These emphases can be viewed as a source of instability since they give rise to expectations in people that often fail to be fulfilled in family relationships (thus contributing, for example, to the modern rise in divorce rates). But they strive to go beyond materialistic values and aspire to close human communion rather than mere co-residence and practical co-operation as the heart of family life. As such, these values have a strong ethical character and make a moral demand on the individual that effort be applied in the attempt to fulfill them.

5.      ### Emergence of egalitarian individualism

It is impossible to pinpoint a particular date at which the beginnings of a paradigm shift in public policy away from patriarchal familism towards egalitarian individualism began to take place in Ireland. It was certainly well under way by the 1970s but more tentative indications can be traced back to earlier decades. For example, the celebrated Supreme Court Judgement in the Tilson case was issued in 1951. This judgement represented a blow for gender equality in that it finally laid to rest the old common law idea of 'supremacy of paternal rights' in regard to children and established that mothers' and fathers' rights and duties in relation to their children were equal. One could step back further in time and point to the presence of Article 40.3 in the Constitution, which pledges the state to defend and vindicate the personal rights of citizens, as a manifestation of liberal individualism within a document which was otherwise dominated by Catholic teaching as far as social issues were concerned. Though the challenge to core aspects of patriarchal familism which was implicit in Article 40.3 remained moribund until the liberal and activist Supreme Court of the late 1960s and 1970s began to draw out its potential,[3] the very fact that it was there at all indicates that the growing emphasis on individualism in family law in recent years has not been utterly without historical background.

### Gender equality

An important strand of the shift towards egalitarian individualism can be traced in the emergence of gender equality as a issue for public policy and in the effects this had in the family field. Historical precursors of this development can be traced back to the married women's property acts and the child custody acts in the nineteenth century. These statutes eliminated a number of gross disabilities suffered by married women under the common law, particularly the prohibition on married women's ownership of property and the ascription of absolute rights of custody of children to fathers. However, these improvements in married women's legal status took place in the midst of a strengthening cult of domesticity which limited married women's role to the home (Bourke 1993 examines the manifestations of this cult in public policy in late nineteenth and early twentieth century Ireland). The pressure on married women to withdraw from paid work, which culminated in the 'marriage bar' in the public service and in many white-collar occupations in the 1930s, was part of this move, as was the obeisance paid to women's 'life within the home' in Article 41 in the 1937 Constitution.

The Succession Act of 1965 serves as an important symbolic marker in the emergence of the modern gender equality era. This act imposed constraints on the traditional freedom of testation enjoyed by Irish property owners by establishing a legal right for spouses and, in certain circumstances, children to share in a property owner's estate. The principal intention of this act was to make it impossible for a male household head to cut his wife out of his will after she had contributed years of effort to building up the family property. Discretionary inheritance had long been one of the key foundations of patriarchal power in Irish family life, particularly in rural areas. The change in direction represented by the Succession Act was thus symbolic of the diminution of rural patriarchal traditions, both as a social ideal and as a daily reality in Irish life.

A more concerted move towards gender equality was promoted by the report of the First Commission on the Status of Women (1972) and Ireland's accession to the European

---

3    The key judgement was *Ryan V Attorney General* (1965) which laid down that the personal rights referred to in Article 40.3 extended beyond those explicitly listed in the Constitution to include 'unenumerated rights' which it was open to the Supreme Court to discover. This judgement laid the foundation for a number of important subsequent 'rights' judgements, most notable in the *McGee* case on contraception in 1973.

Economic Community in 1973 (by virtue of which Ireland committed itself to the provisions on gender equality in the Treaty of Rome). The principal effects were seen in the elimination of formal discrimination against women in the workplace, along with attempts to remove gender biases in social welfare and certain aspects of marital property.

## 6.     Children's rights

The development of the state's role in relation to children echoes in some ways the history of the state's role in constructing gender. We can trace the history of legislative efforts to improve the status of children back to the early nineteenth century, but within this history we can also detect countervailing developments which tended to constrain children within strict and often oppressive modes of behaviour. Overall, the state's role in this area provided shifting and not always coherent definitions of what childhood meant. Within those definitions, the principle of respect for children's needs and rights gradually emerged as a major influence, but that principle was often compromised by the demand that children 'be seen and not heard', that they be obedient and submit to adult expectations both inside and outside the family. As in the case of women, a more sustained questioning of what children's rights should mean has begun to emerge in recent decades. Indeed, it is in regard to children that the principles of egalitarian individualism have been most widely accepted in principle but quite often most difficult to work out and apply in practice. While much has happened in consequence of the new approach, we are far from a final consensus and we can expect further working through of the implications for public policy in the years to come.

An important symbolic marker of the recent strengthening of children's rights is the Status of Children Act 1987 which abolished legal discrimination against non-marital children. Centuries of legal and moral reasoning had judged that the legal down-grading of children born outside of marriage, however harsh on the innocent children involved, was an acceptable price to pay for safeguarding the institution of marriage. In 1984, the Supreme Court had reaffirmed this traditional approach in a judgement which dismissed a claim by the illegitimate daughter of a bachelor farmer to a legal share in his estate under the 1965 Succession Act (the case of *O'B v. S*). Despite this judgement, the Oireachtas three years later passed the Status of Children Act (1987) which, with certain limitations, abolished legal discrimination against children born outside of marriage. The import of the 1987 act was, in effect, to make illegal the kind of discrimination against non-marital children which the Supreme Court had appeared to interpret almost as a constitutional obligation a short time before. While the constitutional basis of the 1987 Act has never been tested in court, it would seem to represent movement away from Article 41 (which deals with the protection of marriage) as a constitutional guide to this area of family policy and a movement towards Article 40, which asserts that all citizens be held equal before the law and commits the state to protect the personal rights of citizens. It is thus characteristic of a broader movement away from a concern with the protection of the social unit towards a concern for individual rights as a basis for social policy which had begun to emerge over the preceding years.

### Weaknesses in children's rights

Alongside this promotion of children's rights, some contradictory trends are still evident. This is so especially in that as the regulatory framework of childhood has grown more benign, the redistributive system has in some ways become less rather than more favourable to children. Income tax allowances for children declined from the 1960s onwards and were abolished in 1986. The value of child benefit (formerly children's allowances) has had a mixed record. While it has been increased in recent years, over the long term it has not been enough to compensate for the loss of tax-free allowances (Kennedy and McCormack 1994). The level of support for child dependants of those on unemployment benefit and unemployment assistance has been low and generally has not been enough to keep the children of unemployed parents out of poverty. Given the growth in unemployment over the last decade, inadequate support for children in the social welfare system has contributed to a sharp increase in the incidence of child poverty. The poverty rate among children in Ireland in the late 1980s was the worst in Europe (Rainwater and Smeeding 1995) and was markedly worse than it had been in Ireland in the early 1970s (Callan *et al.* 1989).

A further concern about children's rights arises from the weakness of the position of children in the legal regulation of marital breakdown. Marital breakdown is universally acknowledged as an issue of vital interest to children. Yet, in Ireland as in other countries, the legal procedures for dealing with marital breakdown lack adequate mechanisms for taking account of the child's interests. Disputes concerning children appear to form a significant part of marital separation cases which reach the courts in Ireland (Fahey and Lyons 1995, pp. 78-79). Yet, in those cases, 'it seems that the child's voice is heard only through the parents, sometimes in the context of bitter conflict between the father and the mother as to what is best for the child' (*ibid.*, pp. 135-6).

The Law Reform Commission, in its report on the Family Courts, considers a number of mechanisms by which this defect in the law on marital breakdown might be resolved (Law Reform Commission, 1996, pp. 104-13). It recommended that the court should have power to appoint a legal representative to act on the child's behalf in family law hearings, and that it should also have the power to appoint guardians *ad litem* to act in a broader manner on behalf of the child's welfare where that might be necessary.

A further difficulty arises at the level of the Constitution. Although the Constitution gives considerable emphasis to the rights of the family and of parents, it makes no explicit reference to the rights of children. As Kiely and Richardson (1995, p. 38) note, 'the Kilkenny Incest Investigation concluded that the very high emphasis on the rights of the family in the Constitution may consciously or unconsciously be interpreted as giving a higher value to the rights of parents than to the rights of children'. In the Kilkenny incest case, the state seemed to be unable to intervene in a situation where a child was known to be at risk because of the strength of parents' powers in relation to children. The Kilkenny Incest Investigation recommended that Articles 41 and 42 of the Constitution be amended to include a statement on the constitutional rights of children.

## 7.     The demographic perspective on family policy

Demographic trends are part of the social context in which paradigms of family policy evolve and offer a perspective from which the general shape of family policy can be viewed. Demographic data are also often read as a commentary on those paradigms since they provide indicators of family behaviour. Concerns about 'family decline' today are often fuelled by statistics on such things as non-marital births, the overall decline in fertility, marital breakdown and the fall in the marriage rate. They thus become part of the debate about family policy as much as an objective reflection of family conditions. However, different ways of reading the same demographic landscape are possible. One can choose what to notice and what to overlook, and one can assess the significance of particular features in divergent ways. Interpretations of demographic trends can thus add to rather than resolve conflict about family issues in public debate. This has been very much the case in Ireland and makes it worthwhile to look at broad demographic developments both as 'objective' indicators of the changing social context of family policy and as the raw material for ideological conflict about family issues.

**Decline and progress as themes in family demography**

Twentieth century population history has been marked by sharply changing patterns of failure and success. Post-famine population decline, and its persistence in the twentieth century, has been read as the outstanding marker of social and economic weakness in Irish society up to the 1960s. Conversely, population recovery since the 1960s, though halting and modest for much of that period, has been taken as a sign that Ireland is finally finding its feet. We thus have a well-defined image of decline and subsequent recovery as a way of characterising the evolution of Ireland's population in modern times.

The family is one of the key institutions of population reproduction and so might be thought to have shared in the same sequence of decline and recovery. However, there is no consensus that this is so. Some read demographic data to suggest that the strong traditional family of the first half of the twentieth century has begun to fall apart in recent decades. This suggests an image of strength and stability giving way to decline. Others will read the same data in the opposite way, finding signs of weakness in the supposedly strong and stable traditional family and signs of advance in the emergence of new patterns in recent decades.

These conflicts of interpretation arise in connection with all major periods in the evolution of family demography in the present century. The patriarchal family in the first half of the century ascribed great importance to family stability and cohesion and in many ways fulfilled those ideals. Marital breakdown scarcely existed as a socially recognised problem (though it may have existed as a hidden reality for some families), child-bearing outside of marriage was exceptional, women's roles had a strong family orientation (as evidenced in the low rates of married women's participation in work outside the home), and men rarely walked out on their responsibilities to their wives and children (at least not overtly). All these can be taken to indicate that the family was a strong, effective social institution which brought men and women together in an orderly, well-understood way in order to provide a stable framework for mutual co-operation and the rearing of children. In this view, to the degree that the patriarchal family had a negative side in such things as hierarchy and rigidity, these faults could be counted as an acceptable price to pay for stability and cohesion in family life.

Signs of weakness which can be seen on the other side of this coin are traceable in a number of aspects of the patriarchal system. One of the most striking is the extraordinarily low incidence of family formation which accompanied it. By the 1920s and 1930s, marriage rates in Ireland had fallen to exceptionally low levels. Those who married tended to do so very late the average age at marriage in the early 1930s was about 34 for men and 29 for women, and some 74 percent of 25-34 year old men and 56 percent of 25-34 year old women were single. Many never married at all. Among 45-54 year olds, 29 per cent of men and 24 per cent of women were single and unlikely every to marry. Given that limited access to marriage was coupled with strict social and cultural sanctions against sex outside of marriage, the result was that at any given time large proportions of the adult population were sexually inactive, and many of these went to their graves without having had a substantial sexual relationship in their lives.

Irish society at the time could thus be considered as marriage-averse to an unusual degree and as the carrier of an extreme regime of mass sexual denial. Though the family system was stable and cohesive in many ways, it could thus be counted as having failed to provide widely for some of the most central of human needs, The 1937 Constitution echoed this paradox. its strongly pro- family provisions were adopted at a time when the actual rate of family formation was among the lowest recorded in human history.

Similar paradoxes were evident in other areas. Though marital fertility was relatively high by European standards, the large proportions who were not married meant that overall fertility was below the European average. The result was a comparatively low rate of natural increase, which contributed to the general weakness in reproductive performance at the national level. Similarly, the ideal of family cohesion was dented by emigration: as children entered adulthood, they were dispersed abroad to an exceptional degree, thus straining the capacity of family members to maintain contact. The concentration of emigration among young adults meant that the age-structure was both top-heavy and bottom heavy - there were large numbers of elderly and children and comparatively few in the ages in between. This in turn led to exceptionally high dependency ratios, and these strained society's capacity to provide adequate support to dependent sections of the population.

### Developments since the 1960s
Population recovery after 1960 has been driven in part by a turnaround in some of the weaknesses in family demography of earlier decades. There was thus some recovery in the family in basic demographic terms. Marriage rates surged, and the 1970s proved to be the boom years for marriage in twentieth century Ireland. The annual number of marriages reached a peak for the century in 1974 (at 23,000), and average age of marriage fell to the lowest of the century in 1977-78 (at 26.2 years for men and 24.0 for women). This marriage surge had a strong positive effect on the overall number of births, even though average family size continued to decline. As a result, the annual number of births also rose and reached a twentieth century peak in 1980 (with 74,000 births in that year). At the same time, emigration eased and turned into a large net inward flow in the early 1970s.

The marriage surge of the 1960s and 1970s proved to be temporary and by the early 1990s had fallen back to the levels of the 1960s in absolute terms and the 1930s in terms of rates per 1000 of the population. When combined with further declines in average family size, falling marriage rates led to a sharp fall in birth rates. The period fertility rate fell below population replacement rates (conventionally estimated at 2.1 births per woman) in 1989 and has hovered around that level since. For a time in the late 1980s, emigration soared again, total population began to fall and it seemed that the demographic gloom of the 1950s had returned.

In the 1990s, the demographic depression of the late 1980s has cleared. Economic boom brought an end to net emigration and by 1997 has begun to yield a substantial net inward flow (estimated by the CSO at 15,000 in the year to April 1997). Population growth has resumed. Furthermore, the age structure of the population has taken on a more positive shape, with fewer in the dependent ages (children and elderly) and more in the active ages. Dependency ratios are now falling sharply and hold the promise of an unprecedentedly strong basis for the support of dependent age-groups in the years ahead. Despite the fall in fertility, overall reproductive performance has improved. Though fewer children are now being born, the prospect that they will be retained in Ireland (and perhaps added to by net inward migration) is greatly increased. In consequence, the small birth cohorts of today are likely to yield larger cohorts of adults in the years ahead than did the large birth cohorts of the past. Apart from raw totals of people, present reproduction patterns also yield what economists often regard as a higher population 'quality', in that young people now are healthier and better educated than ever before and have a markedly higher economic potential than earlier generations.

While the family as an institution might have been thought to deserve some of the credit for this improvement in reproductive performance, the paradox is that much of the public discussion of family life in Ireland today is dominated by the themes of crisis and decline, particularly in connection with child-rearing and child welfare. The increase in unmarried motherhood and in marital breakdown are most often pointed to as evidence in support of these themes. In the early 1960s, less than one birth in thirty took place outside of marriage. In 1996, one birth in four (24.7 per cent) took place outside of marriage, and in 1992 (the most recent year for which relevant data are available), 34.6 per cent of *first* births (that is, of new family formations) took place outside of marriage. Marriage has thus lost much of its traditional function as a gateway to sex and reproduction.

Marriage has also lost much of its former stability. While there is no comprehensive, reliable data on the incidence of marital breakdown, Census of Population data on marital status, which provide the best approximation, show that it has become more widespread (Table 1).[4] In 1996, separated women accounted for 6.6 per cent of ever-married women, in comparison to 3.3 per cent ten years earlier. It is also notable from these data that legally formalised marital breakdowns (in the form of legal separation or divorce in another country) by no means account for all marital breakdowns. In the case of women, more separated women reported themselves under the headings 'desertion' and 'other separated' than under 'legally separated' and 'divorced in another country'.

---

4    These data do not take account of those who have entered second unions following a marriage breakdown. Nor do they make clear why the number of separated women (47,118 in 1996) should be so much higher than the number of separated men (30,887 in 1996). However, the data do provide a lower-bound indication.

Non-marital births and marital breakdown have together caused an increase in lone parenthood in families with dependent children (though widowhood also plays a role in this area). In 1996, 13.8 per cent of family units with children aged under 15 were headed by a lone parent (of these, 85 per cent were headed by lone mothers and 15 per cent by lone fathers) (CSO, *Census 96*, Vol. 3, Table 34).

## Table 1.

Marital Status of Ever-married Women and Men, 1986-1996.

| Marital status | Women | | | Men | | |
|---|---|---|---|---|---|---|
| | 1986 | 1991 | 1996 | 1986 | 1991 | 1996 |
| Ever-married (excl. widowed) | 676,193 | 700,844 | 733,789 | 700,844 | 683,727 | 710,616 |
| Separated | 22,607 | 33,793 | 52,131 | 14,638 | 21,350 | 35,661 |
| *Deserted* | *9,038* | *16,904* | *16,785* | *2,584* | *6,781* | *6,363* |
| *Marriage annulled* | *540* | *722* | *1,287* | *443* | *499* | *920* |
| *Legally separated* | *3,888* | *5,974* | *14,616* | *3,299* | *5,178* | *11,863* |
| *Other separated* | *6,792* | *7,195* | *14,430* | *6,090* | *5,787* | *11,741* |
| *Divorced in another country* | *2,169* | *2,998* | *5,013* | *2,222* | *3,105* | *4,774* |
| Inter-censal increase in numbers separated | - | 11,186 | 13,325 | - | 6,712 | 9,537 |
| Annual average increase | | 2,237 | 2,665 | | 1,342 | 1,970 |
| Separated as % of total | 3.30 | 4.80 | 6.40 | 2.20 | 3.10 | 4.30 |

*Source: Census of Population, Vol. II, 1986, 1991;Census 96 Principal Demographic Results*

It is possible also to point to failures in the principles of egalitarianism in present developments in family life. These relate not only to the persistence of inequalities between men and women, but also to inequalities across social class in the conditions of family life, particularly as these affect children. The majority of children today may be provided with good standards of education and opportunities for personal development but large minorities are not. Children now comprise the largest segment of the population in poverty, and some 15 per cent continue to suffer from serious educational disadvantage (Kellaghan *et al.* 1995). Apart from being unjust, the disadvantage suffered by children could be considered as a waste of national resources. In the past, high emigration and poor educational provision for the majority were the principal forms of such waste - Ireland either exported its children as they reached adulthood or did little to draw out the best from those who remained at home. Today, it could be said that widespread childhood poverty continues the tradition of profligacy in relation to children which was represented by high emigration and poor education in the past.

For some commentators, negative trends and patterns such as these reflect failures in present-day developments in family life. In this view, these failures raise questions about the validity of the modern, individualist model of the family, or at least about the capacity of that model to deliver the beneficial outcomes it promises. On the other hand, the overall social, economic and demographic vitality which prevails today contrasts with the weaknesses in family formation and poor reproductive performance which prevailed in the past. It is thus difficult to talk unambiguously of either progress or decline in the evolution of family demographic patterns. Rather, we have a complex mixture of indicators which can be used to tell a variety of stories and which can be drawn into debate about paradigms of family life in conflicting ways.

8.      **Implications for the future**
The analysis of the underlying paradigms which guided state action on the family up to now does not of itself tell us how family policy is likely to or ought to develop in the future. Nevertheless it is possible to draw out some general points about the direction of developments which provide the context within which future strategic objectives will be established.

The most general such point derives from the unspoken, paradigmatic nature of the strategic aspects of family policy. While underlying principles and objectives can be discerned in present family policy, they lack coherence and clarity, are sometimes in conflict with each other and are nowhere set out in a formal way. The implication arising from this assessment is that the foundations of family policy, the principles and objectives which underlie and guide it, need to be formulated and set out clearly. In other words, the strategic dimension of family policy must be made explicit and, as far as possible, must also be made coherent and rational. It may not always be possible to reconcile the conflicts of principle which might emerge from such a process. For the sake of formal consistency, for example, it might be desirable to move further in the direction of egalitarian individualism, but it might be more realistic and more acceptable to public opinion to strike balances between the competing claims of individualistic and familistic values. In any event, it should be possible to spell out those areas where consensus can be achieved, to identify the conflicts that cannot easily be reconciled, and to indicate what working compromises might be sought in those areas.

The principles and objectives of family policy which should emerge from such a process of clarification need not be radically new. Rather, they could attempt to capture and project forward the essence of developments which have emerged in Ireland in recent decades and are valued by Irish people. As a general rule, family policy should retain a strong popular base, while at the same time protecting minority rights and recognising the real diversity of family life. It should acknowledge and reflect the social worth of long-established traditions of family-centredness and family cohesion in social life in Ireland, while at the same time taking cognisance of new awareness and new concerns about the requirements for individual well-being in the family which have emerged in recent years.

**Overall issues for family policy**
Reasoning from recent trends in this way points to a number of key issues concerning the

*kind of family life* to be promoted by public policy which have emerged in recent developments and merit close attention in framing overall objectives of family policy.  These issues include:

1. The high priority to be attached to *individual well-being* as a measure of family effectiveness  and as a goal of family policy.

2. A recognition of the *diversity* of family forms and relationships which may serve individual well-being and  of the right of individuals to construct family relationships according to their sincerely held views as to what best suits their individual nature and circumstances.

3. As a qualification of (2), the importance of *equality of well-being* between family members as a principle of family organisation and as a primary and necessary constraint on individuals' freedom of behaviour and expression within family life.  This means in particular that legal guarantees for children's rights should properly serve as a limitation on the freedom of behaviour of adults within family life.

4. As an extension of (3) and a further qualification of (2), a recognition of the fundamental requirement for *reciprocity and mutuality* as prerequisites of healthy family relationships and as a fundamental source of obligation on family members to recognise and serve each other's interests as well as their own.

5 . The recognition that continuity and stability in family relationships has a major, though not over-riding, value for individual well-being and social stability, especially, though not solely, as far as children are concerned. This means that family policy should support the institution of marriage and, even outside of marriage, should encourage joint parenthood rather than lone parenthood, while at the same time recognising that failures of marriage and of joint parenthood occur and should be allowed for in public policy.

### Role of the state

A persistent feature of state-family relations in Ireland in the present century has been the strong role of the state in promoting certain models of family life.  Though the nature of those models and the kinds of state intervention used to promote them has changed over time, the underlying fact of state intervention has not. Policy should also recognise and assert the necessary and valid *role of the state* in supporting family life and promoting forms of the family that best serve the welfare of individual members. This role is properly limited in a number of ways - by the principles of family and personal privacy and autonomy, by the practical limits to what state action can achieve as far as certain difficult aspects of family life are concerned (e.g. in limiting the extent of marital conflict), and by public expenditure constraints.  However, these limits leave a great deal of scope for an active state role in the family.  In addition, the limits themselves and their implications in particular policy areas are not always clear-cut and need to be kept under constant critical review.

Without attempting to spell out the proper role of the state in any detail, the following general points can be made.

6. Family policy up to now has played a fundamental role in expressing and affirming the nation's values and ideals concerning family life, at the symbolic as well as the practical levels. This expressive, moral and symbolic dimension of family policy has been an important part of its overall function. There is no reason to expect that this situation will change in the future. In consequence, family policy measures should properly be evaluated not only by reference to their practical efficacy (though this is a key concern) but also by reference to the aspirations and ideals of family life which they entail. Furthermore, the moral, value-laden character of family policy means that moral discourse about family issues (including that inspired by religious belief systems or secular moral philosophies) has a valid role in public debate about how the state should act in family life. The validity of that type of discourse should be acknowledged alongside other forms of discourse such as those based on scientific research or technical professional expertise.

7. The *state transfer system* (social welfare, social services, taxation, etc.) should be recognised as a key means for pursuing the principles and objectives of family policy. While support for the family has long been a major focus of social provision, there are areas of social provision where the concerns of family policy should be accorded greater importance in policy-making than has been the case to date. In particular, 'family incentives', such as the incentive to marry and to provide joint parenthood to children, should be accorded a greater prominence in evaluating social welfare policy, similar to that at present accorded to such things as work incentives and other economic effects of welfare provision.

8. Constitutional and civil law should be recognised as a means for pursuing the principles and objectives of family policy which parallels that represented by social provision. While the courts are necessarily an independent branch of government, the legislative framework of family law should evolve as part of an integrated family policy, where social provision for families and developments in family law (including reform of constitutional provisions on the family) should be planned and developed in tandem with each other. At present, there are a number of areas where the Constitution and family law are out of step either with each other or with the concerns and objectives of social provision (See further under 'Particular Issues' below).

9. Family policy should have a particular concern with protecting the vulnerable within families, on the principle that weaker family members are most at risk of family relationships which threaten well-being and equality. This concern points especially to the role of public policy in protecting and enhancing the position of children within families, as well as that of other vulnerable family members such as economically dependent wives or physically dependent elderly or handicapped. Principles of family privacy and family autonomy should not be open to misuse as a cloak for abuse and oppression of weaker members by the strong within the family.

10. The institutional framework of family policy needs to be strengthened, so that the various areas of family policy acquire a greater degree of coherence and rationality. The precise shape of this institutional framework is open to debate. The possibilities range, for example, from the setting up of a permanent government department of the family to the holding of periodic review exercises such as that currently being conducted by the Commission on the Family. In any event, the absence up to now of institutional mechanisms for integrating the various areas of family policy needs to be rectified in some way.

## The Constitution

The provisions of the Constitution on the family have recently been thoroughly reviewed by the Constitution Review Group, and it is beyond the scope of the present overview to comment in any detail on that review or on the recommendations for reform of the Constitution which emerged from it. It is, however, possible to point to a number of features of the Constitution as far as the family is concerned which strain at the limits of what is now broadly accepted as normal in policy and practice. These features are:

11. The excessive emphasis on the protection of the family as a unit and insufficient emphasis on the protection of individual members of the family. In the terminology of the present report, the Constitution is excessively familist and insufficiently individualist. That aspect of the Constitution reflects a balance which was accepted in the past but which has been widely departed from in many recent practical developments in family policy and which therefore leaves the spirit of the Constitution at odds with current accepted practice.

12. As a parallel to the previous point, the excessive emphasis of the rights of parents and insufficient protection for the rights of children. This aspect of the Constitution is in conflict with the growing concern for child protection in Irish law and social services, and may in certain circumstances amount to an obstacle to the effective implementation of child protection procedures.

13. The excessive emphasis on the marital family as opposed to other family forms. While constitutional protection for the institution of marriage is justified, this should not extend to the exclusion from constitutional recognition of family forms not based on marriage. Again, as far as this issue is concerned, practice in many areas of family policy has departed from the spirit, if not the letter, of Constitutional provision - for example, in the provision of social support for unmarried parents, in the prohibition of legal discrimination against non-marital children and in the legal recognition of the guardianship rights of unmarried fathers.

14. Outdated and ineffective provisions regarding women in the home. Article 41.2 of the Constitution, which deals with women's life and duties in the home, reflect a traditional patriarchal notion of women's position in life which has been abandoned by recent developments in gender equality policy. The section of that article which obliges the State to 'endeavour to ensure that mothers shall not be obliged by economic necessity to engage in labour to the neglect of their duties in the home' also suffers from having had so little impact on government practice.

# References

Barrington, R. (1987), *Health, Medicine and Politics in Ireland, 1900-1970.*
Dublin: Institute of Public Administration.

Bourke, J. (1993) *Husbandry to Housewifery. Women, Economic Change and Housework in Ireland, 1890-1914.* Oxford: Clarendon Press.

Callan, T, B Nolan, and B.J Whelan, D F Hannan, with S Creighton, 1989. *Poverty, Income and Welfare in Ireland.* Dublin: Economic and Social Research Institute

Fahey, T. and M. Lyons, 1995. *Marital Breakdown in Ireland. A Sociological Study.* Dublin: Oak Tree Press.

Hannan, D.F. (1979). *Displacement and Development. Class, Kinship and Social Change in Irish Rural Communities.* Dublin: Economic and Social Research Institute.

Hannan, D. F, and L. Katsiaouri, (1977) *Traditional Families? From Culturally Prescribed to Negotiated Roles in Farm Families.* Dublin: Economic and Social Research Institute.

Kellaghan, T., S. Weir, S. Ó hUallacháin and M. Morgan, (1995). *Educational Disadvantage in Ireland.* Dublin: Department of Education and Combat Poverty Agency.

Kennedy, F. and K. McCormack, (1994) 'Family life and family policy in Ireland - The changes in the 1980s' (typescript)

Kiely, G. and V. Richardson, (1995) *'Family policy in Ireland' in I.Colgan McCarthy (ed.), Irish Family Studies: Selected Papers.* Dublin: Family Studies Centre, University College Dublin.

O'Sullivan, D. (1993). 'The concept of policy paradigm: elaboration and illumination'. *The Journal of Educational Thought 27*, 3 (December).

Rainwater, L. and T. M. Smeeding, 1995. 'Doing Poorly- The Real Income of American Children in Comparative Perspective', Luxembourg Income Study, Working Paper Series, No. 127.

Chapter Eighteen **Fathers: Irish experience in an International context -
An abstract of a report to the Commission on the Family - Kieran
McKeown, Harry Ferguson, Dermot Rooney.**

1.      **Introduction**

The word "father" has many different meanings.  It means the biological father, the
symbolic father, and the person who engages in the practical act of fathering. The word
"father" also has many different images.  There is the image of the "traditional" father who
is a hard working breadwinner but is often absent, both physically and emotionally, from his
children.  There is the "modern" father who pushes prams and changes nappies, takes his
children to school and plays with them in the park, reads to them at night and discusses
the events of the day.  There is the "non-resident" father - be he single, separated or
married - who may see his children regularly, or he may make an appearance only once or
twice a year, or he may lose contact with his children completely.

There are also images of the father which depict particular qualities.  There are loving
fathers, dependable fathers, involved fathers, committed fathers, strong fathers, adoring
fathers.  Equally, there are images which depict negative qualities.  There are disinterested
fathers, unreliable fathers, workaholic fathers, abusive fathers, weak fathers, violent
fathers.  These different images are also part of the way in which men are seen in society.

Expectations are changing about what it is to be a good father. Good fathers are
increasingly expected to be emotionally involved with their children. They are expected to
share housework and take an interest in the children's schooling  It is no longer presumed
that the father is the sole breadwinner or that his role is simply to supply the weekly wage
packet.  There is a presumption that fathers will want to be at the birth of their children and
that they will have the same practical skills of child rearing - apart from breast-feeding - as
the mother.  We are not in a position to judge how fathers measure up to these standards.
However we suspect that few contemporary fathers have actually experienced this type of
fathering themselves.  As a result, many of them cannot rely on their own fathers as models
of good fathers, even if they were good fathers by the standards of their time.

All of the contemporary images of the father - both the positive and the negative - are true
in the sense that they reflect some aspect of  how fathers are experienced.  Just as there
are many different ways of being a man, so there are many different ways of being a father
(see Connell, 1995; Ferguson, 1997a).  The public imagery associated with fatherhood
tends to be contradictory and to involve both positive and negative aspects.  These
contradictory images are, in our view, a reflection of the change and uncertainty affecting
the cultural meaning of men and fatherhood.  By contrast, the public imagery associated
with motherhood tends to be consistent and positive  - sometimes to the point of veneration
- although some writers have drawn attention to ambiguities within the role of mother (see
for example, Featherstone and Holloway, 1997; Hooper, 1992).

One commentator has attributed this change and uncertainty to the "demise of cultural
consensus on the meaning of manhood [which] has left men in a no man's land, searching
for new meanings and definitions of maturity" (Gerson, 1993, p.5). The contemporary

experience of fatherhood in the United States, as described by one writer, is probably not very different to that in Ireland: "fatherhood in recent decades has become a kaleidoscope of images and trends, a sure sign that it has lost cultural coherence. .... Buffeted by powerful demographic, economic, and political changes, fatherhood in American culture is now fraught with ambiguity and confusion. Not surprisingly, so, too, are fathers themselves" (Griswold, 1993, p. 244).

The public imagery and private experience of fathers mutually influence each other. In view of this it is worth looking at how a number of leading commentators have depicted the contemporary image of the father. In the United States, a Jungian analyst has made the following observations about the public image of fathers: "when we watch Dad on TV sitcoms and the accompanying ads, he's a rather foolish man. He's not quite with it; a piece of him is astray. Commentators on contemporary fatherhood complain that he is being deliberately made to look foolish and antiquated, because this weakened image helps take down the stuffed shirt power of the patriarchy, makes more equal the relations between the genders, and blurs the hierarchical differences between fathers and children. Therefore wives are shown to be more practical and connected, children to be more with it and savvy. Even if he's a good guy, Dad is a little dumb" (Hillman, 1996, p.80). In Britain, another commentator has written about the negative image of fathers: "many of the images we have of fatherhood today are negative. Fathers are seen as absurd, pitiable, marginal, violent, abusive, uncaring and delinquent. ... As it has become more difficult to give emotional meaning to paternal absence, the image of the absent father has gathered force and negativity, and father-absence associated with the rising tide of out-of-wedlock births has become a symbol of moral degeneration" (Burgess, 1997, pp.19-20). Some of the literature compounds these negative stereotypes by characterising men's motivations as rational and selfish in contrast to women's motivations which are seen as selfless and altruistic: "male individualism is counterbalanced by female altruism, ..... rational economic man is taken care of by irrational altruistic woman" (Folbre, 1994, p.119).

The negative imagery associated with men and fatherhood also appears in discussions about how to involve men in child care. For example, a seminar on Men as Carers for Children which was organised by the European Commission Network on Childcare in 1990, raised a number of concerns about the prospect of greater involvement by men in childcare: "The prospect [of men being more involved in the care of children] raised a number of anxieties and concerns - for example, about child abuse, about men invading 'women's space' and being too dominant, about fathers taking over the more rewarding and pleasant childcare tasks" (European Commission Network on Childcare, 1990). At the same conference, one commentator even suggested, as a reason why men should participate in the care of children, that "closer contact with children will help men to express themselves in less aggressive and abusive ways" (Ibid, p.5). Does this imply that men normally express themselves in aggressive and abusive ways?

This negative imagery is not just bad publicity for men and fathers, although it is certainly that. It has a base in the experiences of men and women and, in turn, helps to mould that experience. The imagery, even if it is truly representative of the lives of only a small minority of men and fathers - who knows? - is now part of our collective consciousness and seems to "go with the territory" of being a man and a father in our time.

This negative imagery is both dismaying and challenging to men because it asks questions of every man and father: is this a true image of me? am I a good man and a good father? For society generally, it raises questions which are just as serious: does society want men and fathers to be characterised in this negative way? what images of men and role models of fathers does society wish to promote and facilitate? what impact is this negative imagery having on men and fathers? with what ideals and values are boys to grow into men and fathers? These questions cannot be avoided, either individually and collectively. Indeed, the negative imagery may become even more negative if these questions are ignored and the consequences for men and society may become even more negative. Accordingly, the theme of fatherhood touches deeply on matters that are personal as well as political, private as well as public. They concern men first, and fathers second, since no one can become a father without first becoming a man. In other words, a "good father" must first become a "good man" and must search for the meaning of those terms in his life.

It is our view that promoting the active involvement of fathers in the care and upbringing of their children is an ideal worth aspiring to, irrespective of whether the father is married or not, separated or not, resident with his child or not, heterosexual or not. We agree with the Commission on the Family on the importance of joint parenting: "Joint parenting should be encouraged with a view to ensuring as far as possible that children have the opportunity of developing close relationships with both parents which is in the interests both of children and their parents. The option of joint parenting may not always be available or indeed optimal (for example, when violence, abuse or extremes of conflict are involved). In cases where children's interest is best served by joint parenting, public policy has a key role in promoting this interest" (Commission on the Family, 1996, p.14).

In forming this perspective, we have sought to understand the significance that fathers can play in the lives of children as well as the different factors - in the home, in work, in law, in services, in cultural expectations - which have inhibited fathers from being more involved in the care and upbringing of their children. We see the caring relationship between fathers and children - itself a major issue - as part of the broader issue of what it is to be a man and to be a carer of others. Men, like women, have obligations to care for others throughout their adult lives, including care for frail parents and older relatives, care for older children as well as for grandchildren. In our view, men need to actively negotiate these caring responsibilities and share them with women at each of the different stages over the course of a life.

The kernel of our analysis is that the ideal of greater involvement by fathers in the care and upbringing of their children - which is increasingly presented as the ideal and standard towards which the modern father should aspire - is either opposed or not supported by many of the structures, policies and practices which directly impact on fathers. Our analysis shows this in many spheres of public and private life:

- in the symbolic sphere, where the father-child relationship is treated as secondary to the mother-child relationship and the crucial role of the father - as seem in the psychoanalytic perspective of Freud, Lacan and others - is ignored. In this perspective, the father's role is crucial in drawing attention to the fact that mother and child must desire and connect with a world outside of each other if they are to live and grow as separate independent persons;

- in the sphere surrounding the birth of children - including preparation for parenthood - where the father is treated, often unwittingly, as a secondary, supporting parent;
- in the sphere of work, where some fathers work very long hours thereby reducing the time and energy available for involvement with the children but also, at a deeper level, sustaining the self-image of father as the principal breadwinner;
- in the legal sphere, which confers greater parental rights on mothers than fathers, particularly pronounced in the case of separated and unmarried fathers;
- in the sphere of State services and supports which often treats parenting as synonymous with mothering and ignores fathers or fails to make the necessary contact with them.

The net effect of these forces is that the overall involvement by men in the care and upbringing of children may actually be declining precisely at a time when a growing number of fathers appear interested in having closer emotional involvement with their children. This is so for a number reasons. First, a growing number of children are placed in childcare facilities each working day, where virtually all the staff are women, thereby reducing their contact with men and fathers. Second, a growing number of children are in lone parent families under the sole custody of the mother and the amount of access by fathers to these children - whether because the mothers restrict access or because the fathers do not wish to have more access - may be on the decline.

In this scenario, it is hardly surprising that children learn to perceive caring as women's rather than men's work and, out of these experiences, are formed the attitudes that sustain the distancing of men from children for the coming generation. In our view, this pattern will not change unless there is a concerted and sustained effort to support those fathers who wish to be more involved with their children as well as supporting those men who wish to work with children in the caring professions.

It is possible to advance four different reasons or perspectives for promoting the greater involvement of fathers in the lives of their children: (i) benefits to children's development as a result of being emotionally close to both parents and (ii) benefits to families in supporting the interdependent relationships - economic, social and emotional - which hold its members together, including members of the extended family (iii) benefits to women in the form of greater equality in the labour market and in the domestic division of labour (iv) benefits to men in the form of greater involvement as fathers with their children which can lead to their own and their children's personal development and growth. Many of the arguments, both in Ireland and elsewhere, tend to cite the benefits for women and children of greater involvement by fathers (see for example, Second Commission on the Status of Women, 1993, Chapter Three; Employment Equality Agency, 1996; Moss, 1993). However there are fewer arguments citing the benefits for fathers from being more involved with their children - although there is plenty of criticism for their failing to do so - and there are fewer arguments still from the perspective of the needs of the family as an interdependent unit of relationships. We wish to broaden the agenda about fathers' involvement with children by including all these perspectives as ways of looking at relationships within families.

The scale and scope of the agenda involved in promoting men's greater involvement in caring for children and others should not be underestimated. The traditional division of labour between men as providers and women as carers has deep roots in our values and attitudes about the nature of men and women and in the structures of society which express and support those values. These structures have created inequalities in power, property and other resources between men and women. We agree with the feminist analysis that this system has not been in the best interests of women; but we would also argue that it has not been in the best interests of many men or children either. It is our belief that men and women have a shared interest in working for change and developing relationships - personal, social, economic, legal - which allow the full potential of each person to be discovered and expressed.

We now address the following key questions about the role of fathers in society:
• what changes are affecting the role of fathers?
• what is the function of a father?
• what differences do fathers make to the development of children?
• what do fathers do at home?
• how does work impact on the fathering role?
• are the rights and responsibilities of fathers adequately promoted in the Irish Constitution and the law generally?
• what services and supports facilitate good fathering?

2.    **Fathers in a Time of Change**
The concept of father, in its most basic form, involves a relationship with a child that is both biological and psycho-social. Fatherhood, like motherhood, is a social construct which, in Western society, has traditionally been built around marriage. Traditionally, the marriage contract has involved a division of labour between fathers and mothers such that fathers worked as the bread-winners outside the home while mothers worked as carers inside the home. This arrangement, whose ideal is embodied in the Irish Constitution, gave fathers control over the family's subsistence resources while distancing them physically and emotionally from their children. In this way, men expressed their masculinity and their love for wife and children by going out to work and providing for the family. In this value system, "good fathers" were essentially "good providers" and they were esteemed accordingly; their role was more about "investment" than "involvement".

This traditional model of the family - and its related roles of father and mother - remains strong in Ireland but is changing. In order to throw light on the overall structure of families in Ireland, a special analysis of the 1996 Labour Force Survey was carried out. Table 1 is derived from this analysis and shows the proportion of adults who are parents in Ireland in 1996.

## Table 1

**Proportion of Adults Who are Parents in Ireland in 1996**

| Parent / Not a Parent [1] | Men [4] | Women [5] | Total |
|---|---|---|---|
| | % | % | % |
| Parent [2] | 47 | 51 | 49 |
| Not a parent [3] | 53 | 49 | 51 |
| Total | 100 | 100 | 100 |

Source: 1996 Labour Force Survey, Special Tabulations.

(1)  The Labour Force Survey defines parents as those adults who are living with their children of any age.  This has three limitations.  First it includes children over the age of 18 and who, while living with a parent(s), are not children in the legal sense of the term.  Second, it excludes a number of men who are fathers but are not living with their children.  Third, it excludes men who are stepfathers or boyfriends but not fathers but who play fathering roles within the family.  In our analysis, we have added a fourth limitation by defining as adult any person aged 20 or over; this will exclude a very small number of fathers but was necessary since the next available statistical cut-off point, at 15 years, includes too many children.  It also includes a relatively small number of parents (83,000 comprising 43,000 women and 40,000 men) - equivalent to less than 1% of all parents - who are 65 years or over and who are unlikely to be active parents.

(2)  The total number of adults who are parents is approximately 1.2 million.

(3)  The total number of adults who are not parents is approximately 1.2 million.

(4)  The total number of men aged 20 and over in Ireland in 1996 was 1.1 million.

(5)  The total number of women aged 20 and over in Ireland in 1996 was 1.2 million.

This reveals that half the adult population (49%) - defined in this instance as persons aged 20 and over - in Ireland in 1996 were parents. Correspondingly, the proportion of adults who were not parents was 51%. It is also worth noting that the number of mothers exceeds the number of fathers.  The reason for this is that a parent is defined as someone who lives with her or his child and mothers are more likely to live with their children; the reasons for this, in turn, are discussed below.

In order to find out more about parents, a more detailed analysis was undertaken of the distribution of parents between different household types (Table 2).  The analysis distinguishes between older families (where none of the children are under 15) and younger families (where at least one of the children is under 15) and, within these categories, between one and two parent families.  From this it emerges that in 1996 two thirds of parents (68%) lived in younger families and one third (32%) lived in older families.  Most parents live in two parent families (90%); one parent families are more common among older families because many of them involve widows or widowers living with an adult child.

## Table 2

**Distribution of Adults by Type of Household in Ireland in 1996**

| Type of Family [1] | N ('000) | % | One Earner % | Two Earner % | No Earner % | Total % |
|---|---|---|---|---|---|---|
| **Older Families** [2] | **370** | **100** | **45** | **17** | **38** | **100** |
| • Two Parent Families | 304 | 82 | 50 [6] | 20 | 30 | 100 |
| • One Parent Families | 66 [4] | 18 | 23 | - | 77 | 100 |
| **Younger Families** [3] | **786** | **100** | **49** | **36** | **15** | **100** |
| • Two Parent Families | 734 | 93 | 50 [6] | 39 | 11 | 100 |
| • One Parent Families | 52 [5] | 7 | 36 | - | 64 | 100 |
| **Total** N | **1,156** | **100** | **550** | **345** [7] | **260** | **-** |
| % | 100 | 100 | 48 | 30 | 22 | - |

Source: 1996 Labour Force Survey, Special Tabulations by Anthony Murphy at University College Dublin.

(1) The Labour Force Survey defines parents as those adults who are living with their children of any age. This has three limitations. First it includes children over the age of 18 and who, while living with a parent(s), are not children in the legal sense of the term. Second, it excludes a number of men who are fathers but are not living with their children. Third, it excludes men who are stepfathers or boyfriends but not fathers but who play fathering roles within the family. In our analysis, we have added a fourth limitation by defining as adult any person aged 20 or over; this will exclude a very small number of fathers but was necessary since the next available statistical cut-off point, at 15 years, includes too many children. It also includes a relatively small number of parents (83,000 comprising 43,000 women and 40,000 men) - equivalent to less than 1% of all parents - who are 65 years or over and who are unlikely to be active parents.

(2) In this analysis, an older family is defined as a family which has no children under the age of 15 years.

(3) In this analysis, a younger family is defined as a family which has any child under the age of 15 years.

(4) This comprises 53,000 mothers (80% of older lone parents) of whom 19% are earners and 13,000 fathers (20% of older lone parents) of whom 31% are earners.

(5) This comprises 47,000 mothers (90% of younger lone parents) of whom 36% are earners and 5,000 fathers (10% of younger lone parents) of whom 60% are earners.

(6) In the vast majority of cases (93%), the one earner in two parent families is the father.

(7) The proportion of dual earners where the partner is employed part-time is 18%.

Table 2 also distinguishes between the number of earners within each family type. Both older and younger families are similar in that approximately half of each type are one earner families. However they differ dramatically in that younger families were twice as likely to have two earners (39%) compared to older families: one in three of younger families (36%)

are dual earners compared to one in six of older families (17%).   They also differ dramatically in that older families were twice as likely to have no earners compared to younger families: more than one in three of older families (39%) have no earners compared to nearly one in six of younger families (15%).

These results are significant because they reveal that only half of all families - irrespective of whether they are younger or older - conform to the traditional image of having one breadwinner.  In younger two parent families, a very substantial proportion (39%)  are in fact two earner families. At the same time it is also worth noting that a significant minority of younger two parent families (11%) are no earner families and are therefore likely to be living at or below the poverty line. The same applies to the majority of one parent families (64%) which also are no earner families. These families and their children are likely to be living in poverty; it has been estimated that between 26% and 39% of all children in Ireland in 1987 were living in households below the poverty line, defined as either 50% or 60% of average household income respectively (Nolan and Callan, 1990).

The various types of families depicted in Table 2 also highlight the emergence of a polarisation between "work rich" and work poor" families which has been observed in other EU countries.  In Britain, for example, it has been found that the proportion of dual-earner and no-earner families has grown at the expense of one-earner families (Gregg and Wassworth, 1995). No comparable data exists in Ireland on the trend over time. It has also been found that dual-earner families in Britain tend to be better qualified and to have higher status and higher paid jobs while those with no earner tended to be the opposite (Ferri and Smith, 1996).  This is also the case in Ireland, particularly among younger families. Table 3 reveals that two parent, dual earner families tend to be of higher socio-economic status than one earner families and higher still than no earner families.  As regards one parent families, Table 3 reveals that those with one earner tend to be of higher socio-economic status than those with no earner.

From the perspective of fathers, the changing family structure in Ireland has a twofold significance.  First, more than half of all families do not rely on fathers as the exclusive breadwinner; many of these rely on income earned by both parents or on income transfers from the State in the form of social welfare payments.  In other words, breadwinning is no longer the monopoly of fathers and this clearly signals a change in their power and status within families. Second, a significant minority of families live without a father since the vast majority of one parent families are in fact families where the father is absent. These families are symbolically important in showing that families can exist without fathers being present thereby making fathers appear dispensable, at least for this type of family.

## Table 3

**Distribution of One, Two and No Earner Families by Socio-Economic Status in Ireland in 1996**

| Type of Family [1] | Two Parent Families | | | One Parent Families | |
|---|---|---|---|---|---|
| **Older Families** [2] | One Earner % | Two Earner % | No Earner % | One Earner % | No Earner % |
| Farmers, relatives assisting, etc | 19 | 10 | 19 | 16 | 20 |
| Professionals, employers, managers | 21 | 33 | 12 | 21 | 13 |
| Non-manual employees | 29 | 37 | 29 | 42 | 34 |
| Manual-employees | 31 | 20 | 40 | 21 | 33 |
| **Total (%)** | **100 (50)** | **100 (20)** | **100 (30)** | **100 (23)** | **100 (77)** |
| **Younger Families** [3] | One Earner % | Two Earner % | No Earner % | One Earner % | No Earner % |
| Farmers, relatives assisting, etc | 13 | 8 | 7 | 5 | 4 |
| Professionals, employers, managers | 21 | 31 | 4 | 24 | 8 |
| Non-manual employees | 30 | 41 | 24 | 53 | 50 |
| Manual-employees | 36 | 20 | 65 | 18 | 38 |
| **Total %** | **100 (50)** | **100 (40)** | **100 (10)** | **100 (36)** | **100 (64)** |

Source: 1996 Labour Force Survey, Special Tabulations by Anthony Murphy at University College Dublin.

(1) The Labour Force Survey defines parents as those adults who are living with their children of any age. This has three limitations. First it includes children over the age of 18 and who, while living with a parent(s), are not children in the legal sense of the term. Second, it excludes a number of men who are fathers but are not living with their children. Third, it excludes men who are stepfathers or boyfriends but not fathers but who play fathering roles within the family. In our analysis, we have added a fourth limitation by defining as adult any person aged 20 or over; this will exclude a very small number of fathers but was necessary since the next available statistical cut-off point, at 15 years, includes too many children. It also includes a relatively small number of parents (83,000 comprising 43,000 women and 40,000 men) - equivalent to less than 1% of all parents - who are 65 years or over and who are unlikely to be active parents.

(2) In this analysis, an older family is defined as a family which has no children under the age of 15 years.

(3) In this analysis, a younger family is defined as a family which has any child under the age of 15 years.

It is worth teasing out in more detail the factors which have contributed to the declining significance of fathers within families since they are central to understanding the present situation in which fathers find themselves. In our view, there are four main factors which have affected fathering in recent decades. The first is the growth in the number of women, especially married women, working outside the home. In the 25 years between 1971 and 1996, the proportion of women in the Irish labour force - the labour force participation rate - increased from 28% to 36%; in the same period, the labour force participation rate of men fell from 81% to 69% (Department of Enterprise and Employment, 1996, p.28). In 1996, just under half (47%) of all women in the labour force were married compared to just over half (58%) for men. The projection is that these trends will continue: "Male labour force growth is forecast to be about half the female forecast trend, due in part to the dramatic increase in the participation of married women in the labour force" (Ibid, p. 29). These developments are helping to break the mould which sustains the gendered division of labour in the work place and thereby reduces - perhaps more symbolically than practically - the role of the father as the sole breadwinner by showing that women can be both breadwinners and care givers. This development contains a challenge to fathers - at least implicitly - to combine breadwinning with caregiving.

The second factor is that the breadwinning role of many men is severely threatened by the persistence of high levels of unemployment in Ireland, particularly since the 1980s. Unemployment makes it difficult for young men to make the transition to adulthood and fatherhood (Hannan and O'Riain, 1993) and there is evidence that some women may prefer the prospect of lone parenthood than sharing child rearing responsibilities with a young unemployed father (Wilson and Neckerman, 1986; Roberts, 1996). Older established fathers have also seen their breadwinning role wiped out through unemployment and the prospects of returning to that role diminish with each passing year of long-term unemployment since the prospects of employment diminish rapidly with each additional year of long-term unemployment (see Department of Enterprise and Employment, 1996, pp. 42-43). One study of the psychological impact of unemployment in Ireland found that unemployment causes a higher level of psychological distress among men than among women and higher still among married men than among single men due essentially to the erosion of their role as breadwinners, itself undermining their self image as men (see Whelan, Hannan and Creighton, 1991, pp. 41-44).

The third factor is the growth in the number of one parent families. In the 15 year period between 1981 and 1996, lone parent families as a percentage of all families with children under the age of 15 years increased from 7% in 1981 to 11% in 1991 to 18% in 1996 (Census of Population, 1981, 1991 and 1996, Volume 3). This is due mainly to marital breakdown and births outside marriage. In a narrow economic sense, the welfare state, through the One Parent Family Payment and other measures, may have helped replace the breadwinning role of the traditional father and made these families economically viable, even if only barely so (see McCashin, 1993; 1996). For the mothers concerned, the dynamics of the social welfare system are such as to make the father's absence a condition of receiving payment thereby helping to compound the separation of fathers from their children. As already indicated, some young women, particularly in disadvantaged areas, may be choosing to bring up their children with the support of the One Parent Family Payment because the fathers of those children are unable or unwilling to play the breadwinner role of husband and father. Moreover, since most one parent families (87%) are headed by a mother this is sometimes taken to prove - both symbolically and practically - that families can exist without fathers. Our review of the evidence in Chapter Three suggests that children can grow up normally without their biological fathers, although the memory of the biological father may never be totally erased; more importantly, as argued in Chapter Two, we believe that every child needs a "father figure" in its life to grow into a normal adult.

The growth of one parent families has also served to break the link, at least conceptually, between marriage and parenthood by showing that marriage is not a necessary condition of parenthood, even if many people enter marriage with a view to parenthood (Millar and Warman, 1996, p.48; Bjornberg, 1992). The severing of parenthood from marriage also serves to crystallise the definition of mother and father as involving a relationship with their child rather than with each other. The implications of this for fathers - particularly for separated and unmarried fathers - are still being worked out and the legal implications have still not been addressed.

The fourth factor is less quantifiable but no less real and involves changes in expectations about what constitutes a "good father". Parenting can be seen as having two interrelated aspects: the provider or "investment" role and the caring or "involvement" role. Traditionally, the father's role was defined by investment while the mother's role was defined by involvement. However, involvement is increasingly perceived much more highly than investment, particularly by children but often by both fathers and mothers themselves (see, for example, O'Brien and Jones, 1996). The rising status of children within families - and the corresponding changes in norms about good parenting - have made it less easy for fathers to be exclusively preoccupied with investment at the expense of involvement (see Ferguson, 1996a). Indeed, the vast majority (87%) of Europeans - according to a 1993 European-wide survey of 13,000 men and women aged 15 and over - believe that fathers should take a hand in bringing up their children right from birth while three quarters (75%) believe that both parents should share all aspects of the childcare work (Eurobarometer 39.0, 1993, pp. 89 and 93; see also Social Europe, 1994, p.24). Other research suggests that Irish attitudes on these matters are "not consistently more traditional than those of the economically more advanced countries" (Whelan and Fahey, 1994, p.79).

These developments place fathers - particularly those who are sole breadwinners - in an awkward psychological position because investment without involvement no longer carries the esteem that it once did. Ironically, the father's investment role may be esteemed by the mother but not the children and its effect, however unintentional, may be to strengthen the mother's relationship with the children while weakening the father's relationship with his children. Many fathers are experiencing the stress of having to combine both investment with involvement roles and, being unable to rely on the role model of their own father, are having to learn new ways of being a father. At the same time, there appears to be a growing receptivity to the idea that the breadwinner role should not be the sole defining characteristic of a man's worth as a man and a father (Marsiglio, 1995).

These changes have caused confusion about the role of fathers in a wide variety of situations. For men in employment, there is a growing expectation that they will become more involved with their children, even if the demands of work can make that difficult. For men who are unemployed, there is an enforced loss of the traditional provider role which challenges their self-image as both men and fathers. For men who are separated or divorced, there can be a loss of contact with children which threatens to undermine if not erase their role as fathers. For fathers who neither marry nor cohabit with the mother of their child, the practical role of father is often non-existent.

The emergence of men's groups and men's gatherings in Ireland in recent years is evidence that some men are responding to the changed circumstances in which men find themselves. Since 1994, the Department of Social, Community and Family Affairs (formerly the Department of Social Welfare until June 1997) has funded men's groups in disadvantaged areas; women's groups in disadvantaged areas have received funding since 1990. Table 4 reveals that, in 1996, 792 women's groups received IR£1.17 million compared to IR£0.15 million for 103 men's groups. This reflects the fact that there are eight times more women's groups than men's groups throughout the country since the average grant to each group is broadly similar at IR£1,400 each.

## Table 4

**Funding for Men's and Women's Groups by the Department of Social, Community and Family Affairs in 1996**

| Category | Women's Groups | Men's Groups |
| --- | --- | --- |
| Number of Applications from Groups | 1,177 | 152 |
| Number of Groups Funded | 792 | 103 |
| % of Applications Funded | 67 | 68 |
| Average Amount Received by Each Group | IR£1,476 | IR£1,438 |
| Total Amount Received by All Groups | IR£1,168,930 | IR£148,135 |

Source: Department of Social, Community and Family Affairs, 1997.

Our analysis of the process by which men become fathers - both before and after the child's birth - suggests that it is heavily laced with signals to indicate that the primary parent is the mother and the secondary parent is the father. Many mothers and fathers subscribe to, and reinforce, this division of labour. If, as we believe, that fathers are equal parents of the child and should be encouraged to be more actively involved in child-rearing, then some of the existing conventions surrounding pregnancy, childbirth and child rearing need re-examination. For example, are ante-natal classes sufficiently inclusive of and sympathetic to men? Does the information provided through text, pictures, and videos portray a full and positive role for fathers? Is it appropriate that there is no paternity leave for fathers which would facilitate bonding with their new-born child just as there is maternity leave for mothers in recognition of the physical demands of childbearing and breast-feeding? Much of the research evidence suggests that, with better preparation for fatherhood and parenthood, the attachment between father and child - as well as between father and mother - can be greatly strengthened; in addition, fathers become more involved with the child after its birth.

All fathers are not the same. The way in which men play the role of father varies according to a wide range of variables including their own personal experience of being men and of being fathered, their marital and residential status, the number and ages of their children, their social class and employment status, and the relative importance which they attribute - consciously or unconsciously - to work and to fathering and to seeing fathering as valuable work. Inevitably, in view of such complexity, there are many ways to be a good father just as there are many ways to be a good mother. Conversely, as one commentator has pointed out, "there is nothing intrinsically good about family values or about the father as one of the embodiments of these values. A good father is a good thing, a bad father is a bad thing" (French, 1995, p.5).

Before entering the difficult terrain of how to define a "good father", we suggest that being a good father is essentially a derivative of being a "good man". Each man is called, by virtue of his existence, to be a good man in a way that is unique to each and to take the journey of discovering his purpose in life that this entails (McKeown, 1997). A good man, in this sense, will always be a good father. The reverse process - of presenting fathering as the raison d'etre of a man's existence - carries the danger that a father's purpose in life becomes substituted for his child's purpose in life.

In our endeavours to define what is a "good enough" father, we have come to the somewhat minimalist conclusion that the good enough father must: (i) be physically present on a reasonably regular basis to his child and (ii) have a positive and not a negative influence on his child. A reasonably regular basis, even for a separated father, according to one leading psychologist in Dublin, "probably means at least once a week" (Andrews, 1994). Resident fathers will normally see their children once a day.

A positive rather than a negative influence is less easy to define but it involves protecting the child from harm through a bond of attachment between the parents and the child. Beyond that, as one psychiatrist at the Tavistock Clinic in London has pointed, "we need to be careful not to be too certain about what we think is right for children. ... the truth is that there are no rules about child care but there are some principles that we can be fairly confident are universal" (Kraemer, 1995, p.14). The most important of these principles, according to the same psychiatrist, is attachment which is taken to mean protection from physical and emotional harm: "A secure attachment is like an invisible elastic which can stretch and contract depending on the need for protection. So when you are ill or in pain, tired or afraid, you move towards the person with whom you feel secure and when all is well you can move away to explore the world around. Clearly this applies to all of us, but most of all to small children" (Ibid).

The importance of attachment and the associated flexibility which allows both closeness and distance has been emphasised by other commentators: "A father who is too close or too remote will not be good enough. ... In contrast, the good father is able to successfully maintain the golden mean. Such a father is close but not too close, strong but not overwhelming, loving but not seductive, supportive but able to discipline, caring but encouraging autonomy" (Abramovitch, 1997, p.31).

The practical application of these principles has been used to inform a Government-backed publicity campaign in South Australia called "Six Ways to be a Better Dad!". The six ways are summarised in Table 5.

## Table 5
### Six Ways to be a Better Dad

**1. BEING A ROLE MODEL**

As a dad, you are a role model whether you realise it or not. How you act teaches your kids how to act when they grow up. For example, if you talk problems through, your kids will probably grow up to do the same. If you lose your temper, get abusive or become violent, your kids will probably grow up to do the same.

- Kids learn mainly from what you do, not what you say.
- Treat your daughter with love and respect so she grows up expecting to be treated the same by boys and men.
- Teach your son that a man is caring, fair, a mate to his kids and treats women with respect.

**2. SHOW THEM YOU CARE**

Getting involved in your kids' lives is a terrific way to show your kids you care.

- Do things that they want you to do.
- Give them a hug and tell them they're great.
- Help out with their homework.
- Play footy or basketball.
- Go to a school function, go to parent / teacher interviews, watch them play sport.
- Learn their friends and teachers names.

**3. WORK AND FAMILY**

Let's face it, work can be tiring, stressful, and create worries. No doubt these worries are for real, but it isn't fair or useful to pass them on to your kids.

- Put aside some time just for you to recharge your batteries.
- Look after your health through diet and exercise.
- Try and leave your work hassles at work.

**4. WHAT TO DO WHEN YOUR KID'S BEHAVIOUR IS NOT O.K.**

- As hard as it is, try and stay calm!
- When you feel stressed and feel that you might lash out - walk away.
- Leave the room and do something to distract yourself.
- Don't act in anger or you will probably regret what you do.

Kids need to learn right from wrong. Set rules and stick to them. Be clear about what will happen when the rules are broken. This could include not letting your kids watch their favourite TV program. If they break the rules, do what you said would happen.

**5. PARENTING AND PARTNERSHIPS**

Being a parent is a partnership - whether you and your children's mother are together or not.

- Respect your kid's mother.
- Don't argue in front of the kids.
- Do something about relationship problems.
- Get professional advice if you can't sort out problems together.

Kids can't cope with their parents putting each other down.

**6. SPEND TIME WITH YOUR KIDS**

The time you spend with your kids is a good investment in their future. Show your love by getting involved with their sports or hobbies or involving them in your interests. Kids grow up so quickly, so don't miss out!

- Share a regular meal.
- Talk to your kids.
- Listen to their views without criticising.
- Praise their efforts.
- Encourage them and help them make decisions.

Source: The Office for Families and Children, South Australia.

We make four recommendations on foot of our analysis. First, we recommend that the ideal of "good fathering" and "good enough fathering" become matters of public and private debate and discussion. The objective of such debates should be (1) to help elevate the status and importance of fatherhood in society (2) to give men, women and children an opportunity to talk about their ideals of fatherhood (3) to allow fathers - and potential fathers - an opportunity to reflect on their experiences of fathering and the issues which arise for fathers in trying to meet the competing demands of work and family, of being a carer as well as a breadwinner. We see this objective being pursued in three ways: (1) through education, both second level and second-chance, in the form of fathering and relationship courses; appropriate resource materials would need to be prepared to service these courses (2) through the media, both electronic and print, where informed and constructive comment meets with the recorded experiences of fathering by men, women and children in different situations (3) through research on fathering ideals and practices in differing settings, taking into account differences in family types, stage in the family cycle, social class, employment, marital status, geographical location.

The second recommendation is that support for men's groups by the Department of Social, Community and Family should continue and be expanded. We see men's groups as an important fora in which men and fathers can meet to discuss their experiences. It is our experience that men will only engage in discussion about their role as men and fathers if their vulnerabilities are respected and if they are given a safe space to have their voices heard without being automatically criticised for not being good enough. We agree with the existing concentration of support for men's groups in disadvantaged areas. It should also include financial support for groups of men who are endeavouring to address specific issues such as parenting alone or separation from their children.

Third, we recommend that the process leading up to, and following, the birth of a child should be more inclusive of fathers. In order to achieve this objective, we recommend that an examination be carried out of the conventions and practices which take place before, during and after childbirth to identify areas where fathers could be more involved in the preparation for fatherhood. We recommend, subject to the outcome of detailed examination, that these conventions and practices should be modified where they do not promote the objective of joint parenting. This examination should be wide ranging and should include pregnancy, ante-natal classes, childbirth, child rearing, home visitation as well as information and publicity materials about these topics in the form of text, pictures and videos.

Fourth, we recognise that young men and young fathers who are unemployed or otherwise disadvantaged have special needs which require urgent attention. We recommend that services be developed to help them overcome the obstacles which currently hinder their transition to adulthood and fatherhood. This will require increased investment in a range of services for disadvantaged adolescents and young people covering education, training, personal development, and parenting education. These services need to be delivered with skill and sensitivity in each local area so that young men can value the importance of being a role model in their child's life.

3.      **The Psychoanalytic Perspective on Fathers**

Contemporary psychoanalysis, like the majority of human sciences, has primarily emphasised the importance of the mother-child relationship for the healthy development of the child (Bowlby, 1969; 1973; 1980; Winnicott, 1964). This has largely been to the virtual exclusion of any discussion or debate on the father-child relationship (Frosh, 1994). However many psychoanalysts are increasingly drawing attention to the destructive effects of ignoring the function of the father in the child's psychological and emotional development. Some analysts have argued that the decline of the paternal image and the marginalisation of the father are among the causes of neuroses and pathologies in individuals, families and society (Lacan, 1977; Hillman, 1994; Frosh, 1994). Some of these illnesses can be traced back to the relationship and separation process between mother and child, and the role of the father in that transition.

The exclusion of fathers from the child development paradigm that dominates contemporary social science, child psychology and psychoanalysis has served to obscure Freud's insights on the role of fathers in families and in the development of personality (Gallagher, 1986). Freud revolutionised human psychology when he unearthed and named the two key tenets of psychoanalysis: the unconscious and the Oedipus complex. Freud emphasised the notion of the 'unconscious' in order to display that there exists mental activity of which the person is unaware but nonetheless exerts a profound effect on his/her behaviour. In making the unconscious 'conscious', one picture that invariably emerges for a person is their family drama. This involves uncovering where your are situated in relationship to your father and mother, and the influences that this has on your present relationships, including the relationship that you have with yourself.

The Oedipus complex, which Freud first described in 1897, draws on the Greek myth of Oedipus, to explain the intricate relationship of father - child - mother into which every infant is born. Every child takes on a particular significance for both parents, just as the father and the mother (be they absent or present, dead or alive) take on a complex significance for the child. The map of these relationships constitutes the Oedipus complex; it is every child's rite of passage into the world which must be passed through. According to Freud, "every new arrival on this planet is faced with the task of mastering the Oedipus complex; anyone who fails to do so falls victim to neuroses".

The Oedipus complex can be seen as referring to a group of largely unconscious ideas and feelings expressing both the loving and hostile wishes which the child experiences towards each of its parents. The mother-child relationship is described by Freud as the 'first relationship' and the prototype of all other relationships that the child will have. Nonetheless, he drew upon his clinical work to emphasise the importance of the child's need to separate from the mother. For Freud, the child's independence and personality development depended on this process of separation.

Freud saw the mother's relationship with the child as fundamental to the child's survival because it allows the child to internalise a model of safety and trust which is the basis of healthy development and of future relationships. Despite the importance and intensity of this relationship, it needs to enter a process of separation in order to avoid its potentially destructive closeness. For the child, separation allows new identifications and new possibilities in the world. For the mother, separation gives back her sense of self, separateness and independence.

The father, in the vast majority of cases, is the key player in this process of separation, acting as the 'other' or the third person to the mother. He moves the two person mother-child relationship into a three person "triangular" relationship of mother-child-father. This allows the child to move away from a potentially alienating imaginary world (mother-child) and to enter the social and cultural symbolic order (mother-child-father).

The father is seen as fundamental to the child letting go of the mother because (1) he symbolically prohibits too close an attachment between the child and the mother and (2) he symbolically promises and represents new and more exciting ways of being in the world. The father is also fundamental to the mother in her letting go of the child: he is the person who sustains part of the mother's desire and meets this desire. Psychoanalysis teaches that unless the father takes up his position representing the symbolic order for the child and the mother, the separation process can become frustrated resulting in various neuroses and disturbances for the child and indeed for the relationship, the family and society.

Jacques Lacan (1901-1981) offers a contemporary reading of Freud's Oedipus Complex, one that again places both father and mother at the forefront of family and individual development. For Lacan the child is born totally dependent on the primary relationship with the mother. Lacan calls this stage the 'Imaginary order' because the child sees or imagines itself as the focus of the mother's desire and sees her as the all-enveloping object of desire. The child tries to become everything for the mother and sees the mother as having everything it needs.

For her part, the mother tries to provide the necessary caring, feeding and satisfaction of the infant's needs. At the same time, because she was a child herself, there also remains within her the desire for something other than satisfying the infant's needs. All human beings are lacking and are constantly trying to fill this lack. Unconsciously the mother may come to see the child as potentially filling this lack for her, and hence the child can take on a meaning for the mother which has nothing to do with the child itself.

For many psychoanalysts, this relationship of mother-child does not, on its own, provide the child with an appropriate structure or healthy environment for the development of personality. This is where the father becomes crucially important as the symbolic figure who ignites the separation process for both mother and child.

The father's position in our present family structure represents the 'other' to the mother and introduces otherness or difference to the child. Simply, one can see it as a three stage separation process. Firstly, the mother's desire must be directed or focused outside of herself; something other than the child must be in her life. Secondly, the father stands in the crucial position of this 'other' and he must be significant enough so as to capture the desire of the mother. Thirdly, the child follows the mother's desire outside of herself thus moving towards otherness. Thus the father must be 'present', at the very least metaphorically, so as to symbolically engage both the child's and the mother's desire.

The psychoanalytic perspective, particularly as articulated by Lacan and others, restores fathers - and the father figure - to a central place within family life. Within the present structure of the nuclear family in the Western world, the father is normally the biological father; however it is possible that the father figure is neither a father nor even a man. What is essential from the psychoanalytic perspective is that the father figure must be someone other than the mother. The 'other' must be a person who engages the mother's desire enough to create a sense of 'otherness' and difference for the child.

The reason why the father is given such a prominent role in the psychoanalytic perspective is simply due to the fact that the nuclear family of mother-child-father is central to the organisation of society in the Western world. It is crucial that the child experiences, at the deepest level of its being, an awareness of these structures and is initiated into the world through the key figures of mother and father.

In the majority of families in our society, the symbolic position of the father is largely dependent on the character and desire of the person in that role, including the circumstances of his own fathering and mothering. It is also dependent on the character and desire of the mother. Overlapping both of these is the cultural status and standing of fatherhood and manhood. If a society places a high value on fatherhood, then individual fathers are more likely to respond positively to those values and to desire them.

An important implication of this analysis is that a man must first desire to be a good father - whether consciously or unconsciously - before he can be one. It may seem strange, but every father and aspirant father needs to ask: "do I want to be a father?" If fatherhood is not valued - especially by men themselves - then it will not be desired and its symbolic importance is thereby undermined.

There are no quick-fix solutions.  Our understanding of the psychoanalytic process leads us to the view that a man cannot be shown or taught how to be a good father, any more than he can be taught how to be a good person; this can only be educated - in the sense of being brought out or led out - of the person.  Likewise, no father can be shown how to take up his symbolic position in the family since no one fully understands the inscrutable processes of the unconscious. However he can be supported and encouraged in his desire to be a good father and in trying to understand the symbolic position which fatherhood confers on him within the family.  We think this support and encouragement can happen in two ways: through increasing self-awareness among men and fathers and through increasing the symbolic importance which society attaches to fatherhood.

**4.**　　**Fathers and Children**

The involvement of fathers with their children has become the subject of a good deal of research in recent years.  A number of studies have suggested that "there is almost no evidence" (Lewis, 1993, p.95) for the claim that "today's fathers are caring for their children in radically different ways to their older counterparts" (Ibid; Lewis and O'Brien, 1978; Brannen and Moss, 1991; Kiernan, 1992; Kempeneers and Lelievre, 1992).  The same finding has also emerged from a number of longitudinal studies (Coverman and Sheley, 1986; Lewis, 1986; Sanik, 1981). Even the efforts in Sweden at changing the division of labour between mothers and fathers in the home have had relatively little impact (Sandqvist, 1987; 1992).  In English-speaking countries, especially the United States, attempts at teaching fathers the skills of childcare - where these have been evaluated - have not demonstrated clear long-term increases in paternal involvement (Lewis, 1993; Hawkins and Roberts, 1992).  The main exception to this general picture occurs in families where both father and mother are employed and in families where the father is unemployed. One of the features which both these exceptions have in common - the employed father in dual earner families and the unemployed father - is that the involvement of fathers seems to be driven more by the structural characteristics of the situation rather than by any ideological commitment - for or against - equalising the domestic division of labour between men and women. In other words, the fathers' involvement in housework and childcare seems to be negotiated with the mother, taking into account the work and other circumstances in which both find themselves.

The impact of fathers on children is mediated by his parenting relationship with the child. This may appear obvious but for many years it had been thought that it was the father's characteristics as a man rather than his characteristics as a parent which mediated his impact on child development, particularly among boys.  In other words, it is the quality of the parent-child relationship rather than the gender of the parent that is most important in child development (see Lamb, 1997, p.9).  The fact that good fathering and good mothering involve broadly similar behaviours has important implications for fathers, as Burgess (1997, p.188) has pointed out: "The message emanating from this is that there is no free ride for fatherhood, no magical role for fathers just because they are fathers or just because they are men.  It is what each man gives on a personal level that makes him a key player in his child's development.  And, in the wider world, it is what men as a group will give to children in respect of intimate care and attention that will enable males to play a key role in their development. Otherwise a father's main value is limited to a pay-cheque and to a lesser extent a support system, and although these are valuable functions they in no way satisfy the aspirations of today's fathers, or their children".

There appears to be virtual unanimity among researchers that the more extensive a father's involvement with his children the more beneficial it is for them in terms of cognitive competence and performance at school as well as for empathy, self-esteem, self-control, life skills and social competence; these children also have less sex-stereotyped beliefs and a more internal locus of control (see Pleck, 1997; Pruett, 1983; 1985; Radin, 1982; 1994). Conversely, children are less likely to become involved in delinquent behaviour or substance misuse if their fathers are sensitive and attentive to them; even the children of fathers who have a criminal record are less likely to become delinquent if the father spends a lot of time with them.

Some children grow up with little or no contact with their fathers. The research suggests that these children do not fare worse than children who have contact with their fathers, when all the other factors affecting the child's development are taken into account (see Lamb, 1997). The most significant of these other factors is the process by which a child loses its father. Children who lose a father through separation or divorce, possibly after a period of sustained parental conflict, will tend to be more adversely affected than children who have never had a father living with them. As Lamb (1996, p.11) has pointed out, "since many single-parent families are produced by divorce and since divorce is often preceded and accompanied by periods of overt and covert spousal hostility, parental conflict may play a major role in explaining the problems of fatherless children"

Every child - almost without exception - will want to know its biological parents and, in this sense, it is hard to imagine any child remaining entirely unaffected by its biological parents. Moreover, even children who have no contact with their biological fathers still need fathers and male role models. This implies that even "fatherless" children can find in other men - and in their imaginations - the fathering that might otherwise be supplied by the biological father. There is no hard determinism therefore that turns a biological father into a psychologically real father either for the child or the man. Being a father therefore involves choosing to become physically and psychologically connected with the child's life and development in whatever way seems appropriate given the norms and circumstances of one's life.

In assessing the impact of father's involvement with his children, some research distinguishes between two types of involvement: (i) involvement through primary caretaking such as preparing food, changing nappies, cleaning and clearing up; and (ii) involvement through shared activities with the children. The research evidence suggests that fathers tend to be more involved in the second sense and that this is the type of involvement that has the most positive impact on the development of the child (Drago Piechowski, 1992; Owen and Cox, 1988). Indeed it has been suggested that the first type of involvement may be inversely related to the second, particularly in very busy families where both parents work and time is scarce (Morgan, 1996, pp.100-101).

Weak parent-child relationships can occur in a variety of settings and are influenced by a variety of factors. Where children become involved in crime these settings tend to be characterised by poverty and other stresses such as unemployment and poor environment. The development of parent-child relationships in this context involves supporting families who lack the knowledge, skills and self-confidence to make them more effective parents, particularly when their children are young. This type of support would involve a range of measures to reduce poverty, increase childcare, establish family centres and neighbourhood projects, provide intensive support and education to vulnerable parents with pre-adolescent children as well as specific measures to ensure that fathers are involved. The involvement of fathers in this type of work would probably require outreach work, particularly in disadvantaged areas, and a sensitive approach which addresses the obstacles constraining fathers - including obstacles such as skills, attitudes, time, relationships with partner, relationship with child - from being more involved with their children. Beyond the family and its immediate environment, it is also necessary to consider how the education of young people prepares them for their future role as parents and to do this by raising their awareness, understanding and skills for living in satisfying, intimate and respectful relationships.

Researching the impact of fathers on children is clearly important. Of equal interest is the impact which children have on fathers. There is considerably less research on this aspect of the relationship although some researchers have suggested that its impact on the development of fathers could be just as significant as the impact on the development of children (European Commission Network on Childcare, 1990; 1993).

Our analysis suggests that two broad recommendations are required to maximise the beneficial impact which fathers can have on their children. The first is to promote the ideal of good fathering among all fathers and potential fathers through the education system and through public education. This should be done in a variety of fora - family resource centres, parenting programmes, media awareness programmes - according to the needs of different categories of father and should elicit the active participation of fathers in discussing their own experiences of fathering and being fathered. We believe that being a father is not just a skill; it is a way of being a man and requires engagement with one's own life. Education about fathering needs to be sensitive to vulnerabilities and strengths need to be supported and affirmed. We suggest that any initiatives in the area of education should be piloted beforehand.

Our second recommendation concerns the specific needs of fathers and potential fathers in disadvantaged areas. We suggest that measures to facilitate fathers in these areas need to be accompanied by a general improvement in the infrastructure of services in those areas; this could include employment and environmental improvements, increased childcare, family centres, neighbourhood projects, youth services for pre-adolescent and adolescent children. The involvement of fathers will require sensitive out-reach work and a forum for participation. We are not in a position to prescribe how this intervention should be designed and developed but we are aware that it is highly skilled work and will required substantial resources and skills, if it is to be effective. We are also aware that it is extremely necessary and urgent.

## 5. Fathers and Home

The international evidence on father's involvement in families suggests that, broadly speaking, there has been some increase over time in fathers' level of active involvement in child care and domestic tasks. However there appears to be broad agreement that fathers' behaviour has not kept pace with changing attitudes and cultural expectations that fathers should become more involved in child care and domestic tasks.

Only one study has examined what Irish fathers do in families, albeit based on data supplied by mothers (Kiely, 1996). Almost 70% of the mothers said that their partners participated in household tasks as much as they (the mothers) would like. The evidence presented in Table 6 shows that, with the exception of household repairs, fathers took responsibility for relatively few household tasks.

## Table 6
### Who is Responsible for Household Tasks

| Task | Father | Mother | Both | Children | Family |
|------|--------|--------|------|----------|--------|
| Breakfast | 16.2 | 51.2 | 14.8 | 2.1 | 14.8 |
| Dishes | 4.7 | 48.1 | 17.3 | 13.6 | 15.0 |
| Shopping | 4.7 | 69.0 | 22.2 | 1.6 | 2.1 |
| Ironing | 1.2 | 78.1 | 4.9 | 4.1 | 8.6 |
| Hoovering | 5.7 | 51.6 | 18.9 | 6.4 | 12.5 |
| Repairs | 75.7 | 9.7 | 0.6 | 1.8 | 2.5 |

Source: Kiely, 1996, p.149.

With regard to actual child care tasks, Table 7 shows that fathers did quite a lot, and in some activities - such as playing and going on outings - took more responsibility than mothers, according to the mothers themselves.

**Table 7**

**Who is Mostly Responsible for Childcare Tasks**

| Task | Father Only | Mother Only | Both | Other |
|------|-------------|-------------|------|-------|
| Putting to Bed | 11.7 | 42.7 | 41.7 | 4.0 |
| Home Work | 23.0 | 43.3 | 30.4 | 3.4 |
| Playing | 18.9 | 13.1 | 66.1 | 2.0 |
| Outings | 15.5 | 10.7 | 72.1 | 1.6 |
| Discipline | 16.1 | 25.6 | 57.9 | 0.4 |
| School Meetings | 3.4 | 52.7 | 43.1 | 1.0 |

Source: Kiely, 1996, p.149.

It is perhaps understandable that minimally involved fathers get relatively large amounts of attention in public discourse given that child welfare, gender justice and social order itself is reported to be so adversely affected by their lack of contribution. Yet it is crucial also to focus on those actively involved fathers who do exist, to acknowledge their presence, and attempt to learn from them and produce knowledge that can benefit other men and families as well as child care professionals and society. It appears that involved fathers are not inversely related to committed workers as has sometimes been thought. One commentator has pointed out that having a strong commitment to work identity does not preclude men from having a similar commitment to non-provider father roles too (Marsiglio, 1995, p. 17). Another has found that the fathers who were most successful at work were those who were most involved and had quality relationships with their children. They were better time-managers and communicators at work (Burgess, 1997).

There are two perspectives which have sought to account for fathers' roles in the home. The fairness perspective - developed out of a feminist paradigm in the 1970s - suggests that fathers tend to be under-involved at home, leaving the bulk of responsibility with their partners. This perspective emphasises the promotion of equality and "domestic democracy". The developmental perspective - which emerged in the 1990s - emphasises that a man's role in the home needs to be understood in terms of stages in the adult life-cycle that is characterised by change, growth, development and the capacity to care for the next generation. This perspective places the emphasis on what fathers - no less than mothers - need in order to make a successful developmental transition into parenthood.

Parenthood is a developmental transition characterised by periods of uncertainty, confusion and significant disequilibrium for individuals as their inner, psychological worlds are reorganised and their behaviour patterns altered accordingly. This transition can be more or less successful, depending on how it is managed. Exponents of the developmental perspective acknowledge that women have a certain 'biological advantage', so to speak, over men in the transition to parenthood because they have an opportunity to form some kind of emotional relationship with the baby as it develops during pregnancy. Women are also better prepared psychologically and socially to make the transition because - for better or worse - girls are socialised for care-giving and boys for providing. Once the baby arrives, mothers tend to have social supports to help them adjust to their roles, whereas society provides few supports for fathers (Hawkins, et al, 1995, p.51).

The reason many men do not make a successful transition into being active fathers is not simply because they choose to exploit their wives, but because their energy and capacity to care gets focused outside of their direct intimate relationships and they end up caring for the next generation through paid work and forms of altruistic endeavour. It has been argued that men's capacity to nurture and their motivation to become involved with their children increases dramatically around the time of birth (Hawkins, et al, 1995). This emotional energy can be capitalised on by health care professionals and other potential support networks for men. The more that secure bonding and attachment occurs between father and child at this formative time, the greater the likelihood that the man will focus his capacity for caring within the family through active involvement with his children throughout the life-cycle.

We consider that an integration of the fairness perspective and the developmental perspective provides important insights into the question of what it is to be a good father. A good father is a man who is open to developing his capacity for emotional communication and is active in nurturing, care work and being *fully* present for his partner and children within the parameters of what they have openly and honestly negotiated as constituting fairness and domestic democracy in this family.

The overall implication of this analysis is that public policy should seek to create family friendly measures, especially in the workplace, which maximise the choices men and women have to negotiate roles and responsibilities and will allow fathers as well as mothers the time and space for child care. This will require that greater value is placed on child care. Increased involvement of men in child care will not become a widespread reality until and unless there is real economic equality for women which makes it possible for couples to make affordable choices about which partner should stay at home. Care work needs to be valued and rewarded so that it will be seen as a positive choice for men as well as women, whether that work is done in the private domain of the family or in the public provision of child care. Social intervention needs to be strategically focused on promoting men's caring capacities to make the successful transition into fatherhood. Achieving this will depend on individual men's motivation and their capacities for intimacy and open negotiation with women. It will also depend on the provision of adequate supports for fathers and on the willingness and ability of the State's family support services to include fathers in its work.

6.     **Fathers and Work**

Working outside the home is a central part of the way in which men have been fathers and continue to be fathers. It is also one of the greatest determinants of a father's involvement with his children since it determines, inter alia, the amount of time he can spend with them. The traditional breadwinning role required little or no involvement by fathers in the physical or emotional care of children. This pattern is changing, not just for economic reasons but also because expectations about what constitutes a good father are changing. The physical and emotional absences of fathers are less acceptable to both their children and partners and this is obliging some men to reflect on their respective commitments to work and family.

It is against this background that a special analysis of the 1996 Labour Force Survey was undertaken in order to find out about the characteristics of men and fathers at work, as well as women and mothers at work (see the Appendix for the tables). The analysis distinguished two types of father: younger fathers, at least one of whose children is under the age of 15 and older fathers, all of whose children are over the age of 15. Both categories of father are older than non-fathers; half of non-fathers are under the age of 35 (Table A1a reveals). The majority of younger fathers (62%) are aged 35-49 compared to the majority of older fathers (57%) who are in the age group 50-64. In general, fathers tend to be a little older than mothers and this suggests that women tend to enter motherhood at a slightly younger age than men enter fatherhood (Table A1b). This is influenced by the age at marriage, even if marriage and parenthood are not as closely tied as formerly: in 1990, the average age at marriage for men (28.6 years) was two years older than for women (26.6 years) (Department of Health, 1993, p.11).

### Housing Status

Around four fifths of the dwellings in Ireland are owner-occupied. In view of this, it is not surprising that the majority of men and women - irrespective of whether they are parents or not - live in a house which they are buying or have bought. Nevertheless it is worth noting that fathers and mothers are more likely to be in the owner-occupied sector than non-fathers and non-mothers (Tables A2a and A2b). This reflects the fact that buying a house is usually part of the process of preparing for parenthood and, as will be seen, the ensuing financial responsibility seems to affect their overall participation in the world of work. As might be expected, younger fathers and mothers are more likely to be buying than to have bought their house. A minority of both younger fathers (8%) and older fathers (5%) live in local authority houses. Due to the higher incidence of lone parenting among women, a higher proportion of both younger mothers (11%) and older mothers (6%) also live in local authority houses.

### Employment Status

Parenthood brings with it financial as well as other responsibilities. In practice, this means that work outside the home is an extremely important aspect of being a responsible parent. This is particularly the case for fathers whose breadwinning role is important to the family finances as well as to their own self-image as a father. As shown above, the father is the sole earner in about half of all households in Ireland (see Table 2). It is noteworthy that younger fathers are more likely to be in full-time employment than any other category of men: 81% of them are in full-time employment compared to 60% of older fathers and 55%

of non-fathers (Table A3). This clearly suggests a connection between the financial responsibilities of younger fathers and their participation in employment.

The employment status of mothers differ from fathers in two important respects.  First, the proportion of mothers in full-time employment is much lower than for fathers (Table A3b). However it is significant that the proportion of younger mothers in full-time employment (28%) is nearly twice as high as the corresponding proportion for older mothers (15%). Second, the proportion of mothers in part-time employment is much higher than for fathers. Younger mothers are more than four times as likely to be in part-time employment as younger fathers (14% compared to 3%) but are also nearly twice as likely to be in part-time employment as older mothers (14% compared to 9%). It is clear from this that the financial pressure on younger parents - both mothers and fathers - is making itself felt in their higher employment rates.

### Hours Worked

The level of contact between parents and children is affected less by employment rates per se and more by the number of hours which they spend at work outside the home each week.  In general, there is a tendency for fathers to work slightly longer hours than non-fathers even if the overall average is around 46 hours per week (Table A4a).  It is noteworthy that a third of fathers (33%) work 50 hours per week or more compared to only a quarter of non-fathers (27%).   This is significant in view of the fact that, under The Organisation of Working Time Act, 1997, the maximum working week is 48 hours.

Mothers, where they are employed, work an average of 31-32 hours per week outside the home (Table A4b). This is exactly 15 hours less than the number of hours worked outside the home by fathers. By contrast with men, non-mothers work longer hours than mothers.

It is particularly interesting to note that fathers whose partners are working outside the home spend less hours at work than fathers whose partners are not working (see Table A4a).  This suggests that the hours worked by fathers are influenced by the employment status, and therefore the earnings, of their partners. The reverse however is the case with mothers: mothers whose partners are employed work longer hours than mothers whose partners are unemployed or inactive (see Table A4b).  One reason for this is that mothers and fathers may have different ways of looking at work outside the home but this would require further investigation.

Irish men work the same average number of hours as British men - about 45 hours per week - but both categories work significantly longer than the average for the 15 EU Member States which stood at 42 hours in 1995 (Eurostat, 1996, p.164). The usual working hours of Irish women, by contrast, is much closer to the EU norm (Ibid). Data on the hours worked by fathers and mothers is not available at EU level.  However, selected studies indicate that Irish fathers work longer hours than some of their EU counterparts.  In Denmark - where the maximum working week is 37 hours - fathers of young children work an average of 41 hours per week, five hours less than Irish fathers. However Danish mothers worked longer hours than Irish mothers at 34 hours per week (Pruzan, 1993, pp.168-.170; Council of Europe, p.104). Irish fathers also work longer hours than British fathers: 27% of fathers in Britain but 33% of fathers in Ireland work 50 hours a week or more (Ferri and Smith, 1996, p.18). Irish mothers also work longer hours than British mothers: 23% of mothers in Britain but 51% of mothers in Ireland work 35 hours a week or more (Ibid). The tendency for Irish fathers to work longer hours than non-fathers is also replicated in the Norwegian experience (Jensen, 1993, p.160).

The hours which parents spend in work outside the home are a useful indicator of how they meet their financial responsibilities. However they do not capture the distribution of those hours over the week, particularly where the parents may be involved in shift work, evening work, night work, Saturday work or Sunday work. Our analysis revealed that a small proportion of fathers do shift work, nearly half do evening work, a quarter do night work, two thirds do Saturday work and two fifths do Sunday work (Table A5a). In this respect, there is almost no difference between younger and older fathers or between fathers and non-fathers. However there are significant differences between fathers and mothers with fathers being much more likely to work unsocial hours than mothers (Table A5b). British fathers do more evening and night work than Irish fathers but less Saturday work and similar Sunday work (Ferri and Smith, 1996, p.19). British working mothers are more similar to Irish working mothers except that they do more evening work than Irish mothers (Ibid).

One way of overcoming the enforced absences of work outside the home - and one that is increasingly feasible in sectors which utilise modern telecommunications - is to work from home. In view of this, it is worth noting that a significant minority (15%) of younger fathers usually or sometimes work at home; this rises to 19% for older fathers (see Table A6a). However this trend does not seem to be influenced by fathering per se since the proportion of non-fathers who work at home is very similar to young fathers. However it is noteworthy that men are twice as likely as women to work from home, irrespective of whether they are parents or not (Table A5b). This however needs to be seen in the context that a much higher proportion of women "work" in the home, albeit without pay.

In analysing the 1996 Labour Force Survey, we distinguished between fathers and non-fathers and between mothers and non-mothers. Beneath this distinction lies an assumption that parenting makes a difference to the way in which men and women participate in the world of work. Our analysis effectively confirms this while also bringing out significant differences between fathers and mothers. Fathers are much more involved in the world of work outside the home than mothers and work much longer and more unsocial hours. This clearly reflects the gendered division of labour both inside and outside the home, even if that division is becoming much less clear-cut. From the perspective of fathers, the analysis raises the question as to why some of them - particularly the 33% who work 50 hours a week or more - work such long hours. Are they constrained to do it by financial commitments, job insecurity and the pressures of the job? Do they want to do it because their employment role is central to their aspirations, ambitions and satisfactions? Do they experience any tension between their role as worker and their role as father? Is it even conceivable that some men prefer to stay at work in order to avoid the responsibilities of fathering and family life? The answers to these questions are unknown and require further research if we are to understand how men live out their role as fathers. The attitudes of mothers to the long hours worked by fathers and their role in negotiating and deciding on those hours would also have to be considered to understand how families share their parenting roles and responsibilities.

There is a growing recognition in policy circles that many parents have difficulty in reconciling the competing demands of work and family to the satisfaction of their employers, their children and their partners. At the same time, these difficulties are not insurmountable and some research evidence suggests how parents - both mothers and fathers - manage to reconcile the conflict. According to Burgess: "When we began our interviews with fathers for this book, one surprising finding was how often our most involved fathers also turned out to be successful in career terms and conversely how often our least involved fathers seemed to be struggling" (1997, pp.160-161). Among the reasons suggested for this are good time-management, communication and people skills; in addition, "not one [father] had a consuming hobby or played much sport or was very involved in the community. These working fathers, like so many working mothers, seemed to focus on just two main areas; their work and their children" (Ibid, p.163).

In recognition of the need to reconcile the competing demands of work and family, a number of EU countries have introduced - or are introducing - measures designed to make the workplace more family-friendly and flexible so that parents can become more involved in the care of their children. Family-friendly initiatives cover a wide range of measures, as Table 8 illustrates.

In 1996, the Irish Government and the social partners agreed - in Partnership 2000 for Inclusion, Employment and Competitiveness - to support the growth of "family friendly policies in employment, in line with the recommendations contained in the policy document issued by the Employment Equality Agency in 1996" (Government of Ireland, 1996, p.30).

These measures have the potential to facilitate greater involvement by fathers in the care of their children and families. However the realisation of this potential will not be easy because fathers - and men generally - are less likely to avail of them than women and mothers. This was amply confirmed in a recent study of flexible working in Ireland which showed that "job sharing, career breaks and extended parental leave encourage more women than men to trade full-time continuous jobs and careers for extra time off" (Fynes, Morrissey, Roche, Whelan and Williams, 1996, p.227). As a result, flexible working arrangements can leave men's working lives almost untouched and can reinforce existing gender differences between men and women both at work and at home, as fathers work full-time and mothers work part-time.

**Table 8**

**Summary of Family-Friendly Initiatives**

| Category of Family-Friendly Initiative | Category of Family-Friendly initiative |
|---|---|
| **Flexible Working**<br>• job-sharing<br>• flexitime<br>• flexiplace (working from home)<br>• part-time working<br>• term-time working | **Leave Arrangements**<br>• maternity leave<br>• paternity leave<br>• adoption leave<br>• compassionate / berevement leave<br>• emergency leave<br>• eldercare<br>• care for people with disabilities |
| **Breaks**<br>• employment breaks<br>• sabbaticals<br>• secondments | **Other Initiatives**<br>• childcare support<br>• employee assistance programmes<br>• parenting workshops<br>• family days<br>• health care |

Derived from Employment Equality Agency, 1996, p.11.

The response of men and fathers to flexible working arrangements may itself be influenced by the way in which those measures are presented and promoted. In Ireland, most of the arguments in favour of family-friendly measures in the workplace are advanced from the perspective of women's equality in the labour market (see for example, Second Commission on the Status of Women, 1993, Chapter Three; Employment Equality Agency, 1996). The same also appears to be the case in other countries and this may help to explain why women rather than men make most use of these measures.

One of the lessons to emerge from this is that the agenda behind the introduction and implementation of family-friendly measures in the workplace needs to broadened. This agenda needs to include men and children as well as women and the benefits that can accrue, over the course of a life, of sharing work and caring responsibilities more equitably. It should not be assumed that men and women will see the benefits of family-friendly measures in the workplace in exactly the same way.

We also wish to draw attention to the use of gender-neutral language in discussions of family-friendly measures. There is very little usage of the terms "father" or "mother" in this literature even though it is precisely by virtue of being fathers and mothers that the need for family-friendly measures in the workplace arises. For example, a recent report on family-friendly initiatives in the workplace refers mainly to "employees" and "workers", occasionally to "men" and "women", but seldom to "fathers" and "mothers" (Employment Equality Agency, 1996). A similar gender-neutral language is used by the government and the social partners: for example, in Partnership 2000 for Inclusion, Employment and Competitiveness, their commitment to childcare and family-friendly policies in the workplace are cited without making any reference to "fathers" and "mothers" (Government of Ireland, 1996, p.30). The issue here is not just pedantic; if it is an objective of government policy to promote greater involvement of fathers in the care of their children while also promoting the involvement of mothers in the world of paid work, then the inherent value of those roles needs to be explicitly named. The absence of any references to fathers and mothers in matters designed specifically to support those roles is a little contradictory and may even undermine the potential of those measures to achieve their objectives. Both Government and the social partners have a shared responsibility in ensuring that joint parenting is perceived as the ideal for both fathers and mothers and that the workplace must change to accommodate this ideal.

These considerations suggest that the manner in which family-friendly measures are implemented and promoted could be just as important as the measures themselves. Accordingly, we recommend that the Government and the social partners give serious consideration to ensuring that family-friendly measures in the workplace are promoted as measures designed to facilitate both fathers and mothers in meeting their parenting responsibilities. In this regard, we would also recommend that the language used to promote family-friendly measures is less gender-neutral and neutered and uses terms like "father" and "mother" to indicate that it is precisely for them and their children that the measures are being introduced.

Childcare is an extremely important initiative within the overall context of family friendly measures in the workplace. From the beginning of 1997, the Irish government and the social partners have committed themselves to "develop a strategy which integrates the different strands of the current arrangements for the development and delivery of childcare and early educational services" (Government of Ireland, 1996, p.30). As with other family friendly measures in the workplace, our analysis revealed that childcare tends to be seen as a women's issue and this can reduce its overall effectiveness from the point of view of breaking down the gendered division of labour in the home and at work. We acknowledge that change in this area appears to be slow and complex but it would be helped if the arguments in favour of childcare addressed themselves specifically to the needs and benefits of fathers rather than assuming that what is of benefit to mothers is automatically of benefit to fathers. In other words, we recommend that more attention be given to the way in which childcare is presented and delivered with a view to ensuring that it is seen as relevant and of benefit not only to children and mothers but to fathers as well.

Our analysis drew attention to the virtual absence of men from childcare work. The reasons for this are many and inter-related. They involve low pay, the attitude which sees it as inappropriate work for men and the fears of some men about entering a world that is presently the almost exclusive domain of women. However we also suspect that many men have become alienated from childcare because the wholly justified reporting of child abuse cases involving men has created a more generalised perception that all men are dangerous in the context of childcare. Whatever the reasons, we believe that the consequences of gender imbalance in the childcare sector are likely to have long-term consequences in terms of perpetuating, in the minds of children, the image that women, but not men, are the "natural" carers of children. As a result, the gender imbalance in the delivery of childcare may itself undermine the objective which it is trying to promote, namely, reducing the gendered division of labour between home and work. In our opinion, this gender imbalance is also a loss for the children who miss the benefit of having caring men in these services. Accordingly, we recommend that a discussion document should be prepared on gender imbalances in the childcare sector with a view to developing a strategy for addressing the barriers inhibiting men's involvement in this sector and the measures required to overcome them, consistent with maintaining the highest level of service for children.

7.    **Fathers and the Law**

The Irish Constitution makes no reference to fathers; unlike mothers, they do not have a constitutionally-protected right to their children. However the position of unmarried fathers is particularly weak since, under the Irish Constitution, they are not recognised as either a parent or as part of a family and have no constitutional rights to their child. Both the Constitution Review Group and the Commission on the Family have considered this issue and have suggested that the adoption of Article 8 of European Convention on Human Rights - which guarantees every person respect for 'family life,' this being interpreted to include non-marital family life - would be one way of granting constitutional rights to unmarried or "natural" fathers. An alternative approach, and one which we favour, would involve drafting a constitutional provision to guarantee that a mother and a father have equal rights to a child where the child is conceived through their mutual consent. The right of each child to know and be cared for by both its parents, whether living together or not, should also be enshrined in the Constitution. The exercise of these rights would be regulated by law and would always be applied in the best interests of the child.

Moving from the Constitution to statute law, our analysis revealed that unmarried fathers do not have automatic guardianship rights to their children. Our view is that this legal situation - which was confirmed in law by the Children Act, 1997 - is not conducive to joint parenting and is not sufficiently supportive of the child's right - as enshrined in both Article 8 of European Convention on Human Rights and Articles 7 and 9 of the UN Convention on the Rights of the Child - to be brought up by both its parents. Nor is it sufficiently supportive of the child's right to have paternity legally established. We have also considered the evidence - albeit much of it anecdotal in Ireland - concerning separated fathers and the apparent low rates of joint custody of children. This effectively undermines joint parenting since it gives the mother total responsibility for bringing up the child and leaves the father's access to his child almost entirely at the discretion of the child's mother.

The law relating to guardianship, custody and access has an important impact on the level of contact between children and their non-resident fathers. Our analysis suggested that many non-resident fathers in Ireland want to be involved in the care and upbringing of their children but have difficulty in affirming their right as an equal parent of their child. This has been articulated in the work of Treoir: Federation of Services for Unmarried Parents and their Children and more recently in the work of Parental Equality: The Shared Parenting and Joint Custody Support Group.

Marital breakdown is one of the ways in which fathers and families come in contact with the law and the courts. In 1996, around 6% of the ever-married population described themselves as separated or divorced (Table 9). However only two fifths (41%) of these appear to be legally separated or divorced thus indicating that the majority of ever-married men and women involved in family breakup do not have recourse to the court system in Ireland.

Table 9

**Marital Status of Ever-Married Men and Women in Ireland in 1996**

| Marital Status | Men | Women | Total |
|---|---|---|---|
| Total Ever Married[1] | 710,616 | 733,789 | 1,444,405 |
| Total Separated / Divorced | 35,661 | 52,131 | 87,792 |
| *Deserted* | *6,363* | *16,785* | *23,148* |
| *Marriage annulled* | *920* | *1,287* | *2,207* |
| *Legally separated* | *11,863* | *14,616* | *26,479* |
| *Other separated* | *11,741* | *14,430* | *26,171* |
| *Divorced* | *4,774* | *5,013* | *9,787* |
| Separated/divorced as % of ever married | 5 | 7 | 6 |
| Legally separated/divorced as % of separated | 47 | 38 | 41 |

1.   Total ever-married includes all married, re-married and separated persons and excludes widows.
     Source: Census of Population, 1996.

In order to look at the uses which fathers make of the family law system in Ireland we drew upon an existing study of family law cases through the courts in 1993 / 1994 (see Fahey and Lyons, 1995). From this we discovered that only a small proportion of family disputes and separations are resolved in the courts. Most family law cases are initiated by women and many of them are against men in the sense that they involve barring and protection orders (Table 10). Guardianship is effectively the only area where fathers use - or can use - the family law system to redress family disputes.

## Table 10

### Size and Composition of Family Law Cases in the District Courts in Ireland in 1993 / 1994

| Category | Numbers | | Characteristics of Applicant | | |
|---|---|---|---|---|---|
| Type of Application | N | % | Gender Status | Parental Status | Marital Status |
| Barring/Protection Order | 4,500 | 56 | Women | Mothers (75%)* Not Mothers (25%)* | All married** |
| Maintenance Order | 1,750 | 22 | Women | Mothers (100%) | Married (75%) Unmarried (25%) |
| Guardianship | 1,750 | 22 | Men (66%) Women (33%) | Fathers (66%) Mothers (33%) | Married (60%) Unmarried (40%) |
| Total | 8,000 | 100 | Women (85%) Men (15%) | Mothers (71%) Not Mothers (14%) Fathers (15%) | Married (86%) Unmarried (14%) |

\*    Estimated according to the proportion of married women who have children (75%) and who have not children (25%), using the 1994 Labour Force Survey (Table 43). Main Source: Derived from Fahey and Lyons, 1995, Chapter Two.

\*\*   Prior to the Domestic Violence Act 1996 which extended the scope of the Law on barring and protection orders, these orders were not available to cohabiting couples

Table 11 shows that applications for guardianship have increased significantly in recent years - possibly reflecting an increased interest by unmarried fathers in their children - although they still amount to only 6% of all registered births outside marriage.

In general, our analysis suggests that the court system needs to do more to be supportive of fathers who are separating or unmarried. A Family Commission - which would effectively remove family cases from the remit of the courts - could be the best way to proceed.

## Table 11

**Applications for Guardianship by Unmarried Fathers, 1989-1996**

| Year | Applications for Guardianship N | Applications for Guardianship Granted N | Applications for Guardianship Granted % |
|------|------|------|------|
| 1989 | 76 | 25 | 33 |
| 1990 | 215 | 190 | 88 |
| 1991 | 276 | 251 | 91 |
| 1992 | 347 | 312 | 90 |
| 1993 | 531 | 477 | 90 |
| 1994 | 562 | 436 | 76 |
| 1995 | 727 | 556 | 76 |
| 1996 | 700 | 400 | 57 |
| % Change 89-96 | 821 | 1,500 | - |

Source: Department of Justice, Equality and Law Reform.

We have considered the question of joint custody and are of the view that joint custody should be the norm for all parents who are legally separating - with the presumption that parents have equal rights of custody and access - and that the onus should be on the courts, in the exercise of their discretion in these matters, to show why joint custody would not be in the best interests of the child and its parents. This view leaves in place the best interests of the child as the organising principle on which decisions must be based, while at the same time establishing joint custody as the appropriate option for the court to consider, unless the evidence and the circumstances suggest otherwise.

Evidence from elsewhere suggests that the concept of "joint legal custody" may not be sufficient to promote contact between non-resident fathers and their children unless it actually means "joint physical custody". Moreover other measures which impact on families - such as income support payments by the Department of Social, Community and Family Affairs, particularly Child Benefit (Children's Allowance) and the One Parent Family Payment - may need to be re-adjusted to make joint custody a viable option.

Following separation, the issue of contact between children and their non-resident father arises. A number of studies have shown that a key factor affecting the level of contact between non-resident fathers and their children is the level of contact established in the years immediately following separation; if a pattern of regular contact is established and reinforced by shared physical custody and children staying overnight, then the level of contact is likely to be much higher (Wallerstein and Kelly, 1980; Leupnitz, 1986; Maccoby, Depner and Mnookin, 1990; Albiston, Maccoby, and Mnookin, 1990; Ottosen, 1996). One implication of this is that contact between non-resident fathers and their children may not be simply a matter of the father's interest or disinterest in his children but may be more affected by the access to his children which is afforded to him. In this regard, a mediated process of separation - particularly in situations of intense conflict - could help to ensure that the children's need for regular contact with their father is maintained and could be much less damaging for the children (see Law Reform Commission, 1996). Where possible and appropriate, father-children contact needs to be promoted separately as a relationship in its own right which is distinct from the dynamics of the post-separation spousal relationship.

In summary then, our analysis revealed a number of areas within the law where the rights of fathers - particularly the rights of unmarried fathers - require attention. It is our impression that the rights of separated fathers to joint custody of their children may not receive the enthusiastic support from the courts that it deserves and this needs to be addressed. Within the Constitution, we favour a declaration which enshrines the equal rights of father and mother to the guardianship of their child where the child is conceived through consent, irrespective of whether both parents live together. Our analysis is informed by the primacy of the best interests of the child and our belief that this is usually best served when the child knows and is cared for by both its parents, irrespective of the legal or personal relationship between those parents.

8.     **State Services and Supports for Fathers**

State intervention in families - particularly by health care, family care and child care professionals - has a significant impact on fathers by shaping and reinforcing the existing parenting roles of mothers and fathers. Our analysis revealed that fathers tend to be largely ignored or avoided by State social services. These services still tend to assume that mothers take responsibility for childcare and, by making this assumption, they help to ensure that fathers do not. The State's health and social services have made little effort to get men directly involved in fatherhood, a neglect which plays into men's traditional reluctance to define themselves in terms of nurturing and caring roles. The result is an almost total absence of supports for fathers from all social backgrounds.

One of the reasons why professional caring services avoid fathers is that there is little or no concept of men's vulnerability either in society generally or in the professional caring community specifically. This has much to do with how dominant forms of 'masculinity' are constructed and perceived in Irish society, not least by men and male-dominated institutions themselves. It is necessary therefore to start deconstructing the myth of the invulnerable man and father.

There is a great deal of uncertainty among professionals about how to approach men and work with them. The experience tends to be mutual however: just as professionals avoid men, many fathers tend to resist engaging with welfare practitioners, regarding such encounters as "women's business". In practice, many men are not available due to work and other commitments during the hours when services are being delivered.

One of the consequences of the neglect of fathers by State services is that the resourcefulness of fathers to protect and promote the welfare of children in vulnerable family situations is rarely considered, let alone promoted by State intervention. While child sexual abuse tends to gain more media attention, child 'neglect' is still the most commonly reported problem investigated by Health Boards and this clearly involves mothers as much as fathers. Thus, public policy faces a major challenge in re-focusing practice from its primary concern with the ability of mothers 'to protect' their children and to start working with fathers so that they too can become more involved in the parenting process.

The under-involvement of fathers in parenting and support services is underpinned by perceptions of the 'feminised' nature of child rearing. Within the health care system, men's roles are largely restricted to child care 'managers'. This confers very real administrative power but carries limited involvement in terms of day-to-day child care practice.

We are arguing that the gender bias in State services to families - such as public health nursing services or social work services - creates a situation which does not encourage fathers to get involved with their children. We are also arguing that the professional community must become fully aware of its guiding assumptions and practices around gender roles and needs to re-imagine its relationship to fathers and mothers if it is to genuinely allow for the empowerment of men and women as active parents.

The main recommendation to emerge from this analysis is that professionals involved in support services for families need to re-examine their practices from the perspective of fathers. These professionals include Public Health Nurses, Social Workers, General Practitioners and Childcare Workers. In our view, professionals need to be made aware of how their assumptions and practices are excluding fathers. Equally, professionals need to be supported through training programmes on how to work effectively with fathers.

Some young fathers are particularly vulnerable. They experience exclusion from the labour market as well as from parenting, either because of their own choice and circumstances or their partner's choice and circumstances. We recommend that programmes should be devised for these young men to help them make the transition to manhood and fatherhood. Our suspicion is that some of these young men may themselves have had poor fathering experiences and could benefit greatly from a well resourced programme - possibly a New Opportunities Programme for Men - to explore their experiences, both past and present. Programmes like this have been tried elsewhere and could be adapted to Irish circumstances.

# Appendix

## Table A1a

### Ages of Fathers Compared to All Men in Ireland, 1996

| Age | Younger Fathers (1) % | Older Fathers (2) % | Non-Fathers (3) % | All Men (4) % |
|---|---|---|---|---|
| 20-34 | 24 | 0 | 50 | 34 |
| 35-49 | 62 | 20 | 15 | 31 |
| 50-64 | 13 | 57 | 15 | 21 |
| 64+ | 1 | 23 | 20 | 14 |
| Total | 100 | 100 | 100 | 100 |

Source: 1996 Labour Force Survey, Special Tabulations by Anthony Murphy at University College Dublin.

## Table A1b

### Ages of Mothers Compared to All Women in Ireland, 1996

| Age | Younger Mothers (5) % | Older Mothers (6) % | Non-Mothers (7) % | All Women (8) % |
|---|---|---|---|---|
| 20-34 | 35 | 0 | 43 | 33 |
| 35-49 | 58 | 26 | 11 | 30 |
| 50-64 | 7 | 53 | 17 | 19 |
| 64+ | 0 | 21 | 29 | 18 |
| Total | 100 | 100 | 100 | 100 |

Source: 1996 Labour Force Survey, Special Tabulations by Anthony Murphy at University College Dublin.

(1)  For the purpose of this analysis, a younger father is defined as a man over the age of 20 who has any child under the age of 15 years and lives with that child. Using this definition, there were approximately 373,000 younger fathers in Ireland in 1996, equivalent to 69% of all fathers.

(2)  For the purpose of this analysis, an older father is defined as a man over the age of 20 all of whose children are over the age of 15 years and who lives with these children. Using this definition, there were approximately 166,000 older fathers in Ireland in 1996, equivalent to 31% of all fathers.

(3)  Non-fathers are men over the age of 20 who do not have, or do not live with, their children.

(4)  All men refer to men over the age of 20, both fathers and non-fathers, and amount to 1,156,000 men.

(5)  For the purpose of this analysis, a younger mother is defined as a woman over the age of 20 who has any child under the age of 15 years and lives with that child. Using this definition, there were approximately 412,000 younger mothers in Ireland in 1996, equivalent to 67% of all mothers.

(6)  For the purpose of this analysis, an older mother is defined as a woman over the age of 20 all of whose children are over the age of 15 years and who lives with these children. Using this definition, there were approximately 203,000 older mothers in Ireland in 1996, equivalent to 33% of all mothers.

(7)  Non-mothers are women over the age of 20 who do not have, or do not live with, their children.

(8)  All women refer to women over the age of 20, both mothers and non-mothers, and amount to 1,199,000 women.

## Table A2a

**Housing Tenure of Fathers Compared to All Men in Ireland, 1996**

| Housing Tenure | Younger Fathers (1) % | Older Fathers (2) % | Non-Fathers (3) % | All Men (4) % |
|---|---|---|---|---|
| Local Authority Rented | 8 | 5 | 6 | 6 |
| Private Rented | 5 | 2 | 16 | 10 |
| Buying House | 63 | 39 | 28 | 41 |
| House Bought | 24 | 54 | 50 | 43 |
| Total | 100 | 100 | 100 | 100 |

Source: 1996 Labour Force Survey, Special Tabulations by Anthony Murphy at University College Dublin.

## Table A2b

**Housing Tenure of Mothers and All Women in Ireland, 1996**

| Housing Tenure | Younger Mothers (5) % | Older Mothers (6) % | Non-Mothers (7) % | All Women (8) % |
|---|---|---|---|---|
| Local Authority Rented | 11 | 6 | 5 | 7 |
| Private Rented | 7 | 2 | 18 | 11 |
| Buying House | 59 | 36 | 27 | 40 |
| House Bought | 23 | 56 | 50 | 42 |
| Total | 100 | 100 | 100 | 100 |

Source: 1996 Labour Force Survey, Special Tabulations by Anthony Murphy at University College Dublin.

(1) For the purpose of this analysis, a younger father is defined as a man over the age of 20 who has any child under the age of 15 years and lives with that child. Using this definition, there were approximately 373,000 younger fathers in Ireland in 1996, equivalent to 69% of all fathers.

(2) For the purpose of this analysis, an older father is defined as a man over the age of 20 all of whose children are over the age of 15 years and who lives with these children. Using this definition, there were approximately 166,000 older fathers in Ireland in 1996, equivalent to 31% of all fathers.

(3) Non-fathers are men over the age of 20 who do not have, or do not live with, their children.

(4) All men refer to men over the age of 20, both fathers and non-fathers, and amount to 1,156,000 men.

(5) For the purpose of this analysis, a younger mother is defined as a woman over the age of 20 who has any child under the age of 15 years and lives with that child. Using this definition, there were approximately 412,000 younger mothers in Ireland in 1996, equivalent to 67% of all mothers.

(6) For the purpose of this analysis, an older mother is defined as a woman over the age of 20 all of whose children are over the age of 15 years and who lives with these children. Using this definition, there were approximately 203,000 older mothers in Ireland in 1996, equivalent to 33% of all mothers.

(7) Non-mothers are women over the age of 20 who do not have, or do not live with, their children.

(8) All women refer to women over the age of 20, both mothers and non-mothers, and amount to 1,199,000 women.

## Table A3a

### Employment Status of Fathers Compared to All Men in Ireland, 1996

| Employment Status | Younger Fathers (1) % | Older Fathers (2) % | Non-Fathers (3) % | All Men (4) % |
|---|---|---|---|---|
| Full-time employed | 81 | 60 | 55 | 64 |
| Part-time employed | 3 | 2 | 3 | 3 |
| Unemployed | 10 | 5 | 9 | 9 |
| Not looking for work | 6 | 33 | 33 | 24 |
| Total | 100 | 100 | 100 | 100 |

Source: 1996 Labour Force Survey, Special Tabulations by Anthony Murphy at University College Dublin.

## Table A3b

### Employment Status of Mothers and All Women in Ireland, 1996

| Employment Status | Younger Mothers (5) % | Older Mothers (6) % | Non-Mothers (7) % | All Women (8) % |
|---|---|---|---|---|
| Full-time employed | 28 | 15 | 40 | 31 |
| Part-time employed | 14 | 9 | 4 | 9 |
| Unemployed | 7 | 3 | 5 | 5 |
| Not looking for work | 51 | 73 | 51 | 55 |
| Total | 100 | 100 | 100 | 100 |

Source: 1996 Labour Force Survey, Special Tabulations by Anthony Murphy at University College Dublin.

---

(1) For the purpose of this analysis, a younger father is defined as a man over the age of 20 who has any child under the age of 15 years and lives with that child. Using this definition, there were approximately 373,000 younger fathers in Ireland in 1996, equivalent to 69% of all fathers.

(2) For the purpose of this analysis, an older father is defined as a man over the age of 20 all of whose children are over the age of 15 years and who lives with these children. Using this definition, there were approximately 166,000 older fathers in Ireland in 1996, equivalent to 31% of all fathers.

(3) Non-fathers are men over the age of 20 who do not have, or do not live with, their children.

(4) All men refer to men over the age of 20, both fathers and non-fathers, and amount to 1,156,000 men.

(5) For the purpose of this analysis, a younger mother is defined as a woman over the age of 20 who has any child under the age of 15 years and lives with that child. Using this definition, there were approximately 412,000 younger mothers in Ireland in 1996, equivalent to 67% of all mothers.

(6) For the purpose of this analysis, an older mother is defined as a woman over the age of 20 all of whose children are over the age of 15 years and who lives with these children. Using this definition, there were approximately 203,000 older mothers in Ireland in 1996, equivalent to 33% of all mothers.

(7) Non-mothers are women over the age of 20 who do not have, or do not live with, their children.

(8) All women refer to women over the age of 20, both mothers and non-mothers, and amount to 1,199,000 women.

## Table A4a

**Usual Hours Worked by Fathers and Men in Ireland, 1996**

| Usual Hours | Younger Fathers (1) % | Older Fathers (2) % | Non-Fathers (3) % | All Men (4) % |
|---|---|---|---|---|
| Less than 35 hours | 7 | 8 | 9 | 8 |
| 35-49 hours | 61 | 58 | 64 | 62 |
| 50+ hours | 32 | 34 | 27 | 30 |
| Total | 100 | 100 | 100 | 100 |
| Average hours | 46 | 47 | 45 | 46 |
| Average hours (partner working) | 46 | 46 | - | - |
| Average hours (partner not working) | 47 | 48 | - | - |

Source: 1996 Labour Force Survey, Special Tabulations by Anthony Murphy at University College Dublin.

## Table A4b

**Usual Hours Worked by Mothers and Women in Ireland, 1996**

| Usual Hours | Younger Mothers (5) % | Older Mothers (6) % | Non-Mothers (7) % | All Women (8) % |
|---|---|---|---|---|
| Less than 35 hours | 47 | 50 | 19 | 32 |
| 35-49 hours | 48 | 40 | 74 | 61 |
| 50+ hours | 5 | 10 | 7 | 7 |
| Total | 100 | 100 | 100 | 100 |
| Average hours | 31 | 32 | 38 | 35 |
| Average hours (partner working) | 32 | 32 | - | - |
| Average hours (partner not working) | 30 | 29 | - | - |

Source: 1996 Labour Force Survey, Special Tabulations by Anthony Murphy at University College Dublin.

(1) For the purpose of this analysis, a younger father is defined as a man over the age of 20 who has any child under the age of 15 years and lives with that child. Using this definition, there were approximately 373,000 younger fathers in Ireland in 1996, equivalent to 69% of all fathers.

(2) For the purpose of this analysis, an older father is defined as a man over the age of 20 all of whose children are over the age of 15 years and who lives with these children. Using this definition, there were approximately 166,000 older fathers in Ireland in 1996, equivalent to 31% of all fathers.

(3) Non-fathers are men over the age of 20 who do not have, or do not live with, their children.

(4) All men refer to men over the age of 20, both fathers and non-fathers, and amount to 1,156,000 men.

(5) For the purpose of this analysis, a younger mother is defined as a woman over the age of 20 who has any child under the age of 15 years and lives with that child. Using this definition, there were approximately 412,000 younger mothers in Ireland in 1996, equivalent to 67% of all mothers.

(6) For the purpose of this analysis, an older mother is defined as a woman over the age of 20 all of whose children are over the age of 15 years and who lives with these children. Using this definition, there were approximately 203,000 older mothers in Ireland in 1996, equivalent to 33% of all mothers.

(7) Non-mothers are women over the age of 20 who do not have, or do not live with, their children.

(8) All women refer to women over the age of 20, both mothers and non-mothers, and amount to 1,199,000 women.

## Table A5a

**Unsocial Hours Worked Usually or Sometimes by Fathers and Men in Ireland, 1996**

| Category of Unsocial Hours | Younger Fathers (1) % | Older Fathers (2) % | Non- Fathers (3) % | All Men (4) % |
|---|---|---|---|---|
| Shift Work | 16 | 13 | 15 | 15 |
| Evening Work | 46 | 44 | 43 | 44 |
| Night Work | 28 | 25 | 26 | 26 |
| Saturday Work | 68 | 66 | 67 | 67 |
| Sunday Work | 41 | 41 | 40 | 41 |
| Work at Home | 15 | 19 | 14 | 15 |

Source: 1996 Labour Force Survey, Special Tabulations by Anthony Murphy at University College Dublin.

## Table A5b

**Unsocial Hours Worked Usually or Sometimes by Mothers and Women in Ireland, 1996**

| Category of Unsocial Hours | Younger Mothers (5) % | Older Mothers (6) % | Non- Mothers (7) % | All Women (8) % |
|---|---|---|---|---|
| Shift Work | 13 | 11 | 16 | 14 |
| Evening Work | 24 | 27 | 26 | 25 |
| Night Work | 14 | 14 | 14 | 14 |
| Saturday Work | 44 | 49 | 48 | 46 |
| Sunday Work | 28 | 31 | 28 | 28 |
| Work at Home | 9 | 14 | 7 | 8 |

Source: 1996 Labour Force Survey, Special Tabulations by Anthony Murphy at University College Dublin.

(1)  For the purpose of this analysis, a younger father is defined as a man over the age of 20 who has any child under the age of 15 years and lives with that child.  Using this definition, there were approximately 373,000 younger fathers in Ireland in 1996, equivalent to 69% of all fathers.

(2)  For the purpose of this analysis, an older father is defined as a man over the age of 20 all of whose children are over the age of 15 years and who lives with these children. Using this definition, there were approximately 166,000 older fathers in Ireland in 1996, equivalent to 31% of all fathers.

(3)  Non-fathers are men over the age of 20 who do not have, or do not live with, their children.

(4)  All men refer to men over the age of 20, both fathers and non-fathers, and amount to 1,156,000 men.

(5)  For the purpose of this analysis, a younger mother is defined as a woman over the age of 20 who has any child under the age of 15 years and lives with that child.  Using this definition, there were approximately 412,000 younger mothers in Ireland in 1996, equivalent to 67% of all mothers.

(6)  For the purpose of this analysis, an older mother is defined as a woman over the age of 20 all of whose children are over the age of 15 years and who lives with these children. Using this definition, there were approximately 203,000 older mothers in Ireland in 1996, equivalent to 33% of all mothers.

(7)  Non-mothers are women over the age of 20 who do not have, or do not live with, their children.

(8)  All women refer to women over the age of 20, both mothers and non-mothers, and amount to 1,199,000 women.

# Bibliography

**Abramovitch, H., 1997,** "Images of the 'Father' in Psychology and Religion", in Lamb, M., (Editor), The Role of the Father in Child Development, Third Edition, New York: John Wiley and Sons, pp. 19-32.

**Ackerman-Ross, S., and Khanna, 1989,** "The Relationship of High Quality Day Care to Middle Class 3-Year Olds' Language Performance" in Early Childhood Research Quarterly, Volume 4, pp. 97-166.

**Albiston, C., Maccoby, E., and Mnookin, R., 1990,** "Does Joint Legal Custody Matter?" Stanford Law and Policy Review, Volume 2, pp.167-179.

**Andrews, P., 1994,** "A Separated Dad is Still a Dad", Tuesday 1 November, The Irish Times.

**Arthurs, H., Ferguson, H., and Grace, E., 1995,** "Celibacy, Secrecy and the Lives of Men", Doctrine and Life, Volume 45, pp.459-468.

**Barker, R. W., 1994,** Lone Fathers and Masculinity, Aldershot: Avesbury.

**Belsey, C., and Moore, J., (Editors), 1989,** The Feminist Reader, London: Macmillan.

**Benvenuto, B., Kennedy, R., 1986,** Jacques Lacan: An Introduction, New York: St Martin's Press.

**Bergstrand, G., 1995,** "A Theological Approach to Masculinity and Equality", in Men on Men: Eight Swedish Men's Personal Views on Equality, Masculinity and Parenthood. A Contribution by the Swedish Government to the Fourth World Conference on Women in Beijing 1995. Sweden: Ministry of Health and Social Affairs, pp. 74-91.

**Bertoia, C., E., and Drakich, J., 1995,** '"The Fathers' Rights Movement: Contradictions in Rhetoric and Practice", in W. Marsiglio (Editor), Fatherhood: Contemporary Theory, Research, and Social Policy, London: Sage.

**Bjornberg, U., (Editor), 1992,** European Parents in the 1990s: Contradictions and Comparisons, New Brunswick and London: Transaction Publishers.

**Bly, R., 1992,** "My Father's Wedding 1924" in Bly, R., Hillman, J., and Meade, M., (Editors), The Rag and Bone Shop of the Heart: Poems for Men, New York: HarperCollins Publishers, p. 133.

**Bowlby, J., 1969, 1973, 1980,** Attachment and Loss. Vol. 1,2,3. Hogarth Press.

**Bradshaw J., and Miller, J., 1991,** Lone Parents in the UK, London: HMSO.

**Brannen J., and Moss, P., 1991,** Managing Mothers: Dual Earner Households After Maternity Leave, London: Macmillan.

**Brannon, R., 1976,** "The male sex role - and what it's done for us lately" in Brannon, R., and David, D., (Editors), The Forty-nine Percent Majority, Reading, MA: Addison-Wesley.

**Buckley, H., 1997,** "Child Protection in Ireland" in Harder, M., and Pringle, K., (Editors), Protecting Children in Europe: Towards A New Millennium, Aalborg University Press.

**Burgess, A., 1997,** Fatherhood Reclaimed: The Making of the Modern Father, London: Vermillion.

**Brazelton, T.B., and Cramer, B.G., 1991,** The Earliest Relationship, London: Karnac.

**Carlsen, S., 1993,** "New Scandinavian Experiences" in Fathers in Families of Tomorrow, Report from the Conference held in Copenhagen, 17-18 June 1993, Copenhagen: The Ministry of Social Affairs.

**Carlsson, I., 1995,** "Why is Sweden devoting substantial efforts and money to an anthology on men in its preparations for the World Conference on Women?" in Men on Men: Eight Swedish Men's Personal Views on Equality, Masculinity and Parenthood. A Contribution by the Swedish Government to the Fourth World Conference on Women in Beijing 1995. Sweden: Ministry of Health and Social Affairs, pp. 7-8.

**Clatterbaugh, K., 1997,** Contemporary Perspectives on Masculinity: Men, Women and Politics in Modern Society, Colorado: Westview Press.

**Coltrane, S, and Hickman, N., 1992,** "The rhetoric of rights and needs: Moral discourse in the reform of child custody and child support laws", Social Problems, 39(4), pp. 401-420.

**Cohen, T. E., 1993,** "What do Fathers Provide?", in Hood, J. C., (Editor), Men, Work and Family, Newbury Park, CA: Sage.

**Colgan McCarthy, I., 1996,** Irish Family Studies: Selected Papers, Dublin: Family Studies Centre, University College Dublin.

**Coltrane, S., 1989,** "Household Labour and the Routine Production of Gender", Social Problems, Volume 36, pp. 473-490.

**Commission on the Family, 1996,** Strengthening Families for Life: Interim Report to the Minister for Social Welfare, Dublin: Commission on the Family, Department of Social Welfare.

**Commission on the Family, 1997,** Submission to the All-Party Oireachtas Committee on the Constitution, 25 March, Dublin: Commission on the Family, Department of Social Welfare.

**Connell, R. W., 1995,** Masculinities, Cambridge: Polity.

**Constitution Review Group, 1996,** Report of the Constitution Review Group, Dublin: the Stationery Office.

**Cork and Ross Family Centre 1995,** Domestic Violence Treatment Programme: Treatment for Violent Men, Cork and Ross Male Violence Project, 34 Paul Street, Cork.

**Council for Social Welfare, 1991,** The Rights of the Child: Irish Perspectives on the UN Convention,

Dublin: Council for Social Welfare.

**Council of Churches for Britain and Ireland, 1997,** Unemployment and the Future of Work: An Enquiry for the Churches, London: Council of Churches for Britain and Ireland.

**Council of Europe, 1995,** "Ireland" in Conference of European Ministers Responsible for Family Affairs, Twenty Fourth Session, Helsinki, Finland, 26-28 June, Strasbourg: Council of Europe.

**Coverman, S., and Sheley, J., 1986,** "Change in Men's Housework and Child Care Time, 1965-1975", Journal of Marriage and the Family, Volume 48, pp. 413-422.

**Cowan, C. and P., 1988,** "Working with Men Becoming Fathers: The Impact of a Couples Group Intervention", in Bronstein P., and Cowan C. and P. (Editors), Fatherhood Today, New York: John Wiley and Sons.

**Coward, R., 1983,** Patriarchal Precedents, London: Routledge and Keegan Paul.

**Crouter, A., Perry-Jenkins, M., Huston, T., McHale, S., 1987,** "Processes Underlying Father Involvement in Dual-earner and Single-Earner Families", Developmental Psychology, Volume 23, pp.431-440.

**Daly, K. J., 1995,** "Reshaping Fatherhood: Finding the Models", in Marsiglio, W., (Editor), Fatherhood: Contemporary Theory, Research, and Social Policy, London: Sage.

**Deane, M., 1994,** The Legacy of Locasta - A Maternal Metaphor, Unpublished.

**Department of Enterprise and Employment, 1996,** Growing and Sharing Our Employment: Strategy paper on the Labour Market, Dublin: Stationery Office.

**Department of Health, 1993, Report on Vital Statistics, 1990,** April, Compiled by the Central Statistics Office, Dublin: Stationery Office.

**Department of Health and Social Security 1995,** Child Protection: Messages from Research, London: HMSO.

**DeVault, M., 1991,** Feeding the Family, Chicago: University of Chicago Press.

**Doherty, D., 1996,** "Child Care and Protection: Protecting the Children - Supporting their Service Providers", in Ferguson, H., and McNamara, T., (Editors), Protecting Irish Children: Investigation, Protection and Welfare, special edition of Administration, Volume 44, Number 2, pp. 102-113.

**Drage Piechowski, L., 1992,** "Mental Health and Women's Multiple Roles in Families in Society", The Journal of Contemporary Human Sciences, March, pp.131-138.

**Drew, E., Emerek, R., and Mahon, E., 1995,** "Families, Labour Markets and Gender Roles" A Report on a European Research Workshop, Dublin: European Foundation for the Improvement of Living and Working Conditions.

**Dromey M., and Doherty, M., 1992,** "Fathers' Involvement with their Non-Marital Children", Workshop Conference Paper Presented to the Conference: Surviving Childhood Adversity, Trinity College Dublin, Dublin: Treoir: Federation of Services for Unmarried Parents and their Children.

**Eekelaar, J., and Clive, E., 1977,** Custody After Divorce, Oxford: Centre for Socio-Legal Studies.

**Employment Equality Agency, 1996,** Introducing Family-Friendly Initiatives in the Workplace, Researched and Written by Hugh Fisher, Dublin: Employment Equality Agency.

**Erikson, E., 1963,** Childhood and Society, Toronto: Norton.

**EU Directive on Parental Leave, 1996,** "Council Directive 96/34/EC of 3 June 1996 on the framework agreement on parental leave concluded by UNICE, CEEP and ETUC", Official Journal of the European Communities, No I 145/4, 19.6.96, Luxembourg: Office for Official Publications of the European Communities.

**Eurostat, 1996, Labour Force Survey: Results 1995,** Luxembourg: Office for Official Publications of the European Communities.

**Eurobarometer 39.0, 1993,** Europeans and the Family: Results of an Opinion Survey, December, Brussels: Commission of the European Communities, Directorate General V for Employment, Industrial Relations and Social Affairs.

**European Commission Network on Childcare, 1990,** Men as Carers for Children, Brussels: European Commission Network on Childcare.

**European Commission Network on Childcare, 1993,** Men as Carers: Report of an International Seminar in Ravenna, Italy, 21-22 May, Brussels: European Commission Network on Childcare.

**European Court of Human Rights, 1994,** "Judgement in the Case of Keegan v. Ireland", Strasbourg: European Court of Human Rights.

**Fahey, T., and Lyons, M., 1995,** Marital Breakdown and Family Law in Ireland, Oak Tree Press in association with The Economic and Social Research Institute.

**Farrington, D., P., and Hawkin, J.D.,** "Predicting Participation, Early Onset and Later Persistence in Officially Recorded Offending" in Criminal Behaviour and Mental Health, Volume 1, pp. 1-33.

**Featherstone, B., and Holloway, W., (Editors), 1997,** Motherhood and Ambivalence, London: Routledge.

**Ferguson, H., 1996a,** "Men's Issues and Changing Experiences of Masculinity in Ireland", in McCarthy, D., and Lewis R., (Editors), Man And Now: Changing Perspectives, Cork: Togher Family Centre.

**Ferguson, H., 1996b,** "Child Abuse as a Social Problem and the Development of the Child Protection System in the Republic of Ireland", in Ferguson, H., and McNamara, T., (Editors), Protecting Irish Children: Investigation, Protection and Welfare, Special Edition of Administration, Volume 44, Number 2.

**Ferguson, H., 1997a,** "Understanding Men and Masculinities", Paper presented at the Men and Intimacy Conference, St Patrick's College, Carlow, 22 February 1997.

**Ferguson, H. ,1997b,** "Woman Protection, Child Protection and the Implications of the Domestic Violence Act 1996 for Health Boards". A paper based on the findings of a research study commissioned by the Mid-Western Health Board, Department of Applied Social Studies, University College Cork.

**Ferguson, H., 1997c,** "Vicious circle: domestic violence and the law", Gazette: Journal of the Law Society of Ireland, Vol. 91, no 3.

**Ferguson, H., and Kenny, P., (Editors), 1995,** On Behalf of the Child: Child Welfare, Child Protection and the Child Care Act 1991, Dublin: A. & A. Farmar.

**Ferguson, H., and Synott, P., 1995,** "Intervention into Domestic Violence in Ireland: Developing Policy and Practice with Men who Batter", Administration, Volume 43, Number 3.

**Ferri, E., and Smith, K., 1996,** Parenting in the 1990s, London: Family Policy Studies Centre.

**Flower, P, and MacCannell, J., 1986,** Figuring Lacan: Criticism and the Cultural Unconscious, London and Sydney: Croom Helm.

**French, S., 1993,** "Introduction", in French, S., (Editor), Fatherhood, London: Virago Press, pp. 1-8.

**French, S., 1995,** "The Fallen Idol" in Moss, P., (Editor), Father Figures: Fathers in the Families of the 1990s, Edinburgh: HMSAO, pp. 1-6.

**Freud, S., 1954,** The Interpretation of Dreams, Standard Edition, Volumes 3,4, Hogarth Press.: London.

**Freud, S., 1966,** Standard Edition of the Complete Psychological Works of Sigmund Freud , The Hogarth Press and the Institute of Psychoanalysis: London.

**Freud, S., 1977,** On Sexuality, Vol. 7, Penguin Books.

**Freud, S., 1977,** 'The Infantile Genital Organisation: An Interpolation into the Theory of Sexuality'(1923), On Sexuality, Penguin Books.

**Freud, S., 1977,** 'The Dissolution of the Oedipus Complex' (1924) On Sexuality, Penguin Books.

**Freud, S., 1977,** 'Some Psychical Consequences of the Anatomical Distinction Between the Sexes', (1925) On Sexuality, Penguin Books.

Freud, S., 1977, 'Female Sexuality', (1931) On Sexuality, Penguin Books.

Freud, S., 1984, 'A Note on the Unconscious in Psychoanalysis' (1912), P.F.L. Vol. 11, London: Pelican Books.

Freud, S., 1977, Case Histories II P.F.L. vol. 9, Penguin Books, (first published 1924).

Furstenberg, F., and Cherlin, A., 1991, Divided Families: What Happens to Children When Parents Part?, Cambridge: Harvard University Press.

Furstenberg, F., and Nord, C., 1987, "Parenting Apart", Journal of Marriage and the Family, Volume 47, pp. 893-904.

Furstenberg, F., 1995, "Fathering in the Inner City: Paternal Participation and Public Policy", in Marsiglio, W., (Editor), Fatherhood: Contemporary Theory, Research, and Social Policy, London: Sage.

Fynes, B., Morrissey, T., Roche, W., Whelan, B., Williams, J., 1996, Flexible Working Lives: The Changing Nature of Working Time Arrangements in Ireland, Dublin: Oak Tree Press in association with Graduate School of Business, University College Dublin.

Gallagher C., 1986, The Function of the Father in the Family: Psychoanalytic Notes Studies (Summer).

Gallop, J., 1982, Feminism and Psychoanalysis, Macmillan.

Gallop, J., 1985, Reading Lacan, New York: Cornell.

Gerson, K., 1993, No Man's Land: Men's Changing Commitments to Family and Work, New York: Basic Books.

Gibson, J., 1992, "Non-Custodial Fathers and Access patterns" in Research Report, Family Court of Australia.

Giddens, A., 1991, Modernity and Self-Identity, Cambridge: Polity.

Giddens, A., 1992, The Transformation of Intimacy, Cambridge: Polity.

Giddens, A., 1994, Beyond Left and Right, Cambridge: Polity.

Glueck, S., and Glueck, E., 1950, Unravelling Juvenile Delinquency, Harvard: Harvard University Press.

Government of Ireland, 1996, Partnership 2000 for Inclusion, Employment and Competitiveness, Dublin: The Stationery Office.

Government of Ireland, 1997, Growing Our Employment - Sharing Our Growth: A Comprehensive Policy for Enterprise and Jobs, May, Dublin: The Stationery Office.

**Greenberger, E., and O'Neill, R., 1990,** "Parents' Concerns about their Child's Development: Implications for Fathers' and Mothers' Well-Being and Attitudes Towards Work", in Journal of Marriage and the Family, Volume 52, pp. 621-635.

**Griswold, R. L., 1993,** Fatherhood in America: A History, New York: Basic Books.

**Hanley, D., 1995,** "The Sweet Sorrow of Reconciled Partings" in Hyde, T., (Editor), Fathers and Sons, Dublin: Wolfhound Press, pp. 111-112.

**Hannan, D., and O'Riain, S., 1993,** Pathways to Adulthood in Ireland: Causes and Consequences of Success and Failure in Transitions Amongst Irish Youth, Paper Number 161, December, Dublin: The Economic and Social Research Institute.

**Hawkins, A., Christiansen, S.L., Pond Sargent, K., and Hill, E.J., 1995,** "Rethinking Fathers Involvement in Child Care: A Developmental Perspective", in Marsiglio, W., (Editor), Fatherhood: Contemporary Theory, Research, and Social Policy, London: Sage.

**Hawkins A., and Roberts, T-A., 1992,** "Designing a Primary Intervention to Help Dual-Earner Couples Share Housework and Childcare" in Family Relations, Volume 41, pp. 169-177.

**Hillman, J., 1996,** The Soul's Code: In Search of Character and Calling, New York: Random House.

**Hillman, J., 1994,** We've Had a Hundred Years of Psychotherapy and the World's Getting Worse, New York: Random House.

**Hochschild, A. R., with Manning A., 1989,** The Second Shift: Working Parents and the Revolution at Home, New York: Viking.

**Hooper, C., A., 1992,** Mothers Surviving Child Sexual Abuse, London: Routledge.

**Hornsby-Smith, M., and Whelan, C., 1994,** "Religious and Moral Values", in Whelan, C., (Editor), Values and Social Change in Ireland, Dublin: Gill and Macmillan, pp. 7-44.

**Hyde, T., (Editor), 1996,** Fathers and Sons, Dublin: Wolfhound.

**Ireland, 1997,** Labour Force Survey 1996, January, Dublin: Stationery Office.

**Ishii-Kuntz, M., 1995,** "Paternal Involvement and Perception toward Fathers' Roles: A comparison between Japan and the United States", in Marsiglio, W., (Editor), Fatherhood: Contemporary Theory, Research, and Social Policy, London: Sage.

**Ishii-Kuntz, M., and Coltrane, S., 1992,** "Predicting the Sharing of Household Labour: Are Parenting and Housework Distinct?", Sociological Perspectives, Volume 35, pp. 629-647.

**Jackson, B., 1984,** Fatherhood, London: Allen and Unwin.

**Jensen, A-M., 1993,** "Fathers and Children - the Paradox of Closeness and Distance" in Fathers in Families of Tomorrow, Report from the Conference held in Copenhagen, 17-18 June 1993, Copenhagen: The Ministry of Social Affairs.

**Kempeneers, M., and Lelievre, E., 1992,** Work and the Family in the Twelve EC States, Eurobarometer Number 34, Eurostat, Luxembourg: Office for the Official Publications of the European Community.

**Kelleher and Associates and O'Connor, M., 1995,** Making the Links, Dublin: Women's Aid.

**Kelly, N., 1995,** "Father's Legacy" in Hyde, T., (Editor), Fathers and Sons, Dublin: Wolfhound Press, p. 156.

**Kiernan, K., 1992,** "Men and Women at Work and at Home", in Jowell, R., et al (Editors), British Social Attitudes: the Ninth Report, Dartmouth: SCPR.

**Kiely, G., 1996,** "Fathers in Families" in Colgan McCarthy, I., (Editor), Irish Family Studies: Selected Papers, University College Dublin, pp. 147-158.

**Kimmel, M., 1994,** "Masculinity as Homophobia: Fear, Shame, and Silence in the Construction of Gender Identity", in Brod, H., and Kaufman, M., (Editors), Theorising Masculinities, London: Sage.

**Kimmel, M., (Editor) 1995,** The Politics of Manhood, Philadelphia: Temple University Press.

**Koch-Nielsen, 1987,** New Family Patterns: Divorces in Denmark, Booklet Number 23, Copenhagen: The Danish Institute for Social Research.

**Kolvin, I., Miller, F., Scott, D., Gatzanis, S., Fleeting, M., 1990,** Continuities of Deprivation, ESRC / DHSS Studies in Deprivation and Disadvantage Number 15, London: Avebury.

**Kraemer, S., 1995,** "Parenting Yesterday, Today and Tomorrow, in Utting, D., (Editor), Families and Parenting Conference Report: Proceedings of a Conference held in London, 26 September 1995, London: Family Policy Studies Centre.

**Lacan, J., 1977,** Ecrits: A selection, Tavistock, Routledge.

**Lacan, J.,1951,** "Intervention on Transference", in Mitchell, J., and Rose, J., (Editors) 1982, Feminine Sexuality, London: Macmillan.

**Lacan, J., 1958,** The Family, Unpublished , Translated by Cormac Gallagher.

**Lacan, J., 1953,** The Neurotics Individual Myth, Psych Quat, 1979 Trs. Evans.

**Lacan, J., 1973,** The Four Fundamental Concepts (Le Seminaire de Jacques Lacan, Paris) 1979, London: Penguin.

**Lamb, M., 1997,** "Fathers and Child Development: An Introductory Overview and Guide", in Lamb, M., (Editor), The Role of the Father in Child Development, Third Edition, New York: John Wiley and Sons, pp.1-18.

**Laplanche, J., and Pontalis, J.B., 1988,** The Language of Psychoanalysis, Karnac Books.

**Law Reform Commission, 1982,** Report on Illegitimacy, Dublin: Law Reform Commission.

**Law Reform Commission, 1996,** Family Courts, Dublin: Law Reform Commission.

**Leonard, H., 1995,** "The Stroke of a Pen" in Hyde, T., (Editor), Fathers and Sons, Dublin: Wolfhound Press, pp. 36-38.

**Leupnitz, D., 1986,** "A Comparison of Maternal, Paternal and Joint Custody", Journal of Divorce, Volume 9, Number 3, pp. 1-12.

**Lewis, C., 1986,** Becoming a Father, Milton Keynes: Open University Press.

**Lewis, C., et al, 1982,** "Father Participation through Childhood and its Relation to Career Aspirations of Delinquency" in, N., and McGuire, J., (Editors) Fathers: Psychological Perspectives, London: Junction Books.

**Lewis, C., 1993,** "Mother's and Fathers' Roles: Similar or Different?", in Fathers in Families of Tomorrow, Report from the Conference held in Copenhagen, 17-18 June 1993, Copenhagen: The Ministry of Social Affairs.

**Lewis, C., and O'Brien, M., 1987,** "Constraints on Fathers: Research, Theory and Clinical Practice", in Lewis, C., and O'Brien, M., (Editors), Reassessing Fatherhood, London: Sage, pp. 1-22.

**Louv, R., 1994,** Reinventing Fatherhood, Vienna: United Nations.

**Lowe, N., 1982,** "The Legal Status of Fathers - Past and Present" in McKee, L., and O'Brien, M., (Editors), The Father Figure.

**Maccoby EE., Depner, C., and Mnookin, RH., 1990,** "Co-Parenting in the Second Year after Divorce", Journal of Marriage and the Family, Volume 52, pp.141-155.

**Maccoby EE., and Mnookin, RH., 1992,** Dividing the Child: Social and Legal Dilemmas of Custody, Cambridge Massachusetts: Harvard University Press.

**Marks, E., de Courtivron, I (Ed), 1981,** New French Feminisms, Schocken Books.

**Marsiglio, W., 1995,** "Fathers' Diverse Life Course Patterns and Roles", in Marsiglio W., (Editor), Fatherhood: Contemporary Theory, Research, and Social Policy, London: Sage.

**McCarthy, D., and Lewis, R., 1996,** Man And Now: Changing Perspectives, Cork: Togher Family Centre.

**McCashin, A., 1993,** Lone Parents in the Republic of Ireland: Enumeration, Description and Implications for Social Security, Broadsheet Series, Paper Number 29, September, Dublin: The Economic and Social Research Institute.

**McCashin, A., 1996,** Lone Mothers in Ireland: A Local Study, Dublin: Oak Tree Press in association with the Combat Poverty Agency.

**McGuinness, C., 1993,** Report of the Kilkenny Incest Investigation, Dublin: Stationery Office.

**McKeown, K., 1997,** "Vocation Re-Defined" in McKeown K., and Arthurs, H., (Editors), Soul Searching: Personal Stories of the Search for Meaning in Modern Ireland, Dublin: Columba Press, pp. 91-97.

**McKeown, K., and Gilligan, R., 1991,** "Child Sexual Abuse in the Eastern Health Board Region of Ireland in 1988: An Analysis of 512 Confirmed Cases", in The Economic and Social Review, Volume 22, Number 2, January, pp.101-134.

**McKeown, K., Gilligan, R., Brannick, T., McGuane, B., Riordan, S., 1993,** Child Sexual Abuse in the Eastern Health Board Region, Ireland, 1988: A Statistical Analysis of all Suspected and Confirmed Cases of Child Sexual Abuse Known to the Social Work Teams in the Community Care Areas of the Eastern Health Board which were Open at any time in 1988. Dublin: Eastern Health Board.

**McLoyd, V., 1989,** "Socialisation and Development in a Changing Economy: The Effects of Paternal Job and Income Loss on Children" American Psychologist, Volume 44, pp.293-302.

**Milotte, M., 1997,** Banished Babies, Ireland: New Island Books.

**Millar, J., and Warman, A., 1996,** Family Obligations in Europe, , London: Family Policy Studies Centre.

**Milner, J., 1993,** "Avoiding Violent Men: The Gendered Nature of Child Protection Policy and Practice", in Ferguson, H., Gilligan, R., and Torode, R., (Editors), Surviving Childhood Adversity: Issues for Policy and Practice, Dublin: Social Studies Press.

**Milner, J., 1996,** "Men's Resistance to Social Workers", in Fawcett, B., Featherstone, B., Hearn, J., and Toft, C., (Editors), Violence and Gender Relations: Theories and Interventions, London: Sage.

**Mintel International Group Ltd, 1994,** Men 2000, London: Mintel International Group Ltd.

**Mitchell, J., 1974,** Psychoanalysis and Feminism, Penguin Books.

**Mitchell, J., Rose, J., 1982,** Jacques Lacan and the Ecole Freudienne: Female Sexuality, Macmillan Press Ltd.

**Moore, R., and Gilette, D., 1990,** King, Warrior, Magician, Lover: Rediscovering the Archtypes of the Mature Masculine, New York: HarperCollins Publishers.

**Morgan, P., 1966,** Who Needs Parents? The Effects of Childcare and Early Education on Children in Britain and the USA, London: the IEA Health and Welfare Unit.

**Moss, P., 1992,** "Foreword" to Ruxton, S., 'What's he doing at the family centre?': The dilemmas of men who care for children, A Research Report, London: National Children's Home.

**Moss, P., 1993,** "Strategies to Promote Fathers' Involvement in the Care and Upbringing of their Children: Placing Leave Arrangements in a Wider Context", in Fathers in Families of Tomorrow, Report from the Conference held in Copenhagen, 17-18 June 1993, Copenhagen: The Ministry of Social Affairs.

**Muller, J. P. and Richardson, W.J.,1982,** Lacan and Language: A Readers Guide to Ecrits, New York: International Universities Press, Inc.

**Murphy, M. ,1996,** "From Prevention to 'Family Support' and Beyond: Promoting the Welfare of Irish Children", in Ferguson, H., and McNamara T., (Editors), Protecting Irish Children: Investigation, Protection and Welfare, special edition of Administration, Volume 44, Number 2.

**National Economic and Social Council, 1996,** Strategy into the 21st Century, Report Number 99, Dublin: National Economic and Social Council.

**Newburn, T., and Stanko, B., 1994,** Just Boys Doing Business? Masculinities and Crime, London: Sage.

**Newsweek, 1997,** "The Death of Marriage? More European Women are having Children Out of Wedlock, and No One Seems to Mind", 20 January, New York: Newsweek.

**Nickel H., and Kocher, N., 1987,** "West Germany and German Speaking Countries" in Lamb, ME, The Father's Role: Cross Cultural Comparisons, Hillsdale NJ: Lawrence Erlbaum.

**Nolan, B., and Farrell, B., 1990,** Child Poverty in Ireland, Dublin: Combat Poverty Agency.

**O'Brien, M., and Jones, D., 1996,** "Fathers Through the Eyes of Their Children", in Bjrnberg U., and Kollind, A-K., (Editors), Men's Family Relations, Stockholm: Almqvist and Wiksell International.

**O'Hagan, K., 1997,** "The Problem of Engaging Men in Child Protection Work", British Journal of Social Work, Volume 27, pp. 25-42.

**Olds, S., 1992,** "Saturn" in Bly, R., Hillman, J., and Meade, M., (Editors), The Rag and Bone Shop of the Heart: Poems for Men, New York: HarperCollins Publishers, p. 128.

**O'Mahony, P., 1997,** Mountjoy Prisoners: A Sociological and Criminological Profile, Dublin: Stationery Office.

**Ottosen, 1996,** "Relationships Between Non-Resident Fathers and Their Children in Denmark" in Bjrnberg U., and Kollind, A-K., (Editors), Men's Family Relations, Stockholm: Almqvist and Wiksell International.

**Owen, M., and Cox, M., 1988,** "The Transition to Parenthood", in Gottfried, A., Gottfried, A., and Bathurst, K., (Editors), Maternal Employment, Family Environment and Children's Development: Infancy Through the School Years, Plenum Press.

**Parental Equality, 1997,** The Custody Crisis: A Submission to the Minister for Equality and Law Reform, February, Dundalk: Parental Equality.

**Pleck, E., and Pleck, J., 1997,** "Fatherhood Ideals in the United States: Historical Dimensions", in Lamb, M., (Editor), The Role of the Father in Child Development, Third Edition, New York: John Wiley and Sons, pp. 33-48.

**Pleck, J., 1997,** "Paternal Involvement: Levels, Sources and Consequences", in Lamb, M., (Editor), The Role of the Father in Child Development, Third Edition, New York: John Wiley and Sons, pp. 66-103.

**Pleck, J., 1993,** "Are 'family-supportive' employer policies relevant to men?", in Hood, J. C., (Editor), Men, Work and Family, Newbury Park, CA: Sage.

**Polikoff, N., 1983,** "Gender and child-custody determinants: Exploding the myths", in Diamond, I., (Editor), Families, politics and public policy: A feminist dialogue on women and the state, New York: Longman.

**Pruett, K., 1983,** "Infants of Primary Nurturing Fathers" in Psychoanalytic Study of the Child, Volume 38, pp. 257-277.

**Pruett, K., 1985,** "Children of the fathermothers: Infants of Primary Nurturing Fathers" in Call, J., Galenson, E., Tyson, R., (Editors), Frontiers of Infant Psychiatry, Volume 2, New York: Basic Books, pp.375-380.

**Pruzan, V., 1993,** "The Modern Family - A New Generation of Parents?", in Fathers in Families of Tomorrow, Report from the Conference held in Copenhagen, 17-18 June 1993, Copenhagen: The Ministry of Social Affairs.

**Radin, N., 1982,** "Primary Care-giving and Role-Sharing Fathers", in Lamb, M., (Editor), Non-traditional Families: Parenting and Child Development, pp. 173-204, Hillsdale, NJ: Erlbaum.

**Radin, N., 1994,** "Primary Care-giving Fathers in Intact Families", in Gottfried, A., and Gottfried, A., (Editors), Redefining Families: Implications for Children's Development, New York: Plenum, pp. 11-54.

**Real, T., 1997,** I Don't Want to Talk About It: Overcoming The Secret Legacy of Male Depression, New York: Scribner.

**Richards, M., 1982,** "Post-Divorce Arrangements for Children: A Psychological Perspective", Journal of Social Welfare Law, pp133-151.

**Richardson, V., 1991,** "Decision-Making by Unmarried Mothers, The Irish Journal of Psychology, Volume 12, Number 2, pp. 165-181.

**Richardson, V., 1995,** "Reconciliation of Family Life and Working Life", in Colgan McCarthy, I., (Editor), Irish Family Studies: Selected Papers, University College Dublin, pp. 127-146.

**Roberts, C., 1996,** "The Place of Marriage in a Changing Society", Presentation to the Lord Chancellor's Conference: Supporting Marriage into the Next Century, 3 April, Working Paper Number 2, London: Family Policy Studies Centre.

**Robins, L., 1966,** Deviant Children Growing Up, New York: Robert E., Krieger.

**Robinson, M., 1995,** Family Transformation Through Divorce and Re-Marriage, London: Routledge (Quoted in The Irish Times, Tuesday 28 March 1995).

**Rooney, D., 1994,** Dora, Desire and the Oedipus Complex. Unpublished.

**Rutter, M., 1994,** Clinical Implications of Attachment Concepts, Retrospect and Prospect, Bowlby Memorial Lecturer.

**Ruxton, S., 1992,** 'What's he doing at the family centre?': The dilemmas of men who care for children, A Research Report, London: National Children's Home.

**Rylands, J., 1995**, A Study of Parenting Programmes in Ireland: Exploration of Needs and Current Provision, Dublin: National Children's Centre/Department of Health.

**Sanik, M., 1981**, "Division of Household Work: A Decade Comparison, 1967-1977", Home Economics Journal, Volume 10, pp.175-180.

**Sandqvist, K., 1987,** "Swedish Family Policy and the Attempt to Change Paternal Roles, in Lewis, C., and O'Brien, M., (Editors), Reassessing Fatherhood, London: Sage, pp. 144-160.

**Sandqvist, K., 1992,** "Sweden's Sex-Role Scheme and the Attempt to Change Paternal Roles", in Lewis, S., and Israeli, D., and Hootsmans, H., (Editors), Dual-Earner Families: International Perspectives, London: Sage, pp. 80-98.

**Schneiderman, S., 1986,** Returning to Freud, Clinical Psychoanalysis in the School of Lacan, Ed. S Schneiderman, New York: Yale University Press.

**Schultheis, F., 1993**, "Perspectives: Towards Socio-Political Recognition of Paternity in the Countries of the Community" in Fathers in Families of Tomorrow, Report from the Conference held in Copenhagen, 17-18 June 1993, Copenhagen: The Ministry of Social Affairs, pp.230-237.

**Second Commission on the Status of Women, 1993,** Report to Government, January, Dublin: Stationery Office.

**Segal, L., 1990,** Slow Motion: Changing masculinities, changing men, ...

**Seltzer, J., 1991,** "Relationships Between Fathers and Children Who Live Apart", Journal of Marriage and the Family, Volume 53, pp.79-102.

**Shiel, D., 1995,** "My Father" in Hyde, T., (Editor), Fathers and Sons, Dublin: Wolfhound Press, pp. 157-169.

**Skynner, R., 1995,** Family Matters: A Guide to Healthier and Happier Relationships, London: Methuen.

**Smith, R., 1996,** "The Life of a Men's Group", in McCarthy, D., and Lewis, R., (Editors), Man And Now: Changing Perspectives, Cork: Togher Family Centre.

**Social Europe, 1994,** The European Union and the Family, 1/94, Brussels: Directorate-General for Employment, Industrial Relations and Social Affairs, European Commission.

**Sternberg, K. J., 1997,** "Fathers: the Missing Parents in Research on Family Violence" in Lamb ME., (Editor), The Role of the Father in Child Development, New York: Wiley.

**Swedin, G., 1995,** "Modern Swedish Fatherhood: Challenges Which Offer Great Opportunities" in Men on Men: Eight Swedish Men's Personal Views on Equality, Masculinity and Parenthood. A Contribution by the Swedish Government to the Fourth World Conference on Women in Beijing 1995. Sweden: Ministry of Health and Social Affairs, pp. 112-131.

**Task Force on Violence Against Women, 1997,** Report, Office of the Tánaiste, Dublin: Stationery Office.

**Tolson, A., 1977,** The Limits to Masculinity, London: Tavistock.

**Utting, D., Bright, J., and Henricson, C., 1993,** Crime and the Family: Improving Child-Rearing and Preventing Delinquency, Occasional paper 16, London: Family Policy Studies Centre.

**Volling, B., and Belsky, J., 1991,** "Multiple Determinants of Father Involvement During Infancy in Dual-Earner and Single-Earner Families", Journal of Marriage and the Family, Volume 53, pp. 461-474.

**Wadsworth, M., 1979,** The Roots of Delinquency, London: Martin Robertson.

**Wallerstein, J., and Kelly, J., 1980,** Surviving the Break-up, New York: Basic Books.

**Walzer, S., 1996,** Thinking About the Baby: Gender and Divisions of Infant Care, Social Problems, Volume 43, Number 2.

**Weitzman, L., 1985,** The divorce revolution: The unexpected social and economic consequences for women and children in America, New York: Free Press.

**West, D., 1982,** Delinquency: Its Roots, Careers and Prospects, London: Heineman.

**West, D., and Farrington, D., 1973,** Who Becomes Delinquent, London: Heinemann.

**Wheelock, J., 1991,** Husbands at Home: The Domestic Economy in a Post-Industrial Society, London: Routledge.

**Whelan C., and Fahey, T., 1994,** "Marriage and the Family", in Whelan, C., (Editor), Values and Social Change in Ireland, Dublin: Gill and Macmillian, pp. 45-81.

**Whelan, C., Hannan, D., and Creighton, S., 1991,** Unemployment, Poverty and Psychological Distress, Dublin: The Economic and Social Research Institute.

**Wilson, J., and Neckerman, K., 1986,** "Poverty and Family Structure: The Widening Gap Between Evidence and Public Policy Issues", in Danzinger, S., and Weinberg, D., (Editors), Fighting Poverty, Cambridge, MA: Harvard university Press.

**Winnicott, D., 1964,** The Child, the Family and the Outside World. Penguin Books.

**Zorza, J., 1992,** "Friendly Parent Provisions in Custody Determinations", Clearing House Review, US: National Centre on Women and Family Law Inc.

Chapter Nineteen **Child-care Arrangments in Ireland - A Report to the Commission on the Family June 1997 - James Williams and Claire Collins Economic and Social Research Institute**

CONTENTS | Page

# CHAPTER ONE BACKGROUND AND METHODOLOGY

## 1.1      Introduction

In this chapter we consider the background to the report as well as the methodology adopted for collecting and analysing the data. In section 1.2 we discuss the objectives of the study before moving on in section 1.3 to contextualise the report by providing some details on the most recently available figures regarding the number of children in each single year group aged 0-12 years as well as the structure of the total household population with reference to the total number of children in the relevant age category. In section 1.4 we discuss methodological issues including the questionnaire; sample design; sample size; and the re-weighting of the data prior to analysis.

## 1.2      Objectives

The purpose of the report is to provide the Commission on the Family (the Commission) with background information on the care arrangements of children and their families focusing in particular on the child-care services used by parents who work full-time in the home as well as by those who work outside the home. Of particular interest is the back-up child-care arrangements used by households in the event of their usual arrangements not being available. The Commission's interest is restricted to children aged 12 years or less.

Central to this exercise was the collection of information on the child-care arrangements at various points throughout the day in respect of each child in the household who was aged 12 years or less. This required that interviews be carried out with the parents of children in the relevant age category and that a detailed diary of each child's whereabouts on each weekday be recorded. From the outset of the study the completion of the time diaries was seen as the key to much of the information in which the Commission had an interest.

## 1.3      Size and Structure of the Population

The relevant population is the set of children aged 12 years or less as well as the households in which they reside. The most recently available information on the size and structure of the population aged 12 years or less comes from the 1991 *Census of Population*. Table 1.1 presents a breakdown of the total number of children by single year of age and gender. From this we can see that there was a total of 805,087 children recorded in the 1991 *Census of Population*. Just over 51.3 per cent of these were male, 48.7 per cent female. One can see that each of the youngest three age groups accounted for approximately 6.5 per cent of all children in the relevant age group while each year group 3 to 7 accounted for between 7 and 7.8 per cent. Finally, the remaining single year age groups aged 8 to 12 each accounted for between 8-9 per cent of the relevant population. In general, there is little difference between boys and girls in terms of their age structure.

Table 1.2 considers the total population of households classified by the number of children aged 12 years or less who reside therein. There is a total of 1,155,000 households in the population as a whole. From the table we can see that just over two-thirds (772,000) of the households have no children aged 12 years or less. A further 25.7 per cent has 1 or 2 children in the relevant age category and the 7.5 per cent contain 3 or more. This means that there is a total of 383,200 *households* in the country which contain children aged 12 years or less and it is to this subset of the population that the data collected in the course of the survey have been re-weighted.

**Table 1.1:**

**Number of Children Aged 0-12 years in 1991**

| Age Last Birthday (Years) | Males No. | % | Females No. | % | Persons No. | % |
|---|---|---|---|---|---|---|
| 0 | 27,390 | 6.6 | 25,654 | 6.5 | 53,044 | 6.6 |
| 1 | 27,110 | 6.6 | 25,837 | 6.6 | 52,947 | 6.6 |
| 2 | 27,054 | 6.5 | 25,668 | 6.5 | 52,722 | 6.5 |
| 3 | 28,574 | 6.9 | 27,512 | 7.0 | 56,086 | 7.0 |
| 4 | 30,436 | 7.4 | 28,508 | 7.3 | 58,944 | 7.3 |
| 5 | 30,799 | 7.4 | 29,522 | 7.5 | 60,321 | 7.5 |
| 6 | 31,417 | 7.6 | 29,499 | 7.5 | 60,916 | 7.6 |
| 7 | 32,420 | 7.8 | 30,692 | 7.8 | 63,112 | 7.8 |
| 8 | 33,727 | 8.2 | 32,181 | 8.2 | 65,908 | 8.2 |
| 9 | 34,983 | 8.5 | 33,263 | 8.5 | 68,246 | 8.5 |
| 10 | 36,829 | 8.9 | 34,556 | 8.8 | 71,385 | 8.9 |
| 11 | 37,201 | 9.0 | 34,806 | 8.9 | 72,007 | 8.9 |
| 12 | 35,240 | 8.5 | 34,209 | 8.7 | 69,449 | 8.6 |
| Total | 413,180 | 100.0 | 391,907 | 100.0 | 805,087 | 100.0 |

Source: Census of Population, 1991.

## Table 1.2

**Distribution of Households Classified by Number of Children Aged 12 Years or Less**

| Children Aged 12 Years or Less | Number of Households | % |
|---|---|---|
| | (000's) | |
| None | 771.8 | 66.8 |
| One | 162.5 | 14.1 |
| Two | 133.9 | 11.6 |
| Three | 61.7 | 5.3 |
| Four | 18.9 | 1.6 |
| Five | 4.4 | 0.4 |
| Six or More | 1.8 | 0.2 |
| Total | 1,155 | 100.0 |

## 1.4 Methodology

### 1.4.1 The Questionnaire

The questionnaire was designed with a view to collecting information in seven broad areas. First, we recorded details on the number, age and name of all children aged 12 years or less who lived in the household. Second, we completed the time-diary in respect of each of these children. In completing this the parent was presented with a list of 8 possible response codes for child-care arrangements as follows:

A.  At school;

B.  Parent and Child or Mother and Toddler group (parent stays with the child);

C.  Any form of nursery, crèche, kindergarten, Montessori or other pre-school (child is left);

D.  Child-Minder's home;

E.  At home with a child-minder, nanny, au pair or other non-relative;

F.  Being cared for in a relative's home - not the child's home;

G.  At home with their parent or other relative;

H.  At home on their own.

The parent was then asked to say into which category each of their children aged 12 years or less fell during various periods on each weekday preceding the survey. The periods in question were 9.00 a.m.-1.00 p.m.; 1.00-3.00 p.m.; 3.00-5.00 p.m. and 5.00-7.00 p.m. In cases where the child-care code changed at some point in the course of the time periods in question the parent was instructed to assign the code which was relevant throughout the plurality of the period. For example, if a child attended school between 9.00 a.m. to 1.30 p.m. after which (s)he was cared for at home by a parent, Code A (At School) would have been assigned for the 9.00 a.m.-1.00 p.m. period and code G (At home with their parent or other relative) for the 1.00-3.00 p.m. period, even though the first 30 minutes of that period would actually have been spent in school. Third, we collected details on who usually minded the child(ren) during school holidays (in cases where there were school-going children aged 12 years or less in the household). Fourth, we recorded information on the incidence of households using child-minding services in a child-minder's home as well as details on back-up care arrangements in the event of the child-minder not being able to look after the child(ren) due to the minder's illness or other unforeseen events. Fifth, the questionnaire considered the extent to which households used the services of a child-minder, nanny or other non-relative in the child's own home, as well as back-up care arrangements. Sixth, several aspects of the use of nursery/crèche/kindergarten/Montessori or other pre-school were considered. These included the number of children and pupils in the nursery/crèche etc.; the costs involved and back-up care arrangements used in the event of the pre-school not being able to provide care arrangements due to unforeseen circumstances. Finally, standard classificatory details on age, economic status, level of educational attainment etc. of the parents were collected.

### 1.4.2    Sample Design and Sample Size

The questionnaire used in the survey was administered as a supplement to the ESRI's on-going monthly EU Consumer Survey. The Consumer Survey has been carried out at the Institute since the mid-1970s on behalf of DGII (Economic and Financial Affairs). The purpose of that survey is to measure people's opinion about current economic trends and to assess consumer's short- and medium-term purchasing intentions. Issues addressed include perception of past and future trends in the general economic situation; in consumer prices; in the financial situation in respondent households etc. For the last 15 years the survey has been used very successfully as a vehicle for carrying out supplementary surveys on a wide range of issues. It was on this basis that it was used to collect the information for the Commission on the Family.

The sample design used in the monthly survey is based on a two-stage clustered sample using the electoral register as a population frame. A preliminary sample is selected using the ESRI's computerised random sampling system known as RANSAM.[1] A total of 46 primary sampling points or clusters are selected in each of the monthly rounds of the survey. The electoral register is used as the population frame. The basic unit in the register is the polling book. Each book is made up of a collection of portions of District Electoral Divisions (DEDs). At the first stage of sample selection the electoral register is essentially re-written so that the case becomes the DEDs. The population across DEDs is aggregated up to a pre-specified minimum cluster-size threshold. These initial clusters form the Primary Sampling Units (PSUs) for the first stage of sample selection. The second stage of sample selection relates to the individuals (electors) from within each of the primary selection units (aggregates of DEDs).

The survey for the Commission on the Family was carried with the Consumer Survey in November and December 1996 as well as February 1997. It was necessary to conduct the survey in three rounds because the target population of households which are of relevance to the Commission's interests represent only one-third of all households in the State. We saw from Table 1.2 above that two-thirds of households do not contain children aged 12

---

1    For a description of this system see Whelan B.J. (1979). "RANSAM: A Random Sample Design for Ireland". The Economic and Social Review, Vol 10, No., 2, pp. 169-174

years or less. Consequently, the Commission's survey is not of relevance to just over two-thirds of households in the country as a whole. One would expect, therefore, that although the total achieved sample in *each* round of the survey is of the order of 1,425 households, approximately two-thirds of these would not contain children in the relevant age category. It was necessary, therefore, to carry out the survey over three months so as to generate a sufficiently large sample of households which contained children in the relevant age group. Table 1.3 shows that over the three months of November, December and February[2] the total number of households interviewed was 4,276. A total of 1,278 of these contained children aged 12 years or less and it was this subgroup which was analysed for the report.

## Table 1.3
### Achieved Sample Size in Each of the Three Rounds of the Survey

|  | Total Households Interviewed | Households With Children 0-12 Years |
|---|---|---|
| November | 1450 | 485 |
| December | 1300 | 378 |
| February | 1526 | 415 |
| Total | 4276 | 1278 |

1.4.3   Interviewing Methodology and Timing

The survey was carried out by the Institute's own panel of interviewers on a so-called mixed-mode basis. This means interviewing is carried out by a mix of both telephone surveying and personally administered face-to-face interviewing. Each of the 46 primary sampling units represents a geographically restricted area. Each is inspected and linked to the telephone directory. A telephone stem or root for each of the areas in question is then selected. This stem is generated at random for the area in question. The stem represents a valid number for the area, minus the last two digits. In Dublin, for example, 'phone numbers contain seven digits. Consequently, the stem in Dublin would be a randomly selected five-digit number. The last two digits of the number are added to the stem. These run in sequence from 00 to 99. This provides the interviewer with a potential maximum of 100 'phone numbers for each of the geographical clusters in question. The interviewer 'phones these numbers until a total of 34 interviews are completed on the 'phone.[3] If an interviewer exhausts his/her supply of 'phone numbers,[4] a second random stem is supplied and the procedure continues. When conducting the 'phone interviews, the interviewer also enforces a set of quota controls on potential respondents. These controls ensure that the sample of persons conforms with the structure of the population according to age, sex and principal economic status. This helps to minimise bias according to the characteristics of the respondent. For example, females may have a higher probability than males of completing a survey over the 'phone etc. Telephone interviews are conducted in the evenings and also at weekends to avoid under-sampling of those whose principal economic status is "at work

---

2    The survey was not conducted in January as the Christmas school holidays would disrupt the care arrangments for the first week or so in the New Year.

3    This number may fluctuate up or down by a few interviews

4    This could happen if, by chance, the stem was located in a highly industrialised area and most of the numbers formed by it were not those of private households

outside the home". The third dimension of the quota controls mentioned above also helps to minimise bias from this source.

In addition to conducting the 'phone interviews in the selected clusters, interviewers also attempt to carry out personally administered questionnaires on the respondents directly sampled from the electoral register. A total of 32 respondents were selected from each of 46 clusters. Each of the named respondents is contacted by the interviewer. A filter question on whether or not the respondent owns a 'phone is asked. If he/she owns a 'phone (i.e., lives in a private household which had a 'phone) then the personally administered interview is not carried out. If the named elector does not have a 'phone the interview is completed on a face to face basis.

Interviewing was conducted on the survey between the 1st and 16th of each of the months in question.

### 1.4.4    Re-weighting the Data

All sample surveys can be adversely affected by bias from a number of sources. Among the more important of these are bias resulting from sample design effects and that related to differential non-response among various subgroups in the target sample. In other words, certain subgroups may display a greater propensity than others to participate in the survey. To ensure representativeness of the data it is necessary to adjust the composition of the effective sample in such a way as to eliminate any identifiable bias which may have arisen from either of these two sources. This is achieved by re-weighting the data so as to ensure that the structure of the sample (according to key classificatory variables which are known to be most closely correlated with our research objectives) corresponds with the known structure of the population as derived from external independent sources. In analysing the data collected in the Commission's survey it was most important that the size and structure of households in the sample conformed with that of the population as a whole. Accordingly, the data were re-weighted on the basis of number of adults in the household and number of children aged 12 years or less. This weight was used in deriving the household-level estimates discussed in Chapter 3, 4 and 5.

The analysis outlined in Chapter 2 is presented at the level of the *child* rather than the *household*. In other words, the unit of analysis was changed from the household to the children aged 12 years or less who lived in the households. In undertaking this analysis the *household-level* weight mentioned above was associated with each *child* in the household. After this *household-level* weight was applied to the *child-level data* a minor adjustment was made to the corresponding grossed totals for single year of age to ensure that the re-weighted *child-level* figures were consistent with those published in the *1991 Census of Population*.[5] This type of re-weighting procedure is standard statistical practice in quantitative surveys of this nature.

All figures presented in the report - at both household and child-levels - have thus been re-weighted to ensure that the structure of the sample (at both household and child levels) conforms with the corresponding population structure.

---

5    The 1991 Census of Population, is as yet, the most recently available service of information on total number of children by single year of age.

We now turn in Chapter 2 to a consideration of the child-care arrangements at the level of the child based on the time diaries collected in the questionnaire.

## CHAPTER 2   CARE ARRANGEMENTS FOR CHILDREN AGED 12 YEARS OR LESS

### 2.1.   Introduction

In this chapter we examine where children aged 12 years or less are cared for at various times throughout the day in the week preceding the survey. In the course of the questionnaire parents were asked to say where each of their children aged 12 years or less were being cared for over the periods 9.00 a.m. - 1.00 p.m; 1.00 - 3.00 p.m.; 3.00 - 5.00 p.m. and 5.00 - 7.00 p.m. on each weekday in the week preceding the survey. Respondents were presented with a range of eight potential outcome categories as follows:

A.     At school;

B.     In Parent & Child or Mother & Toddler Group (where parent stays with child);

C.     In any form of Nursery, Crèche, Kindergarten, Montessori or Other Pre-School (where child is left);

D.     In a Child-Minder's Home;

E.     At home with a Child-Minder, Nanny, Au-Pair or Other Non-Relative;

F.     Being cared for in a Relative's Home - not the child's home;

G.     At home with their parent or other relative;

H.     At home on their own.

When the range of outcome codes was explained to the parent (s)he was asked to say into which category each of his/her child(ren) aged 12 years or less fell in each of the time periods over the five days in question. In cases where a child's activity status code changed in the course of one of the time periods in question the parent was instructed to assign the activity which was relevant throughout the plurality of the period. For example, if a child attended school between 9.00 a.m. to 1.30 p.m., after which (s)he was cared for at home by a parent, Code A (At School) would have been assigned for the 9.00 a.m. - 1.00 p.m. period and Code G (At home with their parent or other relative) for the 1.00 -3.00 p.m. period, even though the first 30 minutes of that period would actually have been spent in school. As noted in Section 1.4.4 above, all data in the report have been grossed in line with figures from the most recently available Labour Force Survey and Census of Population as outlined in Table 2.1 below.[6]

Two main aspects of the activity patterns of children in the relevant age groups are presented below. First, we examine variations in care/activity patterns by age of child and, secondly, we consider broad regional variations as between Dublin and the rest of the country. To facilitate presentation and discussion, the figures presented below relate only to the Monday preceding the survey. This is taken as representative of activity patterns in any day of the week. The reader is advised that a full breakdown of activity patterns in each of the other four days of the week preceding the survey can be found in Appendix Tables 2.2A to 2.2D at the back of the report.

---

6    The grossed sample totals presented in some of the following tables may diverge marginally from the figures in Table 2.1 due to a small number of missing values in respect of some of the classificatory variables.

**Table 2.1**

**Total Number of Children Aged 12 Years or Less in Each Single Year Age Category in 1991**

| Age Last Birthday | Number | Per Cent of Those Aged 12 Yrs or less | Age Last Birthday | Number | Per Cent of Those Aged 12 Yrs or less |
|---|---|---|---|---|---|
| | | (Per Cent) | | | (Per Cent) |
| 0 | 53,044 | 6.6 | 7 | 63,112 | 7.8 |
| 1 | 52,947 | 6.6 | 8 | 65,908 | 8.2 |
| 2 | 52,722 | 6.5 | 9 | 68,246 | 8.5 |
| 3 | 56,086 | 7.0 | 10 | 71,385 | 8.9 |
| 4 | 58,944 | 7.3 | 11 | 72,007 | 8.9 |
| 5 | 60,321 | 7.5 | 12 | 69,449 | 8.6 |
| 6 | 60,916 | 7.6 | Total | 805,087 | 100.0 |

Source:  Census of Population, 1991.

## 2.2 Variations in Care Arrangements by Age of Child

Table 2.2 provides information on the distribution of children aged 12 years or less classified by age cohort and activity pattern on the Monday preceding the survey. A five-fold breakdown by age cohort is presented as follows: 0-1 year; 2-3 years; 4 years; 5 years; 6-12 years. The eight-fold activity classification discussed in the previous section is used. It is clear from the table, however, that virtually none of the respondents opted for the Mother & Toddler category when describing the activity pattern of their children. One possible explanation for this may be that this type of activity (in which the parent stays with the child(ren)) may be of such a short-term nature (e.g. 30-60 minutes) that it would fail to register as the plurality of any of the time periods specified in the questionnaire.

### 2.2.1 Children Aged 0-1 Years

From Table 2.2 one can see that in the period 9.00 a.m. - 1.00 p.m. a total of 74.7 per cent (79,200) of children in this age category were being cared for in their own home by their parent or other relative. The next most frequently occurring response category was Child-Minder's home which accounted for 12.5 per cent (13,200) of children in the age group while a further 5.1 per cent (5,400) were being cared for in their own home by a non-relative - child minder/nanny etc. A total of 4.7 per cent (5,000) were being minded in a relative's home, while only 3.1 per cent (3,300) of the children in this youngest age-group were being cared for in some form of nursery/crèche/kindergarten or other pre-school.

In general, if one examines changes in this pattern throughout the day one can see that the

FINAL REPORT OF THE COMMISSION ON THE FAMILY

numbers in care categories outside the home decrease slightly between 1.00 - 3.00 and 3.00 - 5.00 p.m. with a marked fall in the incidence of care arrangements outside the home in all categories by 5.00 - 7.00 p.m. By that period just over 96 per cent (102,000) of children aged 0-1 year are at home with a parent or relative while a further 1.6 per cent (1,700) are at home with a non relative. The remaining 1.8 per cent (1,900) are being cared for in a child-minder's home.

### 2.2.2 Children Aged 2-3 years

The table shows that almost two-thirds (69,600) of children in the age group 2-3 years are at home with their parent(s) or other relative between 9.00 a.m. - 1.00 p.m. One can see, however, that the nursery/crèche/kindergarten/montessori or other pre-school arrangement assumes a much greater importance for children in this age category accounting for a total of 19.9 per cent (21,600). The role of child-minders (particularly those who work in the child's home) has fallen somewhat for this age-group as compared with the 0-1 year old. Just under 2 per cent (2,175) children aged 2-3 years are cared for in their own home by a minder, compared with 5.1 per cent of children in the youngest age category.

The data show that there is a sharp drop in the use of nursery/crèche etc. facilities by the 1.00-3.00 period (by which time they account for 5.7 per cent (6,200) of children in the relevant age group). The numbers being cared for in a child-minder's home or in the home of a relative increase marginally between 1.00 - 3.00 p.m.

### 2.2.3 Children Aged 4 Years

From this section of the table one can see that a total of 49.1 per cent of 4 year olds were classified as being "At School" by their parent in the period 9.00 a.m. - 1.00 p.m. This represents 28,900 children in this age category. A further 25.6 per cent (15,100) are in nursery, crèche, kindergarten etc. while 4.2 per cent (2,500) are being minded outside the home in a child-minder's home and 1.5 per cent (900) in their own home by a non-relative or child-minder. A total of 17.6 per cent (10,400) were being cared for at home by their parent or relative and the remaining 2.0 per cent (1,200) in a relative's home.

One can see that as the day progresses the percentage "At School" falls to 30 per cent by the 1.00 - 3.00 p.m. period while the percentage at nursery/crèche etc. falls to 3.6 per cent - just over 2,100. The role of child minding services (both within and without the child's home) assumes an increased importance - rising from 4.2 per cent to 8.2 per cent for child minding services outside the home and from 1.5 to 3.2 per cent for similar such services within the child's own home. Just over half (30,300) of the children in this age group are cared for at home by a parent or other relative in the 1.00 - 3.00 p.m. period.

By the 3.00 - 5.00 p.m. period we can see that a total of 13.6 per cent (8,000) of 4 year olds are being cared for by minders - 10.3 per cent in their own home and 3.3 per cent in the child-minder's home. At this time just under 82 per cent of children in this age group are being cared for at home.

**Table 2.2**

**Distribution of CHILDREN Aged 12 Years or Less Classified by (i) Age Cohort and (ii) Where They Were Cared for At Different Times of the Day in the Monday Preceding the Survey**

AGE COHORT OF CHILD

| | 0-1 Year (Per Cent) | | | | 2-3 Years (Per Cent) | | | | 4 Years (Per Cent) | | | | 5 Years (Per Cent) | | | | 6-12 Years (Per Cent) | | | |
|---|---|---|---|---|---|---|---|---|---|---|---|---|---|---|---|---|---|---|---|---|
| | 9.00-1.00 | 1.00-3.00 | 3.00-5.00 | 5.00-7.00 | 9.00-1.00 | 1.00-3.00 | 3.00-5.00 | 5.00-7.00 | 9.00-1.00 | 1.00-3.00 | 3.00-5.00 | 5.00-7.00 | 9.00-1.00 | 1.00-3.00 | 3.00-5.00 | 5.00-7.00 | 9.00-1.00 | 1.00-3.00 | 3.00-5.00 | 5.00-7.00 |
| At School | 0.0 | 0.0 | 0.0 | 0.0 | 0.3 | 0.0 | 0.0 | 0.0 | 49.1 | 30.0 | 0.0 | 0.0 | 99.3 | 78.4 | 1.1 | 0.0 | 99.3 | 97.6 | 3.1 | 0.0 |
| Mother & Toddler Group | 0.0 | 0.0 | 0.0 | 0.0 | 0.7 | 0.0 | 0.0 | 0.0 | 0.0 | 0.0 | 0.0 | 0.0 | 0.0 | 0.0 | 0.0 | 0.0 | 0.0 | 0.0 | 0.0 | 0.0 |
| Nursery/Crèche/Kindergarten/Montessori/Other Pre-School | 3.1 | 1.8 | 1.4 | 0.0 | 19.9 | 5.7 | 3.1 | 0.8 | 25.6 | 3.6 | 1.0 | 0.0 | 0.0 | 0.5 | 1.6 | 0.5 | 0.0 | 0.0 | 0.1 | 0.0 |
| Child Minder's Home | 12.5 | 12.1 | 11.3 | 1.8 | 10.1 | 12.5 | 9.3 | 1.3 | 4.2 | 8.2 | 10.3 | 2.5 | 0.0 | 1.6 | 4.6 | 1.1 | 0.0 | 0.1 | 2.9 | 0.8 |
| At Home with Non-Relative | 5.1 | 4.6 | 4.3 | 1.6 | 1.9 | 1.9 | 1.9 | 1.0 | 1.5 | 3.2 | 3.3 | 0.6 | 0.0 | 0.5 | 3.9 | 2.2 | 0.1 | 0.1 | 3.7 | 1.5 |
| Relative's Home | 4.7 | 5.1 | 3.9 | 0.0 | 3.1 | 5.0 | 4.4 | 0.3 | 2.0 | 3.7 | 3.7 | 0.6 | 0.0 | 1.0 | 3.1 | 1.0 | 0.1 | 0.3 | 2.9 | 0.4 |
| At Home with Parent/Relative | 74.7 | 76.4 | 79.1 | 96.2 | 64.0 | 74.6 | 81.2 | 96.6 | 17.6 | 51.4 | 81.7 | 96.4 | 0.7 | 18.1 | 85.8 | 95.3 | 0.5 | 1.8 | 87.1 | 96.9 |
| Home Alone | 0.0 | 0.0 | 0.0 | 0.0 | 0.0 | 0.0 | 0.0 | 0.0 | 0.0 | 0.0 | 0.0 | 0.0 | 0.0 | 0.0 | 0.0 | 0.0 | 0.0 | 0.0 | 0.2 | 0.0 |
| Total | 100.0 | 100.0 | 100.0 | 100.0 | 100.0 | 100.0 | 100.0 | 100.0 | 100.0 | 100.0 | 100.0 | 100.0 | 100.0 | 100.0 | 100.0 | 100.0 | 100.0 | 100.0 | 100.0 | 100.0 |
| Weighted Total | 106,000 | 106,000 | 106,000 | 106,000 | 108,800 | 108,800 | 108,800 | 108,800 | 58,900 | 58,900 | 58,900 | 58,900 | 60,300 | 60,300 | 60,300 | 60,300 | 471,000 | 471,000 | 471,000 | 471,000 |
| (Un-weighted n) | (261) | (261) | (261) | (261) | (325) | (325) | (325) | (325) | (186) | (186) | (186) | (186) | (196) | (196) | (196) | (196) | (1364) | (1364) | (1346) | (1346) |

FINAL REPORT OF THE COMMISSION ON THE FAMILY

By 5.00 - 7.00 p.m. a total of 97 per cent of 4 year olds are being cared for by parent/relatives - 96.4 per cent in their own home, 0.6 per cent in a relative's home. The remaining 3 per cent (1,800) are being cared for by a child-minder or other non-relative - 80 per cent of this relatively small group are being minded in a child-minder's home.

### 2.2.4 Children Aged 5 Years

By 5 years of age one can see that almost all children are reported as being "At School" in the period 9.00 a.m.-1.00 p.m. The very small percentage who are not recorded as being at school may represent those who were absent due to illness or similar such reason.

By 1.00 - 3.00 p.m. a total of 78.4 per cent (47,300) are still at school. The contrast between this and the 30 per cent for the corresponding figure for the 4 year olds clearly reflects the move from Junior to Senior infants and the slightly longer school day. As a corollary to this effect the incidence of being at home with parent or relative - at just over 18 per cent - is much lower than that for their 4 year old counterparts.

We can see, however, that by 3.00 - 5.00 p.m. the percentage of 5 year olds being cared for at home by a parent or relative is almost 86 per cent (51,700) while a further 3.1 per cent (1,800) are in a relative's home. Care by child-minders or other non-relative accounts for only 8.5 per cent of this age group by later afternoon with external minder care occurring with a slightly higher frequency (4.6 per cent) than similar such care within the child's home (3.9 per cent).

By the 5.00 - 7.00 p.m. period just over 95 per cent of 5 year olds are being cared for at home by parents or other relatives while a further 1 per cent is being cared for at a relative's home.

### 2.2.5 Children Aged 6 - 12 Years

For obvious reasons "At School" accounts for almost all children aged 6-12 up until 3.00 p.m. Illness or similar such absenteeism may be assumed to account for the very small percentage of children in this age group who are not at school between 9.00 a.m.- 3.00 p.m.

By 3.00 - 5.00 p.m. just over 3 per cent (14,600) of 6-12 year olds were classified as still being At School while 90 per cent are being cared for by relatives - 87 per cent in their own home, 3 per cent in the home of a relative. A further 2.9 per cent are being minded in a child-minder's home while the remaining 3.7 per cent are classified as being at home with a non-relative. One can see that a very small percentage of 6 - 12 year olds - 0.2 per cent representing just over 900 children - were classified as being at home by themselves in this period. The reader is cautioned that the absolute number of unweighted cases in this category is extremely small.

By the 5.00-7.00 p.m. period almost 97 per cent of children in this age group are at home with their parent(s) or relatives.

**Table 2.3**

Distribution of CHILDREN Aged 12 Years or Less Classified by (i) Age Cohort and (ii) Where They Were Cared for At Different Times of the Day on the Monday Preceding the Survey and (iii) broad region (Dublin vs. Rest of the Country)

AGE COHORT OF CHILD

**DUBLIN** (Per Cent)

| | 0-1 Year | | | | 2-3 Years | | | | 4 Years | | | | 5 Years | | | | 6-12 Years | | | |
|---|---|---|---|---|---|---|---|---|---|---|---|---|---|---|---|---|---|---|---|---|
| | 9.00-1.00 | 1.00-3.00 | 3.00-5.00 | 5.00-7.00 | 9.00-1.00 | 1.00-3.00 | 3.00-5.00 | 5.00-7.00 | 9.00-1.00 | 1.00-3.00 | 3.00-5.00 | 5.00-7.00 | 9.00-1.00 | 1.00-3.00 | 3.00-5.00 | 5.00-7.00 | 9.00-1.00 | 1.00-3.00 | 3.00-5.00 | 5.00-7.00 |
| At School | 0.0 | 0.0 | 0.0 | 0.0 | 1.2 | 0.0 | 0.0 | 0.0 | 49.2 | 17.8 | 0.0 | 0.0 | 100.0 | 70.5 | 0.0 | 0.0 | 98.8 | 95.1 | 0.9 | 0.0 |
| Mother & Toddler Group | 0.0 | 0.0 | 0.0 | 0.0 | 2.5 | 0.0 | 0.0 | 0.0 | 0.0 | 0.0 | 0.0 | 0.0 | 0.0 | 0.0 | 0.0 | 0.0 | 0.0 | 0.0 | 0.0 | 0.0 |
| Nursery/Crèche/Kindergarten/Montessori/Other Pre-School | 9.1 | 7.4 | 5.9 | 0.0 | 31.2 | 12.0 | 8.5 | 2.2 | 36.0 | 7.5 | 3.8 | 0.0 | 0.0 | 1.6 | 3.1 | 1.6 | 0.0 | 0.0 | 0.2 | 0.0 |
| Child Minder's Home | 11.1 | 11.1 | 11.0 | 1.4 | 6.9 | 10.5 | 8.1 | 1.1 | 0.0 | 3.8 | 5.3 | 3.5 | 0.0 | 1.6 | 1.6 | 0.0 | 0.0 | 0.0 | 2.6 | 1.1 |
| At Home with Non-Relative | 4.7 | 4.7 | 4.7 | 3.3 | 2.5 | 2.5 | 2.5 | 2.5 | 0.0 | 0.0 | 0.0 | 0.0 | 0.0 | 0.0 | 5.4 | 5.4 | 0.0 | 0.0 | 3.0 | 3.4 |
| Relative's Home | 5.0 | 6.8 | 4.9 | 0.0 | 2.4 | 2.4 | 1.0 | 0.0 | 1.8 | 1.8 | 3.9 | 0.0 | 0.0 | 1.6 | 4.6 | 3.0 | 0.5 | 1.2 | 2.7 | 1.0 |
| At Home with Parent/Relative | 70.2 | 70.0 | 73.5 | 95.3 | 53.3 | 72.6 | 79.9 | 94.3 | 13.0 | 69.1 | 87.0 | 96.5 | 0.0 | 24.8 | 85.3 | 90.0 | 0.7 | 3.7 | 87.6 | 94.5 |
| Home Alone | 0.0 | 0.0 | 0.0 | 0.0 | 0.0 | 0.0 | 0.0 | 0.0 | 0.0 | 0.0 | 0.0 | 0.0 | 0.0 | 0.0 | 0.0 | 0.0 | 0.0 | 0.0 | 0.0 | 0.0 |
| Total | 100.0 | 100.0 | 100.0 | 100.0 | 100.0 | 100.0 | 100.0 | 100.0 | 100.0 | 100.0 | 100.0 | 100.0 | 100.0 | 100.0 | 100.0 | 100.0 | 100.0 | 100.0 | 100.0 | 100.0 |
| Weighted Total | 25,600 | 25,600 | 25,600 | 25,600 | 28,700 | 28,700 | 28,700 | 28,700 | 15,700 | 15,700 | 15,700 | 15,700 | 19,200 | 19,200 | 19,200 | 19,200 | 122,700 | 122,700 | 122,700 | 122,700 |
| (Unweighted n) | (65) | (65) | (65) | (65) | (86) | (86) | (86) | (86) | (49) | (49) | (49) | (49) | (62) | (62) | (62) | (62) | (351) | (351) | (351) | (351) |

**REST OF THE COUNTRY** (Per Cent)

| | 0-1 Year | | | | 2-3 Years | | | | 4 Years | | | | 5 Years | | | | 6-12 Years | | | |
|---|---|---|---|---|---|---|---|---|---|---|---|---|---|---|---|---|---|---|---|---|
| | 9.00-1.00 | 1.00-3.00 | 3.00-5.00 | 5.00-7.00 | 9.00-1.00 | 1.00-3.00 | 3.00-5.00 | 5.00-7.00 | 9.00-1.00 | 1.00-3.00 | 3.00-5.00 | 5.00-7.00 | 9.00-1.00 | 1.00-3.00 | 3.00-5.00 | 5.00-7.00 | 9.00-1.00 | 1.00-3.00 | 3.00-5.00 | 5.00-7.00 |
| At School | 0.0 | 0.0 | 0.0 | 0.0 | 0.0 | 0.0 | 0.0 | 0.0 | 49.0 | 34.4 | 0.0 | 0.0 | 98.9 | 82.1 | 1.6 | 0.0 | 99.5 | 98.5 | 3.9 | 0.0 |
| Mother & Toddler Group | 0.0 | 0.0 | 0.0 | 0.0 | 0.0 | 0.0 | 0.0 | 0.0 | 0.0 | 0.0 | 0.0 | 0.0 | 0.0 | 0.0 | 0.0 | 0.0 | 0.0 | 0.0 | 0.0 | 0.0 |
| Nursery/Crèche/Kindergarten/Montessori/Other Pre-School | 1.1 | 0.0 | 0.0 | 0.0 | 15.9 | 3.5 | 1.2 | 0.3 | 21.8 | 2.1 | 0.0 | 0.0 | 0.0 | 0.0 | 0.8 | 0.0 | 0.0 | 0.0 | 0.0 | 0.0 |
| Child Minder's Home | 12.9 | 12.4 | 11.4 | 2.0 | 11.3 | 13.1 | 9.7 | 1.3 | 5.8 | 9.8 | 12.1 | 2.0 | 0.0 | 1.5 | 6.0 | 1.5 | 0.0 | 0.2 | 3.1 | 1.0 |
| At Home with Non-Relative | 5.3 | 4.6 | 4.1 | 1.0 | 1.8 | 1.8 | 1.8 | 0.5 | 2.1 | 4.3 | 4.4 | 0.8 | 0.0 | 0.7 | 3.2 | 0.7 | 0.1 | 0.2 | 2.9 | 1.2 |
| Relative's Home | 4.6 | 4.6 | 3.6 | 0.0 | 3.3 | 5.9 | 5.7 | 0.5 | 2.1 | 4.4 | 3.6 | 0.8 | 0.0 | 0.7 | 2.4 | 0.0 | 0.0 | 0.0 | 3.0 | 0.2 |
| At Home with Parent/Relative | 76.1 | 78.4 | 80.9 | 97.0 | 67.8 | 75.7 | 81.7 | 97.4 | 19.3 | 44.9 | 79.8 | 96.4 | 1.1 | 14.9 | 86.0 | 97.7 | 0.4 | 1.1 | 87.0 | 97.7 |
| Home Alone | 0.0 | 0.0 | 0.0 | 0.0 | 0.0 | 0.0 | 0.0 | 0.0 | 0.0 | 0.0 | 0.0 | 0.0 | 0.0 | 0.0 | 0.0 | 0.0 | 0.0 | 0.0 | 0.2 | 0.0 |
| Total | 100.0 | 100.0 | 100.0 | 100.0 | 100.0 | 100.0 | 100.0 | 100.0 | 100.0 | 100.0 | 100.0 | 100.0 | 100.0 | 100.0 | 100.0 | 100.0 | 100.0 | 100.0 | 100.0 | 100.0 |
| Weighted Total | 80,400 | 80,400 | 80,400 | 80,400 | 80,100 | 80,100 | 80,100 | 80,100 | 43,200 | 43,200 | 43,200 | 43,200 | 41,200 | 41,200 | 41,200 | 41,200 | 348,300 | 348,300 | 348,300 | 348,300 |
| (Unweighted n) | (196) | (196) | (196) | (196) | (239) | (239) | (239) | (239) | (137) | (137) | (137) | (137) | (134) | (134) | (134) | (134) | (1013) | (1013) | (1013) | (1013) |

## 2.3   Regional Variations in Care Arrangements

Table 2.3 presents details on broad regional variations in care arrangements as between Dublin and the rest of the country.[7]  Dublin is here defined to include all of the city and county areas. The main regional contrast in the child-care experience of the three youngest age categories (0-1; 2-3 and 4 year age group) is in the much higher use of nursery, crèche, kindergarten etc. services in Dublin as compared with the rest of the country. For example, in Dublin in the 9.00 - 1.00 period a total of 9.1 per cent of 0-1 year olds; 31.2 per cent of 2-3 year olds and 36.0 cent of 4 year olds avail of the option. Comparable figures for the rest of the country are 1.1 per cent; 15.9 per cent and 21.8 per cent respectively. This trend is to some degree (though by no means completely) counterbalanced by a higher propensity to use the services of a child-minder in areas outside Dublin than in the capital itself. This is particularly the case in respect of children in the 2-3 year old and 4 year old categories. In Dublin, for example, 6.9 per cent of children in the 2-3 year age group were cared for in a child-minder's home between 9.00 - 1.00 p.m. while 10.5 per cent of this age group were cared for in a minder's home between 1.00 - 3.00 p.m. Comparable figures for the rest of the country were 11.3 per cent and 13.1 per cent respectively.

Reflecting these regional trends in the use (or availability) of nursery, crèche, kindergarten etc. services in Dublin and the rest of the country one finds that a higher proportion of children in the three youngest age categories are cared for at home with a parent or relative in areas outside Dublin city and county.

The other main regional contrast which appears from the table is the substantially lower percentage of both 4 and 5 year olds in Dublin who are classified as being at school between 1.00 - 3.00 p.m. One can see from Table 2.3 that just under 18 per cent of 4 year olds in Dublin were at school in the period 1.00 - 3.00 p.m. The comparable figure for the rest of the country is 34.4 per cent. A similar, though less substantial, differential is maintained in respect of 5 year olds. One can see that a total of 70.5 per cent of 5 year olds in Dublin were classified as being at school between 1.00 - 3.00 p.m. compared with 82.1 per cent in the rest of the country. The reader is cautioned that although these regional trends are substantial it is clear from the table that the absolute number of unweighted cases upon which they are based in in fact smaller than desirable.

In general, there appears to be little systematic regional differences in the child-care arrangements of 6 - 12 year olds between Dublin and the remainder of the country.

## 2.4   Summary

In this chapter we have considered variations in child care arrangements throughout the day by age of child. We saw that approximately three-quarters of the 0 - 1 year olds were at home with their parent(s) or other relative(s) over the period 9.00 a.m. - 5.00 p.m. with this figure rising to 96 per cent in the period 5.00 - 7.00 p.m. A further 4-5 per cent of the youngest category of child were being cared for in a relative's home over the period 9.00 a.m. - 5.00 p.m. The services of nurseries, crèches, kindergartens etc. were not of major importance for this age group accounting for 3 per cent of children in the period 9.00 a.m. - 1.00 p.m., falling to 1.4 - 1.8 per cent between 1.00 - 5.00 p.m.

FINAL REPORT OF THE COMMISSION ON THE FAMILY

---

7    Sample size did not allow further regional disaggregation of the data. Indeed, the reader is advised to note the relatively small number of cases in some cells in Table 2.3, especially the 4 year old category in Dublin

In contrast, nurseries, crèches, kindergartens etc. became an important option for 2-3 year olds, especially in the period 9.00 a.m. - 1.00 p.m. where 20 per cent of children in the relevant age category (representing 21,900 children) were in the care of such facilities. This fell off sharply to 5.7 per cent between 1.00 - 3.00 p.m., 3.1 per cent between 3.00 - 5.00 p.m. and 0.8 per cent in the period 5.00 - 7.00 p.m. The importance of child-minders (especially care arrangements in the child-minder's home) was about equal to that for 0-1 year olds.

For 4 year olds the increasingly important role of school becomes apparent, with 49.1 per cent being in school between 9.00 a.m.- 1.00 p.m. and 30.0 per cent between 1.00 - 3.00 p.m. Nursery, crèche, kindergarten etc. services are also an important element in the care arrangements of this age category, especially in the period 9.00 a.m. - 1.00 p.m. where just over one-quarter of children availed of this service. Child-minding services in the minder's home are relatively less important for this age group than either of their younger counterparts.

For children in the 5 years and 6 - 12 year categories the importance of school is very apparent with a certain level of flow from the school to a minder in the period 3.00 - 5.00 p.m. for both groups. For example, 4.6 per cent of 5 year olds and 2.9 per cent of 6 - 12 year olds were cared for in a child-minder's home between 3.00 - 5.00 p.m. Comparable figures in respect of children who were at home with a non-relative in this period were 3.9 per cent and 3.7 per cent respectively.

### CHAPTER 3  CHILDREN ATTENDING SCHOOL

**3.1.**   **Introduction**

In this chapter we examine the nature of back-up care arrangements in relation to who usually looks after the children during school holidays. Respondents were asked the direct question: *Who usually looks after the child(ren) during school holidays?* and were provided with six possible response categories as follows:

1.    Child's mother
2.    Child's father
3.    Parents take it in turn/jointly share responsibility
4.    Other relative
5.    Friend or neighbour
6.    Other

Responses to the question are considered below both at the level of the *household* and also at the level of the *child*.

**3.2**   **Care Arrangements During School Holidays - the Household Level**

In aggregate terms a total of just under 291,000 households in the population of 1,155,000 households throughout the country as a whole contain some school-going children aged 12 years or less. This means that the issue of back-up care arrangements for those households containing children aged 12 years or less (some or all of whom are at school) is of relevance to 25.2 per cent of all households in the State (i.e. 291,000 out of a population of 1,155,000).

Table 3.1 presents information on the distribution of the relevant subset of 291,000 households classified by (a) who usually minds school-going children during school holidays and (b) principal economic status of the parents. The reader should note that the table presents information at the level of the *household*, not at the level of the child.
The table shows, for example, that in aggregate terms in 71.4 of relevant households it is the child's mother who minds the school-going child(ren) during school holidays; in 4.0 per cent of households it is the child's father; in 9.5 per cent of households the parents share responsibility; in 9.7 per cent of households the children are cared for by a relative (not the parent); and finally in 5.4 per cent of households school-going children are cared for by someone else.

These aggregate figures clearly mask a substantial degree of internal variation between one household type and another. The most important classificatory variable to be considered in this context is possibly the economic status of the parents. Table 3.1 presents the relevant details on the principal economic status for both the mother and the father. For example, in column one of the table we provide information in respect of households in which the mother's status is Full-time Home Duties while that of the Father is Working Outside the Home (on a full-time or part-time basis)[8]. The figures show that in 94.4 per cent of households in which the mother was on home duties and the father worked outside the home the responsibility for minding children during school holidays rested with the child(ren)'s mother. In 3.2 per cent of households the responsibility was shared jointly by both parents.

One can see from the second column in the table that there is a substantially higher degree of joint sharing of responsibility among parents for the caring of their school-going children on holidays in households in which the mother is engaged in full-time home duties and the father is classified in the "Other"[9] economic status category. In a total of 20 per cent of such households the responsibility is shared jointly by the parents.

Of perhaps greater interest from a policy perspective is the situation relating to households in which the mother works on either a full-time or part-time basis outside the home. Column 3 in the table provides details on who minds school-going children during school holidays in those households in which both parents work outside the home. From this one can see that in almost one-quarter of such households (23.5 per cent) the responsibility rests with the mother; in 9.3 per cent with the father and in 11.3 per cent it is shared jointly by both parents. The importance to this group of households of "Other Relatives" (mentioned by 29 per cent) and "Other" (26.9 per cent) is clear from the table. In situations where the mother works full-time outside the household and the father's status is "other" (Column 4 in the table) one can see that a greater share of the responsibility is taken on by the father. A

---

8   We identified only a very small percentage of households in which the father's status was part-time work outside the home.

9   "Other" includes unemployed as well as ill, permanently disabled etc.

## Table 3.1

Distribution of HOUSEHOLDS Which Contain School-going Children Aged 12 Years or Less Classified by (i) Who Usually Minds School-going Children During School Holidays and (ii) Principal Economic Status of Parents

| Who Minds Child(ren) During School Holidays? — Mother / Father | Home Duties / Works outside Home | Home Duties / Other | F-T Outside Home / Works outside Home | F-T Outside Home / Other | P-T Outside Home / Works outside Home | P-T Outside Home / Other | Other / Other | Father Not in Household | Total |
|---|---|---|---|---|---|---|---|---|---|
| | | | | (Per Cent) | | | | | |
| Child's Mother | 94.4 | 78.3 | 23.5 | 46.1 | 53.2 | 8.3 | 50.3 | 65.9 | 71.4 |
| Child's Father | 0.6 | 1.3 | 9.3 | 36.5 | 4.1 | 21.9 | 18.7 | - | 4.0 |
| Parents Share Responsibility | 3.2 | 20.4 | 11.3 | 17.4 | 21.1 | 53.9 | 13.2 | - | 9.5 |
| Other Relative | 1.4 | 0.0 | 29.0 | 0.0 | 16.8 | 7.5 | 14.4 | 28.1 | 9.7 |
| Other | 0.5 | 0.0 | 26.9 | 0.0 | 4.8 | 8.4 | 5.4 | 6.0 | 5.4 |
| Total | 100.0 | 100.0 | 100.0 | 100.0 | 100.0 | 100.0 | 100.0 | 100.0 | 100.0 |
| Est. Wgt'd No. hsds. | 146,300 | 23,000 | 40,400 | 6,400 | 37,200 | 7,300 | 6,500 | 23,700 | 290,900 |
| (Unweighted n of hsds.) | (492) | (78) | (137) | (22) | (127) | (24) | (21) | (64) | (965) |

total of 36.5 per cent of such households say the father will mind the children on school holiday while a further 17.4 per cent say the responsibility will be shared jointly by both parents[10].

In situations in which the mother works on a part-time basis outside the home and the father also works outside the home, it would appear that the majority of the responsibility for minding children during school holidays is with the mother (53.2 per cent of households). In 21 per cent of households it is jointly shared by both parents and in only 4.1 per cent is it taken on by the father. The importance of "Other Relatives" as compared to "Other" for this category of household is clear from the table. In other words, there is a much greater back-up child-caring role for relatives (as compared with non-relatives) in situations in which the mother works part-time outside the home and the father also works outside the home than in the case where the mother works full-time outside the home (with her spouse also working outside the home). One can compare, for example, the figures of 29 and 27 per cent respectively for "other relatives" and "other" in column 3 of the table with 17 per cent and 5 per cent in column 5. In situations in which the mother works part-time outside the home and the father is defined as "other" one can see that the role played by fathers in sharing the responsibility for child-minding during school holidays increases substantially. In such cases a total of 22 per cent of households cite the father as minding the child(ren) during holidays while a further 54 per cent say the responsibility is shared jointly by both parents.

10   The reader's attention is drawn to the small number of unweighted cases in this section of the table.

FINAL REPORT OF THE COMMISSION ON THE FAMILY

In column 8 in Table 3.1 we can see that the responsibility of caring for children during the school holidays falls on the mother in almost two-thirds of households in which the father is not resident. In 28 per cent of such households "Other Relatives" take on this responsibility. It would clearly be of interest to examine the situation in this subgroup of households according to principal economic status of the mother. One is prevented from doing so, however, due to the relatively small number of cases involved.

### 3.3 Care Arrangements During School Holidays - The Child Level

In the previous section we considered child-care arrangements for school-going children during school holidays in terms of the percentage of *households* in question. In Table 3.2 we change the focus from the *household* to the *child* and ask what percentage of school-going *children* are minded by their mother, father, jointly etc. during school holidays.

Perhaps not surprisingly the story told by Table 3.2 is remarkably similar to that told by Table 3.1. For example, one can see that 72.3 per cent of the 521,000 school-going *children* in the relevant age category are minded by their mother during school holidays; 4.5 per cent by their fathers; 9.6 per cent by their parents in turn (the parents share the responsibility); 8.4 per cent by "Other relatives" and the remaining 5.2 per cent by "Other" non-relatives.

**Table 3.2**

**Distribution of School-going CHILDREN Aged 12 Years or Less Classified by (i) Who Usually Minds Them During School Holidays and (ii) Principal Economic Status of Parents**

| Who Minds Children During School Holidays? | Mother | Principal Economic Status of Mother and Father | | | | | | | Father Not in Household | Total |
|---|---|---|---|---|---|---|---|---|---|---|
| | | Home Duties | Home Duties | FT Outside Home | FT Outside Home | P-T Outside Home | P-T Outside Home | Other | | |
| | Father | Works outside Home | Other | Works outside Home | Other | Works outside Home | Other | Other | | |
| | | | | | (Per Cent) | | | | | |
| Child's Mother | | 94.7 | 75.3 | 22.0 | 48.5 | 56.6 | 6.8 | 50.7 | 71.0 | 72.3 |
| Child's Father | | 0.6 | 1.4 | 12.8 | 41.7 | 4.7 | 20.0 | 10.6 | 0.0 | 4.5 |
| Parents Share Responsibility | | 3.2 | 23.2 | 11.5 | 9.8 | 20.5 | 60.0 | 8.9 | 0.0 | 9.6 |
| Other Relative | | 1.0 | 0.0 | 26.9 | 0.0 | 13.9 | 3.8 | 19.1 | 24.7 | 8.4 |
| Other | | 0.4 | 0.0 | 26.7 | 0.0 | 4.3 | 9.1 | 10.7 | 4.3 | 5.2 |
| Total | | 100.0 | 100.0 | 100.0 | 100.0 | 100.0 | 100.0 | 100.0 | 100.0 | 100.0 |
| Est. Wgt'd No. children | | 265,400 | 42,600 | 70,600 | 11,500 | 61,600 | 14,400 | 13,300 | 41,600 | 520,900 |
| (Unweighted n of hsds.) | | (788) | (129) | (212) | (36) | (188) | (44) | (35) | (101) | (1,533) |

As was the case with Table 3.1, we can see that the bulk of the responsibility for minding children during school holidays rested with the mother, even in cases where she worked outside the home. We can see from Table 3.2, for example, that 22 per cent of school-going children whose mother and father both work full-time outside the home are cared for by their mother on school holidays. This compares with 12.8 per cent of school-going children who are cared for by their father and 11.5 per cent whose care is shared jointly by both parents. Just under 27 per cent of all school going children in the relevant age category are cared for by "Other relatives" and a further 27 per cent by "Other" non-relatives.

In situations where the mother works outside the home on a part-time basis and the father also works outside the home, the responsibility for minding school-going children rests substantially with the mother. A total of 57 per cent of school-children in such circumstances are cared for by the child's mother; 20.5 per cent are cared jointly or in turn by both parents and just under 5 per cent are cared for by their father. Non-parental child-care arrangements in such circumstances is heavily oriented towards "Other Relatives" in contrast to "Other" Non-Relatives. We can see that just under 14 per cent of school-going children whose mother works part-time outside the home and whose father also works outside the home are cared for by "Other Relatives". The comparable figure for non-relatives is just over 4 per cent.

## 3.4    Summary

In this chapter we considered who minded school-going children during school holidays, concentrating, in particular, on variations in the combined or joint principal economic status of parents. Tables were presented at both the household and child levels.

In general, the picture emerging from the data is one in which the mother is primarily responsible for minding the children during school holidays. As one would expect, this is especially true in situations in which the mother is classified as being engaged in full-time home duties. For example, in 94 per cent of *households* in which the mother was engaged in home duties and the father worked outside the home the responsibility for minding the children on school holidays rested with the mother. The situation was somewhat different in households where the mother worked full-time outside the home and the father also worked outside the home. In such cases the responsibility for minding school-going children on school holidays was strongly oriented towards the mother. In 23.5 per cent of such households the children were minded by the mother. This contrasts with 9.3 per cent of households in which the responsibility rested with the father and with 11.3 per cent of households in which it was shared jointly by both parents. The story told by the data at the level of the child is, as one would expect, entirely consistent with that at the household level.

## 4.1   Introduction

In this chapter we consider the incidence of child-minding services as well as issues relating to average number of hours of such services consumed by relevant households and also the cost associated with this form of child-care arrangement. In addition, we consider the back-up care arrangements used by households which avail of child-minder services. The two main types of child-minding are examined separately viz. child-minding in the minder's home as well as minding in the child's home.

## 4.2   Caring for Children in a Child-Minder's Home

Table 4.1 presents information on the distribution of households which contain children aged 12 years or less classified according to whether or not they leave any of their children with a child-minder in his/her home as well as the economic status of the mother. From this one can see that in aggregate terms a total of 8.4 per cent of all households which contain children aged 12 years or less availed of these services. This represents 31,900 of the 382,600 households in the State which contained a child or children in the relevant age category. We can see from the upper section in the table that just under 29 per cent of households in which the mother worked on a full-time basis outside the home availed of external[11] child-minding services while these arrangements were used in just over 12 per cent of households in which she worked outside the home on a part-time basis.

The lower section of the table shows the percentage of households which used these services classified by principal economic status of the mother. This indicates, for example, that in just under 71 per cent of households using these arrangements the mother worked full-time outside the home while in 26 per cent of such households she worked on a part-time basis.

### Table 4.1

Distribution of Households Containing Children Aged 12 Years or Less Classified by (i) Whether or Not They Leave Any of Their Children to be Cared for in a Child-Minders Home and (ii) Economic Status of Mother

| Use Child Minders Home | Principal Economic Status of Mother and Father | | | | Total |
|---|---|---|---|---|---|
| | Home Duties | Full-time Work Outside Home | Part-time Work Outside Home | Other | |
| | (Column Percentages) | | | | |
| Yes | 0.5 | 28.8 | 12.4 | 0.0 | 8.4 |
| No | 99.5 | 71.2 | 87.6 | 100.0 | 91.6 |
| Total | 100.0 | 100.0 | 100.0 | 100.0 | 100.0 |
| | (Row Percentages) | | | | |
| Yes | 3.7 | 70.7 | 25.6 | 0.0 | 100.0 |
| No | 63.7 | 16.0 | 16.5 | 3.8 | 100.0 |
| Total | 58.7 | 20.5 | 17.3 | 3.5 | 100.0 |
| Est.Wgt'd no. of households | 1,200 | 22,500 | 8,200 | 0 | 31,900 |
| (Unweighted) No. of cases availing of services | (4) | (72) | (27) | (0) | (103) |

11   External to the home of the child being cared for i.e., child-minding in the minder's home.

## Table 4.2

Distribution of Households which leave their children to be cared for in a Child-minder's home Classified by time of day children are cared for by the Minder.

| TIME OF DAY | | | | (a) Per Cent of those households which use minder services | (b) Estimated Number of Households | (c) Unweighted Number of cases |
|---|---|---|---|---|---|---|
| 9.00-1.00 | 1.00-3.00 | 3.00-5.00 | 5.00-7.00 | (Per Cent) | | |
| Yes | Yes | Yes | No | 48.3 | 15,400 | |
| No | No | Yes | No | 15.6 | 5,000 | |
| Yes | Yes | No | No | 8.8 | 2,800 | |
| No | No | Yes | Yes | 8.2 | 2,600 | |
| Yes | Yes | Yes | Yes | 7.5 | 2,400 | |
| No | Yes | Yes | No | 6.6 | 2,100 | |
| | | | All Other | 5.0 | 1,600 | |
| | | | Total | 100.0 | 31,900 | |

Table 4.2 provides details on the various periods throughout the day when external child-minding services are used. The combination of time periods are presented in order of frequency of occurrence. For example, the plurality of households which use this service (just over 48 per cent or 15,400) do so between 9.00am - 5.00pm. A further 16 per cent (approximately 5,000 households) use them only in the period 3.00 - 5.00pm. This clearly reflects children leaving school and being cared for in a minder's home until parents who work outside the home return from work at some time around 5.00 p.m. The fourth row in the table shows that in a further 8 per cent of households external minding arrangements are used between 3.00 - 7.00 p.m., presumably by parents who return somewhat later from work. Just under 9 per cent of households which use these services do so between 9.00 a.m.-3.00 p.m. (third row in the table) while 7.5 per cent of relevant households (representing an estimated total of 2,400) used external minding arrangements throughout the day from 9.00 a.m. - 7.00 p.m.

In Table 4.3 we consider the back-up care arrangements used by households which avail of external minding arrangements classified by the principal economic status of the mother.[12] This shows that in aggregate back-up care (which could be availed of if the child-minder were unavailable to mind the children due to illness etc.) is provided by the child's mother in just over 22 per cent of households whose primary arrangement is an external minder.

---

12    The unweighted number of cases which use external minding arrangements is too small to allow an analysis by the joint economic status of both parents. With this caveat in mind we estimate that both parents work outside the home on either a full-time or part-time basis in approximately 85 per cent of the 31,900 households which use this service.

Table 4.3

**Distribution of Households which use the services of a Childminder in his/her own home classified by (i) who minds the children if the minder is unable to do so and (ii) Economic Status of Mother.**

| Backup Care Provided by: | Principal Economic Status of Mother and Father | | | Total |
| | Home Duties | Full-time Work Outside Home | Part-time Work Outside Home | |
|---|---|---|---|---|
| | (Per Cent) | | | |
| Child's Mother | * | 21.3 | 20.1 | 22.4 |
| Child's Father | * | 4.2 | 3.7 | 3.9 |
| Child's Parents Share Responsibility | * | 22.0 | 26.2 | 23.0 |
| Other Relative | * | 35.1 | 32.5 | 34.0 |
| Other | * | 17.4 | 17.4 | 16.8 |
| Total | * | 100.0 | 100.0 | 100.0 |
| Est.Wgt'd no. of households | 1,200 | 22,500 | 8,200 | 31,900 |
| (Unweighted) | (4) | (72) | (27) | (103) |

In 23 per cent of cases the parents jointly share the responsibility of providing back-up cover for their child-minder. In only 4 per cent of cases, however, does the father provide the primary back-up arrangement. One can see from the table that there is very little variation from this aggregate picture as between households in which the mother works outside the home on either a full-time or part-time basis.

Table 4.4 presents information on some descriptive statistics regarding external child-minding arrangements. This table relates only to those households which avail of external child-care services. Columns A and B in Table 4.4 provide a breakdown of the number of households using these services classified by the number of children in the household being minded (1; 2; 3 or more). From this one can see that an estimated 17,500 (55 per cent) of households which use such services do so in respect of 1 child; a further 35 per cent of the relevant households (just over 11,000) do so in respect of 2 children; and the remaining 10 per cent of households (approximately 3,300) do so in respect of 3 or more children.

Table 4.4

**Summary Descriptive Statistics on Hours of External Child-minding Services Consumed by Households and Average Cost Per Hour Per Child Minded Classified by Number of Children from the Household Who Are Left With a Minder**

| No. of Children Being Minded | A Est. No. of Households | B Per Cent of Households | C Ave. No. Hours Minded Per Child | D Ave. Cost Per Hour Per Child Minded | E Unweight-ed n of Cases |
|---|---|---|---|---|---|
| 1 | 17,500 | 54.9 | 24.6 | £1.77 | (58) |
| 2 | 11,100 | 34.8 | 21.5 | £1.32 | (37) |
| 3+ | 3,300 | 10.3 | 24.2 | - | (10) |
| Total | 31,900 | 100.0 | 23.5 | - | (105) |

Overall, the average number of children minded per household which used external child minding services had 1.57 children cared for by a minder in the minder's home.

Column C presents details on the average number of hours minded per child. This is the average number of external child minding hours per child per week which is consumed by the relevant group of households. It is calculated as an average across all households of the *total* number of hours minded for all children within the household divided by the total number of children in the household who are minded. From the table we can see that, in aggregate, the average number of hours for which each child is cared for in a minder's home is 23.5 hours per child minded per week. The table shows that there is relatively little variation in this figure with number of children minded. For obvious reasons there is, as one would expect, substantial variation in this figure in terms of the mother's principal economic status. In relevant households in which the mother is working full-time outside the home the figure rises to just over 27 hours per week and where the mother is working on a part-time basis outside the home the figure is 15 hours per week.[13]

Finally, in Column D in the table we present information on the average cost per hour per child minded classified by number of children from the household who are left with a minder outside the home. The figures are disaggregated by number of children from the household who are being minded so as to reflect as accurately as possible the assumed pricing structure adopted by child-minders. This assumes that the marginal cost to the parents of having an additional child minded falls as the number of children minded increases. Pricing arrangements are agreed (consciously or subconsciously) between household and minder which incorporate this pricing structure. In discussing the information on costs, therefore, one should do so on the basis of the average cost per hour per child minded within each of the categories of number of children minded. The data in the table indicate that in circumstances where only one child is being minded the cost per hour is in the order of £1.77 In circumstances in which two children are being minded this falls to approximately £1.32 per child per hour.

## 4.3 Caring for Children by a Child-Minder in the Child's Home

A further aspect of child-minding is caring for the child(ren) in the child(ren)'s own home i.e., where the minder comes to the home of the child(ren). Only 47 unweighted cases in the sample availed of this service and so one is severely constrained in the degree to which one can provide quantitative estimates of usage levels and the characteristics of households which use them. With this caveat in mind, we would estimate that approximately 4 per cent of households which contain children aged 12 years or less arrange for some or all of those children to be cared for in the child(ren)'s home. This represents approximately 14,800 households in the country as a whole. These child-care arrangements are used predominantly by households in which the mother works outside the house, either on a full-time or part-time basis.

In terms of back-up care arrangements in the event of the child-minder not being able to come to the child's home due to illness etc. we found that, overall, in approximately 15 per cent of households the back-up arrangement was provided by the mother. In 5 per cent of

---

13  Estimate of full-time outside the home based on 59 unweighted cases; part-time outside the home is based on 26 unweighted cases.

households it was provided by the father and in a further 15 per cent of households it was provided jointly by both parents in turn. The notable aspect of back-up care arrangements associated with this form of child-care, however, is the importance of "Other Relatives". Approximately 45 per cent of households in total said they relied on "Other relatives" in the event of their minder not being able to come to their home for a few days because of illness or other unexpected event. As one would expect, the "Other relative" option is particularly important for households in which the mother works on a *part-time* basis outside the home.

## 4.4    Summary

In this chapter we considered the incidence of child-care arrangements using the services of a child-minder as well as some of the characteristics of the households which availed of such services. Overall, we found that 8.4 per cent of households which contained children aged 0-12 years used the services of a child-minder in the minder's own home. This represents approximately 31,900 households. The highest incidence of this service was among households in which the mother worked full-time outside the home with 29 per cent of such households using an external child-minder. A total of 12.4 per cent of households in which the mother worked outside the home on a part-time basis used the services of a child-minder in the minder's own home.

In terms of time of the day in which the services of the external minder is used we saw that 48.3 per cent of the households which left children in a minder's home did so in the period 9.00 a.m.-5.00 p.m. while a further 7.5 per cent did so in the period 9.00 a.m.-7.00 p.m. This obviously reflects the work patterns of households in which both parents work full-time outside the home. A total of 9 per cent of the households using this service did so in the period 9.00 a.m.-3.00 p.m.; 16 per cent in the period 3.00-5.00 p.m. and 8 per cent in the period 3.00-7.00 p.m. It seems reasonable to attribute the pattern displayed by the latter two groups as largely characterising use of child-minders after school by households in which the parents work full-time outside the home.

As regards back-up care arrangements we saw that in 22 per cent of households this was provided by the mother; in a further 23 per cent it was shared jointly by both parents and in 4 per cent was provided by the father. The role of "Other Relatives" as back-up care providers was very important for those households which used the services of an external child-minder. A total of 34 per cent of such households cited "Other Relatives" when asked who would care for their children in the event of their minder not being able to do so due to illness or similar such unforeseen event.

The chapter also considered the role played by what we described as internal child-minders i.e., minders who care for children in the children's own home. The number of unweighted cases of households which used the services of the internal minder was relatively small and so one must be slightly more circumspect than desirable in terms of what can be said about this group of households. Nonetheless, the survey suggests that 4 per cent of households which contain 0-12 year olds use the services of a minder in the child's own home. This represents some 14,800 households. This form of care arrangement was used predominantly in households in which the mother worked outside the home. It was notable that back-up care arrangements were provided in 45 per cent of these households by "Other Relatives". In a further 15 per cent of households they were provided by the mother; in 5 per cent they were provided by the father and in 15 per cent they were shared jointly by both parents.

## CHAPTER 5   NURSERY, CRÈCHE, KINDERGARTEN, MONTESSORI, OTHER PRE-SCHOOL

### 5.1   Introduction

In this chapter we examine the use of nursery, crèche, kindergarten, montessori or other forms of pre-school care arrangement. In this context we consider the distribution of households according to the number of children which they contain aged 0-2 years and 3-4 years as these can be seen as the valid target group for the services in question. Among this target group we consider incidence levels classified by principal economic status of the mother and father in the households; back-up care arrangements as well as the average pupil/teacher ratio and average cost per child-hour.

### 5.2   Households in the Nursery/Crèche Market

Table 5.1 presents details on the distribution of all households classified by whether or not

**Table 5.1**

**Distribution of All Households Classified by Whether or Not they Contained Children in the 0-2 year, 3-4 year, and 5-12 year cohorts**

| | Contain Children Aged | | | All Households | Est. Number of Households | Unweighted No. of Cases |
|---|---|---|---|---|---|---|
| | 0-2 years | 3-4 years | 5-12 years | | | |
| | | | | (Per Cent) | ('000s) | |
| a. | No | No | No | 67.0 | 774 | 3005 |
| b. | No | No | Yes | 17.4 | 201 | 690 |
| c. | No | Yes | No | 1.5 | 17 | 57 |
| d. | No | Yes | Yes | 3.7 | 43 | 136 |
| e. | Yes | No | No | 3.5 | 40 | 138 |
| f. | Yes | No | Yes | 3.2 | 37 | 118 |
| g. | Yes | Yes | No | 1.9 | 22 | 73 |
| h. | Yes | Yes | Yes | 1.7 | 20 | 59 |
| | | | Total | 100.0 | 1154 | 4276 |

they contain children in the age groups 0-2 years; 3-4 years and 5-12 years. From this one can see that just over 84 per cent of all households in the population as a whole did not contain children aged 4 years or less. This means that just under 16 per cent of all households (representing 179,000 households) contained children who were aged 4 years or less on their last birthday. These 179,000 households can be thought of as representing the "target market" for the services provided by the nursery/crèche/kindergarten/montessori/other pre-school sector.[14]

## 5.3    The Use of Nursery, Crèche, Kindergarten, Montessori Other Pre-School

Table 5.2 provides information on the use made of nursery/crèche services among the 179,000 target households classified by joint economic status of the mother and father. From the top section of the table one can see that in aggregate terms 21 per cent of target households use the services of nurseries, crèches etc[15].

Highest use levels occur in households in which the mother works on a part-time basis outside the home and the father also works outside the home with 32.5 per cent of such households using these services. This represents a total of 6,900 households. Approximately 25 per cent of target households in which the mother works full-time outside the home use the nursery/crèche etc. option, representing 10,400 households.

### Table 5.2

Distribution of "Target" Households for Services of Nursery/Crèche/Kindergarten/Montessori/Other Pre-School Classified According to (i) Economic Status of Parents and (ii) Whether or Not They Use the Services Provided by Nursery/Crèches etc.

| Use Nursery /Crèche? | Mother | Principal Economic Status of Mother and Father | | | | | | | Total |
|---|---|---|---|---|---|---|---|---|---|
| | | Home Duties | Home Duties | F-T Outside Home | F-T Outside Home | P-T Outside Home | P-T Outside Home | Other | |
| | Father | Works outside Home | Other | Works outside Home | Other | Works outside Home | Other | Other | |
| | | (Column Percentages) | | | | | | | |
| Yes | | 17.1 | 18.2 | 24.7 | 26.4 | 32.5 | 15.8 | 28.3 | 21.3 |
| No | | 82.9 | 81.8 | 75.3 | 73.6 | 67.5 | 84.2 | 71.7 | 78.7 |
| Total | | 100.0 | 100.0 | 100. | 100.0 | 100.0 | 100.0 | 100.0 | 100.0 |
| | | (Row Percentages) | | | | | | | |
| Yes | | 36.0 | 10.1 | 22.8 | 4.8 | 18.3 | 3.0 | 5.0 | 100.0 |
| No | | 47.3 | 12.3 | 18.8 | 3.6 | 10.3 | 4.3 | 3.4 | 100.0 |
| Total | | 44.9 | 11.8 | 19.7 | 3.9 | 12.0 | 4.0 | 3.8 | 100.0 |
| Est. Wgt'd households | | 79,200 | 20,800 | 34,700 | 6,900 | 21,200 | 7,000 | 6,700 | 176,400 |
| (Unwgt'd n) | | | | | | | | | |

14   Although we would have assumed that a small percentage of households might have used the services of nurseries/crèches for 5 year olds and even 6-7 year olds after school we in fact find a trivial number of households in the reweighted sample (in the order of 700-800) in fact do so. Consequently it seems best to concentrate on the relevant target group of households as those with children aged 4 years or less.

15   Because the target population of 179,000 households represents only 47.1 per cent of all households in the country containing children aged 12 years or less, the 21 per cent of target households containing children aged 4 years or less represents 9.9 per cent of all households which contain children aged 12 years or less (ie. 0.471 x 0.21).

It is interesting to note that just over 17 per cent of households in which the mother is engaged on full-time home duties (representing 17,300 households) leave their child(ren) in a nursery/crèche etc. at some time in the day. Indeed, from the lower section of the table one can see that in 46 per cent of households using a nursery/crèche etc. the mother is on full-time home duties. This clearly indicates that one of the primary motivations for any pre-school activity is the pre-school socialisation and related educational experience which it can provide.

## 5.4 Time of Day in Which Nursery/Crèche etc. Services Utilised

Table 5.3 provides information on the time of day in which the nursery/crèche etc. arrangements are used by households. From this one can see that almost 80 per cent of the households which use these services do so in the period 9.00 a.m. - 1.00 p.m.; 9 per cent in the period 9.00 a.m. - 3.00 p.m.; 8 per cent between 9.00 a.m. - 5.00 p.m. and just over 2 per cent throughout the day from 9.00 a.m. - 7.00 p.m. The remainder of households which used the service did so at other times of the day 1.00 - 3.00 p.m. or 1.00 - 5.00 p.m.

### Table 5.3

**Distribution of Households Which Leave Their Children to be Cared for in a Nursery etc. Classified by Time of Day Children are Cared for by the Nursery etc.**

| TIME OF DAY | | | | Per Cent of those households which use services | Estimated Number of Households |
|---|---|---|---|---|---|
| 9.00-1.00 | 1.00-3.00 | 3.00-5.00 | 5.00-7.00 | (Per Cent) | |
| Yes | No | No | No | 79.5 | 30,100 |
| Yes | Yes | No | No | 8.9 | 3,600 |
| Yes | Yes | Yes | No | 7.9 | 3,000 |
| Yes | Yes | Yes | Yes | 2.3 | 900 |
| | | | All Other | 1.3 | 500 |
| | | | Total | 100.0 | 38,100 |

## 5.5 Back-up Care Arrangements Among Households Using Nursery/Crèche Services

Table 5.4 presents details on the back-up care arrangements used by households in the event of the nursery/crèche not being able to care for the child(ren) due to the teacher's illness or other unexpected event. The information is classified by economic status of the mother in the household. From this we can see that the back-up care is primarily provided by the child(ren)'s mother in households in which she is on full-time home duties - with a very small incidence of "Other Relative" and "Others" providing some cover. In households in which the mother works full-time outside the home the back-up care seems to be provided on an equitable basis as between the father and the mother - approximately 17 per cent of relevant households cite each parent. In a further 24 per cent of households in which the mother works full-time outside the home the responsibility for providing back-up arrangements is shared jointly by both parents. In a further 25 per cent of such households the back-up cover is provided by "Other relatives" and in the remaining 18 per cent of relevant households by "Other" non-relatives.

In situations in which the mother is working on a part-time basis outside the home the increased importance of the role played by "Other Relatives" in providing back-up care arrangements is evident - mentioned by 43.5 per cent of the households in question. The "Child's Mother" and "Shared Jointly by Parents" are each mentioned in just over one-quarter of the households in question.[16]

**Table 5.4**

Distribution of Households Which Use the Services of Nursery/Crèche/Kindergarten/Montessori/Other Pre-School Classified by (i) Who Would Mind the Children if either (s)he/they were too ill to attend or the Teacher/Supervisor in the Nursery etc. Facility Were Unable to Mind the Child(ren) and (ii) Principal Economic Status of Mother

| Backup Care Provided by: | Principal Economic Status of Mother | | | | |
| --- | --- | --- | --- | --- | --- |
| | Home Duties | Full-time Work Outside Home | Part-time Work Outside Home | Other | Total |
| | (Per Cent) | | | | |
| Child's Mother | 95.0 | 16.3 | 27.0 | * | 58.9 |
| Child's Father | 0.0 | 17.1 | 0.0 | * | 4.3 |
| Child's Parents Share Responsibility | 0.0 | 23.6 | 25.5 | * | 11.8 |
| Other Relative | 3.0 | 25.0 | 43.5 | * | 18.7 |
| Other | 2.0 | 17.9 | 4.0 | * | 6.3 |
| Total | 100.0 | 100.0 | 100.0 | * | 100.0 |
| Est. Wgt'd. No. of Hsds. | 16,700 | 8,900 | 8,300 | 1,900 | 35,800 |
| (Unweight'd No.) | (51) | (30) | (26) | (6) | (113) |

## 5.6 Costs of Nursery/Crèche etc.

The questionnaire recorded details on the total amount paid per week by the household for the services of a nursery, crèche, kindergarten, Montessori, other pre-school etc. From the activity diaries it was possible to calculate both the number of children in the household availing of this service as well as the total number of hours which they spent each week in a nursery, crèche etc. From this it was possible to calculate the average cost per child-hour for this form of child-care arrangement. When the cost per hour is averaged across all households we found that the overall cost is £1.27 per child hour. Because this is calculated across all households it includes all types of nurseries, crèches, kindergartens etc. as well as different levels of usage throughout the day of this service. In other words, it includes households which use them in the morning only; those which use them, for example, only between 3-5 p.m. for after-school care, as well as those which use them on an all-day basis. One could assume that households which use the services of the nursery/crèche etc. at some point only in the period 9.00-1.00 p.m. and not in the afternoon may represent a different type of user than those households which use them throughout the day from, for example, 9.00-3.00 pm or 9.00-5.00 pm or later. This latter type of household is much more likely to use crèches etc. which are in the strictly

16    The readers attention is drawn to the relative small number of unweighted cases in this section of the tables.

commercial market than would many of those which would use these care arrangements only at some time in the period 9.00-1.00 p.m. As we saw in Table 5.3 above, almost 80 per cent of households which use these services do so only in the period 9.00 - 1.00 pm. This means that a correspondingly small number of unweighted cases in fact fall into the longer care-period category - a total of 21 respondent households. This is clearly smaller than desirable as the basis for making strong statements regarding costs. With this caveat in mind, however, one can note that the average child-hour cost is lower for those households which use these services only at some point in the period 9.00 - 1.00 p.m. than for those which use them for some time into the afternoon in addition to the morning period. The average child-hour cost figures for the two groups are £1.24 and £1.39 respectively.

## 5.7     Summary

In this chapter we considered several aspects of child-care arrangements in a nursery, crèche, kindergarten, Montessori or other pre-school. We saw that almost all households which used these arrangements do so in respect of children aged 4 years or less. Consequently, we concentrated on households containing children aged 4 years or less as the target group of households for this chapter. This represents 179,000 households and this is the base to which the percentage incidence figures relate.

Overall we saw that just over 21 per cent of this group of households (38,100) used the services of a nursery, crèche, etc. In 27.6 per cent of the households which used them the mother worked outside the home. This compared with a figure of 23.6 per cent of such households in the target population, indicating an over-representation in the order of 17 per cent among this group of households using a nursery, crèche, etc. The fact that households in which the mother is working outside the home are represented on an above average basis (relative to their representation in the population as a whole) is as one would expect. It is noteworthy, however, that in 46 per cent (17,300) of the households which use a nursery, crèche, etc. the mother is engaged in full-time home duties. Such households constitute 56.7 per cent of the relevant population[17]. Consequently, although they are under-represented among the households which use nurseries, crèches, etc. they still represent a sizeable population of households which use these services. The principle motivation in such households for using nurseries, crèches etc. can be presumed to be oriented towards socialisation. In general, nurseries, crèches etc. are used primarily between 9.00 a.m. - 1.00 p.m. with over 80 per cent of the households which use them doing so only during this period.

In terms of back-up care arrangements in the event of the crèche etc. not being able to mind the children, we saw that these were provided almost exclusively by the mother in households in which she is engaged on home duties. In those households in which she works outside the home the back-up arrangements are provided on a reasonably equitable basis by the father and the mother with approximately 17 per cent of relevant households citing each parent. In households in which the mother worked part-time outside the home there was clear evidence to indicate the increased role played by "other relatives" in providing back-up care arrangements.

17     As noted throughout the chapter the "relevant population" is the estimated 179,000 households which contain children aged 4 years or less.

## CHAPTER 6 SUMMARY

In this chapter we provide a summary of the main findings from the report. As noted in Chapter 1, the data were collected in a supplementary questionnaire which was conducted as part of the on-going Consumer Survey carried out by the ESRI on a monthly basis on behalf of the European Commission. The focus of the survey was care arrangements for children, concentrating in particular on the child-care services used by parents who work full-time in the home as well as by those who work outside the home. Of special interest was the back-up child-care arrangements used by households in the event of their usual arrangements not being available. The key to much of the information in which the Commission on the Family had an interest lay in the completion of the time diaries which recorded child-care arrangements in respect of each child aged 12 years or less at various periods throughout the day.

In Chapter 2 we considered the variations in these child-care arrangements at different points in the day according to age of child. We saw that approximately three-quarters of 0-1 year olds were at home with their parent(s) or other relative(s) over the period 9.00 a.m. - 5.00 p.m. This figure rose to 96 per cent in the period 5.00 - 7.00 p.m. Nurseries/crèches etc. are not of major importance to this age group at any time of the day - accounting for only 3.1 per cent of relevant children between 9.00 a.m.- 1.00 p.m., this figure progressively falling to 1.8 per cent, 1.4 per cent and 0.0 per cent by the 5.00 - 7.00 p.m. period. The most important non-parental arrangement for this youngest age category is a child-minder in the minder's home (accounting for approximately 11-12 per cent up until 5.00 p.m. and less than 2 per cent thereafter until 7.00 p.m.) followed by a child-minder in the child's home (accounting for 4.5 - 5.0 per cent until 5.00 p.m. and just under 2 per cent thereafter until 7.00 p.m.).

In contrast, nurseries/crèches etc. have a more important role for 2-3 year olds, especially in the period 9.00 a.m.- 1.00 p.m.. At some stage through that period in the order of 20 per cent of the relevant age category (approximately 21,900 children) are cared for in a nursery/crèche etc. There is a sharp decrease in the relevant percentage figures (to 5.7 per cent) between 1.00 - 3.00 p.m. The importance of child-minders (especially care arrangements provided in the child-minder's home) is approximately equal to that of the 0-1 year olds. As a corollary of these trends the percentage of the 2-3 year olds in the care of parents in their own home is lower than for 0-1 year olds. In the period 9.00 a.m.- 1.00 p.m. just under two-thirds of the age group are at home with their parents; three quarters in the period 1.00 - 3.00 p.m.; 81 per cent between 3.00 - 5.00 p.m. and 97 per cent between 5.00 - 7.00 p.m.

The importance of school becomes apparent for 4 year olds with 49.1 per cent being in school in the period 9.00a.m.-1.00 p.m. and 30 per cent between 1.00-3.00 p.m. Nurseries/crèches etc. are also an important element in the care arrangements for this group, especially in the 9.00 a.m.- 1.00 p.m. period. At some stage through that period just over one-quarter of children avail of this service. Child-minding services are consequently of less significance for 4 year olds than for their younger counterparts. This is especially so in the period 9.00 a.m.- 3.00 p.m. Between 3.00 - 5.00 p.m. they are of approximately the same importance to 4 year olds as to the two younger age groups.

For children aged 5 years and over the role of school is obviously predominant, especially until 3.00 p.m. (somewhat earlier for 5 year olds, reflecting the influence of junior infants in their ranks). There is a certain flow from school to child-minder in the period 3.00 - 5.00 pm.

Chapter 3 considered care arrangements during school holiday periods for school-going children. At the household level it would appear that the responsibility for minding school children during holiday periods primarily rests with the mother. This is, for obvious reasons, particularly so in cases where the mother is engaged full-time on home duties. Even in cases in which the mother works full-time outside the home the responsibility for providing child-care arrangements during school holidays was strongly oriented towards her. For example, in 23.5 per cent of such households the children were minded by the mother. The comparable figure for the father taking primary responsibility for child-care arrangements was 9.3 per cent of households and in 11.3 per cent of households the responsibility was shared jointly.

As one would expect, the story told by the data at the level of the child is entirely consistent with that at the household level.

In Chapter 4 we discussed the role played by child-minder's. We examined in detail the incidence of this service at the household level, as well as the back-up arrangements in the event of the minder not being able to provide the service due to illness or other unanticipated event. The provision of child-minding services in the minder's home as well as in the child(ren)'s home was considered. We found that 8.4 per cent of households which contained children aged 0-12 years used the services of a child-minder in the minder's own home. This represents approximately 31,900 households. The highest incidence of this service was among households in which the mother worked full-time outside the home with 29 per cent of such households using an external child-minder. A total of 12.4 per cent of households in which the mother worked outside the home on a part-time basis used the services of a child-minder in the minder's own home.

In terms of time of the day in which the services of the external minder are used we saw that 48.3 per cent of the households which left children in a minder's home did so in the period 9.00 a.m.- 5.00 p.m. while a further 7.5 per cent did so in the period 9.00 a.m.-7.00 p.m. This obviously reflects the work patterns of households in which both parents work full-time outside the home. A total of 9 per cent of the households using this service did so in the period 9.00 a.m.-3.00 p.m.; 16 per cent in the period 3.00 - 5.00 p.m. and 8 per cent in the period 3.00 - 7.00 p.m. It seems reasonable to attribute the pattern displayed by the latter two groups as largely characterising use of child-minders after school by households in which the parents work full-time outside the home.

As regards back-up care arrangements we saw that in 24 per cent of households this was provided by the mother; in a further 23 per cent it was shared jointly by both parents and in 4 per cent was provided by the father. The role of "Other Relatives" as back-up care providers was very important for those households which used the services of an external child-minder. A total of 34 per cent of such households cited "Other Relatives" when asked who would care for their children in the event of their minder not being able to do so due to illness or similar such unforeseen event.

The chapter also considered the role played by what we described as internal child-minders i.e., minders who care for children in the children's own home. The number of unweighted cases of households which used the services of the internal minder was relatively small and so one must be slightly more circumspect than desirable in terms of what can be said about this group of households. Nonetheless, the survey suggests that 4 per cent of households which contain 0-12 year olds use the services of a minder in the child's own home. This represents some 14,800 households. This form of care arrangements was used predominantly in households in which the mother worked outside the home. It was notable that back-up care arrangements were provided in 45 per cent of these households by "Other Relatives". In a further 15 per cent of households they were provided by the mother; in 5 per cent they were provided by the father and in 15 per cent they were shared jointly by both parents.

Finally, we considered in Chapter 5 the role played by nurseries, crèches, kindergarten, Montessori and other pre-school in the provision of care services to children aged 12 years or less. From the sample we found almost all households which used these arrangements did so in respect of children aged 4 years or less. Consequently, we focused on that subset of the household population which contained children aged 4 years or less. This represented a total of 179,000 households and it was to this base that the figures presented in the chapter related.

In aggregate terms we saw that just over 21 per cent (representing 38,100 households) used the services of a nursery, crèche, etc. In 28 per cent of the households which used them the mother worked outside the home. It is noteworthy, however, that in 46 per cent of households (17,300) which use a nursery, crèche, etc. the mother was engaged in full-time home duties. This implies that almost one-half of the households which use nurseries, creches etc. can be presumed to do so for pre-school socialisation and related early educational benefits rather than primarily as a result of necessity imposed by working outside the home.

In general, nurseries, crèches etc. are used primarily between 9.00 a.m.- 1.00 p.m. with 80 per cent of the households which use them doing so only during that period.

In terms of back-up care arrangements in the event of the crèche not being able to mind the children, we saw that these were provided almost exclusively by the mother in households in which she is engaged on home duties. In those households in which she works outside the home the back-up arrangements are provided on a reasonably equitable basis by the father and the mother with approximately 17 per cent of relevant households citing each parent. In households in which the mother worked part-time outside the home there was clear evidence to indicate the increased role played by "Other Relatives" in providing back-up care arrangements.

# APPENDIX TABLES

## Appendix Table 2.2A

**Distribution of CHILDREN Aged 12 Years or Less Classified by (i) Age Cohort and (ii) Where They Were Cared for At Different Times of the Day in the Tuesday Preceding the Survey**

AGE COHORT OF CHILD

| | 0-1 Year (Per Cent) | | | | 2-3 Years (Per Cent) | | | | 4 Years (Per Cent) | | | | 5 Years (Per Cent) | | | | 6-12 Years (Per Cent) | | | |
|---|---|---|---|---|---|---|---|---|---|---|---|---|---|---|---|---|---|---|---|---|
| | 9.00-1.00 | 1.00-3.00 | 3.00-5.00 | 5.00-7.00 | 9.00-1.00 | 1.00-3.00 | 3.00-5.00 | 5.00-7.00 | 9.00-1.00 | 1.00-3.00 | 3.00-5.00 | 5.00-7.00 | 9.00-1.00 | 1.00-3.00 | 3.00-5.00 | 5.00-7.00 | 9.00-1.00 | 1.00-3.00 | 3.00-5.00 | 5.00-7.00 |
| At School | 0.0 | 0.0 | 0.0 | 0.0 | 0.6 | 0.2 | 0.2 | 0.0 | 48.6 | 31.6 | 0.0 | 0.0 | 98.8 | 78.4 | 1.1 | 0.0 | 99.1 | 97.6 | 3.3 | 0.2 |
| Mother & Toddler Group | 0.0 | 0.0 | 0.0 | 0.0 | 0.7 | 0.0 | 0.0 | 0.0 | 0.0 | 0.0 | 0.0 | 0.5 | 0.0 | 0.0 | 0.0 | 0.0 | 0.0 | 0.0 | 0.0 | 0.0 |
| Nursery/Crèche/Kindergarten/Montessori/Other Pre-School | 3.5 | 2.2 | 1.9 | 0.0 | 18.3 | 5.4 | 3.1 | 0.8 | 25.5 | 3.6 | 1.0 | 0.0 | 0.0 | 0.5 | 1.6 | 0.5 | 0.0 | 0.0 | 0.0 | 0.0 |
| Child Minder's Home | 12.5 | 11.7 | 11.3 | 1.8 | 10.2 | 11.8 | 8.7 | 1.3 | 4.7 | 7.7 | 9.8 | 2.0 | 0.0 | 1.6 | 5.6 | 1.1 | 0.0 | 0.1 | 3.0 | 0.8 |
| At Home with Non-Relative | 5.1 | 4.6 | 4.3 | 1.6 | 1.9 | 2.3 | 2.3 | 1.4 | 2.1 | 3.2 | 3.3 | 0.6 | 0.0 | 0.0 | 4.5 | 2.8 | 0.1 | 0.2 | 3.8 | 1.5 |
| Relative's Home | 5.0 | 5.0 | 3.5 | 0.0 | 3.7 | 5.3 | 5.0 | 0.3 | 1.5 | 3.1 | 3.1 | 0.6 | 0.0 | 1.0 | 3.1 | 1.0 | 0.1 | 0.3 | 3.0 | 0.5 |
| At Home with Parent/Relative | 73.8 | 76.4 | 79.0 | 96.6 | 64.6 | 74.9 | 80.6 | 96.2 | 17.7 | 50.8 | 82.8 | 96.4 | 1.2 | 18.6 | 84.1 | 94.7 | 0.7 | 1.8 | 86.7 | 96.9 |
| Home Alone | 0.0 | 0.0 | 0.0 | 0.0 | 0.0 | 0.0 | 0.0 | 0.0 | 0.0 | 0.0 | 0.0 | 0.0 | 0.0 | 0.0 | 6.3 | 0.0 | 0.0 | 0.0 | 0.2 | 0.1 |
| Total | 100.0 | 100.0 | 100.0 | 100.0 | 100.0 | 100.0 | 100.0 | 100.0 | 100.0 | 100.0 | 100.0 | 100.0 | 100.0 | 100.0 | 100.0 | 100.0 | 100.0 | 100.0 | 100.0 | 100.0 |
| Weighted Total | 106,000 | 106,000 | 106,000 | 106,000 | 108,800 | 108,800 | 108,800 | 108,800 | 58,900 | 58,900 | 58,900 | 58,900 | 60,300 | 60,300 | 60,300 | 60,300 | 471,000 | 471,000 | 471,000 | 471,000 |
| (Unweighted n) | (261) | (261) | (261) | (261) | (325) | (325) | (325) | (325) | (186) | (186) | (186) | (186) | (196) | (196) | (196) | (196) | (1364) | (1364) | (1346) | (1346) |

# Appendix Table 2.2B

## Distribution of CHILDREN Aged 12 Years or Less Classified by (i) Age Cohort and (ii) Where They Were Cared for At Different Times of the Day in the Wednesday Preceding the Survey

AGE COHORT OF CHILD

| | 0-1 Year (Per Cent) | | | | 2-3 Years (Per Cent) | | | | 4 Years (Per Cent) | | | | 5 Years (Per Cent) | | | | 6-12 Years (Per Cent) | | | |
|---|---|---|---|---|---|---|---|---|---|---|---|---|---|---|---|---|---|---|---|---|
| | 9.00-1.00 | 1.00-3.00 | 3.00-5.00 | 5.00-7.00 | 9.00-1.00 | 1.00-3.00 | 3.00-5.00 | 5.00-7.00 | 9.00-1.00 | 1.00-3.00 | 3.00-5.00 | 5.00-7.00 | 9.00-1.00 | 1.00-3.00 | 3.00-5.00 | 5.00-7.00 | 9.00-1.00 | 1.00-3.00 | 3.00-5.00 | 5.00-7.00 |
| At School | 0.0 | 0.0 | 0.0 | 0.0 | 0.6 | 0.2 | 0.2 | 0.0 | 48.1 | 30.6 | 0.0 | 0.0 | 97.3 | 76.9 | 1.1 | 0.0 | 98.4 | 96.7 | 3.2 | 0.2 |
| Mother & Toddler Group | 0.0 | 0.0 | 0.0 | 0.0 | 0.7 | 0.0 | 0.0 | 0.0 | 0.0 | 0.0 | 0.0 | 0.5 | 0.0 | 0.0 | 0.0 | 0.0 | 0.0. | 0.0 | 0.0 | 0.0 |
| Nursery/Crèche/Kindergarten/Montessori/Other Pre-School | 3.1 | 1.9 | 1.5 | 0.0 | 20.2 | 5.1 | 2.8 | 0.8 | 25.9 | 3.6 | 1.0 | 0.0 | 0.0 | 0.5 | 1.6 | 0.5 | 0.0 | 0.0 | 0.0 | 0.0 |
| Child Minder's Home | 13.7 | 13.3 | 12.4 | 1.8 | 9.6 | 11.9 | 8.4 | 1.3 | 4.2 | 8.2 | 10.3 | 2.0 | 0.0 | 1.6 | 5.1 | 1.1 | 0.0 | 0.1 | 3.1 | 0.7 |
| At Home with Non-Relative | 5.1 | 4.6 | 4.3 | 1.6 | 1.9 | 2.5 | 2.5 | 1.6 | 1.5 | 3.2 | 3.3 | 0.6 | 0.0 | 0.5 | 3.9 | 1.7 | 0.1 | 0.2 | 4.0 | 1.6 |
| Relative's Home | 4.6 | 4.6 | 3.9 | 0.0 | 3.1 | 4.7 | 4.4 | 0.3 | 1.5 | 3.1 | 3.7 | 0.6 | 0.0 | 1.0 | 3.1 | 1.0 | 0.1 | 0.3 | 2.9 | 0.4 |
| At Home with Parent/Relative | 73.5 | 75.6 | 77.8 | 96.6 | 64.0 | 75.6 | 81.6 | 96.0 | 18.9 | 51.3 | 81.7 | 96.4 | 2.7 | 19.5 | 85.2 | 95.8 | 1.3 | 2.6 | 86.6 | 97.1 |
| Home Alone | 0.0 | 0.0 | 0.0 | 0.0 | 0.0 | 0.0 | 0.0 | 0.0 | 0.0 | 0.0 | 0.0 | 0.0 | 0.0 | 0.0 | 0.0 | 0.0 | 0.0 | 0.0 | 0.2 | 0.0 |
| Total | 100.0 | 100.0 | 100.0 | 100.0 | 100.0 | 100.0 | 100.0 | 100.0 | 100.0 | 100.0 | 100.0 | 100.0 | 100.0 | 100.0 | 100.0 | 100.0 | 100.0 | 100.0 | 100.0 | 100.0 |
| Weighted Total | 106,000 | 106,000 | 106,000 | 106,000 | 108,800 | 108,800 | 108,800 | 108,800 | 58,900 | 58,900 | 58,900 | 58,900 | 60,300 | 60,300 | 60,300 | 60,300 | 471,000 | 471,000 | 471,000 | 471,000 |
| (Unweighted n) | (261) | (261) | (261) | (261) | (325) | (325) | (325) | (325) | (186) | (186) | (186) | (186) | (196) | (196) | (196) | (196) | (1364) | (1364) | (1346) | (1346) |

## Appendix Table 2.2C

**Distribution of CHILDREN Aged 12 Years or Less Classified by (i) Age Cohort and (ii) Where They Were Cared for At Different Times of the Day in the Thursday Preceding the Survey**

AGE COHORT OF CHILD

|  | 0-1 Year (Per Cent) | | | | 2-3 Years (Per Cent) | | | | 4 Years (Per Cent) | | | | 5 Years (Per Cent) | | | | 6-12 Years (Per Cent) | | | |
|---|---|---|---|---|---|---|---|---|---|---|---|---|---|---|---|---|---|---|---|---|
|  | 9.00-1.00 | 1.00-3.00 | 3.00-5.00 | 5.00-7.00 | 9.00-1.00 | 1.00-3.00 | 3.00-5.00 | 5.00-7.00 | 9.00-1.00 | 1.00-3.00 | 3.00-5.00 | 5.00-7.00 | 9.00-1.00 | 1.00-3.00 | 3.00-5.00 | 5.00-7.00 | 9.00-1.00 | 1.00-3.00 | 3.00-5.00 | 5.00-7.00 |
| At School | 0.0 | 0.0 | 0.0 | 0.0 | 0.6 | 0.2 | 0.2 | 0.0 | 47.6 | 30.6 | 0.0 | 0.0 | 97.3 | 77.4 | 1.1 | 0.0 | 98.1 | 96.5 | 3.2 | 0.2 |
| Mother & Toddler Group | 0.0 | 0.0 | 0.0 | 0.0 | 0.7 | 0.0 | 0.0 | 0.0 | 0.0 | 0.0 | 0.0 | 0.5 | 0.0 | 0.0 | 0.0 | 0.0 | 0.0 | 0.0 | 0.0 | 0.0 |
| Nursery/Crèche/Kindergarten/Montessori/Other Pre-School | 3.1 | 1.8 | 1.1 | 0.0 | 18.3 | 5.1 | 2.8 | 0.8 | 23.4 | 3.6 | 1.0 | 0.0 | 0.0 | 0.5 | 1.6 | 0.5 | 0.0 | 0.0 | 0.0 | 0.0 |
| Child Minder's Home | 12.0 | 11.6 | 11.2 | 1.8 | 10.2 | 11.5 | 8.4 | 1.3 | 4.7 | 6.7 | 8.8 | 2.0 | 0.0 | 1.6 | 4.6 | 1.1 | 0.0 | 0.1 | 2.9 | 0.7 |
| At Home with Non-Relative | 4.7 | 4.2 | 4.2 | 1.9 | 1.6 | 2.0 | 2.0 | 1.4 | 2.1 | 3.2 | 3.3 | 0.6 | 0.0 | 0.0 | 4.5 | 2.8 | 0.1 | 0.2 | 3.8 | 1.5 |
| Relative's Home | 5.4 | 5.4 | 4.2 | 0.0 | 3.7 | 5.3 | 5.0 | 0.6 | 1.5 | 3.1 | 3.7 | 1.1 | 0.0 | 1.0 | 3.1 | 1.0 | 0.1 | 0.3 | 2.8 | 0.3 |
| At Home with Parent/Relative | 74.8 | 77.1 | 79.3 | 96.2 | 64.9 | 75.9 | 81.5 | 95.9 | 20.8 | 52.8 | 83.2 | 95.9 | 2.7 | 19.5 | 85.2 | 94.7 | 1.7 | 2.9 | 87.0 | 97.2 |
| Home Alone | 0.0 | 0.0 | 0.0 | 0.0 | 0.0 | 0.0 | 0.0 | 0.0 | 0.0 | 0.0 | 0.0 | 0.0 | 0.0 | 0.0 | 0.0 | 0.0 | 0.0 | 0.0 | 0.0 | 0.0 |
| Total | 100.0 | 100.0 | 100.0 | 100.0 | 100.0 | 100.0 | 100.0 | 100.0 | 100.0 | 100.0 | 100.0 | 100.0 | 100.0 | 100.0 | 100.0 | 100.0 | 100.0 | 100.0 | 100.0 | 100.0 |
| Weighted Total | 106,000 | 106,000 | 106,000 | 106,000 | 108,800 | 108,800 | 108,800 | 108,800 | 58,900 | 58,900 | 58,900 | 58,900 | 60,300 | 60,300 | 60,300 | 60,300 | 471,000 | 471,000 | 471,000 | 471,000 |
| (Unweighted n) | (261) | (261) | (261) | (261) | (325) | (325) | (325) | (325) | (186) | (186) | (186) | (186) | (196) | (196) | (196) | (196) | (1364) | (1364) | (1346) | (1346) |

# Appendix Table 2.2D

## Distribution of CHILDREN Aged 12 Years or Less Classified by (i) Age Cohort and (ii) Where They Were Cared for At Different Times of the Day in the Friday Preceding the Survey

AGE COHORT OF CHILD

| | 0-1 Year (Per Cent) | | | | 2-3 Years (Per Cent) | | | | 4 Years (Per Cent) | | | | 5 Years (Per Cent) | | | | 6-12 Years (Per Cent) | | | |
|---|---|---|---|---|---|---|---|---|---|---|---|---|---|---|---|---|---|---|---|---|
| | 9.00-1.00 | 1.00-3.00 | 3.00-5.00 | 5.00-7.00 | 9.00-1.00 | 1.00-3.00 | 3.00-5.00 | 5.00-7.00 | 9.00-1.00 | 1.00-3.00 | 3.00-5.00 | 5.00-7.00 | 9.00-1.00 | 1.00-3.00 | 3.00-5.00 | 5.00-7.00 | 9.00-1.00 | 1.00-3.00 | 3.00-5.00 | 5.00-7.00 |
| At School | 0.0 | 0.0 | 0.0 | 0.0 | 0.6 | 0.2 | 0.2 | 0.0 | 46.5 | 28.0 | 0.0 | 0.0 | 97.3 | 76.9 | 1.1 | 0.0 | 96.2 | 94.6 | 3.1 | 0.2 |
| Mother & Toddler Group | 0.0 | 0.0 | 0.0 | 0.0 | 0.7 | 0.0 | 0.0 | 0.0 | 0.0 | 0.0 | 0.0 | 0.5 | 0.0 | 0.0 | 0.0 | 0.0 | 0.0 | 0.0 | 0.0 | 0.0 |
| Nursery/Crèche/Kindergarten/Montessori/Other Pre-School | 2.7 | 1.4 | 1.1 | 0.0 | 16.5 | 4.8 | 2.8 | 0.6 | 23.7 | 3.6 | 1.0 | 0.0 | 0.0 | 0.5 | 1.6 | 0.5 | 0.0 | 0.0 | 0.0 | 0.0 |
| Child Minder's Home | 12.4 | 12.4 | 11.6 | 1.8 | 10.2 | 12.2 | 8.7 | 1.3 | 4.2 | 7.2 | 9.3 | 2.0 | 0.0 | 2.0 | 4.6 | 1.1 | 0.1 | 0.3 | 2.9 | 0.7 |
| At Home with Non-Relative | 5.1 | 4.6 | 4.6 | 1.9 | 1.9 | 1.9 | 1.9 | 1.0 | 1.5 | 2.6 | 3.3 | 1.1 | 0.0 | 0.5 | 3.9 | 2.2 | 0.1 | 0.2 | 4.0 | 1.6 |
| Relative's Home | 5.0 | 4.6 | 3.8 | 0.3 | 3.4 | 5.2 | 4.7 | 0.6 | 1.5 | 3.7 | 3.7 | 0.6 | 0.0 | 1.0 | 3.1 | 1.0 | 0.1 | 0.3 | 2.9 | 0.5 |
| At Home with Parent/Relative | 74.8 | 76.9 | 78.9 | 95.9 | 66.7 | 75.6 | 81.6 | 96.6 | 27.6 | 54.9 | 82.7 | 95.9 | 2.7 | 19.0 | 85.8 | 95.3 | 3.3 | 4.6 | 86.9 | 96.9 |
| Home Alone | 0.0 | 0.0 | 0.0 | 0.0 | 0.0 | 0.0 | 0.0 | 0.0 | 0.0 | 0.0 | 0.0 | 0.0 | 0.0 | 0.0 | 0.0 | 0.0 | 0.0 | 0.0 | 0.2 | 0.0 |
| Total | 100.0 | 100.0 | 100.0 | 100.0 | 100.0 | 100.0 | 100.0 | 100.0 | 100.0 | 100.0 | 100.0 | 100.0 | 100.0 | 100.0 | 100.0 | 100.0 | 100.0 | 100.0 | 100.0 | 100.0 |
| Weighted Total | 106,000 | 106,000 | 106,000 | 106,000 | 108,800 | 108,800 | 108,800 | 108,800 | 58,900 | 58,900 | 58,900 | 58,900 | 60,300 | 60,300 | 60,300 | 60,300 | 471,000 | 471,000 | 471,000 | 471,000 |
| (Unweighted n) | (261) | (261) | (261) | (261) | (325) | (325) | (325) | (325) | (186) | (186) | (186) | (186) | (196) | (196) | (196) | (196) | (1364) | (1364) | (1346) | (1346) |

**The Economic and Social Research Institute**

Limited Company No. 18269  CHY 5335    **4 Burlington Road  Dublin 4  Ireland**

Telephone: (353-1) 6671525          Fax: (353-1) 6686231

## *Supplement on Child Caring Arrangement for Commission on the Family - December 1996*

Interviewer No. ☐☐☐   Area Code: ☐☐☐   Respondent Code: ☐☐☐   Date of Interview_____Day_____ Mth

The Commission on the Family has asked us to collect some information on childcare arrangements used by parents who work full-time in the home or who go out to the workplace.

Q1   First, could you tell me how many children aged 12 years or less live in your household?

_____ Children aged 12 or less

No child aged 12 years or less ...90--->End interview

Refused to answer........91

Q.2   Could you tell me just the first name and age last birthday of each child aged 12 years or less in your household as well as the first name of either the father or mother of each of these children?

| First Name of Child 12 years or less | Age last Birthday | First Name of Mother or Father | First Name of child 12 years or less | Age last Birthday | First Name of Mother or Father |
|---|---|---|---|---|---|
| 1 _____ | _____ yrs | _____ | 4 _____ | _____ yrs | _____ |
| 2 _____ | _____ yrs | _____ | 5 _____ | _____ yrs | _____ |
| 3 _____ | _____ yrs | _____ | 6 _____ | _____ yrs | _____ |

[Interviewer: You should now try to speak to the parent of each child aged 12 years or less in the household.]

To complete the questionnaire I would like to speak to _____(*parent's name*) and_____ (*other parent's name*) if *children from more than one family reside in the household*. [Int. Remember that you should complete this supplementary questionnaire with either the mother of father of each family unit in the household, even if this means 'phoning back to the household at another time]

Parent's First Name:_____

Q3  Do you work:

Full-time in the home
(On home duties) ...1        Full-time Outside the home ...2        Part-time Outside the home ...3

Unemployed ...4        Other (specify) _____ ...5

Q.4 Does your partner/spouse work:

Full-time in the home
(On home duties) ...1        Full-time Outside the home ...2        Part-time Outside the home ...3

Partner/Spouse Unemployed ...4        No partner/spouse in h'hold ...5

Q.5 Interviewer: Sex of respondent?

Male ... 1                Female ... 2

Q. 6 You said that you have_____children aged 12 years or less (see Q1) living in your household. I would like to collect some information on each of them in terms of where and with whom they spent their time last week. For example, they could have spent their time:

    A. At School . . . . . . . . . . . . . . . . . . . . . . . . . . . . . . . . . . . . . . . . . . . . . . . . . . . . . . . . . . . . . . 1
    B Parent & Child or Mother & toddler group (parent stays with child) . . . . . . . . . . . . . . . . . . . . . . . 2
    C Any form of nursery, crèche, kindergarten, montessori or other pre-school (child left) . . . . . . . . . . . . . . . . . . . . 3
    D Child-Minder's Home . . . . . . . . . . . . . . . . . . . . . . . . . . . . . . . . . . . . . . . . . . . . . . . . . . . . . 4
    E At home with a child-minder, nanny, au pair or other NON-RELATIVE . . . . . . . . . . . . . . . . . . . . . . . 5
    F Being cared for in a relative's home - not the child's home . . . . . . . . . . . . . . . . . . . . . . . . . . . . . . 6
    G At home with their parent or other relative . . . . . . . . . . . . . . . . . . . . . . . . . . . . . . . . . . . . . . . 7
    H At home on their own . . . . . . . . . . . . . . . . . . . . . . . . . . . . . . . . . . . . . . . . . . . . . . . . . . . . 8

So, if we could think of where your children spent time during last week. Lets start with (Child No. 1 at Q 2) and where he/she spent time last Monday morning between 9.00am - 1.00 pm. And between 1.00 pm - 3.00pm and between 3.00pm - 5.00om. and between 5.00pm - 7.00pm. And on Tuesday, Wednesday...etc.

[Int: Insert Code A, B, C, D, E, F, G, or H in each of the boxes below in respect of each child aged 12 years or less in the household.]

**Child No. 1** (From Q.2) Name: _____

|  | Mon. | Tues. | Wed. | Thurs. | Fri. |
|---|---|---|---|---|---|
| 9.00-1.00 |  |  |  |  |  |
| 1.00-3.00 |  |  |  |  |  |
| 3.00-5.00 |  |  |  |  |  |
| 5.00-7.00 |  |  |  |  |  |

**Child No. 4** (From Q.2) Name: _____

|  | Mon. | Tues. | Wed. | Thurs. | Fri. |
|---|---|---|---|---|---|
| 9.00-1.00 |  |  |  |  |  |
| 1.00-3.00 |  |  |  |  |  |
| 3.00-5.00 |  |  |  |  |  |
| 5.00-7.00 |  |  |  |  |  |

**Child No. 2** (From Q.2) Name: _____

|  | Mon. | Tues. | Wed. | Thurs. | Fri. |
|---|---|---|---|---|---|
| 9.00-1.00 |  |  |  |  |  |
| 1.00-3.00 |  |  |  |  |  |
| 3.00-5.00 |  |  |  |  |  |
| 5.00-7.00 |  |  |  |  |  |

**Child No. 5** (From Q.2) Name: _____

|  | Mon. | Tues. | Wed. | Thurs. | Fri. |
|---|---|---|---|---|---|
| 9.00-1.00 |  |  |  |  |  |
| 1.00-3.00 |  |  |  |  |  |
| 3.00-5.00 |  |  |  |  |  |
| 5.00-7.00 |  |  |  |  |  |

**Child No. 3** (From Q.2) Name: _____

|  | Mon. | Tues. | Wed. | Thurs. | Fri. |
|---|---|---|---|---|---|
| 9.00-1.00 |  |  |  |  |  |
| 1.00-3.00 |  |  |  |  |  |
| 3.00-5.00 |  |  |  |  |  |
| 5.00-7.00 |  |  |  |  |  |

**Child No. 6** (From Q.2) Name: _____

|  | Mon. | Tues. | Wed. | Thurs. | Fri. |
|---|---|---|---|---|---|
| 9.00-1.00 |  |  |  |  |  |
| 1.00-3.00 |  |  |  |  |  |
| 3.00-5.00 |  |  |  |  |  |
| 5.00-7.00 |  |  |  |  |  |

FINAL REPORT OF THE COMMISSION ON THE FAMILY

**CODE A: 'At School'**

Q.7 Interviewer: Does Code A ("At School") occur in *any* part of the table in Q.6?

Yes ... 1          No...2 --->Go to Q.10

---

Q. 8 Who usually looks after the child(ren) during school holidays?

Child's Mother ..1   Child's Father ...2   Parents take it in turn ...3   Other Relative ...4   Friend or Neighbour ...5  Other ...6

Q.9 Who usually minds the child(ren) if he/she is too sick to attend school?

Child's Mother ..1   Child's Father ...2   Parents take it in turn ...3   Other Relative ...4   Friend or Neighbour ...5  Other ...6

---

**CODE C: Any form of nursery, crèche, kindergarten, Montessori, other pre-school**

Q 10 Interviewer: Does Code C (i.e., 'any form of nursery, crèche, kindergarten, Montessori, other pre-school') occur in *any* part of the table in Q.6?

Yes ... 1          No...2 --->Go to Q.15

---

Q 11 Approximately how many children IN TOTAL are looked after in the nursery, crèche, kindergarten, Montessori, other pre-school which _____attends (name(s) of child(ren))
                    A total of _____children

Q12 And how many teachers or supervisors are there in total in this nursery, crèche, kindergarten,  Montessori, pre-school?
                    A total of _____teachers/supervisors

Q13 How much IN TOTAL do you pay for this nursery, crèche, kindergarten, Montessori, pre-school per week, fortnight etc.?
          A TOTAL OF IR£ _____per_____(week, forthnight, month, etc)

Q14 Who would mind the child(ren) if either he/she were ill and could not attend the nursery, crèche, kindergarten, Montessori, or pre-school or if the teacher were ill and could not mind your childl(ren)

Child's Mother ..1   Child's Father ...2   Parents take it in turn ...3   Other Relative ...4   Friend or Neighbour ...5  Other ...6

---

**CODE D: In a child-minder's home**

Q15 Interviewer: Does CODE D occur in *any* part of the table in Q 6?

Yes ... 1          No...2 --->Go to Q.18

---

Q16 How much de you pay per week for the child-minder to mind your children? IR£ _____per week

Q17 Who would mind your child(ren) if your child-minder was unable to do so for a few days because of illness or some other unexpected event?

Child's Mother ..1   Child's Father ...2   Parents take it in turn ...3   Other Relative ...4   Friend or Neighbour ...5  Other ...6

---

**CODE E: At home with a child-minder, nanny, au pair or other NON-RELATIVE**

Q 18 Interviewer: Does Code E occur in *any* part of the table in Q 6?

Yes ... 1          No...2 --->Go to Q.21

---

Q 19 Who would mind your child(ren) if your child-minder, nanny, au pair etc. was unable to come to your home for a few days because of illness or some other unexpected event?

Child's Mother ..1   Child's Father ...2   Parents take it in turn ...3   Other Relative ...4   Friend or Neighbour ...5  Other ...6

Q 20 How much do you pay per week for the child-minder, nanny, au pair etc. to come to mind your children?
                              IR£_____per week

**CODES F OR G: 'Being cared for in a relative's home' or 'in the child's home by child's parent or other relative"**

Q21 Interviewer: Do Codes F or G occur in any part of the table at Q 6?

Yes ... 1       No...2 --->Go to Q.26

Q 22 Who usually minds _____(name(s) of child(ren) Is it?

Child's Mother ...1 -->Go to Q25    Child's Father ...2-->Go to Q25    Parents take it in turn ...3-->Go to Q25    Other Relative ... 4

Q23 Do you have to pay this relative for minding the child(ren)?   Yes ... 1   No ...2--->Go to Q25

Q24 How much do you usually pay per week?   IR£_____per week

Q25 Who minds them if that person (Child's Mother, Child's Father or Other Relative at Q.22) is too ill or needs to attend to other commitments outside the home and is unable to care for the child(ren)?

| | |
|---|---|
| Other Parent ............1 | Friend or neighbour.........5 |
| Other Relative .........2 | Other...............................6 |
| Child minder .............3 | Please specify _____ |
| Crèche, nursery, etc..4 | _____ |

**ONLY codes A, G OR H in table at Q 6 ('At School';'At home with parent or relative'; 'At home on their own')**
INT. IF ONLY CODES A,G OR H OCCUR IN THE TABLE AT Q6 ASK Q 26. IF ANY OTHER CODE OCCURS IN *ANY* PART OF THE TABLE AT Q6 GO TO Q27.

Q26 What is your MAIN reason for not using any alternative child-care arrangements such as a playgroup, nursery, crèche, kindergarten, Montessori, other pre-school, child-minder etc. (Int. Circle ONE only)

| | |
|---|---|
| I'm at home anyway ............................1 | No transport available to get to |
| I'd prefer to mind the children myself....2 | alternative minding arrangements ......................................4 |
| Too dear.................................................3 | Other (specify) _____5 |

Q27 Int: Did this respondent complete the Consumer Survey? Yes ...1--->End Interview No ... 2

Q28 Respondent's age group    16-29 yrs ...1    30-49 yrs ...2   50-64 yrs...3   65 or more ...4   Don't Know ...5

Q29 What is (or was) your main occupation? If retired or unemployed please give previous occupation. If never worked or housewife, give occupation of main earner in household (Int: Write full title and code).

_____

Self-employed(not farmer) ...1    Farmer ...2    Professional/Senior Managerial ...3   Other non-manual worker ..4

Skilled manual worker ...5    Unskilled manual worker ...6    Don't know ...9

Q30 What type of school or college did you last attend?

| | | |
|---|---|---|
| Primary School ...1 | Other Second Level (nursing, agric or | Third Level (univ., college of tech., art college, teacher |
| Group/Inter/Junior ...2 | commercial college etc ..4 | training, professional qualifications etc.) ...5 |
| Leaving Cert ...3 | | |

INTERVIEWER: If there is another family unit (or unitsl) in the household which have children aged 12 years or less you should interview one parent of each of these other families about their childcare arrangements, even if this means telephoning back to the household. Use a blue questionnaire to record the information on each of these <u>additional</u> family units

Total number of family units in the household (incl. above) _____family units

Total number successfully interviewed (incl.above)_____family units interviewed

4

## 20.1 Introduction

The Commission's examination of the effects of policy programmes and services on families has highlighted the dearth of research into families, family members and how children from different backgrounds fare in the longer term. There is very little research into the lives of children in Ireland. In this chapter the Commission sets out the case for a National Child Development Study. The proposal for the study was submitted to the Commission by TREOIR ( Federation for Unmarried Parents and their Children).

## 20.2 A study of Irish children

A large scale study which includes all children has not been undertaken in Ireland. Children may experience a variety of changing circumstances from birth to adulthood. It is not known how children from different family types function in the long-term. Neither is it known how children from particular family backgrounds, such as single-parent families, achieve, compared to children in general or to their peers from similar socio-economic backgrounds. By studying large numbers of children it is possible to compile information about children's experience in Irish society.

To date, studies of children which have been undertaken in Ireland have in the main concentrated on what are generally regarded as adverse circumstances. For example, many small-scale studies have focused on families headed by unmarried parents, mainly mothers. These families tend to be studied in isolation from the broader society. A study which includes children from different strands of society and different home situations should concentrate on all aspects of the life of children and should be able to identify the combination of circumstances in which children succeed as well as highlighting the difficulties for children in adverse circumstances. Much can be learned from studying what works, as well as studying what does not work. This would contribute to the debate about values and which values or contribution of values serve to underpin the better functioning of society. It would help in the more effective shaping of policy responses to particular social needs.

## 20.3 What would be involved in a National Study

A national child development study would involve having a large cross-section of Irish children studied at various crucial intervals from birth to adulthood.

The study would, of its nature, be multidisciplinary and would produce findings which could be used by all government departments, health boards and other interested parties. Sub-studies into particular groups, such as children in care or those in foster homes, where background information already exists would be facilitated and the database developed for the study could be used as a sampling frame for policy-makers and analysts wishing to undertake independent research.

The best known study of the type proposed is the British National Child Development Study

(1958 cohort) which was conducted between 1964 and 1991. In that study 17,000 children were studied at birth and at ages 7, 11, 16, 23 and 33. Policy-makers still refer to the National Child Development Study in the UK.

### Longitudinal studies

There are two types of longitudinal research: trend studies and panel studies. In trend studies, a piece of research is repeated a number of times but with a different sample each time. In panel studies (such as is proposed here) the same original respondents are interviewed more than once and usually several times over a period of years. For example, the annual ESRI, Living in Ireland household surveys are part of a European Union panel survey.

One of the main advantages of a panel study, therefore, is that over a period of time very reliable information is collected to which the researcher can refer back without being dependent on the subjective memory of respondents. This allows for significant events to be identified in retrospect and cause and effect examined.

Longitudinal studies enable one to follow the transition from the birth of the child to later life cycles. In Ireland no major examination has been made of the movement between different family types and the impact this has at different stages in the life of the child. It is already known that many mothers who are unmarried at the birth of their children marry afterwards. The study would facilitate an examination of the effects of marital separation and divorce and the growing trend toward cohabitation outside of marriage, referred to in Chapter 9. The effects of policies and practices in all aspects of social policy can be monitored and the need for changes highlighted.

Longitudinal studies enable one to identify risk factors and to put early interventions in place. Research into the findings which emerge in longitudinal studies holds out the possibility of identifying some of the circumstances which might counteract a potentially damaging tendency; for example, the risk of being involved in drug abuse or criminal activity.

A national study would allow for regional comparisons, and its findings will be able to highlight gaps in services and possible inequalities in different areas of the country.

A longitudinal panel study of this sort would be an invaluable resource for policy-makers, researchers and those with an interest in the social and related needs of children in Ireland, as well as the policy response to those needs.

The Commission recommends that the possibility of undertaking a national child development study should be examined with a view to advancing the proposal.

## 20.4    Cost

The Commission has been advised that to maximise the full potential of the study, the sample size would have to be sufficiently large as to allow a focus on specific policy-relevant sub-groups. An initial minimum sample of 15,000-20,000 children should be considered. Resources necessary for this sort of study are estimated to be in the approximate region of £0.8-1 million per round of the study.

The Commission suggests that the potential of a trust fund currently under examination by the Minister for Social, Community and Family Affairs to fund such a study be explored.

# Summary of Part 7

The Commission presents the main findings in the research projects which it has undertaken

# Making a start Part 7

## Recommendation 44

The Commission recommends

- **that the possibility of undertaking a national child development study should be examined.**

**Cost:** It is estimated that the cost of a study would be in the region of £0.8 million to £1 million per survey 'round'.

The Commission suggests that the potential of a trust fund, currently under examination by the Minister for Social, Community and Family Affairs, to fund such a study should be explored.

part 8

"to raise public awareness and improve understanding of issues affecting families"

**In Part 8 the Commission**

- describes a number of initiatives undertaken to raise awareness and promote understanding of family matters
- presents a summary of the main issues, concerns, comments and suggestions made in submissions received

# Overview of Part 8

**The terms of reference required the Commission *inter alia*, "to raise public awareness and improve understanding of issues affecting families".**

In Part 8 the Commission presents details of a number of initiatives which it has taken over the past two years to raise awareness about family interests and promote understanding about issues of concern to families.

The Commission began its task with the launch of an ambitious programme to encourage submissions from the public.

The Commission on the Family programme to invite submissions was launched in the Royal Hospital, Kilmainham, on 15 February 1996 by the Minister for Social Welfare. Some 250 representatives from government departments, state agencies and national voluntary organisations who work with families attended the launch.

Advertisements were placed in national and provincial newspapers and information leaflets about the Commission were widely distributed. A freephone helpdesk was set up to advise callers about the work of the Commission and how they might contribute. There was a huge response from the public, with over 450 calls to the freephone helpdesk. Nearly half of all callers went on to send in written submissions. In all, over 530 submissions were received from individuals and families and national and local voluntary organisations who work with families. The majority of submissions came from individuals, families and from small groups, many of whom came together to make a submission telling the Commission about their experiences and what they would like to see put in place to better support families.

On UN International Day of Families, 15 May 1996, the Commission hosted a forum to hear what local community groups and families themselves see as the priorities. The forum was particularly aimed at local and community groups which have practical experience of working with families.

UN International Day of Families 1997 was marked with a special exhibition, in the National Gallery of Ireland, of the winning entries in the sculpture category of a national art competition for students in second-level Transition Year. In addition, the Commission hosted an expert workshop for the key providers of marriage and relationship counselling to explore the priorities for these services in the years ahead.

The Commission together with the Transition Year Support Team has developed a module of studies related to family issues. The module is designed for teenage students in the 15-to-16 year age group who are taking the transition year at second-level school. "Family Studies" is now available as an option to some 26,000 students throughout the country.

The publication of the Commission's interim report, in November 1996 presented a further opportunity to highlight the importance of family issues and to elicit views in relation to the future direction of State support for families.

Over 530 submissions were made to the Commission. Over half of the submissions, 56 per cent, came from families and individuals. The rest, 44 per cent, came from national and local organisations that work with families. Submissions covered a range of topics. Almost half of all submissions commented on the importance of education in relation to a range of family concerns. Other very significant topics were: counselling support (including marriage counselling), which was raised in nearly 40 per cent of submissions; childcare arrangements and facilities (36 per cent of submissions), health and social welfare and legal matters (some 30 per cent ), and the effects of changes in families and in society, (23 per cent), the family and the Constitution (20 per cent) and support for mothers who work full-time in the home (20 per cent).

**Percentage of submissions on different topics**

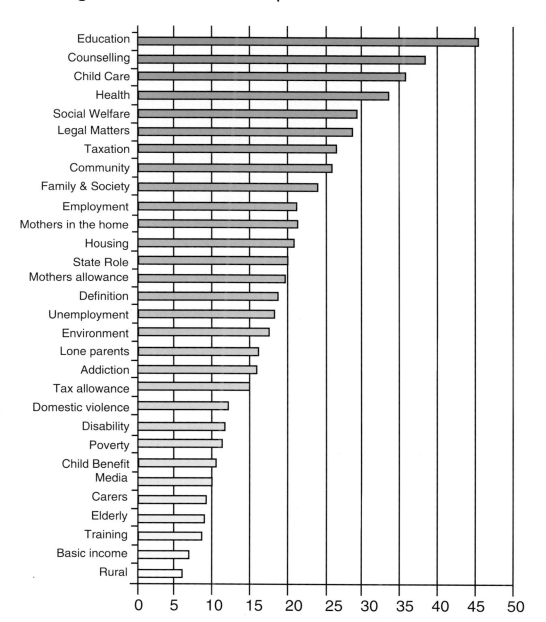

# Chapter 21 Some highlights from the Commission's programme to raise public awareness and improve understanding of issues affecting families.

## 21.1 Introduction

The Commission has been overwhelmed by the response from the public to its work. The goodwill extended to the Commission in pursuing its task is indicative of the level of interest in family matters. This interest has been very evident in the response to the initiatives which the Commission has undertaken. In this chapter, details are presented about some of the initiatives which it has undertaken to raise awareness about family issues.

## 21.2 Forum for voluntary and community groups who work with families

*UN International Day of Families, 15 May 1996*

Some 250 people participated in the Forum. These were representative of voluntary and local community groups, including family resource centres, those who work with lone parents, people with disabilities and their carers, women's and men's development groups and support groups who assist people coping with marital breakdown, parenting difficulties and unemployment. Representatives of 13 local communities gave presentations about the issues which they had identified as being important to the future support of families. There was a strong emphasis in the presentations on the potential within families and their local communities to meet their own needs and on the role of state and voluntary agencies in building up the capacities of local communities and empowering families in carrying out their responsibilities to themselves and their children.

Presentations covered the very different experiences of families in contending with modern-day problems; for example, parenting alone, marital breakdown and addiction problems. There were suggestions in relation to the support services provided by the State and those available in the local community.

Some of the main issues raised in the presentations included:
- the difficulties in establishing and running a voluntary support service for families
- the complexities of the social welfare and taxation systems and eligibility for medical services for families that have members who are unemployed and for older people and carers
- the supports needed for lone parents to assist them in getting access to employment and the importance of childminding services
- carers and their needs for support, information and access to respite services
- the loss and grief experienced by children and by grandparents when marital breakdown separates a family.

The presentations were followed by a lively discussion with many different points of view being expressed.

## 21.3    Family studies at second level (Transition Year)

The family awareness module of studies has been developed by the Commission on the Family with the Transition Year Support Team of the Department of Education and Science. The module[1] is a first  in the Irish school curriculum. The new studies, are for students in the 15-to-16 year age-group who are taking the Transition Year at second level. The studies provide an opportunity for young people to explore topics such as roles and responsibilities in families, the media and its influence on family life, managing the family finances, the law and families and communication between the generations.

The Family Awareness Studies module is now available as an option for some 26,000 Transition Year pupils throughout the country.

The following extracts from the Family Awareness Studies Handbook give an indication of the studies involved for young people.

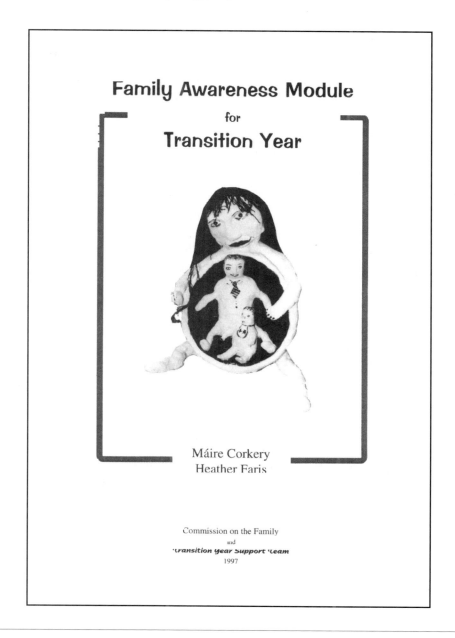

**Family Awareness Module**
for
**Transition Year**

Máire Corkery
Heather Faris

Commission on the Family
and
Transition Year Support Team
1997

---

1    The Commission wishes to acknowledge the work of Máire Corkery and Heather Faris in compiling the module of studies.

## Unit 1

Definitions

Aims: *To provide the students with an opportunity to :*

- name some of the existing definitions of family with which they are familiar
- explore new definitions
- link definition to experience
- create their own definition, with the emphasis on relationship. ( It might be helpful here to concentrate on the notion of families rather than on that of 'the family'.)

## Unit 2

Literature

Aims:

- To create an awareness of the breadth of literature portraying family life
- To understand how literature reflects and analyses emotional complexity in the context of the family.

*Resources:*

- Maeve Binchy:      *Circle of Friends; The Glass Lake; Light a Penny Candle; Echoes*
- Jung Chang:      *Wild Swans*
- Roddy Doyle:      *The Commitments; The Snapper; The Van*
- Fergal Keane:      *Despatches from the Heart- Letter to Daniel (pp 35-38)*
- Joan Lingard:      *The Twelfth of July*
- Brendan O' Carroll:      *The Mammy; The Chislers*
- Joan O' Neill:      *The Daisychain War; Bread and Sugar*
- Patricia Scanlan:      *City Girl ; Appt. 3B*
- The Old Testament:      *The story of Jacob and Esau (Genesis: Chapters 25, 27 and 28.)*
- The New Testament:      *The story of the Prodigal Son (Luke : Chapter 15: verses 11-32)*

## Unit 3

Who Says What ?

*"When I was a boy of fourteen, my father was so ignorant I could hardly stand to have the man around. But when I got to be twenty-one I was astonished at how much he had learnt in seven years."*
Mark Twain

*Aims :*

- To explore the issue of communication within the family in a general way.
- To make students aware that there is a type of communication which is conducive to the maintenance of a healthy environment within the family unit, whatever its make-up. What should be kept in mind here is the flourishing of both individual family members and of the family unit itself.

*Methodology*

Questions which could be followed up in subsequent discussion could be :

- What did you notice about this family, about yourself, about silences, sulks, talk, politeness, rudeness, abruptness, honesty, masking?

- How do you feel when other family members communicate inadequately with you?
- Are you able to imagine how other members of the family feel when faced with sulks, anger, rudeness from you ?

## Unit 4

### Who Says What?
### Roles and Responsibilities

*Aims:*

- To look at the issue of responsibility within the family unit.
- To look at the variety of tasks in any household.
- To point to the danger of stereotyping.
- To allow students to express their feelings about the roles they play.

## Unit 5

### Family Finances

*Aims :*

- To help students come to an awareness of the different financial circumstances which exist for families within society.
- To give students a realisation of what is involved in the managing of family finances without giving them a sense of guilt or indeed without making them feel that they are in any way primarily responsible for the running of the family finances.
- To draw attention to the implications of money matters for individuals and for the family unit as a whole.

*Note to the Teacher*

The emphasis here is on the attitude to and management of money by individual family members and by the family as a whole. The issue is how families cope with financial dilemmas rather than the exact amount involved in any budgeting situation.

The teacher should emphasise that help is available for families in financial difficulties, for example: St. Vincent de Paul, Citizens Information Centres, Credit Unions, Family Income Supplement. In this context, reference can also be made to Unit 8 where the students will be asked to put together a resource pack for families for their local area.

## Unit 6

### The Family in the Media

*Methodology*

1. Why are soap operas so popular ? What is their appeal ?
2. In the soap that you have chosen, how are the characters drawn up ? Is the characterisation too simplistic, too plastic, too stereotypical? Are there individuals who are portrayed as being more important than others ? On what grounds ?
3. Is there a message or agenda ?
4. What issues are surfacing in the portrayal of family life ?

**Unit 7**

The Family and the Law in Ireland

*Aims :*

- To remind students of the significance of the Family in the Irish Constitution.
- To give basic legal information about the family in Ireland.
- To create a general awareness of the legal issues which are relevant to family life in Ireland.

**Unit 8**

Support for the Family- Resources

The immediate aim then is to involve the students in a bit of detective work with a view to putting together a catalogue of all agencies, support and help groups in their locality that would respond to some of the crises that beset families. In this way the students will become very aware that such support does exist, will learn how to name problems and will see that there is always someone else out there with the same or a similar problem. How the situation is experienced and lived, however, will be different for each family.

**Unit 9**

Conclusion

*Aims:*

- To invite the students to assess whether or not there has been any change in their attitude to and knowledge of family life and issues.
- To reflect again on the definition of 'family' which the students decided on in Unit 1 and to decide now if they are still happy with that definition.

# Chapter 22 A summary of the main issues raised in submissions to the Commission on the Family

## Introduction

The Commission's programme to encourage submissions from the public was carried out from February 1996 to May 1996. During that time some 540 submissions were received. This report gives an overview of the main topics which arose in the submissions.

**The Commission would like to acknowledge the work of Ms. Judith Kiernan in assisting with the Commission's examination of the issues raised in submissions.**

*Summary of the submissions to the Commission on the Family*

Contents                                                                 Page

# Section I

### Introduction
This report is a summary of the issues raised in submissions to the Commission on the Family (the Commission). The purpose of this summary of submissions is to record the range of views expressed. Sections II to X of this report present the issues, concerns and views raised. Some submissions addressed short-term solutions to current difficulties experienced by families or categories of families. Some centred on medium and long-term strategies to improve various aspects of family life. This report notes instances of unanimity of view. In cases of substantial agreement, a distillation of view is presented. In certain instances there was no general agreement and this summary records the main differences of view, with an attempt to identify the principal arguments, in relation to each such issue.

### Background to the submissions
Early in 1996, the Commission launched a campaign to encourage submissions from the public. Advertisements were placed in the national and provincial press. The advertising campaign was augmented by a free phone telephone advice line providing further information for people and groups interested in making a submission.

An information leaflet was circulated to a total of 6,000 national and local groups. These were State and semi-State bodies, professional associations, and voluntary organisations working at national and local level including community and parish groups, women's and  men's groups and support groups working with lone parents, people with disabilities, elderly people and carers. At the Commission's request, the Department of Social Welfare sent the information leaflet to a total of 1,100 families in receipt of child benefit, including families living in Gaeltacht areas.

Organisations and individuals with a particular interest in issues relating to families were invited to contribute to the Commission's work by making a submission. These included members of the Oireachtas, political parties represented in Dail Eireann, government departments, statutory bodies, e.g. health boards, the Combat Poverty Agency and Bord na Gaeilge, trades unions, employers' organisations, professional associations, farming bodies, national voluntary organisations, the main churches and academic and research institutions.

### Submissions received
At the time of writing, 536 submissions had been received by the Commission, of which 485 form the basis of this report. There were 448 phone calls to the free phone advice desk. Many of these callers went on to make written submissions to the Commission. A short description of the issues raised by callers is set out at the end of this section of the report.

## Analysis of Submissions

Submissions were analysed in terms of whether they came from individuals or organisations (source of submissions). Submissions from organisations were categorised in terms of the size of organisations and the primary focus of activity of organisations. All submissions were analysed in terms of their geographic source, of the number of issues raised in each submission and of the type of main issues raised in submissions. All percentages presented throughout the text are approximate.

## Source of submissions

The submissions were categorised on the basis of whether they came from individuals or from organisations (see Table I). A total of 273 individuals made submissions to the Commission, comprising 56% of all submissions. There were 212 submissions (44% of total) from organisations.

**Table I: Individuals and organisations making submissions**

| Source | No. | % of total |
|---|---|---|
| Individuals | 273 | 56% |
| Organisations | 212 | 44% |
| Total | 485 | 100% |

## Size of organisations

Organisations were categorised as national, regional, county or local (see Table II). Submissions came mainly from national or local organisations.

**Table II: Size and number of organisations making submissions**

| Organisation | No. | % of total |
|---|---|---|
| National | 82 | 17% |
| Regional | 6 | 1% |
| County | 33 | 7% |
| Local | 91 | 19% |
| Total | 212 | 44% |

## Areas of activity of organisations

The primary area of activity of the organisations contributing submissions was analysed. It should be noted that the issue(s) raised in the submission of any given organisation did not necessarily reflect the main area of activity of that organisation. Table III shows the wide range of organisations represented in submissions.

**Table III: Activity of organisations making submissions**

| Activity | No. | % of total |
|---|---|---|
| Community centres | 47 | 10% |
| Women | 37 | 8% |
| Education | 17 | 3% |
| Counselling and guidance | 16 | 3% |
| Religious | 13 | 3% |
| Disability | 11 | 2% |
| Children | 9 | 2% |
| Elderly and carers | 8 | 2% |
| Health | 7 | 1% |
| Family resource centres | 7 | 1% |
| Youth and drugs | 7 | 1% |
| Legal | 6 | 1% |
| Poverty | 5 | 1% |
| Lone parents | 3 | 1% |
| Gay and lesbian | 3 | 1% |
| Travellers | 2 | 1% |
| Refugees | 2 | 1% |
| Unemployed | 1 | — |
| Other | 11 | 2% |
| **Total** | **212** | **44%** |

## Geographic source of submissions

The geographic source of submissions was examined. National organisations were frequently based in Dublin. Regional organisations were categorised by province. As Table IV indicates there was a wide spread of geographic source of submissions. Dublin was the source of the largest number of contributions with 127 (26% of total). National organisations, most of which are based in Dublin, accounted for 82 submissions (17% of total).

**Table IV: Geographic source of submissions**

| Geographic source | No. |
|---|---|
| Dublin | 127 |
| National | 82 |
| Cork | 45 |
| No address given | 31 |
| Donegal | 26 |
| Sligo | 14 |
| Tipperary | 11 |
| Mayo | 11 |
| Galway | 11 |
| Waterford | 10 |
| Louth | 10 |
| Kildare | 10 |
| Kerry | 9 |
| Clare | 9 |
| Cavan | 9 |
| Meath | 8 |
| Limerick | 8 |
| Kilkenny | 8 |
| Wicklow | 7 |
| Roscommon | 7 |
| Westmeath | 5 |
| Offaly | 5 |
| Wexford | 4 |
| Connacht | 4 |
| Monaghan | 3 |
| Longford | 3 |
| Laois | 3 |
| Leinster | 2 |
| Carlow | 2 |
| International | 1 |
| Leitrim | 0 |
| Munster | 0 |
| **Total** | **485** |

## Numbers of issues raised in submissions

Most submissions, (367 or 76% in all), from both individuals and organisations, referred to more than one issue affecting the family (see Table V).

### Table V: Numbers of issues raised in submissions

| Number of issues raised | No. | % of total |
|---|---|---|
| Submissions from individuals, raising only one issue | 83 | 17% |
| Submissions from individuals, raising more than one issue | 190 | 39% |
| Submissions from organisations, raising only one issue | 35 | 7% |
| Submissions from organisations, raising more than one issue | 177 | 37% |
| Total | 485 | 100% |

## Most frequently mentioned issues

A count of the issues most frequently cited was undertaken to provide a broad sense of their relative importance in the submissions. Issues and concerns discussed in more than 5% of submissions are listed in summary form in Table VI. The list below contains a short description of the range of issues covered within each issue and the section of this report dealing with the content of the relevant submissions.

**Education:** any reference to formal education for any age group, **section IV;**

**Counselling:** any reference to any form of counselling, **section VI;**

**Child care:** any reference to child care facilities or crèches, **sections II, IV and V;**

**Health:** any reference to general concerns of the health system, **section V;**

**Social welfare:** any reference to the social welfare system, including child benefit, **section VII;**

**Legal matters:** any reference to family law or other legal concerns, **section X;**

**Taxation:** any reference to taxation matters, **section VIII;**

**Community:** any reference to matters such as community development, community facilities or community organisations, **section IX;**

**Family and society:** any reference to concerns regarding ethical, religious or broadly philosophical themes relating to the individual, the family and society, presented in **section II** and throughout the report;

**Employment:** any reference to employment, **section VIII;**

**Mothers in the home:** any reference to mothers who work full-time in the home, **section III;**

**Housing :** any reference to housing, **section IX;**

**State role:** any reference to matters to do with government and suggestions regarding the State response to the family, **section II** and throughout the report;

**Mothers in the home allowance:** any reference to financial assistance for mothers working full-time in the home, **section III;**

**Definition of the family:** any reference to concerns regarding constitutional and other definitions of the family for legal and social purposes, **section II.**

**Unemployment:** any reference to unemployment, **section VII;**

**Environment:** any reference to the environment, **section IX;**

**Lone parents:** any reference to lone parents, **section III** and throughout the report;

**Addiction:** any reference to matters in relation to alcohol and drug addiction, **section III** and throughout the report.

**Tax-free allowances for children:** any reference to requests for tax-free allowances for dependent children, **section VIII;**

**Domestic violence:** any reference to domestic violence, **section III** and throughout the report.

**Disability:** any reference to disability issues, **section III** and throughout the report;

**Poverty:** any reference to poverty, **section VII;**

**Child benefit:** any reference to child benefit, **section VII;**

**Media:** any reference to the media, **sections II, III** and throughout the report;

**Carers:** any reference to carers, **section V;**

**Elderly:** any reference to elderly people, **sections III, V** and throughout the report;

**Training:** any reference to State funded training schemes, **section VI;**

**Minimum income:** any reference to a minimum income for all, **section VII;**

**Rural:** any reference to rural living, throughout the report.


Table VI shows the main issues identified and the number of submissions in which each of these issues was raised.

**Table VI: Main issues of submissions**

| Issue | No. | % of total |
|---|---|---|
| Education | 225 | 46% |
| Counselling | 185 | 38% |
| Child care | 173 | 36% |
| Health | 160 | 33% |
| Social welfare | 143 | 29% |
| Legal matters | 142 | 29% |
| Taxation | 127 | 26% |
| Community | 123 | 25% |
| Family and society | 113 | 23% |
| Employment | 104 | 21% |
| Mothers working in the home | 104 | 21% |
| Housing | 102 | 21% |
| State role | 97 | 20% |
| Mothers allowance | 96 | 20% |
| Definition of family | 91 | 19% |
| Unemployment | 90 | 18% |
| Environment | 85 | 17% |
| Lone parents | 77 | 16% |
| Addiction | 76 | 16% |
| Tax allowance | 73 | 15% |
| Domestic violence | 62 | 13% |
| Disability | 60 | 12% |
| Poverty | 58 | 12% |
| Child benefit | 50 | 10% |
| Media | 48 | 10% |
| Carers | 45 | 9% |
| Elderly | 45 | 9% |
| Training | 43 | 9% |
| Basic income | 33 | 7% |
| Rural | 31 | 6% |

## Calls to the free phone advice line

More than 450 callers contacted the Commission's free phone advice desk. Most of the calls were from individuals with families who particularly welcomed the opportunity to express their views to the Commission.

Callers generally expressed deep concern about the issues affecting families today. A large number of callers placed great emphasis on the importance of the family in society. These callers went on to stress the importance of strengthening families for the future by providing necessary support structures, such as counselling services. Many people also felt that society has undergone considerable changes in recent years and were concerned that some of these changes have had negative effects on families.

Lone parents were also mentioned. Callers generally felt that lone parents are doing an excellent job of rearing their children in difficult circumstances. However, some callers expressed reservations about social welfare and other benefits for lone parents. Housing and the environment were discussed in some detail. Callers believed that housing facilities should be more family-friendly and should take account of the diversity of family needs. Nearly 5% of callers (both male and female) asked for financial recognition and support for mothers working in the home.

# Changing society, changing roles

## Section II

**Families in a changing society**

**Introduction**

Many of the submissions discussed changes perceived to have occurred in Irish society and in the Irish family in the recent past. These submissions reflected on themes such as ethical and religious considerations in relation to the family and society (113 submissions, 23% of total), with frequent reference to the changing role of women; the role of the State in relation to the family (97 submissions, 20% of total); how the family should be defined for constitutional and State purposes (91 submissions, 19% of total); and the influence of the media (48 submissions, 10% of total). The percentage of submissions which examined each of these issues is shown in Figure 1.

Figure 1: Percentage of submissions on ethical and religious concerns relating to the family in society, the role of the State, the definition of the family and the influence of the media.

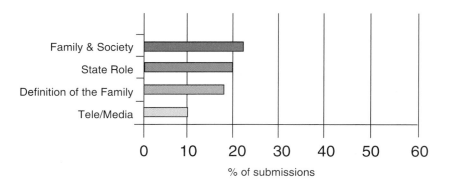

This section of the report presents a concise overview of the significant societal, familial and individual changes, as described in these submissions, which have brought us to the present day. In addition to these main themes, other issues of significant concern in the submissions are noted here. These will be discussed in greater detail in subsequent sections of this report. A complex picture emerges, involving a critical appraisal of changing norms and values in society and of people's reactions to these changes, both positive and negative.

## Families and society

In all, 113 submissions (23% of total) commented on changes in mores and expectations in our society. Contributing factors were identified as the growth of individualism and as changes in the roles of women, in the social climate, in social legislation, in attitudes to religion, and in the economic climate and demography.

### Growth of individualism

Submissions noted the rise of individualism, often viewed as consequent upon relative affluence and upon the effect of advertising and other media influences. Individualism was deemed to have both positive and negative outcomes. The accompanying sense of self worth, which was often discussed in terms of rights to fair treatment, was considered to be a positive development, especially in the context of women. Negative perceptions of individualism included its association with consumerism and with a lack of regard for other people's rights or for personal responsibilities. Numerous submissions observed that increased individualism may lead to fracturing of the family bond. A common view was that the collective requirements of family life necessarily supersede individual autonomy. Teenagers and young adults were identified as particularly vulnerable to the negative outcomes of individualism. The problems of drug use and addiction among the young were prominent concerns.

## Changing roles of women

A principal theme of submissions was the central role of women in the family and the effect of the changing societal opportunities and expectations of women on the family. Women's lives, their work, their health and their protection were all deemed crucial to the viability of the family. Changes in women's lives were thought to have affected expectations of family life, of marriage and of the individual lives of men and children. Submissions also reflected on the different, and sometimes conflicting, views held by women and on their lack of recognition and integration at the higher levels of decision making in society.

## Changing social climate

Submissions identified changes in the social climate. These were generally characterised in terms of increased openness of public discussion and changed social behaviour. The increased openness of discussion of previously unmentioned and hidden issues such as domestic violence, incest and rape was perceived to be positive. Recent public debate on marriage breakdown and its consequences had disturbed many contributors who sought to put forward suggestions to alleviate both the causes and outcomes of such problems. The public awareness campaigns on the human immundodeficiency virus (HIV) and the acquired immune deficiency syndrome (AIDS) informed some of the submissions.

Changes in social behaviour were noted in child rearing practices, in increased teenage sexual activity and unplanned pregnancies, in the rising numbers of unmarried parents and of legally separated people and in the growing acceptance of homosexuality. Some submissions attributed some changes in social and personal behaviour to the stress of modern living.

## Changing social legislation

Submissions commented on changing social legislation in relation to marriage breakdown, separation and the introduction of divorce. Numerous submissions reiterated continuing  principled opposition to divorce and warned of the social and familial consequences of its introduction. Others believed that divorce legislation, now inevitable, should be constructed in such a way as to minimise possible negative effects. The legalisation of male homosexual acts and the legalisation of provision of information regarding the termination of pregnancy were viewed as significant issues. The possibility of the introduction of euthanasia was mentioned as an issue of concern.

There was general welcome for the proposed equal status legislation as giving support to minority groups such as Travellers and people with disabilities. Acknowledgment of the rights of people with disabilities was strongly reiterated. A number of submissions suggested that the equality provisions of the Constitution of Ireland should be strengthened to include named vulnerable groups.

Some submissions focused on the changes brought about by Ireland's participation in the European Union which have opened us to new influences and to increased affluence. For some, European involvement has brought about an intellectual, cultural, social and political expansion. For others, it has brought about unwelcome changes and has damaged our traditional values.

### Changing economic climate and demography

The changes in the workforce in recent years were the concern of some submissions. Patterns of employment mobility and working conditions were considered not always to be to the advantage of families. The increased participation of mothers in the labour force was examined in some submissions.

Unemployment, notably long-term and inter-generation unemployment, was identified as a significant social problem, especially in the context of family and child poverty. Some submissions reflected on the social causes of and solutions to poverty.

The changes in the economic infrastructure of the country, the increase in national and international labour mobility and the effects of migration on the national demography were examined in some submissions. Many of these stated that such changes have decreased the role of the extended family, with its supportive net. Many young people are now without support in the early years of marriage or of child-rearing. In some submissions the growth of urban centres was viewed as having led to problems of isolation and of a sense of loss of neighbourhood and community. Other submissions raised the problems of rural Ireland.

### Changing attitudes to religion

One set of submissions within this category pointed to the increasingly secular nature of Irish society and to changing attitudes to values and moral standards. Many submissions viewed the churches as a mainstay of Irish life. These submissions stressed the importance of religious perspectives and observance and of the power of prayer as a force of personal, familial and community strength. New age and alternative philosophies were also mentioned.

### Changing families

Most submissions argued that family life has changed. Some suggested that this has resulted from societal pressures on the family. Others suggested that family changes are altering society. Many submissions commented on the alteration of the Irish family in terms of the declining birthrate and rate of marriage, the growing incidence of marital breakdown, the expected effects of divorce, the increased number of unmarried parents and the decreased rate of adoption. These changes were thought to affect how adult partners perceive themselves as individuals and in relationships; how parents perceive and respond to their children; and how children perceive and respond to their parents.

### Children and parents

There was a predominant focus on children in families throughout the submissions. Particular and repeated concern was expressed for children living in poverty and for children with special needs. There was frequent reiteration of the need for improved parenting, of the important and underdeveloped role of fathers in parenting, and of concerns for and supports needed by lone parents. Many submissions commented on the changing notions of the concept of the family. The gradual erosion of the extended family and the decreased influence and involvement of older family members in the life of the nuclear family were notable themes.

# State role

In all, 97 submissions (20% of total) referred to the State's role in relation to the family and to changes brought about by legislation and by government policy and practice. The State's role was identified as supporting the family and laying down the minimum standards for the common social good. In general, submissions considered that successive governments had singularly failed to protect the family. For many submissions, there was an absence of State support for marriage and the family. For others, the lack of support to mother and child and the lack of inclusiveness in existing legislation were the source of dissatisfaction.

Submissions considered the State's response to be fragmentary, lacking coordination or focus. Typical complaints were the lack of coherence of the family support system, its arbitrary nature and the lack of adequate information. A small number of submissions suggested that the State should confine its interventions with the family to eliminating prejudices, restrictions and obstructions, in order to provide a general climate which allows the family to flourish. These submissions also affirmed inviolable parental rights and responsibilities. These views were based on the family having special legitimacy and autonomy.

### Perspective of submissions on the Commission on the Family

Many submissions welcomed the establishment of the Commission on the Family. These submissions valued the opportunity to explore the issues surrounding Irish family life at the end of the twentieth century. For some, there was optimism that the Commission on the Family would be a strategic body of benefit to the family in Ireland. For others, the establishment of the Commission stood in contrast to changing social legislation perceived to be damaging to the fabric of the family and society.

**How the Family is defined in the Constitution and for State purposes**

In all, 91 submissions (19% of total) raised the issue of how the family is defined in the Constitution or for other purposes. The terms of reference[1] of the Commission on the Family refer to the constitutional provisions[2] in relation to the family and to the United Nations definition[3] of the family. Submissions commented on the inherent difficulties of harmonizing different potential definitions.

Numerous submissions expressed a preference for the maintenance of the constitutional provisions in their present terms. These submissions typically focused on the need for a stable lifelong family structure, based on marriage, to give children the best chance in life. These submissions were unanimous in asking for reinvigorated State support for marriage as a unique social institution which has substantial internal familial and extended societal benefits. Many submissions came from individuals and groups with a strong religious sense. These submissions focused on the role of God in the creation and sustaining of marriage and on the Christian notion of marriage as a partnership based on irrevocable consent. The value of premarital celibacy and lifelong marital fidelity were seen as the best option for individuals, couples, children, society and the State. Some submissions gave support to marriage without reference to either religious values or constitutional definitions.

Some submissions noted the high rate of births outside marriage, the increased incidence of non-marital unions of separated people and expressed concern for second families following the introduction of divorce. The general thrust of these submissions was that existing legislation discriminates against unmarried parents and their children and derives from an outdated and singular

---

1    Extract from the terms of reference of the Commission on the Family

"The Commission is expected to make proposals to the all-party Committee on the Constitution on any changes which it believes might be necessary in the constitutional provisions in relation to the family" ;

"in carrying out its work, the Commission while having due regard to the provisions on the family in the Constitution of Ireland intended to support the family unit, should reflect also in its deliberation the definition of the family outlined by the United Nations".

2    Constitution of Ireland

Art 41.1.1 The State recognises the Family as the natural primary and fundamental unit group of Society, and as a moral institution possessing inalienable and imprescriptible rights, antecedent and superior to all positive law.

Art 41.1.2 The State, therefore, guarantees to protect the Family in its Constitution and authority, as the necessary basis of social order and as indispensable to the welfare of the Nation and the State.

Art 41.2.1 In particular, the State recognises that by her life within the home, woman gives to the State a support without which the common good cannot be achieved.

Art 41.2.2 The State shall, therefore, endeavour to ensure that mothers shall not be obliged by economic necessity to engage in labour to the neglect of their duties in the home.

Art 41.3.1 The State pledges itself to guard with special care the institution of Marriage, on which the Family is founded, and to protect it against attack.

3    United Nations definition

The United Nations considered that the fundamental principle underlying the celebration of the International Year of the Family in 1994 was that the family constitutes the basic unit of society. The United Nations focused on a broad definition of the family as the basic unit of society in all its forms, whether traditional, biological, common law, extended or one parent.

The definition used by the United Nations is:

"Any combination of two or more persons who are bound together by ties of mutual consent, birth and/or adoption or placement and who, together, assume responsibility for, inter alia, the care and maintenance of group members through procreation or adoption, the socialisation of children and the social control of members".

view of the family unit. These submissions considered that couples and individuals with children outside marriage have a legitimate call on the term family and all the protection and preference of legislation that this may entail. The varied life experiences of different people were considered to require a modified and inclusive definition of family and a revision of existing legislation to promote inclusion.

## Suggested new definitions of the family

Some submissions viewed the Commission on the Family as having the potential to propose changes to the constitutional definition and hence to the understanding of and protection of the nuclear family in Ireland. Many of these submissions put forward suggestions on a new definition of the family. The dominant concern, within this group, was for constitutional recognition of unmarried parents to ensure policies and provision to support them in their dual role of parent and breadwinner.

Some submissions, while perceiving a need to change the definition of the family, sought that any new definition should include an intention that every family should be permanent and have economic responsibility for its members. Another suggestion was that families coming within any new definition should be obliged to register as families, with a full disclosure of information as to the parties involved. A further suggestion was that the rights of any partnerships which might fall outside any new definition of the family should also be formalised by the State.

Another group of submissions focused on redefining the family based on the rights of, provision for and protection of the child as the principal concern. One preferred option was that of constitutional protection for citizenship, including that of children, as the most appropriate means of ensuring societal progress.

A small number of submissions discussed pragmatic alterations to the definition of the family such as the number of children to be included on family tickets or concessions at public facilities, or the provision of a clear definition of the terms adult or child to be used for all purposes within the State.

## United Nations definition of the family

The majority of submissions expressing a view on the United Nations definition indicated that the United Nations definition was inappropriate for Irish society at this juncture. A small number of submissions sought the adoption of the United Nations definition. This proposal reflected a preference for inclusion of a wide range of domestic arrangements including those of homosexual relationships. These submissions presented detailed analyses of existing legal structures and processes which exclude gay and lesbian couples from rights and services taken for granted by married couples and from those available to unmarried heterosexual couples. These submissions called for the extension to homosexual couples of the right to marry, to adopt and foster children, to share and transfer custody of children and to transfer property and pensions. A number of submissions warned of the danger of creating a definition so inclusive that it is meaningless.

## Influence of the media

In all, 48 submissions (10% of total) expressed concern regarding the role and influence of the media in Irish society. The dominant view was that the media portray a value system diametrically opposed to the traditional family values of stability, interdependence and fidelity. The main concern of submissions on this issue was that of sexually explicit material. Many submissions described the difficulty of raising children with appropriate moral values when television, film and other media portray families and family values in a negative light. Advertisements were considered to promote a culture of materialism as the only worthwhile goal and to place strains on family resources and relationships. Some submissions suggested that television and computer interaction has replaced productive family exchange.

Violent material was less frequently discussed. An association between violence in the media and in society was reiterated. Pornography was deemed worthless and tight media controls on its availability were sought.

## Conclusion

In summary, submissions described how numerous intermeshed factors have given rise to a changed society where there is now less deference to authority and an increased practice and acceptance of diverse lifestyles. Wide-ranging changes have occurred in families and family life. Submissions were unanimous that the family is the basic unit of society, although there were sharply contrasting views on the appropriate definition of the family. There was widespread agreement that the family, however defined, is under threat and needs substantial State assistance. A preeminent concern was that children must be nurtured and protected to become active citizens, and parents, of tomorrow.

The remaining sections of this report present a synopsis of how submissions to the Commission on the Family described the present day situation of Irish families and the strategies put forward for their support.

# Section III

## Mothers, fathers, parenting and children

### Introduction

A large number of submissions addressed a broad range of issues relating to the many functions of families. These issues included rearing children and child care (173 submissions, 36% of total), the roles of individual family members, especially mothers (104 submissions, 21% of total), whether mothers in the home should receive an allowance (96 submissions, 20% of total), and lone parent families (77 submissions, 16% of total). Other significant issues described in this section of the report include addiction (76 submissions, 16% of total), domestic violence (62 submissions, 13% of total), family members with disabilities (60 submissions, 12% of total), older people (45 submissions, 9% of total), and the media (48 submissions, 10% of total). Traveller families, refugee families and others with special needs are also discussed. The percentage of submissions focusing on each of the main issues is shown in Figure 2.

Figure 2: Percentage of submissions on issues relating to the functions of families

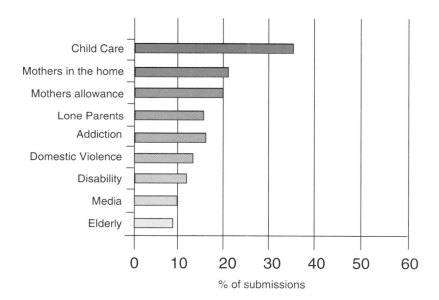

% of submissions

## Child care

Fully 173 submissions (36% of total) referred to concerns regarding crèche and child care facilities. The consensus was that crèche and preschool facilities and after-school hours child care are urgently required throughout the country, not only for children whose parent(s) work but also to assist shopping and other activities. Quality child care was often perceived to be vital to family life in that it supports the development, education, care and welfare of the child.

There were calls for crèche facilities in small urban areas and to cater for rural families and farm women in particular. Special concern was raised regarding the importance of the provision of child care facilities for children being reared through Irish. The child care needs of the Traveller community were identified.

### Child care as a woman's issue

Women's changing roles were seen to bring calls for child care facilities. A predominant view was that, while many mothers now remain in work, neither the State nor fathers concern themselves with the social and economic burden of child care. This was considered to place a double burden on those women who work both outside and in the home.

Some submissions expressed concerns about child care practices. For example, child minding by family members may place more work on the older generation. Equally, there was a view that non-parental child care may lead to clashes of discipline for children. The Commission was asked to study child care provision outside of the home and its effects on the emotional health of children and parents in the long- and short-term.

### Child care provision

There were distinct differences of opinion expressed in submissions regarding the preferred organisation of child care facilities. For some, State crèches in local communities were the appropriate way forward, giving guaranteed access to parents who might otherwise be caught in the poverty trap of unemployment. Privately run crèches were judged not to be easily accessible for many parents, due to costs and other factors. There was a suggestion that the Commission examine the European child care system, that of Belgium in particular.

### Cost of child care

Many submissions considered that the cost of child care should be borne solely by those who use it and should not be an added tax burden on one-earner families. A policy of subsidising child care was seen to have the potential to put further pressure on mothers working in the home to go out to work. This view was sometimes aligned with the proposal that mothers working full-time in the home should receive financial recognition from the State. A related suggestion was that a childminder allowance should be given to every mother, to spend as she sees fit.

Other submissions viewed subsidised child care as essential and stated that charges should be based on the ability to pay. The point was made that subsidised child care is a prerequisite to obtaining work for many lone parents and low income parents. Submissions from families with two working parents often focused on the need for assistance with child care costs. A number of possible approaches were presented, including the use of a voucher system to the parent, a subsidy to those providing child care, and various tax proposals.

### Monitoring of child care and child carers

Submissions commenting on the monitoring and control of child care facilities were dissatisfied with the existing situation where child care remains unregulated, operating without licence or inspection.

The general view was that official certification and registration of all crèche and childminder personnel, and the appropriate inspection of premises and facilities, should be established immediately. Some submissions wished to see the suitability of all people dealing with children, excepting relatives, but including babysitters, to be investigated. A legal age for babysitting was requested. There was concern that regulation might make child care more expensive and that those caring for less than three preschool children will not be subject to childcare legislation.

# Women's role in the family

Fully 104 submissions (21% of total) discussed concerns regarding mothers working in the home. The consensus was that women in the home are performing one of the most important social functions possible, in the face of lack of appreciation from government, society and the media. Numerous submissions concurred that the mother is the core of the family as child bearer, rearer and educator, sometimes the main discipliner, and almost always the main care giver. Many submissions expressed the opinion that it is easier to go out to work than to rear children. This view was almost always raised in the context that children need time, love and care, which material goods will not satisfy, and which can be provided in a unique way by mothers.

Many submissions remarked that women's roles often lead to stress, ill-health and financial worries. Some submissions considered that Irish family life is built on the personal, social and economic sacrifice of the mother. Some submissions viewed the family as an asymmetrical social arrangement whereby the State has its child care needs met on a privatised basis.

### Recognition of women working in the home
Numerous submissions reiterated the constitutional protection of the woman's role in the home and judged successive governments and administrations to have ignored this protection or to have deliberately undermined it. Numerous submissions gave detailed descriptions of how the legal and taxation systems operate to penalise and discriminate against women working in the home. In the perspective of these submissions, the married woman finds that her work within the home gives her no legal right to a share in family resources, be it tax allowances, property, share income or pension. Some submissions pointed out that from the moment a woman leaves work there is a loss of tax allowances which means that the family is affected adversely. If the mother has an additional child there is no maternity benefit or allowance payable to her, and if the mother goes into hospital, no benefit is payable.

A number of submissions argued that women's unwaged work in the home may be the largest industry in the country and that, even though some women may work the same hours as men, their work is not valued. The premise of these submissions was that the State is wholly dependent on women's unpaid work. These submissions proposed that the Irish government should count, measure and value the unwaged work of women in national accounts and satellite accounts of Gross Domestic Product (GDP). Defining the unwaged worker as a worker in the system of national accounts could give a corrected view of spending on such concerns as social services, urban planning, transportation, education etc. Measuring this work could alter women's perceptions of themselves in the family and in society. A number of submissions noted that the contribution of women on the farm has yet to be fully acknowledged by government.

# Financial recognition of mothers working in the home

In all 96 submissions (20% of total) suggested some form of direct payment to mothers working full-time in the home. This was sometimes put forward in the context of the provision of financial supports to enable at least one parent to remain full-time in the family home.

A number of different proposals were put forward. By far the most popular suggestion was for a realistic allowance to be paid weekly to the woman, similar to unemployment assistance. For some, an allowance for mothers could come through weekly payment of an increased child benefit. This proposal was often linked with the provision of a series of additional benefits including Christmas bonuses, back to school allowances, dental and medical care for the mother and her children up to the age of eighteen and a pension in her own right. Other proposals included a tax allowance for the woman in her own right and a formal structure of credited Pay Related Social Insurance (PRSI) contributions for mothers, in full time employment, who give up a job to provide full time care for a disabled child. There was a suggestion that payments to a mother at home should be given only if she has completed an approved parenting course.

Some submissions sought a legal entitlement for each spouse to half the family income, half of all acquisitions from the date of marriage and half the value of the family home. Others requested the reintroduction of the matrimonial home bill.

### Women who wish to be at home

The majority of submissions focusing on women working in the home took the view that most women, if given a real choice, would prefer to rear their own children at home. Most of these submissions considered that the pressures on mothers to work, particularly when their children are young, are largely negative. Many of these submissions stated that women are often in low paid employment and that following deduction of taxes, travel costs and child minding expenses, they are only marginally better off working. The dominant view was that the State should assist them to stay at home. Many submissions observed that there are pressures on women who work both inside and outside the home and that they may miss out on many of the positive aspects of rearing their children. Many submissions asked how many mothers actually want to work outside the home and sought to reaffirm family-based child care as a fundamental human right.

The expected benefits of a return to maternal child care were increased family stability, fewer family problems, and more jobs available for school leavers and unemployed people. Some submissions requested financial incentives for parents to leave work in the form of marriage gratuities, voluntary redundancy, paid career breaks and unemployment benefit. Others suggested ways in which genuine societal recognition could be given to foster equally the esteem of mothers working in the home with other women in the workforce.

### Expectations of women working in the home

Some of the submissions focusing on women in the home gave details of the support required by mothers, particularly those with very young children. The sense of isolation often experienced by young mothers, especially in urban environments where the majority of neighbours continue to work, was noted. The view was expressed that women who work in the home have the right to obtain services of support, to recreation and to education.

Mothers in the home were stated to need a break from their children, for relaxation and for education. Community-based crèches and drop-in centres were suggested. It was stated that opportunities for relaxation are often denied to women because of their lack of disposal income, their own prioritising of income for family and not personal purposes, and the absence of public transport. The transport problem for women was deemed particularly acute in rural areas, where public transport is effectively unavailable and the family car is typically viewed as a husband's personal property.

Many submissions focused on the rights of women in the home to further education and to "second chance" education. A suggestion was made that opportunities for further education should be available through daytime television. The cost of further education was a repeated theme also. It was pointed out that, unless availing of a full-time third level course, women working in the home must pay all educational fees, with no tax relief and no grant assistance. Women may be unable to attend night classes because of unequal resource distribution in the family and insufficient funds.

### Representing women in the home

Many submissions, particularly those from women working in the home, expressed a deep sense of isolation from the dominant trends in national women's representative bodies. In the matter of women who stay at home to rear children, a number of these submissions considered that the recommendations of the report of the Second Commission on the Status of Women do not acknowledge the maternal role of women or the benefit to children of being reared by their own mother. These submissions asked that such recommendations not be the basis of the response of the Commission on the Family. Some submissions also sought the establishment of a State-sponsored council for women in the home, to represent the voice and values of this group in the national debate. A number of other submissions considered that many of the recommendations of the report of the Second Commission on the Status of Women have positive implications for the future of the family.

### Reintegration into the workforce following child rearing

The reintegration of women into the workforce following full-time home making was an issue of substantial interest in some submissions. It was noted that State assisted training schemes are reserved for people signing on the live register and that women who work in the home are precluded from signing on the register at present. These submissions objected to this ruling and stated that women should be able to sign on the live register in their own right. Other submissions noted that potential employers do not regard time spent parenting as skilled work. This means that on return to the workforce mothers often experience downward job mobility. Accreditation of prior learning and of transferable skills was viewed as one means of public validation for the work of parenting.

## Men's role in the family

Submissions on this issue reflected the conflicting societal perspectives of men's role as fathers. On the one hand, the view was put forward that the father is the head of household. This was often identified with the notion of financial responsibility for family members. At the same time, submissions noted the social perceptions which see the father as the lesser of the two parents. This was particularly evident in submissions dealing with the custody and access elements of marital separation. There was general acknowledgement that the father's role is changing and will continue to change.

Some submissions suggested that women's evolving roles have altered men's roles in the family. Submissions indicated that changes in the law and the social climate have come as a shock to many men, particularly to those who believe in traditional roles within marriage. Some submissions expressed the view that there is a lack of responsibility of the male partner in some relationships and often a basic lack of respect for the woman as a person, a spouse, a parent or a partner. The resulting exploitative relationships were sometimes linked with a demeaning view of women in the media. There was also a strongly argued view that men, as a group, are being criticised without just cause, as a result of the actions of a few.

Many submissions on the issue of men and the family raised concerns about the absence of parental responsibility by those men who abandon a child or children whom they have fathered. Repeated complaints were made that such men are under no compulsion to provide support and that the State effectively steps in to pay for their irresponsible behaviour. Some submissions viewed the mother in some of these instances as being irresponsible also.

### Parenting

Many of these submissions went on to focus on parenting. The general view was that parenting is a challenging task and the need for assistance at certain times is normal. The dominant thrust of these submissions was that active and shared parenting, inside and out of marriage, is to be preferred. There was a special focus on the needs of new parents and on supports for couples who marry at an early age.

There was a consensus that parenting courses and support groups for parents should be available in both rural and urban areas. Submissions described numerous benefits of such courses including improved child language development and greater bonding between child and parent. A number of submissions called for compulsory parenting courses, some suggesting that social welfare payments should be withheld until these were satisfactorily completed. Another suggestion was that groups endeavouring to promote and teach responsible parenting by both the father and mother should be given State financial support.

There was a sense, from these submissions, that parenting has become a more difficult and uncertain task. Some submissions commented on the prevalence of poor parenting, instancing lack of basic child care skills. Some submissions expressed concern that parents under stress may not come forward for help because of fears of their child(ren) being taken from them.

### Parenting after marital breakdown

Some submissions stressed that parenthood does not end with the termination of a marital partnership. Marriage breakdown was characterised in these submissions as resulting in the removal of the father to a peripheral position in the lives of children. The dominant opinion expressed in these submissions, many of which came from separated men, was that fathers are an integral part of families and should remain so even after marital separation. Such submissions sought that State institutions should not be responsible for cutting fathers off from their children. The loss of contact with families was also keenly felt by grandparents who, in cases of marital separation, may find their relationship with grandchildren severed.

There was a call for a public information campaign on responsible and productive parenting, with direction to more specialist information and expertise when required. A national free phone facility for parents to obtain information and to deal with problems, including those which may arise in parenting children with disabilities, was suggested.

## Lone parents

Fully 77 submissions (16% of total) discussed a variety of issues affecting lone parents. Some of these submissions came from lone parents, widows and widowers, separated parents and unmarried mothers. All of these submissions expressed concerns regarding the difficult task of lone parenthood. A number of submissions noted the common belief that Ireland has the highest percentage of lone parents in Europe. Some of these submissions considered that this is an artifact of the categorisation system used.

## Children

A number of submissions sought the placing of a clear statement of children's rights, independent of the rights or responsibilities of parents, in the Constitution of Ireland. There were repeated requests for another referendum to ensure a constitutional pro-life guarantee. There was significant support for all matters relating to children to be amalgamated into a single government department. Some submissions called for the establishment of a body to assist in the implementation and assurance of children's rights, for example, an ombudsman for children. Some submissions asked for a national children's council, independent of government, with advisory, monitoring and research functions. This would act as an impartial body to aid communication between government and those nonstatutory agencies working with children and young people, to provide a coordinated response. There was a proposal for a national longitudinal study of children to ascertain how Irish children fare and to indicate appropriate policy responses to particular needs.

Some submissions considered that children are gifts from God and that parents and society at large are accountable to God for raising, shaping and preparing them for a life of service to God and to humanity. Other submissions focused on the need of children for love and/or discipline within the family. Some others detected a lack of respect for children and a lack of respect from children.

A small number of submissions concentrated on the UN Convention of the Rights of the Child, ratified by Ireland in 1992. Most of these submissions considered that there are many areas of a child's life where the State is not fulfilling its obligations under the convention and asked that the convention be applied to ensure the rights of Irish children, with specific mention of Traveller children. Other submissions suggested that Ireland withdraw from the convention on the grounds that children do not have unfettered rights of self-determination and that to suggest that they do undermines parents' natural authority.

### Children's safety

A range of safety concerns was raised in some submissions. Fears regarding drug abuse were to the forefront and there was a consensus that a national policy for family protection against drugs is needed. Submissions also referred to the safety of children in the context of domestic violence and sexual abuse. Other issues raised included the dangers of accidents on the road, with suggestions that speed limits should be observed, that bicycle lanes should be used and that cycle helmets should be worn. The problem of accidents in the home was also raised.

The autonomy of parents was stressed in many submissions. The dominant view from these submissions was that parents have the right to discipline their children. Some of these submissions expressed the view that recent exposure of issues, particularly in relation to physical punishment of children and the potential effects of the Child Care Act 1991, were encouraging mistrust between parents and children. A small number of submissions rejected physical disciplining of children.

## Addiction

In the 76 submissions (16% of total) discussing addiction there was a consensus that the State has a responsibility to protect its citizens from the dangers of drugs and alcohol. Abuse of substances, including alcohol, was described as a serious and growing problem, destroying families and individuals, and with enormous repercussions for society at large.

### Alcohol abuse

Submissions focusing on addiction were unanimous in viewing alcohol as a hard drug. Alcohol misuse and addiction were frequently cited as greater problems than drug addiction, particularly in rural areas. A large number of the submissions focused on the anti-family aspects of alcohol. The problem of domestic violence was seen to be intimately related to alcohol abuse. There was substantial concern regarding women's drinking and underage drinking. Submissions indicated that resources must be put into the prevention, limitation and treatment of alcohol-related problems. Submissions proposed that drunkenness must be seen as antisocial and that educational programmes should start in primary school. An identity card system for young people was suggested. There were calls to ban alcohol from discos and children from pubs and to stop the advertising of alcohol.

### Drug abuse

There was general agreement, in the submissions focusing on addiction issues, that the drug problem is out of control and is now part of the youth culture. Many submissions considered drug use as a problem affecting an entire family and not merely the addict. Some submissions stressed that drug use is a genuine problem in rural areas, particularly in the larger housing estates. There was a call for the establishment of a government commission on the effects of addiction on the family and for strategies for the treatment of addicts and the control of this social problem.

# Domestic violence

Fully 62 submissions (13% of total) referred to domestic violence. The main non-governmental organisations dealing with domestic violence put forward detailed submissions characterising the problem as a denial of human rights; a serious health problem; a criminal offence with legal and judicial consequences; and as having repercussions on children's education and welfare. Many of these submissions put forward wide ranging proposals on all aspects of society's response to domestic violence.

The general consensus of all submissions dealing with the issue was that women are the usual victims of domestic violence and men its perpetrators. A number of submissions while accepting that most physical violence was against women and children considered that women too can be physically and emotionally abusive in relationships. Children are also potential victims of physical and emotional abuse and may be emotionally disturbed by witnessing violence. Some submissions stated that elderly parents and single parents are at risk of abuse from their children. Violence in gay and lesbian relationships was also noted.

Many submissions suggested that combinations of abuse of alcohol, financial problems and unemployment were underlying reasons for domestic violence. Others stressed that the problem is not confined to any particular social grouping and occurs in rural and urban areas. Many submissions stated that women remain in violent situations because they have nowhere to go and are economically dependent. In rural areas, in particular, women may feel that there is no confidential source to turn to for assistance.

For many submissions, education is the key to confronting and beginning to overcome domestic violence. Submissions sought a national information and advice service, including funding and advertisement of the national free phone help line. One suggestion was that an intense sharp media message condemning violence be issued at times of greater incidence (for example, Christmas and holiday periods).

# Families with a disabled member(s)

In all, 60 submissions (12% of total) discussed the issue of disability. Many of these came from organisations representing people with disabilities, from individuals with disabilities or with a spouse or child with a disability. The overwhelming sense from these submissions was the need for immediate action to improve the quality of life of people with disabilities and their families. There was call for a bill of rights for disabled people. Equal status legislation and employment equality legislation were seen as necessary requisites for genuine inclusion of people with disabilities in the life of society. Groups also asked for disability awareness campaigns and a system of disability proofing to be developed and applied. Particular calls were made that all funding and financial decisions, made at national and local level, should always include disabled people at a consultative and distributive level.

These submissions pointed out that there is no necessary coincidence of illness with disability per se. The sidelining of the disability agenda into the health area was strongly rejected and the need to mainstream all disability issues was repeatedly stressed. This was seen to require access to therapies, recreation, employment and independence options including a choice of assistance services. Submissions sought standardised services throughout the country.

There was a proposal that organisations providing services for people with disabilities should have representatives with a disability on management boards. Other proposals included that there should be consultative procedures in organisations to involve people with disabilities in decision-making.

There was also strong support for the enfranchisement of people with disabilities. Submissions proposed that the special voter's list should be replaced by a postal vote and that only accessible buildings should be used as polling stations. There were calls for a voting system for people with visual impairment or with literacy problems, and for a section on the next census form to give details of the lives of families and of disabled members.

### Families with a member with mental illness

A number of submissions described how families with a member with mental illness may be socially ostracised. A comprehensive, State-funded campaign to increase awareness and understanding of mental illness was suggested. Many people with serious mental illness are being cared for by elderly relatives. There was a view that there has been no real attempt to assist people with mental illness to live meaningful lives in the community.

## The media and the family

Fully 48 submissions (10% of total) discussed issues relating to the media and families. A large number of suggestions were made with the aim of improving the quality of media. The main proposal from these submissions was for the establishment of an independent statutory commission for complaints regarding all media. Another popular suggestion was the use of public decency laws and the powers of the Censorship Board to control material deemed to be offensive, including advertising.

Submissions focusing on the media sought to encourage those involved in popular entertainment to promote a more positive picture of marriage and family life. Numerous submissions were concerned to limit the sale and rent of certain videos to adult shops and of pornographic books to areas of restricted access in a small number of outlets. Use of the media for campaigns to alert families to the danger of drugs and to encourage positive parenting practices was requested.

A range of other suggestions included that Radio Teilifís Eireann (RTE) should establish and operate a code of ethics, including the appropriate rating of all programmes, that a TV soap opera with family values should be commissioned and televised and that switching off the television benefits family and social interaction.

### Children and the media

A number of submissions asked the Commission to give indications publicly of the amount of time children should watch television, to adjudicate on whether television is affecting family life and to investigate whether technological advances such as CD ROMs and the internet are fit for children. There was a call to censor children's programmes containing violence.

**Teilifís na Gaeilge**

There was welcome for the establishment of Teilifís na Gaeilge as a support for parents who are rearing their children through Irish, for children attending all-Irish schools, and for all learners of the national language.

# Elderly people and families

Some 45 submissions (9% of total) focused on issues in relation to elderly people. The promotion of self-esteem among older people was considered a priority. The point was stressed repeatedly that most older people live as part of a family household, are often the leading members of the extended family, are healthy and independent, and are satisfied with their home. Concerns were raised regarding the prevalent negative perceptions of older people and of the process of aging. Submissions asked for public policy initiatives to identify and validate the cultural and practical resources that older people bring to bear on society.

**Travellers**

A small number of submissions dealt with issues in relation to Travellers. Most of these considered that the introduction of equal status legislation and the ratification of the UN convention on the elimination of racial discrimination must be priority tasks for government. There was a series of calls to implement the recommendations of the Task Force on the Travelling community. Many of these submissions argued that the Travellers' way of life must be recognised, accepted and given the necessary resources. Some submissions noted the child care needs of Travellers, and special concern was expressed for Traveller's health and for Traveller children's rights and education. Some of the submissions pointed out that there are problems of violence and exploitation within the Traveller community. A number of submissions expressed concerns about the Traveller way of life, especially in relation to Traveller women and children.

**Refugees**

A small number of wide ranging submissions called for the integration of refugees into Irish society. The Vietnamese, as one of the longest settled communities, were given special mention. Submissions sought progress on the matter of family reunification for Vietnamese immigrants. The need for translation assistance and bilingual support for refugees when dealing with all of the aspects of the public system, particularly for older members of the community, was stressed.

**Families of homosexual people**

A small number of submissions dealt with issues relating to homosexuality. Submissions from homosexual representative groups sought parity with heterosexual individuals and partnerships. This request was strongly rejected in other submissions. Some submissions focused on the process of coming to terms with homosexuality for an individual and his or her family. Policies and services to support families and to resource the voluntary sector response were requested.

### Family information service

Numerous submissions requested a comprehensive and coordinated impartial information service on all matters relating to the family. This service might also act as a referral agency to professional services and might be available in health clinics, community centres, pharmacies and supermarkets. A number of disability organisations stressed that information on disability issues, benefits and entitlements should be accessible from mainstream information providers, including help lines.

There was a strong call for the availability of information and assistance through the medium of Irish. There was criticism of the failure of some State organisations to explicitly advertise or publicise the availability of services through Irish. Ongoing emphasis on the provision of bilingual services was sought.

## The function of the family

The primary function of the family was typically described in submissions as the provision of mutual support and mutual benefit and the nurturing, socialising and educating of children. Many submissions described the positive sense of family life. Many submissions sought the public promotion of desirable values of family life. Many submissions stressed that security of rights for all family members must be guaranteed in legislation.

Throughout the submissions certain families were identified as having special needs. There was a general view that if we are to build a just society we must ensure equality of opportunity and participation for all. Many submissions focused on the need for equality proofing, training and education to promote an awareness and acceptance of the need for participation of all.

### A Department of the Family

Many submissions in this vein wished to see the establishment of a government department for the family. Other proposals included that a family impact report should be prepared and made public on all legislation prior to approval. Another suggestion was for the setting up of a State-funded council of the family, as a recognised social partner.

### Economic policies to promote marriage

Some submissions commented that young people of marriageable age, faced with serious economic uncertainties, are frequently tempted to postpone the time to marry and start a family. These submissions proposed that State economic policies should promote the effective freedom necessary to enter marriage and found a family. There was also a suggestion that State investment in the family should be cost effective and a priority.

## Conclusion

This section has outlined the views presented in submissions on a number of important issues affecting family structure and life. Child care provision and funding were prominent concerns for many submissions. The role of the mother in the home was highly valued and seen to be underrated by society as a whole. There was strong support for the payment of an allowance for mothers working full-time in the home and for measures to encourage women to stay at home to rear children. The role of men as fathers outside, in and after marriage was critically reviewed. Particular concerns were voiced about the role of fathers following marital separation and about some men who do not support the children they have fathered. Diverse concerns and differing perspectives on issues relating to children were presented.

The problems posed for families by substance addiction and by domestic violence were examined. Submissions also commented on some of the issues facing lone parents, families with special needs, family members with disabilities and on the role of elderly people. The influence of the media on the family was perceived to be largely negative, and many proposals were put forward to ameliorate this situation.

# Educational and social services and families

# Section IV

**Education and families**

**Introduction**

This section examines the issue of formal education for all age groups, the preeminent concern of submissions to the Commission on the Family. In all, 225 submissions (46% of total) discussed some aspect of the formal educational system in this country. This percentage is shown in Figure 3 below.

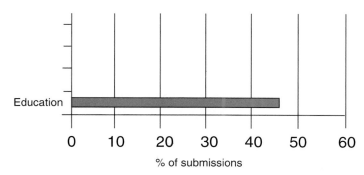

Education

0    10    20    30    40    50    60

% of submissions

The issues addressed in the submissions dealing with education spanned a wide ambit, from the ethos of the educational system to concerns regarding costs and to the education of specific groups. This section first examines broad issues surrounding the education system as a whole and then focuses on preschool, primary, secondary and third level education in turn.

# The role of parents in education

Numerous submissions focusing on education supported the acknowledgement of the parent as the primary educator of the child, as enunciated in the Constitution of Ireland[1]. These submissions voiced concerns over aspects of the educational system considered to be intrusive on parental rights to determine the educational content presented to their children, particularly in the matter of moral guidance. For this group, the basis for a successful family is a successful education, with schools playing an enormous part in reinforcing the work already done in the home or compensating for its lack. There were calls for more accountability for teachers and a formally recognised method of complaint.

### A religious ethos in education

For a large number of submissions, education is as much a matter of the spiritual well-being of children as of their social or intellectual development. Submissions commented frequently that a Christian-based education contributes in a positive way to the individual, the family and to society, establishing the child on a firm foundation of truth, knowledge, love, discipline and guidance. These submissions considered that the ethos of any school should be decided by the school management

---

1    Constitution of Ireland

Art 42.1.The State acknowledges that the primary and natural educator of the child is the Family and guarantees to respect the inalienable right and duty of parents to provide, according to their means, for the religious and moral, intellectual, physical and social education of their children.

and the community served by the school and that the State should not interfere in their choice. These submissions sought to oppose the secularisation of schools and asked for greater emphasis on spiritual and moral education, especially in the second level curriculum.

Particular concerns were raised about the election of parents to school boards. The dominant sense was that elected parents should reflect the views of the parents of children attending the school and not merely a single, and possibly unrepresentative, organisational perspective. Regarding discipline, submissions considered that children should obey reasonable directions of teachers, and other adults, unless they are convinced that an instruction is morally wrong.

### Multidenominational and nondenominational schools

A small set of submissions stated that Roman Catholicism should not be imposed within the educational system and that other faiths should be studied. Increased access to and a choice of multidenominational and nondenominational schools were also suggested.

## The cost of education

Another main issue of concern, in the submissions focusing on education, was the cost of education. The consensus was that free education does not exist. It was pointed out that free education should mean that all items required for schooling are provided free of charge. Submissions gave lengthy lists of school costs including voluntary contributions, school transport, examination fees, lockers, photocopies, books, uniforms, materials, outings, games, trips and extra curricular activities.

There were strong objections to the purchase of school books and to new editions of books being required almost every year, sometimes with minimal changes in the overall content. It was proposed that school books should be provided by the Department of Education or that school books should be loaned or rented. There was widespread agreement that examination fees should be abolished, especially for low income families. Social welfare assistance with schooling costs, through the "back to school" scheme, was acknowledged to be of some assistance but was considered not to cover costs in a realistic fashion.

There was agreement that it is a continuous struggle to meet education expenses, especially for parents who are long-term unemployed or on low incomes. A number of submissions noted that the current system places children living in deprived areas at a double disadvantage, as their parents cannot provide in the same way as parents in more affluent areas. There was a call to target schools in these areas with more financial and other resources. There was a suggestion that the Department of Education, in consultation with schools, should calculate the yearly cost of all educational items and make a weekly charge during the school year. Some submissions criticised the physical condition of school buildings, with complaints of insufficient sanitation and heating and of the lack of provision of basic equipment, including computers.

# Educating all children

Another prominent perception of educated-related submissions was that the system in this country is geared towards the bright child. There was overwhelming support for the provision of an education which is not merely academic but promotes the self esteem of all pupils. There was a substantial focus on the need for a composite educational programme to ensure learning by all children in the school system. There was an emphasis on the role of staff in developing and affirming the self-esteem of students at all levels of schooling. Adequate resources, particularly in-service training, were seen as a first step to ensuring positive teaching outcomes. Some submissions sought an improved joint health and education strategy. Criticism was levelled at the points system for entry into third level education, which was characterised as destroying students. There was a proposal for the adoption of an alternative aptitude or ability testing system to provide two complementary bases of assessment.

### Educational disadvantage

Numerous submissions discussed the matter of educational disadvantage in Ireland. Tackling this problem was seen to require altered expectations of and attitudes towards children from disadvantaged areas. A number of different strategies were proposed including a national policy to combat disadvantage in all aspects of education. There was a call for more targeted resources and for intensive assistance for schools in areas of severe urban disadvantage There were special requests for literacy development programmes for parents and children. Concern was raised regarding children arriving at school undernourished and underfed, and the provision of a school meal was suggested. Other proposals were for the development of closer links between mainstream education and community and youth groups. Some submissions sought that teachers should be aware of the diversity of families and that this should be reflected in all resource materials used in schools.

### Special rural concerns

The decline in the national birthrate has major policy implications for schools and was seen, in some submissions, to have marked implications for rural schools. New approaches were considered necessary to deal with disadvantage in rural areas, perceived to receive inadequate attention in existing schemes. The closure of small primary and secondary schools in rural Ireland was described as one of the many ways in which the fabric of rural Ireland is being destroyed. The experience of France, where no primary or secondary school in a rural area may be closed, was cited as a means of sustaining families in rural areas. Local consultation and support were seen as basic rights. There were a number of calls for third level colleges in specific county areas, to keep families together and to offer young people the opportunity to remain in rural Ireland.

The issue of school transport in rural areas was also a concern. Various anomalies in the free school transport scheme were considered to create a sense of injustice. Overall, the costs of school transport were believed to be excessive. There was a special plea for school meals for children, attending schools in rural areas, who are away from home for long hours due to distances travelled.

### Educating children with special needs

The consensus of submissions dealing with the issue of education for children with disabilities was that most children benefit from, and are entitled to, mainstream education in the ordinary classroom, with suitable personal and educational support. The prevalent view was that each child with a disability should have an educational training programme tailored to his or her individual needs. This should be established alongside education programmes for the families of these children to help them cope with the additional needs of the child, with emphasis on the involvement of the father.

Submissions called for the introduction of personal assistants and special technology to give access to children with physical disabilities to integrated education in their own communities. Submissions noted that both school and public transport are inaccessible to many children with physical disabilities and were insistent that this should be rectified. Other requested supports included extra time in examinations, the use of computers, flexible courses and guidance counselling. There were detailed proposals to improve educational attitudes to people with disabilities. For example, there was a call for compulsory disability equality training of professional educators. The introduction of legislation to require schools to be inclusive, the appointment of disability equality officers and the incorporation of disability studies as part of all school curricula were also suggested.

### Special schools

Some children were identified as needing special schools, often as part of an evolving response to learning disability. It was stated that all persons with a learning disability should have the right to integrated, community-based facilities, providing quality day placement whether it is preschool, educational, training or employment and, when required, the full range of specialist intervention.

A number of submissions considered that grants should be available to assist parents with children in specialised schools. There was a proposal for ongoing use of special education facilities during the summer holidays, as the break from routine often leads to loss of skills and to difficulties for families. Another suggestion was that children with learning difficulties should not be required to learn Irish. Many submissions deplored the fact that when education is completed there is nothing for many of these young people but to remain with elderly parents, or with siblings who have their own family commitments, or to live in institutional care.

### Traveller children

Some submissions focused on the educational needs of Traveller children. The consensus was that intercultural education is necessary and that too many young Travellers are dropping out of school with no qualifications. Special intervention was requested to assist with literacy problems among Travellers. Submissions also sought the implementation of the recommendations of the Task Force on Travelling community.

### After school hours child care

There was significant support for the development of after-hours clubs in schools to enable children to stay to do homework. There were proposals for longer school hours to suit working parents, often mentioned in the context of preschool and after school hours care, at nominal cost to parents. There were also a number of calls to continue school terms during the summer months to aid working parents.

### Community resource

Some submissions remarked that schools should be used outside hours as a community resource, providing educational and social opportunities for each family member. Particular emphasis was placed on adult education. There was also a call to recognise and fund voluntary groups associated with education.

There was specific discussion of the importance of return to education for people in long-term unemployment. There was a suggestion that social welfare regulations be further relaxed to encourage attendance at approved courses for personal development or other education. A suggestion was made for more places on the Vocational Training Opportunities Scheme (VTOS). Increased funding for adult literacy schemes was also deemed a priority and the institution of pilot projects was suggested.

### All-Irish education

There were repeated calls for support of all-Irish schools and of the educational system in Gaeltacht areas. Requests included the establishment of a coordinating body for the advancement and provision of facilities and training for all-Irish education.

## Preschool education

The development of a nursery education policy, separate but related to crèche and child care facilities, was proposed. There was preference for community preschools as opposed to fee-paying ones and demands for more preschools in low income housing estates. Many of these submissions suggested that these facilities should also provide parental development courses and opportunities, including literacy classes, while children are at school.

In the submissions focusing on preschool and early education, there was general support for the Early Start programme. Some submissions asked for its implementation in all areas designated as disadvantaged, with special emphasis on rural areas. Some wished to see it introduced for all children. Other submissions raised concerns that the Early Start programme might undermine the already existing community and private playgroups; that programmes to involve parents, to a greater extent, in the education of their children might be more appropriate; and that primary school facilities are not always suitable for preschool education.

## Primary level education

Submissions were broadly critical of the existing primary education system. Complaints included overcrowded classrooms, insufficient teaching staff and excessive homework creating strains on parents, particularly mothers. There was general agreement that the State should invest money in primary, and not third level, education. There were calls for a reduction of the pupil/teacher ratio.

There was a proposal that, before school enrolment of a child is accepted, the parent(s) should attend a parenting course. There was a suggestion that children be assessed more frequently at primary school level. A pilot project in which children from a designated disadvantaged area would receive every possible advantage available to other children was also proposed. Additional subjects proposed for the primary school syllabus included nature study, a foreign language, science and technology and civics. The importance of the inclusion of physical education, music, dance and elocution in school was stressed. Other submissions asked for a simple curriculum of core subjects to give basic literacy and numeracy to children.

### The school medical examination

Some submissions criticised the existing arrangements regarding the school medical examination. Most of these submissions considered that such examinations should be continued through the secondary educational system. Submissions also expressed concern that the school dental examination now occurs only every two years.

### The stay safe programme

The importance of this programme was stressed and there was a suggestion that schools not supporting it should be given a lower per capita subvention than others. Some submissions expressed the view that it was potentially an interference in parental rights in education.

### Remedial education

Submissions on remedial education were unanimous in their call for early recognition of and intervention with learning problems. This was seen to require the active involvement of parents and the provision, to them, of information and advice. Clear referral procedures and frequent, regular remedial classes were suggested. Many submissions indicated a preference for a remedial teacher in every school, irrespective of pupil numbers. Others wished to see remedial teachers in schools in disadvantaged areas, where some parents are paying for remedial classes at the present.

### Bullying

A number of submissions referred to the problem of bullying in primary and secondary schools. The dominant view was that this problem is growing, and is not fully understood by teachers or parents. Suggestions were made to increase training of teachers in this area and to establish mandatory reporting of cases. The involvement of parents was also sought.

## Secondary level education

Problems of secondary education were high on the agenda of submissions to the Commission. Educational attainments were the issue of numerous submissions. Some of these believed that low pass rates in State examinations from one school or one teacher should be investigated. There was a proposal that parents should be made accountable for children who do not stay in school to complete examinations.

A common theme was that there should be increased provision and coordination of services for young people unable to cope with the educational or behavioural demands of the mainstream school. Submissions stated that many of these children lack basic literacy skills, that school offers little for them and is often seen by themselves, and sometimes their parents, as a waste of time. For many, the cycle of failure, non-attendance and suspensions mean they do not receive an education.

### Disruptive behaviour in class
The growing problem of disruptive children in class was a source of considerable concern. Many submissions commented that disruptive pupils may commit serious offences, but may go unpunished.

### Truancy
Some submissions commented on school truants and on the apparent absence of concern about these children's educational needs. These submissions noted that there is no standard system or adequate funding to deal with truancy. It was proposed that the gardaí should be informed of truancy and that cases should be followed up by health board social workers. Suggested means of dealing with the problem included legislation to deal comprehensively with poor school attendance and truancy, residential correction schools and increased numbers of school inspectors.

### School exclusion and expulsion
Most of the submissions focusing on school exclusion and expulsion stated that these sanctions should be avoided if at all possible. Many of these submissions noted that time out of school and lack of alternative educational placements are directly linked to antisocial behaviour and resulting family stress. A number of submissions instanced cases of expulsion and requested a different, more positive, approach.

Some submissions about the problems of classroom disruption, truancy, exclusion and expulsion asked for psychological services at preschool and school levels and the establishment of an expulsion tribunal along the lines of that in Northern Ireland.

### Home school liaison
The underlying concept of the home school liaison service was deemed valuable. However, many submissions viewed the current situation as less than effective as there is insufficient parental involvement. Suggestions to improve the scheme included the use of mailshots and the involvement of local tenants' associations. Another view was that every school should have a community worker resident in the catchment area of that school, in order to target children in need.

### Early school leavers
The problem of early school leavers was noted in many submissions. Reasons put forward for this problem included uninterested or overly ambitious parents and disturbed, disruptive or bullied children. Particular concern was voiced about the children of unemployed people leaving school early.

Suggestions included the use of a coordinated approach by youth workers, parents, attendance officers, home-school liaison staff, teachers, gardaí and health board staff to overcome the problem. Some submissions sought that skills for living, to include budgeting, shopping, basic cooking and home making skills, should be taught to young people who are at risk of early school leaving. Special supports were sought to enable teenage mothers to stay in school and complete their education. Other submissions requested better links between students and work schemes and local clubs, to help build community leadership and involvement. There was a call for training programmes to encourage the establishment of community based cooperative enterprises in second and third level schools and colleges.

### Counselling

Some submissions considered that counselling should be developed in all schools, for children and parents, and acknowledged that special staff may be necessary. Counselling was seen to be valuable in instances of early school leaving, school attendance problems, educational progress concerns, family difficulties, teenage pregnancy and drug addiction. There was a call for early detection and follow up of educational difficulties with the comment that referral to specialist agencies takes too long.

### Relationship and sexuality education

Divergent views were expressed on the issue of sex education in schools. A large body of submissions welcomed the introduction of relationship and sexuality education. Many of these submissions proposed that it should be a compulsory programme at both primary and secondary levels. However, others felt the issue was being introduced to children at too young an age.

Suggestions were made on how to improve existing courses. Numerous submissions focused on ways in which a programme can reduce teenage pregnancies. Many of these submissions stated that sex education must be taught within a moral or religious context in terms of primary values, namely that chastity, marriage, fidelity and family rearing are positive choices for young people. Other submissions stated that there should be no discussion of artificial contraception. There was a call for careful monitoring to ensure that these programmes make a difference.

Various submissions sought that issues of parenting, the benefits of breast feeding, the futility of violence, the effects of crime and sexist role modelling should be included in these courses. A small number of submissions called for awareness and acceptance of homosexuality, as a legitimate expression of sexual nature, to be cultivated at all educational levels.

In another group of submissions there was a widely held view that sex education should be taught by parents and not by schools. A number of these submissions suggested that the starting point must be a parent education programme aimed at equipping them to carry out their responsibilities to their children. Associated with this view was the call to leave the matter to each individual school, in consultation with parents, who should be made aware of their rights on this issue.

### Drugs education

There was general welcome in the 76 submissions (16% of total) focusing on addiction for the recognition by the Department of Education of the need for a coordinated approach to drugs education. Many of these submissions called for integration of alcohol and drugs education at every level of schooling, using appropriate methods for different age groups. It was considered that such education should include the skills necessary for young people to resist peer and adult pressure, to find pleasure and excitement in ways which do not harm them, to seek out constructive occupations and to resist the attractions that drugs hold for people. In contrast, there was a view that education in relationships and drugs was best done with teenagers outside of the school environment in local youth clubs.

## Third level education

The main proposal of the submissions focusing on third level education was for government action to relieve the competition for, and cost of, third level education. For many, this meant increasing the numbers of third level places so that everyone who is eligible may attend and widening the criteria for grant payments. There was considerable criticism of the lack of tax allowances or other benefits to assist people in employment to pay for their children's education. A particular bone of contention was that many tax payers are unable to afford to send their children to third level institutions but pay taxes to support the attendance of other people's children.

For some submissions, the emphasis was on the inclusion of students from lower socioeconomic groups through the targeting of grants, particularly maintenance grants. Others requested improved links between third level colleges and second level schools in disadvantaged areas, including courses for these students to become familiar with the notion and benefits of third level education.

Prompt payment of grants was sought. There was a call for grants to be made available for all post-leaving certificate courses, including correspondence and open university courses. There was a suggestion that students should be allowed to have some earnings tax free, without affecting means test limits.

## Conclusion

This section has looked at the views of submissions in relation to formal education. Almost half of all submissions to the Commission commented on this issue. The range of concerns raised was extensive and spanned all aspects of the educational system, from preschool through primary, secondary, third level and adult education opportunities. There was unanimity that education should be broad ranging and address the development of the whole person. Many submissions were strongly critical of the cost of education. Diverse views on the appropriate ethos of schools and curricula were presented.

Special concern was expressed repeatedly in relation to the education needs of children and young people living in poverty and for children with disabilities. Rural areas were identified as in need of special assistance and resources.

# Section V

**Health and families**

## Introduction

A large number of submissions considered the effect of various aspects of the health system on the family. The range of concerns amply reflected the wide ambit of the health service, and in particular, the extensive operations of the health boards in service provision, the administration of the general medical service ("the medical card") and the payment of a series of allowances. Special health and medical concerns for people with disabilities, for elderly people and for carers are also presented in this section.

In all 160 submissions (33% of total) focused on general health issues, 60 submissions (12% of total) discussed disability concerns, 45 submissions (9% of total) raised issues about elderly people and 45 submissions (9% of total) discussed issues in relation to carers. The relevant percentages of submissions concerned with the main issues presented in this section are shown in Figure 4.

Figure 4: Percentage of submissions on health, disability, the elderly and carers

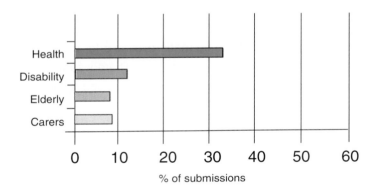

% of submissions

## The health service

The general issues raised in the 160 submissions (33% of total) on health included criticisms of the delivery of health services, proposals for their improvement, community and local health services, the cost of medical services, women and the health services and children and the health services.

## Criticisms of the delivery of health services

Numerous concerns were expressed about the range of health board services. Criticisms included lack of funding and understaffing of services. Numerous submissions identified pressures on doctors and other health care staff, overcrowded hospitals, extended waiting time for appointments and inadequacy or absence of core services. Many submissions stated that help was not available out of hours in an emergency. Some submissions considered that public patients and medical card holders experience inordinate delays and inferior treatment.

There were complaints about the inconsistency of application of legislation and regulations from one health board area to another, including the interpretation of the Child Care Act 1991, and the operation of means testing and discretionary payments. Many submissions commented on the difficulty of obtaining precise information about the entire range of their health service entitlements.

Criticisms focused on the inadequacy of local health centre facilities and on the difficulties experienced by parents with children when attending centralised services, due to the cost of travel and subsistence. Other criticisms included the length of waiting times and the absence of facilities for children and adults in waiting areas.

A particular criticism was that the health service ethos tends to shore up families rather than tackle real problems and provide long-lasting solutions. Disability groups objected to the medical approach to their needs as frequently inappropriate. Special concerns were voiced for people in rural areas where problems are compounded by the absence of public transport and by long distances to travel. There was criticism of health board management for not collaborating with local communities and groups in rural areas.

Submissions from health board managements described existing health services and proposed improvements to health and other social services. A number of these submissions gave detailed figures on demographic and social trends in the relevant health board areas. The main areas of interest of these submissions was on income level, income supports and poverty, education, child care and family supports, the abuse of children and women, drug misuse, family support and intervention services, fostering services, parents and parenting, services for the elderly and intersectoral liaison and cooperation.

## Proposals for improvements to the health service

A wide range of proposals was put forward to improve the operation of the health services. There was a widespread preference for truly local intervention in terms of free phone information and advice, home visiting, mobile information, screening, diagnostic and treatment facilities, community-based family centres, hospital services within reasonable distance of communities, respite services and residential care. The importance of counselling for a wide variety of issues was stressed repeatedly.

### Preventive health education
Many submissions identified the importance of preventive education for heathy living and some wished to see the appointment of health promotion officers in each area. Some submissions wished to see public education campaigns on a range of issues including good parenting skills, the dangers of addiction to alcohol, tobacco and illegal drugs, the importance of exercise and a healthy diet. Some submissions were concerned about junk food, irradiation of food, the need for nutrition information and the advertisement of certain foods on children's television programmes.

## Community and local services

There were calls for resources to decrease waiting lists and to employ additional staff in all branches of the health services particularly to deal with people's problems "out of hours".

### The public health nurse service

The public health nurse service was generally well received. Many submissions asked for more frequent visits from the public health nurse and for an increased focus on groups deemed to be at risk, including mothers with young children, widows and widowers, families with a member who is seriously ill, people with disabilities and the elderly living alone. Other suggestions included the creation of a 24-hour community nursing service.

### The home help service

The home help service was also appreciated. There was a general consensus, in the submissions discussing the issue, that the number of home helps should be increased, that they should be better paid and their role should be upgraded. Some of these submissions requested that home helps be available outside working hours. Others noted that there were wide variations between different health boards in terms of the tasks performed by home helps. The homemaker service was also identified as offering valuable support.

### Local health centres

Some submissions asked for more health centres in disadvantaged urban and rural areas. There were proposals for family-friendly health centres and hospital reception facilities with play, breastfeeding and babychanging areas. A number of submissions sought the introduction of an appointment system with different days for different clinics. There was demand for increased speech therapy services nationally, for both adults and children.

Community-based drop-in or day centres were suggested for people with mental illness, who often have no social contact except with their family. Other local services deemed to be in short supply for people with mental illness included psychiatric social workers and community psychiatric nurses. There were calls for the clarification of the responsibilities of the geriatric and psychiatric services in the management of pregeriatric dementia.

### Community services for drug addiction

Submissions called for more detoxification and prescribing services, residential drug free services and respite services for families under stress because of a family member with a drug problem. Two distinct views were represented in submissions in relation to mothers with drug problems. Some submissions considered that mothers who are addicts should be supported to keep their children and avoid family breakups. The alternative view was that there should be mandatory supervision of drug addicts with children, including removal of the child into care if necessary and active use of foster care services in such instances.

The problems of families with a member with HIV were addressed in a small number of submissions. The main call was for families affected by HIV to be given a range of support services in a coordinated network. These would include health care for the infected person, access to counselling and support for the extended family and child care planning and arrangement. One submission considered that the rights of children affected by AIDS and HIV to information, consultation, treatment and services should be a priority.

**Hospital services**

Some submissions stated that patients generally, and specifically those with medical cards, are discharged early from hospital without a community support service. There were requests for increased support for hospices and home-based care for people who are terminally ill and for overnight facilities for relatives of seriously ill patients.

A patient's charter was requested, to include the rights of the family and non-marital partners to information, privacy and participation in decision-making. There was a proposal that all people should have personal access to their own or dependent children's medical records and other files. Homosexual couples sought the same rights as other couples to visitation and consultation, when one partner is hospitalised. It was also commented that people who are committed to psychiatric hospitals are entitled to a quality of service and approach.

**Health services for Irish speakers**

There was a proposal that all health information and services be made bilingual to assist families who chose to use Irish when dealing with the system. The importance of the provision of speech therapy in Irish was stressed.

# Dental care

Submissions which referred to dental care were unanimous in their criticism of the length of waiting lists. Concerns were also raised about women's dental care needs, about social welfare entitlements to dentistry services for women and the dental services for children.

# The cost of medical services

There was significant criticism of the cost of all medical services in the 160 submissions (33% of total) dealing with the health service. Special concerns were expressed regarding the effect of the costs of medical services on the health of mothers. Numerous submissions recounted how mothers without a medical card prioritise the health needs of their children and are therefore unable to afford to attend doctors when ill themselves.

Families in low paid employment were noted to be at high risk of poor health, but often unable to afford proper care. Some submissions considered that in order to obtain a reasonable level of medical care it is necessary to have private medical insurance and that this is unfair on workers who have already paid Pay Related Social Insurance (PRSI). Individual submissions described instances of inability to attend a doctor due to lack of money and also of large annual medical bills for ongoing illness or disability not covered by medical cards. Suggestions included that health insurance should reward people for looking after their own health and that medical insurance schemes and hospital cash plans should be monitored to avoid discrimination against people with disabilities, including people with mental illness, and against homosexuals.

# The general medical service (the medical card)

A series of submissions criticised the operation of the medical card system. There was a general consensus that means testing causes great hardship. Frequently repeated complaints were that the criteria for eligibility are not easily understandable and that many needy people feel degraded, humiliated and demoralised rather than helped. Some submissions discussed the fact that people with a significant degree of disability may not be eligible for free medical care due to means testing, and that this places strains on family finances and should be reviewed.

Numerous submissions proposed the extension of general medical services to various groups. The most popular suggestion was for free medical and dental care for children under a stated age. For some submissions this was five years, for others sixteen or eighteen years of age. Some submissions suggested that such moves could be gradual, with initial application to the newborn and children up to five years. The main benefit anticipated was the potential financial saving, as a result of early identification of problems.

Other suggestions were that free medical care should be available to all families regardless of income, to all children with a disability, or to all elderly people. Another proposal was that mothers and children should have a free medical check up every 2 years. Some submissions sought additional services for medical card holders including alternative medicine, eye care and prescription glasses, counselling, including genetic counselling and family planning services. There was a suggestion that a fee of £5 should be charged for each consultation.

A number of submissions noted that the loss of free general medical services has been a considerable disincentive to the taking up of employment. This was taken to illustrate the value people place on the services. Some submissions sought phased medical entitlements on the basis of income thresholds. A small number of submissions were critical of the medical card system on the grounds that it encouraged recipients to seek assistance for minor complaints and that it was a drain on tax payers.

# Women and the health services

Women's health needs were a dominant focus of many of the submissions on health. The consensus was that the health system does not adequately recognise the health implications of a woman's life cycle.

### Women's general health care
The importance of reducing the incidence of women's diseases, such as breast and cervical cancer, postnatal depression and osteoporosis was stressed. It was noted that well-woman and other clinics tend to be at city hospitals, which precludes many women from availing of these services. A national screening programme for common diseases was sought, using mobile units, and with specific emphasis on farm and rural dwelling women. More female doctors and the choice of a female doctor to be available to women were suggested.

### The health service response to domestic violence
Numerous submissions pointed out that the service for victims of domestic violence should be

available seven days a week. There were calls for increased training of accident and emergency staff and of health workers generally and social workers in particular, in recognising, assisting disclosure by and supporting victims of domestic violence. Suggested improvements included that a good practice code should be implemented throughout the services and that an interdepartmental policy team should be established to work in partnership with the voluntary sector to develop an overall strategy, policies and procedure on domestic violence. Another suggestion was for the use of treatment programmes with perpetrators, designed in consultation with professionals and organisations working with victims of violence.

Special concerns were voiced for women victims who are addicts, psychiatrically ill or chronically homeless. Some submissions focused on the needs of child victims of domestic violence in terms of schools, nursing, medical and social work services, child psychiatry, clothing and child care work assistance.

## Family planning services

The majority of submissions on family planning issues requested that family planning clinics be set up in all local areas and be available free of charge to medical card holders. Certain groups sought the provision of extensive information and services to young people. Such provision was strongly rejected by other submissions. A small number of submissions sought full and equal access to alternative forms of conception for lesbian women who wish to conceive a child. A number of submissions noted that family planning or contraception is not solely a woman's issue.

## Women with disabilities

There were calls for gynaecologists and obstetricians to receive training on the entire range of sexual, contraceptive and reproductive health issues in the context of disability and for genetic counselling to be available free of charge.

## Antenatal care

A significant number of submissions on women's health commented on the problems many women have in attending for antenatal care due to transport, time and cost factors and child care demands. The solution put forward was to bring services closer to communities, including the use of district hospital maternity units in rural areas. The importance of contact with the same midwife during antenatal, perinatal and postnatal clinical care was stressed. Another suggestion was that prenatal classes should give information on child rearing and parenting programmes.

Many submissions expressed implacable opposition to abortion. A number of submissions called for a new constitutional referendum to enact a pro-life guarantee. This contrasted with the call for introduction of legislation for termination of pregnancies considered to put a woman's life or well-being at risk. Moral objections were also expressed in relation to euthanasia.

The possible distress of an unplanned pregnancy was considered in relation to married and unmarried women. Greater community support was suggested for pregnant married women who may have difficulties coping with another child. In relation to teenage pregnancies there was a preference for the non-directive discussion of adoption as an option, particularly as an alternative to abortion. There was also a call to strengthen the support for the whole family where a teenager becomes pregnant - the expectant mother, the father and their parents. The importance of support and help for mothers who keep their babies and for young mothers who live with their families was noted.

### Maternity units

For many, the preferred birth is in a hospital setting and some submissions sought that the father's right to be present during birth be written policy. There was a call for the physical environment where birth takes place to be conducive and for birthing pools to be available. Early discharge from hospital was seen as a problem, particularly in the case of first time mothers, because of the lack of community health support. This problem was considered to be compounded by the increasing incidence of smaller families, both immediate and extended, by the rising number of unmarried parents and the pressures on mothers to return to work. Concerns were voiced about the practice whereby most pregnant single women are automatically referred to a social worker in the maternity unit. This was perceived to be discriminatory.

There was a call for government support of home birth policies, for training of midwives and for financial assistance to be given to organisations involved in the promotion of home birth options. Discrepancies in payments of home birth midwives by different health boards were noted. Concerns were raised in relation to the institutionalisation of nearly all births with some submissions expressing the view that this leads to families being split at an important time.

Submissions requested increased funding of intensive care units for infants. Special concern was also raised for new born children who live for only a short time. The importance of support for parents and their representative organisations in all these matters was stressed. A number of submissions wished to see the extension of the register of stillbirths be extended, in acknowledgement of the sense of loss and need to grieve in cases of miscarriage.

### Breastfeeding

Some submissions focused on breastfeeding in the context that Ireland has one of the lowest rates of breastfeeding in Europe. The main proposal was for more positive information and support for mothers who wish to breastfeed. Some submissions suggested that all maternity hospitals should have a policy in favour of breastfeeding. To aid mothers who are breastfeeding, submissions sought 24 hour feeding assistance telephone help lines. There was a call for the implementation of a national policy on breastfeeding.

### Post-natal care service

There was a consensus that the public health nursing service is a significant first and ongoing contact with new mothers. Suggested roles of the public health nurse included the detection of post-natal depression, the relief of anxiety in the new mother and the detection of illness or failure to thrive in the child or mother. Calls were made for public health nurses to inform all new mothers of the supports and services available and that there be daily visits by a maternity trained health visitor to support and complement the work of the public health nurse for the first few weeks. There was a call for improved communication between hospitals and the public heath service regarding the mother's and baby's well being on discharge from hospital.

## Home help service
Many submissions sought that the home help service should assist new mothers with cooking or cleaning for the first few weeks after the birth and for longer periods in the case of a mother with a child who is ill or has a disability.

## Other services for mother and child
There was a positive view of the Homestart programme, which offers support, friendship and practical help to families with children under the age of five years in their own homes. Continued funding and extension of this service were sought on the grounds that it is a valuable intervention in the lives of young families. The Community mothers scheme was also well received and further expansion was requested. There were calls for the number of community child care workers to be increased, for psychotherapeutic intervention with mothers and infants up to age of two years and for support and advice for lone parents.

A number of submissions complained that inoculation for infants now takes place at a general practitioner's surgery or clinic which means waiting with a young baby. The preference was to return to the system of inoculation at home.

# Children and the health services

The importance of prevention was a dominant theme of the submissions focusing on children's health and medical problems. Suggestions included that the public health nurse should have access to children in their own home up to end of primary school, and particularly to children deemed to be at risk. There was a proposal that there should be an improved followup system when children are sent home from hospital. Another suggestion was that a social worker be assigned to each town/area so families may build up trust and a sense of continuity.

## The Child Care Act (1991)
There was general agreement that the State should develop a comprehensive range of child care services in Ireland in partnership with the voluntary sector. A group of submissions believed that children should not be taken into care except as a last resort, particularly if the cause of removal from the home is associated with financial difficulties. Some submissions considered that written information on their legal rights should be made available to every parent whose child is admitted to care. A number of submissions asked that independent monitoring be introduced to ensure adherence to Department of Health guidelines and current legislation.

Differing viewpoints were expressed regarding the growing numbers of reports of suspected child abuse. Mandatory reporting of all child sex abuse cases was a popular view. Some submissions stated that there is a need for urgent responses, including immediate provision of more psychologists and social workers in each health board, to deal with the large number of new allegations. Other proposals included a national paedophile register to assist gardaí, teachers, carers and voluntary groups organising events for children, scouts, sports and youth clubs. There was a proposal that the gardaí should have strong links with the police force in Britain to share information on suspected or actual cases. There was a call for family group conferences rather than the current case conference format, to obtain decisions and support family generally. Concern was expressed about the high rate of suspected neglect, in addition to physical and sexual abuse.

Some submissions urged caution for fear of wrongful accusation or to ensure that the rights of parents cannot be indiscriminately undermined by health board personnel or structures. Many of these submissions considered that evidence should come from cooperation and interacting agencies, rather than from an individual professional. A number of submissions stated that women are making false claims regarding child abuse in order to further their cases for marital separation. The treatment of abusers was also a focus of submissions, with a number of innovative projects suggested.

### Fostering

Some submissions called for improved payments to foster families. Others sought innovative uses of fostering for the accommodation of children visiting hospitals for treatment, for provision of alternative homes to homeless children, for periods of emotional upheaval in the family, and to provide permanent substitute care in the event of death of a parent.

A number of submissions stated that more imaginative use of fostering options should be used for the children of teenage mothers, to allow time for the adolescent parent to complete her education or to mature sufficiently to act as a parent. Some submissions sought halfway houses for children awaiting fostering and that hospitalisation as a short-term placement should cease. Concerns were raised about discriminatory attitudes and behaviour towards lesbian and gay youths in foster placements.

### Traveller children

Some submissions noted that the mortality rates of infant Travellers are three times higher that the national average and that Travellers have a low life expectancy. Health boards accepted the need for culturally appropriate health education programmes for Travellers. One health board noted that Traveller children are at increased risk of gastroenteritis and other enteric infections, due to unsatisfactory living conditions such as overcrowding, lack of clean drinking water and poor sanitary conditions. All of these figures were seen to be a challenge to health services and local authorities.

## People with disabilities and the health services

Fully 60 submissions (12% of total) dealt with various aspects of disability, including health and medical service provision for family members with disabilities. The overwhelming majority of these submissions called for improved income support for this group as a whole.

### Disabled Person's Maintenance Allowance (DPMA)

Prominent suggestions were that the payment rates of the Disabled Person's Maintenance Allowance

(DPMA) should be equal to unemployment benefit. Another suggestion was that the level of dependency or disability should be considered and that allowances should be made on that basis.

Many submissions from individuals and organisations stated that DPMA payments should not be withdrawn when the claimant is in hospital or in temporary residential care as it places considerable burdens on families to maintain accommodation and to provide necessary requisites. Some submissions suggested that a reduced payment should be made while a recipient is hospitalised and that a similar payment should be made to recipients of unemployment assistance while they are hospitalised.

Anomalies in the DPMA scheme were also instanced. A call was made for people who have been diagnosed with certain long-term conditions, and who are currently ineligible, to be entitled to the DPMA.

Some submissions sought extension of the long-term illness scheme to a wider group of conditions than at present. A number of additional services were requested for inclusion on the long-term illness scheme. These included the community physiotherapy service, continence advice service and technical aids. On the related issue of the drugs repayment schemes, it was suggested that the total to be paid by elderly people should be reduced.

Some submissions sought that existing disability should not to be used to delay treatment for unrelated difficulties and that new drug treatments be made available free of charge to those who need them. There was a view that children should not help with personal care and that adequate home assistance should be available, with special emphasis on the importance of this service in rural areas. Specific mention was made of the importance of improved and increased respite facilities.

There was widespread support for a national genetic counselling service for people with disabilities and their families. There were calls for research to be carried out in the areas of diagnosis and treatment of disabilities including multiple sclerosis, schizophrenia and Alzheimer's disease.

**Long term residential care**
Numerous submissions on disability issues criticised the inappropriate placement of people with disabilities in residential care and indicated a preference for independent living in the community with personal assistance back up. Some submissions, focusing on the needs of people with learning disabilities (mental handicap), stressed the importance of residential care, if and when the family can no longer cope, or the person with a learning disability wishes to avail of it.

**Children with disabilities**
Some submissions focused on disability, both physical disability and learning disability (mental handicap) and some on specific diagnostic groups (including cerebral palsy, autism and Asperger syndrome). These submissions pointed out that families with a member with a disability should have the right to expect help with the emotional, financial and practical issues involved with care, education and living a full life. There was a consensus that services for children with disabilities and

their families should be designed and developed in partnership with families, to acknowledge their expertise and to meet their needs.

A prominent concern was for the provision of respite services, emergency and planned, residential and home-based. Other services were sought including diagnostic services, genetic counselling, home support services, day services, access to comprehensive, multi-disciplinary clinical support and long-term residential care services. Some submissions considered that paediatricians, doctors, nurses and social workers should be trained specifically in the area of giving diagnostic information and prognosis in an empathetic manner. There were calls for support for parents and families and improved information and counselling services at times of need. The establishment and funding of support groups for parents with children with disabilities was stressed. Complaints were made that home adaptation and appliances are nearly impossible to obtain.

### Domiciliary Care Allowance (DCA)

A number of submissions pointed out that the DCA is not payable if a child is in five day weekly residential care. There was a proposal that some financial assistance should be given in these instances and also to assist in paying for transport to and from the centres. Another suggestion was that the DCA should be administered by the Department of Social Welfare.

## Elderly people and the health services

In all, 45 submissions (9% of total) discussed issues relating to elderly people. Submissions pointed out that some elderly people are vulnerable because of their health, social isolation or inadequate financial resources. Figures were presented to show that the elderly population is rising steadily both in absolute and relative terms. It was predicted that this increase will pose a significant challenge to the State in the future.

There was a general opinion that existing home care and support services for frail elderly people are not sufficiently comprehensive to enable them to live in dignity and independence. Some submissions stated that certain services for the elderly should be designated as core services and should be available by statutory entitlement. Other submissions considered that voluntary bodies should be encouraged to provide social services for the elderly in their communities. A number of submissions focused on supports for families to assist them in continuing to provide support for elderly relatives and saw this as the preferred avenue.

General suggestions included more State investment in community support services, with increased home visits of elderly people living alone by public health nurses, general practitioners, chiropodists and alternative medical practitioners. Improved and expanded home help and meals-on-wheels services and holidays for the elderly were proposed. Other submissions asked for the provision of transport for outpatient treatment and for elderly people to be made aware of day care centres and services. It was suggested that information on the range of services should be available to elderly people when they collect their pension payments.

There was a view that for some elderly people the best option may be long-term residential care. The main proposal put forward in these submissions was for the provision of high quality hospital and residential care for elderly people when they can no longer be maintained in dignity and independence at home. Submissions focused on the importance of suitable accommodation, assistance with aspects of daily living and personal care, specialised nursing care and opportunities for stimulating daily activities. There were calls to set up quality nursing home care, without means testing criteria, to monitor standards in private nursing homes and to stop the closure of long-term geriatric wards.

# Carers and the health services

In all, 45 submissions (9% of total) detailed the concerns of carers along a wide range of issues. Throughout these submissions there was a sense of isolation from ongoing or emergency support of the health services. The dominant view was that women in the community take care of relatives with little backup from the State, while saving the State the cost of alternative, usually residential, care. Special concerns were raised about children caring for sick parents, lone parents caring for a disabled child, spouses caring for a dementing partner and carers of people who are terminally ill, including children who are dying.

### Farm carers

There was discussion of the special isolation and loneliness of carers living on farms. The dearth of services in rural areas, from home visiting to meals on wheels, was noted. It was stated that the system of family inheritance places responsibilities for elderly parents on the inheritor and sometimes the care of an older husband on a young wife with a young family. There was a comment that the older type of farmhouse is unsuitable for many elderly people.

### Caring for carers

A number of the submissions on carers discussed how the Carer's charter promotes the right of carers to lead full and independent lives and to continue to provide care without undue cost to their own way of life. The charter lists the information, training and support services needed to give carers assistance and relief such as day centres, home nursing, home helps and both emergency and planned, short-term care.

Some of these submissions outlined the financial support and involvement in policy making necessary for the effective inclusion of carers within the community care process. One of the issues identified was the need to strengthen the family's ability to meet its own needs and to clarify and understand the balance between how the family can satisfy its needs and what it can expect through public provision of services. Submissions sought the establishment of a 24-hour "care line" to give advice to carers and carers' support groups. The community alert groups were described as a lifeline to carers and more funding was requested for them.

### Carer's Allowance

There was unanimity among the submissions on carers that taking care of people in their own homes and family environment means a cost to the care giver, who is entitled to financial recognition in his or her own right. There were proposals that credits should be given to carers towards pension rights and other social welfare benefits.

Numerous suggestions were made to improve the Carer's Allowance. These included the abolition of means testing and the use of a "cost of care" allocation. Other proposals were that the dependency level of the person being cared should be taken into account when assessing entitlement and that the carer should be permitted other part-time employment. Other suggestions were that, at minimum, the Carer's Allowance should be paid at the same rate as unemployment assistance, and that carers in receipt of the Carer's Allowance should not be discriminated against when they undertake FAS and other training schemes. There was also a proposal that a carer's allowance should be paid to carers who are not residing with the person being cared for.

### Health board funding of voluntary groups

Some submissions stated that voluntary and community organisations should not have to rely on local fundraising efforts. There was widespread support, in these submissions, for improved State funding of voluntary groups to cover operating and administration costs. Grant application processing and payment were described as too slow and suggestions were made to facilitate applications and to bring payments into line with organisations' financial years. Other proposals were that grants should continue beyond one year to permit continuity of service. There was a suggestion that grants from sources other than the health boards should not have to go through the health board payment system and that national groups should make applications to central government departments.

### Medical research

Suggested issues for research included the attitudes and behaviour of domestic abusers, sexual activity of teenagers, suicide, the effects of unemployment on health, and the effects of disability on marriage and relationships. There was a proposal for the introduction of a unique identification number for every person in the State to facilitate tracking of the health careers of people and to improve statistics and research and development.

# Conclusion

The complexity of the health service was exemplified in the vast range of issues addressed in submissions to the Commission. The primary proposal was that the health services should plan and provide holistic and locally-based family services. Central importance was attached to improving a wide range of health services for women. Particular emphasis was also placed in submissions on the importance of protecting children. A number of submissions sought the introduction of free medical treatment, particularly for young children. Means testing requirements were often criticised and the wide remit of the health boards in terms of certain payments was questioned.

The special needs of certain groups including people with disabilities, elderly people and carers were voiced in terms of the importance of a mainstream service response and of the system responding to the person and not merely the problem.

# Section VI

## Counselling and families

### Introduction

Fully 185 submissions (38% of total) made specific reference to the importance of increased and improved nationwide, locally-based and comprehensive counselling provision
(see Figure 5).

Figure 5: Percentage of submissions on counselling

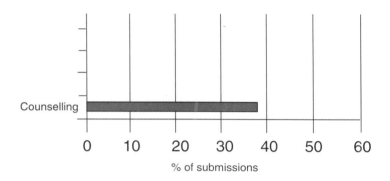

% of submissions

The need for counselling was considered to reflect the decreasing role of the extended family, as a result of relocation of families from rural to urban areas, and from city locations to new suburban housing estates, and to the declining role of the church in providing ethical or personal support.

## Importance of counselling

Submissions focusing on counselling put forward the unanimous view that counselling may assist people to understand their situation and help them react positively to change. Many of these submissions commented that families and individuals may reach out and may be reached at crisis times. The focus of these submissions was the need for continuous development of counselling services capable of responding to all crisis calls. For other submissions, counselling was too heavily focused on crisis management and intervention, in part due to long waiting lists and complicated referral procedures which act as a deterrent for many families. Counselling was perceived to have a preventive role and submissions identified the need for the provision of confidential facilities where any family with problems may get necessary advice and attention.

### Benefits of counselling
The potential benefits of counselling were identified as a reduction in the incidence of hospitalisation and in financial expenses for medication and in decreased numbers of sick days in the workplace.

### Regulation of counselling services

A number of submissions noted that counselling and therapy services are unregulated in this country at the moment. Proposals were put forward to end this unregulated situation and to control the setting up of counselling services.

### Preferred means of service delivery

Numerous submissions demanded the establishment of a professional counselling service, freely available to everyone who requires it. This would involve increased numbers of community-based centres where family counselling was easily accessible and readily available at all stages of family development. Special emphasis was laid in some submissions on the real counselling needs of rural communities and on the importance of local facilities to eliminate travel problems. Other submissions requested greater publicity of available services and increased awareness of such services by general medical practitioners.

There was a strong preference that counselling should be State-sponsored and funded. A number of counselling organisations specifically commented that the full cost of counsellors, reception staff and premises should be considered in any funding allocation. The State's role was identified as ensuring minimum standards of counselling and of service management.

Another repeated suggestion was for a national help line for families under stress, specifically a free phone, staffed by personnel trained to listen and offer concrete suggestions. Some submissions proposed that counselling should be available through the GMS (medical card system) or through private health insurance. Others asked for time off work to attend counselling.

One view was that the counselling needs of the family can only be met by counsellors who have had similar experiences and perhaps who have come from similar backgrounds.

## Specific counselling needs

Many of the submissions focused on particular groups or particular problems requiring counselling assistance.

### Pre-marriage courses

There was general support in the submissions for the introduction of the increased notice of marriage regulation. A small number of submissions did not support this alteration on the grounds that it was an intrusion into the private affairs of individuals. Many submissions argued for legislation to ensure that people may not enter marriage without first undergoing a professionally devised course dealing with all aspects of relationships and responsibilities. Subjects considered appropriate for such courses included childbearing and rearing, marriage preparation, communication, sexuality, conflict management and spirituality and morality in relationships. There was a call for specialised programmes for emotionally and socially deprived people entering marriage.

## Marriage and relationship counselling

The importance of attempting to heal wounds and to promote continuance of marriage was stressed in many submissions. At the same time, there was an appreciation that counsellors need to be knowledgeable about the legal aspects of divorce. Marriage and relationship counsellors were considered to need specialist training in areas such as psychosexual problems, bereavement and child abuse all of which place an enormous strain on relationships. A number of submissions considered that marriage guidance should be professional and not left to voluntary groups. There were suggestions for public awareness campaigns and courses to assist young people to adjust to early marriage.

## Marriage and relationship breakdown

Submissions commented on the painful experience of marriage breakdown and made a general plea for counselling and non-adversarial mediation. The benefits of mediation were identified as the use of a problem-solving and non-confrontational approach. Many submissions differentiated between parental and marital relationships. The general consensus in these submissions was that the family mediation service should be expanded to the whole country and should be advertised. Improved referral to mediation by both the medical and legal professions was also proposed. The needs of rural families were particularly noted. Submissions from mediators sought greater recognition for their work and the introduction of professional standards.

## Illness and bereavement counselling

A number of submissions dealt with the concerns of long-term illness, terminal illness and bereavement. There was general support for the establishment of a national bereavement counselling service. Submissions were agreed that bereavement counselling should be offered in a normalised environment in local centres and should include courses for young people in local schools to develop an understanding of death. There was a call that people living in rural areas should have locally available services.

A small number of submissions comprised broad ranging overviews of the impact of illness on the family life cycle and called for State policies and funding to deal with the psychosocial, physical, financial and bereavement impacts on families and for support and funding of the hospice movement. A number of submissions from individuals described the immense personal hurt, loneliness and absence of support they had experienced following bereavement. The bereavement following suicide was identified as special concern.

Some submissions described how caring for a child with limited life expectancy places enormous strain on the family members, parents and siblings. A number of suggestions regarding home-based nursing assistance, continuity of care and respite care were put forward. Stillbirths and perinatal deaths were the issue of some submissions. All of these submissions asked for the bereaved parents and siblings to be given assistance in coming to terms with loss.

It was observed that approximately 50,000 Irish women have had abortions in the last decade and that many of these women may have post-abortion syndrome and may require counselling.

### Adolescent counselling

Some submissions observed that children and adolescents may need counselling assistance at times of parental marital conflict and in the event of the breakdown of their parents' marriage. Other submissions considered that adolescents may experience their own difficulties, not solely in conjunction with family upset. Isolated young people may be at risk of suicide and need supportive intervention. Counselling services for the sixteen to eighteen year age groups were stated to need immediate financial support. There was also a call for counselling of young lesbians and gay men and their families.

### Addiction counselling

Many of the 76 submissions (16% of total) focusing on addiction concerns considered that alcohol use was related to the stress of modern living, along with addiction to gambling, smoking and drugs. Submissions called for the establishment and funding of appropriate levels of specialised counselling services for all of these problems in all areas, urban and rural.

### Disability counselling

Many of the 60 submissions (12% of total) focusing on disability called for the provision of counselling for people with disabilities and their families. This included counselling at the time of diagnosis for the person, his or her parents and/or spouse, with some submissions giving detailed accounts of the upheavals in their lives and marriages when first told of significant illness or disability. Children with disabilities or special needs were identified as requiring counselling input also. There was a perceived need for psychosexual counselling of young people and adults with disabilities.

There was a suggestion for counselling support for carers of people who are disabled, or chronically or terminally ill.

### Other concerns

Other areas in which counselling was requested included depression, stress related problems, domestic violence, rape, child abuse, life trauma of refugees, and bullying.

## Conclusion

Provision of improved and expanded counselling services nationwide was one of the most frequent requests in submissions to the Commission. There was a widespread sense that existing counselling services are oversubscribed, underresourced and accessible only to urban dwellers with sufficient money. There was a unified demand for a nationwide State-funded comprehensive counselling service in local urban and rural community settings which assists individuals and families with difficulties.

# Financing families

# Section VII

**Social welfare, child benefit, unemployment, training for employment, poverty and families**

### Introduction

This section deals with the issues of social welfare services, unemployment, poverty, training for employment and minimum income. In all, 143 submissions (29% of total) addressed the issue of social welfare services, with 50 submissions (10% of total) discussing child benefit. A further 90 submissions (18% of total) raised issues relating to unemployment and 43 submissions (9% of total) dealt with training for employment. Fully 58 submissions (12%) focused on poverty and 33 submissions (7% of total) discussed the concept of a minimum income.

Figure 6: Percentages of submissions on social welfare services, unemployment, poverty, child benefit, training for employment and a minimum income

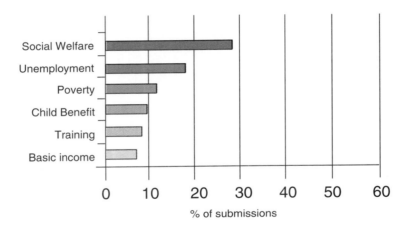

% of submissions

## Social welfare

In all, 143 submissions (29% of total) focused on social welfare entitlements, payments and other benefits. The main emphasis in these submissions was on social welfare payments. Numerous submissions focused on discrepancies and anomalies within various parts of the social welfare system. Many submissions, from individuals who are dependent on a variety of social welfare payments, described the day-to-day financial pressures on them. These submissions gave a perspective on how difficult it is for two parents, and even more difficult for lone parents, dependent on social welfare, to raise a family. Submissions holding to this general view described how people have little chance to escape dependency on social welfare. Particular concerns were raised regarding people living in rural areas.

There were calls to increase social welfare payments to the levels recommended by the Report of the Commission on Social Welfare, as the minimum adequate payment necessary to alleviate the poverty suffered by families dependent on these payments. There was also some comment on the cost of the social welfare system to tax payers.

Many submissions stated that the role of the social welfare system and of employment policies must be to encourage real improvements in the standard of living and at the same time promote passage into work. Phasing of entitlements on the basis of level of income, including the full range of secondary benefits, was suggested as a positive measure to assist people in low paid employment.

Some submissions remarked on the arbitrary nature of the community welfare system and proposed that a single payment be provided to each claimant. Means testing was also criticised. Comments included that there should be regular updates of the limits, that some savings should be excluded from the capital assessment, and that interest payments on small compensation awards should not be counted.

## Social welfare service delivery

A series of criticisms was levelled at the delivery of social welfare entitlements. A recurrent theme of submissions was that public servants need customer care courses in order to provide user-centred information and services. The payment of social welfare entitlements at post offices was criticised on the grounds of lengthy queuing. There was a suggestion that the system of voluntary direct deductions from social welfare payments should be expanded. Another suggestion was for greater use of computerised systems to modernise payment approaches.

## Unemployment benefit

Some submissions indicated that it should be mandatory for those fit for work and claiming social welfare to carry out some useful public or community service tasks in return. This view was often put forward in the context of helping families to help themselves, putting a value on the benefit received, encouraging a work ethic and reducing the element of black economy activity.

There was a call for the system of signing on the live register and of the operation of rules regarding availability for work to be abolished. Suggestions included the introduction of a single payment to amalgamate the various allowances and discretionary payments, and the supplementing of the social welfare income of men who attend parenting, cookery or academic courses.

## Individualising family payments

The consensus from the submissions dealing with social welfare concerns was that women should be treated equally with men within the social welfare code, through the introduction of an adult allowance and the abolition of the dependent allowance. The present system was characterised as anti-woman and anti-family in that it encourages the man to believe that the payment is his and forces the woman to cope for her family on a lower payment than her male partner.

Some submissions observed that equality should also mean equality of men with women and sought that State support of fathers should be at the same level and in same ways as for mothers. Other suggestions included that the Department of Social Welfare should advertise and encourage the use of the payment arrangements whereby both partners may split payments and benefits and that the child dependent rate should be the same for all social welfare payments.

# Lone parenting

An issue raised in many of the 77 submissions (16% of total) on lone parents was that of lone parents within the social welfare code. Many submissions noted the significantly different criteria for certain entitlements for unmarried and married parents. The majority of these submissions expressed strong criticism of the current system.

### Financial support of unmarried mothers by fathers

Many of the submissions on social welfare stated that the fathers of the children of unmarried mothers should be required to support them financially. Other submissions considered that young unmarried mothers should be encouraged to live in their parental family home without loss of either party's social welfare entitlements, in order to encourage greater support for the young mother.

Some submissions noted that families headed by one parent are twice as likely to live in poverty as the two parent model. Such submissions also observed that social welfare income support is the only source of income for many lone parents, particularly women. There were calls for the implementation of the recommendations of the report of the second Commission on the Status of Women, in relation to child care, to assist lone parents to return to work. Some submissions considered that lone parents are often unaware of their entitlements and need improved information services and adequately funded support groups.

There was concern raised regarding lone parents in receipt of payments and rent allowances. If a woman in this position earns additional income, she may lose some or all of her rent allowance. Such rules were seen to operate to prevent people from improving their situation. It was also noted that lone parents may fall into debt while waiting for their social welfare claim to be accepted and suggested that the supplementary welfare system should be fully integrated into mainstream social welfare services and administered at a single local office.

Plans to abolish the deserted wife's benefit were criticised. Deserted husbands pointed out that the rules with regard to social welfare payments discriminate against them and that many deserted husbands have little choice but to place their children in care.

### Marriage versus cohabitation

Most of the submissions dealing with this issue believed that the current social welfare regulations encourage and support unmarried couples to live together and to claim more social welfare payments than they could if they were married. Submissions stated that not only are couples discriminated against for being married, but that many couples feel unable to marry because of social welfare regulations. This situation was viewed universally as unsatisfactory.

A number of submissions pointed out that, in legal terms, because women are treated as dependents within the social welfare system, women lone parents cohabiting with men are ineligible for any of the lone parent payments. Another group, while appreciating that the rules prohibit cohabitation, considered that it is a common occurrence. A number of lone parent organisations pointed out that the rules surrounding cohabitation encourage deceit and fraud.

# Child benefit

Fully 50 submissions (10% of total) raised issues about child benefit. The consensus was that the current social welfare provision for children falls short of the actual cost of rearing a child.

### Children over the age of sixteen years

Almost all submissions focusing on child benefit sought that it be payable for unemployed young people, living at home, until the age of eighteen years. The present situation was universally depicted as anti-family, encouraging young people to leave home before they are sufficiently mature to live on their own. On leaving home the young person may be entitled to subsidised rent allowances, a medical card and other benefits. Some submissions proposed that child benefit should be payable for as long as the young person is a dependent on their parent(s). There was also a suggestion that the State should continue child benefit payments to attempt to support the young person and family in the case of school dropout. Other suggestions included that child benefit should continue for young people in low wage apprenticeships.

A large number of submissions requested that child benefit payments increase with the age of the child. This was on the basis that teenagers have many more needs than younger children. A number of submissions instanced anomalies in the way the State views the cost of a child. For example, some allowances, other than child benefit, are paid until the child is eighteen. Another example cited was that of an unemployed young person living at home being deemed to obtain a board and lodging benefit greater than the existing level of child benefit payment.

There was a call for increased child benefit for families with more than two children. A small number of submissions proposed the increase of child benefit rates alongside the taxation of the benefit or the placement of an income threshold on eligibility.

# Other social welfare concerns

### Unemployment assistance

Another group of submissions sought that children under the age of eighteen years should be entitled to claim unemployment assistance without having their parents' means taken into account. Various anomalies that encourage children to leave school to claim this payment were described. Concerns were raised in relation to the financial support of young women during pregnancy or illness.

### Family Income Supplement (FIS)

In submissions on FIS, the rules regarding the income thresholds for this payment were criticised unanimously and the suggestion was made that FIS should be based on net and not on gross income. There were requests for a proactive information drive to ensure full take-up of the FIS scheme and for clarification of the eligibility criteria for the scheme. Comments on FIS included that the scheme assists some employers to continue to pay low wages. Another view was that the FIS should be phased out and replaced by increased child benefit.

### Pensions

Some submissions considered that the income of pensioners living alone, following the death of a spouse, is inadequate to meet their needs. In particular, many widows wrote to express their sense of being treated unfairly. There was discussion of the problems for women who stayed at home to rear families and now depend on their husbands for a pension. There was criticism of the existing rules whereby the old age pension, in respect of spouses, and some other benefits are not available to non-marital partnerships.

Some submissions discussed the financial problems stemming from taking a grandparent or other elderly relative into the home of his or her children. This may lead to the elderly person's entitlements being terminated. This was considered to be an anti-family measure and these submissions suggested that not only should the allowances and entitlements be continued, but that integration into the younger generation household should be encouraged. Some submissions raised cases where the Department of Social Welfare has claimed an elderly person's savings, on death, as repayment of a pension.

A number of suggestions were made in relation to improving the social welfare system. A free bus pass for all social welfare recipients and for chronically ill or disabled persons was suggested. The view was expressed that free travel for the elderly is not available in rural areas and it was also proposed that free travel should not be limited to off-peak times.

Free phone rental was requested for unemployed people and for carers of people with disabilities. There were also requests for financial assistance for holidays for families on social welfare. There was a call to abolish the television licence fees for low income families. The rate of fuel allowance was viewed as insufficient and submissions sought an increase in this allowance.

### Supplementary Welfare Allowance

Some submissions dealt with the supplementary welfare allowances administered by the health board community welfare officers. Most of these submissions considered that this discretionary scheme was best amalgamated into the mainstream social welfare payment system. The means tested and discretionary elements of these payments were criticised in many submissions. A few submissions called for the continued development of the allowance.

### Social welfare appeals system

There was criticism of the social welfare appeals system and proposals made for the use of an independent complaints adjudicator and for free legal aid assistance.

## Unemployment

In all, 90 submissions (18% of total) identified unemployment, especially long-term unemployment, as the most important cause of poverty. Numerous submissions described how unemployment damages the family and creates genuine inequality in society. Some submissions focused on the stigma of unemployment and suggested that the attitudes of others towards unemployed people need to be changed. Some submissions considered that unemployment was being perpetuated by the social welfare system, creating additional burdens for tax payers.

The need to tackle inter-generational unemployment was identified as a central aim in nearly all of the submissions addressing the issue. The prevalence of early school leaving by children whose parents are unemployed was raised as a source of concern in many of these submissions. Other submissions commented that the pressure to avoid unemployment creates severe educational pressures on young people.

**Unemployment and men**

Some submissions focused on the effects of unemployment on men. These suggested that men without work have no obvious role in society and that the consequent lowering of their self esteem, and their fears for the future, make it difficult for them to involve themselves creatively in the search for new job opportunities or in community activities. Unemployed men were considered to need assistance to enable them to progress. Concern was expressed about people over the age of sixty years having to compete for work until the age of sixty-six.

**Creating employment**

Most submissions expected the government to create work. Many submissions focused on the perceived circularity and ineffectiveness of State funding or on unfairness of European Union (EU) funding allocation. Submissions referred to the potential for work in libraries, leisure centres, play and sports grounds, on buses and in the tourist industry, where there are existing staff shortages or where full-time employment may not be justified. Part-time, taxed, self-employed work for people who are currently unemployed was also suggested. Comments included that each family in Ireland has a right to charge the Irish government with the responsibility of providing work for at least one member, so that each family has a breadwinner.

Many submissions alluded to the black economy. The general view was that it is endemic and that too many employers are willing to employ people who continue to draw unemployment benefit. Some submissions commented on the need to encourage groups out of the black economy. A number of submissions called for assertiveness courses for the unemployed. Some submissions asked for a national debate on the meaning of work.

The main reasons put forward for unemployment were low educational qualifications and perceived unemployability because of the applicant's home address. Other suggested reasons included the lack of employment in certain areas, especially rural areas.

Suggested ways to tackle unemployment included a rights-based approach to give information and provide a system that respects the individual. Local job centres to provide information on entitlements and to develop support structures and mentoring programmes were also suggested. Comments included that there should be greater intervention with newly unemployed people, who were perceived to have no avenue of return to the workforce or into retraining schemes until they are classified as being long-term unemployed.

# Training for employment

In all, 43 submissions (9% of total) discussed training issues. Most of these submissions noted the difficulty of obtaining information and the lack of coherence of the delivery of the training service as a whole. There was repeated criticism that marginal rates of taxation and loss of benefits mean that unemployed people are worse off on schemes and in low paid employment than on benefit. Maintenance of the medical card and other secondary benefits were seen as positive steps forward in this regard. Suggested improvements included the publication of FAS job vacancies in community centres and other public places. The cost of travelling to obtain information was a source of concern, particularly in rural areas. The nature of the work and of the supervision on schemes was criticised in a number of submissions.

### Women and training for employment

Some submissions requested that women in the home, who wish to return to paid work, should be included on training schemes. Widows asked to be treated in the same way as unmarried parents in respect of training schemes. The small number of places on some schemes for lone parents was criticised. There was general criticism of the lack of child care provision and flexible hours on training schemes, identified as further obstacles to women's (re)integration to the workforce. There was also a call to include people entitled to receive benefit but not actually doing so and people out of work for a shorter period than one year.

### Disability and training for employment

Disability representative organisations were unanimous in their call for equal access to pre-training, training and mentoring programmes. There were demands for physical access and transport provision, flexible training courses and appropriate allowances. There was a request for additional training of personal assistants to work for people with disabilities, with special emphasis on the non-Dublin and rural areas, to increase independent living opportunities.

### Community Employment Programme

A number of submissions remarked that trainees need more than 20 hours per week on employment schemes and that there should be some academic content in the training. Anomalies regarding the loss of benefits, particularly disability benefit, as a result of participation on the schemes were also identified. Other comments included that the schemes should be directed at those most in need, that the age eligibility threshold should be lowered, that the pay rates are insufficient and that more follow up and improved employment prospects are required.

There was widespread support for a part-time job opportunities programme in the area of socially useful work. A number of submissions asked for funding for community associations to provide work schemes. Submissions called for provision of training to provide home care and for respite services for carers. Other suggestions included that allotments should be made available to train people in gardening, especially the young unemployed, that there should be bilingual training schemes in the arts and that Gaeltacht area schemes should be used as a model for rural enterprise and cottage industry.

In all, 76 submissions (16% of total) dealt in depth with the problems surrounding drug addiction. Some of these submissions considered that a vital part of the stabilisation and rehabilitation process for drug users was preparation for and reintegration into the workforce. Problems in obtaining release of drug offenders from prison to avail of existing training programmes were noted.

FÁS, the national training and employment authority, gave details of its activities to the Commission. These included descriptions of the Community Employment Scheme (CES), the main vehicle through which the State supports the provision of temporary employment for unemployed people. Among its many programmes, FÁS operates training for unemployed people in the areas of industry and local enterprise, seeks to reintegrate early school leavers into training, supports certain employee training measures and provides an employment service.

# Family poverty

Fully 58 submissions (12% of total) discussed poverty and the family. A small number of submissions focused in depth on this concern. Some submissions noted that 1996 is the United Nations year for the eradication of poverty. Some suggested that the Commission on the Family should work with the National Anti-Poverty Strategy.

### Existing research on family poverty

A number of detailed submissions on the issue of poverty gave overviews of existing research on poverty in Ireland. This research indicates that the cost of rearing a family is substantial, with the incomes of families being lower than those of other households. These submissions identified groups at the greatest risk of poverty including people who are unemployed, children, especially in large families, small farmers, women, especially lone mothers, people who are ill or disabled, and elderly people. The highest risk of poverty for families was stated to occur in two parent families with three or more children and in lone parent families.

Submissions noted the research indicating that children have a higher risk of poverty than do adults. Figures were presented to show that 40% of all Irish children live in households with insufficient income to maintain a minimally adequate standard of living. Unemployment and consequent poverty were identified as the main reasons for the high level of child poverty. Submissions stated that the needs of children living in poverty should be identified, early intervention undertaken and outcomes monitored. There was a suggestion that the State should intervene to utilise a family's disposal income to ensure children's care in cases where the parents are not doing so adequately. It was also suggested that families are victims of poverty and at the same time potential powerful agents in its eradication.

### Debt and family poverty

Some submissions focused on the problem of debt associated with family poverty and hardship. Curbs on the activities of moneylenders and on exorbitant interest rates were demanded. The Money Advice and Budgeting Service (MABS), a combined approach of government departmental, church, community and credit union organisations to tackle debt, was highly commended. Criticisms were directed at advertising, the lottery, credit policies and the legal and judicial response to debt.

### Divorce and poverty

Some submissions stated that divorce may create family impoverishment through loss of the main breadwinner or of the family business or farm in dividing assets and through legal expenses. A number of submissions expressed their dissatisfaction with the introduction of divorce on the grounds that tax payers would inevitably have to support families impoverished by the process.

### Financial vulnerability of women

Some submissions noted that shortage of money leads to stress and strained relationships. In this regard, women's lives were viewed as particularly stressful, partly as a result of their traditional role of home money management, partly as a result of their traditional economic dependence on men and partly as a result of their lifestyle which involves shopping and queuing. The family needs, the demands of children, the provision of an adequate family diet were all viewed as inevitably leading to budgeting difficulties, which, in turn, may lead to debt and sometimes to the use of moneylenders. It was suggested that women should be involved in policy making for the family to ensure that their perspective is understood and their position improved.

### A minimum income

Thirty-three submissions (7% of total) suggested that each adult in every family be paid a guaranteed minimum income, indexed to the cost of living. Some submissions also suggested that each child be guaranteed an income commensurate with his or her age and paid through his or her parent.

## Conclusion

The content of submissions examined in this section was wide ranging. Many aspects of the social welfare system were criticised, but its importance in providing financial support for the most vulnerable in society was generally recognised. The principal proposals coming from submissions focusing on the social welfare system were the introduction of phased benefits so that people do not lose all benefits on taking up employment and the use of individualised payments for men and women. The difficulties of lone parents were acknowledged but reservations were expressed about specific benefits being available to them and not to others on low incomes. There were calls for equal treatment of all groups throughout the system. In relation to child benefit, the main focus of submissions was on continued payments for older teenagers who are ineligible at present.

Unemployment was viewed as one of the most serious problems affecting families and various suggestions were put forward to improve the current situation. Regarding training for employment the main proposal was that women in the home should be entitled to sign on the live register. Poverty was the focus of some submissions, with particular concerns expressed for children living in poverty. The introduction of a minimum income for all was promoted by a small number of submissions.

# Section VIII

**Taxation, employment and families**

## Introduction

In all 127 submissions (26% of total) commented on taxation issues, 104 submissions (21% of total) discussed aspects of employment and 73 submissions (15% of total) called for the reintroduction of tax allowances for children. The percentages of submissions are presented in Figure 7.

Figure 7: Percentages of submissions on taxation, employment and the re-introduction of tax-free allowances for children

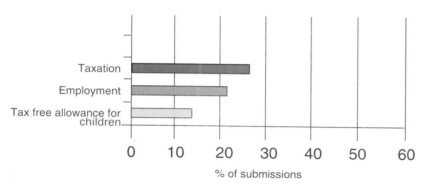

% of submissions

## Taxation

Some 127 submissions (26% of total) discussed taxation. The dominant view was that tax reform must focus on increasing tax-free allowances for people on low incomes. Many of these submissions stated that taxation is applied on too low a level of income and that as a result it may be a deterrent for parents entering or returning to the workforce. Some submissions considered that medium income earners and self-employed families have financial difficulties due to taxation rates and lack of welfare benefits.

## Tax relief for dependent children

A total of 73 submissions (15%) singled out tax relief for dependent children as a particular issue and called for its reinstatement. The abolition of covenanting arrangements was also viewed as a negative development.

## Other taxation concerns

### Child care and tax

Numerous submissions discussed the issue of tax relief on child care costs. Many of these raised objections in principle to paying tax to subvent State-funded child care facilities. Other proposals included tax relief for employers who provide child care services and tax relief on child care fees and private employment of childminders.

## Tax allowances for women working in the home

Many submissions sought special income tax incentives to support one spouse at home. There were a number of different proposals for the taxation system to be used to reward all that is done for families by a parent who is full-time in the home. Suggestions included that the spouse of a full-time home working wife or husband should be exempt from income tax. There was a prevalent view that the characterisation of women as dependent spouses in the tax and social welfare codes is outdated and its removal is long overdue.

## Taxation and the family home

Mortgage tax relief was a particular concern of many submissions, with calls for various forms of taxation assistance with housing costs. A number of submissions discussed property tax which was viewed as inequitable and anti-family in its operation. Examples were given of older homes, where families have lived for many years being subject to property tax, because the area has become fashionable to live in, with a consequent rise in house prices. Other submissions considered that the liability for tax, aggregated on the income of all people living in the home, is encouraging the break up of families. Suggestions put forward included that initiatives should be directed towards family home renewal schemes, that a family affairs section in the Department of Finance should ensure that families are not adversely affected by taxation policies and that stamp duty liability on house purchase should take account of family size.

## Marriage and tax

Some submissions sought taxation policies to support marriage and tax concessions for married couples. These submissions criticised taxation policies which may encourage cohabitation rather than marriage. Some submissions looked for the extension to non-marital partnerships of the tax benefits accruing to married persons. Suggestions included that the married person's income tax exemption limit should be extended to lone parents, that widows and widowers should be taxed as married persons indefinitely and that the Revenue Commissioners should not require separated couples to use separate tax assessment against both their wishes. A number of submissions stated that couples are financially better off when separated. The instance given was that, if a parent has custody of a child for even one day of the year, he or she receives the full lone parent family allowance for that year.

## Carers and tax

Some submissions commented on problems of taxation in relation to carers. Most of these made the general point that the taxation system should seek to assist carers to continue in their role. The present system requiring the invalided person to register as employers and to deduct taxes on behalf of the carer/employee was perceived as virtually unworkable. The point was made that many people who need a carer are not in a position to avail of the existing tax-free allowance of £8.500(6th April 1998) towards the cost of employing people to provide care services for them.

Regarding people with disabilities and tax there was a call to review disabled drivers' tax concessions.

**Death and taxes**

A number of submissions dealt with concerns regarding probate and inheritance. The general consensus was that excessive fees and taxes are payable on death and that certain aspects of the inheritance laws have negative consequences for relatives and for long-term carers. A number of submissions raised questions about the effect of divorce on the inheritance rights on second families.

Concerns were expressed that elderly people may have worries regarding funeral expenses. The provision of a well publicised financial holding service in which the elderly may hold money for this purpose was suggested.

A number of submissions focused on probate tax and on the sale of property to pay for taxes when the beneficiary is not the spouse of the testator. There was a suggestion that payment of probate tax by those on low incomes should be abolished.

**Cross border dual taxation**

A number of submissions dealt with various aspects of the dual taxation laws affecting people who work in Northern Ireland but live in Ireland. The problem was described in terms of the low salaries and low taxation rates available in Northern Ireland. Such salaries are subject to additional tax when declared in this country. Submissions argued that this situation was leading to families being separated and to young people emigrating to the United Kingdom.

**Family business and tax**

A small number of submissions raised issues relating to the taxation of family firms. There was criticism of the earned income allowances of employed wives and children of the owners and of the taxation rules on land leasing to a third party.

Other submissions criticised the interest rates charged by the Revenue Commissioners and asked for compensation for mistakes made by them.

# Pay Related Social Insurance (PRSI)

Submissions that raised issues relating to PRSI expressed the view that social insurance contributions without entitlement are inequitable. Some submissions indicated that everyone should have the choice of paying the full social insurance levies and of obtaining full benefit while others considered that benefits should be pro rata. Other suggestions on the issue of PRSI included that all mothers working full-time in the home and all carers should have PRSI entitlements and pension rights.

### PRSI for farmers and other self-employed persons

Some submissions related to a specific problem regarding PRSI for farmers and the self-employed. These submissions described how PRSI came into force in 1988 for these groups and included the stipulation that contributory pension entitlements were conditional on payments having been made prior to the age of 56 years. Some people have therefore made contributions but can never claim a contributory pension under the scheme. This was viewed unanimously as unjust and the suggestion was made that such persons should be permitted to claim a partial pension.

Other PRSI issues raised included the situation where a separated man makes PRSI contributions on his income and his wife also contributes on her maintenance payments. Concerns were also put forward about the situation of State employees who emigrated, worked abroad, returned later to Ireland and as a result are not entitled to a full contributory pension.

## Employment

A wide range of employment issues, as they affect the family, were raised in 104 submissions (21% of total). These included the creation of employment, family responsibilities and employment, low pay; women and employment, men and employment, lone parents and employment, disability and employment, and retirement.

### The creation of employment

Submissions on this issue focused on the need for State resources and support. Submissions stated that increased production was the key to the nation's economic success. There were repeated calls to bring together local employers and potential employees. Other suggestions included that businesses in deprived areas should be required to assist local voluntary and community organisations and to gain tax relief for such donations. Support should be available for employers of first time workers and incentives should be given to small employers to increase their workforce. Share ownership by employees in firms was viewed positively.

### Creating rural employment

There were numerous calls to bring employment into rural areas by supporting job creation outside the major cities. Policies of State and semi-State organisations were deemed bureaucratic and unresponsive to local needs. Many submissions noted the development of partnership companies, facilitating local and regional empowerment. There were suggestions that partnership structures should be extended nationally to establish and support manufacturing enterprises within each region. Other suggestions included tax exemptions for setting up small rural-based enterprises or self-employment projects and grant aid to be made available to foster handcrafts. Comments were made about the benefits of the Common Agricultural Policy (CAP) and there was a call for land and quotas to be given to young farmers to keep them in rural Ireland.

### Family responsibilities and employment

Some submissions focused on working conditions that affect family life. The consensus was that family responsibilities of employees are part and parcel of an employer's concern. Parental leave was the issue of many of these submissions. The view was that parental leave is an important facility and should be extended for both parents. Maternity leave for periods up to three years was suggested, as was paid paternity leave. A number of submissions suggested that parents should be entitled legally to take time off work to care for sick children. Parents and carers sought to avail of flexitime and job sharing. A system of family leave to permit carers to take leave for family needs was also suggested. Long working hours, overtime and substantial travel requirements of certain types of employment were considered to have negative effects on family life. A number of submissions dealt in depth with the matter of transfers of staff to different locations and to the disruption this brings to families. A number of submissions rejected the introduction of Sunday trading as an imposition on workers and families and inappropriate for a Christian country.

Some submissions addressed the issue of discrimination and bullying in the work place. Proposals were made for the implementation of equality legislation for work and training and for the mandatory reporting of cases. The extension of free legal aid to employment tribunals was also proposed.

## Low pay

Submissions on this issue considered that cheap labour is subsidising industry. There was a general consensus that there is little incentive to work in low paid jobs due to existing social welfare rules, which make low paid workers and their families worse off than if they were in receipt of unemployment benefit. There was a comment that bank charges on wage payments should be curbed. The number of women in low paid occupations was a source of concern.

## Women and employment

Most submissions on the issue of women's employment sought the extension of part-time work to facilitate mothers. The dominant view expressed in these submissions was that work hours should be flexible to accommodate children's school times and needs. The State was urged to lead the way by providing part-time and flexitime opportunities for parents. Numerous individual submissions came from mothers who wished to avail of part-time working but were precluded from doing so by their employers. It was noted that companies, including semi-State companies, have limits on the numbers of staff permitted to avail of part-time work. There was concern that mothers, in such situations, are forced to resign with the consequent saving to the employer of pension contributions and worker benefits.

Many submissions commented that contract labour and "zero hours" contracts are negatively affecting women's employment. There were a number of calls for a compulsory minimum wage and minimum contract policy in the service industries. Other suggestions included improving employment facilities in the interests of women's occupational health and the provision of breaks and suitable facilities for women who are breastfeeding.

## Men and employment

Submissions on the issue of men and work generally focused on the need to improve the environment of paid work to give men the opportunity to fulfil their role within the family as a breadwinner. There was general agreement that full-time employment, rather than part time or contract work should be the aim for the adult male population. Some submissions suggested that fathers who support families should be given priority in the workforce.

### Lone parents and employment

A point made repeatedly in submissions was that there is little incentive to work due to social welfare regulations, particularly those in relation to secondary benefits. A number of submissions gave figures on the number of lone parents, male and female in paid employment. The thrust of these submissions was that the life chances and status conferred on a person by labour market participation are impossible goals for many lone parents.

The matter of the employment and social welfare treatment of lone parents was also addressed in these submissions. In relation to employment, some lone parents are entitled to certain allowances to assist them to go out to work. Submissions from lone parents in receipt of such allowances suggested that the rate of assistance could be improved. However, a large number of submissions from other parents considered these allowances to be inequitable.

### Disability and employment

The extension of employment equality legislation to assist people with disabilities was a dominant concern in submissions on the issue of disability and employment. There was a demand that the employment quota for people with disabilities be enforced within the public service and extended to all employment. There were calls for employment creation for people with disabilities, in particular for people with learning disabilities (mental handicap) and for appropriate disability leave.

### Retirement

Some submissions concentrated on the issue of retirement. The concept of planning for retirement was deemed to be undervalued and underresourced. Suggestions included that every worker contemplating retirement should have access to pre-retirement information and education, that spouses should also attend courses, that employers should actively inform their employees of pension and retirement issues, and that phased or gradual retirement should be explored.

The financial problems caused by forced retirement due to ill health were the focus of a small number of submissions. People affected in this way have no opportunities to better their position and this may place a strain on family relationships. Access to alternative training and employment was sought in such instances.

## Conclusion

Taxation was an issue of considerable interest, with the dominant theme being the call for the reinstatement of child dependent tax allowances. Other proposed taxation changes sought to assist families, particularly those on low incomes. Other concerns raised in this section including retirement, inheritance and probate are matters which often affect people and families at vulnerable times of life and this was deeply felt by many contributors.

Submissions were also concerned to improve working conditions for all people, but especially for women. The payment of allowances to some parents and not to others was a source of repeated criticism. Innovative and flexible approaches to employment creation and maintenance were suggested.

# Families in the community

# Section IX

**Local communities, housing, the environment and families**

### Introduction

The issues of the community, housing and the environment were central concerns of submissions to the Commission. A total of 123 submissions (25% of total), gave views on community life, 102 submissions (21% of total) dealt with concerns about housing and 35 (17% of total) discussed issues relating to the environment. These percentages are presented in Figure 8.

Figure 8: Percentages of submissions focusing on community life, housing and the environment.

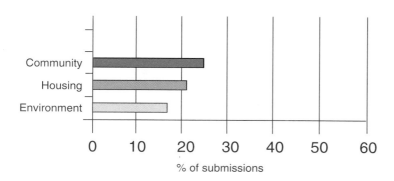

## Local communities

The promotion and protection of community life were discussed in 123 submissions (25% of total). The importance of involvement and representation of people at local level was a reiterated concern. It was suggested that a vibrant community life keeps the family unit together and provides the best foundation for its members. There were calls for the provision for all of the family needs within the local community, with special emphasis on facilities for teenagers who were identified as most at risk. There were suggestions on the development of prevention and support services for local communities where families are affected by drug use. There was a call for the establishment of a community approach to information on and prevention of domestic violence.

A wide range of suggestions was made with the aim of securing community integration. Family resource centres were described as a positive adjunct and ongoing, increased State funding was requested. A number of submissions valued the community youth work schemes, with their emphasis on volunteering.

Some submissions looked for the establishment of local community councils with representation from professional bodies, voluntary groups and elected local representatives. This was sometimes proposed as part of a revised local authority structure. Other suggestions included parish drop-in centres in each community to include crÍches, overnight facilities and adult education, giving practical local support for families in crisis. Another proposal was that estate management courses should be provided for residents and council personnel.

Many submissions commented on the need to provide a suitable social infrastructure in urban areas with problems. The thrust of these submissions was that there must be concerted State support for groups with a community ethos, to give a sense of purpose to people living in these areas. A number of comments were made on the role of the churches in fostering and focusing community spirit and identity.

A number of submissions from religious groups identified the importance of parish support and the relevance of religious and moral values for the vitality of families and communities. Other issues alluded to were the sense of growing isolation of people in middle class estates and neighbourhoods. There was also a suggestion for policing within communities to avoid vandalism and to protect property.

A number of submissions instanced examples of cultural discrimination on housing estates. There were descriptions of harassment in some neighbourhoods. There were concerns about lone mothers, foreigners, members of non-Christian religions and new age life stylists.

Some submissions stated that there is continuing discrimination against Travellers by the settled community. A small number of submissions mentioned difficulties with some Travellers on environmental matters. The refugee community and their representatives identified serious discrimination against them in many aspects of life.

### Maintaining rural communities
In all, 31 submissions (6% of total) focused on the services needed for families in rural areas. Suggestions included the provision of street lighting, footpaths and cycle paths along roads in populated areas, including safe paths for pushchairs and buggies, regular public bus services and more post boxes, roadside cleanups and tree planting.

## Public facilities

The consensus was that public buildings and public transport facilities should be accessible to people with mobility problems and to parents with children in buggies. Suggestions were made for improved access to shopping facilities, e.g. the children's department on the ground floor level and for breastfeeding area in all big stores and shopping centres. There was a proposal that planning permission for public buildings should be given only when crèche facilities are included. A number of submissions asked for better stocking, longer opening hours and play facilities in public libraries. Another issue of concern was the provision and accessibility of public toilet facilities for families.

### Public facilities and disabled access
In a detailed submission one of the organisations representing people with disabilities gave a critical overview of the existing situation regarding access to public facilities by people with disabilities. This detailed analysis proposed that all buildings in State ownership should be accessible to all people with physical disabilities and that a full review of health and safety regulations should be undertaken.

Another suggestion was that local authorities should employ access officers to advise about access for the disabled.

# Public transport

The main focus in submissions relating to public transport was the absence of service in rural areas. Numerous submissions commented on the resulting isolation, the loss of opportunity and experience for members of the rural community. There were proposals for better utilisation of school buses and postal vans and increased numbers of bus routes and frequency of service in rural areas. Other suggestions focused on insurance cover for transport services by the local community, on allowance to individuals to purchase transport in rural areas and on innovative approaches to taxi services in rural areas.

### Transport and disability

Special mention of transport difficulties was a feature of all submissions on physical disability. There were demands that all public transport be accessible and that companion passes be available for escorts of people with disabilities. There were calls for more dedicated wheelchair-accessible car parking and for proper regulation of disabled parking entitlements. Other suggestions included the review of the motorised transport grant system, the removal of loadings by motor insurance companies on people with disabilities and the provision of hire cars with hand controls. The recent introduction of a fully accessible transport service in Dublin by a disability rights group, supported through the Community Employment Scheme, was welcomed. Continuation and expansion of this type of service, with State funding support, was proposed.

### Recreational facilities

Most submissions expressing a view stated that there was a chronic lack of finance for recreational facilities generally and for disadvantaged families specifically. Many submissions drew attention to the problems surrounding public liability insurance for public playgrounds. Young people were seen to be poorly catered for in terms of recreation, with the possible exception of some sports for boys. Facilities for girls and for women were considered to be exceptionally poor. Improved family recreation options were requested to promote greater positive interaction between parents and teenagers. Quality recreation was considered to provide a positive alternatives to drugs. There was a demand that recreational facilities should cater for families who use Irish as a means of communication.

Suggestions included that the State should undertake a leisure centre building programme to benefit communities in the long-term and to create short-term employment in construction. There was a proposal that leisure centres in receipt of State grants should be available for members of the public who cannot afford the membership fees. Another suggestion was that community leaders should be appointed to coordinate recreation.

### Recreational facilities and people with disabilities

Many submissions looked forward to the implementation of anti-discrimination legislation which would ensure access rights of people with disabilities to leisure centres. Some submissions stated that lottery funding should only be available for leisure centres with full access and support services for people with disabilities. A further suggestion was for escort schemes for people with disabilities to attend leisure centres.

## Voluntary community involvement

There was almost unanimous support for voluntary organisations working within the community and numerous submissions asked for increased and ongoing State funding of their activities, particularly of women's and community groups. A commonly expressed view was that the State should not become directly involved in the provision of a service where a voluntary organisation or agency shows it has the capacity to provide that service. The State role was envisaged as establishing standards for these services in consultation with them. Other comments relating to State activity included that many voluntary organisations operate FÁS schemes which have limitations, in particular the absence of continuity as a result of regular personnel changes. There were criticisms of the methods of disposal of Lottery funds.

One proposal was for government tax breaks for "empty nest" parents, midlife people who are available for paid community work. The role of elderly people in voluntary and community work and the need to encourage men to participate in their communities were also mentioned.

## Youth work and youth groups

A detailed submission regarding youth services considered that youth work and the youth service should be recognised as having a valuable contribution to make to family life and should be encouraged and supported in doing so. This submission observed that youth groups provide safe, enjoyable socialising, recreation and education and promote the development of healthy friendships and social skills. The point was also made that youth activities provide an opportunity for the involvement of parents acting as youth leaders.

## Housing

In all, 102 submissions (21% of total) referred to the central importance of adequate and appropriate family housing. Most of these were concerned about the preplanning of communities. There was a consensus that new estates should have attractive layouts, bus routes, schools, shops, public telephones and a community infrastructure in place. A prominent concern was to have a social and age mix in all housing. Submissions sought green areas in all towns and cities. Some submissions commented that the built environment may assist in creating conditions for criminal activities and drug use.

Training for planners and designers, architects and engineers in the matter of family appropriate housing was suggested. Some submissions sought that living areas in houses should be larger and more family-friendly. Special concern was expressed for the provision of study space in homes to permit children to complete homework in a quiet environment. There were calls for research into the housing needs of different family compositions to provide a planned response. A number of submissions asked for environmental studies of high density housing and for intervention to reduce problems. There was a demand for greater awareness of energy conservation.

Innovative approaches to housing provision, for example housing associations and cooperatives were viewed positively in most submissions, although some lone parents and low income families felt themselves excluded from such schemes.

## Owner occupied housing

Many submissions from individuals dealt with the cost of purchase of homes and the associated mortgage problems. Some submissions considered that dual incomes are now necessary to pay for private housing. Urban families were identified as particularly affected by higher mortgages, with resulting effects on their disposable income. It was noted that urban family homes are also potentially liable to property tax.

Another view was that dual incomes have helped to inflate house prices. Proposed ways to reduce financial pressure on people buying homes included tax incentives and grants for first time buyers on second-hand homes. Other suggestions included that land banks held by local authorities should be offered to people at reasonable prices to build their own private homes and that the sale of land rezoned for housing should be heavily taxed. There was criticism of water rates, viewed as double taxation.

## Owner occupied housing and marital separation

There was a prevalent view that, in cases of marital separation, the spouse with day-to-day care of the children should be given the family home as part of the other spouse's contribution to the support of the children. The children's right to remain in the family home was seen as essential.

Some submissions pointed out that following marital separation two places of residence are now required, but that it is not possible to take a second mortgage, using part of the equity in the original home as security. These submissions looked for the use of tangible assets as security for loan purposes.

Questions were raised about the role of lending institutions in consenting to the transfer of the family home to a dependent spouse on separation or divorce. Other comments related to the mortgage relief refunds following marital separation, to the mortgage support scheme and to the way that mortgage institutions treat homosexual couples in long-term relationships on application for a mortgage. A number of submissions from unmarried couples looked for the extension to them of existing legislation which confers rights on married couples regarding property ownership, transfer and inheritance.

# Local authority housing

A common view was that the local authorities should be given increased funding to build more and better quality housing, with an improved infrastructure, including public transport and that the authorities should allocate houses more quickly. The potential for employment from an expanded housing programme was viewed positively.

A number of submissions described how towns often have old council houses lacking indoor toilet/shower facilities, with poor quality heating and with dampness, all leading to health problems. A repeated criticism was that repairs and maintenance are often delayed and inadequate. A number of submissions considered that home maintenance is too costly for people on low income and that the local authorities should undertake decoration and general maintenance of housing free of charge.

There was a complaint that, in certain local authority areas, dwellings previously categorised as one person dwellings are now being redesignated "special housing for small families". There was support for changes in building regulations to ensure privacy is afforded in homes. Other suggestions included that small groups of housing, rather than large estates, should be the norm and that houses should have gardens, central heating, fitted kitchens, floor coverings, built-in furniture and storage as people living on social welfare payments cannot afford these necessities.

### Flat complexes
Flat complexes were viewed as anti-family with many reasons cited. These included that lifts do not operate and children must be taken up and down flights of stairs, that dangerous areas in basements and on corridors encourage crime and drug dealing, that safety features are largely absent, that refuse collection and removal services are poor and that there are too few caretakers in buildings.

### Local authority housing applications and allocation criteria
There was a commonly held view that the criteria for obtaining a local authority home are often unclear and seem discriminatory. In particular, some lone parents were often believed to obtain preferential treatment. Other submissions stated that people are having children in order to get out of unsuitable accommodation. This was viewed as a failure of public housing policy, leading to impoverishment of families and requiring immediate action.

Some submissions proposed that every effort should be made to accommodate people in their own areas near their parents or other relatives. Local authorities were requested to purchase housing in existing housing estates. Some submissions stated that people and families with serious social problems are all housed in the same area, leading to problems, and settlement help was sought to assist these families when a house is allocated.

### Rents and arrears
The method of calculating differential rents on the basis of the principal earner, as opposed to the named tenant's income, was seen as inappropriate and potentially leading to family disputes. The system whereby increases in social welfare are partly offset by increases in rent was criticised. There was a call for rent free accommodation whilst the children of a family are in education.

There was a call for a concerted policy by local authorities to assist tenants to avoid rent arrears. The adversarial court system was deemed unsuitable for dealing with such problems. Another tier of the court system, based on mediation, was proposed.

Instances of difficulty in relation to local authority housing in marital separation were described. The instances related to the statement of resignation required from the spouse who leaves the family home and to local authority legislation regarding the sale of the family home, designed to preserve the housing stock from speculators.

## Private rented accommodation

In the submissions dealing with this issue, there was general criticism of the rent allowance scheme. The rule whereby minimal earned income leads to reduction in rent subsidies was universally condemned. There was considerable criticism of the private rented accommodation sector. The accommodation was described as often substandard. New legislation was considered inadequate. The high cost and shortage of rented accommodation were seen to place stress on couples at the crucial initial stage of marriage. Submissions asked that landlord-tenant legislation be enforced to prevent private landlords choosing not to accept health board payments, particularly in the case of lone parents.

## Homelessness and emergency accommodation

A number of dominant concerns were expressed in the submissions discussing homelessness. In the first instance some submissions sought to prevent homelessness. They proposed that local authorities should not make their tenants homeless and sought assistance for tenants in arrears. Equally the view was expressed that financial institutions should be prohibited from repossessing homes from mortgage holders.

The second prominent demand from these submissions was the provision of temporary accommodation for families in distress. Essential features of any emergency accommodation were judged to include the ability to remain in the accommodation during the day, facilities to prepare and eat food, day services such as kitchen and laundry facilities and play areas. There was also a call for nursery/crèche facilities for homeless families and for the provision of family support services, including outreach workers. All of this was seen as part of a settlement strategy to move people from emergency accommodation back into homes. Special assistance was requested for people barred from hostels or from bed and breakfast accommodation.

There was a strong call to end reliance on bed and breakfast accommodation. A preferred option was the provision of hostel accommodation for families in crisis. There was consensus that the whole family, including the father, should be housed or placed together.

Some submissions sought that all major urban areas should have a 24-hour "one stop shop" to give advice and support to homeless people on all welfare matters as well as to provide booking facilities for emergency accommodation. There was a suggestion that a clear working arrangement be set up whereby families and family members who are homeless, on leaving hospital, should be given housing immediately. There were also proposals that the health boards should be obliged to provide comprehensive psychiatric and community care services for homeless persons and that persons with mental illness should be entitled to the full range of services. Other comments related to insurance for families against the loss of their home and the role of the voluntary sector in providing housing services.

### Homeless young people

The consensus in the relevant submissions was that young people should be supported in approved shelters and hostels and should not be placed in private rented accommodation. Some submissions stated that the provision of temporary accommodation should be conditional on an attempt to restore normality to the life of the young person.

## Housing needs of specific groups

### Lone parents

Some of the 77 submissions (16% of total) focusing on lone parents stated that this group may be offered accommodation in private rented flats in areas unsuitable for raising children. The view was expressed that short-term tenancy arrangements do not enable families to establish roots. Concern was expressed about overcrowding when a young mother, and possibly her partner, remains living with her parents.

Suggestions in this area included that young lone parents should be housed close to the maternal or paternal grandparents in mixed housing schemes. There was also a call for supervised accommodation in hostels for young mothers, to include courses in parenting and crèche facilities to assist continuing education, training or work.

### Women's refuges

All of the 62 submissions (13% of total) on the issue of domestic violence sought more resources for women's support organisations. There was a call for increased refuge provision for all women, including Traveller women. Submissions stated that there are insufficient numbers and inadequate funding of refuges in urban and rural areas. There were also demands for a funding policy and setting of minimum standards of staffing, service support and information in all refuges. There was a focus too, on the rebuilding of women's and children's lives through supportive housing, training, employment, child care, and ongoing support and counselling.

Some submissions called for the removal of the perpetrator of the crime from the family home and for practical and emotional support within the home and in the community for the victim.

One of the main organisations associated with the refuge movement requested the establishment of a domestic violence resource unit to facilitate the development of an area based inter-agency task force. The unit's functions would include the assistance of local agencies to train service providers, the development of drop-in centres including a 24-hour crisis assistance service, the provision of outreach services, and the assistance of local schools in developing appropriate educational policies.

### People with disabilities

The main proposal in relation to housing, in submissions discussing physical disability, was for the establishment of a national policy focusing on the options of independent living, independent living with supports and quality residential care. There were calls for building access regulations to be extended to domestic housing. Submissions sought that the concept of a "lifetime home", one suitable for use by a person who has a disability, should become the norm. There were also suggestions that priority for housing allocation be given to people with disabilities and their families and that housing of people with disabilities should receive full State funding. Housing associations were asked to provide suitable accommodation for people with disabilities. The problem of homelessness among people with mental illness was stressed. Hostel accommodation specifically designed and suited to their needs was requested.

Some submissions commented that people with drug problems need assistance to access housing when they leave treatment or prison and accepted that such needs must be balanced with the fears of communities. There was a call for information and training of communities in this regard. A need for a range of housing options to support family relationships in cases of HIV was also identified.

### Elderly people

Many of the 45 submissions (9% of total) discussing specific concerns of the elderly suggested the development of multipurpose ground floor facilities at local level to meet the needs of individuals whether they are older people or people with disabilities of all ages. Developers in the private sector were encouraged to build sheltered accommodation. A number of submissions considered that there should be a requirement on developers to include housing for elderly people in any new project. Some submissions discussed the inadequate living conditions of some elderly people whose houses are cold and damp. These submissions called for an examination of the housing needs of the elderly. Suggested services to assist elderly people living alone were day care and local drop-in facilities, sheltered and serviced accommodation. It was noted that local pubs and restaurants could provide low cost meals to pensioners.

The announcement of a government grant to provide security systems for elderly people was welcomed. Suggestions included that the good neighbour scheme should be extended to cover all areas. Provision of a rural link phone service, similar to the medical alert system ,for the most vulnerable people in rural areas was also seen as an option.

### Travellers

The dominant view expressed in submissions was that the Travellers have a right to suitable accommodation and that due regard should be given to their cultural preferences in terms of the extended family. There was a general appreciation that Travellers should be included in local communities and that more and better halting sites are required nationally. Concern was expressed for women and children living in unacceptable conditions. A particular concern voiced in many submissions was for Traveller children, especially those in families lacking basic facilities on unofficial or inadequate sites. It was argued that these children are being denied the rights and possibilities taken for granted by other children.

### Refugees

Submissions on the issue of refugees proposed that refugees should be given appropriate housing. In addition, it was suggested that transfers out of certain areas should be considered for this group if racism was a problem.

**Rural resettlement**

A small number of submissions focused positively on the innovative project to move families from urban to rural homes. There was a call for increased financial assistance for the scheme.

## Environmental concerns

Fully 85 submissions (17% of total) dealt with a variety of environmental concerns many of which have been referred to in the context of housing policy and the built environment. A large number of these submissions commented on the problem of illegal refuse dumping and of litter. Recycling programmes were seen as positive. Many submissions stated that parents should teach their children not to litter. In addition, there were calls for a more developed sense of conservation and heritage, greater emphasis on the revitalisation of inner cities and towns and monitoring of rezoning to avoid urban sprawl and ribbon development. Specific suggestions were made to increase green areas in towns and cities and for the elimination of sewerage problems.

## Conclusion

A wide range of community issues was examined and the thrust of submissions was that the State must provide the necessary community structures and supports, with a particular emphasis on recreation facilities and must also ensure funds for community organisations. Submissions stressed the central role of quality housing and infrastructure, in a clean environment, for active communities. These were deemed to require a coordinated, multifaceted and flexible approach from central and local government. The housing requirements of families in need were also raised, with special emphasis on parents and children fleeing domestic violence, on homelessness and on the needs of people with disabilities and of the elderly. The environmental nuisances of dumping and litter were the focus of some submissions and there were numerous suggestions on how to improve our countryside and urban areas.

# Section X

**The law and families**

## Introduction

In all, 142 submissions (29% of the total) addressed legal issues (see Figure 9). The great majority of these focused on the operation of the family law system and, in particular, on marital separation. A small number of submissions addressed certain aspects of criminal law, sentencing and imprisonment.

Figure 9: Percentage of submissions on legal matters

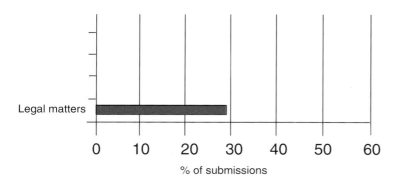

% of submissions

## The family law court system

Submissions on the issue of family law agreed that within the family court system there are overcrowded lists, long delays and frequent adjournments, all of which add to the distress of litigants. Many court procedures were viewed as archaic and contributory to the delays within the judicial system.

Submissions cited particular problems in the regions. There was a consensus that more time should be allotted to family law in rural areas at circuit court level, with fixed dates for hearings to give certainty to litigants who, at present, turn up time after time for the one family law day per term and often leave without their case being heard.

Some of the submissions focusing on legal matters gave detailed proposals for the overhaul of the entire judicial system. The changes most frequently advised included that:
- the recommendations of the Law Reform Commission on family law should be implemented;
- more circuit court judges should be appointed in Dublin and on circuit;
- there should be use of experienced family lawyers, sitting outside their own areas, to act as substitute judges to clear backlogs;

- investigative family tribunals should be set up outside the existing court system;
- separate days should be provided for family law cases;
- large urban areas should have locally situated courts; and
- applications for adjournments on consent should be by written form to the court registrar prior to the hearing date.

There was a suggestion that any family wishing to deal with the courts through the medium of Irish should be able to do so.

**Alternative structures for family law matters**
One detailed submission proposed the establishment of a family commission with five aspects

- a national counselling service;
- a national mediation service;
- family tribunals;
- a commissioner for children; and
- a research and information office.

It was envisaged that this structure would improve the development and application of family law in Ireland. Another proposal was for a new court structure for children.

# Family law in the courts

### The in camera rule
Some submissions discussed the matter of the in camera rule, which means that family law cases cannot be reported. The consensus view was that this rule must stay. At the same time, there was recognition of the need to provide the general public with factual information on family law cases and decisions.

A number of contributors with legal training stated that, at present, the absence of case law in the area makes it difficult to obtain consistency of judgements. This group as a whole sought relaxation of the rules to permit the presence of bona fide researchers, reasoned reporting of in camera cases and/or the publication of an edited annual report of family law cases.

Other submissions noted that no transcript of the court proceedings is taken in a family law case. This was universally considered to be negative. A prominent concern was that it allowed, and perhaps encouraged, some litigants to embellish their presentation or even to tell lies. There was a proposal that the problems of litigants in family law cases who tell lies in court for their own reasons should be investigated.
A number of submissions observed that cases between unmarried people may be heard in open court and reported in the media, leading to considerable potential embarrassment for the couple.

### Training of legal and judicial personnel
A number of submissions felt that the judge in family law cases should have the skills of a mediator. Areas in which judges were considered to require ongoing training and refresher courses included

counselling, women's issues, men's responsibilities, rape, sexual abuse, including incest, and the effects of sentencing policies.

Suggestions were also made for the provision of an in-court conciliation and welfare service; a probation and welfare service for family cases; and greater access to the services of social workers, psychologists and psychiatrists.

## Costs of legal action

There was a consensus that family law charges are too high and that free civil legal aid should be available throughout the country. The legal aid system itself was criticised, with litigants not eligible to obtain assistance with the cost of reports and assessments of private practitioners. It was noted that the increased level of work, following on the phased introduction of the Child Care Act 1991, means that these reports may be slow to obtain. There was a proposal that full family assessment services should be made available to all.

## Children in the family courts

In the submissions which expressed a view there was a consensus that children's needs must be the deciding factor in all family law cases and that children's progress must be monitored for some time after the decision, to ensure all is well. Other suggestions were that children should have access to a panel of children's solicitors and that a guardian ad litem should be available to those involved in the legal process. There was agreement that children's court cases should be heard separately and children should be accorded the same dignity as their parents.

## The courts

The circuit and district courts were described as badly maintained, poorly heated, with insufficient lighting, no toilet facilities, no consultation facilities, minimal staff facilities, no fax machines, no photocopying, severely restricted telephone service and no up to date computer facilities.

District courts were perceived to be under an enormous burden of work, with the example given that an emergency application in the district court takes ten weeks to process. Suggestions in this area included that there should be a family division of the district court; that additional judges should be appointed to ensure a speedy service; and that judgements in the district court should be made orders of the court. There was a proposal for the establishment of new divisions of the high and circuit courts, one part of which would deal exclusively with family matters within each court jurisdiction.

# Marital separation

The main proposal was the replacement of the existing adversarial system by a mediation-based approach. Acrimonious separations were considered to cause long-term damage to children. Another view was that mediation should be a precondition of all proceedings for separation or divorce. Other suggestions included that legal aid personnel should represent both sides equally and that custody of children proceedings should be distinct from the separation proceedings.

### Children and separation

Among the submissions on the issue of separation there was unanimity that there should be discrete representation of children at separation proceedings with free legal aid in their own right. Some submissions considered that the ratification of the Hague Convention should be a priority. Among other benefits it was believed that this would assist children with separated or divorced parents living in different countries.

### Custody of children following separation

There was general dissatisfaction with custody judgements, with many submissions considering that the father has to prove his fitness to maintain his involvement with his children and that there is a judicial assumption that the mother is blameless. There was overwhelming support for joint custody and joint guardianship, viewed as natural rights which should not be taken away in separation. Sole custody was seen to be an option only in exceptional circumstances. There was strong support for the view that the non-custodial parents' rights should be set out clearly by the courts. There was a request for research to evaluate custody decisions.

### Custody and guardianship

A number of submissions dealt with specific aspects of the custody and guardianship laws. Various situations were described where the acting or effective parent is not the birth mother or the father. Submissions sought that guardianship laws should be amended to allow such a person to apply for guardianship.

### Parental access

There was considerable interest in the issue of access to children by the non-custodial parent. The current situation was seen to be problematic and to deny many fathers sufficient contact with their children to enable them to have healthy and mutually beneficial relationships. Many submissions remarked that the non-residential parent may feel an excessive negative influence on the children by the custodial parent.

Regarding access orders, the prominent view was that, in practice, access orders are not enforced. However, this perception was not shared by all and a small number of submissions requested that a limit be placed on the number of possible appeals of access orders by fathers.

### Grandparental access

A number of submissions focused on the concerns of grandparents, aunts and uncles to obtain access rights to their grandchildren, nieces or nephews. Following separation there may be a total cessation of the relationship of the non-custodial parent's family with the children of the marriage. At present, there is no procedure for grandparents, aunts or uncles to apply in their own right for access.[1] These submissions pointed to the child's rights to continued involvement with the extended family and considered that grandparents in particular should have the right to apply for and obtain access to their grandchildren.

---

1    At the time submissions were received (1996) there was no procedure for relatives to apply in their own right for access. However, under the Children Act 1997 (Section 9) relatives may now apply for access.

## Family access centres

The establishment of family access or meeting centres was proposed as a mechanism to ensure access rights and to diffuse potentially distressing situations. These access centres were seen to have the potential to facilitate, and where necessary, supervise access. Supervision by probation officers was put forward as an option.

## Maintenance payments

There was substantial criticism of the maintenance payments system. The view was expressed that judges often refrain from making orders relating to maintenance and take the parties back to court time and again when the agreed sums have not been paid. Many different suggestions were made to overcome this problem. These included that the State should guarantee a payment without obliging women to trace and pursue the partner; that maintenance payments should be limited to a specified number of years; and that the specified grounds of judicial separation should be taken into consideration in deciding payments.

# Divorce

A large number of the submissions which expressed reservations about divorce focused on the possibility of a "no fault clause" in proposed legislation. This was widely assumed to operate to the benefit of one partner and was equated with women and children being divorced against their will. Other interpretations of the term were that the innocent party was the outright victor in any settlement. The instigator of divorce was frequently assumed to be the husband and a number of contributors objected, as tax payers, to paying for the infidelity of a spouse and parent. Some submissions questioned the number of times a person may be permitted to divorce.

Submissions raised questions regarding the preparations in the courts to deal with volume of applications for divorce. In some submissions, the important concern was that the courts should be accessible to all. A series of improvements was proposed including a properly functioning legal aid system, specialist judges, better court facilities and an improved family court structure. Additional services requested included an extension of the family mediation service and court powers to give pension adjustment orders and financial compensation orders. There was a call to ensure that there will be no loss of social welfare rights following divorce and that, when property is divided, the spouse who has been a full-time homemaker will be considered to have made an equal contribution.

## Divorce and children

There was a strongly held view that both parents should be made accountable for the upbringing of their children following divorce. There was a call for separate representation of children at divorce proceedings. Questions were also raised about the family home in divorce situations and about the children of annulled marriages.

# Domestic violence

In all, 62 submissions (13% of total) addressed the issue of domestic violence. Most of these stipulated that there should be garda in-service and ongoing training to ensure a pro-arrest policy.

### Protection orders, barring orders and injunctions

The dominant view was that the long delays and frequent adjournments in domestic violence cases coming to court are unacceptable, as they mean that women and children are under stress for weeks and even months. A number of submissions stated that the system whereby the victim is in full view of the accused person in court is unsatisfactory. Judges were frequently thought to be unsympathetic to the plight of the battered woman and her children. There was a view that women should not be expected to or encouraged to represent themselves. A suggestion was made for a court accompaniment service.

The view was expressed that the Domestic Violence Act 1996 gives the court great powers and these should not be exercised against unrepresented litigants who cannot afford legal representation. There was a suggestion that legal aid should be available for test cases and group cases.

### Barring orders

The view of most submissions on the issue was that the perpetrator of violence must vacate the family home. A number of submissions asked that barring orders by children should be allowed. The view was also expressed that barring orders may be a destructive measure in terms of the possibility of reform or reconciliation and that they may be used wrongly by women in certain circumstances. Proponents of this view considered that protection orders are a better interim measure to indicate clearly that certain behaviours are not acceptable under the law, while at the same time affording the couple an opportunity to evaluate their situation and seek help. The comment was made that the seeking of a barring order or similar legal device indicates that a family is in serious trouble and should be the signal to alert and involve the social services that a family is in need of assistance.

Concerns were raised in relation to couples who are not married and their right to go to court for a barring order. Other concerns focused on the Domestic Violence Act 1996 which excludes an application for a barring order by a person who has a child in common with a respondent, where the couple have never resided together but have had a relationship. In such a case if violence occurs, the only redress is the use of an injunction.

# Sexual abuse

Three main points were raised regarding the judicial system and cases of child sexual abuse. First, it was pointed out that the child victim is obliged to give evidence on two occasions, on disposition and at the time of trial. This was considered to be unnecessarily traumatic and a suggestion was made that the child give evidence only at the trial.

Second, it was stated that at present if a spouse or mother makes any allegations, usually against a husband or father, most courts feel constrained to suspend access by the accused parent until some investigation or report is completed. This may take months and in the meantime the accused parent has no access. To respond to this problem, the proposal was for supervised access, with either a neutral family member present or the use of access centres. Third, a number of submissions objected to the short sentences received by perpetrators of child sex abuse.

# Adoption

A number of submissions dealt in depth with adoption. Issues raised included the need to ensure that the adopted child has the same rights as natural children; that the Adoption Board be replaced by an adoption court; and that any new system of registration requires that agencies keep adequate records.

Some submissions commented on the situation where a mother marries a man who is not the father of her child(ren). The husband may wish to adopt his wife's child. There was discussion of the fact that present legislation requires that the mother also adopt her own child and of recent court cases which had acknowledged the rights of biological fathers in such instances. A number of different solutions were put forward. Some submissions suggested that provision should be made in legislation to allow such parents to adopt the child while still permitting the biological father the right of access to his child. Others proposed a new procedure of adoption to retain both birth parents' legal relationship with the child, while giving the husband rights and duties of joint parenthood.

### Private placement

Particular concerns were expressed regarding the process known as private placement whereby some birth mothers place their children for adoption with couples who are not members of the extended family and who have not undergone assessment by an adoption agency as to their suitability to adopt. Submissions generally held the view that the detailed assessment involved in applying to an adoption agency provides a safeguard for the welfare of the child which is inevitably circumvented by a birth mother who places her child directly. A further feature of concern in these instances was the lack of professional counselling and support of the birth mother.

### Foreign adoption

It was pointed out that for any foreign adoption to be recognised in this State it must comply with the definition of a foreign adoption as prescribed in legislation. Suggestions were that the government and the health boards monitor and prepare followup reports on all children adopted from abroad. There was a request for the State to assist financially in adopting children from other countries.

### A national adoption register

In the submissions focusing on adoption, there was general support for the proposal that an adoptee on reaching the age of eighteen years should have access to his or her original birth certificates, after appropriate counselling. The majority of these submissions called for the immediate introduction of a national contact register, open to all birth mothers and children. There was criticism of people providing tracing services in the absence of any guidelines, protection or appropriate counselling from professionals.

### Adoption by homosexual couples

There were calls for adoption to be made available to homosexual couples, male and female. Numerous submissions expressed implacable opposition to such a move.

## Criminal, judicial and penal matters

Most individual submissions on the issue of crime, took the view that crime rates are excessive and that communities require garda stations and personnel to restore community confidence. Criminality was seen to be associated with youth, particularly teenage vandalism, petty crime and drug use. There was support for the view that the right to remain silent should be abolished; that sentencing is too lax; and that parole is inappropriate. A common view was that there is too much emphasis on the criminal and insufficient concern for the victim.

A small number of submissions complained about access to legal representation and advice and disagreed with possible further restrictions of bail. These submissions considered that court cases may be too public and that a court may be a frightening place.

### Drugs and crime

A strong sense of the importance of tackling the supply of drugs as a criminal activity was put forward in many of the 76 submissions (16% of total) on addiction, particularly those from individuals. Vigilantism was depicted as an inevitable reaction. There was a call that the assets of convicted drug dealers should be confiscated and put back into society in the form of rehabilitation centres for drug addicts and victims. Some submissions requested increased cooperation between the gardaí and the Revenue Commissioners in an attempt to reduce criminal activities.

### Children and crime

The prominent perspective from submissions was that parents should be made responsible for the actions of their children and where relevant should be made to pay financial damages to the victim on behalf of the child. Other submissions focused on the inappropriateness of the court system for juveniles and some sought the use of a statutory juvenile liaison scheme. There was a suggestion that community workers should have a role in identifying the needs of the defendant so that he or she might be dealt with in a positive and appropriate manner.

### Prison

Some submissions requested increased prison places while others focused on the importance of non-custodial sentences for nonviolent offenders. The reduction of recidivism was itemised as a key goal. Suggestions to achieve this end included training in employment-related skills as a compulsory part of any prison sentence. There was a strong focus on reparation to the victim and society with the suggestion that first time offenders should work on community projects visible to the community, as opposed to community service. Submissions were also concerned about prison visiting conditions. There were comments that the probation services lack resources and are understaffed.

A number of submissions observed that criminal convictions for women are mainly drugs related.

Concern was expressed that many of these women have children and are therefore separated from them in prison and afterwards. There was a recommendation for supportive child care, particularly at the early stages of criminality and convictions.

Some submissions cited instances of what they perceived was discrimination by gardaí, the legal profession and judges against certain groups including Travellers, people with mental illness and refugees. There were suggestions that these professional groups should partake in training programmes to increase awareness and empathy.

## Conclusion

This section has described the main views of submissions on a diverse range of legal matters. The family experiences described in this section were seen to need special legal and judicial responses, particularly in relation to the welfare of children. The problems arising from marital separation proceedings gave rise to a number of suggestions to improve the present system. There was unanimity that the court system, as it affects families, is in need of a substantial overhaul. Submissions differed on how best to approach certain problems and the need for alterations in legislation and in practice was a repeated theme. There were divided views on some non-family legal issues, with different perspectives on the appropriate societal responses to crime and to criminals.

# Appendix 1

**Organisations who made submissions to the Commission.**

Abbey Park and District Residents Association
Accord, Head Office, All Hallows College, Drumcondra
Accord, Harcourt St, Dublin
Accord, Newbridge, Kildare
Accord, Waterford
Adoption Board
Adoptive Parents Association
Adult Children Breaking the Cycle, Dublin
Age & Opportunity
AIM Family Services
Alzheimer Society of Ireland
Artane Active Retirment Group
Askea Parish Pastoral Council
ASPIRE Ltd. (Asperger Syndrome Association of Ireland)
Association of Community & Comprehensive Schools
Association of Community Welfare Officers
Association of Remedial Teachers of Ireland
Athlone Youth Community Council
Ballygall Womens' Group
Ballymote Community Care Council
Ballymun Comprehensive Schools Parents Association
Ballymun Youth Action Project
Ballyroan Family Ministry Group
Bar of Ireland & Family Lawyers Association
Barnardo's
Bord Na Gaeilge
Bray Old Folks Association
Bray Women's Refuge
Business Spouses Association
Cabhair, Interdenominanational Women's Group, Mayo
Campaign Against Bullying
Cashel Social Services
Catholic Secondary Schools Parents Association (CSPA)
Centre for Independent Living
Cerebal Palsy Ireland
Cheeverstown House Ltd.
Cherish, Dublin
Childminders Union
Childrens Rights Alliance
Christian Family Movement
Christian Initiatives, Dublin
Church of Ireland, Rathmines
Citywise, Dublin
Clanwilliam Institute

Clare Family Learning Project

Clare Parents Awareness Group

Cobh Youth Services

Combat Poverty Agency

Comhdail Naisiúnta Na Gaeilge

Comhludar, Dublin

Community Action Network

Community Education Centre, Arklow

Community Group Delvin, Co. Westmeath

Conference of Religious of Ireland, Dublin

Congress of Catholic Secondary Schools Parents Association

Coolock Community Law Centre

Corduff Counselling Centre, Dublin

Cork Association for Autism

Cork Domestic Violence Project

Cork Federation of Women's Associations

Cork Women's Political Association

Cosaint na Beatha agus an Teaghlaigh

Council for the Status of the Family

Counselling Centre, Fr. Matthew St. Cork

Covey Leadership Centre Ltd.

Crosscare

Cuidiú, Irish Childbirth Trust

Cuidiú- Cork Branch

Department of Agriculture, Food and Forestry

Donaghmede Community Development Association

Donegal Womens Refuge Group

Dr. Sean Denyer, Director of Public Health, North Western Health Board

Dublin Corporation Pensioned Officers' Association

Dundalk Social Service Council

Eastern Health Board

FÁS

Family Centre, St. Vincents, Dublin

Family Federation for Unification and World Peace, Dublin

Family Life Centre, Model Farm Road, Cork

Family Life Centre, Sligo

Family Resource Centre, Ballaly, Dublin

Fermoy Social Analysis Group

Filemore Parents Council

First Year Masters Social Science, Trinity College

Foróige, Dublin

FORUM, Letterfrack, Co. Galway

Franciscan Social Justice Initiatives

Galway Adult Literacy Group

Gay and Lesbian Equality Network (GLEN)

Good Shepherd Pastoral Centre

Grand Parents Obliterated

Group of Psychiatric Nurses, Midland Health Board

Group of Social Workers, Housing Welfare, Dublin Corporation

Holy Trinity Rainbow Bereavement Group

Homestart Blanchardstown

Huntstown Development Group

ICA, Strandhill Guild

ICA, Ballydehob

ICA, Carrick -On-Suir

ICA, Central Office, 58, Merrion Road, Dublin

ICA, Kilcormac Guild, Offaly

ICA, Kildare Federation

ICA, Longford Federation

ICA, Moore Guild, Wexford

ICA, Offaly Federation

ICA, Clonbeirne Guild

Integrated Services Initiative, Dublin

Irish Bank Officials Association

Irish College of General Practitioners

Irish Family Planning Association

Irish Farmers Association - Farm Families Committee

Irish Federation of Women's Refuges

Irish Mental Patients' Educational and Representative Organisation

Irish National Organisation of the Unemployed

Irish Practice Nurses Association

Irish Pre-school Playgroups Association (Wexford)

Irish Society of Autism

Irish Wheelchair Association

Irish Widowers and Deserted Husbands Association

Kilbrin Family Resource Centre

Kilkenny Women's Refuge

Knights of Columbanas

Knockanrawley Resource Centre Ltd., Tipperary

La Leche League of Ireland

Ladies Lifestyle Development, Ardee, Co. Louth

Law Society of Ireland

Legal Aid Board

Legal Aid Board, Longford

Lesbian Equality Network

Life Pregnancy Care

Marist Resource Centre, Dublin

Marriage and Relationship Counselling Service Ltd., Grafton St., Dublin

Mater Dei Counselling Centre, Dublin

Mater Dei Counselling Centre, Teen Counselling

Maternity & Paediatric Dept., University Hospital Galway

Matt Talbot Community Trust, Dublin 20

Meath Women's Aid

Mediators Institute Ireland

Merchants Quay Project

Mercy Family Centre Womens Education Groups

Mid-South Roscommon Rural Development Company Ltd.

Mid- Western Health Board (Central Offices)

Midland Health Board

Midwives Association of Ireland

Money Advice and Budgeting Service, Dungarvan, Co. Waterford

Mothers Union, Ireland

Multiple Sclerosis Association of Ireland

National Association for Parent Support

National Association of the Mentally Handicapped, Ireland

National Association of the Ovulation Method Ireland

National Children's Nurseries Association

National Council for Curriculum and Assessment

National Council for the Elderly

National Federation of Pensioners Associations

National Parents Council (Post-primary)

National Social Service Board

National Womens Council of Ireland

National Youth Federation

Newbury House Family Centre

North Clondalkin Community Development Association

North Eastern Health Board

North West Hospice Sligo

North Western Health Board

OASIS House, Waterford

One Parent Exchange and Network, Dublin

Our Lady's Hospice, Harolds Cross, Dublin

Parental Equality

Parentline

Parents' Support

Parents Alone Resource Centre, Coolock

Parents Association, St. Mullins, Carlow

Past Students Union, St. Catherines College for Home Economics

Patient Advisory Council, Coombe Womens Hospital

Paul Partnership, Limerick

Pavee Point Travellers Centre

Public Policy Institute of Ireland

Redemptorist Retreat House, Athenry, Co. Galway

Rescue Trust

Retirement Planning Council of Ireland

Ringsend & District Community Centre

Roscommon and Boyle Active Age Group

Rowlagh Womens Group, Dublin

Rural Resettlement Kerry

Schizophrenia Association of Ireland

SIPTU Office, Dublin Airport

Sligo Social Service Council

Social Justice Initiative, Waterford

Society of St. Vincent De Paul (Mount Carmel)

Society of St. Vincent De Paul (Clonmany, Donegal)

Society of St. Vincent De Paul (Donegal)

Society of St. Vincent De Paul, Head Office, Dublin 7

Soroptimist International (Ennis & District)

Soroptimist International (Mullingar & District)

Soroptimist International (Drogheda)

Soroptimist International, Ireland

South Dublin County Council, Community Department

South Dublin Family Solidarity

South Inner City Community Development Association

South West Womens Shelter

Southern Health Board

St. Brigids Family & Community Centre, Waterford

St. Catherines College of Education for Home Economics, Blackrock, Co. Dublin

St. Josephs College Parents Association, Lucan, Co. Dublin

St. Vincents Family Centre, Dublin

The Family Education Group, Knocklyon, Dublin 16

The Other Place, Lesbian and Gay Community Centre, Cork

Threshold

Tralee Community Development Project

TREOIR, Dublin

Vietnamese Irish Association

Waterford Womens Federation

Women In Media & Entertainment, Galway

Women in the Home, Dublin

Women of the North West

Womens Aid, Dublin 7

Youth New Ross Ltd.

A number of organisations made oral presentations to the Commission. These include: the Irish Congress of Trade Unions, the Irish Business and Employers Confederation, Area Development Management Ltd., AONTAS and the Childminders Association.

A public seminar entitled "Family matters" was convened in St. Patrick's College, Maynooth, Co. Kildare on April 27th 1997. The event was hosted by one of the Commission's members, Cllr. Catherine Murphy. Ms. Liz McManus TD opened proceedings. A wide selection of groups and organisations from the surrounding north Kildare area attended. These included Veronica Lawlor and Marie Daly from Marriage Counselling Services, Ann O' Connor Of AIM, Harry Marsden , Irish National Organisation of the Unemployed and Ann Cox National Social Services Board, Deirdre Kelly of the Living City Group, Paul Gilligan of the Irish Society of the Prevention of Cruelty to Children, and Jim Walsh of the Combat Poverty Agency.

The outcome of the seminar, made an important contribution in highlighting the importance of family concerns and the potential of a review such as that undertaken by the Commission on the Family.

# Appendix 2

**Individuals who made submissions to the Commission on the Family.**

S. Allen - Hamilton.

M. Ashe.

M. Bane - Corbett.

R. Barr.

B. Baxter.

A.G. Beirne.

G. Beirne.

Dr. A. Bell.

Bell Family.

K. Berry.

H. Blanchfield.

M. Bolger.

J.A . Boyle.

Sr. C. Bradley.

E. Brady.

T. Brady.

A. Browne.

W.B. Bryan.

K. Burke.

E. Burns.

B. Byrne.

C. Byrne.

C. Byrne Fallon.

F. Byrne.

S. Byrne.

T. Byrne.

M. and G. Callan.

M. Callinan.

G. Callis.

I. Cantwell.

H. Cardogan.

M. Carey.

S. Carrick.

J. Carroll.

C. Cauldwell.

A. Charlton - Cruite.

A. Clancy.

N. Clarke.

O. Clince.

R. Cochran.

M. Comberton.

P. and A. Conneally.

P. Connick.

A. Connolly.

J. Connolly.

R. Connolly.

T. Corish.

P. Corr.

J. Costello

Fr. L. Coughlan.

J. Cox.

G. Creighton.

M. and T. Cuddy.

C. Cullen.

M. Cullen.

T. Commins.

J. Curran.

T. Dalton.

R. Darcy.

P. Dawson.

A. De. Chlair.

V. Denafle.

E. Devine.

C. Doherty.

F.F. Doherty.

J. Doherty.

M. Doherty.

M. Doherty.

B. Donoghue.

Sr. P. Donovan.

M. Dooley.

D. Doran.

R. Duffy.

S. Duffin.

N. Dwyer.

J. Earnshaw.

R. Egan.

S. Fagan.

S.C. Fair.

K. Feehely.

K. Feeney.

J. Fergus.

M. Fergus.

D. Fitzgerald.

P. Fitzgerald.

B. Flanagan.

M. Flannigan.

M. Foley.

H. Forde - Myers.

Sr. K. Friel.

S. Frost.

M.T. Furey.

A. Gannon.

F. Gartland.

V. Geirin.

A. Ghee.

E. Giblin.

B. Gilligan.

K. Gilmartin

B. Gogarty.

C. and L. Golden.

A. Gormley.

E.D. Graham.

M. Graham

M. Greene.

T. Guschulla.

R. Hanley.

D. Harkin.

K. Harkin.

G.A. Harold - Barry.

P. Harte.

Sr. M. Hartley.

J. and Y. Hartnett.

Sr. M. Hassett.

G. Hastings.

P. Haughey.

H. Haughton.

S.G. Hawkins

A. and E. Hayes.

J. Healy.

T.A. Hennessy.

A. Hill.

V. Holmes.

P. Hopkins.

R. Horgan.

V. Hunt.

C. Hurwitz.

D. Hynes.

M.J. Johnston.

Fr. J. Joyce.

P. Joyce.

A. Kavanagh.

B. Keane.

L. Keane.

Sr. N. Keane.

C. Kearns.

E. Kelleher.

P. Kelleher.

J. Kelly.

J. Kennedy.

M Kenrick.

M.B. Kerr.

P. Killen.

C. King.

L. and M. Kirwan.

J. Lawless.

J. Ledwidge.

N. Lenihan.

K. Lewis.

M. Leydon.

Prof. B.G. Loftus.

N. Looney.

A. Lore.

G. Lowe.

M. Lowry - Ryan.

T. Lynam.

C. Lynch.

F. Mac Aodha Bhui.

B. Mc Cabe.

G. Mc Carthy.

P. Mc Closkey.

J. Mc Cormick.

P. Mc Curtin.

Rev. G. Cusack.

B. Mc Gaffin.

D. Mc Gleen.

Fr. G. Mc Greevey (pp)

Fr. M. Mc Keown.

M. Mc Loughlin.

M. Maher.

A. Mangan.

T. Martin.

H. Massup

K. Maxwell.

B. Meade.

G. Merrifield.

M. Merriman.

J. Moore.

S. Molloy-Fagan

C. Moriarty.

K. Mullaney.

Sr. H. Mulroy.

L. Murnaghan.

A. Murphy.

B. Murphy.

H. Myers

C. and E. Nolan.

Rev. A. O' Brien.

C. O' Brien.

Dr. E.J. O' Brien.

T. O' Brien.

B. O'Byrne.

M. O'Byrne.

M. Ó Chonghaile.

B. O'Connell.

C. O'Connell.

R. O'Connell

O'Connor Family.

L. O'Connor.

M. O'Connor.

An tAthair P. O Cuill.

M. and L. O'Donnell.

J. O' Donoghue.

P. O' Donovan.

G. Ó Dubhtaigh.

Dr. E. O'Flynn.

E.H.J. O'Flynn.

C. Ó Gallachain.

M. O'Grady.

O. O'Hagan.

Mr. and Mrs. O' Hara.

P. Ó hAodha.

M. O' Keefe.

Sr. S. O' Kelly.

T. O' Leary.

F. O' Neill.

M. O' Neill.

S. Ó Raghallaigh.

K. O' Reilly.

P. O' Riordan.

B. O' Shaughnessy.

J. O' Sullivan.

T. O' Sullivan.

C. Phelan.

J. Phelan.

Mr. and Mrs. Plunkett.

K. F. Quinlan.

H. Quinn.

M. Quinn.

A. Reidy.

J. Reilly.

B. Reynolds.

C. Riordan.

M. Robbins.

M. Roberts.

W. Roche.

G. Ryan.

J. Ryan.

L. Ryan.

P. Ryan.

S. Ryan.

P. Schutte.

B. Seligman.

G. Shenan.

S. Smith.

D. Smith.

Prof. L. P. F. Smith.

F. Smyth.

M. Somers.

M. Stewart.

J. Stack

C. Talbot.

Dr. M.A. Tierney.

Fr. M. Tierney.

J. Travers.

Fr. C. T. Twohig.

R. Twohig.

K. Walker.

P. Walsh.

J. Waters.

M. Woods.

R. Wynne.

The Commission also received 25 submissions set out in a particular format which allowed Contributors, in each case, to set out their views on various issues in relation to the family.

The Commission also received some 34 submissions from individuals who did not wish their names to be published.

part 9

"proposals to the all-party committee
on the constitution"

**In Part 9 the Commission**

- publishes its submission to the All-Party Oireachtas Committee on the Constitution.

# Overview of Part 9

**The terms of reference require the Commission, *inter alia*, to make proposals to the All-Party Committee on the Constitution on any changes which it believes might be necessary in the constitutional provisions in relation to the family.**

The Commission presented its submission to the All-Party Committee in March 1997.[1]

In its submission to the All-Party Committee, Article 41 of the Constitution is the focus of the Commission's attention with some reference to Article 42.5. The Commission sets out views in relation to:

- The provisions on the family in the Constitution in general.
- Recognition of the family in the Constitution.
- Constitutional protection of the institution of marriage, the right to marry and to found a family.
- The right to family life and the balance between the rights of the family unit and those of individual members.
- Constitutional guarantees for the rights of a child.
- Constitutional protection for the rights of natural parents
- Role of women and mothers or other persons within the home.

The All-Party Committee's attention was drawn to the findings in the Commission's interim report, *Strengthening Families for Life*, (November 1996) in relation to the principles which should underlie and guide the development of the State's response to families in the future. The Commission also drew attention to issues which arose in submissions made to the Commission and which are relevant to the work of the All-Party Committee.

Chapter 23 presents the main body of the Commission's submission to the All- Party Oireachtas Committee.

*In developing its submission to the All-Party Oireachtas Committee, the Commission was guided by the analyses and recommendations of the Constitution Review Group whose report was published in May 1996.*
*In addition, the Commission would like to thank:*
*Dr. T K Whitaker, Chairman of the Constitution Review Group*
*William Duncan, Professor of Law and Jurisprudence, Trinity College, Dublin, and*
*Mr. Gerry Mangan, Principal Officer, Planning Unit, Department of Social, Community and Family Affairs,*
*for their contribution to the Commission's examination of these important legal issues for families.*

---

1    An All-Party Committee on the Constitution was established by the Houses of the Oireachtas in July 1996. Following the dissolution of Dáil Eireann in May 1997, the All-Party Oireachtas Committee on the Constitution was also dissolved. It was reconstituted in October 1997. For details of terms of reference and membership of the Committee, see Appendix 1 to this chapter.

## Chapter 23 Submission of the Commission on the Family to the All-Party Oireachtas Committee on the Constitution (March 1997)

**2.** **Provisions on the Family in the Constitution - General Considerations**

**2.1.** The Constitution is a public text. It is highly visible and accessible to people in a way that the details of legislative provisions are not. The core principles and aspirations in relation to society which are valued by people must be expressed in a way which will endure for a long time. The Commission is of the view that there is a role for the Constitution in underpinning and affirming society's values and ideals concerning family life.

**2.2.** The Commission on the Family in its Interim Report sets out a series of statements for consideration in the development of family policy. These include the following which are of particular relevance to the provisions of the family in the Constitution.

*"the foundations of family policy and the principles and objectives which underlie and guide it, need to be formulated and set out clearly (Statement No 1)."*

*"Family policy has a fundamental role in expressing and affirming society's values and ideals concerning family life, at the symbolic as well as the practical levels" (Statement No 2).*

*"Family policy must have a particular concern with protecting the vulnerable members within families" (Statement No 6).*

*"The legislative framework of family law should evolve as part of an integrated family policy. Social supports for families and ongoing developments in family law (including reform of the constitutional provisions on the family) should be planned and developed in tandem with each other." (Statement No 5).*

*- Commission on the Family Interim Report Chap.2*

**The Constitution contains the basic law of the State. The Commission considers that it should provide a clear foundation for the development of the law and policy in relation to the family. The Constitution should acknowledge that there are responsibilities implicit in the exercise of rights contained in it. This is particularly relevant in the constitutional provisions in relation to the rights of parents and individual family members.**

**2.3.** The Commission in its examination of the challenges families are facing, has also been guided by the "*principles*" which it considers should underpin a family policy[2]. It has also taken into account the major social and economic changes and the changes in mores which

---

2    The principles referred to are set out in Chapter 1 of this report.

have occurred in recent decades which have had a profound effect on the family. These realities are also very much reflected in the submissions it has received. Many submissions to the Commission expressed concern about changes in society and the impact these could have on families now and for the future. The State's role, it was generally agreed, was to support families, ensure access to services for all and put in place the framework for promoting the well being of families and society.

**In the light of these considerations, the Commission has concluded that Articles 41 and 42.5 of the Constitution need to be revised to reflect both those long established traditions relating to family life which are still valued by Irish people and the new realities referred to above.**

**2.4.**    Some of the changes proposed will raise difficult issues in relation to fundamental values we hold as a people. The Commission considers that one of its tasks is to identify and develop consensus about the principles and objectives which should be adopted for the future development of family policy. In discharging this task we would hope to make a significant contribution to raising awareness about the importance of the family provisions in the Constitution.

**3.**    **Recognition of the family in the Constitution.**

**3.1.**    In all, 91 submissions received, or 19% of the total, raised the issue of how the family is defined in the Constitution or for other purposes. A summary of the views on the matter expressed in these submissions is given in pages 56/57 of the Interim Report.

It is clear from the submissions to the Commission that there are divided views on the provisions on the family in the Constitution. Some would wish to retain the current provisions which they see as giving support to the family based on marriage and the stable lifelong family structure which it generally provides. Others consider that recognition should also be given to other family arrangements, in particular families where the parents are unmarried, with the main focus being on the need for the protection of children in the family context. In a majority of submissions it was considered that the UN definition of the Family[3] was inappropriate for Irish society at this juncture, but a small number favoured this definition.

---

3    **Extract from the terms of reference and the Commission on the Family.**

The terms of reference for the Commission direct that "in carrying out its work, the Commission while having due regard to the provisions on the family in the Constitution of Ireland intended to support the family unit, should reflect also in its deliberations the definition of the family outlined by the United Nations."

**United Nations definition**

The United Nations considered that the fundamental principle underlying the celebration of the International Year of the Family, in 1994 was that the family constitutes the basic unit of society. The United Nations focused on a broad definition of the family as a basic unit of society in all its forms, whether traditional, biological, common-law, extended or one parent. The definition used by the United Nations is:

"Any combination of two or more persons who are bound together by ties of mutual consent, birth and/or adoption or placement and who, together assume responsibility for, *inter alia*, the care and maintenance of group members through procreation or adoption, the socialisation of children and the social control of members."

A number of submissions warned of the danger of creating a definition so inclusive that it is meaningless.

3.2.    The first " *principle* " which the Commission puts forward in its report is that

*" The family unit is a fundamental unit providing stability and well being in our society."* *(Principle No. 1)*

This recognition is reflected in Article 41 of the Constitution, but is confined to the family based on marriage.

The Commission also considers

*"A  diversity of family forms and relationships should be recognised"* *(Principle No. 6)*

and that

*"The fundamental human activities of care, intimacy and belongingness can take place in a variety of family forms".*

*Commission on the Family, Interim Report, Chap. 2*

**3.3.    The Commission has concluded in light of the principles set out in Paragraph 3.2 above that Article 41 should be revised to give  constitutional recognition to all family units, including families not based on marriage.**

**The Commission also recommends in this context that provision should be made in a revised Article 41 for recognition of the right to respect for family life (Section 5 below) and for the protection of the institution of marriage (Section 4 below).**

**4.    Constitutional Protection of the Institution of Marriage, the right to marry and found a family**

**4.1.    The Commission considers that " continuity and stability in family relationships" have  a major value for individual well-being especially as far as children are concerned. The Commission's thinking on the matter is described in Chapter 2 of the Interim Report. The Commission in its consideration of the issues involved for families concludes;**

*"For many people marriage represents the expression of their commitment to long-term continuity and stability. In this context the Commission feels that marriage should be supported in public policy."*
*Commission on the Family Interim Report Chap.2*

A man and woman in getting married make a clear and public commitment to live together and to support each other, with the intention of their union being for life. Marriage is a legal contract. It is afforded a clear legal status by the State and both parties have legally enforceable rights and duties.

These features of marriage result in a majority of cases in the union being permanent or at least continuing for a relatively long period. They facilitate, in particular, joint parenting and a stable family life for the children of married couples, which is conducive to their overall development. Marriage also provides legal protection for the spouse who undertakes the main responsibility of caring for home and family (usually the wife/mother) and who can, as a result lose out in terms of acquiring an adequate income and other benefits related to work in his/her own right, which could be obtained from being available for work consistently on a full time basis.

4.2.    **The Commission supports the retention of Article 41.3.1. in the Constitution by which the State pledges to guard with special care the institution of marriage and to protect it against attack.**

This should require the State to specifically support marriage in public policy.

**The Commission, also agrees with the Review Group[4] that the pledge by the State on marriage should not prevent the Oireachtas from legislating for the benefit of families not based on marriage and that a clear constitutional basis for this should be provided in Article 41.**

4.3.    **The Commission notes that the right to marry in accordance with the requirements of law and to found a family have been held by the Courts to be personal rights guaranteed by Article 40.3.**

**The Commission supports the Review Group's recommendation 4 ii) that express provision for this right be made in a revised Article 41.**

5.    **The Right to Family Life and the Balance between the Rights of the Family Unit and those of Individual Members.**

5.1.    The Commission considers that

" *An equality of well-being is recognised between individual family members.*" (Principle No. 4)

and that

" *Individual well-being has a high priority as a measure of family effectiveness and as an*

4    Reference is to the Report of the Constitution Review Group, published in May 1996.

FINAL REPORT OF THE COMMISSION ON THE FAMILY

*objective of family policy."(See Principle No. 2)*

*Commission on the Family Interim Report Chap.2*

The Commission shares the concern of the Review Group that "the present focus of Articles 41 and 42 emphasises the rights of the family as a unit to the possible detriment of individual members", particularly children.

**5.2.**    **The Commission considers, in particular that it is no longer appropriate to provide for recognition of the family in the Constitution, including the family based on marriage, as "a moral institution possessing inalienable and imprescriptable rights, antecedent and superior to all positive law." Instead of giving such recognition, as at present in Article 41.1, to the rights of the family unit, the Commission recommends that provision should be made affording individuals the right to respect for their family life.**

**5.3.**    It is important, however, to clarify what is meant by "family life" in this context. For a unit of people to constitute a "family unit", there would  normally be family links between the members of the unit. In the case of adults these would include links by marriage, parenthood, or kin, e.g. brothers/sisters. In the case of children, the links would be by birth and/or adoption or placement. Family life within such units would be characterised by its members together assuming responsibility for the care and support of each other, particularly children and other dependent family members, and by the sharing of time and resources which promotes intimacy and belongingness.

**5.4.**    **The Commission also considers that there must be a necessary limitation and constraint on an individual's freedom of behaviour and expression within family life. Family membership and the concept of  family privacy and autonomy should not be used to cloak oppression of weaker members by the strong within the family. Children are particularly vulnerable in this regard and the Commission considers that special provision for the rights of children in relation to their family should be made in the Constitution (see section 6).**

**5.5.**    **The Commission agrees with the Review Group that general criteria for State interference with the right to respect for family life should be set out in the Constitution and that Article 8.2 of the European Convention on Human Rights [5] might be an appropriate model in that regard. It also wishes to emphasise the importance in drawing up such a text of ensuring that State interference in family life is permitted, where necessary, to safeguard the welfare of the elderly, those with disabilities, or other family members who are vulnerable as is recommended in the case of children.**

---

5    **Article 8.2 of ECHR**

"There shall be no interference by a public authority with the exercise of this right except such as is in accordance with the law and is necessary in a democratic society in the interests of national security, public safety or economic well-being of the country, for the prevention of disorder or crime, for the protection of health or morals, or the protection of the rights and freedom of others".

## 6. Constitutional Guarantees for the Rights of a Child

**6.1.** The Commission considers that the best interests of children must be a paramount concern in public policy; in areas of conflicting rights children because of their vulnerability, must be particularly protected; and public policy has a role in protecting and enhancing the position of children within families.

**The Commission fully supports the approach recommended by the Review Group that an express statement be included in any revised Article 41 that in all actions concerning children the best interests of the child should be a paramount consideration. Such a provision should also have due regard to the rights and duties of parents in respect of the welfare of their children.**

It notes that such a constitutional provision would be consistent with the UN Convention on the Rights of the Child specifically Article 3.1 of the Convention[6] which Ireland ratified in September 1992, with Sections 3 and 17(2) of the Guardianship of Infants Act, 1964[7] and with Section 3(2) (b) of the Child Care Act, 1991[8] and that the provision would oblige those making decisions in relation to children to take into account not only the child's right to be cared for by his or her parents but also such matters as the desirability of continuity in a child's upbringing.

**6.2.** The Commission considers that the report of the Review Group contains a clear and comprehensive analysis of the current constitutional and legal protection for the rights of children generally and that provided for in the UN Convention on the Rights of the Child.

---

6    **Article 3.1 of the UN Convention of the Rights of the Child.**

"In all actions concerning children, whether undertaken by public or private social welfare institutions, courts of law, administrative authorities or legislative bodies, the best interests of the child shall be a primary consideration".

7    **Section 3 of the Guardianship of Infants Act, 1964**

" Where, in any proceedings before any court the custody, guardianship or upbringing of an infant, or the administration of any property belonging to or held on trust for an infant, or the application of the income thereof,  is in question, the court, in deciding that question, shall  regard the welfare of the child as the first and paramount consideration.

**Section 17(2) of the Guardianship of Infants Act, 1964**

"Nothing in this Act shall interfere with or affect the power of the court to consult the wishes of the infant in considering what order to be made or diminish the right which any infant now possesses to the exercise of his own free choice."

8    **Section 3(2) (b) of the Child Care Act 1991.**

"Having regard to the rights and duties of parents, whether under the Constitution or otherwise-

(i) regard the welfare of the child as the first and paramount consideration, and

(ii) in so far as is practicable, give due consideration, having regard to his age and understanding, to the wishes of the child".

**The Commission fully supports the Review Group's Recommendation 4 (vi) that an express guarantee of certain rights of the child related to family life be included in a revised Article 41 and that the specified rights should include;**

b) **" the right of every child, as far as practicable, to know his or her parents, subject to the provision that such right should be subject to regulation by law in the interests of the child;**

c) **the right of every child, as far as practicable, to be cared for by his or her parents**

d) **the right to be reared with due regard to his or her welfare."**

## 7. Constitutional protection for the rights of natural parents

**7.1.** The Commission in Chapter 2 of its Interim Report stresses the importance of joint parenting as follows ;

*"Continuity and stability are major requirements in family relationships". (Principle No. 3)*

*"Continuity and stability in family relationships should be recognised as having a major value for individual well-being and social stability especially as far as children are concerned. Joint parenting should be encouraged with a view to ensuring as far as possible that children have the opportunity of developing close relationships with both parents which is in the interests both of children and their parents." (See Principle No.3)*

*Commission on the Family Interim Report, Chap. 2*

**7.2.** An unmarried mother who wishes to keep her child normally has custody of the child and her rights in this regard have already been recognised as personal rights protected by Article 40.3 of the Constitution. A natural father, however, does not have any constitutionally protected rights in relation to his child *(The State (Nicolaou) v An Bord Uchtála)*. The Commission notes that the natural father is entitled under Section 12 of the Status of Children Act 1987 to apply to the court for an order for his appointment as a guardian of his infant. If he is thus appointed guardian, he is entitled to the custody of the child jointly with any other guardian, usually the mother[9]. It is also the case that under the Adoption Act his child may not be adopted without his consent unless the Court makes an order dispensing with his consent.

---

9   Since the submission was prepared in March 1997, provision has been made in the Children Act, 1997 whereby a father can become joint guardian of his child by agreement with the mother upon the making of a statutory declaration without having to go to court.

**7.3.** The Commission also notes that the European Court of Human Rights found in the *Keegan* Case that Ireland was in breach of Article 8 of the European Convention on Human Rights in failing to respect the family life of an unmarried father who had a stable relationship with the mother of his child by permitting the placement of the child for adoption without his knowledge or consent.

**7.4.** **The Commission agrees with the Review Group that providing in the Constitution for a guarantee of respect for family life, to include non marital family life, may be a way, *inter alia*, of granting natural parents rights in relation to access to and/or custody of their children or consent to their adoption. Such rights would be subject to what is the best interests of the child (section 6 above refers).**

**8.** **Role of Women and Mothers or Other Persons within the Home**

**8.1.** The Commission agrees with the Review Group that Article 41.2 which assigns to women a domestic role as wives and mothers is a dated provision and no longer reflects current realities or the aspirations of many women.

**8.2.** **The Commission agrees with the Review Group that the caring function in the home makes a major contribution to the well-being of society and should be granted constitutional recognition. The Commission, fully supports the Review Group's recommendation for the replacement of the existing Article 41.2 with a provision in a gender-neutral form that would afford constitutional recognition to the caring function in the home as exercised by both men and women.**

# Summary

**9.**     **Constitutional Basis for Family Policy**

**9.1.**     As the Constitution is the basic law of the State, the Commission considers that it should provide a clear foundation for the development of the law and policy in relation to the family. Article 41 should reflect the long established traditions relating to family which are still valued by Irish people and the new realities of Irish society today.

**9.2.**     The changes recommended are in the first instance designed to give constitutional recognition and protection to all families and a guarantee to all individuals of respect for their family life in our society.

Special protection, however, would still be given to marriage and the family based on marriage in recognition of its key role in promoting long term continuity and stability in family life, but this would not prevent the Oireachtas from legislating for the benefit of families not based on marriage and their individual members.

**9.3.**     Express provision would be made for the protection of the rights of every child to family life and, in particular, to know his or her parents and, as far as practicable, to be cared for by them. Provision would also be made, however, that in all actions concerning children the best interests of the child would be a paramount concern.

**9.4.**     A guarantee of respect for family life to include non-marital families may be a way of granting natural parents' rights in relation to access to and/or custody of their children, subject to what is in the best interests of the child.

**9.5.**     One of the main functions of families is to care for members, especially children, and other vulnerable members; those who are ill, people with disabilities and elderly people. Provision should continue to be made for Constitutional recognition of and support for this caring function, but in gender neutral form.

**9.6.**     The Commission on the Family considers that the constitutional framework outlined would greatly facilitate and underpin the development of a coherent family policy in which the State can better respond to the needs of families in the changing environment of today and in the future".

# Appendix 1

## All- Party Oireachtas Committee on the Constitution

**1.** **Terms of reference**

In order to provide focus to the place and relevance of the Constitution and to establish those areas where Constitutional change may be desirable or necessary, the All-Party Committee will undertake a full review of the Constitution. In undertaking this review, the All-Party Committee will have regard to the following :

a   the Report of the Constitution Review Group

b   participation in the All-Party Committee would involve no obligation to support any recommendations which might be made, even if made unanimously

c   members of the All-Party Committee, either as individuals or as Party representatives, would not be regarded as committed in any way to support such recommendations

d   members of the All-Party Committee shall keep their respective Party Leaders informed from time to time of the progress of the Committee's work

e   none of the parties, in Government or Opposition, would be precluded from dealing with matters within the All-Party Committee's terms of reference while it is sitting, and

f   whether there might be a single draft of non-controversial amendments to the Constitution to deal with technical matters.

**2.** **Members**

The members of the All-Party Committee are;
Brian Lenihan, TD (Chairman), Jim O' Keeffe, TD (Vice-Chairman), Brendan Daly, TD, Senator John Dardis, Thomas Enright, TD, Séamus Kirk, TD, Derek McDowell, TD, Marian McGennis, TD, Liz McManus, TD, Senator Denis O' Donovan, Senator Fergus O' Dowd, Senator Kathleen O' Meara. The Secretariat is provided by the Institute of Public Administration: Jim O' Donnell, Secretary and Karen Cullen, Assistant Secretary.

# part 10

**Making it happen**

**In Part 10 the Commission presents its findings in relation to:**

- strengthening the institutional framework within which the State's response to families is developed and delivered and facilitating the development of a coherent policy approach to families across Government departments and services.

# Overview of Part 10

Throughout this report, the Commission has considered ways of strengthening the State's response to families. The recommendations put forward by the Commission thus far provide the basis for the development of an integrated family policy to strengthen and assist families coping with change and to put in place the supports to prevent family breakdown.

In Part 10 of the report, the Commission considers ways of strengthening the institutional framework within which the State's response to families is developed and delivered.

The Commission concludes that the institutional framework which is recommended must aim to put families centre-stage at political, executive and administrative levels. In this context, the Commission recommends that family well-being should be singled out as a matter of critical importance for Government in the years ahead.

The Commission goes on to recommend the establishment of a separate unit within the Department of Social, Community and Family Affairs with responsibility for family issues. The Family Affairs Unit would co-ordinate family policy, pursue the findings in the Commission's final report, undertake research and promote awareness about family issues.

The Commission notes that the building up of expertise and close relationships with other key departments such as the Departments of Health and Children, Education and Science, and Justice, Equality and Law Reform will be essential to success in achieving shared family objectives. The Commission suggests that an inter-departmental committee would facilitate the achievement of co-ordination objectives.

The Commission recommends the introduction of a Family Impact Statement which would set out clearly the consequences of policies, programmes and services for families in all major facets of Government activity, central and local. The adoption of this statement would put a focus on supporting and strengthening families in all actions taken by the Government and facilitate development of a coherent policy approach to families across government departments and services.

## Chapter 24 Strengthening the institutional framework within which the State's response to families is developed and delivered.

### 24.1 Introduction

The Commission has considered ways in which the institutional framework within which the State's response to families is developed and delivered can be strengthened. The precise shape of an appropriate institutional framework for the promotion of family well-being has been discussed on several occasions in recent years. The possibilities range from the setting up of a permanent Government Department of the Family to the holding of periodic review exercises, such as that which has been undertaken by the Commission on the Family over the past two years.

An 1989 ESRI study[1] proposed the establishment of a Family Affairs Unit in the Department of Finance within the context of national economic and social planning, which would co-ordinate taxation with social welfare policies and assess housing, health, education and other policies from the viewpoint of families. This approach was recommended by the Joint Committee on the Family. [2] A separate Ministry for the Family and a State-funded independent co-ordinating body for families was suggested by the National Steering Committee for the International Year of the Family (1994).

It is the Commission's view that the institutional framework which is recommended to pursue the work of the Commission in support of families must aim to place families centre-stage at political, executive and administrative levels.

### 24.2 Strategic Management Initiative - an opportunity

The Commission has considered the different mechanisms which other working groups have used and has considered the recommendations made by various experts in relation to this issue. Overall, the Commission is of the view that the Strategic Management Initiative, which is underpinned by major public sector reform, presents the best opportunity to achieve an objective to place families centre-stage.

Central to the Strategic Management Initiative is the delivery of the highest quality of service to the customers of the civil service. These are the public and the Government. The aim is to provide quality services in an open and transparent way, avoiding unnecessary regulation and dealing systematically with key issues that cross the boundaries of departments and of agencies. [3] The Public Service Management Act 1997 gives a statutory basis to this major reform of Ireland's public services. The Act provides new authority and structures for dealing with questions of critical importance that cross departmental boundaries. It heralds a more results and performance-oriented civil service within a structure that emphasises teamwork within and between departments and agencies to achieve excellence in public service.

Based on the core principles of the Strategic Management Initiative which have been adopted by Government and the public service, the Commission's proposals to strengthen

---

1    Finola Kennedy, *Family Economy and Government in Ireland,* ESRI, Dublin 1989

2    *Impact of State, Tax and Social Welfare Schemes on the Family,* Houses of the Oireachtas, February 1996.

3    Draws on *Delivering Better Government ,a programme of change for the Irish Civil Service,* 1996, Government Publications Office.

the institutional framework within which the State responds to families cover the political, legislative, executive and administrative levels of public service with a participatory monitoring and advisory role for voluntary and community and other expert interests.

### 24.3 Political level - the Government and the Houses of the Oireachtas

Part of the strategic management process suggests that the Government singles out areas of critical importance in relation to the programme of the Government for its term of office. It is evident that there is a strong commitment to the promotion of families throughout the current Government programme. [4] The Commission recommends that family well-being should be a matter of critical importance in this way in the years ahead. It is suggested that the Cabinet Subcommittee on Social Inclusion might include in its remit this family objective.

The Commission acknowledges the work undertaken by the Joint Committee on the Family. [5] The Joint Committee on the Family, established by the Oireachtas in March 1995 to consider the impact of social change and State policies on the family, provided a new focus in the Houses of the Oireachtas on families. Reports produced by the Joint Committee on the effects of Social Welfare and taxation on families and on older people have informed the Commission's report. Public hearings have highlighted the issues affecting families in a changing social and economic environment and provided a voice for family interests in the legislature. The Commission welcomes the recent establishment of a new Joint Committee with a remit in relation to family, community and social affairs, continuing the focus on family interests in the Houses of the Oireachtas.

### 24.4 Executive and administrative level - Family Affairs Unit

The Commission recommends the establishment of a separate and distinct Family Affairs Unit within the Department of Social, Community and Family Affairs.

Suggested functions for the Family Affairs Unit might include the following:
- To *co-ordinate family policy* and facilitate the effort across different departments and agencies, including the voluntary and community sector, to achieve shared objectives in relation to families.
- To *pursue the findings* in the Commission's report.
- To *evaluate the effects of legislation and policies* on families and to promote the adoption of the family impact statement as a means of auditing the impact of initiatives on families.[6]
- To *pioneer new approaches* to the provision of services for families. These might include:
  - development of the *Family and Community Services Resource Centres;* and the evaluation of their effectiveness in terms of outcomes for families.
  - the refocusing of the delivery of State services at local level and the development of the *one-stop-shop services for families.*
- To initiate the policy response to new and emerging issues by undertaking *specific*

---

4  Programme for Government *An Action Programme for the Millennium.*

5  The term of office of the committee ended in March 1997.

6  In *Strengthening Families for Life,* Interim report of the Commission on the Family to the Minister for Social Welfare, November 1996, the Commission recommended the introduction of a Family Impact Statement which would set out clearly the consequences of policies, programmes and services for families in all major aspects of Government activity, central and local. The Commission's recommendation for the Family Impact Statement is reproduced in Appendix 1 to this chapter.

*activities* in support of families, i.e. parent support programmes, parent information and education, strategies to redress barriers to employment and training encountered by low income families with children, including lone-parent families.

- To develop the policy framework for support for the *Marriage Counselling Services* and the *Family Mediation Service.*
- To promote *awareness* about new and emerging issues affecting families.
- To undertake *research* to inform policy development.

A *budget for research* in relation to family issues is recommended. Initially a budget of £100,000 would allow for three or four research projects in the first year of operation.

It is the Commission's view that the Family Affairs Unit should have a distinct and separate identity within the Department of Social, Community and Family Affairs. It should be led by a senior manager (at principal officer level) dedicated to the unit with a number of staff. It is envisaged that the unit would work to strategic management principles. It is suggested that the core staffing of the unit would be augmented from time to time by staff from other key departments or agencies on a full or part-time basis, i.e. the team approach as promoted under strategic management to develop and co-ordinate specific strategies within a given timescale.

The building up of expertise and close relationships with other key departments, such as the Departments of Health and Children, Education and Science, and Justice, Equality and Law Reform will be essential to the success of the unit. In this context, an inter-departmental committee which would meet periodically would be appropriate.

*Costs*
The establishment of the Family Affairs Unit in the Department of Social, Community and Family Affairs would have implications for that Department's administrative budget.

Following the Commission's pre-budget submission, the Government has announced the establishment of a Family Affairs Unit in the Department of Social, Community and Family Affairs. An allocation of £850,000 has been provided for the unit in the 1998 budget, to include administration costs, a research budget, an information programme to raise awareness about family and parenting issues, and a pilot project in local offices of the Department to provide improved services for families. Important functions of the unit are to co-ordinate family policy in consultation with other departments and to pursue the recommendations of the Commission on the Family following their consideration by the Government.

**24.5    Monitoring and evaluation**
In order to monitor progress, it is suggested that the Family Affairs Unit produce an *annual/biennial report* (to be laid before the Houses of the Oireachtas).

It is suggested that an advisory committee, comprised of experts in family matters and representatives of the voluntary and community groups, should be considered to support the work of the unit. Experts in family matters would advise on the development of policy responses to emerging needs and on research initiatives. The advisory committee would

## Placing Families Centre-stage

**Strengthing the framework within which the State Responds to Families**

Government

- **family well-being** a matter of critical importance

Joint Committee on **Family,** Community & Social Affairs

*Cabinet Subcommittee*

Secretary-General, Department of Social, Community & **Family Affairs**

### Family Affairs Unit
- to co-ordinate family policy
- to undertake research
- to promote awareness about family issues
- **family impact statement**

*Expert Advisory Committee*
Experts in **family matters,**
voluntary, community interests

*Inter-Departmental Policy Committee*
Departments of Social, Community and Family Affairs, Education and Science, Health and Children, Justice, Equality and Law Reform

provide independent commentary in relation to the annual/biennial reports.

## 24.6 Family Impact Statement

In the context of the functions of the Family Affairs Unit, the Commission would like to highlight the significance of a Family Impact Statement.

The importance of measuring the impact on families of policies and programmes is increasingly being recognised in European and in international fora. Family auditing or family impact statements are instruments which have been suggested as ways of routinely assessing the impact on families at all stages of policy development and implementation.[7]

## 24.7 Role of the Department of Social, Community and Family Affairs

As Chapters 2 and 3 have described, the Department of Social, Community and Family Affairs is well placed to develop a coherent platform of strategic policy, linking its own service responsibilities with those of other Government departments and agencies and community and voluntary organisations with a shared concern for families.

The Department already has a significant responsibility in relation to support for families. A significant part of its budget of £4.4 billion (1996) is accounted for by expenditure on families, including the One-Parent Family Payments, payments for unemployed families and families who are out of work through illness. It includes child benefit for over one million children in almost five hundred thousand families.

The Department's contact with families spans their lifecycle from maternity payments through income support during illness or unemployment, providing payments to families on low wages, through active age adults who are working and paying PRSI and older people who are retired.

The Department's network of local offices throughout the country and the taxpayers' investment in information technology over the years have provided the infrastructure to underpin the local customised service proposed in Chapter 3.  The Department's wider remit in relation to supporting the voluntary and community sector, has the potential for a dynamic partnership which would add value to its core income maintenance responsibilities and harness communities in working towards positive outcomes for families. This is proving to be the case in the 'cross agency' approach taken to tackling the difficulty of families having recourse to illegal money-lenders. Working with local communities and the credit unions, the initiative successfully halted the rise in recourse to illegal money-lending. Similar cross-agency initiatives are underway in pursuing the National Anti-Poverty Strategy.

Close working relationships with the Departments of Health and Children, Education and Science and Justice, Equality and Law  Reform in pursuit of shared family objectives provide opportunities to harness the synergies of the statutory functions and responsibilities of each department, to bring about a new focus on strengthening families for life.

---

7    Appendix 2 to this chapter sets out a rationale for family impact considerations, as described in *Indicative Guide for Action on Family Issues:* United Nations, Department for Policy Co-ordination and Sustainable Development, Secretariat for the International Year of the Family, Vienna, 1995.

# Appendix 1

**Family Impact Statement**

**In its interim report, November, 1996 the Commission recommends the introduction of a Family Impact Statement which would set out clearly the consequences of policies, programmes and services for families in all major aspects of Government activity, central and local. As an initial step, the Commission considers that the Family Impact Statement should be included in all proposals put forward for consideration by the Government and in the terms of reference for committees of the Houses of the Oireachtas.**

The adoption of the statement would:
- highlight awareness of how Government affects families; increase sensitivity about family issues at each level of Government, from the consideration of proposals through to the delivery of services
- put a focus on supporting and strengthening families in all actions taken by Government and
- facilitate the development of a coherent policy approach to families across Government departments and services.

The Commission suggests that the Government rules which set out the procedures and instructions in relation to submitting proposals for the consideration and decision of the Government should be amended to require the inclusion of the Family Impact Statement.

The objective in time should be the publication of the Family Impact Statement so that it is available for public scrutiny. The statement, could be included in the published explanatory memoranda which accompany proposed new legislation, in public consultative papers, and, where appropriate, as part of information and promotional material produced by Government departments and state agencies in relation to new policy and legislative developments.

Further development of the Family Impact Statement would involve the adoption of the key principles suggested by the Commission in Chapter 1 of this report, to guide policy and programmes, which are being developed to support families, the measurement of existing policies and programmes against those principles, and the unintended consequences of policies for families being addressed. Ultimately, the goal should be to bring all policies, programmes and services in line with the principles and to extend the use of the Family Impact Statement to local Government, State agencies and community organisations.

# Appendix 2

**Extract from Indicative Guide for Action on Family Issues[1]**

*Rationale for action, family impact considerations.*
Many policies and programmes other than those directed specifically at families deal with issues that have direct consequences for families, even though those consequences are generally not acknowledged. It is important to realise that policies and programmes in many spheres of activity are likely to have an impact on families, on how they are formed and on whether they will thrive and be able to carry out their functions. Because family concerns span all levels of society and reach across generations, many policies that are not explicitly regarded as relevant to families may have unseen or long-range implications. It is important, therefore, to pay attention to the impact of all policies on families, throughout the process of policy development, implementation, monitoring and evaluation, while taking measures to minimise the long-term negative effects on family well-being.

*Objective*
The objective is to promote consideration of the impact on families of all policies, programmes and legislation that affect them and avoid any negative consequences to family well-being and ability to contribute to society.

*Suggestions for action*
Suggested actions include the following :
(a) Make families a focus of public concerns by officially recognising that decisions and actions will usually have an impact on families
(b) Routinely assess the impact on families at all stages of policy development, implementation, monitoring and evaluation and alleviate any negative consequences for families. Prepare family impact statements for each proposed law or policy or specify situations when such statements are required.

1    United Nations Department for Policy Co-ordination and Sustainable Development: Secretariat for the International Year of the Family, Vienna, 1995.

# Summary of Recommendations in Part 10

*In relation to strengthening the institutional framework within which the State's response to families is developed and delivered.*

The Commission recommends

- **that the Government consider extending the remit of the Cabinet Subcommittee on Social Inclusion to include the promotion of family well-being as an area of critical importance to its work,**
- **the establishment of a Family Affairs Unit in the Department of Social, Community and Family Affairs**

- To co-ordinate family policy and facilitate the effort across different departments and agencies including the voluntary and community sector to achieve shared objectives in relation to families.
- To pursue the findings in the Commission's report.
- To evaluate the effects of policies on families and promote the adoption of a Family Impact Statement as a means of routinely auditing the effects of proposals on families.
- To pioneer new approaches to the provision of services for families.
- To develop the policy framework for support for marriage counselling services and the Family Mediation Service.
- To promote awareness about family issues.
- To undertake research.

**Costs:** The establishment of a Family Affairs Unit in the Department of Social, Community and Family Affairs will have implications for that department's administration budget.

*An allocation of £850,000 has been provided by the Government in the 1998 budget for a new Family Affairs Unit to include administration costs, a research budget, an information programme to raise awareness about parenting issues and a pilot project to improve family services at a number of local offices of the Department of Social, Community and Family Affairs.*

# Index to the report

Travellers, 7-8, 24, 39, 248, 261, 269, 292-3,
        295-7, 360-1, 543, 550, 564, 599
TREOIR (Federation for Unmarried Parents and
        their Children), 111, 121-2, 504

## U

UN Convention on the Rights of the Child, 85,
        434
UN Fourth World Conference, 62-3
UN International Day of Families, 5, 202, 211,
        274, 510, 512
UN on Family Issues, 2, 531, 539, 622, 626,
        641
unemployment, 23, 147-9, 578-9
    educational initiatives and, 167
    families and, 148-9, 156-7, 575, 606-9
    income support and, 151-5, 166, 575, 577
    labour market measures and, 148, 165
    priority groups for support, 151, 155-7
    programmes to tackle, 155
    social inclusion and, 149-50, 151
Universities Act **1997**, 264
unmarried parents, 97, 98-9, 107, 116-7,
        121-3, 187 *see also* lone parent families

## V

violence against women, task force on, 350-2
violence, domestic
Vocational Training Opportunities Scheme,
        106, 167

## W

women, 535-7
    and employment, 64, 64, 138-9, 80, 130-1,
        249, 580, 587
    unpaid home care work and, 62, 79, 535-7
    violence against, 350-2 *see also* domestic
        violence
women's groups, 415 *see also* men's groups
*Women's Participation in the Labour Market,*
        64, 74, 80, 249
working groups *see* expert working groups

## Y

young lone mothers, 109-11
youth services, 33, 38, 111-14, 289-92, 594
    funding for, 289, 290, 291, 292
    teenage health and, 112-13
Youthreach, 106-7, 261, 276, 291-3, 372